Burying Mao

Burying Mao

CHINESE POLITICS IN THE AGE

OF DENG XIAOPING

• *RICHARD BAUM* •

PRINCETON UNIVERSITY PRESS

PRINCETON, NEW JERSEY

Library of Congress Cataloging-in-Publication Data

Baum, Richard, 1940–
Burying Mao : Chinese politics in the age of Deng Xiaoping /
Richard Baum.
p. cm.
Includes bibliographical references and index.
ISBN 0-691-03639-X
ISBN 0-691-03637-3 (pbk.)
1. China—Politics and government—1976– 2. Teng, Hsiao-p'ing, 1904– I. Title.
DS779.26.B38 1994 951.05′8—dc20 94-9892 CIP

This book has been composed in Adobe Times Roman

Princeton University Press books are printed
on acid-free paper and meet the guidelines
for permanence and durability of the Committee
on Production Guidelines for Book Longevity
of the Council on Library Resources

Fourth printing, and first paperback printing,
with additions and corrections, 1996

Printed in the United States of America by Princeton Academic Press

5   7   9   10   8   6   4

• *C O N T E N T S* •

LIST OF TABLES AND ILLUSTRATIONS   ix

PREFACE   xi

ACKNOWLEDGMENTS   xv

A NOTE ON SOURCES AND METHODS   xvii

ABBREVIATIONS USED IN THE TEXT   xix

INTRODUCTION
The Age of Deng Xiaoping   3

PART I: THE ROOTS OF REFORM, 1976–1980   25

CHAPTER 1
Burying Mao: April 1976–July 1977   27

CHAPTER 2
Deng Takes Command: August 1977–December 1978   48

CHAPTER 3
The First Fang/Shou Cycle: November 1978–August 1980   66

CHAPTER 4
High Tide of Reform: *Gengshen*, 1980   94

PART II: THE ROAD TO TIANANMEN, 1981–1989   119

CHAPTER 5
Polarization and Paralysis: January 1981–April 1982   121

CHAPTER 6
Defining the Spirit of Socialism: Summer 1982–December 1983   143

CHAPTER 7
The Rebirth of Liberal Reform: January 1984–Summer 1985   164

CHAPTER 8
Social Origins of Student Protest: Summer 1985–December 1986   189

CHAPTER 9
Combating Bourgeois Liberalization: January 1987–Spring 1988   206

CHAPTER 10
Bittersweet Fruits of Reform: March 1988–April 1989   225

PART III: THE BEIJING SPRING, 1989   245

CHAPTER 11
The Beijing Spring: April–May 1989   247

CHAPTER 12
Cracking Down: June 1989–February 1990   275

PART IV: THE OLD ORDER CHANGES, 1990–1995   311

CHAPTER 13
Picking Up the Pieces: Winter 1990–Autumn 1991   313

CHAPTER 14
Deng's Final Offensive: January–October 1992   341

CHAPTER 15
The Last Cycle: October 1992–Summer 1993   369

CHAPTER 16
The Mandate of Heaven: Summer 1993–Summer 1995   377

EPILOGUE
Burying Deng   391

ABBREVIATIONS USED IN THE NOTES   395

NOTES   397

REFERENCES   473

INDEX   491

TABLE

Deng Liqun's Ten-Year Cyclical Model   6

ILLUSTRATIONS

Memorial service for Mao Zedong. *China Pictorial* (November 1976).   28

Tiananmen Square, April 4, 1976. *Renminde daonian* (People's grief) (Beijing: Beijing Chubanshe, 1979).   33

"With you in charge, I'm at ease." *China Pictorial* (May 1977); mural by Peng Pin and Qin Shangyi.   38

Tiananmen Poems go on sale, November 1978. *Zhongguo Gongchandang qishinian* (The CCP's seventy years) (Jilin: Meishu Chubanshe, 1991).   70

Democracy Wall, December 1978. Photo by Richard Baum.   75

"Trial of the Gang of Four" and "Lin Biao clique." *China Pictorial* (January 1981).   114

The Gang of Four in the dock. *China Pictorial* (April 1981).   115

Old and new party leaders chat, June 1981. *China Reconstructs* (September 1981).   133

Central Committee adopts resolution, June 1981. *China Reconstructs* (September 1981).   137

Old comrades reminisce at Twelfth Party Congress. *Zhongguo Gongchandang qishinian.*   146

First plenary session of Central Advisory Committee. *Zhongguo Gongchandang qishinian.*   147

Deng Xiaoping and Hu Yaobang review PLA units. *China Reconstructs* (December 1981).   187

Deng Xiaoping cools off at Beidaihe. *Flashback: A Decade of Changes, 1976–86* (Beijing: China Photographic Publishing House, 1986). Photo by Yang Shaoming.   197

Deng Xiaoping plays bridge. *Beijing Review*, February 9, 1987. Photo by Yang Shaoming.   212

Students present petition to government. *The Truth about the Beijing Turmoil* (Beijing: Beijing Publishing House, 1991).   249

Students march to Tiananmen Square. *The Truth about the Beijing Turmoil.*   252

Hunger strike at Tiananmen Square. Photo by Robert Lum.   257

Li Peng visits hunger strikers in hospital. *The Truth about the Beijing Turmoil.*   259

Zhao Ziyang tearfully bids farewell to students. *Huo yü hsieh chih chen-hsiang* (The truth of fire and blood) (Taipei: Chung-kung Yen-chiu Tsa-chih She, 1989).   262

Li Peng declares state of emergency. *The Truth about the Beijing Turmoil.*   263

Beijing citizens block army convoy. *Beijing Spring* (Boston: Little, Brown, 1989). Photo by Peter Turnley.   264

Demonstrators carry banners. Photo by Steve Futterman.   266

The Goddess of Democracy. Photo by Steve Futterman.   274

Central Beijing. Timothy Brook, *Quelling the People* (Oxford: Oxford University Press, 1992).   277

Citizens display captured military hardware. *The Truth about the Beijing Turmoil.*   280

Demonstrators confront riot police. *The Truth about the Beijing Turmoil.*   281

Armored personnel carriers set afire. *The Truth about the Beijing Turmoil.*   284

Charred corpse of PLA soldier. *The Truth about the Beijing Turmoil.*   285

Army units reoccupy Tiananmen Square. *The Truth about the Beijing Turmoil.*   288

Old comrades dominate leadership meeting. *Zhongguo Gongchandang qishinian.*   293

Deng Xiaoping congratulates army leaders. *The Truth about the Beijing Turmoil.*   294

New Politburo Standing Committee selected. *Zhongguo Gongchandang qishinian.*   297

Deng Xiaoping pauses for photo opportunity in Shenzhen. *Zhongguo* (China) (June 1992). Photo by Xue Wen.   343

Deng Xiaoping greets workers at steel mill. *Beijing Review*, August 17–23, 1992. Photo by Yang Guozhu.   354

Chen Yun greets government officials in Shanghai. *Beijing Review*, May 11–17, 1992.   355

Jiang Zemin introduces new Politburo Standing Committee. *Zhongguo* (December 1992). Photo by Huang Taopeng.   366

IN THE SUMMER of 1993, an enterprising Chinese businessman took out a full-page ad in the *Liberation Army Daily* to announce the offering of a limited edition of diamond-studded, eighteen-carat gold pocket watches bearing Mao Zedong's distinctive profile—at a cash price of U.S. $16,000. The entire supply reportedly sold out in a matter of days. At about the same time, tens of thousands of farmers in twenty Chinese provinces rioted in protest over steadily declining farm incomes and chronic fiscal predation on the part of greedy local officials.

As a result of Deng Xiaoping's reform initiatives, the austere and colorless collectivism of the Maoist era was supplanted by an upscale entrepreneurial ethos labeled "socialism with Chinese characteristics." For some Chinese this meant new and unprecedented opportunities for upward mobility; for others it meant rising personal vulnerability and marginalization.

Today, a scant two decades after Mao's death, few traces of the Chairman's essential zeitgeist remain. Mao*ism*—the spartan, puritanical credo fashioned by a small band of dedicated revolutionaries in the 1930s and 1940s—is moribund. Though "Marxism-Leninism-Mao Zedong thought" remains the official state religion, it is a religion largely devoid of both faith and faithful, its true believers having dwindled to a mere handful of senescent old men.

This book is about how China got from there to here. It is the story of a country—and a Communist Party leadership—forced to confront far-reaching socioeconomic changes and painful political choices. Far from being smooth or steady, the course of reform in post-Mao China has been complex and convoluted, filled with obstacles and subject to frequent false starts and sudden stops. On one terrifying occasion, the reform process was frozen in a fearsome hail of machine-gun fire.

When I first began working on this project, my intent was to write a straightforward, hundred-page narrative essay on Chinese politics in the 1980s, centering on the causes and consequences of the 1989 Tiananmen disaster.[1] As I began peeling back the outer layers of this extraordinary decade, however, my attention was increasingly drawn to the uneven, oscillating nature of the reform process and to a series of deep-seated ideological and factional schisms that appeared to fuel its periodic fluctuations. Probing more deeply the nature and dynamics of these fluctuations, I gradually enlarged and intensified my research. What emerged, finally, was a political history of the entire post-Mao era, from the 1976 deaths of Chairman Mao and Premier Zhou Enlai to the waning moments of Deng Xiaoping's controversy-filled career in 1995.

Although the book's twenty-year time span encompasses a wide range of issues, events, and actors, its primary focus is the political behavior of approximately three dozen top-level Chinese Communist Party (CCP) leaders, including policymakers, theoreticians, and propagandists. At times acting in harmony, but more often deeply divided among themselves, these three dozen leaders, together with their various clients, cohorts, and constituents, occupied the primary pathways of power and influence in post-Mao China. Under the watchful eye of "paramount leader" Deng Xiaoping, they pursued diverse policy agendas and carved out divergent spheres of interest. Collectively they determined, in Harold Lasswell's classic phrase, "Who got what, when, and how."

In the years following Mao's death some of these leaders—generally the younger, better educated ones—vigorously embraced the cause of economic and political reform and modernization; a bold few went so far as to advocate "wholesale Westernization." Others—principally older cadres with revolutionary roots in the Yan'an period—stubbornly resisted all change, clinging tenaciously to the myths and icons of a bygone age. The majority, however, positioned themselves in between these two extremes, selectively embracing some reforms while rejecting others. Over time, competition and conflict among these various groups and factions helped give the reform process its wavelike, oscillatory character.

Although a substantial number of party leaders shared the spotlight at various points, one man commanded the supreme political heights. More than any other single individual, Deng Xiaoping shaped the politics and policies of the post-Mao era. Principal coalition-builder and architect of China's market reforms, Deng was also, paradoxically, the principal author of the brutal Beijing massacre. Vigorously extolling the growth-inducing effects of market competition in the economic sphere, Deng strongly eschewed the chaotic potential of democratic competition in the political arena. The tension inherent in this dualism—between Deng Xiaoping the bold, pragmatic economic innovator and Deng Xiaoping the unyielding, hard-line political Leninist—helped set in motion the periodic policy swings that were a hallmark of the reform era. Not coincidentally, the sharp policy oscillations engendered by Deng's ambivalent dualism contributed mightily to the genesis of China's traumatic Tiananmen crisis. In the aftermath of that crisis, Deng's attempt to rescue his endangered regime and revive his stalled economic reforms proved to be the most difficult test of his seventy-five-year political career.

The book's narrative is divided into four parts, organized chronologically. Following a general thematic introduction, Part I (chapters 1–4) explores the political and ideological roots of reform, from Mao's last days in 1976 to Deng's final triumph over Hua Guofeng, Mao's designated successor, some four years later. Among other subjects, these chapters examine the complex three-way struggle for power triggered by Mao's death; the formation of a broad-based reform coalition under Deng's leadership; Deng's sharpening rivalry with Hua Guofeng; his initial triumph over Hua at the historic Third Plenum of the Eleventh Central Committee; and the subsequent emergence of internal ideological frictions within Deng's victorious coalition.

In analyzing these unfolding events, the chapters in Part I also explore the roots of sociopolitical unrest in post-Mao China, as the initial victory of the reformers gave rise to a dramatic popular display of rising expectations at

Beijing's newly christened "Democracy Wall." It was the party center's decision to restrict the scope of permissible dissent at Democracy Wall in the spring of 1979 that ushered in the first major policy oscillations of the Deng Xiaoping era.

Part II (chapters 5–10) explores the social origins and political antecedents of the 1989 Tiananmen crisis. Detailing the intensification of reform-induced socioeconomic stresses and ideological antagonisms in the 1980s, the chapters in Part II analyze, inter alia, the emerging controversy over "spiritual pollution"; the mood of heightened anxiety occasioned by spiraling urban inflation and economic inequality; the spread of cadre-centered economic crime and corruption; the growing activism of China's university students; and the personal and factional cleavages that increasingly threatened to split apart Deng's reform coalition. Owing to such deepening stresses and schisms, the 1980s witnessed a series of sharp, spasmodic policy shifts, as rival leaders and factions maneuvered—and sometimes openly struggled—to seize (and retain) control over the instruments of power and policy.

Part III (chapters 11–12) examines the anatomy of the Beijing Spring of 1989. These chapters analyze the catalytic chemistry of student political activism, touched off by the sudden death of liberal party reformer Hu Yaobang; the internal divisions within the party leadership over how to deal with the student movement; the escalating moral righteousness, on both sides, that made peaceful accommodation increasingly difficult; and the return to active duty of a small group of hard-line, semiretired gerontocrats, whose declaration of martial law and subsequent sacking of CCP General Secretary Zhao Ziyang pushed the escalating conflict beyond the point of combustion.

Chronicling the government's bloody June 3 assault on Tiananmen Square and the ensuing crackdown against "bourgeois liberalism," Part III assays, finally, the reasons why China's embattled party and military leaders were able to regain control of the political situation in the months after the June debacle, thus avoiding the fate suffered by Communist regimes in East and Central Europe in the "gentle revolution" of 1989.

Part IV (chapters 13–16) examines the CCP's attempt to pick up the pieces in the early and mid-1990s. Detailing Deng's race to restore a shattered public trust and breathe new life into his endangered reform program before going to "meet Marx," this section documents the travails of a regime struggling to ensure its survival—and a leader struggling to assure his own future posterity—in a world turned upside down by the cascading collapse of communism. The chapters in Part IV also examine Deng's high-stakes showdown with hard-line conservative ideologues in the aftermath of the failed Soviet coup attempt of August 1991, culminating in Deng's strategic "southern tour" of 1992 and his subsequent, stunning victory over the opponents of economic reform. An epilogue provides an overview of Chinese politics at the twilight of the Deng Xiaoping era and a retrospective assessment of Deng's legacy.

Los Angeles, California
August 1995

• A C K N O W L E D G M E N T S •

IN WRITING this book I have benefited from the advice, assistance, and good-will of a number of people. Roderick MacFarquhar planted the first seeds when he invited me to contribute the concluding chapter to his Cambridge University Press anthology, *The Politics of China, 1949–1989*. Pursuant to this commission, in the fall of 1990 the Faculty of Letters at the University of Leiden offered me an appointment as visiting scholar, enabling me to work on the project in an intellectually stimulating environment. The director of the Leiden Sinology Institute, Tony Saich, provided an office and ready access to the institute's exceptional research facilities, professional staff, and students; he also graciously shared with me his vast knowledge of Chinese politics—and Dutch pubs—while providing much valuable feedback on my draft chapters, right up to the afternoon of his wedding.

In Leiden, and later in Los Angeles, I profited greatly from the encyclopedic Sino-memory of Geor Hintzen, who caught and corrected numerous minor (and some major) errors in my original manuscript. In Beijing, David and Fumiyo Holley, Regina Piovesana, and He Di shared their rich experiences and insights with me on a number of occasions. Back in Los Angeles, my University of California colleagues Dorothy Solinger and James Tong graciously read successive drafts of the manuscript, offering many valuable comments and suggestions.

At UCLA, Richard Siao gave generously of his time and talents, checking facts, providing vital Chinese-language documentation, and offering bibliographic support. Supplemental research assistance was provided by graduate students Hongyi Lai, Chi-ho Chan, and James Mulvenon, and by my undergraduate aides, Jon-Erik Holty and Cecil Prado. The students in my Chinese politics seminar served as a sounding board for many of the ideas and arguments advanced in these pages. Jean Hung, Ted Pritikin, Robert Lum, and Steve Futterman all generously provided me with photographs for use in this book.

Several anonymous press reviewers carefully critiqued the manuscript in its submission stage. Though they are by no means responsible for the finished product, the book is, I believe, considerably stronger as a result of their criticisms. I am particularly indebted to the unknown reviewer who saved me great embarrassment by pointing out that one reason Tao Zhu may have failed to attend Mao Zedong's 1976 funeral was that he had been dead for seven years. Many thanks! (You know who you are.)

Malcolm DeBevoise, political science and law editor at Princeton University Press, offered timely advice and encouragement at various stages of the editorial process, helping to demonstrate that electronic mail can be a relatively pleasant and productive way for author and editor to communicate.

Anita O'Brien expertly copyedited the manuscript, cheerfully fielding a steady stream of nit-picking auteurial inquiries.

I would like to express my appreciation, finally, to Trudy Wilcox, who helped to share my travail and sharpen my thinking at a critical juncture in my writing.

IN PREPARING this book I have relied extensively on documentary sources, including a large number of media reports originating from China, Taiwan, and Hong Kong. I have also incorporated into the book a substantial number of personal observations and anecdotes gleaned from periodic visits to China, from interviews with Chinese scholars and officials, and from the experiences and observations of various Western journalists and scholars. In piecing together the book's narrative argument, I have made frequent use of statements attributed to Chinese political leaders by various Hong Kong- and Taiwan-based China-watching journals. As anyone who regularly reads such publications is undoubtedly aware, this is an enterprise fraught with peril. Given that such journals trade extensively in rumors, gossip, and inside information garnered from unofficial Chinese sources, some of which are notoriously less reliable than others, one must always allow a reasonable margin of error in assessing the accuracy and authenticity of attributed statements.

After weighing the possibilities of distortion and error, I decided that on balance it is better to risk occasional misquotation and misinformation than to avoid using all unconfirmed or questionably sourced materials. To have done otherwise would have significantly weakened the book's argument and undermined its narrative structure. I have, however, taken pains to avoid using source materials that I had reason to believe were fabricated or otherwise embellished. On occasion, to ensure fidelity to original texts or to provide greater idiomatic fluency and coherence, I have retranslated certain Chinese phrases cited in secondary English sources.

Whenever I became aware of questions concerning the veracity of sources or the authenticity of cited materials, I have endeavored to indicate this, either in the text itself or in an accompanying endnote. I have also made frequent use of such irritating journalistic conventions and caveats as "allegedly" and "reportedly" and "it was rumored" to highlight the vital (if elusive) distinction between fact and conjecture. The reader's indulgence is hereby begged with respect to such awkward literary devices. Finally, notwithstanding my best efforts to reduce the margin of error, it is virtually certain that there remain mistakes of fact, attribution, and interpretation. Though I would strongly prefer to beg the reader's indulgence with respect to these also, I fear that I am not entitled to do so.

By choosing to focus primarily on key political actors, ideological issues, factional controversies, and events at the center of the Chinese political system in Beijing, I have opened myself to the possible reproach that this book is essentially an exercise in the analysis of elite political behavior and is insufficiently attentive to the underlying systemic structures and processes of Chinese politics. I have not, for example, devoted a great deal of time or space to the institutional mechanics of policy making, bureaucratic bargaining, or policy implementation.[1] Nor have I attempted systematically to assay the political economy of China's post-Mao reforms, at either the macro or the micro level.[2] I have instead chosen to view the vicissitudes of China's recent political history through the prismatic lens of elite conflict. Though I readily concede that this approach is capable of illuminating only part of the bigger picture of Chinese politics, it is a vital part of that picture. On this question I find myself wholly in agreement with Frederick Teiwes who, in a recent discussion of the pitfalls inherent in studying elite behavior in China, concluded that because "major difficulties exist in the analysis of reform era elite politics . . . [the analyst] must be especially tentative, restrained in the use of unverifiable sources, and explicit concerning what is speculative and what cannot be known. But for all its uncertainties, the exercise is necessary."[3]

ACFTU All-China Federation of Trade Unions
APC   armored personnel carrier
BSAF   Beijing Students' Autonomous Federation
CAC   Central Advisory Committee
CASS   Chinese Academy of Social Sciences
CC   Central Committee
CCP   Chinese Communist Party
CDIC   Central Discipline Inspection Committee
CITIC China International Trust and Investment Corporation
CPPCC Chinese People's Political Consultative Conference
CUST   Chinese University of Science and Technology
CYL   Communist Youth League
GPD   General Political Department
MAC   Military Affairs Commission
NPC   National People's Congress
PAP   People's Armed Police
PLA   People's Liberation Army
PRC   People's Republic of China
SC   Standing Committee
SEZ   special economic zone
VOA   Voice of America

Burying Mao

The Age of Deng Xiaoping

[We] announce with deepest grief . . . Comrade Mao Zedong,

our esteemed and beloved great leader . . .

passed away at 00:10 hours.

—Xinhua, September 9, 1976

SIC TRANSIT Mao Zedong: peasant, revolutionary, philosopher-king. Mao's life had been deeply paradoxical and self-contradictory. His millennarian vision of a world without egotism and greed, without mandarins, landlords, or bureaucrats, had inspired legendary feats of revolutionary heroism and endurance. Yet the very radicalism of Mao's vision, and the draconian means used to implement it, had visited great suffering upon the Chinese people.

Mao's death, following a long struggle with Lou Gehrig's disease compounded by assorted respiratory, heart, and kidney ailments, came a few short months after the passing of Premier Zhou Enlai, who succumbed to bladder cancer in January 1976.[1] The demise of China's two top leaders left the country rudderless and adrift. Widespread dismay over the cruelty and chaos of the Cultural Revolution had spawned a deep "crisis of faith" among the people. Reacting to two decades of economic stagnation and political repression, ordinary Chinese openly questioned the benefits conferred on them by a rigid, aloof, and seemingly insensitive Communist Party.

Superimposed upon this societywide crisis of faith were a series of intense political rivalries and personal antagonisms that split the Chinese Communist leadership into a number of contending factions. At one level, these intraparty cleavages centered on such issues as the extent of Mao Zedong's personal responsibility for the Cultural Revolution and the overall quality of Mao's leadership during his declining years. At another level they concerned more primitive, rudimentary questions of political power: Who would win the struggle to succeed Mao? Who would lose? And equally important, what would the winners do with—or *to*—the losers?

The post-Mao succession crisis lasted more than three years. At first a group of loyalists, led by Acting Premier Hua Guofeng, laid claim to the Chairman's mantle on the basis of Mao's purported deathbed bequest: "With you in charge, I'm at ease." This put them on a collision course with a small group of left-wing Cultural Revolution ideologues led by Mao's widow, Jiang Qing, who sought to claim Mao's legacy as her own. With a struggle for power imminent, the loyalists struck first. Less than a month after Mao's death, they preemptively arrested Mme. Mao and her three top lieutenants—pejoratively known as the Gang of Four—on charges of conspiring to usurp party and state power.

Notwithstanding their triumph over Jiang Qing and her radical clique, the loyalists had a sizable skeleton in their own closet, one that eventually precluded them from consolidating power. A few months before Mao's death, in April 1976, Hua Guofeng and his lieutenants had collaborated with the Gang of Four to effect the removal of a rival claimant to power, former CCP general secretary Deng Xiaoping, whom they falsely accused of stirring up a "counterrevolutionary incident" at Tiananmen Square. Refusing to take his removal lying down, however, the tenacious Deng rallied supporters on the party Central Committee (CC) to fight for his exoneration, setting the stage for a showdown with the loyalists.

Toward the end of 1978 Deng, relying on an extensive network of personal ties to an influential group of senior party and military leaders, gained the upper hand. The verdict on the Tiananmen incident was reversed, and Deng was formally cleared of all charges of wrongdoing. Over the next two years, Hua Guofeng and his supporters, now cynically referred to as the "whatever faction" because of their unswerving public devotion to whatever Mao said or did, were gradually eased out of power.

With Deng at the helm and Chen Yun as principal economic strategist, China's new leaders, sensing the great magnitude and urgency of the crisis confronting the country, began to think the unthinkable. Many had only recently been rehabilitated after suffering prolonged personal humiliation and abuse during the Cultural Revolution. Constituting a strong force for institutional change, leading members of this reform group began forthrightly to jettison key components of Mao Zedong's legacy. They repudiated Mao's Cultural Revolution, renounced most of his economic theories, and reinstated virtually all of his purged opponents. In place of Mao's insistence on austerity, egalitarianism, self-sacrifice, self-reliance, and perpetual class struggle, they advocated incentive-driven production responsibility systems, decentralized state administration, expanded use of market mechanisms (euphemistically known as "economic methods"), and sharply increased international economic and technological involvement.

Although members of the reform coalition could agree among themselves, in principle, on the need for economic modernization and "opening up" to the outside world, they lacked a coherent plan or blueprint for reform. Within the coalition there were frequent debates over how much (or how little) tampering with the basic structures of socialism was needed to raise economic efficiency and promote political/administrative rationality. In these debates, middle-aged intellectuals and technocrats (including China's new premier, Zhao Ziyang, and the new Communist Party chief, Hu Yaobang) tended to support relatively bold, aggressive structural reforms, while members of the older generation of Marxist revolutionaries (including such notables as Peng Zhen, Chen Yun, Wang Zhen, Bo Yibo, and Hu Qiaomu) generally proved more cautious and conservative. Perhaps most important, members of the reform coalition differed among themselves over just how much "bourgeois liberalization"—if any—could be tolerated in a country that continued to call itself Marxist-Leninist.

Sometimes disagreement took the form of esoteric academic debates over such issues as the nature and special characteristics of China's "socialist spiritual civilization," or the relevance to China of such foreign concepts as "universal humanism" and "alienation." More often than not, however, academic debates served to mask highly contentious policy disputes, such as those over the tolerable limits of free-market activity and private accumulation of wealth, the severity of the problem of "spiritual pollution" posed by the influx of Western ideas and influences, and the proper boundaries of free expression for artists, writers, and other creative intellectuals whose contributions were deemed essential to the success of China's modernization drive.

CYCLES OF REFORM: THE "FANG/SHOU" FLUX

Just beneath the surface of these debates lay the potent issue of stability versus chaos. Throughout the initial decade of post-Mao reform, China's new leaders repeatedly tempered their desire for modernization and change with a deep concern for maintaining political order and discipline. Wanting the benefits of modernity without the destabilizing effects of spontaneous, uncontrolled social mobilization, they tended to follow each new round of liberalizing reform with an attempt to retain—or regain —control. Letting go (*fang*) with one hand, they instinctively tightened up (*shou*) with the other. Over time, the conflicting pressures and imperatives associated with fang and shou produced an oscillating pattern of policy initiative and response, as phases of reform and relaxation alternated with phases of relative restriction and retrenchment. The fluid ebb and flow of this recursive "fang/shou cycle" lent the process of political and economic reform a discontinuous, pulsating quality.[2]

Chinese economists were among the first to recognize the existence of a recurrent pattern of reform and retrenchment. By 1982 they had identified four stages in a sequential reform cycle: "On many occasions . . . we have witnessed the spectacle of 'flexibility immediately followed by disorder, disorder immediately followed by control, control immediately followed by rigidity, and rigidity again followed by flexibility,' in a 'flexibility-disorder-control-rigidity' cycle."[3]

Elaborating upon the concept of cyclical flux, early in 1987 Chinese Communist theoretician Deng Liqun posited the existence of a biennial relaxation/contraction cycle spanning the ten years 1978–1987. According to this model, proactive pressures for "bourgeois liberalization" were strongest in even-numbered years, while conservative counterpressures peaked in odd-numbered years. The basic contours of Deng Liqun's model are presented in the accompanying table.

Deng Liqun's Ten-Year Cyclical Model

Year/Phase	Key Events
First Round: 1978–79	
1978 (fang)	"Criterion of truth" debate
	Democracy Wall
	Third Plenum of Eleventh Central Committee
1979 (shou)	Wei Jingsheng arrested
	Four cardinal principles
Second Round: 1980–81	
1980 (fang)	Gengshen reforms
	Local elections
1981 (shou)	Economic readjustment
	Bai Hua criticized
Third Round: 1982–83	
1982 (fang)	Constitution revised
	"Humanism" and "alienation" debated
1983 (shou)	Anti-spiritual pollution campaign
Fourth Round: 1984–85	
1984 (fang)	Urban reform and "open cities"
	Cultural and artistic freedom
1985 (shou)	Economic retrenchment
	Critique of bourgeois liberalization
Fifth Round: 1986–87	
1986: (fang)	Revival of Gengshen reforms
	Student demonstrations
1987: (shou)	Hu Yaobang dismissed
	Campaign against "bourgeois liberalization"
Sixth Round: 1988–89[a]	
1988: (fang)	Neo-authoritarianism (late 1987)
	Administrative reform
1989: (shou)	Economic reform frozen (late 1988)
	Tiananmen crackdown

Source: Ruan Ming, *Deng Xiaoping diguo*, 168–71.
[a] The sixth round represents the author's extrapolation from Deng Liqun's 1987 model.

Insofar as observed phase changes in the fang/shou cycle were neither so neatly symmetrical nor so precisely biennial in periodicity as suggested by Deng Liqun's model, the model was clearly oversimplified. Moreover, the model demonstrably lacked a dynamic engine, or motive force, driving its cyclical fluctuations. Addressing these deficiencies, Susan Shirk elaborated a more sophisticated cyclical schema.[4] According to Shirk's conception, with the introduction of partial economic reforms in the late 1970s China's economy began to lurch erratically between alternating phases of expansion and contraction. Backlash from these "boom and bust" economic oscillations served to amplify preexisting political and ideological cleavages among rival elite factions. The intensification of factional conflict, in turn, necessitated periodic personal intervention by "paramount leader" Deng Xiaoping, who, to mollify conservative party elders and relieve the buildup of antireform pressures, was compelled to follow each new surge of economic reform with an ideological swing back in the direction of Leninist orthodoxy.[5] In Shirk's schema, the engine driving the entire fang/shou flux was the jerky rhythm of heating and cooling displayed by China's semireformed, semiplanned economy.

Charting the course of China's first decade of post-Mao economic reform, Shirk found (not unlike Deng Liqun) that expansion (fang) predominated in 1979–80, 1984, 1986–87, and 1988, while contraction (shou) predominated in 1981, 1985–86, 1987, and 1988–89. As anticipated, she also found that these economic fluctuations closely paralleled policy shifts in other areas, such as ideological relaxation/control and administrative decentralization/recentralization. For this reason, she described the pattern of alternating political and economic cycles as essentially "synchronous" in nature.[6]

While accepting the underlying logic of Shirk's model, my own understanding of the nature and dynamics of reform cycles differs somewhat. For one thing, the observed pattern of cyclical flux in post-Mao China has sometimes been quite irregular and asynchronous, involving partially crosscutting (or noncongruent) forces and phase changes. Political, economic, and ideological currents have not always neatly coincided or covaried. At times, their effects have been highly turbulent and cross-pressured, rather than mutually reinforcing. For example, the anti–bourgeois-liberal ideological backlash of spring 1987, which followed close on the heels of prodemocracy demonstrations on Chinese college campuses, was not accompanied by any significant contraction of economic reforms. As a result, conflicting signals of fang and shou were simultaneously generated in different policy arenas, lending an element of incoherence to the reform cycle—akin to a riptide effect in fluid dynamics.[7]

In addition to turbulence produced by noncongruent or asynchronous policy fluxes, a second source of irregularity in the fang/shou cycles were the unforeseen exogenous forces and events—that is, occurrences unrelated to the internal dynamics of the reform process itself—that periodically impinged upon that process, altering its course and its contours. Examples of such external influences include the Polish Solidarnosç crisis of 1980–81 (which triggered a strong antireform backlash among CCP conservatives); the sudden death of liberal reform leader Hu Yaobang in April 1989 (which touched off a firestorm of student protest, culminating in the Tiananmen crisis); and the 1991 collapse of communism in the Soviet Union (which prompted Chinese hard-liners to attempt sharply to curtail China's economic reforms and "open policy"). While ostensibly idiosyncratic and exogenous in origin, each of these events exerted a powerful impact upon the dynamics of reform in China, exacerbating existing strains and tensions and visibly affecting the rhythms and oscillations of the fang/shou cycle.

Periodic crises of leadership succession constituted a third source of significant variability. Twice since the mid-1970s China experienced prolonged, bitterly divisive succession struggles, as first Mao Zedong and then Deng Xiaoping prepared to "meet Marx." On both occasions, the intensification of factional infighting significantly affected the momentum and trajectory of reform. In the first instance, Mao's approaching death in 1976 triggered a powerful popular backlash against the Cultural Revolution, which translated into broad opposition to the Gang of Four and broad support for the return to power of Deng Xiaoping and his "rehabilitated cadres faction." Utilizing this anti–Cultural Revolution backlash to maximum advantage, Deng ultimately succeeded both in undermining the legitimacy of Hua Guofeng's "whatever faction" and in generating strong political momentum behind his own reform program.[8]

In roughly equal (but opposite) Newtonian fashion, as Deng Xiaoping neared the end of his political career in the late 1980s and early 1990s, competition among rival Communist Party factions intensified once again. This time, however, it was the reformers who were on the defensive, as a strong conservative backlash from the 1989 Tiananmen upheaval, coupled with Deng Xiaoping's visibly declining physical vitality, served to drain the reform movement of much of its previous energy and inspiration. For a considerable period of time, and to a rather harrowing degree, the future of reform after June 1989 seemed to hang on a thread as delicate as the state of Deng's health, and on the related question of who would die first, Deng (who turned eighty-five in August 1989) or his more conservative octogenarian copatriarch, Chen Yun. In the event, Deng's marginally superior physical stamina—demonstrated in his dramatic one-man proreform pilgrimage to the special economic zones (SEZs) of South China in January 1992—helped rescue China's market reforms at their point of maximum peril following the shocking political collapse of the USSR.

A fourth, closely related source of cyclical variation was intergenerational leadership change. During the first decade and a half of reform, many of the aging first- and second-generation revolutionaries who had been most deeply involved in policy making at the outset of the post-Mao period either died or became inactive. In most cases, their places were taken by middle-aged technocrats of the "third echelon" (*disan tidui*), whose educational level was higher and whose outlook (with some notable exceptions) was distinctly more cosmopolitan and pragmatic. Over time, the rejuvenation of party leadership had the effect of reducing the strength of conservative resistance to reform. Although party old-timers periodically dug in their heels, as in the anti–spiritual pollution campaign of 1983 and the anti–bourgeois liberalization campaign of 1987, in the long run not even the Beijing massacre of June 1989 or the ensuing "red terror" could permanently forestall the rise of new leaders who favored fundamental structural change. In this respect, the eventual triumph of reform was ensured as much by actuarial laws as by the sagacity of the reformers themselves.

Reinforcing the secular impact of generational change was the gradual enculturation of China's on-again, off-again market reforms. With each new relaxation phase in the reform cycle, social mobility increased while systemic barriers to the free flow of ideas, information, money, goods, and people were lowered. Disposable income grew, as did personal consumption. Notwithstanding periodic conservative policy contractions, the long-term effect was of a progressive shift in the direction of greater societal openness, affluence, and competitiveness. After a decade and a half of sporadic, halting, halfway reforms, by the mid-1990s it thus appeared that Deng Xiaoping's "second Chinese revolution" had become more or less irreversibly entrained.[9]

THE FLUIDITY OF FACTIONAL ALIGNMENTS

A final source of significant irregularity in reform cycles were the perturbations produced by shifting factional alignments. "Factions" (*zongpai*) in Chinese politics are informal networks of interdependent personal relationships. Neither fixed in membership nor immutable in ideology and policy preference, factions wax and wane, change shape, shift focus, divide, and recombine in fluid, protean fashion. Moreover, their common group identity—often encoded in such arcane symbolic precepts as the "two whatevers" or "practice is the sole criterion for testing truth"—may mask considerable internal dissonance, divisiveness, and disarray.[10]

To give one obvious example of factional fluidity and instability, in the late 1970s the "rehabilitated cadres faction" led by Deng Xiaoping and Chen Yun was composed of a number of individuals whose most vital common characteristic was their intense opposition to the Cultural Revolution, its leaders, and its legacy. With members as diverse in orientation as Zhao Ziyang and Wan Li (economic pragmatists), Hu Yaobang (political liberal), Chen Yun and Bo Yibo (economic neotraditionalists), Hu Qiaomu and Deng Liqun (ideological conservatives), and Wang Zhen (political reactionary), the coalition displayed little internal political or ideological coherence. What held the coalition together were (a) its members' common experience of having been humiliated during the Cultural Revolution and (b) the existence of a powerful and ambitious rival faction—Hua Guofeng's "whateverists."

In the struggle between these two contending camps, a handful of lesser factions—including a "survivors faction" (made up of senior party and military leaders who had avoided purgation during the Cultural Revolution) and a "petroleum clique" (comprised of leading advocates of centralized planning, deficit spending, and an economic strategy of energy-based, export-led development)—played important roles as power balancers and tactical allies of the two major factions. The more evenly matched the principal contenders, the more important the role played by these minor factions. Indeed, throughout much of 1978 and 1979, the "survivors," led by Ye Jianying and Li Xiannian, played a pivotal power-balancing role as swing voters in a Politburo divided more or less evenly between supporters of Deng Xiaoping and Hua Guofeng.[11]

By 1979 virtually all high-level purge victims of the Cultural Revolution had been cleared of charges and restored to positions of power and influence. As the balance thus shifted in favor of Deng's rehabilitated cadres (now renamed the "practice faction" because of their rejection of the rigid dogmas of the Left) and away from Hua's "whateverists," the "survivors" lost some of their political clout. By the same token, however, once Hua Guofeng was successfully shouldered aside, Deng's broad proreform coalition—which included leaders whose views on specific policy issues were quite diverse and wide-ranging—also became susceptible to centrifugal stress. Indeed, the fragmentation of Deng's victorious coalition into a number of divergent opinion groups and subfactions was a major feature of the Chinese political landscape in the 1980s.[12]

Not only was Deng's reform coalition extremely diverse in composition and orientation, its members could not be neatly arrayed along a single, constant left-to-right ideological continuum. In the economic realm, for example, patriarch Chen Yun and Deng protégé Premier Zhao Ziyang, who initially shared a common concern for maintaining central administrative control over the reform process, began to diverge appreciably in 1983–84. Where Chen remained cautious and risk-aversive, Zhao became increasingly bold and experimental. At the same time, however, Chen—a moderate conservative on economic matters—was considerably more permissive *politically* than many of his peers within the reform coalition, including Zhao's own mentor, Deng Xiaoping. On the key issue of how to deal with student demonstrators and political dissidents, for example, Chen repeatedly displayed greater tolerance and forbearance than Deng. In 1979 Chen openly questioned Deng's decision to incarcerate human rights activist Wei Jingsheng; and in the aftermath of the 1989 Beijing massacre, Chen pointed the finger of blame squarely at Deng for issuing the controversial order to use deadly force in the army's assault on Tiananmen Square. Under these circumstances, to label Chen Yun a "hardliner" based solely on his relatively conservative economic views, as some have done without qualification or caveat, is clearly misleading.[13]

It is evident from the above that conventional ideological labels such as "liberal," "hard-liner," "moderate," "pragmatist," "radical," and "conservative," often prove highly problematical in the Chinese political context; to complicate matters further, the factions, opinion clusters, and individual leaders upon whom such labels are affixed may alter their personal views and partisan affiliations over time. For example, in the early to mid-1980s, at around the same time that Chen Yun's economic views began to diverge from those of Zhao Ziyang and Deng Xiaoping, Chen began to attract some of Deng's disillusioned followers to his own camp. A prominent example was

Deng Liqun. In the late 1970s Deng Liqun (no relation to Deng Xiaoping), a party theoretician who had once been Liu Shaoqi's political secretary, became embroiled in an intense rivalry with Hu Yaobang for the political favor of Deng Xiaoping. When the elder Deng selected Hu Yaobang to succeed Hua Guofeng as head of the party apparatus, Deng Liqun reportedly felt bitterly disappointed; he subsequently expressed his displeasure by shifting his primary allegiance from Deng Xiaoping to Chen Yun. Thenceforward, Deng Liqun proved to be a constant thorn in the side of Hu Yaobang and his mentor, Deng Xiaoping, sparing no effort to criticize and humiliate the former while (more subtly) sniping at the programs and policies of the latter. Thereafter, too, Deng Xiaoping and Chen Yun began to go their separate ways until, by the time of the 1989 Tiananmen crisis, they had become, in effect, acting heads of rival gerontocratic factions.

A similar pattern of shifting personal loyalties and political alignments characterized the complex relationship between Deng's two principal reformist protégés, Hu Yaobang and Zhao Ziyang. Although both men belonged to the liberal wing of Deng's "practice faction," they frequently failed to see eye to eye. In the early and mid-1980s, Hu was clearly the more free-spirited and populistic of the two, being more inclined to take political risks in pursuit of fundamental structural reform; Zhao, on the other hand, tended, at least initially, to hew more closely to the established conventions of reform socialism. Where Zhao, for example, generally backed Chen Yun's strategy of cautious, centrally controlled economic reform (at least until 1984), Hu showed a greater willingness radically to empower local authorities and enterprise managers, allowing them to assume substantial operational autonomy—generally at the expense of central planners. Hu also displayed greater capacity than Zhao for tolerating periodic outbursts of free, unfettered expression on the part of Chinese journalists, writers, and artists.

To a considerable extent, the differences between Hu Yaobang and Zhao Ziyang could be attributed to their growing competition as rival claimants to inherit Deng Xiaoping's leadership mantle. Through the early and mid-1980s, Deng's two protégés jockeyed for political position, sometimes directly opposing each other (as in the 1982–83 debate over how to apportion enterprise revenues), while at other times collaborating to repel conservative challenges to reform policies (as in the 1983 anti–spiritual pollution campaign). At one point, Zhao openly complained that he could no longer work with Hu.[14]

When Hu Yaobang was removed from office at the insistence of angry party elders in January 1987 (for the alleged offense of being soft on "bourgeois liberalism" and for having the audacity to suggest that the offspring of certain senior party conservatives should be criminally indicted on charges of corruption), Zhao Ziyang carefully distanced himself from the general secretary, speaking out in support of Hu's removal. Zhao's discretion did not go unrewarded by party elders: shortly after Hu's forced resignation, Zhao was named to succeed him as general secretary. In light of the past rivalry between the two, there is no small irony in the fact that two years later, at the height of the 1989 Tiananmen crisis, Zhao Ziyang himself fell victim to the wrath of the very same elderly conservatives who had scuttled his predecessor—and for some of the very same reasons, including his excessive indulgence of bourgeois liberalism and his insistence on fully exposing corruption on the part of the offspring of senior party leaders.[15]

THE IMPORTANCE OF LANGUAGE

With the dynamics of factional composition, coherence, and conflict subject to such frequently shifting vicissitudes and idiosyncracies, the task of identifying, tracking, and labeling factions in Chinese politics is extremely challenging.[16] In such a situation, one key to unraveling the complexities of factional alignment lies in the analysis of terminological shifts and distinctions that periodically creep into the language of political discourse in China. As Lucian Pye has convincingly demonstrated, in a society where real power is almost always masked, where personal influence is seldom exercised through formally institutionalized channels and chains of command, and where rival leaders vie for factional advantage behind closed doors, the external signs of factional conflict and cleavage are often quite subtle and may be difficult for outsiders (and sometimes even for insiders) to detect and decipher.[17] Typically, emergent Chinese factional disputes first appear publicly in the form of subtle rhetorical distinctions. While often intended to mask the underlying sources of conflict, shifts in the language or terminology of political discourse convey vital information to Chinese political actors, for example, portending changes in the prevailing party line, signaling shifts in the alignment of factional forces, or providing other important behavioral cues to members of a particular factional constituency.

Ever sensitive to the potential ramifications of even the most innocuous-sounding terminological distinctions, Chinese leaders and followers alike place great emphasis on defining and interpreting the "correct" political line—and rejecting (at times mercilessly attacking) all other lines, which are by definition "incorrect" or even heretical. When even seemingly minor changes in phraseology can signal important shifts in factional fortunes, words matter a great deal. During the Cultural Revolution, the widely noted Maoist penchant for stereotyped linguistic hyperbole (the CCP was "great, glorious, and correct"; Liu Shaoqi was a "renegade, traitor, and scab") led some observers to view the party's compulsive attention to line-orientation as some sort of ultra-Leftist aberration or idiosyncracy. In fact, however, Mao Zedong's "pragmatic" successors have continued to pay extraordinarily close attention to minute terminological distinctions in matters pertaining to party line.[18]

During Hua Guofeng's brief interregnum in the late 1970s, an intense debate raged for many months over the arcane question of whether the Communist Party's "fine tradition and style" should be "restored" (*huifu*) or merely "upheld" (*jianchi*). When the Central Committee endorsed the former interpretation in 1978, it was the first clear sign of Deng Xiaoping's impending triumph over Hua Guofeng. More recently, in the aftermath of the Tiananmen crackdown, a linguistic dispute simmered between Deng and China's hard-line vice-president, Wang Zhen, over how to define the essential "core" (*hexin*) of the party's new leadership. Where Deng called for a one-man leadership core in the person of newly promoted CCP General Secretary Jiang Zemin, Wang, distrustful of Jiang's centrist tendencies, sought to enlarge the definition of the core by including within it the entire "third-echelon" group of younger Politburo Standing Committee members, most notably hard-line Premier Li Peng.

Similarly, in the course of a 1979 intraparty debate between pragmatic reformers such as Hu Yaobang and more orthodox theoreticians such as Hu Qiaomu and Deng Liqun, the question arose as to whether "feudal influences" or "bourgeois influences" posed the greater danger to the party and the country. This dispute preoccupied a small army of theoreticians and propagandists for the better part of a year before Deng Xiaoping—apparently acting as much out of sheer exasperation as out of firm conviction—rendered the point moot by declaring that there could be "no single answer" that was valid at all times and under all circumstances. With increasing difficulty, Deng hewed to this ambivalent position throughout the 1980s and well into the 1990s, tacking first one way and then the other in the face of brisk, frequently shifting political and ideological winds.

Closely related to the ongoing dispute over the relative dangers of Leftism and Rightism was the nagging question of what kind of terminology to employ in describing the Tiananmen crisis. For almost three years after the June 1989 crackdown, a debate raged between hard-liners and moderates over whether the crisis had been a full-scale "counterrevolutionary rebellion" (*fan'geming baoluan*), a more limited "turmoil" (*dongluan*), or merely an "event" (*shijian*). Upon the outcome of this rhetorical debate hinged such weighty matters as the future rehabilitation of the disgraced General Secretary Zhao Ziyang, the political future of Premier Li Peng, and the fate of dozens (perhaps hundreds) of imprisoned political dissidents. In a country like China, where the rigid discipline of democratic centralism has been superimposed upon strong Confucian traditions of patriarchal authority and group conformity, party members and cadres are constantly—indeed compulsively—constrained to look to higher levels for cues as to what is necessary, appropriate, or even permissible language. Under such circumstances, even seemingly minor shifts in prevailing terminology may prove extremely important.[19]

As a final example of the importance of terminology, consider the controversy that raged in the early 1990s between Deng Xiaoping and Chen Yun (and their respective supporters) over the question of how to define the central task of the CCP in the age of reform. According to Deng's "theory of one center," economic construction was the country's categorical imperative, the ultimate yardstick against which all programs and policies had to be measured. For Chen Yun, on the other hand, economic construction, while extremely important, had to be pursued in tandem with "another center," namely, *ideological* construction, which involved giving coequal status to the "four cardinal principles"—the CCP's benchmark political commandments, first articulated in 1979, mandating unwavering allegiance to socialism, the people's democratic dictatorship, Communist Party leadership, and Marxism–Leninism–Mao Zedong Thought. For almost two years, the Deng and Chen camps traded verbal salvoes on the linguistic battlefield, employing such devices as photo-opportunity sessions, inspection visits, and media commentaries to score points. The issue was not resolved until the winter of 1992, when Deng trumped his rival by undertaking a spectacular four-week southern tour, visiting China's free-wheeling SEZs to drum up support for his program of accelerated economic reform and "opening up." Thereafter, a bandwagon effect quickly took shape, as a number of erstwhile CCP conservatives and fence-straddlers, including Li Peng, fell into line and declared their undying allegiance to Deng's "theory of one center," thus shifting the balance of power decisively in Deng's favor.[20]

THE HAZARDS OF LABELING

As indicated earlier, due to the highly complex, fluid interplay of linguistic, factional, and cyclical phenomena it is extremely hazardous to attempt to apply constant, unchanging ideological labels to individuals and groups in Chinese politics. While there have always existed left-wing, centrist, and right-wing tendencies within the CCP, these terms have varied widely in their meanings and referents, depending on time, place, and policy context. To give one salient example of such variability, Deng Xiaoping's twin proposals to introduce managerial responsibility systems and expand acquisition of foreign technology were widely denounced as "Rightist" in 1976; two years later they were officially incorporated into the government's ten-year plan for economic development.

Compounding the difficulty posed by changing policy contexts is the fact that individual party leaders have been known to shift from one position to another along the ideological/economic spectrum. For example, senior party theorist Hu Qiaomu was a vocal advocate of economic modernization in the late 1970s; by 1980, however, his endorsement of structural reform was tempered by a mounting concern for the dangers posed by a rising tide of political dissent and instability. Over the next decade, Hu acquired a reputation as one of China's leading ideological conservatives. Just before his death in 1992, however, Hu Qiaomu recanted his hard-line views and once again embraced the goal of fundamental economic reform.

A final source of confusion surrounding the use of ideological labels is the fact that in China the policy orientations indicated by the terms "Left" and "Right" are generally the reverse of their conventional Western referents. Since the advent of post-Mao reforms in 1978–79, Leftism in China has generally stood for *conservatism*, that is, devotion to traditional CCP institutions and values, while Rightism has connoted *liberalism*, meaning support for market reforms and/or democratic institutions and values.[21]

Since individual leaders can and do alter their opinions and allegiances over time, and since they sometimes hold noncongruent (and even mutually inconsistent) views on different issues at the same time, it is obviously hazardous to attempt to divide Chinese political elites into clear, constant categories such as pragmatists versus hard-liners, liberals versus conservatives, or moderates versus Leftists (or some similar cross-pairing of dichotomous labels). The relative fluidity of the ideological spectrum, in turn, further complicates the understanding of the oscillations of the reform process, which, as I have noted, are most commonly described as alternating phases of "liberal" relaxation and "conservative" contraction.

The difficulty of categorization is compounded still further by the problem of China's "floating fulcrum." Since 1979 Deng Xiaoping has sought to occupy the strategic middle ground between contending "liberal" and "conservative" wings of his reform coalition. Shifting his stance periodically in order to retain (or restore) overall balance within the discontinuous policy flux of the fang/shou cycle, Deng by his actions has continually redefined the operational center of the policy spectrum; that is, at any given time, the terms "Left," "Right," "liberal," and "conservative" (among others) derive their meaning in relation to Deng's floating center.

Having said all this, it can be argued that conventional ideological labels, though far from precise or constant, may, if used with a modicum of contextual discretion and care, have considerable utility as indicators of the relative location of individual leaders in ideological/political/economic space, with respect to particular issues at particular points in time. Provided that the policy context is well established and understood, it thus makes good sense to describe *some* Chinese leaders, on *some* issues, *some* of the time (indeed, on many issues much of the time), as reformers or conservatives or Leftists or liberals or neo-Maoists or moderates or hard-liners. Recognizing the risk of oversimplification inherent in such stereotypy, I have freely employed these (and a few other) labeling conventions whenever it appeared that doing so added clarity to the descriptions and analyses of particular events, individuals, or processes. Where labels (or individuals) changed their identities or alignments over time, I have endeavored to make clear the nature of such alterations.

DENG'S ELUSIVE QUEST

Throughout the entire post-Mao epoch, from 1976 to 1993, the dynamics of faction formation, competition, and recombination interacted with the dynamics of fang/shou fluctuations and the vicissitudes of leadership succession to produce an extremely complex pattern of Chinese political development.

Standing at the epicenter of this richly marbled developmental mosaic, personifying its manifold political convolutions and complexities, was the diminutive figure of China's "paramount leader," Deng Xiaoping. Delicately maneuvering his way through successive economic cycles, ideological struggles, terminological disputes, and political wind shifts, Deng came to encompass and embody virtually all the complex antinomies of fang and shou. Seeking to contain and manage the deep personal rivalries and political antagonisms that periodically threatened to shatter the delicate unity and stability of his reform coalition, Deng became, of necessity, a consummate improviser and balancer.

Lacking a coherent, integrated blueprint or theory of reform, Deng initially sought to fashion a hybrid, syncretic model of "socialism with Chinese characteristics." He apparently believed that China could develop robust, competitive markets under noncompetitive Leninist institutional auspices; he believed that a vigorous, creative intelligentsia could thrive under the four cardinal principles; he believed that special economic zones could be infused with the values of "socialist spiritual civilization." Yet as the decade of the 1980s wore on, and these various goals began to collide rather than converge, Deng found it increasingly difficult to steer a balanced course. He—and China—began to swerve, first one way and then the other, as he searched, in vain, for a coherent, viable center.[22]

For the better part of a decade, Deng tried to overhaul China's inefficient command economy, create a rationalized structure of governance, and effect the orderly empowerment of a younger generation of leaders. Four times—in 1980, 1984, 1986, and 1988—he either personally initiated or endorsed major efforts to overhaul China's overcentralized, ossified leadership system; in all four instances intense factional strife, combined with mounting economic difficulties, compelled him to abort the project. Twice, in 1982 and again in 1987, Deng tried to leave the political stage, designating pragmatic, reform-oriented heirs apparent to succeed him; both times his choices were eventually rejected, as first Hu Yaobang and then Zhao Ziyang ran afoul of party hardliners. Three times—in 1979, 1984, and 1988—Deng backed the introduction of wide-ranging structural and/or price reforms in China's urban economy; all three times a rising tide of inflation, corruption, and resultant social unrest forced him to back down.

With the middle path of orderly, institutionalized reform becoming ever more elusive, Deng was repeatedly forced to rely upon his personal prestige and authority to preserve a semblance of political stability and unity. Unable to create a viable structure of authority that reconciled fang and shou, and unable to locate a successor acceptable to all major political groups and factions, he was unable to retire from active duty. Each time he retreated to the "second line" of party leadership, leaving the initiative for policy making in the hands of younger cadres, veteran conservatives, finding new cause for complaint, pressured Deng to return to the front line. As a result, Deng was unable to transfer power successfully to the third echelon. Over time, his personal authority thus became more, rather than less, critical to the coherence—perhaps the very survival—of the regime. Yet the more he intervened in the decision process ex cathedra, the more elusive became his quest for a routinized, rationalized political order. Therein, perhaps, lay the supreme paradox of Deng's political stewardship; for in his quest to lead China out of the "feudal autocracy" of the Maoist era toward a more highly developed, institutionalized political-legal system, Deng increasingly resorted to highly personalized instruments of control—instruments that were in many ways the very antithesis of the system he sought to create.[23] By the early 1990s, a little more than a decade after he first criticized Mao Zedong's cult of personality as a "feudal remnant," Deng had begun to cloak himself in a personality cult all his own. *Plus ça change, plus c'est la même chose.*

Lacking a viable blueprint for systematic institutional reform, Deng was compelled to "cross the river by groping for stepping stones" (*mozhe shitou guohe*). Improvising as he went along, he introduced a series of ad hoc, piecemeal measures designed to facilitate smooth, orderly change. In the early 1980s, when elderly party cadres proved reluctant to retire and turn power over to younger leaders, Deng gave the old-timers their very own Central Advisory Committee (CAC) to help ease them into inactivity. Yet many still refused to leave the stage voluntarily; and Deng could not (or would not) force them off. Consequently, the temporary became permanent: the CAC became a virtual shadow cabinet, parallel and powerful. Still active until the early 1990s, this "sitting committee," as it was sometimes derisively known, played a key role in fashioning the June 1989 military crackdown at Tiananmen Square.[24]

Over time, some of Deng's stepping stones became millstones. As part of his campaign to modernize and professionalize China's outmoded military establishment, Deng tried to move the People's Liberation Army (PLA) out from under the command of a few dozen superannuated Long March veterans by placing the army directly under the jurisdiction of the central government. But since outright abolition of the party's powerful Central Military Affairs Commission (MAC) would have alienated China's conservative old guard, Deng improvised once again. He created a governmental MAC alongside the existing party MAC, allowing the latter to remain wholly intact. He then proceeded to staff the new body with virtually the same elderly veterans who controlled the old one, thereby ensuring both the redundancy and the irrelevancy of the new governmental commission. Although Deng repeatedly expressed a personal wish to retire from his chairmanship of the two MACs, his inability to locate a successor acceptable to elderly conservatives in the PLA high command prevented him from doing so. Thus, when PLA troops were called in to Beijing to put down student protests in May–June 1989, it was the old-timers on the party MAC—led by Deng himself—who gave the order.

When China's urban consumers balked at the prospect of reform-induced commodity price hikes in the late 1980s, Deng once again offered an expedient compromise: he slowed down the decontrol of prices and granted city dwellers a series of temporary food and housing subsidies to help ease the painful transition to market-regulated pricing. Shortly thereafter, a combination of consumer panic and conservative criticism forced the government to halt price decontrol altogether; as a result, another temporary expedient was frozen in place, and China was forced to limp along for two more years with a semireformed, two-tiered price structure that retained many of the worst irrationalities of the old system while perpetuating the costly transitional subsidies of the new one. More than one observer likened the government's indecisive, start-and-stop approach toward price reform to an attempt to leap over the Grand Canyon in a series of small jumps.

In each of the above examples, an ad hoc policy improvisation, originally intended to serve as a temporary bridge, or stepping stone, en route to more fundamental structural reform was frozen in place due to conservative backlash, becoming in the process an impediment to further systemic change. Cumulatively, the effect was to exacerbate existing structural tensions and stresses, rather than to resolve them.[25]

Notwithstanding the frequent policy improvisations and increasing turbulence of the 1980s, for a brief period in 1987–88 it appeared that a viable developmental path might, after all, be found. Under Zhao Ziyang's leadership, a new formula for China's political development was devised, one that was neither totalitarian nor libertarian, but which contained the first ideological and institutional sprouts of emergent pluralism. This was the "new authoritarianism" (*xin quanweizhuyi*), a hybrid system that sought to combine the economic openness and market vitality of fang with the centralized political authority of shou. The proposed system was characterized by continued one-party tutelage and a consultative structure of limited political participation by non-Communist groups, on the one hand, and a state-induced shift toward market regulation of the economy and the recognition of diverse, pluralistic societal interests and aspirations, on the other.[26]

Unhappily for China, the new formula was never adequately tested. Mounting urban anxiety over surging inflation, made worse by rumors of impending price decontrol and rendered politically volatile by deepening public resentment over flagrant official profiteering, triggered a wave of consumer panic in the summer of 1988. Communist Party conservatives, afraid of incipient political instability, reacted instinctively by halting price deregulation, freezing structural reform, and attempting—with only limited success—to reassert central control over local economic activity.

THE TIANANMEN CRISIS

By the spring of 1989, reform-related stresses had reached critical levels. With economy and society seemingly stalled midway between plan and market, between bureaucrats and entrepreneurs, between shou and fang, China continued to suffer from some of the worst distortions of the old system without enjoying the full fruits of the new. It was truly a "crisis of incomplete reform."[27] Following the unexpected death of Hu Yaobang in mid-April 1989, the political center began to crumble, as a student-led, inflation-bred, corruption-fed protest movement in Beijing brought the Chinese capital to the very brink of governmental paralysis. Faced with a mounting urban revolt against a government whose authority was being openly defied—even ridiculed—by its own citizens, in early June a group of elderly, semiretired party conservatives, supported now by a clearly exasperated Deng Xiaoping, reentered the political arena with a vengeance and played their trump card, the PLA.

The bloody crackdown and repression that followed put an end, temporarily, to the developmental dynamism of the 1980s. With the massacre of several hundred—perhaps more than a thousand—civilians in the streets of Beijing in early June, the fang/shou cycle ceased oscillating. Under the cumulative stresses engendered by a decade of reform-induced sociopolitical mobilization, Deng Xiaoping's carefully crafted coalition came unglued. The center dissolved. Zhao Ziyang was dismissed and placed under house arrest for aiding and abetting a "counterrevolutionary rebellion"; a number of his more liberal supporters were sacked, arrested, or driven into exile; and a new wave of repression, recrimination, and regimentation spread throughout China. Though party leaders made energetic efforts to keep up the appearance of political unity and consensus, the extreme rigidity of government policy bespoke the existence of deep, painful political wounds that mere words of self-congratulation and self-assurance could not assuage. By the late spring of 1989, Deng appeared on the verge of losing his biggest gamble, namely, that socioeconomic reform and modernization could be achieved without fatally undermining the country's political stability.

The 1980s, which began in China amid great optimism and high hopes for reform and renewal, thus ended on a bitter, discordant note. Far from being acclaimed as China's savior, Deng Xiaoping was now widely reviled as the "Butcher of Beijing." Yet for all China's national agony and distress, the country did not disintegrate politically, as some had predicted at the time of the June massacre; nor did China go the way of Eastern Europe and the Soviet Union, where communism was overwhelmingly repudiated in the cascading "gentle revolution" that began in 1989.

With the benefit of hindsight, it is possible to identify several factors that were instrumental in preventing the post-Tiananmen collapse of China's Communist regime. These included: (1) the cumulative effects of a decade of reform-induced economic growth, which—despite numerous gaps and inequities, and despite widespread urban alarm over rising inflation and corruption—gave most Chinese, producers and consumers alike, a visible if uneven stake in the survival of the system; (2) the forceful assertion of party discipline after June 4, which gave a strong (if somewhat misleading) impression of elite solidarity at the top; (3) the loyalty and obedience to civilian command displayed by the Chinese armed forces throughout the spring crisis, which, notwithstanding severe military morale problems, reinforced the prevailing public impression of harmony between the PLA and the Communist Party; (4) the absence of such viable institutions of "civil society" as autonomous trade unions, newspapers, and professional associations capable of serving as focal points for ongoing political debate and dissent in the aftermath of the government crackdown; (5) the existence of significant schisms within the student movement, over the means as well as the ends of political action; (6) an elitist attitude on the part of student leaders, many of whom refused to engage in joint action with factory workers and other urban groups and strata until the very end, thus fragmenting the movement and limiting its overall effectiveness; and (7) a widespread fear of chaos, summed up in Deng Xiaoping's classic paraphrase of the warning issued by Mme. de Pompadour after the defeat of the French Army at the Battle of Rossback: "Après moi le déluge." Mindful of the devastating social disorder of the Cultural Revolution, and intensely fearful of any new descent into uncontrolled anarchy, after June 4 the citizens of Beijing and other major Chinese cities backed away from the brink of civil war.[28]

CHANGING THE GUARD: THE POST-DENG ORDER

As China regained its balance politically and economically in the early 1990s, Deng Xiaoping, now nearing ninety, made one final, concerted effort to overcome hard-line resistance and to forge a new, progressive ruling coalition capable of holding the country on the path of modernization and reform after his passing. In the course of his well-publicized tour of China's coastal SEZs early in 1992, Deng insisted that any party leaders or cadres who could not wholeheartedly support the policies of accelerated reform and opening up should "go to sleep"—that is, resign from office. Pressing his point, Deng abandoned his decade-long neutral stance on the question of which was worse, Leftism or Rightism, declaring that Leftist obstruction was the principal threat to the commonweal. With the fang/shou flux having lost most of its forward thrust after June 4, and with party conservatives taking advantage of the collapse of the USSR to spread fears of bourgeois liberalism, Deng felt it necessary to jump-start the reform process.

Even as Deng stepped up his support for accelerated market reforms, a series of deaths began to deplete the ranks of China's elderly hard-liners. In the twelve months surrounding the Fourteenth Party Congress, from March 1992 to March 1993, four of the most influential conservatives on the CAC— Deng Yingchao (eighty-eight), Li Xiannian (eighty-six), Hu Qiaomu (eighty), and Wang Zhen (eighty-five)—died of natural causes, as did the left-wing former director of party propaganda, Wang Renzhong (seventy-five). In addition, Deng's rivalrous copatriarch Chen Yun (eighty-eight) was reported to be in seriously failing health. This sequence of events lent added impetus to the new relaxation phase of the fang/shou cycle, helping to push the prevailing balance of political forces farther in the direction of accelerated reform. Although Deng's health had also deteriorated, to the point where he could not walk or talk without assistance, and though he was unable to take part in his customary twice-weekly bridge game for more than one hour at a sitting (down from his usual four hours), he remained, at eighty-eight years of age, relatively alert.

At the Fourteenth Party Congress in October 1992, Deng's policies appeared to carry the day: economic reform was declared to be the principal focus of party policy for the next one hundred years; the "theory of one center" was formally endorsed; the remaining conservative gerontocrats retired from active political life; the CAC was finally and formally abolished; and the way was cleared for a younger group of third-echelon technocrats to assume the reins of power.

Combining a general preference for rapid economic reform with a strong dose of political authoritarianism, the new leadership coalition, much like Deng himself, was a hybrid composed of contradictory elements. Centrist CCP General Secretary Jiang Zemin (who also assumed the presidency of the PRC following Yang Shangkun's March 1993 retirement) and hard-line Premier Li Peng—arguably the two greatest beneficiaries of the Tiananmen crackdown—now presided over a Politburo Standing Committee whose majority strongly favored accelerated market reform of the economy and renewed commitment to China's global economic engagement.

Although Premier Li remained highly unpopular in Beijing (it was he who had imposed martial law in May 1989), Deng Xiaoping's strong commitment to stability and unity and his continued deference to his elderly comrades precluded Li Peng's early removal from office, just as it also precluded Zhao Ziyang's political rehabilitation. In this connection, on the eve of the Fourteenth Party Congress Deng reportedly began to exert great pressure on his comrades to refrain from undertaking an official reassessment of the events of spring 1989. Said to be deeply concerned about preserving for posterity his reputation as principal architect of China's post-Mao reforms, Deng in the last few months of 1992 consented to the fashioning of a new personality cult, centering around the canonization of his own theories.

Deng's concern with preserving his posterity reportedly played a key role in his belated decision to part company with his long-time friend and colleague, PRC President and Deputy Military Commission Chairman Yang Shangkun. Yang had apparently boasted that he was in possession of documents proving that it was Deng, and not he, who had given the order for the PLA to open fire on civilians on the night of June 3–4, 1989. Responding to the peril implicit in Yang's claim, an obviously alarmed Deng Xiaoping moved, during and after the Fourteenth Congress, to have President Yang, his family members, and their supporters ousted from key party, state, and military leadership posts. At the same time, Deng firmly instructed his own supporters that there was to be absolutely no "reversal of verdicts" on the June 1989 massacre—posthumously or otherwise.

TIANANMEN REVISITED: DENG'S DÉJÀ VU

There was no small irony in the fact that Deng should feel compelled, three years after the Tiananmen debacle, to exert intense political pressure to prevent any reconsideration of the 1989 disturbance. Thirteen years earlier, in the aftermath of the first Tiananmen incident of April 1976, Deng had strongly lobbied his colleagues to *remove* the "counterrevolutionary" label. Now he lobbied, with equal vigor, to *retain* it.

Although Deng's role in the second Tiananmen incident was virtually the reverse of his role in the first, the two events were strikingly similar. Each began as a peaceful display of mourning for a recently deceased, highly popular Chinese leader; each became inflamed when party hard-liners, seeking to delegitimize the demonstrations, impugned the patriotic motives of participants; and each culminated in the purge of a popular, proreform leader who was blamed for inciting a "counterrevolutionary riot."

The irony is striking: having defeated Hua Guofeng and ascended to power on the strength of his own belated vindication in the first Tiananmen verdict reversal, Deng now stood to have his reputation tarnished forever through a similar reversal, à la Hua Guofeng. It was to forestall such an ironic denouement—and to avoid being hoist by his own petard—that Deng took the calculated risk of shattering his reform coalition in the winter of 1992–93, putting the brakes on the anti-Leftist campaign and moving to restrict the political authority of those party and military leaders who advocated a reassessment of June 1989. It was also for this reason that China's patriarch belatedly sanctioned the eleventh-hour campaign to canonize his theoretical contributions to socialist modernization.

Although Deng's posterity thus remained uncertain, many of the most significant reforms enacted under his stewardship seemed, finally, to have become essentially irreversible. By 1995 Beijing had relinquished so much control over the economic life of the country that no amount of periodic tough talk from central government leaders—about the need to curtail new investment, regulate financial markets, restrict the money supply, and control inflation—seemed significantly to affect economic behavior in the provinces, where *enrichissez-vouz* had clearly become the prevailing social ethic. This was particularly true along China's southeastern seaboard, where the vibrant, pulsating rhythms of the marketplace threatened totally to overwhelm the dull, droning voices of socialist caution, and where the four cardinal principles went increasingly unenforced or, even worse, unnoticed. With China's doors to the outside world open wide, with economic power devolved to the provinces and localities, and with elderly conservatives no longer able to exert a significant braking influence, Mao Zedong's warning, issued some thirty years earlier, now seemed prophetic: "If socialism doesn't occupy the battlefront, capitalism surely will." Though capitalism, Chinese style, differed in important respects from its Western prototype, the 1993 constitutional enshrinement of market principles appeared to put an end to a decade and a half of fang/shou fluctuations. For better or worse, China had opted to become the next East Asian "little dragon." For better or worse, Mao's revolution had come to an end.

PART I

The Roots of Reform, 1976–1980

Burying Mao: April 1976–July 1977

Chairman Mao himself initiated and led the Great Proletarian
Cultural Revolution, which smashed the schemes of Liu
Shaoqi, Lin Biao and Deng Xiaoping for restoration, criticized
their counterrevolutionary revisionist line, and enabled us to
seize back that portion of leading power in the party and state
they had usurped. . . . Eternal glory to the great leader and
teacher Chairman Mao Zedong!

—Hua Guofeng, memorial speech for
Mao Zedong, September 18, 1976

AMONG the "Who's Who" of Chinese Communist Party elites who gathered
at Tiananmen Square to pay last respects to Mao Zedong on September 18,
1976, were leading figures from each of China's four principal political factions. Entrusted with delivering the key eulogy at the memorial service was
the newly designated party first vice-chairman and premier of the State Council, fifty-five-year-old Hua Guofeng. The latest in a growing line of Maoist
acolytes to be named heir apparent to the party chairman, Hua was accompanied at the memorial service by leading members of his loyalist faction, including Beijing Mayor Wu De (age sixty-three), Beijing military commander
Chen Xilian (sixty-one), Mao's long-time personal bodyguard Wang Dongxing (sixty), Politburo member Ji Dengkui (fifty-eight), and Vice-Premier
Chen Yonggui (sixty-three).

Occupying positions of equal prominence among the elite mourners at
Mao's memorial service were the loyalists' principal adversaries, a group of
left-wing ideologues led by Mao's sixty-three-year-old widow, Jiang Qing,
and including Deputy Premier Zhang Chunqiao (fifty-nine), Party Vice-
Chairman Wang Hongwen (forty-one), and Politburo member Yao Wenyuan
(forty-five). Soon to be reviled collectively as the "Gang of Four," their im-
ages crudely air-brushed out of all official photos, the four Leftists had engineered, along with China's shadowy former security chief, the recently deceased Kang Sheng, and Mao's former secretary and ghost writer, Chen Boda,
the persecution and torture of countless party and government officials during
the Cultural Revolution.[1]

Hua Guofeng (*center*) conducts memorial service for Mao Zedong, September 18, 1976. Gaps in mourners' ranks at left center and right center indicate position of the Gang of Four, who were airbrushed out of all official photos after their arrest.

Rounding out the front line of mourners were members of two other important political groups. The first was a group of senior government and military leaders who had survived the purges of the Cultural Revolution (hence the sobriquet "survivors faction"). The ranks of the survivors included China's seventy-nine-year-old defense minister, Marshal Ye Jianying, Vice-Premier Li Xiannian (sixty-seven), People's Liberation Army generals Xu Shiyou (seventy-one) and Wei Guoqing (sixty-three), and Vice-Premier Wang Zhen (sixty-eight).[2] Finally, confined to the outer fringe of elite mourners at Mao's funeral, were members of the "rehabilitated cadres faction," consisting of veteran party leaders who had been restored to power after falling from grace in the Cultural Revolution. Key members of the latter group in attendance at the September 18 memorial service included former Politburo members Chen Yun (seventy-one), Tan Zhenlin (seventy-four), and Li Jingquan (sixty-seven).[3]

Conspicuous by their absence from the memorial service were a handful of high-level Cultural Revolution purge victims who remained in disrepute, including Beijing's ex-mayor Peng Zhen (seventy-four), former director of the General Office of the CCP Central Committee Yang Shangkun (sixty-nine), and senior economic strategist Bo Yibo (sixty-eight). The most prominent of China's senior no-shows, however, was seventy-two-year-old former CCP general secretary Deng Xiaoping. A practical Marxist, Deng had run afoul of the more doctrinaire Mao in the early 1960s when Deng, together with Chen Yun and Party Vice-Chairman Liu Shaoqi, among others, supported the introduction of incentive-based production responsibility systems, the expansion of household sideline occupations and rural free markets, and the enlargement of private plots to halt the agricultural crisis induced by Mao's calamitous Great Leap Forward. At the time, Deng had justified such innovations by claiming that "It doesn't matter if the cat is white or black, so long as it catches rats." To Mao, on the other hand, the color of the cat was of paramount importance, and both Deng and Liu were subsequently stripped of all power and position, while Chen was removed from the Politburo.[4]

After spending seven years in Cultural Revolution ignominy, Deng Xiaoping was rehabilitated and restored to favor at the Tenth Party Congress in 1973. On the joint recommendation of Ye Jianying and Zhou Enlai, and with the explicit approval of Chairman Mao, Deng was elevated to the concurrent posts of vice-chairman of the party's Military Affairs Commission and vice-premier of the State Council. In January 1975 he was also named PLA chief of staff and vice-chairman of the party Central Committee.

Deng's restoration was deemed necessary to help bolster China's fragile political-military stability. In the highly charged aftermath of the 1971 "Lin Biao affair,"[5] China's regional military commanders had displayed an alarming tendency to defy Beijing's political authority. Visibly concerned, Mao, Ye, and Zhou agreed that Deng Xiaoping's prestige and influence among senior army leaders could prove useful in counteracting regional PLA defiance.[6] Shortly after his rehabilitation, in December 1973, Deng was instrumental, along with Zhou Enlai, in engineering the transfers of eight of China's eleven regional military commanders to new regional assignments; in the process, the eight generals were stripped of their concurrent posts in provincial party and government organs, thereby losing control over their "independent kingdoms."

For Zhou Enlai, who was suffering from bladder cancer, an added consideration in the rehabilitation of Deng Xiaoping was the latter's long experience in economic administration. Deng had played a major role in overseeing China's post–Great Leap economic recovery. Convinced that the country once again needed fresh ideas to jump-start its stagnant economy, Zhou late in 1974 revived the concept of "four modernizations" as the centerpiece of his economic agenda.[7] At the same time, he began to groom Deng as his successor. Although Mao may have entertained reservations about Deng's economic preferences and priorities, the Chairman concurred, and in October 1974, with Zhou's cancer getting progressively worse, Mao proposed that Deng should be given the title of first deputy premier. Partially to offset Deng's rising power, Leftist Zhang Chunqiao was appointed second deputy premier.[8]

DENG XIAOPING'S "THREE POISONOUS WEEDS"

Wasting little time, Deng set about trying to dismantle some of the more radical policy innovations of the Cultural Revolution. At a series of high-level conferences convened by Deng under the State Council's auspices in 1975, he put forward three major policy initiatives, calling for broad changes in the country's development strategy and for wholesale structural reforms in scientific research and industrial management. The three documents—"On the General Program of Work for the Whole Party and the Country," "On Some Problems Concerning the Work of Science and Technology," and "Some Problems in Accelerating Industrial Development"—were drafted by a group of Deng's supporters that included his sometime bridge partner and former chairman of the Communist Youth League (CYL), Hu Yaobang (age sixty); Mao Zedong's former political secretary and confidant, Hu Qiaomu (sixty-three); and Liu Shaoqi's former chief aide, Deng Liqun (sixty).

Stressing the primacy of practical results over political correctness, economic development over ideological purity, these three initiatives, if adopted as official policy, would have had the effect of reversing the main thrust of the Cultural Revolution. For this reason, Deng Xiaoping once again ran afoul of party Leftists, who viewed him as a threat to their own political agenda, if not their political survival. Accordingly, the radicals began to refer disparagingly to Deng's three 1975 policy initiatives as the "three poisonous weeds."[9]

Throughout the latter half of 1975, Deng and his Leftist rivals engaged in a complex game of cat-and-mouse, with each side seeking to exploit the other's weaknesses. Deng's main advantage in this political chess game lay in the patronage of the ever-popular Zhou Enlai and the support of powerful members of the survivors faction; through them, Deng also enjoyed access to the considerable resources of the State Council and the PLA. In contrast, the Leftists' chief strengths lay in their control over the party's propaganda organs and the presumed patronage of Jiang Qing's illustrious, if no longer particularly enamored, husband. With the game being played for extremely high stakes, the contest heated up rapidly.

By dint of circumstance—Zhou Enlai died before Mao, in early January 1976—the Leftists drew first blood. Emboldened by the demise of Deng's chief patron and benefactor, the radicals quickly set about trying to block Deng's promotion to premier.[10] They were assisted in this effort by Chairman Mao himself, who belatedly withdrew his support from Deng after having been persuaded by several close associates, including the ailing, sinister Kang Sheng, that Deng was involved in a "Right deviationist plot" to reverse the verdicts of the Cultural Revolution. This perception was reinforced by Mao's nephew, Mao Yuanxin, a trusted ally of the Leftists who served as Mao's constant companion and confidant throughout the last year of his life, and who reportedly fed his ailing uncle a steady stream of anti–Deng Xiaoping gossip in the late autumn and early winter of 1975.[11]

Backing Wang Hongwen as their candidate for the premiership, the Leftists sought Mao's endorsement. However, the Chairman had grown increasingly impatient with the four radicals as well. On more than one previous occasion he had rebuked them for their heavy-handed political machinations. "Don't flaunt yourself in public," he wrote to Jiang Qing in November 1974; "Don't write instructions on documents. . . . You've already got too many complaints against you." On another occasion, in the spring of 1975, Mao chastised the four Leftists: "Don't function as a gang of four. Stop doing that any more. Why do you keep on doing so?"[12] According to the Beijing rumor mill, Mao's anger at his wife had been piqued, among other things, by her display of extreme vanity and self-promotion in granting a week-long interview to the American historian Roxane Witke in 1972. Recounting this incident, Harrison Salisbury writes that when certain translated passages from Witke's manuscript were read aloud to Chairman Mao, he became enraged, vowing to drive Jiang Qing out of his bed and out of the Politburo.[13]

Whatever the source of Mao's anger at his wife and her associates, he now withheld his support from them. In the words of a key participant in the January 1976 deliberations, "Chairman Mao was most emphatic and resolute. He just wouldn't brook any [member] of the Gang of Four assuming the premiership."[14] With neither side able to muster a supportive consensus in the Politburo, stalemate ensued. Mao eventually broke the deadlock by proposing the name of a darkhorse candidate—Minister of Public Security Hua Guofeng.[15]

A relative newcomer to the Beijing political scene, Hua Guofeng had survived the Cultural Revolution to become party first secretary of Mao's native Hunan Province in 1970. Hua first gained national attention in 1971, when Mao nominated him to serve on a blue-ribbon panel assigned to investigate the conspiracy and death of Lin Biao. As a result of his work on this commission, Hua, with Mao's strong backing, was elevated to the Politburo in 1973. Two years later, at the Fourth National People's Congress, he was concurrently appointed public security minister and sixth deputy premier. In the latter post he ranked well below both Deng Xiaoping and Zhang Chunqiao, the State Council's two senior vice-premiers. A competent administrator who lacked strong factional ties to either Deng or the Leftists, who enjoyed Mao Zedong's personal confidence, and who lacked a powerful organizational base of his own, Hua made an ideal compromise candidate. His unexpected designation as "acting premier" in late January—leapfrogging over the better-known Deng, Zhang, and Wang—broke the stalemate.[16]

Although the radicals were reportedly furious over Mao's belated intervention on behalf of Hua Guofeng, they had succeeded in thwarting Deng Xiaoping's political ambitions. Striking while the iron was hot, the four Leftists next sought publicly to demean and discredit Deng. In a series of pseudonymous newspaper articles and unsigned editorials that appeared in the mass media in February and March 1976, the Leftists savagely vilified an unnamed "unrepentant capitalist roader" who, among other allegedly ignoble deeds, had promulgated "three poisonous weeds" in 1975 in an attempt to "whip up a Right deviationist wind of reversing correct verdicts." Exhorting the Chinese people to "beat back" the evil wind, the radicals skewered Deng with inflammatory charges of anti-Maoist, anti–Cultural Revolution heresy.[17] Their spirits buoyed by Zhou Enlai's demise and by Mao Zedong's visible rancor over Deng Xiaoping's recent behavior, the Leftists now went straight for Deng's political jugular.

THE TIANANMEN INCIDENT

On Sunday morning, April 4, 1976, people across China arose earlier than usual to perform the ancient rites of sweeping and decorating their ancestors' graves. The occasion was Qingming, an annual festival dedicated to currying favor with the departed spirits of family forebears. At the Heroes' Monument in Tiananmen Square—a massive, multi-tiered concrete cenotaph erected in the late 1950s to honor those who sacrificed their lives for the revolution—the spirit of Qingming was very much in evidence.[18]

Ten days earlier, on March 25, an article appearing in the Leftist-controlled Shanghai *Wenhui bao* (Wenhui daily) had savagely attacked the late Premier Zhou Enlai, accusing him of having been a "capitalist roader." In nearby Nanjing, angry crowds of Zhou's admirers gathered the next day at the city center to protest publication of the article and avow allegiance to the late premier. Although China's official media carried no report of the event, news spread by word of mouth and via inscriptions scrawled indelibly in black tar on the side of railroad cars on the Nanjing-Beijing railway.

By the end of March, floral wreaths and streamers began to appear at the foot of the Heroes' Monument in Tiananmen Square. Many bore inscriptions dedicated to the memory of Zhou Enlai; some contained photographic likenesses of the late premier. Most had been collectively donated by industrial enterprises and other work units (*danwei*) in and around the nation's capital. In the days that followed, a large number of unsigned poems and elegies were posted on the monument's balustrades, in memoriam Zhou Enlai.

On April 2 a sharply worded directive was distributed to work units throughout Beijing. Promulgated at the behest of the Gang of Four, the directive referred to Qingming mockingly as a "festival of ghosts" and cautioned Beijing's workers not to participate in any unauthorized displays of mourning at Tiananmen Square. Those who disobeyed, it said, would be "severely punished."

The directive had little apparent effect. By April 4—Qingming—the Heroes' Monument was awash with thousands of wreaths, poems, and elegiac remembrances celebrating Zhou's life, lamenting his death, and angrily berating his ultra-Leftist detractors. Some of the elegies were inflammatory, bordering on political heresy: "If there are monsters who spit out poisonous fire, there will be men who dare to seize them," declared one. "Devils howl as we pour out our grief / we spill our blood in memory of the hero / the people are no longer wrapped in sheer ignorance / gone for good is Qinshihuang's feudal society," proclaimed another. "Down with the Empress Dowager! Down with Qinshihuang!" exhorted a third.[19] Altogether more than a million people visited Tiananmen Square that day, milling solemnly around the monument, reading the missives posted around its base and balustrades. Many mourners wept openly; others nodded their heads in grim concordance as they read;

Mourners place funeral wreaths in honor of Zhou Enlai at the Heroes' Monument in Tiananmen Square, April 4, 1976.

some meticulously hand-copied poems and elegies to share with friends and family. As much as for Zhou Enlai, the people seemed to be grieving for themselves and their country.[20]

Sensing the profound emotional resonances being evoked among the mourning masses, nervous party leaders convened a meeting of the Politburo on the late afternoon of April 4. Several members of the CCP old guard— including Mao, Ye Jianying, and Xu Shiyou—failed to attend the meeting, which was dominated by the combined forces of the loyalists and the Left.[21] At the meeting, Jiang Qing insisted that the placing of funeral wreaths at the Heroes' Monument had been the work of class enemies. Zhang Chunqiao and Wang Hongwen agreed. Wang proposed a way of dealing with the problem: "If we were to make a bonfire out of the wreaths," he urged, "I don't believe anyone would dare to resist." Calling the wreaths "artillery shells aimed against us," Chen Xilian called for their immediate removal. Mayor Wu De, after initially calling for a thorough investigation of the matter, was persuaded that immediate action was necessary and offered to use municipal public security forces to accomplish the task. Sensing an emerging consensus, Hua Guofeng introduced a resolution calling for the immediate removal of the wreaths. With Mao's concurrence relayed by messenger, the decision was approved. Under cover of darkness, after midnight, some two hundred trucks belonging to the Beijing municipal government rolled into Tiananmen

Square. By daybreak, the Heroes' Monument had been stripped clean of all visible evidence of memorial activity.[22]

Incensed by the actions of the authorities, tens of thousands of Beijing residents flocked to Tiananmen Square on Monday morning, April 5. Demanding the return of the confiscated wreaths and poems, the crowd angrily confronted local security forces, who had cordoned off the Heroes' Monument. Tempers flared as plainclothes police began photographing demonstrators for purposes of identification. Fistfights broke out and a police car was overturned. Several protesters were arrested. Later in the day an irate crowd surrounded the Tiananmen public security station, once again demanding the return of confiscated materials and urging the release of arrested comrades. When their demands were rejected, the crowd set fire to military vehicles and burned down a police command post. Film clips of the day's events, narrated by government spokespersons and broadcast later on public television, pinned responsibility for the violence on "a few bad elements [who] took turns inciting the people." One person in particular—a smallish young man derisively dubbed "crewcut shorty" (*xiao pingtou*)—was shown in the film urging the crowd to storm the Great Hall of the People.[23]

Observing these events from an upper-story window inside the Great Hall of the People, several members of the Politburo reacted with alarm. "Counter-revolutionaries are murdering people!" exclaimed Jiang Qing. "They're trying to burn down the Great Hall." General Chen Xilian proposed that units from the 66th and 38th armies be brought in from nearby Tianjin and Baoding to deal with the disturbance. Wang Hongwen suggested to Mayor Wu that units of the Beijing workers' militia could be mobilized to handle the situation.[24] The conversation then turned to the question of whether guns and live ammunition should be used to quell the turmoil. Listening to all this, Deng Xiaoping remained silent. Of the remaining Politburo participants, only Vice-Premier Li Xiannian raised objections to the use of force against demonstrators, arguing that the consequences could be serious. In the end, Hua Guofeng proposed sending a messenger to inform Chairman Mao of the latest developments and to request the Chairman's further instructions.[25]

Terminally ill and living in virtual seclusion in his "swimming pool residence" in Zhongnanhai, not far from the Great Hall of the People, eighty-three-year-old Mao Zedong listened with alarm as his nephew, Mao Yuanxin, relayed to him the latest reports of the mounting turmoil at Tiananmen Square. A loyal follower of the radical clique, Mao Yuanxin was the gatekeeper who controlled access to his ailing uncle. On April 5, 1976, the gates were open only to those bearing information acceptable to the Left.

Listening to his nephew's account of recent events at Tiananmen Square, Mao Zedong—whose lucidity at this stage of his illness was so limited that he allegedly interrupted Mao Yuanxin's narrative to inquire "Who are you?"—took an extremely dim view of the Qingming disturbance.[26] According to the Leftists' interpretation, the turmoil had been engineered by Deng Xiaoping, who had secretly instigated the outpouring of grief for Zhou Enlai in order to establish a convenient cover for his plan to discredit the Left, "reverse the verdicts" of the Cultural Revolution, and grasp political power for himself. In their conspiracy-soaked scenario, Deng had cynically masterminded the entire affair.[27]

Mao was evidently prepared to believe the worst. Some months earlier he had grown visibly upset over Deng's efforts to reverse the thrust of the Cultural Revolution. On March 10, for example, the *People's Daily* published an unsigned editorial quoting Mao's recent observation that "reversing verdicts goes against the will of the people. . . . the capitalist roaders are still on the capitalist road." Two weeks later, on March 28, a second *People's Daily* editorial quoted Mao's most recent critique of Deng Xiaoping, obliquely referring to Deng as "the party capitalist roader who has refused to change": "This person does not grasp class struggle; he has never referred to this key link. Still his theme of 'white cat, black cat,' making no distinction between imperialism and Marxism."[28] The Chairman was clearly perturbed.

Predisposed to distrust Deng, Mao reacted to reports of the latter's machinations by issuing three "instructions" on April 5. The first of these referred to the Tiananmen disturbance as a premeditated, organized "counterrevolutionary rebellion" (*fan'geming baoluan*); the second authorized the use of "necessary force" to quell the disturbance—though it pointedly proscribed the use of firearms; and the third, noting Deng's "undeniable responsibility" for the rebellion, recommended that Deng be "isolated" (*geli*) pending a thorough investigation of his role in the affair.

When Mao Yuanxin read his uncle's three instructions aloud to the assembled Politburo, a show of hands was called for. One by one, Zhang Chunqiao, Yao Wenyuan, Jiang Qing, Wang Hongwen, Chen Xilian, Wu De, and Chen Yonggui raised their hands in support of Mao's three initiatives. There were no dissenting voices. Declaring unanimous consent, Hua Guofeng pledged to carry out Chairman Mao's orders. Upon hearing the decision, Deng Xiaoping announced his "wholehearted support" for Mao's instructions and requested permission to go to Tiananmen Square to persuade the crowds to disperse. Zhang Chunqiao coldly replied, "It's too late. Your little drama has already produced its results."[29]

Shortly after dusk, at around 6:30 P.M. on April 5, all the lights in Tiananmen Square were suddenly turned on. Taken by surprise, the milling crowds anxiously began retreating, group by group, toward the northern end of the square. Many spectators left the scene at this point, and within an hour the ranks of the demonstrators had thinned appreciably.

At 9:25 P.M., on orders from the Beijing municipal government, a force numbering over ten thousand workers' militia, wearing red armbands and backed by uniformed municipal police and five battalions of soldiers from the Beijing Garrison Command, cornered the protesters at the north end of the square, herding them into small, isolated groups. Brandishing clubs and truncheons, the workers' militia then charged straight into the ranks of the demonstrators. In the ensuing melee, hundreds of protesters were beaten, and almost four thousand people were arrested.[30]

The next day, when Mao Yuanxin informed his uncle that the operation to quell the counterrevolutionary rebellion in Tiananmen Square had been a success, the Chairman was encouraged. "The morale of the troops has been boosted," he remarked. "Good! Good! Good!"[31]

On April 7 the Politburo, meeting (at Mao's insistence) without Deng Xiaoping, Ye Jianying, or alternate member Su Zhenhua present, unanimously adopted two resolutions. The first, designated "Central Document No. 9 (1976)," announced Hua Guofeng's concurrent appointment as first vice-chairman of the Central Committee and premier of the State Council (thereby removing the "acting" designation from his latter title); the second, designated "Central Document No. 10," formally labeled the Tiananmen disturbance a "counterrevolutionary incident," condemned Deng Xiaoping's recent behavior as an "antagonistic contradiction," and ordered Deng's immediate dismissal from all official posts inside and outside the party.[32]

What happened to Deng Xiaoping immediately after the Qingming incident is a matter of some controversy. According to one widely circulated story, when the Politburo issued its April 7 resolutions, the commander of the PLA's Beijing regional forces, loyalist General Chen Xilian, ordered his troops to blockade all major traffic routes into and out of the city, issuing a command to detain anyone who refused to submit to vehicular inspection. Taiwan sources claim that Deng, now a fugitive, was able to evade the PLA's roadblock with an assist from his old friend Marshal Ye Jianying. According to another version of the same story, shortly after his narrow escape Deng Xiaoping headed south. With the aid (again) of Marshal Ye and General Wang Zhen, Deng reportedly took refuge in Guangzhou under the protective wing of two other long-time military associates, Guangdong regional commander Xu Shiyou and PLA General Political Department (GPD) Director Wei Guoqing.[33] When the Gang of Four tried to have Deng brought back to Beijing for further discipline, General Xu allegedly refused, telling the Leftists "if you want him, come and get him; I'll be waiting for you across the Yangzi."[34]

In the past few years a very different story has emerged, based on sources with reputed access to members of Deng's household. According to these sources, Deng never left Beijing at all, but remained inside the city, living under "control" (a modified form of house arrest) in his spacious, well-guarded family residence on Kuanjie (Broadway), north of the Forbidden City. In this version of events, Deng spent his time after April 5 reading, listening to news broadcasts, and playing bridge, occasionally visiting with Ye Jianying and Wang Zhen, among others. At one point, Ye Jianying reportedly cautioned his old friend to take all necessary precautions to safeguard his health and personal safety for the political trials that lay ahead (*yiding yao zhi hao, yiding yao baowei hao*).[35]

Late in the summer of 1976, around the time of Mao's death, Deng report-edly contracted a potentially serious urinary infection. After securing permis-sion from his Politburo control officer, Wang Dongxing, Deng entered Bei-jing's No. 301 Hospital for emergency surgery. He was still recuperating in the hospital when the Gang of Four were arrested on October 6. News of the radicals' detention reportedly contributed to Deng's speedy recovery.[36]

Regardless of which (if any) of the above accounts is true, it is clear that following Deng's dismissal from office the radicals spared no effort trying to pin responsibility for the Tiananmen incident squarely on him. Yao Wenyuan personally pored over thousands of photographs taken by plainclothes police in Tiananmen Square in an effort to locate a "smoking gun" that might link Deng, his family, or his friends to the Qingming disturbances. Try as they might, however, the Gang could find nothing more incriminating than the meager fact that the work unit to which one of Deng's daughters belonged, the Beijing Transistor Research Institute, had donated one of the more than two thousand wreaths that adorned the Heroes' Monument on April 4.[37]

Though Deng had been framed, he nonetheless suffered an enormous set-back as a result of the Leftist assault. Even his erstwhile friends and support-ers—including Hu Qiaomu and Deng Liqun, who had helped him draft the "three poisonous weeds" in 1975—were now under intense pressure to de-nounce him. Some caved in; others resisted.[38] With the mass media conduct-ing a frenzied campaign of character assassination against him, the situation looked anything but promising. This time, the radicals seemingly had Deng where they wanted him; this time, Zhou Enlai was not around to come to his rescue; this time, there would be no timely "reversal of verdicts."

MAO TO HUA: "WITH YOU IN CHARGE, I'M AT EASE"

In the event, the radicals' victory celebration proved premature. No sooner had Deng been shunted to the sidelines than a major new obstacle presented itself. To the dismay of the Leftists, Hua Guofeng appeared to be enjoying his new prominence; more worrisome still, he appeared to enjoy Mao Zedong's complete trust and confidence. With the Chairman's physical condition dete-riorating rapidly, his public appearances grew fewer and farther between. In mid-June he stopped greeting visitors altogether. As Mao weakened, Hua Guofeng visibly began to grow in political stature and self-confidence. Under the circumstances, his four radical rivals were far from pleased.

Although the Leftists had reluctantly agreed to support Hua in late January in order to thwart Deng's bid to become premier, subsequently collaborating with the loyalists to purge Deng after the Tiananmen incident, they had done so in the belief that Hua was unlikely to present an insurmountable obstacle to their own ambitions. As Hua dug in, however, the tactical entente between the two groups began to show signs of strain.

"With you in charge, I'm at ease." Mural depicts Mao Zedong anointing his chosen successor, Hua Guofeng.

Months later, after Mao's death, the Chinese media reported that during the terminal stages of Mao's illness in the spring of 1976, at a private meeting with Hua Guofeng, Chairman Mao had jotted down a six-character phrase conveying his wish to have Hua succeed him as chairman of the party Central Committee. "With you in charge, I'm at ease" (*Ni banshi, wo fangxin*) were the words Mao allegedly scrawled. Whether such a dramatic investiture actually occurred or was simply a piece of public relations apocrypha cooked up by the loyalists after the fact to buttress Hua's otherwise shaky claim to inherit Mao's mantle is not entirely clear.[39] Authentic or not, however, "With you in charge, I'm at ease" soon became Hua's major—indeed virtually his *only*—claim to glory. It was a perilously thin claim, and one that would later be expertly undermined by no less a master political tactician than Deng Xiaoping. At the time, however, it was Jiang Qing and her radical colleagues who were most adversely affected by Mao's behest. Mme. Mao had succession plans of her own, and her plans did not include Hua Guofeng.[40] Thus, by the early summer of 1976 the marriage of convenience between the radicals and the loyalists began to unravel.

Sometimes their growing rivalry took subtle forms. In July a major earthquake in Tangshan, North China, killed 242,000 people and left more than one million homeless. Vigorously asserting his authority as premier of the State Council, Hua immediately took personal charge of the national earthquake relief effort, managing in the process to generate a great deal of favorable publicity for himself—including several flattering photo opportunities.[41] With the succession to Chairman Mao hanging in the balance, Hua's role in earthquake relief would help establish his credentials as a decisive, caring leader capable of filling Mao's enormous shoes.

Lacking the superior administrative and financial resources of the premier's office, the Leftists responded to the Tangshan earthquake by issuing a series of press releases urging quake victims and relief workers to "vigorously study Chairman Mao's important directives" concerning the necessity of "taking class struggle as the key link" in times of national emergency. Under the headline, "Deepen Criticism of Deng Xiaoping in Anti-Quake and Relief Work," the Leftist-controlled *People's Daily* went so far as to assert that in order to achieve complete success in earthquake relief it was necessary to "take the criticism of Deng Xiaoping's counterrevolutionary line . . . as the motive force."[42]

Such jockeying for partisan advantage between Hua and the radicals was accompanied by other, less subtle maneuvers. According to allegations made several months later, after the fact, Jiang Qing sought to counteract Hua Guofeng's potent six-character trump card by contriving to discover a second, hitherto unknown Maoist "last testament" of her own. In the course of perusing documents housed in the Central Committee's archives, Mme. Mao purportedly unearthed a statement made by her husband in April 1976, exhorting his comrades, after his death, to continue to "act according to established principles" (*an jiding fangzhen ban*). Armed with this convenient new behest, the Gang of Four prepared to join the battle of dueling testaments.[43]

MAO'S DEATH AND THE OCTOBER COUP

When Mao died on September 9, factional infighting quickly intensified. The memorial service at Tiananmen, held nine days later, provided the last occasion upon which all Chinese factions and leaders—minus the pariah Deng Xiaoping—would engage in a public display of contrived unity and solidarity. Thereafter, it was everyone for him/herself.

In his eulogy at the memorial service at Tiananmen Square, Hua Guofeng spoke glowingly of Chairman Mao's heroic contributions to the Chinese revolution—and of the necessity to continue to repulse Deng Xiaoping's "Right deviationist wind." Omitting all mention of Mao's controversial adjuration to "act according to established principles," Hua sternly warned that "anyone who tampers with Chairman Mao's directives . . . and anyone who practices splittism or engages in conspiracies is bound to fail." In so speaking, Hua Guofeng laid down the gauntlet for the Gang of Four.[44]

It is extremely difficult to sort out fact from fiction, reality from hyperbole, in the highly charged, intensely partisan accounts of events that transpired in the first weeks after the death of Chairman Mao. Two things are clear, however. First, the increasingly strained united front between the radicals and the loyalists totally disintegrated as the Leftists positioned themselves for a show-down. Second, in the aftermath of Mao's death key members of the survivors faction, including Ye Jianying, Wang Zhen, and a number of other senior PLA officers, decisively cast their lot with Hua Guofeng and the loyalists against the four Leftists.[45]

Even before Mao's death, Ye Jianying and Wang Zhen had met to discuss the possibility of arresting the four radicals. According to party theorist Deng Liqun, the two old military comrades had been deterred from making the arrests by Mao's unpredictability. "The old man was still around," said Ye. "We could act by majority and solve the problem, but the old man was still around, and did he approve of it or not?" Immediately following Mao's death, Wang and Ye consulted with Chen Yun, Deng Yingchao (Mme. Zhou Enlai), Li Xiannian, and several senior army commanders, including Marshal Nie Rong-zhen, General Wang Dongxing, Acting PLA Chief of Staff Yang Chengwu, and Deputy Naval Commander Su Zhenhua concerning tactics to be used in removing the Gang. All reportedly agreed that the time had come to act; they failed, however, to reach an early consensus on just what to do or how to do it.[46]

In the event, the radicals were first to seize the initiative. In mid-September, they blanketed the mass media with articles warning that Rightists and "capi-talist roaders" were seeking to split the party and urging "all supporters of Chairman Mao's proletarian revolutionary line" to heighten their vigilance and to "act according to established principles."[47] At around the same time, the Leftists reportedly issued orders to arm units of the Shanghai and Beijing workers' militia in preparation for a possible clash with regular army units under the control of loyalists and survivors.[48]

Other Leftist actions also suggested, albeit circumstantially, an imminent bid for power. Shortly after Mao's death, Wang Hongwen ordered the General Office of the Central Committee to contact all provincial party committees, directing them to refer all local problems to his office for instruction. On September 12 Yao Wenyuan instructed Leftist supporters at Beijing and Qinghua universities to organize a petition drive urging the Central Committee to name Jiang Qing as party chairperson. A week later Wang Hongwen traveled to Shanghai to check on local militia preparations. Between September 26 and 28, Jiang Qing, Zhang Chunqiao, and Wang Hongwen each paid inspection visits to military units in the Beijing area.[49]

The final straw was the appearance in the October 4 edition of the Leftist-dominated *Guangming ribao* (Guangming daily) of a shrill, strident article enjoining the CCP to "forever act according to the principles established by Chairman Mao." Collectively authored by a radical writing group using the nom de plume "Liang Xiao," the article accused certain unnamed "chiefs of the revisionist road" of "distorting established principles ..., betraying Marxism–Leninism–Mao Zedong Thought ..., and emasculating its revolu-tionary cutting edge." With menacing overtones, the article's authors warned that all such class enemies would inevitably "come to no good end."

Galvanized by the Leftists' words and deeds, which were taken as prima facie evidence of a putsch in the making, Hua's loyalists and their bureaucratic-military allies struck first. Shortly after the appearance of the October 4 *Guangming Daily* article, Nie Rongzhen urged Ye Jianying to make immediate preparations to arrest the four radical leaders. On the night of October 6—after Jiang Qing had made a last, unsuccessful plea to Hua Guofeng to support her candidacy for chair of the Central Committee—Ye launched a preemptive coup. A combined force of elite troops from the State Council home guard and PLA unit 8341, under the joint command of Ye and Wang Dongxing, assisted by Su Zhenhua, arrested the four radical leaders within the walls of the Zhongnanhai state residential compound near Tiananmen.[50] A few days later, units of the Nanjing military region under the temporary command of General Xu Shiyou moved into Shanghai where, after a brief struggle, they disarmed the rebellious workers' militias and arrested several members of the Shanghai CCP municipal committee.[51] In Beijing, workers' militia forces submitted without a struggle. Shortly after the October 6 coup, key Leftists in Beijing and the provinces, including Mao's nephew Mao Yuanxin, were also rounded up and placed under arrest.

These events were not reported to the Chinese public for several weeks; and in the days following the coup, it appeared on the surface to be business as usual in Beijing. On October 8 it was announced that a memorial mausoleum would be built in Tiananmen Square to display Mao's remains, which had been rather hastily embalmed. Concurrently, it was disclosed that a new volume of Chairman Mao's postrevolutionary writings (volume 5) was under editorial preparation. Both projects, it was noted, came under "the direct leadership of the CCP Central Committee Politburo *headed by Comrade Hua Guofeng.*" This low-key announcement was the first public mention of Hua's presumptive claim to succeed Mao Zedong.[52]

Soon afterward the mass media began broadly hinting at a series of grave improprieties committed by the Left. On October 9 the official Xinhua news agency prominently displayed, in boldface type, a 1971 directive attributed to Chairman Mao enjoining party leaders to "unite, and don't split; be open and aboveboard, and don't intrigue and conspire."[53] A day later a joint editorial published in three leading party journals repeated Hua Guofeng's funereal warning that "Anyone who tampers with Chairman Mao's directives . . . and anyone who practices splittism or engages in conspiracies is bound to fail."[54]

Rumors of the purge of the four radicals began to surface in Hong Kong in mid-October. On the 18th the Central Committee informed party organizations at various levels that an "antiparty clique" headed by Wang, Zhang, Jiang, and Yao had been smashed. Two days later, the CC set up a special group to examine the crimes committed by the four radicals.[55] It was not until October 22, however, that word of the arrest reached the people of Beijing. On that date, the first wall posters appeared at two conspicuous places in the nation's capital: the Beijing Languages Institute and the foreign diplomatic quarter at Sanlitun. The posters spoke of "striking down the Gang of Four antiparty clique" (*dadao sirenbang fandang jituan*)—though few people at the time had even the vaguest notion of just what a "gang of four" might be.

The first media report concerning the arrest of the four Leftists was penned by Nigel Wade of the London *Daily Telegraph*. Wade had accidentally stumbled across a hint of the coup at a press briefing in the British Embassy, and when Chinese officials refused to confirm or deny the story, he ran it on speculation. When word of the Gang's arrest reached the university quarter in the Haidian district of northwest Beijing on October 22, all shops in the area quickly sold out of alcoholic beverages, as students and teachers began to celebrate. The first public demonstrations, spontaneous and somewhat chaotic in nature, also occurred at this time and appear to have originated near the headquarters of the Beijing municipal government.[56]

On October 24 a mass rally of one million people featuring several PLA divisions marching in full uniform was held in Tiananmen Square to "warmly celebrate the great victory in shattering the scheme of the antiparty clique of Wang Hongwen, Zhang Chunqiao, Jiang Qing, and Yao Wenyuan to usurp party and state power."[57] At the rally it was announced that Hua Guofeng had been appointed to the concurrent posts of chairman of the CCP Central Committee and chairman of the CCP Central Military Affairs Commission. Exeunt the Gang of Four.

HUA CONSOLIDATES; DENG WAITS

In moving decisively against the four radicals, Hua Guofeng relied heavily upon the cooperation of key military-bureaucratic leaders, especially Ye Jianying and Li Xiannian. In the aftermath of the October coup, Hua, Ye, and Li comprised a de facto ruling troika.

Although the arrest of the Gang significantly shifted the balance of forces in Beijing, it did not immediately redound to Deng Xiaoping's benefit. Having so recently (and so unanimously) painted Deng as a villain, the Politburo now found it extremely difficult to reverse itself without tacitly acknowledging (a) that Mao had made a serious mistake in judgment and (b) that its own members had been badly duped by the Gang of Four. Thus, although both Ye Jianying and Li Xiannian were said to be strongly in favor of bringing Deng "out of the cowshed" (*chu niupeng*), Hua Guofeng and the loyalists adamantly opposed the idea. "How can you suggest this?" demanded Hua. "So many supporters of the Gang of Four are still quite active. Wouldn't people say that [arresting the Gang] was done solely for the purpose of reversing the verdict on Deng Xiaoping?"[58]

Recuperating from his recent urinary tract surgery, Deng now sought to have his case reopened. Advised by his old comrades in the bureaucratic-military group to strike a conciliatory pose, he wrote a personal letter to Hua Guofeng and the Central Committee on October 10, just four days after the arrest of the four radicals. In it, Deng humbly congratulated the party center on its victory against the Gang of Four and enthusiastically hailed Hua's selection as party chairman.

> I sincerely support the decision of the Central Committee on the appointment of Comrade Hua Guofeng to become chairman of the Central Committee and the Central Military Affairs Commission. . . . Comrade Guofeng is the most appropriate successor to Chairman Mao. . . . Considering his age, [his appointment] will guarantee the stability of our proletarian leadership for at least fifteen or twenty years. . . . How jubilant this makes us feel!
>
> The recent struggle against the intrigue of usurping party leadership by those careerists and conspirators occurred . . . at a crucial moment. The Central Committee led by Comrade Guofeng defeated these villains and achieved a great victory. . . . For this victory, I am deeply joyful . . . to the point that I cannot help shouting "Long live! Long live! Long, long live!"[59]

Although Deng's jubilation at the overthrow of the Gang was undoubtedly sincere, his flattery of Hua Guofeng was somewhat more suspect. For his part, Hua had clear and compelling reason to distrust Deng's effusiveness and to oppose, out of hand, any future reconsideration of the Tiananmen affair. Unlike senior members of the survivors group, who had been mere spectators to the unfolding of events of April 4–5, Hua and his fellow loyalists had played an active role in helping to suppress the disturbance. Deeply implicated in the Gang of Four's Qingming chicanery, they thus had good reason to oppose any reconsideration of the affair—or of Deng's putative role in it.

With Hua and his allies adamantly refusing to reverse the verdict on Tiananmen, the Politburo could not act; perforce, Deng Xiaoping remained out in the cold. Conveying the leadership's decision not to reopen Deng's case, Wu De, in the course of the October 24 anti-Gang rally of one million at Tiananmen Square, tersely announced that "We shall continue to criticize Deng."[60] Two days later, on October 26, Hua Guofeng issued a set of four instructions to leading members of the party's propaganda apparatus: (1) the Gang of Four and Deng Xiaoping should be criticized simultaneously; (2) the line pursued by the Gang had been ultra-Rightist rather than Leftist; (3) the media should avoid all mention of the Tiananmen incident; and (4) there should be absolutely no criticism of "whatever Chairman Mao instructed or approved."[61] Hua's final point contained the earliest known reference to the infamous "two whatevers" (*liangge fanshi*), which Hua's critics later used to mock the loyalists' penchant for compulsively glorifying Mao's every word and deed.[62]

Even as the loyalists reaffirmed their determination not to rehabilitate Deng or reverse the Tiananmen verdict, new calls—at first subdued and oblique, later becoming more direct and insistent—began to be heard demanding reconsideration of the cases of veteran cadres who had been wrongfully persecuted by the Gang of Four during the Cultural Revolution. Although ostensibly in line with the party's recent repudiation of the Gang's evil deeds, such demands were inherently problematic for Hua and his allies. Blaming four individuals for an entire decade of persecution and injustice could easily spill over into criticism of Chairman Mao for permitting such things to happen—or even worse, for actually *causing* them to happen. Hence, despite Hua's repeated attempts to place all blame for Cultural Revolution persecution on Jiang Qing and her associates, it became increasingly difficult for the loyalists to preserve the vital bulkhead that separated the "heinous crimes" of the four radicals (now incongruously labeled "ultra-Rightists") from the pristine innocence of an infallible Chairman Mao. Having opened the gates of criticism against the four miscreants, the Huaists now stood in some danger of being overwhelmed by the floodwaters.

The first prominent victim of the Left to have his reputation restored after Mao's death was Marshal He Long, a hero of the Chinese revolution who had died in prison at the hands of radical tormentors in 1969. His posthumous rehabilitation in the winter of 1976–77, promoted by Ye Jianying, Wang Zhen, and other senior military leaders, was followed in succeeding months by the reinstatement of a number of other previously disgraced officials, several of whom were now promoted to leading positions in the State Council and provincial governments, replacing purged collaborators of the Gang of Four.[63]

This first wave of post-Mao rehabilitations underlined the extreme delicacy of Hua Guofeng's position. On the one hand, too much obstruction on Hua's part would render him vulnerable to the charge of covering up the misdeeds of the Left; on the other hand, a blanket exoneration of all previously deposed cadres would, at the very least, cast serious doubt on Chairman Mao's judgment—upon which Hua relied for his leadership mandate. It was a predicament from which Hua Guofeng could not easily escape.

In the late fall and winter of 1976–77, the national media gradually ceased publishing articles critical of Deng Xiaoping's "counterrevolutionary line" and "Right deviationist wind." The last major condemnation of Deng by a central leader appeared in Wu De's speech to the Standing Committee of the National People's Congress, delivered on November 30, 1976.[64] Meanwhile, the first faint whispers of public support for Deng began to be heard. On January 8, 1977—the first anniversary of Zhou Enlai's death—pro-Deng posters appeared at small public mourning ceremonies in Nanjing, Shanghai, Guangzhou, and Beijing. Two days later, at a gathering in Tiananmen Square, a "letter of opinion" was circulated calling for the dismissal of Mayor Wu De and the reinstatement of Deng Xiaoping.[65] At around the same time, foreign visitors to Beijing reported seeing small bottles (in Chinese, *xiaoping*, a homophonic word-play on Deng's given name) atop marble columns near the Gate of Heavenly Peace and dangling from trees lining the main traffic route from the airport to the center of the city.[66]

The movement to rehabilitate Deng gained further momentum in February 1977, when an article appeared in the party's leading theoretical journal, *Red Flag*, accusing the four deposed radicals of "smearing and striking down as 'unrepentant capitalist roaders' a large number of leading cadres at the center . . . who have followed Chairman Mao . . . for several decades, loyally served the people, and persevered in taking the socialist road."[67] Also in February 1977, Deng reportedly received another boost when two of his key military supporters, Xu Shiyou and Wei Guoqing, sent a letter to the party Central Committee alleging that notwithstanding the great victory achieved in the struggle against the Gang of Four, certain serious morale problems remained unresolved within the party and army. In identifying the source of these problems, the two outspoken southern generals openly stated what others had previously only dared to whisper: Chairman Mao had been fallible; Chairman Mao had made mistakes; branding everyone who disagreed with him as a "class enemy" had been wrong.[68]

DENG XIAOPING'S SECOND COMEBACK

Faced with mounting sympathy and support for Deng Xiaoping, the loyalists dug in their heels, redoubling their efforts to block his return to power.[69] At a work conference of the Central Committee held in March 1977, Wu De and Wang Dongxing were especially outspoken in opposing Deng's rehabilitation, citing as justification Mao's personal decision to remove Deng from power following the Tiananmen incident. Any reversal of that decision, they argued, would reflect badly on the Chairman's image.

Rejecting this argument, a number of senior party and military leaders present at the March work conference voiced criticism of the "whateverist" position and expressed support for Deng Xiaoping. These included Li Xiannian, Wang Zhen, Xu Shiyou, Wei Guoqing, and Chen Yun—all of whom agreed that the restoration of Deng's good name and reputation should be linked to an official reconsideration of the Tiananmen incident.

Chen Yun had a personal reason for resenting Hua Guofeng. Immediately after the arrest of the Gang of Four, Wang Zhen had proposed to Li Xiannian that Chen should be restored to the Politburo. Li agreed and passed the suggestion on to Hua, who reportedly remained silent on the matter, thereby effectively blocking Chen's reinstatement. Hua continued to withhold his approval for more than two years, and it was not until the eve of the Third Plenum of the Eleventh Central Committee, in November 1978, that he belatedly endorsed Chen Yun's bid for restoration.[70]

With Chen's reinstatement stalled, Ye Jianying brokered a compromise in the spring of 1977 to resolve the deadlock over Deng Xiaoping's rehabilitation. Under its terms, Hua Guofeng agreed to make two concessions: first, he would acknowledge that Deng's work in 1975 had contained both "successes and shortcomings"; and second, he would concede that the April 4 demonstrations had started out as a peaceful homage to Zhou Enlai and had thus been "reasonable" from the outset. For his part, Deng agreed to write a second letter to the party center, pledging to support Hua and acknowledging that his own work in 1975 had contained some shortcomings. Significantly, Deng was not required to admit any personal wrongdoing in connection with the Qingming disturbance. Once the agreement was implemented, Deng would be formally reinstated to his previous positions.

As per his agreement, Deng Xiaoping wrote a letter to the Central Committee on April 10, 1977. The letter contained four main points: first, Deng expressed his gratitude to Chairman Hua for acknowledging that the Qingming demonstrations had been reasonable and that Deng himself had not been personally involved; second, while conceding that his own work in 1975 had contained shortcomings and mistakes, Deng affirmed that he had also done "some beneficial things" at that time; third, Deng pledged to obey all future Central Committee decisions pertaining to his possible reinstatement and return to work; and fourth, he implicitly challenged the appropriateness of the "two whatevers" by insisting that the party's future policies should be guided by an "accurate and complete" understanding of Mao Zedong's Thought.[71]

Dissatisfied with the last point in Deng's letter, the "whateverists" dispatched a two-man delegation, led by Wang Dongxing, to negotiate further with Deng. According to Deng's personal account of this meeting, which took place in mid-May, he adamantly stuck to his guns on the question of the "two whatevers":

> [W]hen two leading comrades of the General Office of the Central Committee came to see me, I told them that the "two whatevers" are unacceptable. If this principle were correct, there could be no justification for my rehabilitation, nor could there be any for the statement that the activities of the masses at Tiananmen Square in 1976 were reasonable. . . . Comrade Mao Zedong himself said repeatedly that some of his own statements were wrong . . . that he too had made mistakes and that there had never been a person whose statements were all correct.[72]

Notwithstanding Deng's continued defiance, a bargain was struck, under the terms of which Deng agreed in future to refrain from attacking the "two whatevers" or otherwise undermining Mao's reputation and legacy; in return, he would be permitted to attend—and address—the Third Plenary Session of the Tenth Central Committee. With the bargain thus sealed, the plenum was convened in mid-July and Deng was restored to all four posts from which he had been removed in April 1976: CCP vice-chairman, MAC vice-chairman, first deputy premier, and PLA chief of staff.[73]

In his address to the July 1977 CC Plenum, Deng honored his agreement, toning down his criticism of the "two whatevers" and warmly endorsing the broad corpus of Mao's works—with one important caveat: When using Chairman Mao's past instructions as a guide to present policy, Deng averred, it was necessary to treat his writings "as an integral system instead of just citing a few specific words or sentences."[74] Following up on this theme, toward the end of his remarks Deng sounded a novel, subtle challenge to the new orthodoxy of Hua Guofeng and his loyalist allies. Instead of gauging the correctness of policies, words, or actions by their degree of concordance with the literal canon of Mao's writings, Deng now proposed an alternative yardstick. Borrowing a four-character homily from Mao's Yan'an writings, Deng enjoined his comrades to "seek truth from facts" (*shishi qiushi*).[75] Unobjection-able in itself, it was a phrase that would eventually be used as a weapon to disarm the "whateverists" and nullify important parts of the Maoist legacy. Indeed, within sixteen months, "seek truth from facts" would be enshrined as the first commandment of Deng Xiaoping's pragmatic "second Chinese revolution."

Deng Takes Command:
August 1977–December 1978

The plenary session seriously discussed . . . certain historical

questions left over from an earlier period. . . . . The session

emphatically points out that the great feats performed by

Comrade Mao Zedong . . . are indelible. [However] it would

not be Marxist to demand that a revolutionary leader be free of

all shortcomings. . . . As for shortcomings and mistakes, . . .

these should be summed up at an appropriate time.

—Communiqué of the Third Plenum of

the Eleventh Central Committee,

December 22, 1978

DENG XIAOPING'S return to power was formally ratified by the Eleventh National Congress of the CCP, which met in August 1977. The first party congress to be held since 1973, and the first since the deaths of Mao Zedong and Zhou Enlai, the Eleventh Congress formally declared an end to the Cultural Revolution, adopted a revised party constitution, elected a new Central Committee, and installed a new five-member Politburo Standing Committee (SC)—which now included Deng Xiaoping.[1] Deng was given third position on the new Standing Committee, ranking just below Hua Guofeng and Ye Jianying and just ahead of Li Xiannian and Wang Dongxing. For all intents and purposes, China was now ruled by two "whateverists," two "survivors," and the redoubtable Deng Xiaoping. At best a fragile condominium, it was not an arrangement that Deng found to his liking.

THE ELEVENTH PARTY CONGRESS

Reflecting the balance of power between the "whateverists" and the "survivors," the new party constitution bowed deeply in Mao Zedong's direction, reaffirming that the late Chairman's thought had been an indispensable guide to victory in revolution and socialist construction, and stipulating that the party's primary task in the foreseeable future was to "persist in continuing the revolution under the dictatorship of the proletariat, eliminate the bourgeoisie step by step, and bring about the triumph of socialism over capitalism." This reaffirmation of Maoist orthodoxy was accompanied by a new demand for all party members to guard against people who violated Mao's injunction to "unite and don't split; be open and aboveboard, and don't intrigue and conspire."[2]

In a lengthy speech outlining key features of the new party constitution, Vice-Chairman Ye Jianying went out of his way to praise effusively "our wise leader Chairman Hua Guofeng" as "Mao's good student and successor" and "brilliant supreme commander of the army." Ye also recounted with approval Mao's six-character behest to Hua, "With you in charge, I'm at ease," and gave full credit to Hua for heroically exposing and smashing the sinister plot of the Gang of Four:

> When the destiny of our party and our revolution was at stake at the peak of the conspiracy of the Gang of Four to usurp supreme power in the party and state, Comrade Hua Guofeng, carrying out Chairman Mao's behest with a proletarian revolutionary's boldness and vision, took decisive action, led the whole party in smashing the Gang of Four at one blow, spared our party and our country a major split and retrogression, and thus saved the revolution and the party.[3]

On a more chilling note, Ye Jianying defended Mao's Cultural Revolution as a "vital weapon against capitalist restoration," suggesting that if capitalist roaders ever dared to hatch new plots to seize power in the party, more Cultural Revolutions would have to be launched.

In his political report to the Eleventh Party Congress, Chairman Hua Guofeng gave a lengthy, detailed account of the crimes and misdemeanors of the Gang of Four. In the process, he devoted a great deal of space to recounting Chairman Mao's frequent warnings against the "wild ambitions" and "sinister intrigues" of the four radicals.[4] Hua also went out of his way to pacify Deng Xiaoping, noting that it was Chairman Mao himself who initially proposed that Deng be named first deputy premier and vice-chairman of the party CC and MAC in the autumn of 1974. In addition, Hua now tacitly exonerated Deng of the charge of having stirring up a "Right deviationist wind" in 1975, pointing the accusatory finger instead at the four deposed conspirators: "In the days prior to and immediately following the death of our esteemed and beloved Premier Zhou, the Gang of Four ran amok again. . . . Defying Chairman Mao's instructions and going their own way, they attacked Comrade Deng Xiaoping and brought false charges against him."[5]

In a final concession to Deng, Hua retreated from a position taken immediately following the arrest of the Gang of Four, when he had characterized the deposed radicals as "ultra-Rightists." Use of this inflammatory label (which suggested, among other things, a presumptive link between the Gang's criminal conspiracy and Deng's alleged "Right deviationist" policies) had apparently rubbed a number of Politburo members the wrong way; thenceforth, the controversial label was dropped from official discussions of the Gang's misdeeds.[6]

Notwithstanding these exculpatory nods in Deng's direction, Hua Guofeng was strangely silent on the one subject that was presumably uppermost in the minds of many party leaders in attendance at the Eleventh Congress: the Qingming affair. Not once in Hua's political report was the Tiananmen incident even indirectly alluded to. It was as if the entire episode never happened.

The omission was hardly accidental. The Tiananmen incident was the source of Hua's greatest political vulnerability, his Achilles heel. While he could distance himself from most other controversial actions of the Gang of Four, he could never dissociate himself entirely from the Qingming affair. His fingerprints—and those of his key supporters—were all over it.

In his lengthy narrative account of the sins of the Gang, Hua gamely tried to gloss over this glaring gap, claiming that it had been out of respect for Mao Zedong's declining health that he and his colleagues had failed to take timely action to expose (and oppose) the Gang's devious machinations: "In 1976, as Chairman Mao's illness worsened, the Gang of Four became more unscrupulous in their antiparty activities. However, in consideration of Chairman Mao's health and with the overall interest in mind, comrades of the Politburo, while adhering to principle, exercised restraint."[7] Covering himself with this rather thin figleaf, Hua sought to sidestep all questions concerning "whateverist" collaboration with the Gang of Four in suppressing the Qingming demonstrations and securing Deng Xiaoping's removal.

Last to speak at the Eleventh Congress was Deng Xiaoping himself. Operating on a rather short leash, Deng gave a closing address that was considerably more succinct—lasting only eight minutes—and more circumspect than the speeches by Hua Guofeng and Ye Jianying. Containing no overtly combative language, Deng's statement was nonetheless controversial. At the outset, he subtly registered his disapproval of Hua Guofeng's newly exalted status by referring to him as "our wise leader *Comrade* Hua Guofeng."[8] After delivering himself of this slight, Deng devoted the bulk of his remarks to elaborating upon a theme he had initially raised a month earlier at the July Central Committee plenum: the need to "restore and carry forward the practice of seeking truth from facts, the fine tradition and style which Chairman Mao fostered in our party."[9] Here again, Deng's distinctive phrasing masked a subtle challenge to Hua Guofeng and the "whateverists." In Deng's view, the party's "fine tradition and style" had fallen into desuetude since the late 1950s and hence stood in dire need of being "restored" (*huifu*) and revitalized—a point also stressed by Chen Yun. To the "whateverists," on the other hand, there was no fundamental discontinuity between past and present: the party's "fine tradition and style" remained unbroken and hence had only to be "upheld" (*jianchi*). Upon such small, subtle terminological distinctions hinged the future of Mao's revolution.[10]

Toward the end of 1977, a series of high-level personnel changes in key CCP departments signaled trouble ahead for Hua Guofeng, as several of

Deng's supporters were promoted to leading positions in the party organization. Two of the changes were of particular significance: Hu Yaobang, the recently installed vice-president of the Central Party School in Beijing, and at age sixty-two one of the youngest Long March veterans, was picked to head the CC Organization Department and concurrently to serve as deputy director of the party's General Office under Wang Dongxing; and Zhu Muzhi, like Hu Yaobang a rehabilitated cadre, was named deputy director of the Propaganda Department of the Central Committee under "whateverist" Zhang Pinghua. As victims of Cultural Revolution persecution, neither Hu nor Zhu was a great admirer of "whateverism." Indeed, Hu Yaobang had the rare distinction, along with his mentor, Deng Xiaoping, of having been twice sacked by radical Maoists.[11]

To make matters even worse for Hua Guofeng and his associates, in November Politburo member Nie Rongzhen, a PLA marshal and contemporary of Ye Jianying and Mao Zedong, published an important article echoing Deng Xiaoping's plea to "restore" the CCP's fine tradition of "seeking truth from facts."[12]

By the end of the year, outside observers detected the first clear signs of an emerging power struggle between Deng and Hua, centering on reports that Deng's followers had launched a campaign to uncover information pertaining to past collusion between the "whateverists" and the Gang of Four. Hinting at the trouble that lay ahead for Hua Guofeng and his associates, on January 4, 1978, the official military newspaper *Liberation Army Daily* published a scathing analysis of "those who follow the wind." Taking an obvious (if oblique) swipe at the "whateverists," the article denounced those opportunists who sought to curry favor with powerful authority figures. On January 6 the article was reprinted in *People's Daily*. Two days later, on January 8—the second anniversary of Zhou Enlai's death—a wall poster appeared in Beijing calling for an official reexamination of the Tiananmen incident.[13]

THE HUA GUOFENG INTERREGNUM

Painfully aware that his political power rested on a fragile foundation, Hua, in the period immediately following the Eleventh Party Congress, sought to bolster his credentials as Mao's rightful heir. Invoking the "two whatevers" to back up this claim, he wrapped himself in the cloak of Maoist infallibility, complementing this with an all out campaign to fashion a personality cult of his own. Throughout the last half of 1977 and much of 1978, the "whateverists" used all means at their disposal to mold a new public image of Chairman Hua as a "wise leader" and "beloved comrade" in the tradition of Chairman Mao. A new official hagiography appeared, glorifying Hua's past exploits. Numerous popular songs and dances were commissioned as paeans to the putative popularity, warmth, and compassion of the new chairman. Huge billboards depicting Hua receiving Mao Zedong's benediction, "With you in charge, I'm at ease," were erected in dozens of Chinese cities. Side-by-side portraits of Hua and Mao began to appear in public places and private homes throughout the country. In the drive to polish Hua's image, no sartorial details were overlooked, as the new chairman even took to growing his normally close-cropped hair a bit longer, combing it back from the forehead in emulation of Mao's signature hairstyle.

While thus inventing a new image for himself, Hua also sought to fashion a reputation as a forward-thinking leader and economic strategist. Coopting Zhou Enlai's long-dormant "four modernizations" theme as his own, he used the occasion of the opening of the Fifth National People's Congress in February 1978 to introduce a refurbished ten-year plan for economic development.

HUA REVAMPS THE "FOUR MODERNIZATIONS"

In his "Report on the Work of the Government," delivered on February 26, Premier Hua revived Zhou's January 1975 call for "all-around modernization of agriculture, industry, national defense, and science and technology by the end of the century."[14] Spelling out the means by which China would accomplish this objective, Hua borrowed (without attribution) a number of ideas previously advanced by Deng Xiaoping in his three infamous policy initiatives of 1975, now adding to these a rather more orthodox ideological spin.[15] The resulting policy mixture contained elements of both Maoism and Dengism and was thus inherently inconsistent. For example, while urging his comrades to "resolutely implement Chairman Mao's revolutionary line" and "always act on Chairman Mao's instructions," Hua also encouraged them to "seek truth from facts" and "break free from conventions."[16]

Among the Maoist conventions Hua proposed abandoning were the traditional norms of self-reliance, egalitarianism, and reliance on nonmaterial incentives. In their stead he proposed a number of economic and administrative reforms, including accelerated acquisition of advanced foreign technology; decentralization of economic management; adoption of managerial responsibility systems; expansion of household sideline production in agriculture; enlargement of rural free markets; employment of the "law of value" (read: prices and profits) to direct economic activity; and widespread utilization of incentive pay schemes, including bonuses and royalties as rewards for outstanding individual achievement.[17] Previously, Leftists had attacked each of these ideas for abetting a "capitalist restoration."

Equally significant, Hua now urged a policy of "opening wide" with respect to China's intellectuals. To overcome the "cultural poverty and insipidity" that ostensibly resulted from the "fascist dictatorship" of the Left, it was necessary to foster a vigorous, lively environment of "spirited discussion" in science and philosophy, literature and the arts. "Where there is controversy in academic discussions and literary criticism," Hua stated, "we should avoid hasty conclusions. We should seek solutions not through such oversimple measures as administrative orders, but through full discussion and practical experience."[18]

Pursuant to these recommendations, a new Chinese Academy of Social Sciences (CASS) was created in February 1978, under the leadership of Deng associate Hu Qiaomu. Under CASS auspices, social science research underwent a significant renaissance in 1978–79. Many Chinese scholars, including CASS Vice-President Yu Guangyuan, credit Hua Guofeng for having "opened up" the social sciences in China.[19]

Although Hua's report to the Fifth NPC leaned strongly in the direction of intellectual tolerance, his prescriptions for reform were offset by calls for the continued observance of traditional Maoist behavioral constraints and political limits, thus lending his work report its appearance of extraordinary ambivalence—if not outright schizophrenia. A good example was Hua's inconsistent treatment of the controversial question of how to view the CCP's "fine tradition and style of work." At one point in his text, Hua appeared to go out of his way to placate Deng Xiaoping, calling on CCP members to "*restore* and carry forward the party's fine tradition and style of work." Later in the same passage, however, he reverted to contrarian form, entreating his comrades merely to "*uphold*" their fine style of work. Notwithstanding such rhetorical contradictions (which undoubtedly reflected the collective authorship of the speech), Hua's February 1978 work report to the First Session of the Fifth NPC represented a clear break with the dominant ethos and values of the Cultural Revolution. As such, it marked an important watershed in China's post-Mao development.

REVISING THE STATE CONSTITUTION

The second important piece of business transacted at the Fifth NPC was adoption of a revised PRC state constitution. Drafted by a committee headed by Premier Hua, and presented to the NPC by its newly designated Standing Committee chairman, Ye Jianying, the new constitution reflected two primary aims: to restore a measure of institutional authority, accountability, and procedural regularity to government in the wake of the anarchy spread by the Gang of Four; and to enable the new Hua Guofeng-Ye Jianying-Li Xiannian triumvirate to consolidate their joint political hegemony.[20]

One important provision of the new constitution concerned the disposition of the powers and functions formerly exercised by the PRC chairman—a position that no longer existed.[21] Of the fourteen original functions of the state chairman, nine were now redistributed among offices or organs controlled by the Hua-Ye-Li alliance. In addition, the new constitution explicitly affirmed Hua Guofeng's authority over the executive branch, stipulating that "the premier presides over the work of the State Council," while the various deputy premiers (including Deng Xiaoping) were empowered merely to "assist the premier in his work." It was further stipulated that henceforth members of the

State Council other than the premier were to be appointed and removed "on the recommendation of the premier," rather than on the proposal of the party Central Committee, as before. Finally, the powers of the NPC Standing Committee—chaired by Ye Jianying—were enhanced by giving that body the authority to remove members of the State Council upon recommendation of the premier, and to supervise the work of all government ministries and commissions.[22]

In his "Report on the Revision of the Constitution," Ye Jianying stressed the importance of restoring "socialist democracy" in China. In particular, he focused on the newly codified rights of citizens to "speak out freely, air their views fully, engage in great debates, and write big-character posters." By incorporating these so-called four big freedoms into the constitution, Ye argued, China would in the future be able to avoid fascist rule of the type imposed by the Gang of Four.[23]

Turning to the issue of law and order, Ye stressed the need to restore the shattered authority of China's public security and procuratorial organs and people's courts, all of which had been severely damaged by the legal anarchism of the Gang. To prevent future recurrences of wholesale lawlessness, Ye noted, the new constitution explicitly strengthened the powers of specialized judicial bodies and prohibited such things as arbitrary arrest and detention and criminal confessions extracted by coercion. He further stressed that henceforth the "weight of evidence and investigation" would be the primary standards for determining guilt or innocence in judicial hearings, thus enabling courts to strike "accurate blows" at criminal elements.

HUA GUOFENG COURTS THE PETROLEUM CLIQUE

At the heart of the eclectic ten-year economic plan unveiled by Hua Guofeng at the Fifth NPC was a proposal to accelerate the development of heavy industry and related infrastructure through a crash program involving construction of 120 large-scale projects, including iron and steel complexes, coal mines, oil and natural gas fields, power complexes, railroad lines, and harbors. To facilitate completion of these projects, Hua called for opening the country to large-scale technological imports from the West and Japan.[24] In so doing, the premier sharply reversed the "nativism" of Mao's post-1956 developmental model, which had stressed, among other things, the need for economic self-reliance, the primacy of agriculture and light industry over heavy industry, and the intensive use of indigenous technologies of manufacture.

Hua's call for massive new investment in heavy industry received important support from Li Xiannian (who had previously expressed serious reservations about the grandiosity of the new ten-year plan)[25] and from the so-called petroleum clique, whose members included top government officials in the State Economic Commission, the State Planning Commission, and various heavy industrial ministries under the State Council—all of which were slated to play key roles in the implementation of the new development plan. The petroleum clique—so named because of its enthusiastic advocacy of a scheme to use profits from petroleum exports to finance high-technology industrial imports from the West and, not coincidentally, because most of its key members were current (or former) high officials in China's energy bureaucracy— was essentially orthodox and conservative in its economic outlook; its leaders, including Vice-Premier Yu Qiuli, Vice-Premier Kang Shi'en, and Petroleum Minister Song Zhenming, believed strongly in centralized state planning and the preferential development of large-scale heavy industry, à la Stalin. In this respect, the petroleum group differed from the more eclectic "whatever" faction, whose members, including Hua Guofeng, lacked a single clear, coherent economic outlook or strategy.[26]

CHAOS IN THE TEN-YEAR PLAN

In retrospect, it is evident that the very grandiosity of Hua's ten-year economic plan contributed to its eventual failure. By committing himself to the simultaneous pursuit of a series of massive new construction programs whose putative benefits were clear enough to all but whose enormous upstream requirements and downstream costs and complexities were only dimly perceived by any, Hua badly overtaxed China's limited technical and financial capabilities. In the rush to accelerate China's modernization, a number of expensive, state-of-the-art industrial turnkey plants were imported from the West and Japan. In many cases, the plants were designed, sited, and contracted in great haste, without adequate consideration of technical feasibility, infrastructure requirements, or cost-effectiveness. As a result, a series of high-tech industrial fiascos occurred, including a multi-billion-dollar planning boondoggle involving the Baoshan Iron and Steel Works and the collapse of an expensive, imported offshore oil rig in the Bohai Gulf, with substantial loss of life.[27]

Hua Guofeng's "flying leap" approach to modernization and development soon led to serious imbalances in China's national economy. In the first full year of the "four modernizations," China's net capital investment rate exceeded 38 percent of the national budget—the highest figure since Mao's calamitous Great Leap Forward. Expanded capital investment far exceeded the state's resource capacity, leading to huge bottlenecks in capital goods and construction materials. Along with accelerated capital investment came the first substantial across-the-board increases in wages and bonuses since 1956. With the money supply sharply increased, consumer demand rose; in the absence of a collateral expansion in consumer goods production, the result was a steady rise in the rate of inflation.

There was more bad news. In 1977 and 1978 China's foreign imports grew by 85 percent, leading to the largest trade imbalance since the mid-1950s. Compounding the trade deficit was the weakness of the anticipated "flying

leap" in energy exports. Evidently the petroleum group had greatly overesti-
mated China's ability quickly to expand production and delivery of low-cost,
high-quality oil, natural gas, and coal. As a consequence of all these unantici-
pated difficulties, in 1979 China registered a record one-year budget deficit of
RMB ¥17.1 billion—fully 15.5 percent of total revenues.[28]

Such results could hardly boost Hua Guofeng's reputation as an enlight-
ened economic strategist. On the contrary, by eagerly embracing overly ambitious, quick-fix development schemes, Hua severely undermined his own
credibility, further contributing to the erosion of his political authority. And
when several members of the petroleum clique were publicly humiliated and
dismissed from office in the aftermath of the 1979 Bohai Gulf oil-rig disaster,
it signaled the imminent demise of Hua Guofeng's ruling coalition.[29]

There is a certain irony in all of this, insofar as a fair number of Hua's
economic prescriptions had originally been borrowed from Deng Xiaoping's
1975 proposals for industrial and technological development—including recommendations for accelerated industrial growth and for stepping-up petroleum exports to pay for technology imports. When these ideas backfired, however, it was Hua, not Deng, who shouldered the blame.[30]

DENG TAKES THE OFFENSIVE

Even before the first downside effects of Hua's ten-year plan had begun to
materialize, Deng Xiaoping seized the political initiative. At a series of national conferences on education, science, and technology held in the spring of
1978, Deng stepped up his (implied) criticism of the policies of the Maoist
era. In a speech to the National Science Conference on March 18, Deng can-
didly acknowledged that in the past three decades China had fallen farther
behind the advanced industrial nations of the West. Arguing that "backwardness must be perceived before it can be changed," he called for a profound
revolution in the ethos and management of scientific research in China.[31]
While nominally praising Mao Zedong's past contribution to the development
of Chinese science and blaming the Gang of Four for the country's current
state of backwardness, Deng went far beyond a mere critique of the deposed
Leftists. Wholly rejecting the Maoist concept of self-reliance, he urged a new
respect for foreign science and a new determination to learn from other
countries.

Where Hua Guofeng had merely stressed the need for accelerated *trade*
with the West to obtain the most advanced products of Western science and
technology (a prescription that Deng Xiaoping himself had offered in 1975,
and for which he had been heavily criticized), Deng now went much further,
stressing the need urgently and continuously to *learn* from the West: "It is not
just today, when we are technically backward, that we need to learn from other
countries; after we catch up with the advanced world levels in science and
technology, we will still have to learn from the strong points of others." In

taking this controversial position, Deng echoed an argument first made a century earlier by radical Chinese modernizers who had urged wholesale borrowing from the West as an alternative to the more limited prescriptions for "self-strengthening" advanced by neoconservatives in the Qing dynasty.[32]

In his address to the National Science Conference, Deng refuted the Maoist assertion that science and technology possessed distinctive class characteristics and thus belonged to the realm of society's political-ideological "superstructure." Instead, Deng advanced the claim that science and technology were "productive forces" (*shengchan li*) that were inherently class-neutral and universal in nature, that is, "a kind of wealth created in common by all of mankind."[33] As such, they were not properly the objects of political or ideological restriction or restraint. To give full play to the creative energy and initiative of China's scientific and technical workers, Deng called for an across-the-board reclassification of all "brain workers" from the category of petit bourgeoisie (an inherently ambivalent, ideologically unreliable class) to the more politically acceptable category of "working people." He also demanded a fundamental change in the party's style of work to permit scientists and other technical intellectuals greater autonomy in their professional activities. Toward this end, party secretaries in research institutes were urged to give institute directors and deputy directors a free hand to guide and supervise research work, and party cadres were exhorted to release technical intellectuals from excessive political study requirements, thus enabling them to devote at least five days a week to research-related activities.[34]

Deng reiterated many of these same themes in a speech to a National Conference on Education Work in late April. In the latter address Deng denounced the Gang of Four for, among other things, sabotaging China's educational system through their opposition to high school and university entrance examinations, deriding educators as "bourgeois intellectuals," and insisting that "it is preferable to have laborers with no culture; . . . the more knowledge, the more reactionary."[35] To revive and develop China's badly damaged educational institutions, Deng urged adoption of a number of reform measures, including rigorous academic examinations, individual bonuses and other material rewards for outstanding educators, and a two-track school system with special emphasis on preferential development of a limited number of elite "key schools" and universities.[36] He also raised two additional proposals, neither of which appeared in the published version of his speech due to their rather delicate subject matter: a call to send large numbers of Chinese students and scholars abroad to receive advanced training in the West, and a proposal to establish "sister institution" relations between a number of leading Chinese universities and their Western counterparts.[37]

According to a memoir by party theoretician Deng Liqun, the urgency of Deng Xiaoping's 1978 call for systemic reform and "opening up" was given added impetus when a group of party leaders visited Tokyo in the fall of that year to negotiate a peace treaty with Japan. Greatly impressed by the level of industrial development, technological sophistication, and consumer affluence displayed by the Japanese, members of the delegation returned to China strongly determined to modernize China's socialist system as thoroughly and as rapidly as possible.[38]

In almost every respect, Deng Xiaoping's 1978 reform initiatives went well beyond his more modest proposals of 1975—and beyond the ideas put forward by Hua Guofeng at the Fifth NPC as well. But it was not in the realm of debate over proposed reforms in science, technology, or education that the Hua-Deng rivalry showed up most clearly in 1978; rather, it was in the more arcane and esoteric realm of epistemology—the relationship between "doctrine" and "practice" in the quest for truth—that the rivalry showed signs of heating up.

The Debate over Truth and Tradition

In mid-May 1978 China's leading intellectual newspaper, the *Guangming Daily*, published an article by an unnamed "special correspondent" arguing that in the process of formulating policies, ideological precepts had to be put to the test of "experience" (*jingyan*) and "practice" (*shijian*) to ascertain whether or not they corresponded to reality. Insisting that political, economic, and social truth could not be deduced a priori from doctrinal guidelines or dogmas, but had to be derived from practical experience, the author boldly proclaimed that "Practice is the sole criterion for testing truth" (*Shijian shi jianying zhenli de weiyi biaozhun*).[39] In making this assertion, the author clearly intended to expose and exploit the principal theoretical weakness of the "whateverists." According to knowledgeable insiders, the article was approved for publication by Hu Yaobang, who may not have been fully apprised of either the article's significance or the gravity of the debate that surrounded it.[40]

The issue of how best to seek truth was raised again at an all-army political work conference in early June. Addressed by the Politburo's three top leaders—Hua, Ye, and Deng—this high-profile conference provided a key forum for the escalating debate over truth and tradition. In his remarks to the conference, Deng strongly rebuked as "false Marxists" those (unnamed) people who substituted the mechanical recitation of Mao's words for the "Marxist viewpoint" of seeking truth from facts. Focusing his criticism obliquely on "some comrades," Deng launched his sharpest public attack yet on "whateverism":

> Some comrades . . . talk about Mao Zedong Thought every day, but often forget, abandon, or even oppose Comrade Mao's fundamental Marxist viewpoint and method of seeking truth from facts. . . . Some people even go further: they maintain that those who persist in seeking truth from facts . . . are guilty of a heinous crime. In essence, their view is that one need only parrot what was said by Marx, Lenin, and Comrade Mao Zedong—that it is enough to reproduce their words mechanically. . . . This issue . . . is no minor one.[41]

Adroitly selecting several key passages from Chairman Mao's writings to bolster his own argument, Deng next sought to hoist the "whateverists" by their own petard:

> Ever since Comrade Mao Zedong joined the communist movement . . . he fought resolutely against the erroneous tendency to divorce theory from practice. . . . In 1936 and 1937 [he wrote] a series of immortal works in [which] he pointed out: "Marxists hold that man's social practice alone is the criterion of the truth of his knowledge of the external world." . . . Comrade Mao Zedong admonished all comrades in the party not to "regard odd quotations from Marxist-Leninist works as a ready-made panacea which, once acquired, can easily cure all maladies." . . . In 1963 Comrade Mao Zedong pointed out that correct ideas "come from social practice, and from it alone. . . ; there is no other way of testing truth."[42]

In the latter part of his address to the army work conference, Deng repeated his 1977 call to "restore" the PLA's fine tradition in political work, linking it as before to the Maoist admonition to "seek truth from facts."

When Hua Guofeng and Ye Jianying addressed the conference, both men elected to avoid the epistemological minefield of the "seek truth" debate, carefully skirting the issue altogether. Both also stuck to their established position that it was necessary only to "uphold" (*jianchi*) rather than to "restore" (*huifu*) the army's fine tradition in political work.[43]

In the aftermath of the work conference, the "whateverists" tried to deflect Deng's attack, claiming that he had one-sidedly and disingenuously employed Chairman Mao's words to "cut down the banner of Mao Zedong's Thought."[44] The counterattack failed to generate significant thrust, however, and by early summer it was apparent that Deng had succeeded in capturing the canonical high ground with his "seek truth" salvo. Thereafter, his offensive against "whateverism" rapidly gained momentum.

THE ASSAULT ON "WHATEVERISM"

As early as April 4, 1978—the second anniversary of the Qingming incident—a number of wall posters in and around Tiananmen Square and on the campus of Peking University had vigorously denounced certain unnamed "opportunists" and "political clowns" for having used the Qingming disturbances to advance their own careers. Several of the posters demanded full vindication of all those arrested during the April 1976 demonstrations, a few boldly singled out Wu De and Chen Xilian for special condemnation.[45]

The critique of "whateverism" picked up added momentum in late June, when *People's Daily* published an article by a "special correspondent" who argued that it was not necessarily a revisionist sin to update the Thought of Mao Zedong periodically in accordance with the requirements of a changing reality. Indeed, occasional revision of Mao's directives might be both neces-

sary and appropriate.[46] A week later, the same newspaper printed a hitherto
unpublished 1962 speech by Chairman Mao in which he took personal responsibility for certain mistakes made during the Great Leap Forward,
thereby acknowledging his own fallibility.[47] On August 1, 1978, on the occasion of the fifty-first anniversary of the founding of the PLA, an editorial in the
Liberation Army Daily warmly endorsed Deng's positions on both the "seek
truth" and "fine tradition" debates. Thereafter, a bandwagon effect took shape,
as a growing number of party and army leaders began submitting articles to
Chinese newspapers and journals echoing Deng's ideological position in his
struggle with the "whateverists."

Throughout the summer, Deng's supporters pressed the attack against traditional norms and values. On the economic front, Hu Qiaomu, recently installed as president of CASS and a co-author of Deng's notorious "poisonous
weeds" of 1975, gave a major address before the State Council in July. In it he
raised a number of controversial policy recommendations, including proposals to grant enhanced operational authority and autonomy to enterprise managers; to pay greater attention to questions of "comparative advantage"
in promoting regional economic specialization; and to use "economic
methods"—such as legally binding contracts and price adjustments reflecting
the "law of value"—to replace arbitrary administrative fiat as the dominant
mechanism for regulating the nation's economic activity.[48]

Caught off guard by the strength and intensity of Deng's multifront offensive, the "whateverists" tried vainly to blunt the thrust of the attack. Wang
Dongxing, who had gained a measure of influence over the editorial content
of the party's theoretical journal *Red Flag* following the purge of the Gang of
Four, now used his influence to retard the spread of Deng's ideas on truth,
tradition, and economic restructuring. In his new role as media watchdog,
Wang was able to delay publication of Hu Qiaomu's controversial economic
proposals for more than two months; in a similar vein, he tried to suppress
distribution of the inaugural September 1978 issue of the journal *Zhongguo
qingnian* (China youth), which was set to resume publication after twelve
years of Cultural Revolution–enforced silence. The issue in question contained three anti-"whateverism" articles penned by supporters of Hu Yaobang, who dominated the journal's editorial committee. One article carried the
provocative title "Why 'Every Word Is Truth' Is Absurd," while another—
rumored to have been written by Hu Yaobang himself—was entitled "Eliminate Blind Faith, Get a Good Grasp of Science."[49]

China Youth was the house organ of the Communist Youth League, of
which Hu Yaobang was past chairman. The CYL leadership core also included another member of Hu Yaobang's political network, who coincidentally shared his surname, Hu Qili. Along with *People's Daily* chief editor Hu
Jiwei (also unrelated), the "three Hus" formed a strong proreform, anti-"whateverist" contingent; under their leadership, *People's Daily* and *China Youth*
became key outlets for articles critical of China's existing political structure.[50]

In its November 1978 issue, *China Youth* ran a provocative article that bluntly asked, "How could the Gang of Four have run amok in such a way over the past several years? Why did the Chinese people tolerate them?" The answer suggested by the article's authors, Lin Chun and Li Yinhe, was that the Gang had been a product of China's political structure, which lacked "reliable organizations and systems to safeguard socialist democracy." Socialist democracy, in turn, was said to require the existence of an independent judiciary, meaningful popular elections (complete with secret ballot), and limited terms of office for leading officials. A week after appearing in *China Youth*, this controversial article was reprinted in *People's Daily*.[51] Also published in *People's Daily* in November 1978 was an article acknowledging that in the past, constitutional guarantees of free speech and free association had failed to protect people's rights because such guarantees were "mere principles" that could be evaded with impunity. What was needed, the author argued, was a wholesale reform of the legal system, including adoption of a comprehensive civil code putting teeth into constitutional rights.[52]

In the late summer and autumn of 1978, remnant Leftists and their collaborators were dislodged from provincial strongholds around the country, while one after another of China's provincial party and military organs lined up in support of Deng Xiaoping on the twin issues of truth and tradition. Even the quintessential survivor Li Xiannian now began to back away from his earlier support of Hua Guofeng.

In the second week of October the penny dropped, as the Beijing municipal government removed the most strident and abrasive member of the "whatever" faction, Wu De, from his mayoralty post, triggering a rash of celebratory "happy sendoff" posters in the streets of Beijing.[53] Shortly thereafter, speculation began to mount that General Chen Xilian had also been removed from his post as commander of the Beijing Military Region, due, among other things, to his alleged past association with Zhang Chunqiao and Mao Yuanxin.[54] Of China's eleven military region commanders, only Chen Xilian failed to endorse Deng's injunction to "seek truth from facts."[55]

As autumn deepened, the mass media published a number of outspoken articles on sensitive subjects, including a critique of the cult of Mao-worship and a literary allusion to the "blood-soaked legacy" of the Cultural Revolution. A new exhortation to "emancipate thinking" (*jiefang sixiang*) now began to gain currency as a catchword of the new pragmatism. More portentous still, at a congress of the Communist Youth League organized by supporters of Hu Yaobang, two groups of young "heroes of Tiananmen"—men and women who had recently been released from custody after serving prison terms for their role in the 1976 Qingming disturbances—were given an enthusiastic public reception.[56] Toward the end of November, a key member of Hu Yaobang's political network, CASS Vice-President Yu Guangyuan, gave a speech in which he claimed that democracy was a vital prerequisite for successful modernization; without the one, he argued, the other was unattainable.[57]

REVERSING VERDICTS: THE NOVEMBER WORK CONFERENCE

In Beijing the winds of change blew with increasing force as a Central Committee work conference was convened on November 10. At this important meeting, which lasted for more than a month, senior CCP economic strategist Chen Yun made a strong appeal to reverse the verdicts on a group of sixty-one unrehabilitated Cultural Revolution purge victims, including former Beijing mayor Peng Zhen, former central party secretary Yang Shangkun, economic planner Bo Yibo, and (posthumously) Marshal Peng Dehuai and regional party chief Tao Zhu, both of whom had died in disgrace.[58] More provocatively, Chen Yun now strongly affirmed the "revolutionary" nature of the Tiananmen incident and criticized Wang Dongxing for having maintained illicit relations with the Gang of Four. Finally, Chen affixed the blame for much of the organizational paralysis and chaos of the Cultural Revolution on Mao's sinister former internal security chief, Kang Sheng, who died late in 1975. Chen's speech reportedly evoked a wave of affirmative responses from members of the Central Committee, including many who now demanded reassessment of a wide range of Cultural Revolution–related events.[59]

Trying desperately to get out in front of the wave before it overwhelmed him, Hua Guofeng now issued an informal apologia, conceding that the Qingming incident had been "completely revolutionary."[60] With this, the last formal obstacle was removed to reversing this most controversial of verdicts. On November 16 Hua Guofeng's change of heart was symbolically conveyed to the people when the mass media published a photograph of Hua's personal inscription dedicating the first officially approved anthology of poems from the April 5 incident—which included an elegy tacitly likening Mao Zedong to the brutal emperor Qinshihuang.[61]

When the decision to reverse the Tiananmen verdict was first announced informally in the *Guangming Daily* on November 15, it created an immediate sensation. Equally electrifying were two other items that appeared in the same newspaper. One conveyed the party's decision to rehabilitate most of the remaining victims of Mao's 1957 "anti-Rightist rectification campaign"; the other contained a scathing denunciation of an essay written with Mao Zedong's approval in November 1965 by Yao Wenyuan, firing the opening salvo in the Cultural Revolution. With a single stroke, three of Chairman Mao's most controversial initiatives—his 1957 crackdown on "bourgeois intellectuals," his 1965 decision to launch the Cultural Revolution, and his 1976 verdict on the Tiananmen disturbance—were essentially rescinded. Gone, too, was Mao's carefully guarded reputation for wisdom and perspicacity. The person reportedly behind the decision to "reverse the verdicts" from the anti-Rightist movement was Hu Yaobang.[62]

Toward the end of the November–December CC work conference, four leading "whateverists"—Wang Dongxing, Wu De, Chen Xilian, and Vice-Premier Ji Dengkui—were sharply criticized for various mistakes and shortcomings and were required to make self-criticisms. Despite widespread calls to remove the four from the inner core of party leadership, Deng Xiaoping and Li Xiannian argued against such a step, citing the urgent need to preserve inner-party stability and unity.[63]

In his closing address to the work conference on December 13, Deng Xiaoping once again emphasized the need to "emancipate thinking" and "seek truth from facts." Noting wryly that "Engels did not ride on an airplane; Stalin did not wear dacron," Deng urged his comrades to reject the rigid formulas and obsolete dogmas of the past. "Practice is continuously developing," he said. "We must study the new situation and solve new problems."[64] Responding to Deng's challenge, the work conference endorsed his twin proposals to "open up to the outside world" (*kaifang*) and to press ahead with the full normalization of China's diplomatic relations with the United States.

Although Deng stopped short of calling for Hua Guofeng's ouster, Hua was nonetheless badly—perhaps fatally—damaged by the work conference's reversal of several key Maoist verdicts and by the pointed criticism directed at Hua's top lieutenants. Despite his eleventh-hour bid to regain a measure of political legitimacy by affecting the guise of a born-again pragmatist, Hua Guofeng's days as "wise leader Chairman Hua" were now numbered.

In the late fall of 1978 the initial stage of China's post-Mao succession crisis thus came to a close. Mao's wife and her three radical cronies stood imprisoned and powerless; Mao's heir apparent was under fire; Mao's judgment was conceded to be fallible; and Mao's policies were being openly questioned. With Deng Xiaoping gaining steadily in political strength and confidence, the final stage in the succession struggle was about to begin. The pivotal turning point was the Third Plenum of the Eleventh CC, which met in the third week of December 1978.

TURNING POINT: THE THIRD PLENUM

With the path cleared for a fundamental change in the prevailing ethos and policy orientations of the Maoist era, it remained for the Third Plenum to ratify Deng Xiaoping's stunning triumph. Although the meeting, which opened on December 18, was in some respects anticlimactic (groundwork for Deng's victory over the "whateverists" had been laid at the November–December work conference), the plenum nonetheless marked a clear watershed. In addition to formally vindicating Deng, rehabilitating most remaining Maoist purge victims,[65] and opening the door to a future reassessment of Mao's errors and shortcomings, the Third Plenum adopted a number of important changes in the party's political line and economic orientation. These included a shift from criticism of the Gang of Four to the pursuit of "socialist modernization" as the primary focus in party work; a decision to decentralize, rationalize, and reform economic administration and management through introduction of responsibility systems, performance-based rewards and punishments, and the "law of value"; abandonment of mass movements as a preferred means of policy implementation; and a commitment to strengthen the institutions of collective leadership, socialist democracy, and the legal system.[66]

Reflecting the shifting balance of political forces within the party, four of Deng Xiaoping's staunchest senior supporters were added to the Politburo at the Third Plenum: Chen Yun, Hu Yaobang, Wang Zhen, and Deng Yingchao. Chen Yun was concurrently appointed to the Politburo Standing Committee, which was now expanded from five members to six: Hua Guofeng (chairman), Ye Jianying, Deng Xiaoping, Li Xiannian, Chen Yun, and Wang Dongxing. Further strengthening Deng's bid for power, nine rehabilitated cadres were added to the 169-member Central Committee, including Deng's longtime associates Hu Qiaomu, Wang Renzhong, Song Renqiong, and Xi Zhongxun.[67]

In a move designed to curb the organizational power and autonomy of the "whateverists," the post of CC general secretary (*zongshuji*), abolished during the Cultural Revolution, was now reconstituted, with Hu Yaobang designated as "chief secretary" (*mishuzhang*). Hu's promotion gave Deng's reform faction added leverage vis-à-vis the powerful CC General Office.[68] To ensure that pro-Deng forces would exercise control over the editorial policy and content of the party-dominated mass media, Hu Yaobang was concurrently named to head the CC's propaganda department, replacing "whateverist" Zhang Pinghua. Another key Deng associate, Song Renqiong, took Hu's place as director of the party's organization department.

Having severely weakened the hold of the "whateverists" on party organization and operations, Deng stopped short of formally seeking to oust Hua and his supporters from the central leadership. To stabilize his newly empowered reform coalition and to assuage key survivors such as Ye Jianying and Li Xiannian, who wished to avoid a sharp break with China's Maoist past, Deng agreed to permit the "whateverists" to retain their seats on the Central Committee and Politburo. They did not escape unscathed, however: Wang Dongxing was bumped down to the bottom position on the Politburo's Standing Committee, beneath Chen Yun, and was also removed from his posts as commander of PLA unit 8341 and director of the CC General Office. The former position was filled by veteran PLA political commissar Yang Dezhong; the latter went to Yao Yilin, a rehabilitated former minister of commerce with close personal ties to Chen Yun and Peng Zhen.[69] Two other leading "whateverists"—vice-premiers Ji Dengkui and Chen Yonggui—were stripped of responsibility for agricultural policy, which was now placed under the jurisdiction of newly appointed Dengist vice-premier Wang Renzhong.[70]

In a move designed to root out entrenched supporters of the Gang of Four and strengthen the enforcement of party rules and regulations, the Third Plenum created a new internal supervisory organ, the Central Discipline Inspection Commission (CDIC). Under the chairmanship of Chen Yun, with Hu Yaobang and Deng Yingchao serving as principal vice-chairmen, the hundred-member CDIC was charged with the task of exposing and rectifying remnant ultra-Leftists, "factionalists," "anarchists," and "smash-and-grab-bers" within the party organization.[71]

Apart from the key role played by Chen Yun in mobilizing veteran party cadres to oppose the "whateverists," much of the credit for Deng Xiaoping's triumph at the Third Plenum belonged to Hu Yaobang and his network of supporters inside the CYL and the Central Party School. It was they who spearheaded Deng's "criterion of truth" campaign; they who led the drive to desanctify Mao and demystify "whateverism"; they who drafted the Third Plenum's pathbreaking communiqué; and they who, along with such veteran party theorists as Liao Gailong, most ardently championed systemic structural reform.[72] In the aftermath of the Third Plenum, they began to spell out their agenda for China's modernization and development.

The First Fang/Shou Cycle:
November 1978–August 1980

In the China of the seventies

You send out the call of the times.

The cry of a new arrival

Echoes all around, forcefully:

"We want democracy!"

"We want science!"

"We want a legal system!"

"We want the Four Modernizations!"

—*"Ode to Democracy Wall," November 1978*

PROPELLED by pent-up public disillusionment over the chaos of the Cultural Revolution and fueled by frustration over China's prolonged economic stagnation,[1] the victorious "practice faction" (*shijian pai*), as the Deng Xiaoping–Chen Yun–Hu Yaobang alliance was now dubbed, unleashed a flurry of reform initiatives in the winter and spring of 1978–79. In agriculture, commerce, law, foreign policy, literature and the arts, inter alia, it was a time of experimentation and innovation.[2] For Hua Guofeng, on the other hand, it was a time of enforced humility. By order of the Third Plenum, Hua was no longer referred to as "wise leader Chairman Hua," but simply as "Comrade Hua." Henceforth, collective leadership—decision making by consensus—was to replace the long-standing practice of a single, supreme leader issuing Olympian "instructions."[3]

Adding injury to insult, in the spring of 1979 Chen Yun openly criticized Hua Guofeng's ten-year plan for economic development. Addressing a Central Committee work conference in April, Chen argued that the plan was badly unbalanced, leading to serious overinvestment in heavy industrial construction, neglect of light industry, and rampant deficit spending. To remedy these and other defects, Chen proposed a three-year retrenchment under the aegis of an eight-character charter: "readjustment, reform, correction, and improvement" (*tiaozheng, gaige, zhengdun, tigao*). Under Chen's program, Hua Guofeng's "four modernizations" would be drastically overhauled and scaled down.[4]

Also formally proposed at the April 1979 work conference was the concept of special economic zones. Introduced by two of Deng's old comrades, Guangdong provincial party secretaries Xi Zhongxun and Yang Shangkun, the SEZ concept reportedly originated in 1978 in She'kou Township, Guangdong, where an official of the Hong Kong–based China Merchants' Steamship Navigation Company was searching for a suitable location for a new facility to break up old ships for scrap metal. When Deng heard about the proposal to site the plant on Chinese territory across the border from Hong Kong, he reportedly approved of the idea, saying "During the war, wasn't Yan'an a special zone?"[5]

Four SEZs were provisionally approved in the spring of 1979. Three of them—Shenzhen, Shantou, and Zhuhai—were in Guangdong Province, adjacent to Hong Kong and Macao, while the fourth, Xiamen (Amoy), was on the Fujian coast, directly across the straits from Taiwan. Modeled after export processing zones found elsewhere in Asia, the four coastal SEZs were expected to become advanced centers of high-technology manufacturing and industrial processing, geared to a rapid expansion of the country's export trade. Offering reduced taxes and duties, flexible formats for investment, low labor costs, and other managerial incentives, the SEZs were envisioned as the leading edge of China's economic modernization and reform.[6]

Also receiving preliminary government approval in the spring of 1979 was Chen Yun's controversial eight-character charter for economic readjustment. Overcoming considerable initial resistance from the "whateverists" and their sometime allies, the petroleum clique, Chen's proposed retrenchment plan was adopted in principle by the NPC in June 1979.[7] In July Chen was named vice-premier with overall responsibility for China's economic planning. Thereafter, assisted by two newly rehabilitated vice-premiers, Yao Yilin and Bo Yibo, Chen set about dismantling Hua's "flying leap." By the end of the year, more than three hundred previously approved construction projects had been canceled, with hundreds of others placed on hold pending further review and fiscal consolidation.

Along with the "whateverists," members of the petroleum clique were hard hit by the retrenchment policy. Led by State Planning Commissioner Yu Qiuli and State Economic Commissioner Kang Shi'en, the petroleum group had promoted accelerated deficit spending as a means of stimulating rapid growth in heavy industry, a strategy that had putatively caused serious sectoral imbalances, budget deficits, and fiscal disarray; in the latter half of 1979 they found themselves being squeezed progressively out of the decision-making loop by the Chen-Yao-Bo group. By the end of the year the political aspirations of the petroleum clique had been effectively stifled—along with Hua Guofeng's economic program.[8]

There is considerable irony in the fact that Hua's ten-year plan should be discredited by Chen Yun, who would later become Deng's principal competitor within the reform movement. As noted earlier, several key ingredients of Hua's plan had been lifted straight out of Deng Xiaoping's "three poisonous weeds" of 1975. And while Deng is generally credited with having charted the course of China's post-Mao economic development, much of the credit really belongs to Chen Yun. Indeed, a good many "Dengist" policy innovations—such as the production responsibility system, price reform, market regulation, and smashing the "iron rice bowl"—were actually first proposed either by Chen or by other members of Deng's reform coalition, including Zhao Ziyang, Wan Li, Hu Qiaomu, Sun Yefang, and Xue Muqiao.[9]

Notwithstanding Chen Yun's evident success in derailing Hua Guofeng's "flying leap," the readjustment of 1979 failed to achieve its stated goals of restoring economic balance and reducing state budgetary deficits. For one thing, while over seven hundred construction projects were targeted for cancellation in 1979, the vast majority of these were small in size, resulting in only modest savings. In addition, many of the projects initially frozen in 1979 were restarted a year later with funds generated by an inflow of U.S. $4 billion in new foreign loans. And finally, the rising costs of China's agricultural price support program, including an across-the-board increase of 20 to 50 percent in the price paid to farmers for grain delivered to the state, together with substantial wage hikes and bonus payments granted to workers in 1979, quickly offset whatever savings had been realized from the cancellation of construction projects. The net result was a continuing surfeit of capital construction and a budget deficit that reached RMB ¥17.9 billion by the end of 1979—only to climb even higher in 1980.

While Chen Yun, Bo Yibo, and Yao Yilin wrestled with the country's budgetary problems, in agriculture the year 1979 witnessed the launching of a series of experimental reforms that radically altered the face of the Chinese countryside. Stimulated by the Third Plenum's decision to allow the country's five hundred million farmers to engage in various forms of decollectivized, incentive-driven agricultural production and marketing, a number of rural areas began to experiment with household-based production responsibility systems.[10] Although the Third Plenum had, at the initiative of Hu Qiaomu, issued a document urging caution in devolving agricultural responsibility to the level of the individual household, a number of high-level party leaders supported the household responsibility concept—including theoretician Deng Liqun, whose own son, Deng Yingtao, had become a rural cadre after being sent down to the countryside during the Cultural Revolution. With Deng Liqun's patronage, the first embryonic Chinese think tank—the Rural Development Research Group—was formed in Beijing under the leadership of proreform intellectual Chen Yizi.[11]

In the forefront of the drive to reform agriculture in 1978–79 were two provinces headed by rehabilitated cadres allied with Deng Xiaoping's "practice" faction: traditionally prosperous Sichuan, whose party first secretary Zhao Ziyang was Deng's protégé, and perennially poor Anhui, under Deng's long-time friend Wan Li.[12] Both provinces had experienced a decline in rural productivity and welfare under the radical-collectivist agrarian policies of the Cultural Revolution. Consequently, farmers in both provinces were predisposed to respond favorably to the party's decision to permit experimentation with expanded rural free markets, enlarged private plots, decentralized land-ownership and accounting, and household responsibility systems.[13]

Coupled with the central government's decision to grant farmers a substantial across-the-board price increase for grain delivered to the state, the agricultural reforms of 1979 contributed to a significant upturn in rural income and farm production in Sichuan and Anhui. Based on experiences gained in these two provinces, the reforms were extended the following year to a number of other areas.[14] Meanwhile, Zhao Ziyang and Wan Li were rewarded for their achievements in the design and implementation of rural reform. In September 1979 Zhao was promoted to full membership on the Politburo; the following February Wan Li became a member of the refurbished Central Party Secretariat; two months later, in April 1980, both Zhao and Wan became vice-premiers. Wan, whose place in the inner circle of Chinese political elites was symbolized by his membership in Deng Xiaoping's regular Wednesday and Saturday bridge club, took over the State Council's agriculture portfolio, displacing Wang Renzhong, who retired from his vice-premiership shortly thereafter. In September of the same year, Zhao Ziyang replaced Hua Guofeng as premier of the State Council.

Zhao's rapid ascent from provincial party secretary to premier was paralleled by the formation of several high-level economic policy research groups in Beijing. Under the overall supervision of Hu Qiaomu and Deng Liqun, four specialized task forces were organized in the spring of 1979 to investigate the causes of China's past economic failures and to make recommendations for future reform. Two of the four groups—Technology Transfer, under Vice-Minister of Economic Relations with Foreign Countries Wang Daohan, and Economic System Reform, under Finance Minister Zhang Jingfu—were headed by officials who had worked closely with Chen Yun in the 1940s and 1950s; a third group, Structural Readjustment, was headed by CASS Vice-President Ma Hong, a longtime associate of Bo Yibo; the fourth group, Economic Theory, was led by liberal reformer Yu Guangyuan.[15]

Shortly after Zhao Ziyang was promoted to the premiership in October 1980, the four economic research groups were placed directly under the State Council. With Zhao's support and patronage, they became a prime source of reformist policy initiatives on subjects ranging from price decontrol and profit-sharing to privatization of property rights.[16]

THE DEMOCRACY MOVEMENT OF 1978–1979

While reform and readjustment were getting underway on the economic front, important developments were also taking place on the political/ideological front. In the midst of the CC work conference of November–December 1978, a number of *dazibao* (big-character posters) appeared in downtown Beijing, along a two-hundred-meter stretch of wall on Chang'an Boulevard at Xidan, west of Tiananmen Square.[17] Dubbed "Democracy Wall," the edifice at Xidan

Crowds queue up to purchase copies of the *Tiananmen Poems*, November 1978.

soon became the focal point of a remarkable display of free, unfettered public political discourse.

Wall posters had long served in China as pressure valves for the release of political tension and as informal conduits for disseminating "inside" information and opinion.[18] In the spring of 1978, the people's right to post dazibao had been enshrined in the Chinese constitution as one of the so-called four big freedoms (*sida*). Immediately after the Central Committee published its November 15 decision to reverse the verdict on the Tiananmen incident, there was a sudden spurt of poster activity in the vicinity of Xidan Wall. Parked on the sidewalk in front of the wall on November 16, a bus loaded down with copies of a previously restricted book of poems from the Qingming incident quickly sold out its complete stock.[19]

Two themes stood out among the various opinions expressed in the new dazibao at Xidan Wall: intensified criticism of the "whateverists," in particular Wu De, and questions about Mao Zedong's political judgment and his relations with Cultural Revolution ultra-Leftists.[20] One poster, appearing on November 22, warned: "There is a handful of people who were in power during the epoch of the Gang of Four. These people took part in the suppression of the Tiananmen incident. If they do not repent, if they do not publicly admit their crimes, their days will soon be numbered." Another poster, appearing over the weekend of November 18–19, raised a serious allegation concerning Mao Zedong's political acumen: "In 1976, . . . the Gang of Four made use of the prestige and power of Chairman Mao Zedong's mistaken judgment on class struggle to launch an all-out attack on the cause of revolution in China."

As far as anyone at the scene could recall, this was the first time that Chairman Mao had been criticized by name in an open forum. A few days later, an even more serious set of questions concerning Mao's behavior appeared on a dazibao at Xidan:

> Ask yourself: How could Lin Biao reach power without the support of Mao? Ask yourself: Did Mao not know that Jiang Qing . . . [and] Zhang Chunqiao [were] traitors? Ask yourself: Without the consent of Mao, would it have been possible for the Gang of Four to launch the campaign against Deng Xiaoping? Ask yourself: Without the consent of Mao, would it have been possible to label the Tiananmen episode a counterrevolutionary incident?

By late November the posters had begun to attract considerable attention. Individually and in small groups, citizens of Beijing gathered at Xidan Wall and in Tiananmen Square to read the latest political broadsides and to participate in an unprecedented public dialogue on pressing national issues. The vast majority of participants were young workers, clerks, and unemployed intellectual youths in their twenties and thirties. Many had been "sent down" for two years of urban labor after middle school graduation as a prerequisite to seeking university entrance, but had then failed to secure college admission because of either academic shortcomings or lack of acceptable political credentials. Consequently, they became stuck indefinitely performing menial urban jobs or "waiting for work," as unemployment was euphemistically referred to at the time. As a result of their dismal situation, they comprised a politically articulate, disaffected substratum of Beijing's working population.[21] Although most of the participants in the Beijing street dialogue of November 1978 were graduates of junior or senior middle schools, few university students or higher intellectuals played an active role.[22]

At first party leaders, including Deng Xiaoping, were ambivalent about the new rash of wall posters. Although the "practice faction" was the clear beneficiary of much of the political discourse at Xidan Wall, Deng entertained reservations about the burgeoning movement. In an interview with a group of visiting Japanese politicians on November 26, Deng grudgingly supported free speech, but with one important caveat: Chairman Mao should not be criticized by name. "In the beginning," he stated, "we made an attempt to stop the campaign. We thought the masses would oppose attempts to use Mao's name. The leaders were opposed to it and I am not supporting it. But we should not check the demands of the masses to speak."[23]

The following day Deng ostensibly softened his stance on the issue of free expression. In response to a direct question posed by visiting American journalist Robert Novak, Deng now called the appearance of dazibao "a good thing," though he once again expressed reservations about criticizing Chairman Mao.[24] When John Fraser, a Canadian diplomat, relayed word of Deng's approbation to a crowd of several thousand activists and onlookers gathered at Democracy Wall, the excitement was palpable. The crowds at Xidan and other poster sites in and around Tiananmen Square soon swelled; and within a relatively short period of time, what had started out as a rather small fringe movement of disaffected workers, educated youths, and former Red Guards was transformed from the realm of guerrilla theater for the few into participatory politics for the many.

DEALING WITH DISSENT: DENG XIAOPING'S DILEMMA

As November turned to December, and the Central Committee continued to chisel away at Hua Guofeng's power and prestige, Deng Xiaoping could afford to affect a benign, patronizing attitude toward Democracy Wall. Most of the dazibao were, after all, strongly supportive of the spirit of economic and political reform, and many were openly hostile to "whateverism." Yet within the burgeoning poster movement there were signs of a deeper, more fundamental critique of the core political institutions and values of Chinese Marxism—a critique that, if left unchecked, could prove extremely troublesome.

Even before prodemocracy activists received Deng's message of support in late November, a militant, sixty-six-page poster appeared on Mao's memorial hall at the south end of Tiananmen Square, calling on the Chinese people to arise and "settle accounts" with all dictators, "no matter who they are." Also called for was a reassessment of Mao's contributions and shortcomings.[25] In a somewhat less combative mode, in early December participants in an open forum at the Heroes' Monument in Tiananmen Square urged greater freedom and democracy for China. Some speakers criticized Mao's economic strategy, calling on China's new leaders to copy the more liberal Yugoslav model of worker self-management; others urged party leaders to study the positive aspects of American-style democracy, including its system of constitutional checks and balances and its two-party system. One speaker questioned Mao's 1949 decision to "lean to one side" in favor of the Soviet Union against the United States.

Although the criticisms were generally couched in nonconfrontational language, the progressive escalation of public debate from a relatively narrow focus on the misdeeds of the Gang of Four and the mistakes of the "whateverists" to a more fundamental critique of the Chinese political system proved inherently unsettling to party authorities. Schooled in the monocratic Leninist institutional tradition of proletarian dictatorship and democratic centralism, Deng Xiaoping and his associates faced a complex and difficult dilemma: how to end the twenty-year reign of Leftism in China without at the same time opening the door to Rightist agitation, political opposition, and consequent instability.

Spurred by Deng's November expression of support for free speech, Xidan activists became bolder and more outspoken in their criticisms. By early December, as the poster campaign spread from Beijing to Shanghai, Wuhan, Guangzhou, and other major Chinese cities, a unifying theme began to emerge from among the disparate elements participating in the new movement: the call for political democratization and respect for human rights as prerequisites to successful economic modernization. As one Xidan wall poster put it: "China's system of government is modeled on the Russian system [which] produces bureaucracy and a privileged stratum. Without changes in this system, the 'four modernizations' will stop halfway . . . , as in Russia where the state is strong and the people are poor. . . . We need a state where all delegates are elected and responsible to the people." Another poster, written by a group calling itself the China Human Rights League, took the form of an open letter to U.S. President Jimmy Carter. Lauding President Carter's recent speech on universal human rights, the letter's drafters called on him actively to support the drive for human rights in China:

> Your speech . . . has moved the conscience of the world. As Chinese citizens, we think that truth is universal and that . . . the demand for human rights is common to all. Your concern for Sakharov, Shcharansky, and Ginsburg was very moving, but . . . you should not only protest against unsuccessful oppression, because successful oppression is even more fearful. In a country [like China] which regards Marxism as a new religion . . . , anyone who expresses a different opinion may be considered a counterrevolutionary . . . and can be arrested, imprisoned, . . . sent into exile, [or] even executed. . . . We would like to ask you to pay attention to the state of human rights in China. The Chinese people do not want to repeat the tragic life of the Soviet people in the Gulag Archipelago.

Growing visibly perturbed over the newfound brashness of the Democracy Movement, Deng Xiaoping was especially irritated by the appeal to President Carter, which came in the midst of delicate Sino-American negotiations over the normalization of bilateral diplomatic relations,[26] and by the spreading practice of openly criticizing Mao Zedong by name. When Deng's objections were made known in early December, new posters immediately appeared at Xidan. For the first time, movement activists now began openly chastising Deng himself. One poster admonished: "Vice-Premier Deng, you are wrong, completely wrong. . . . There is no doubt that, a long time ago, the Chinese people took note of Chairman Mao's mistakes. Those who hate the Gang of Four cannot fail to have grievances against Chairman Mao."

Other posters openly questioned the motives and intentions of the reformers themselves. One particularly critical assessment came from a twenty-eight-year-old electrician-turned-activist named Wei Jingsheng, whose lengthy wall poster, "The Fifth Modernization," appeared in Beijing on December 5. The poster began by noting that the hopes and aspirations of the Chinese people had been greatly elevated following the arrest of the Gang of Four and the return to power of Deng Xiaoping; but these expectations had been severely dampened when the new leaders turned out to be nearly as rigid and undemocratic as the old ones:

> [When] Vice-Premier Deng finally returned to his leading post . . . how excited people were, how inspired. . . . When Deng Xiaoping raised the slogan of "getting down to business" . . . the people wanted to "seek truth from facts," to investigate

the past. . . . But "some people" warned us: . . . Chairman Mao is the great savior of the Chinese people. . . . If you don't agree with this you will come to no good end! . . . Regrettably, the old political system so hated by the people was not changed, the democracy and freedom they hoped for could not even be mentioned. . . .

. . . When people ask for democracy they are only asking for something they rightfully own. . . . [Under such circumstances] are not the people justified in seizing power from the overlords?

Although Deng was clearly disturbed by the tone of such commentaries, he continued to defend the right of Chinese citizens to express their political views without fear of retaliation. In his closing address to the Central Committee work conference on December 13, Deng coupled a general endorsement of the spirit of the new Democracy Movement ("The masses should be encouraged to offer criticisms; there is nothing to worry about even if a few malcontents take advantage of democracy to make trouble") with a pointed warning to his comrades against the temptation to use coercive methods to stamp out criticism ("We must firmly put a stop to practices such as attacking and trying to silence people who make critical comments").[27] In a demonstration of his sincerity, Deng approved the release from custody of three members of the collective writing group known as "Li Yizhe," who had been detained without trial since December 1974 for having posted a "counter-revolutionary" dazibao at a busy intersection in downtown Guangzhou. The offending poster, a lengthy treatise entitled "On Socialist Democracy and the Legal System," had contained a scathing attack upon the Cultural Revolution and the "feudal autocracy" of the Chinese political-legal system. The decision to free the three members of "Li Yizhe"—*Li* Zhengtian, Chen *Yi*gang, and Wang Xi*zhe*—had been recommended by Xi Zhongxun and Yang Shangkun, with the support of Zhao Ziyang.[28] When the three poster-writing activists were released from labor reform and exonerated of all charges of wrongdoing at the end of December 1978, wall posters in Guangzhou, Beijing, and elsewhere happily greeted them as heroes.[29]

Notwithstanding Deng's display of good will, the voices of public dissent grew more insistent and less restrained in the early winter of 1978–79. By this time, a number of underground journals had sprung up, with names like "Beijing Spring" (*Zhongguo zhichun*), "April Fifth Forum" (*Siwu luntan*), "Enlightenment" (*Qimeng*), "Exploration" (*Tansuo*), "Today" (*Jintian*), and "Masses' Reference News" (*Qunzhong cankao xiaoxi*). Similar in some respects to Soviet *samizdat*, the new publications were printed surreptitiously, generally in production runs of a few hundred copies per issue, often on crude mimeograph machines using hand-stenciled originals and "back-door" supplies of paper and ink. Once printed, copies of the journals were posted at Xidan Wall and in the vicinity of Tiananmen Square, where they could be discussed or hand-copied by interested readers; remaining copies were distributed as handbills around the city.[30]

Beijing residents read the latest dazibao at Democracy Wall, December 1978.

Some of the new journals repeated the latest political rumors and spread gossip about Communist Party leaders; others discoursed more philosophically (or polemically) upon the major political issues of the day, including the relative merits of different leaders and different systems of government; still others provided an outlet for new poetic and literary works by a young generation of alienated, anti-establishment writers. Unlike the Soviet samizdat, which were true underground publications, several of China's most prominent unofficial journals and journalists maintained informal contacts with reform-oriented party officials. In turn, reform politicians apparently found it useful to keep open their lines of communication with the fledgling Democracy Movement. A few leading officials, including Hu Yaobang, even made it a practice to have prodemocracy activists come to their homes to discuss politics and philosophy.[31] Later, when the movement was under fire from orthodox party leaders, Deng Xiaoping would charge that some of the more slickly produced underground journals had received clandestine support from high-level cadres.

NEW SOURCES OF DISCONTENT: THE PETITIONERS' MOVEMENT

As the voices demanding systemic change grew more insistent and more articulate, a new source of popular discontent began to emerge. Alongside the proliferation of wall-poster polemics, political gossip, and anti-establishment poetry, there now appeared a spate of highly personalized appeals for redress of grievances written by (or on behalf of) ordinary citizens who had suffered abuse at the hands of Leftists during the Cultural Revolution. With Hu Yaobang now taking the lead in promoting the reexamination of all reported cases of unjust persecution, tens of thousands of people addressed written appeals to party and government offices in the winter of 1978–79; additional thousands descended upon Beijing personally to press their grievances. With official channels clogged and response times painfully slow, many petitioners took to the streets, posting handwritten appeals (known as *xiaozibao*, or "small-character posters") at Xidan, Tiananmen, and elsewhere. Often, the appeals contained detailed descriptions of horrendous persecution and injustice.[32] Such poignant personal pleas for help were supplemented by a large number of appeals by former Red Guards and educated urban youths who had been sent down to the countryside during the rustication (*xiaxiang*) movement of the late 1960s and early 1970s, and who now flocked illegally to China's largest cities in hopes of having their cases reviewed and their urban household registration restored.

Most of the petitioners who descended on Beijing were poor; many were in dire straits. Some had traveled long distances on foot, carrying their possessions in knotted bundles; others had hitched rides into the cities on freight trains or trucks. Gathering in clusters near railroad stations and in city centers, petitioners took to begging food or peddling small household items while waiting for their cases to be reopened. In Beijing, one group of rural petitioners camped out at the front gate of Zhongnanhai, official residence of party and government leaders, vowing not to leave until their grievances had been heard. A foreign journalist described another group of petitioners, living in squalor at a temporary encampment, as having come "straight out of a Goya painting . . . sick, on crutches, dressed in rags and tatters, wretchedly poverty-stricken."[33]

In all, more than 100,000 out-of-towners descended upon Beijing and Shanghai in 1979, hoping to have their cases reopened. So great was the volume of appeals that the Central Committee and the State Council, under Hu Yaobang's overall supervision, eventually assigned more than 1,000 cadres to spread out across the country to sift through the complaints, the vast majority of which were officially conceded to be "reasonable."[34]

Despite government pledges to review all appeals objectively and impartially, many petitioners complained of receiving unfair treatment. One celebrated case involved a thirty-two-year-old unemployed female worker named Fu Yuehua, who had been fired from her job after reporting that she had been raped by a male cadre. Unable to gain an unbiased hearing for her complaint, Fu stirred up a political storm in early January 1979 by organizing peasant petitioners to hold a demonstration in Tiananmen Square, demanding an end to oppression and hunger in China. Held on January 8—the third anniversary of Zhou Enlai's death—Fu Yuehua's petitioners' protest played to an audience of more than ten thousand people who had come to the Heroes' Monument to pay homage to the memory of Premier Zhou. One week later, on January 14, another demonstration by hundreds of angry petitioners, carrying banners and shouting demands for food, work, human rights, and democracy, marched from Tiananmen Square down Chang'an Boulevard to Zhongnanhai, where they tried unsuccessfully to enter the gates of the state residential compound to present a letter of appeal to Hua Guofeng.

Alarmed by the rising militancy of the petitioners, and unmoved by Deng Xiaoping's exhortation to avoid using coercion to suppress dissent, the Beijing municipal government prepared to respond. On January 18 Beijing police arrested Fu Yuehua, making her the first known political casualty of the Chinese Democracy Movement.[35]

In the face of mounting intraparty pressure to take a firm stand against "troublemakers," Deng Xiaoping continued to urge his comrades to expand their investigation and study of democratic reforms. As late as January 27— ten days after Fu Yuehua's arrest—Deng addressed a party forum on theoretical work. Noting that the bourgeoisie in Western countries had solved the problem of transforming government officials from masters of society into public servants, he called for further study of Western democratic institutions in order to "develop the good points of the bourgeoisie in this respect. . . . So far we have not done this well. . . . We should find a way to let people feel they are the masters of the country."[36] Immediately after delivering these remarks, Deng departed on a ten-day visit to the United States to celebrate the normalization of Sino-American relations.

In Deng's absence, tensions continued to mount between prodemocracy activists and Beijing municipal authorities. When plainclothes police were observed tape recording conversations at Xidan Wall and copying down license numbers of bicyclists who stopped to take part in political discussions there, an underground journalist took note of these events, ominously observing that "Some bigwigs in the Beijing Municipal CCP Committee are afraid that the people might be able truly to enjoy democracy."

THE SPLIT IN DENG'S REFORM COALITION

By the time Deng returned to Beijing in the second week of February, a significant rift had opened within his reform coalition. On one side stood the progressive intellectuals of Hu Yaobang's network, including *People's Daily* Editor Hu Jiwei, Associate Editor Wang Ruoshui, and senior CASS Vice-President Yu Guangyuan, who continued to stress the need for political tolerance and thoroughgoing democratic reform. On the other side were arrayed a group of veteran party theoreticians, including Hu Qiaomu and Deng Liqun, who had come to view the Democracy Movement and associated petitioners' protests as threats to the stability and unity of the country. A group of activists, representing seven different Beijing underground journals, noted the existence of this rift when they met at Xidan Wall on January 29 to discuss the changing political situation and its implications for the future of the Democracy Movement.[37]

Under pressure from conservatives and centrists alike to harden his position

on free speech, Deng Xiaoping temporized. In an unpublished speech to senior cadres on March 16, he acknowledged that "majority opinion" within the
party and military leadership favored the dissolution of human rights organizations, the banning of mass marches on party and government offices, and
the closing of Democracy Wall. Expressing his personal disagreement with
such views, Deng argued that if "the old road of suppressing differing opinion
and not listening to criticism" were taken, "the result will definitely be unfavorable. . . . [It] will make the trust and support of the masses disappear."
Despite such personal reservations, Deng conceded that "if you all want it, I
will go along with the majority opinion. . . . The worst that might happen [to
me] is that the masses might speak badly of me." Appealing for a middle
course, Deng made the following proposal: "Let the people post some
dazibao; catch a few proven evil-doers in the human rights organization; and
let the others do what they want."[38]

Testing the limits of Deng's forbearance, on March 25 Wei Jingsheng, editor of the underground journal *Explorations*, published a biting critique of
Deng's March 16 speech. Entitled "Do We Want a Democracy or a New Dictatorship?" Wei's broadside accused Deng of shedding his mask as protector
of democracy, betraying the people's trust, and metamorphosizing into a "dictatorial fascist" in the mold of the deposed ultra-Leftists.[39]

In Beijing and elsewhere, the months of February and March witnessed an
increase in the scale, volatility, and occasional violence of petitioners' demonstrations and protest marches. In some places, groups of angry demonstrators
entered factory compounds and other work units in an effort to confront cadres and coworkers who had persecuted them; in other instances petitioners
broke into party and government offices in search of records pertaining to
their cases. Violence was reported in a number of cities.[40]

As a result of such developments, the split within Deng's reform coalition
grew wider. Adopting a sympathetic, tolerant attitude toward the petitioners'
movement, Chen Yun traced the roots of the current situation to Leftist-in-
flicted economic hardships of the past two decades. "If people don't have
enough to eat and are not adequately clothed," Chen argued,

> you can offer a million excuses. . . . But no matter how many they are or how
> good they are, nobody will listen. . . . They are impatient and tired of waiting.
> They feel they have been waiting thirty years and now have to wait another thirty
> years. . . . They also claim to raise a point of justice. . . . They say: you cadres
> have already been rewarded for your suffering. Why must we the people go on
> suffering without end? . . . Unless we win the confidence of the entire country
> there can be no resolution.[41]

By contrast, the more conservative members of Deng's coalition, such as
NPC Standing Committee Vice-Chairman Tan Zhenlin, viewed the latest
urban disturbances as part of an insidious attempt by people who "specialize
in making trouble" to disrupt the "calm and discipline" of society. Dismissing
as sheer nonsense the arguments advanced by people like Chen Yun who
were in basic sympathy with the motives and aspirations of the demonstrators,

Tan strongly denounced the permissiveness of the reform coalition's liberal wing:

> The amazing thing is that even among us there are some . . . leading individuals in the party Central Committee who close their eyes . . . and talk a lot of nonsense. . . . They babble such absurdities as: "It is because these people have suffered such grave injustice over the last ten years, have borne intolerable wrongs, that these consequences now occur. It is entirely understandable." Even more ridiculous are such statements as "China needs more democracy" that are brought forth as placation. What utter nonsense! . . . Who among us has not suffered injustice and felt indignation? Every one of you has, my comrades, and so have I. But our suffering and indignation are stronger and deeper than theirs.[42]

With urban violence on the increase, law-and-order elements within the party and the PLA prevailed, spurning Chen Yun's plea for tolerance and rejecting Deng Xiaoping's call for moderation and restraint. Signaling the advent of a new, harder line, a *People's Daily* editorial of March 27 noted that acts of "attacking government offices, beating cadres, . . . and sabotaging work discipline, production, and society" were posing a serious threat to public order. "From now on," the editorial warned, "such actions will be vigorously suppressed." Two days later the Beijing municipal government issued a circular on public order, laying down strict rules governing mass meetings and demonstrations. Henceforth, petitioners and protesters would not be permitted to block traffic, interfere with the work of public offices, or instigate the masses to cause trouble; attacks on organs of the party, government, and army were strictly forbidden, and citizens attending public meetings were required to follow the orders of the people's police; finally, placement of leaflets and wall posters was prohibited on all streets, public places, or buildings outside of "designated areas"—which in Beijing were now limited to a single site at Xidan Wall.[43] Most ominous of all, the March 29 municipal proclamation invoked a series of four political and ideological injunctions that set clear limits on the scope of free speech and expression: "All activities in opposition to socialism, in opposition to proletarian dictatorship, in opposition to leadership by the party, or in opposition to Marxism–Leninism–Mao Zedong Thought . . . are prohibited by law and will be prosecuted."[44] Henceforth these injunctions, known collectively as the "four cardinal principles" (*sixiang jiben yuanze*), were to be employed as a litmus test for judging politically acceptable behavior.

DENG TAKES A STAND: THE 1979 CONFERENCE ON THEORETICAL WORK

Bowing to the proponents of stability and unity, at the end of March Deng delivered a strong law-and-order speech to the closing session of a major party conference on theoretical work.[45] The ten-week conference, run by Hu Yaobang and jointly sponsored by CASS and the CC Propaganda Department, had provided a forum for reform-minded political theorists to lay the intellectual foundations for a revision of party ideology and the reform of China's political and economic institutions. Although dominated by liberal reformers, a scattering of more conventional Marxist theoreticians also attended the conference, including Hu Qiaomu, Zhang Pinghua, Deng Liqun, and NPC Standing Committee member Hu Sheng.[46]

During the latter part of the conference, after Deng Xiaoping had returned from his trip to the United States, Hu Qiaomu reportedly complained to him about a number of antiparty, anti-Maoist statements made by various conference participants, including members of Hu Yaobang's network; he also complained of clandestine collusion between Hu's supporters and certain activists inside the Democracy Movement. Deng reportedly became upset by this disclosure, and for the first time he compared the current situation of "ultrademocracy" to the Rightist challenge of spring 1957, calling the present situation "more dangerous" than the earlier one. He then asked Hu Qiaomu to organize a team of writers to prepare a speech for delivery at the closing session of the conference.

While Deng considered his response, he came under increasing pressure from another quarter. In mid-February China had launched a surprise military attack against Vietnam (euphemistically referred to as a "self-defensive counterattack"), ostensibly in retaliation for Vietnam's autumn 1978 invasion of Cambodia. Personally approved by Deng with the concurrence of the MAC,[47] the Chinese offensive encountered unexpectedly heavy resistance. Instead of inflicting a quick, decisive defeat on Vietnamese defense forces and then pulling back across their own border, as planned, Chinese troops became bogged down inside Vietnam; in just over a month of fighting, the PLA absorbed more than thirty thousand casualties.[48] Although the war ended in a virtual military standoff, China suffered a significant loss of face due to the PLA's inability to "teach a lesson" to Vietnam. As the commander-in-chief of the Vietnam operation, Deng, too, lost face.

Some of Deng's Vietnam policy critics were outspoken democracy activists like Wei Jingsheng, whose wall-poster critique of the February invasion reportedly drew Deng's ire.[49] Other criticism, however, came from senior members of Deng's own reform coalition. Frustrated over the stalemate in Vietnam, Chen Yun, for example, reportedly complained that Vietnam "was only hurt a little" in its war with China. "We didn't break their fingers," he said, "but merely hurt them. In some respects, we actually helped them."[50] In a similar vein, MAC Vice-Chairman Nie Rongzhen, another key Deng ally, allegedly complained that the tactics employed against Vietnam had been unsatisfactory.[51]

Stung by such criticism, and angered by allegations of rampant "Rightism" at the theory conference, Deng endorsed the four cardinal principles in his speech of March 30. While vigorously defending his reform program and repeating previous calls to emancipate thinking and foster socialist democracy, Deng now offered—in the name of the Central Committee—a darker, more pessimistic view of China's Democracy Movement, and of the mounting threat posed by a handful of antisocialist, antiparty elements:

The Central Committee considers that we must now repeatedly emphasize the necessity of upholding the four cardinal principles, because certain people (even if only a handful) are attempting to undermine them. In no way can such attempts be tolerated. . . . Is the Central Committee making a mountain out of a molehill when it takes this view of the matter? No, it is not. In the light of current develop-ments the party has no choice.

In the recent period a small number of persons have provoked incidents in some places . . . , seriously disrupting public order. . . . They have raised such sensa-tional slogans as "Oppose hunger" and "Give us human rights," inciting people to hold demonstrations and . . . [even going] so far as to put up wall posters request-ing the president of the United States to "show concern" for human rights in China. Can we permit such an open call for intervention in China's internal af-fairs? . . . Can we tolerate the kind of freedom of speech which . . . slanders Mao Zedong and proclaims that "proletarian dictatorship is the source of all evil" . . . ?

We have not propagated and practiced democracy enough, and our systems and institutions leave much to be desired. . . . However, while propagating democ-racy, we must strictly distinguish between socialist democracy on the one hand and bourgeois, individualist democracy on the other. We must link democracy for the people with dictatorship over the enemy, and with centralism, legality, disci-pline, and leadership by the Communist Party. . . . To depart from the four cardi-nal principles and talk about democracy in the abstract will inevitably lead to the unchecked spread of ultrademocracy and anarchism, to the complete disruption of political stability and unity, and to the total failure of our modernization pro-gram.[52]

Notwithstanding Deng's attempt to disclaim personal responsibility for the decision to get tough with dissidents,[53] his March 30 speech marked a water-shed in the party's handling of the Democracy Movement. Even as Deng spoke, security police were rounding up a number of vocal prodemocracy activists. First to be arrested was Wei Jingsheng; other detainees included Ren Wanding, whose China Human Rights League had published the notorious "open letter" to President Carter, criticized by Deng in his March 30 speech; garment worker Huang Xiang, cofounder of the "Enlightenment Society" (Qimengshe), whose fiery poems and wall posters denouncing Mao-era injus-tices had served to catalyze the Democracy Movement; and several members of Wei Jingsheng's *Explorations* editorial staff.[54]

On April 5, 1979—the third anniversary of the Qingming incident—*Peo-ple's Daily* pointedly claimed in its lead editorial that the aims of the original April 5 movement had been fully achieved: The Gang of Four had been van-quished; socialist democracy had been restored; thinking had been emanci-pated; and the path had been cleared for China to become a "powerful socialist country with four modernizations." Adopting a tone that was by turns warmly patronizing and coldly cautionary, the editorial first congratulated China's young people on their heartening display of democratic spontaneity during the April 5 movement, then warned them not to take their quest for democracy and spontaneity too far. "Nowadays," the editorial cautioned, "some people want to reject party leadership and believe in spontaneous activities, thinking that democracy means doing whatever one pleases. This is not democracy at all but ultra-democratization."[55] As if to underline the new mood of political sobriety and restraint, an official notice went up near the small mountain of floral wreaths that now encircled the base of the Heroes' Monument in Tiananmen Square, reminding people that wall posters were banned. The freeze had begun.

The arrest of Wei Jingsheng and the ensuing crackdown on dissent, spearheaded by conservatives in the Beijing municipal government, provoked considerable controversy within Deng's coalition. While the majority supported some form of crackdown, a minority, including unlikely collaborators Hu Yaobang and Chen Yun, expressed reservations. Addressing a Central Committee work conference in April, Chen reportedly argued that in some cases arresting political dissidents could be more troublesome than leaving them alone:

> Take Wei Jingsheng, for example. It was a mistake to arrest him, but it would [also] have been a mistake not to arrest him. Comrade Lin Hujia [mayor of Beijing] asked me what I thought he should do. I said, "You arrested him. It's up to you to try him or let him go free. The one who tied the knot must untie it." . . . My personal opinion is that the best thing to do would have been to have a talk with him and invite him to travel all over the country, visit our factories, and see how our workers devote themselves unselfishly to their work. If we could have persuaded him in this way to change his attitude, that would have been the best thing.[56]

Notwithstanding Chen Yun's apparent reservations, in mid-October Wei Jingsheng was tried and sentenced to fifteen years in prison on a series of charges involving "counterrevolutionary incitement" and the conveyance of official secrets concerning China's war with Vietnam to a foreign journalist.[57] At the end of November—almost exactly one year after the Chinese Democracy Movement had been sparked by the reversal of verdicts on the Tiananmen incident—Xidan was placed off limits to poster writers and Democracy Wall was moved, on orders from the Beijing municipal government, to Yuetan Park, a quiet location some two miles from the center of the city. A few weeks later Fu Yuehua was tried, convicted, and sentenced to two years in jail for "violating public order." Ren Wanding was ordered to serve four years in prison, his sentence reportedly lengthened as a result of his refusal to confess his crimes. By the end of the year, the Democracy Movement had been effectively stifled. In January Deng proposed eliminating the "four big freedoms" from the PRC state constitution. Perforce, the first full fang/shou cycle of the post-Mao era was now complete.

DENG AND THE "ADVERSE CURRENT" OF 1979

At one level, Deng Xiaoping's turnabout on the issue of tolerance toward prodemocracy activists reflected his growing impatience with the libertarian excesses committed (or condoned) by members of Hu Yaobang's network, which ostensibly threatened to undermine the party's political control over society. At another level, however, Deng's adoption of a hard line toward dissent represented an attempt to disarm, through preemption, growing criticism by a loose affiliation of antireform forces, who sought to discredit Deng's policies by any means possible, and conservative reformers, who were inherently distrustful of spontaneous political activity.

In the spring of 1979, rumors began to circulate in China about the existence of a new "adverse current," a shadowy opposition group that was allegedly attempting to undermine Deng Xiaoping's prestige, blaming him, among other things, for the recent tide of social and political unrest triggered by the Democracy Movement and charging him with such cardinal sins as "cutting down the banner of Mao Zedong Thought."[58] Varied and diffuse in composition, the "adverse current" reportedly encompassed a substantial number of veteran cadres with "ossified thinking," including unreconstructed "whatever-ists," disgruntled provincial party officials, regional military commanders, and members of the petroleum clique—all of whom had personal axes to grind or vested interests to protect, and all of whom felt disadvantaged by policies introduced at the Third Plenum.

According to Liao Gailong, a senior reform theoretician with close ties to Deng Xiaoping and Hu Yaobang, Deng's March 30 endorsement of the four cardinal principles had specifically been designed to repel this "adverse current." By embracing the opposition critique of Rightism and sacrificing a few activists in the Democracy Movement, Deng ostensibly hoped to ensure the survival of the entire package of reform policies approved at the Third Plenum:

> Comrades whose thinking is ossified . . . and who obstinately support the erroneous line of the "two whatevers" took advantage of the opportunity [presented by the excesses of the Democracy Movement] to attack the correct line of the Third Plenum . . . , saying that the decisions of the Third Plenum had brought about a mad attack by the bourgeois Rightists. . . . Consequently, the party Central Committee considered that . . . in order to continue to implement thoroughly the correct line of the Third Plenum . . . and to continue liquidating the influence of the erroneous line of the "two whatevers," it was necessary to reaffirm the four principles.[59]

For all its circuitous logic, Deng's strategy of preempting conservative criticism met with only limited success. At the Central Committee's April work conference, opposition forces continued to express misgivings over the Third

Plenum's line and policies. For example, when Chen Yun introduced his proposal for a three-year economic retrenchment, the initiative reportedly encountered substantial resistance. Due to the strength of the opposition, the Second Session of the Fifth NPC, originally scheduled for late April, had to be delayed until the end of June.[60]

Although the NPC ultimately adopted Chen Yun's proposal, Deng's opponents did not give up without a struggle. In key policy addresses by Premier Hua Guofeng and State Planning Commission chief Yu Qiuli at the June 1979 NPC meeting, the readjustment program was carefully hemmed and hedged with multiple caveats and conditions—so much so that one observer was led to comment that "neither readjustment nor reform received a full hearing at this time."[61] Indeed, Deng Xiaoping himself later acknowledged the lack of initial enthusiasm for Chen Yun's proposal, noting that it could not be effectively implemented at the time "because party members did not have a profound or unanimous understanding of the issues involved."[62]

REFORMING THE LEGAL SYSTEM

While controversy over economic plans and programs continued to swirl around the June 1979 NPC meeting, Deng's reform coalition managed to score some impressive legislative gains. Reacting to the judicial nihilism of the Cultural Revolution, the Third Plenum had issued a broad mandate to overhaul China's legal system.[63] Pursuant to that mandate, the Second Session of the Fifth NPC approved seven major pieces of new legislation, including a comprehensive criminal code, a code of criminal procedure, an electoral law, and a law on joint ventures.[64]

Introducing the seven statutes to the 3,400 NPC deputies was Peng Zhen, newly installed chairman of the NPC's Legislative Affairs Commission and a close associate of Deng Xiaoping. Making his first public appearance since being purged by Mao and the ultra-Left in 1966, Peng passionately denounced the legal anarchism spawned by the Gang of Four and strongly asserted the need to restore socialist legality and the rule of law.[65]

Of the seven new statutes, the most widely discussed were the comprehensive criminal law and its adjunct, the code of criminal procedure.[66] The criminal law fleshed out recently enacted constitutional prohibitions against unlawful incarceration, extraction of coerced confessions, illegal search and seizure, and willful fabrication of criminal charges—practices that had been commonplace during the Cultural Revolution. In addition, the new law narrowed the definition of "counterrevolutionary crime" and limited the applicability of capital punishment to crimes committed "under particularly odious circumstances" involving "particularly serious danger" to the state.[67]

Companion piece to the criminal law, the 1979 code of criminal procedure affirmed the universality of law, asserting that "the law is equally applicable to all citizens" and stipulating that "no special privilege whatever is permissible before the law." The rights of persons under criminal detention were also spelled out, including the right to retain a lawyer; the right to refuse to answer questions not pertaining to the case at hand; the right to a public trial and a public verdict; the right to review written transcripts of all legal proceedings; and the right to appeal any criminal conviction. Other new procedural safeguards covered the issuance of arrest warrants and criminal indictments; the notification of family members following an arrest; and the fixing of maximum time limits for pretrial detention of criminal suspects. Despite their evident concern for strengthening the rule of law, however, the drafters of the new criminal statutes incorporated into the laws a number of loopholes and exclusions that limited the scope of judicial due process and rendered the legal system potentially susceptible to governmental abuse.[68]

Aside from issues of judicial due process, two other important questions were posed in connection with the new criminal codes: first, would the new laws be applied equally to Communist Party members and cadres, who had traditionally been shielded from judicial scrutiny and criminal accountability? And second, would a reformed, semi-autonomous Chinese legal system extend the full protection of the law to political dissidents and other nonconformists who dared to challenge the status quo? While the first question could not immediately be answered, a clause in the criminal law strongly hinted at the probable answer to the second: In a section specifying categories of counterrevolutionary behavior, it was now deemed illegal to employ slogans, leaflets, or "any other means" to encourage people to question socialism or the proletarian dictatorship. Henceforth, public opposition to the four cardinal principles would constitute a criminal offense.[69]

ELECTORAL REFORM

Along with the drive to revive and strengthen the institutions of socialist legality, another key aim of reformers was to enlarge the scope of socialist democracy at the grass-roots level. In the past, local elections in China had generally been perceived as ritualized displays of rubber-stamp acclamation, controlled and manipulated by local party cadres. "What is an election," asked one skeptical citizen, "but a list of candidates put up by the authorities for voters to endorse?"[70] To alter this perception, and to help restore the public's deeply eroded faith in the integrity and responsiveness of government, Hu Yaobang's supporters drafted a new electoral law for presentation at the Second Session of the Fifth NPC.[71]

Less widely publicized than the new criminal statutes, the 1979 electoral law mandated direct popular election of deputies to local people's congresses at and below the county level. To ensure meaningful choice, the new statute prohibited the customary practice of having only as many names on the ballot as there were deputies to elect. To ensure broad popular input in the electoral process, the code stipulated that any registered voter could, with a minimum of three seconding sponsors, nominate a candidate for people's deputy without having to pass through prescreening by local authorities. Also permitted for the first time under the terms of the new law was active campaigning by or on behalf of citizen-nominated candidates, for example, through electoral rallies, sloganeering, and distribution of campaign literature. Finally, the traditional practice of voting by show of hands was abolished in favor of the institution of the secret ballot. Henceforth, citizens would be free—at least in theory—to vote their preferences without fear of reprisal.[72]

By spelling out and taking concrete steps to institutionalize the guiding principles of "socialist democracy" and "socialist legality," the 1979 electoral law, criminal law, and code of criminal procedure went a long way toward fulfilling the Third Plenum's mandate to address China's post–Cultural Revolution "crisis of faith." What remained to be seen was how well the new laws would translate from paper to policy, from principle to practice.

REASSESSING MAO: THE FOURTH PLENUM

Although Deng's reform coalition was now subject to severe centrifugal stresses, the coalition held together, scoring new gains in the fall of 1979. In September the Fourth Plenum of the Eleventh Central Committee added twelve more rehabilitated veteran cadres to the Central Committee, including Peng Zhen, Yang Shangkun, and Bo Yibo. More important, with the addition of Peng Zhen and Zhao Ziyang to the Politburo, reformers for the first time gained a clear numerical plurality—though not yet a majority—of support on that body.[73]

Reflecting the enhanced voting strength of Deng's coalition, the Fourth Plenum strongly endorsed Chen Yun's eight-character program of "readjustment, restructuring, consolidation, and improvement." In other key actions, the plenum unanimously approved a draft decision to accelerate the reform of agriculture and pushed ahead with the task of reassessing Mao Zedong's contributions and shortcomings.

In the official communiqué of the Fourth Plenum, party members were exhorted to "broaden and deepen" their study of guidelines for policy reform adopted at the Third Plenum, including the priority of modernization, the emancipation of thinking, and the criterion for testing truth. While making strongly worded appeals to accelerate reform and deepen the struggle against the "poisonous influence . . . of the ultra-Left line," the communiqué remained conspicuously silent on two important issues that underlay the deepening split within Deng's reform coalition: the danger posed by Rightist ultrademocracy, and the imperative to uphold the four cardinal principles.[74] Under the circumstances, the omission of all references to these key conservative watchwords bespoke a clear lack of consensus on political and ideological fundamentals within the "practice" faction.

The Fourth Plenum's decisions were conveyed to the public on September 29, in a major speech by Ye Jianying marking the thirtieth anniversary of the founding of the People's Republic.[75] In his address, Ye carefully explained the necessity to undertake economic readjustment, noting that a three-year battle would be needed to overcome problems of excessive capital construction and disproportionality in the national economy. Significantly, while endorsing the policy of readjustment, Ye credited its authorship to Hua Guofeng rather than to Chen Yun.

Reviewing the thirty-year history of the PRC, Ye indirectly confirmed that an official reassessment of Chairman Mao's record, including his mistakes and shortcomings, was under way. In a major departure from past party practice, Ye openly acknowledged that top CCP leaders, including Mao, had made a series of "Leftist errors" in 1957–59, during the anti-Rightist rectification campaign and the Great Leap Forward, and again during the Cultural Revolution. In the past such mistakes generally had been either denied, minimized, or—more commonly—attributed to sabotage by "antiparty elements" such as Liu Shaoqi, the "Lin Biao clique," or the Gang of Four. Now, for the first time, the errors of the late 1950s and 1960s were implicitly laid at the doorstep of the Great Helmsman himself:

> In 1957 . . . the mistake was made of broadening the scope of struggle [against bourgeois Rightists]. In 1958, we . . . violated objective laws in our economic work. We made the mistakes of giving arbitrary directions, being boastful, and stirring up a "communist wind." In 1959, . . . we ineptly carried out the struggle against so-called Right opportunism. These "Leftist" errors plus three years of natural calamities . . . brought about serious economic reverses.[76]

Shielding Mao from direct personal criticism for initiating the policies in question, Ye nonetheless left little room for doubt as to where ultimate responsibility lay: "Leaders are not gods," he said; "they are not infallible and therefore should not be deified." Nor was there much room for doubt with respect to Ye's apportioning of responsibility for the Cultural Revolution, which he now described—in deference to a collective decision taken at the Fourth Plenum—as "an appalling catastrophe suffered by all our people." While directing the brunt of criticism at Lin Biao and the Gang of Four, Ye pointed to Mao's 1962 thesis on class struggle[77] as the ultimate source of China's "decade of suppression, tyranny, and bloodshed":

> The Cultural Revolution was launched with the aim of preventing and combating revisionism. . . . At the time when the Cultural Revolution was launched, the estimate made of the situation [of class struggle] within the party and the country ran counter to reality, no accurate definition was given of revisionism, and an erroneous policy and method of struggle were adopted, deviating from the principle of democratic centralism.[78]

While acknowledging the fallibility of Mao's leadership, Ye nonetheless vigorously defended Mao's ideological contributions, arguing that "what we call Mao Zedong Thought" was not the product of a single mind but rather represented the "crystallization of the collective wisdom" of the party. As such, it had to be upheld against "an erroneous trend of skepticism" that had recently emerged "inside and outside the party." To oppose this trend, Ye called for the moral rebirth of "spiritual civilization" (*jingshen wenming*) in China; he also explicitly invoked the danger of Rightism and reaffirmed the sanctity of the four cardinal principles. In doing so, Ye subtly departed from the straightforward anti-Leftist tone of the Fourth Plenum's communiqué, issued just one day earlier.

DENG COURTS PROVINCIAL CADRES, STRONG-ARMS THE PLA

The subtle differences in tone and language between Ye Jianying's National Day speech and the Fourth Plenum's official communiqué bespoke a serious division within the party. While the "whateverists" and their allies had lost control of the Politburo, they continued to draw support from veteran party cadres and senior military leaders who were visibly upset over the "Rightist" excesses of the Democracy Movement and who remained uneasy over Deng's reform agenda. Seeking to counteract criticism, Deng employed a variety of tactics, from old-fashioned patronage and pork-barrel politicking to imperial arm-twisting.

To firm up support among uncommitted and wavering provincial party secretaries, Deng held out the promise of greater local fiscal autonomy and administrative decentralization. With provincial representatives occupying up to 40 percent of the seats on the Eleventh Central Committee, Deng's strategy of "playing to the provinces" (to borrow Susan Shirk's phrase) evidently proved effective. As one Chinese government official put it, "They decided to give power and money to provincial leaders, which made them happy and made them support reform."[79] Toward disaffected senior military commanders, on the other hand—including Deng's erstwhile old comrades Xu Shiyou and Wei Guoqing, who were said to be unhappy over Deng's handling of the Vietnam invasion and over his failure to back Xu's bid for a promotion—Deng took a harder line.[80] Implying that China's Vietnam debacle was due in large part to the "ossified thinking" of his senior PLA colleagues, Deng proposed to accelerate the promotion of younger officers and apply pressure on elderly ones to retire.[81] In the winter of 1979–80, he underscored his point by engineering the replacement or transfer of seven of China's veteran regional military commanders, along with a substantial number of PLA political commissars.[82] He then approved a 13 percent cut in the PLA's 1980 budgetary appropriation. Adding insult to injury, Deng altered the rank-order of the "four modernizations," dropping military modernization from third to fourth—and last—place.

DENG LEANS TO THE LEFT

Having scuttled Hua Guofeng's economic plan, passed several important pieces of reform legislation, gained a working plurality within the Politburo, and laid down the law to disgruntled regional military commanders, Deng next sought, early in 1980, to dislodge the "whateverists" from their remaining strongholds within the party and government apparatus.

Lacking an absolute majority within the Politburo, Deng needed the continued backing of at least some members of the Ye Jianying–Li Xiannian group to effect the final ouster of Hua Guofeng and his allies. To obtain such backing, and to mollify disaffected centrists and conservatives within the reform coalition, Deng now undertook a calculated turn toward the left. With vivid memories of Cultural Revolution chaos still quite fresh, many party members—reformers and survivors alike—sought credible assurances from Deng that the "turmoil" triggered by the Democracy Movement and petitioners' protests would not be permitted to undermine China's hard-won political stability. To assuage such fears, and to protect his reform program against allegations that he was soft on counterrevolutionaries and troublemakers, Deng delivered a hard-line law-and-order speech at a Central Committee work conference in mid-January 1980.[83]

Unlike his "warning" speech of March 30, 1979, which contained evidence of personal ambivalence, Deng now adopted a harsh, uncompromising attitude toward dissidents. Noting that "our people have just gone through a decade of suffering [and] cannot afford further chaos," Deng decried the increase in social disorder precipitated by "so-called democrats with ulterior motives." Claiming that anarchists and extreme individualists in the Democracy Movement were flagrantly opposed to the socialist system and Communist Party leadership, he accused them of colluding with foreign agents, including the Kuomintang secret service, to sow discord among the Chinese people. Arguing that freedom of speech, press, and assembly were never meant to be extended to such counterrevolutionary elements, Deng urged the constitutional abolition of the four big freedoms and promised greater reliance on the "weapon of law" in the campaign against troublemakers—a campaign that he now characterized as containing elements of class struggle.[84]

Firmly embracing the four cardinal principles on his own behalf (rather than in the name of the Central Committee, as before), Deng also came down hard on unnamed individuals within the "practice" faction who had allegedly provided behind-the-scenes support for prodemocracy activists. Noting sardonically that certain underground journals had been "beautifully produced," Deng demanded to know where they had been printed. Answering his own question, Deng suggested that it was unlikely that underground newspapers owned their own printing presses. "Aren't there party members in the printing houses that turn these things out?" he queried. "Among their supporters there must be some party members or even cadres holding fairly high posts." Warning such people that their stand is "very mistaken, very dangerous," Deng put them on notice that "unless they correct their mistakes immediately they will be subject to party disciplinary measures."[85]

Anticipating criticism from liberals who were opposed in principle to any new "tightening up" (shou) of party policy toward free speech and expression, Deng sternly lectured that such a tightening up was impossible, since there had "never been a loosening up" (fang) in the first place. "Just when," he asked sarcastically, "did we say we would tolerate the activities of counter-revolutionaries and saboteurs? When did we say that the dictatorship of the proletariat was to be abolished?"[86]

Whether Deng's sharp rhetorical reminder reflected an enduring personal change of attitude or merely a tactical decision to trim his sails in the face of a strong political wind (or, more likely, some combination of the two), his January speech achieved its immediate objective of reassuring skittish "survivors" and cementing relations with the conservative wing of his reform coalition. Having firmed up his support at the left-center of the political spectrum, Deng now set out to close the book on Hua Guofeng and the "whatever" faction.

THE FIFTH PLENUM: PURGING THE "LITTLE GANG OF FOUR"

At the Fifth Plenum in late February 1980, Deng secured the resignations of Hua Guofeng's four top associates, the so-called little gang of four—Wang Dongxing, Wu De, Chen Xilian, and Ji Dengkui—from all remaining party and government posts.[87] Reportedly, resignation was chosen over outright dismissal for two reasons: first, because of Deng's ostensible aversion to Cultural Revolution–style putsches or purges; and second—perhaps more important—because of pressure exerted by Ye Jianying and other senior survivors to avoid the stigma of dismissal.

Promoted to the Politburo Standing Committee to occupy the spot vacated by Wang Dongxing were two of Deng's proreform confederates, Hu Yaobang and Zhao Ziyang, thus giving the "practice" faction for the first time a working majority of four members—Deng, Chen, Hu, and Zhao—on the seven-person Standing Committee, with only Ye, Li, and Hua Guofeng—who was permitted to retain his post out of deference to Ye and Li—occupying the back bench. The removal of the four "whateverists" from the Politburo also gave Deng an absolute majority of supporters on that body as well.[88]

In a related action, the Fifth Plenum formally restored the authority of the Central Party Secretariat, which had been undergoing reconstruction since the Third Plenum. With Hu Yaobang as general secretary, the refurbished Secretariat consisted of eleven secretaries, eight of whom were affiliated with Deng's reform coalition.[89] To enable Hu Yaobang to devote full time to his duties as head of the central party apparatus, Hu relinquished his concurrent post as director of the CC Propaganda Department, a position that was now filled by Wang Renzhong.

Aside from these key personnel and organizational changes, the Fifth Plenum also took final action on the posthumous rehabilitation of Liu Shaoqi—the last prominent unliberated victim of the Cultural Revolution. Liu was now praised effusively as a great Marxist and proletarian revolutionary who, despite great mental and physical persecution, had remained "at all times loyal to the party and the people." Liu's 1966 purge by Mao Zedong, Lin Biao, and the ultra-Left was now called the "biggest frame-up our party has ever known."[90] Ye Jianying reportedly objected to such strong language; and when Liu was given posthumous burial honors in May 1980, Ye conspicuously failed to attend the memorial service.[91]

Responding to Hu Yaobang's acknowledgment that the CCP confronted a threefold crisis of faith, belief, and trust in its relations with the Chinese people,[92] the Fifth Plenum adopted a set of "guiding principles for inner-party political life." Designed to provide concrete behavioral norms for party members in the new era of reform and opening up, the twelve-point document was drafted by the Central Discipline Inspection Committee under the supervision of Chen Yun and Hu Yaobang.

Pointing out that the CCP's "fine tradition and style of work" had been seriously impaired under the influence of feudal-fascist practices that flourished during the Cultural Revolution, the new document denounced the practice of "regarding every word of Comrade Mao Zedong as truth, law, and dogma" and called upon all party members to "oppose ossified thinking and the practice of proceeding in all cases from [what is written in] books."[93]

The "guiding principles" directed especially heavy criticism at the phenomenon of autocratic leadership by party secretaries. "No individual is allowed to make arbitrary decisions," said the document. "The relationship between the secretary and the members of the party committee is not like that between superior and inferior. . . . The secretary is not allowed to make a practice of 'what I say goes' or to behave in a patriarchal manner." To deal with such autocratic behavior, the right of party members to criticize any party organization or individual was categorically affirmed, as was their right "to propose removing or replacing cadres who have committed serious mistakes . . . or who are incompetent." All attempts by leading cadres to retaliate against whistle-blowers or "to equate the views of a certain comrade with opposition to the party" were prohibited. To facilitate inner-party democracy, party congresses and committees at all levels were encouraged to replace a "definite number" of their leading members at each session, with elections to be conducted by secret ballot in order to "give genuine expression to the voters' will."

"Factionalism" was another problem that received serious attention in the "guiding principles." "It is absolutely forbidden," said the document, "to band together in cliques. It is impermissible to . . . favor one group of people while suppressing another. [Party members] must not get tangled up in settling old scores. . . ." Cadres who persisted in factionalism "must be removed [from] leading posts."

The lengthiest section of the twelve-point document was devoted to the subject of privilege seeking. Noting that rampant nepotism and corrupt, self-serving behavior on the part of leading cadres were seriously poisoning the party's relations with the people, the document catalogued a number of "abominable tendencies" and called for the resolute strengthening of party discipline to punish offenders:

It is necessary firmly to overcome the abominable tendency among some leading cadres to seek special treatment for themselves and their family members. It is forbidden for leading members . . . to use their position and power to seek preferment for relatives in regard to such matters as enrollment in schools and colleges, transferring from one to another, promotions, employment, and going abroad. The use of public funds for banquets, gifts, and residences for leading members . . . is forbidden. It is impermissible . . . to use public service for private gain, appropriate and squander state and collective property under any pretext. . . . No leading cadre is permitted . . . to promote his family members or relatives to leading positions . . . nor should he place them in key posts on his staff.

Reflecting the predominance of the "practice" faction within the CDIC, the "guiding principles" made only passing, perfunctory reference to upholding the four cardinal principles, and no reference whatever to the need to oppose Rightism. Indeed, the lone mention of the conservatives' two favorite whipping posts—extreme individualism and anarchism—occurred in the document's shortest section, which simply listed, briefly and without comment, a number of miscellaneous errors and evil deeds to be criticized.

Although the "guiding principles" contained little to assuage party hardliners, conservatives were cheered by one measure adopted at the Fifth Plenum: Pursuant to Deng Xiaoping's expressed intention to eliminate the "four bigs," the plenum recommended deleting a provision of Article 45 of the 1978 state constitution which guaranteed citizens "the right to speak out freely, air their views fully, hold great debates, and write big-character posters."[94] Notwithstanding this recommendation, and in striking contrast to Deng's stern anti-Rightist rhetoric of January 16, the Fifth Plenum's final communiqué made no mention of extreme individualism, anarchism, or the four cardinal principles.

In the months following the Fifth Plenum, the "practice" faction moved to consolidate its gains. At a meeting of the NPC Standing Committee in April, Deng confederates Zhao Ziyang and Wan Li were elevated to the position of vice-premier, replacing deposed "whateverists" Ji Dengkui and Chen Xilian. Signaling the significance of the new appointments to the outside world, Deng Xiaoping told a Japanese visitor in late April that Zhao Ziyang "is now in charge of the day-to-day work of the State Council."[95] For all intents and purposes, Hua Guofeng had become a lame-duck premier.

HUA'S LAST STAND

Before the reformers could celebrate their victory, however, Hua Guofeng had one additional card to play. As chairman of the party's Military Affairs Commission, Hua enjoyed organizational access to China's senior army commanders, many of whom, as noted, were seriously unhappy with Deng's policies. With his back to the wall, Hua now actively courted the disaffected generals.

In mid-April, Hua addressed an all-army political work conference, organized by the PLA's General Political Department. In his speech, Hua raised an anti-Rightist banner to counteract the anti-Leftist "guiding principles" adopted by the Fifth Plenum. Using a slogan proposed by Deng's one-time ally and protector, GPD chief Wei Guoqing, Hua exhorted his colleagues in the military to "foster proletarian ideology, eliminate bourgeois ideology" (*xingwu miezi*). The slogan was carefully chosen: It had originally been coined in 1957 by Deng Xiaoping himself, in the course of Mao's anti-Rightist rectification campaign. Here, then, was a Leftist "whatever" that Deng could not easily disavow.[96] Lacing his speech with antibourgeois rhetoric, Hua launched a not-so-subtle attack on Deng's economic reforms, criticizing the reformers' "one-sided emphasis on economic means" and, in a throwback to the Maoist era, calling political work the "lifeblood of all economic work."[97]

Hua's eleventh-hour campaign to forge an anti-Rightist united front with the PLA may have gained him some new friends in the military, but it did not save him. Instead, it galvanized Deng's supporters into action. At the end of May, Deng personally ordered the *People's Daily* and the *Guangming Daily* to cease publicizing Wei Guoqing's controversial antibourgeois slogan.[98] In July and August a media blitz indirectly attacked Hua's presumptive standing as successor to Zhou Enlai and Mao Zedong. In one thinly veiled historical allegory, Hua was likened to the emperor's favorite eunuch in the Eastern Han dynasty, an opportunistic puppet who had achieved power after the emperor's death by conspiring with other court eunuchs to suppress a rival faction headed by "relatives of the empress."[99] In another allegorical article, a Tang dynasty emperor was quoted as having expressed confidence in an unscrupulous eunuch in terms that closely paralleled Mao's deathbed bequest to Hua Guofeng, "With you in charge, I'm at ease."[100]

By midsummer, rumors were circulating in Beijing that Hua Guofeng would soon step down as premier. Imparting a curious spin to such rumors, a Chinese historian, writing in the *Guangming Daily*, implied that Hua's resignation might not be entirely spontaneous or unconstrained. Commenting on the case of an ancient Chinese prime minister who in an act of ostensibly selfless devotion volunteered to relinquish his post to a worthy successor, the historian pointed out that the prime minister in question had been grossly unfit for office in the first place and was later put to death for his misdeeds.[101]

Toward the end of August, Deng Xiaoping stopped beating around the bush. In an interview with an Italian journalist he bluntly declared that "for a leader to pick his own successor is a feudal practice. It is an illustration of the imperfections in our institutions."[102] Thus were the last shreds of political respectability stripped from Hua Guofeng's already badly damaged political persona. Denied Politburo support and shorn of Mao's legitimizing bequest, Hua now stood wholly exposed.

High Tide of Reform: *Gengshen*, 1980

Anything that can best promote the development of the
productive forces . . . may count on the support of Marxists;
anything that does not . . . Marxists will not support.

—Yu Guangyuan, Chinese Academy of
Social Sciences, December 1980

Do people merely need a comfortable life? We also need
extensive freedom and democracy, so that our minds can be at
ease. . . . A high degree of democracy is our ultimate goal.

—Liao Gailong, CCP Central Committee,
Office of Policy Studies, October 1980

WITH Hua Guofeng reduced to lame-duck status, with Leftists in retreat, and
with proreform forces now controlling both the Politburo and the State Council, the last nine months of 1980 witnessed a remarkable outpouring of reform-
oriented ideas and innovations. As the pendulum swung sharply in the direction of fang, new policy initiatives went well beyond previous limits, in some
cases challenging the very foundations of Chinese communism. In terms of
the sheer scope and audacity of proposed structural changes, 1980 represented
the high water mark of post-Mao reform and relaxation.

PROMOTING ECONOMIC REFORM

At the end of 1979, CASS economist Xue Muqiao published a book strongly
critical of China's neo-Stalinist system of centralized economic planning and
unified management. Expanding upon ideas first introduced in the early 1960s
by Sun Yefang, and then revived by Hu Qiaomu in 1978, Xue's critique of the
Stalinist command economy centered on the idea that excessive centralization
of enterprise administration and management had served to "bind enterprises
hand and foot," rendering them unable to bring local initiative and creativity
into play. As a result, many Chinese factories, including those that prided

themselves on their advanced Soviet technology, "lag far behind those of the same type in the capitalist countries."[1]

To remedy this defect, Xue proposed a number of fundamental reforms, including comprehensive price reform—the readjustment of raw material and commodity prices to reflect their actual value—and the elimination of such traditional practices as "eating from the same big pot" (*chi daguofan*), the system whereby state-owned enterprises received their operating funds directly from the state, turned all revenues over to the state, and required state authorization for all expenditures. Also recommended for elimination was the "iron rice bowl" (*tiefanwan*), the system of guaranteed lifetime employment and standardized, lock-step salaries for all Chinese workers and cadres, regardless of individual skill or quality of performance.

Noting that firms in capitalist countries ran their own business and were responsible for their own profits and losses, Xue Muqiao argued for granting China's enterprise managers greater autonomy over such things as hiring, firing, promoting, and punishing workers and staff members. He also strongly supported the practice of permitting managers to retain a portion of enterprise profits for investment in technical innovation and other productivity-enhancing measures, including workers' bonuses. Noting that in capitalist countries the scramble for markets led firms to seek to maximize profits with minimal capital outlays, Xue suggested that the goals of increasing managerial efficiency, productivity, and responsibility were better achieved through the economic discipline of the marketplace than through the administrative discipline of higher-level compulsion. Although he advocated supplanting administrative methods of enterprise management with economic methods, he stopped short of recommending the abolition of central planning, endorsing instead the idea that "to regulate production according to market demand is ideal *as a supplement* to regulation . . . by planning."[2]

Xue clearly recognized the controversial nature of his proposals, and he foresaw that in the effort to change things, "it is very likely that we may be fettered by traditional thinking and meet with resistance of one kind or another. We must emancipate our minds, dare to pioneer, and boldly bring out all sorts of ideas."[3]

Picking up where Xue Muqiao left off, senior reform economist and CASS Vice-President Yu Guangyuan defended the use of individual bonuses and other differential material incentives to encourage and reward meritorious labor performance, arguing that the radical egalitarianism of the ultra-Left had exerted a serious inhibiting effect on labor enthusiasm and productivity: "The advanced gained nothing, the backward lost nothing, and the initiative of the broad masses was seriously dampened."[4] In an even bolder vein, Yu Guangyuan challenged another key Leftist shibboleth, the notion that large, publicly owned enterprises represented the highest form of developed socialism and were superior to all other forms. In criticizing this notion, Yu argued that it was not size or degree of public ownership but rather productivity that determined the superiority or inferiority of any given economic structure or institution. Elaborating upon this idea, Yu Guangyuan gave a concise defense of what has come to be called the "theory of the productive forces": "Anything that can best promote the development of the productive forces . . . may count on the support of Marxists; anything that does not . . . Marxists will not support."[5]

In line with this reformulation of Deng Xiaoping's pragmatic "black cats, white cats" philosophy, reform economists in 1980 argued for expanding the practice, first sanctioned in the 1978 PRC State Constitution, of permitting individuals to go into business for themselves, either singly or in small, family-run collectives. Intended in part as an interim measure to ameliorate the mounting problem of urban unemployment, small-scale private enterprise received an indirect ideological boost from the "theory of the productive forces," which legitimated any form of economic activity that could be shown to make a positive contribution to economic development. So long as they obeyed the law and did not exploit others, private entrepreneurs were henceforth to be permitted to operate their own small businesses.[6]

Throughout 1980, liberal reformers strongly defended the role of market competition under socialism. One commentary argued that "if consumers can freely select what they want on the market, the factories which . . . supply cheap but good commodities will have a better future." As for those enterprises that suffered "serious losses" due to poor management and a consequent lack of market competitiveness, they would be "compelled to improve their business management. . . . Otherwise, these enterprises must be reorganized or even closed down." Here, for the first time, the threat of bankruptcy—Hungarian economist János Kornai's famous "hard budget constraint"—was raised as a means of imposing economic discipline upon chronically unprofitable firms and managers.[7] Other articles applauded the role to be played by "patriotic national capitalists"—such as millionaire former textile manufacturer Rong Yiren—in the development of China's post-Mao economy. Rong's newly established China International Trust and Investment Corporation (CITIC) was singled out for special publicity in connection with its designated role of promoting foreign investment in China under Deng Xiaoping's "open policy."[8]

The year 1980 also witnessed strong criticism of China's past economic preoccupations with "producing for production's sake," "seeking high speed in disregard of objective conditions," and "increasing capital accumulation to the neglect of personal consumption." Asserting that the most important goal of a socialist economy is not to produce more capital goods but rather to "secure the maximum satisfaction of the constantly rising material and cultural requirements of the people," economic theorist Wu Jiang, elaborating upon Chen Yun's earlier expression of concern for the well-being of China's long-suffering consumers, argued for a sharp reduction in the rate of capital accumulation. The accumulation rate had reached levels as high as 40 percent of national income during the Great Leap Forward and had surged to 36.6 percent as recently as 1978, the first year of Hua Guofeng's "flying leap." In the view of Wu and a growing number of other reform economists, a substantially reduced accumulation rate—somewhere in the neighborhood of 25 percent or less—was necessary "so that proper arrangements can be made for people's clothing, food, shelter, transportation, and other necessities." For the first time since the early 1950s, consumer goods were being accorded a priority status equal to or higher than capital goods.[9]

Epitomizing the type of "emancipated thinking" that characterized Chinese economic policy debates in 1980, CC Propaganda Director Wang Renzhong—a cautious Marxist reformer who normally eschewed radical measures—placed his seal of approval on Lenin's famous NEP formulation of the early 1920s: "Soviet government + good order on the Prussian railways + American technology and trusts + national education in the United States, etc., etc. = socialism." "Rightly so," granted Wang, albeit without any particular enthusiasm.[10]

THE CONTROVERSY OVER FEUDAL INFLUENCE

While proposals for economic reform continued to be debated in a lively, free-wheeling atmosphere throughout most of 1980, by midyear attention had shifted to the political arena. The twelve-point "guiding principles" adopted at the Fifth Plenum in February had identified a number of deep-seated flaws in the political, ideological, and organizational life of the Communist Party.[11] The problem now confronting party leaders was how to remedy them.

Within Deng's reform coalition there was considerable disagreement over this question. At a series of party meetings in the spring of 1980, conservative theoreticians such as Hu Qiaomu argued that the key to getting the party back on the right track lay in effectively combatting "bourgeois ideology." For Hu Yaobang and his supporters, on the other hand, the main task, now that the Gang of Four was out of the way and "whateverism" no longer posed a major threat, was combating remnant "feudal influences" (*fengjian yingxiang*) in the political system.[12]

Throughout April and May, Deng Xiaoping reportedly wavered on the question of the "main task." Eventually, however, after some heavy lobbying by one of his old comrades, Li Weihan, Deng sided with Hu Yaobang and the "feudal influence" school.[13] In a speech on May 31, Deng made known his views on the subject. Arguing that the slogan "foster proletarian ideology, eliminate bourgeois ideology" lacked specific content and was therefore "incomplete," he instructed the mass media to cease publicizing the slogan. Turning to the question of feudal influences in party life, Deng agreed with Li Weihan's suggestion that the traditions of patriarchy (*jiazhangzhi*) and lifetime tenure for leading cadres were extremely serious problems that required immediate attention. At all levels of the party, Deng noted, leading cadres acted arbitrarily and autocratically, their subordinates daring to do nothing without their approval. Specifically citing Chen Duxiu and Li Lisan as past party leaders who had displayed serious patriarchal tendencies (but also tac-itly implicating Mao Zedong), Deng noted that when such leaders were in charge, "once a meeting began, no matter what anyone else had to say, . . . the only thing that counted was what 'the old man' said; once 'the old man' spoke, there was no choice but to comply." Deng also decried the feudal ten-dency to worship party leaders as if they were gods, citing the case of leading cadres who "clamor to build memorial halls for Chairman [Mao], Premier [Zhou], and now even for [Liu] Shaoqi." Such behavior, he averred, had "inflicted grave harm upon our people and our party." Toward the end of his statement, Deng rendered his verdict: "Comrade Li Weihan's opinion is very good. . . . Everything must be approached from the point of view of erad-icating feudal influence and gradually stepping-up reform."[14]

When Hu Yaobang learned of Deng's statement, he immediately sought—and received—Ye Jianying's consent to convene a meeting of the Politburo to discuss the eradication of feudal influences. With Ye's blessing, the Politburo met in early June.[15] At the meeting Hu argued that it was necessary to consider two basic issues in connection with feudalism: first, its influence on the polit-ical structure; second, its influence on ideology. With respect to the former, he emphasized the adverse effects of the absence of a routinized mechanism for demoting or dismissing incompetent party cadres. Without "normal" exit pro-cedures, Hu argued, the only way to remove someone was through denun-ciation. As a result, cadres frequently lived in a state of heightened anxiety, "never knowing when some petty mistake or difference of opinion . . . would be seized upon as a pretext for 'rectification.'" Because of this anxiety, lower-level cadres displayed a notable lack of independence and initiative in their work, always waiting for cues from their leaders before taking a position. "How can you manage anything," asked Hu rhetorically, "if you always have to wait for the 'top banana' to nod his head 'yes' or shake his head 'no'?"

Turning to the realm of ideology, Hu Yaobang suggested that because China had never undergone "baptism by bourgeois democracy," bourgeois ideology posed far less of a threat than feudal ideology. Indeed, he claimed, the persistence of feudal influences in the political system meant that bour-geois democracy actually represented "great, great progress" (*weida weidade jinbu*) in the ideological sphere. Pointing out that feudal ideology was deeply rooted and extremely insidious, Hu estimated that it would take at least three years to eradicate it.[16]

In the event, Hu's estimate proved overly optimistic. Shortly after the June Politburo meeting, Li Weihan wrote to Hu Yaobang and Hu Qiaomu, suggest-ing that at a forthcoming NPC meeting, scheduled for late August, Deng Xiaoping might be persuaded to deliver a talk on the subject of eliminating feudal influences. Hu Yaobang was delighted; Hu Qiaomu, on the other hand, was clearly displeased, complaining that unless a great deal of preparatory work were done in advance to specify "exactly what to oppose, what to cor-rect, and how to reform," the most likely result would be "ideological, polit-ical, and even organizational confusion." Besides, he argued testily, it would be improper "to oppose feudalism only, while relaxing opposition to the evil, degenerate phenomena of capitalist profit-mongering and exploitation."[17]

For almost two months the "two Hus" went back and forth in their struggle to control the party's ideological agenda. In the end, a compromise was reached. Deng would give the speech, but he would not take sides on the question of the main task.

On August 18, on the eve of the Third Session of the Fifth NPC, Deng delivered his much-anticipated address to an enlarged session of the Politburo. Assailing both feudal and capitalist influences, Deng argued that there could be no single categorical answer to the question, "Which was worse?" Notwithstanding his declaration of ideological nonalignment, Deng's critique of feudalism was considerably more thoroughgoing and intense than his critique of bourgeois ideology, which was limited for the most part to bemoaning the influence upon China's young people of the "decadent life-style" and "profit-above-everything-else" mentality of the bourgeoisie abroad.

Spelling out in considerable detail a number of undesirable political and ideological tendencies, Deng proposed a series of structural reforms designed to make the political system more functionally specialized, more responsive, more accountable, and more democratic. Known as the "Gengshen reforms" (in accordance with the traditional Chinese lunar calendar designation for the year 1980), Deng's August 18 proposals constituted the boldest manifesto for political change yet articulated by a top-level Chinese leader in the four years since Mao's death.[18]

THE GENGSHEN REFORMS

Deng's speech had two parallel objectives, one manifest and the other more subtle. Overtly, the purpose was to diagnose and propose remedies for certain endemic defects in the Chinese political system. More immediately, Deng's goal was to provide a persuasive rationale for seeking the immediate resignation of Premier Hua Guofeng and the concurrent retirement of a number of superannuated government officials. In Deng's speech, these two goals were neatly wrapped in a single package: reform of the leadership structure.

> First of all, it is not good to have an overconcentration of power. . . . Overconcentration of power is liable to give rise to arbitrary rule by individuals at the expense of collective leadership. . . .
>
> Second, it is not good to have too many people holding two or more posts concurrently, or to have too many deputy posts. . . . If a person holds too many posts . . . , he will find it difficult to come to grips with the problems in his work and, more importantly, he will block the way for other more suitable comrades to take up leading posts. . . .
>
> Third, it is time for us to distinguish between the responsibilities of the party and those of the government, and to stop substituting the former for the latter. Those principal leading comrades of the Central Committee who are to be re-

lieved of their concurrent government posts can concentrate their energies on our party work. . . . This will help . . . strengthen the unified leadership of the Central Committee, . . . and promote a better exercise of government functions and powers.

Fourth, we must . . . solve the problem of the succession in leadership. . . . It is of great strategic importance for us to ensure the continuity and stability of . . . party and state leadership by having younger comrades take "front-line" posts while older comrades give them necessary advice and support.

With this by way of explanation, Deng proceeded to announce the forthcoming resignations of Premier Hua and seven of the State Council's sixteen vice-premiers, including himself, Li Xiannian, Chen Yun, Wang Zhen, Xu Xiangqian, Wang Renzhong, and the sole remaining "whateverist" vice-premier, Chen Yonggui. By tacitly linking Hua Guofeng's resignation to the goal of eliminating feudal influences, and by proposing his own voluntary retirement as an example for other elderly veterans to emulate, Deng was able to secure Hua's exit, prevent a sanguinary power struggle, and clear the way for younger, reform-oriented leaders to rise to positions of governmental power and influence. It was, in short, a classic display of Deng's remarkable skills as a political tactician.

After explaining the reasons for the shake-up in the leadership of the State Council, Deng recapitulated the critique of patriarchy previously articulated in the Fifth Plenum's "guiding principles." To deal with the problem of aging officials who acted autocratically, Deng proposed abolishing the system of lifetime tenure for party and government leaders. "No leading cadres," he said, "should hold any office indefinitely." To ensure that younger, better educated cadres would have an opportunity to fill front-line leadership positions, Deng proposed the introduction of "regular methods" of hiring, promoting, retiring, and removing party officials. In particular, Deng stressed the need to work out "appropriate and explicit regulations" specifying terms of office and conditions of retirement for leading cadres at all levels.

To help induce leading cadres to accept retirement voluntarily, Deng called for creation of a new, high-level CCP advisory committee, to be composed of veteran comrades who had stepped down from the executive bodies of the Central Committee and State Council. With its membership chosen by the National Party Congress, the advisory committee would enable retired leaders to "put their experience to good use" rendering "guidance, advice, and supervision" to regular party and government organs. At the same time, by absorbing elderly, superannuated cadres, the advisory committee would also help reduce the size and lower the average age of leading organs, thus improving their efficiency.

To deal with party officials who habitually sought personal privileges or otherwise abused their authority, Deng called for creation of a system of "mass supervision," with ordinary citizens and rank-and-file party members having the right to "expose, accuse, impeach, replace, and recall" party cadres who habitually engaged in gross misconduct. Notwithstanding such supervision, however, party members were not to be held legally accountable for their actions; although he stressed that "all citizens are equal before the law," Deng made a categorical distinction between citizens and party members. The latter were held accountable only to "the party constitution and regulations on party discipline."

While continuing to shield CCP members from legal accountability, Deng proposed a clear separation of powers and functions between the Communist Party and the government. For its part, the party was to continue exercising political leadership over government bodies; however, party organs were to cease involving themselves directly in state administration. "All matters within the competence of the government," said Deng, must henceforth be "discussed and decided by the relevant governmental bodies alone"; the party should "neither issue directives nor take decisions on such matters."

In a related injunction, Deng called for strengthening collective leadership and adopting "a division of labor with individual responsibility" in all party organizations. Party first secretaries were specifically enjoined from making important decisions unilaterally or arbitrarily. Once a decision was made, each member of the organization was expected to take responsibility for its implementation; buck passing and shirking were not to be tolerated "on any account." These and other endemic manifestations of "bureaucratism"—including such practices as "indulging in empty talk," "being hidebound by convention," "being dilatory and inefficient," "circulating documents endlessly without solving problems," "jockeying for power," and "assuming the airs of a mandarin"—were said to be closely linked to the problem of autocratic leadership and were targeted for rectification.

In a passage of Deng's August 18 speech devoted to the subject of preventing abuses of power and authority, he alluded (as he had in his speech of January 27) to the superior institutional safeguards against autocracy found in the bourgeois democracies of the West. Noting that Stalin's one-man dictatorship had gravely impaired the operation of socialist legality in the USSR, Deng recalled that Mao had once suggested that such personal dictatorship "would have been impossible in Western countries like Britain, France, and the United States." In a tacit critique of Mao, Deng went on to note that "although Comrade Mao was aware of this, he did not in practice solve the problems in our system of leadership."

Mao came in for other criticisms as well. Acknowledging that the Chairman had made mistakes in his later years, Deng echoed Ye Jianying's 1979 National Day speech, labeling Mao's Cultural Revolution "a blunder and a failure" that had caused a decade of destruction. Promising that the party would soon make public a comprehensive assessment of Mao's merits and demerits, Deng nonetheless strongly defended Mao's overall record, saying that Mao had rendered immortal service to the party and to the people, and that his contributions, enshrined as "The Thought of Mao Zedong," were indelible.

While feudal influences received the brunt of Deng's criticism, he also identified himself with Hu Qiaomu's desire to combat the "evil, degenerate phenomena of capitalist profit-mongering and exploitation." Decrying the apparent loss of popular enthusiasm for socialism in China, Deng denounced as absolutely wrong the idea that "just because we have made mistakes, socialism is inferior to capitalism." On the contrary, "although our system is imperfect . . . it is much better than the capitalist system based on the law of the jungle."

Pointing out that China's rapidly expanding contacts with capitalist countries under the open policy had exposed many people to the decadent ideology and life-styles of the bourgeoisie abroad, Deng criticized the growing tendency to "worship things foreign or fawn on foreigners." Enamored of the capitalist West, increasing numbers of young people were said to be putting profit above everything else and seeking to get ahead at the expense of others. The result was an upsurge in economic crime and corruption. "We have some young people now," Deng said, "including children of cadres, and even some cadres themselves, who have . . . engaged in smuggling, speculation, and profiteering so as to make money or find a way to go abroad." Calling such things despicable, Deng linked the rising incidence of economic crime to a recent increase in the smuggling of "pornographic, obscene, filthy, and repulsive" films and publications into China. Demanding urgent action to "ban and destroy this decadent rubbish," Deng enjoined his colleagues to be "constantly on guard against such illegal, antisocialist activities."[19]

Notwithstanding Deng's condemnation of bourgeois decadence, only a single sentence in his August 18 speech was devoted to problems of extreme individualism and anarchism within the Democracy Movement—subjects that had preoccupied him only a few months earlier. Not only did he fail to repeat his earlier critique of China's Democracy Movement, he now made a number of concrete proposals aimed at enhancing grass-roots democracy, calling, for example, for expanded political participation, more effective constitutional and legal safeguards to protect the rights of citizens, and a more active voice for workers in running the affairs of the workplace.

In order "to really ensure the people's right to manage state organs," Deng recommended strengthening the system of people's congresses at all levels. To ensure the healthy growth of industrial democracy, he called for the formation of "representative congresses or conferences of workers and staff members" in all enterprises and institutions. The new organizations were to have the express right to "discuss and take decisions" on all major questions affecting the operations of their unit; eventually, the goal was for the workers' congresses and conferences gradually and "within appropriate limits" to elect their own leaders.

PREEMPTIVE DEMOCRATIZATION AND THE POLISH CRISIS

Deng's motives for seeking to expand grass-roots democracy and worker participation at this particular juncture have been the subject of considerable speculation. According to a former member of Hu Yaobang's entourage, Deng was influenced by the growing political crisis in Poland, which reportedly preoccupied him throughout the summer of 1980.[20] Worried that Polish-style work stoppages and antigovernment demonstrations might occur in China, Deng embraced grass-roots political participation, at least in part, as a means of heading off labor unrest.

A number of contemporaneous Chinese news commentaries dealing with the Polish crisis provided indirect support for this hypothesis. One article published in the late summer of 1980 noted the profound significance of the Polish government's acknowledgment that "economic and political reforms must be introduced rapidly to ameliorate [the country's] unhappy state of affairs"; the same report pointed out (with evident approval) that the initial wave of Polish strikes, occasioned by the government's July 1 decision to raise the price of meat, had begun to subside "only after a major party and government reshuffle and after concessions were made to the workers' political demands," that is, the demand for free trade unions.[21] Another midautumn commentary blamed the Polish crisis primarily on bureaucratism and corruption within the Polish Communist regime:

> The big strike of July was due in large measure to the continuing economic decline in recent years. . . . But the crisis has a deeper political cause. Senior Polish party officials have admitted that some leading party and government officials have arrogant work-styles and hold the public in contempt. There is widespread abuse of office for personal gain. . . . Corruption is quite widespread among officials, who enjoy special privileges and lavish life-styles. . . . Foreign news agencies report that the number of officials engaged in shady practices is quite large and only a very few have been prosecuted so far. It is not going to be easy to improve the image of the party and government leadership with the Polish public.
>
> To defend their own vital interests was what led the Polish people to decide to set up their own organizations. . . . Polish party leader Kania said . . . that the recent wave of strikes "was a large scale workers' protest. It was not directed at socialism but was opposed to the undermining of the principles of socialism; it was not against the party but [against] the mistakes in its policies."[22]

In the above commentary, worker unrest in Poland was seen as an outgrowth of justifiable public anger over bureaucratism, rampant corruption, and the mistaken policies of Polish party leaders. It did not require a great stretch of the imagination in the summer of 1980 to transpose the locale of this scenario from Poland to China, or to conclude that a little preemptive political reform might go a long way toward forestalling a Polish-type crisis in the People's Republic. This, at any rate, was Hu Yaobang's view; from all indications, Deng Xiaoping was inclined to agree.[23]

In late October the connection between political reform and the prevention of political rebellion was made explicit by party theoretician Liao Gailong, a reformer associated with the liberal wing of the "practice" faction and former political secretary to the late Marshal Zhu De:

> Leftist practices breed the type of crisis like the Polish crisis. We all know what has happened in Poland. If we do not change our course, the same things will

happen to us. Will [our] working class not rise in rebellion? Therefore, our trade
unions and mass organizations must be thoroughly reformed and the masses of
workers must be allowed to enjoy freedom and democracy in electing their own
trade union leaders and officials of their leading bodies.[24]

SHOWCASING DEMOCRATIC REFORM:
THE 1980 NATIONAL PEOPLE'S CONGRESS

Although Deng's Gengshen reform speech was not immediately disseminated
outside of party circles, his antifeudal message quickly reverberated throughout the country, providing liberal reformers with a major morale boost.[25] The
first significant showcase for the new policy of political openness and reform
was the Third Session of the Fifth NPC, which met in early September.

At the NPC, Deng pushed ahead on two main fronts: rejuvenation of government leadership (with emphasis on removing his remaining political opponents) and governmental rationalization and democratization. In pursuit of the
former objective, Deng first secured the resignations of Hua Guofeng and a
number of other senior government leaders, replacing them with proreform
leaders.[26] He then used the newly introduced device of legislative interpellation to undermine the political power and influence of his remaining adversaries.

Under the aegis of the party's commitment to greater governmental accountability, Deng's supporters in the NPC launched an "independent" inquiry into the November 1979 collapse of a Japanese-made offshore oil-drill-
ing platform in the Bohai Gulf. At a cost of seventy-two lives and RMB ¥37
million, the Bohai oil-rig disaster was the most serious accident in the history
of China's petroleum industry. After a preliminary investigation by Tianjin
municipal authorities determined that the principal causes of the collapse were
"official negligence" and "bureaucratic arrogance and complacency," it was
subsequently disclosed that authorities within the Ministry of Petroleum had
tried to squelch the investigation—presumably in order to cover up their own
culpability.[27]

At the September 1980 NPC meeting, legislators exercised their new powers of interpellation by questioning leading officials from the Petroleum Ministry and its Bureau of Oceanic Exploration. After conducting a well-publicized hearing, one group of delegates criticized Vice-Premier Kang Shi'en
(whose jurisdiction included the petrochemical industry) and reprimanded Petroleum Minister Song Zhenming. Kang was subsequently demoted, while
Song was removed from his post along with several of his subordinates, four
of whom were tried and sentenced to prison for their roles in the disaster.[28]
The petroleum minister's reputation was further damaged when it was revealed that in 1978 he had attempted to suppress a police investigation into a
brutal kidnap, rape, and murder purportedly committed by his personal
driver.[29]

While exposure of the Bohai oil-rig scandal received a great deal of media publicity as an example of China's new policy of governmental openness and accountability, the political subtext of the Bohai story was even more interesting: both Kang Shi'en and Song Zhenming were leading figures in the petroleum clique, and their disgrace inevitably affected the prestige (and hence the influence) of their chief Politburo patron, Yu Qiuli. Thus, the public airing of the Bohai scandal severely undermined the power base of the petroleum clique. In the reshuffle of personnel that followed the scandal, the biggest winner was Chen Yun.[30]

In a number of other well-publicized ministerial- and subministerial-level interrogations that took place at the 1980 NPC meeting, groups of deputies hammered away at governmental waste, corruption, and inefficiency. Not surprisingly, many (if not most) of the officials targeted for criticism had been actively involved in supporting Hua Guofeng's deficit-spending, heavy-industry-boosting "flying leap" of 1978–79. Examples included the minister and two deputy ministers of the metallurgical industry, who were rebuked for mishandling massive investment projects like the Baoshan iron and steel complex and the Wuhan steel rolling mill—projects that Li Xiannian had personally approved and signed off on;[31] and several high-level officials in the Ministry of Chemical Industry, who were held responsible for mismanaging a number of large-scale capital construction projects. Other problems indirectly linked to Hua Guofeng's economic and political stewardship that came under attack at the NPC included China's high rate of retail inflation (which reached 11 percent in 1980); rampant industrial waste and pollution; uncontrolled population growth; and unreasonable wage and bonus payments to workers.[32]

Notwithstanding the underlying partisan purpose of such legislative inquiries, the exposure of governmental misdeeds by NPC delegates was hailed in the mass media as a demonstration of the seriousness of the party's commitment to political reform. By allowing the NPC to play more than its traditional role as a ritualistic rubber stamp, reformers sought to convince a skeptical public, grown weary of empty slogans and unkept promises, that this time socialist democracy was for real. If such indeed was the objective, it apparently succeeded, at least for the moment. As one NPC delegate remarked, "I found myself pleased by the candidness of the government leaders, who lived up to the commitments to the people by not making false, pompous, meaningless reports pretending that everything was all right and nothing wrong. Haven't we had enough of that in the past?"[33]

While the mass media were loudly trumpeting the democratic virtues of the 1980 NPC meeting, a related event received scant official publicity: On September 2, NPC Standing Committee Vice-Chairman Peng Zhen announced his committee's unanimous decision to accept the Fifth Plenum's proposal to amend Article 45 of the PRC state constitution, deleting the four big freedoms. Peng's report, in which he blamed the "four bigs," among other things, for spawning the chaos and anarchy of the Cultural Revolution, was subsequently approved by the NPC as a whole. Henceforth, wall posters were no longer a constitutionally protected form of speech in China.[34]

In the immediate, ebullient aftermath of the NPC such countercurrents went largely unnoticed, as political reformers associated with the liberal wing of Deng's coalition stepped up their efforts to create a positive environment for political change. In mid-October Hu Yaobang declared that China had reached a "great historical turning point" in its ideology and politics. Noting that Mao's shortcomings and limitations had rendered him unable to achieve socialist democracy in his lifetime, Hu promised that henceforth socialist democracy would be "not only a means, but an end; it is our basic system."[35]

Later that same month, reform theoretician Liao Gailong elaborated on Hu's theme of democratization as an end in itself in a lengthy manifesto on political-institutional reform. Taking as his point of departure Deng Xiaoping's August reform proposals and Hu Yaobang's "turning point" speech, Liao went further than either Deng or Hu in proclaiming a "high degree of democracy" and "extensive freedom" to be the ultimate goals of political reform in China. To circumscribe the power of the party and ensure democratic control of the government, Liao boldly called for several institutional innovations: (1) a strong, bicameral national legislature, reduced in size to make it more effective as a deliberative body, with a full-time, professional standing committee and several functionally specialized subcommittees exercising jurisdiction over legislation within their particular areas of competence; (2) a wholly independent judiciary, no longer subject to interference by party committees; (3) freedom of the press and publication, with journalists assuming independent responsibility for news collection, analysis, commentary, and investigative reporting; (4) free and democratic labor unions and peasant associations, with workers and farmers electing their own leaders to represent their interests; (5) democratic management of enterprises and business firms, with staff members and workers assuming the role of "masters of the house," and with the old system of dictatorship by party committee secretaries totally eliminated; and (6) complete separation of party and state administrative functions at all levels, with organs of the government assuming sole responsibility for doing the government's work. While advancing these proposals, Liao also managed to take a not-so-subtle swipe at Ye Jianying, whose 1979 National Day speech was explicitly criticized for failing to mention two important tasks: achieving a "high degree of democracy in politics" and a "high degree of civility in culture."[36]

Emboldened by the proreform establishment's vocal support for the goal of democratization, the mass media in the late summer and autumn of 1980 published a spate of articles criticizing remnant feudal influences,[37] overconcentration of power,[38] personality cults,[39] and the system of lifetime tenure for cadres.[40] Equal numbers of newspaper and journal articles extolled the virtues of industrial democracy,[41] religious and intellectual freedom,[42] independent courts and lawyers,[43] and even student protest movements.[44]

In mid-October 1980, on the heels of Hu Yaobang's "historical turning point" speech, the *Guangming Daily* invited several liberal political theorists to participate in a symposium on structural reform. Among the participants were a number of people who had taken part in the CCP's winter 1979 conference on theoretical work.[45] In their remarks, participants emphasized the principal themes of the Gengshen reforms. Carefully refraining from criticizing the party's leading role in society, a succession of speakers advocated complete freedom of speech, rapid democratization, and an end to all feudal influences.[46] Excerpts from the symposium were published in the *Guangming Daily* in three installments, on October 16, 17, and 19. In terms of liveliness of public debate and boldness of reform rhetoric, the *Guangming Daily* symposium, along with Liao Gailong's speech, represented the high point of liberal political advocacy, the very apogee of fang.

THE 1980 LOCAL ELECTIONS

Reflecting the high degree of democratic optimism that accompanied reform initiatives in 1980, spirited local election campaigns were held in hundreds of counties across China in the latter half of the year. With the new electoral law as a guide, the 1980 county-level People's Congress elections embodied an unprecedented degree of political openness and grass-roots participation.

When the first experimental elections were conducted in the winter and spring of 1979–80, they were hailed as a milestone in the development of socialist democracy.[47] Although "autocratic" and "patriarchal" cadres in some areas reportedly resisted fully implementing certain provisions of the new law (e.g., its stipulations permitting ordinary citizens to nominate candidates and mandating the use of the secret ballot), central authorities vigorously supported the drive to promote the extension of political participation at the local level.[48] What happened thereafter, however, was a classic instance of a spiraling "revolution of rising expectations" leading, in some cases, to heightened problems of political stability and unity.

Encouraged by the democratic rhetoric of the Gengshen reforms, and given their first real opportunity for meaningful grass-roots political participation, some political activists, most notably in university constituencies, began testing the outer limits of electoral freedom. Invoking officially sanctioned catchphrases of the Third, Fourth, and Fifth Plenums—"emancipate thinking," "seek truth from facts," "oppose ossified thinking," and "leaders are not gods"—they began to question the scientific validity of Marxist doctrines, cast aspersions on Mao's reputation, and challenge the sanctity of the four cardinal principles. In pushing the ethos of fang to new extremes, they eventually ran afoul of older, more conservative members of Deng's reform coalition, including Chen Yun, who was becoming increasingly concerned about the implications of uncontrolled grass-roots political mobilization.

Two local elections, one in Changsha (Hunan) and the other in Beijing, provide cogent illustration of the type of problems encountered in implementing the electoral reforms.[49] At Hunan Teachers' College in Changsha, candidates for the county People's Congress conducted a heated election campaign in the autumn of 1980. Reform of the political structure was a dominant motif in the campaign. One candidate, a twenty-seven-year-old former Red Guard named Liang Heng, campaigned on a platform of opposition to "the kind of Marxism-Leninism propagandized and taught through all China." Decrying the passive, dependent political mentality of the Chinese people, Liang alleged that the "nation's people have sunk into servitude, no different from slavery. . . . How can we speak of a nation of citizens when both people and officials are like this?"[50]

Liang Heng's radical rhetoric, along with that of another rebellious student candidate named Tao Sen, clearly upset university officials, who sought to discourage voters from electing the two dissidents by arbitrarily adding additional names to the candidates' list at the last minute and by placing the names of Tao and Liang at the bottom of the enlarged list. When word of the officials' devious tactics got out, some two thousand students marched in protest across the city to the provincial party headquarters, where they sang the "Internationale," shouted antifeudal, antibureaucratic slogans, and demanded an investigation into the behavior of university authorities. The provincial party committee agreed, and several days later a group of provincial election officials visited the college campus. After completing a one-day investigation, they concluded that school officials had done nothing wrong and that the election should be held as scheduled. Thereupon, Liang, Tao, and one other candidate tried to withdraw their names from the ballot in protest, urging their fellow students to boycott the election.

The school's election committee refused to take the three names off the ballot and ruled that the election should be held as scheduled, on October 14. With supporters of Liang and Tao boycotting the election, less than 60 percent of the eligible voters cast ballots; not surprisingly, the two rebels lost. Angered by the outcome, eighty-seven students began a hunger strike in front of the provincial party committee compound.[51] Other students organized a boycott of classes at the college. Friends of the hunger strikers initiated a campaign to send telegrams to party and government officials and universities around the country, informing them of the situation. An American journalist was also contacted, and within a few days the ordeal of Liang and Tao was being broadcast back to China over the Voice of America.

With the confrontation at Hunan Teachers' College escalating rapidly, and with adverse publicity mushrooming, the central party leadership stepped in, in the person of Politburo member Wang Zhen. Wang, who had been contacted informally by Tao Sen (who reportedly had a "back door" family connection with the old general), called upon the rebellious students to "take stability and unity as the key link," end their hunger strike, and return to classes; he also promised to launch a fresh inquiry into the incident.

In mid-November the central investigation team dispatched by Wang Zhen rendered its verdict. The decision held that university authorities had acted improperly in padding the candidates' list and in going forward with the election in the face of justifiable student protest. The election results were consequently voided, a new election was ordered, and the college vice-president was instructed to issue a self-examination. All of this was quite consistent with the democratic spirit of the Gengshen reforms—or so it seemed.

Meanwhile, in Beijing a similar conflict broke out between student activists and university authorities during the autumn 1980 election campaign. At Peking University, a total of twenty-nine candidates vied for two positions on the Haidian District People's Congress. Several of the candidates campaigned on platforms that either directly or indirectly challenged orthodox Communist Party doctrines. For example, physics student Wang Juntao, a deputy editor of the underground journal *Beijing Spring* and at seventeen years of age reportedly the youngest person arrested during the Qingming incident of April 1976, stirred up a firestorm of controversy by openly questioning whether Mao Zedong had been a true Marxist, and by urging the adoption of Western-style political institutions. In a similar vein, prodemocracy candidate Fang Zhiwen, arguing in favor of an independent press, suggested that because China lacked democracy it could not truly be called a socialist country. A third liberal candidate, philosophy graduate student Hu Ping, boldly declared that free speech was virtually nonexistent in China. Little wonder that university authorities were visibly nervous about the approaching election.[52]

When the election was held in early December, Hu Ping and Wang Juntao finished first and second in the balloting; the third-place finisher was a centrist candidate named Zhang Wei, who represented the official student union. In accordance with existing electoral rules, the three top vote-getters competed in a runoff election to fill the two vacant seats. On the second ballot, Hu Ping and Wang Juntao again finished one-two, with Hu gaining a clear majority of the votes cast, entitling him to fill one of the two vacant seats; Wang, on the other hand, fell just shy of 50 percent, necessitating a second runoff election (between Wang and Zhang Wei) to fill the remaining seat. Embarrassed by the outcome of the first two ballots, university authorities refused either to accredit Hu Ping or to hold a runoff election for the second seat. Instead, Hu and Wang were subjected to a lengthy investigation by university officials. Wang was pressured to write a self criticism renouncing his advocacy of Western democracy, while Hu was accused of having a "bad class background" and of maintaining "suspicious overseas contacts." After a delay of several months, Zhang Wei, the third-place finisher, was quietly installed as people's deputy from Peking University. Meanwhile, at the nearby Chinese Academy of Sciences, prodemocracy activist Chen Ziming—the notorious "crewcut shorty" of the Qingming incident—was similarly barred from occupying his duly elected seat on the local People's Congress.[53]

At Hunan Teachers' College, the postelection fallout was even more disturbing: Despite the mid-November recommendations of Wang Zhen's investigation group, the promise of a new election was never kept; dissident candidates Tao Sen and Liang Heng were severely criticized for violating the four cardinal principles; Tao was expelled from the university—and later sentenced to three years of labor reform—for his "wrecking activities" and "bad morals"; and Liang Heng, under attack for his alleged "bourgeois ideas," left the country to pursue graduate study abroad.[54]

Similar instances of irregular or extralegal tampering with election rules and results, including harassment of liberal activists by local authorities, were reported in Shanghai and other cities.[55] By the onset of winter, party and Youth League branches throughout the country had been instructed to step up their "political and ideological work" in schools, universities, and factories, with a view toward inculcating "socialist discipline" and "socialist morality" among China's young people; by then, however, the 1979 electoral reforms had become a dead letter.[56]

Angrily protesting this state of affairs, Wang Juntao—the second-place finisher in the aborted Peking University elections—issued a statement denouncing electoral manipulation by local authorities. Alleging that the wave of democratic enthusiasm that had greeted the NPC meeting in September 1980 had been premature, Wang chided party and government leaders for betraying the spirit of democracy. "The Third Session of the Fifth NPC was to have been a 'congress of democracy,'" he said, "but what is the actual situation now? The democratic reform movement . . . has been strangled. Mild demands for democracy are not allowed by authorities." Citing the case of Liang Heng in Hunan, he further admonished: "The Chinese people have been enslaved for so long it's in their blood. . . . [But] history does not stand still; democracy is what the people desperately want."[57]

SAFEGUARDING STABILITY AND UNITY: THE CONSERVATIVE BACKLASH

The sudden, midstream decision to suspend implementation of China's electoral law in certain controversial constituencies was the leading edge of a powerful conservative backlash that took shape at the end of 1980. The backlash had at least three components: first, a worsening domestic economic situation, marked by rising inflation, growing sectoral imbalances, and mounting budgetary deficits; second, a general increase in domestic social and political disorder, evidenced in such phenomena as "agitation by illegal organizations," "counterattacks by remnants of the 'Lin Biao clique' and the Gang of Four," and "sabotage by people who want chaos";[58] and third, a serious new flare-up in Poland's political crisis, bringing that country to the brink of chaos. By year's end, the backlash was strong enough—and its diverse assortment of supporters coherent enough—to bring about an indefinite freeze on further reform.

Conservatives began to express their deep concern over the implications of the Gengshen reforms shortly after the conclusion of the September NPC meeting. In a letter to Hu Yaobang dated September 24, 1980, Hu Qiaomu raised the strong possibility that a Polish-style crisis could occur in China. Arguing that the existence of independent labor unions and other autonomous mass organizations would enable a small number of political dissidents and disgruntled workers to stir up a great deal of trouble, Hu Qiaomu strongly opposed the formation of free unions, as recommended, for example, by Liao Gailong and others.[59]

Expressing agreement with Hu Qiaomu, CC Propaganda Director Wang Renzhong, speaking on October 9, called for a moratorium on further discussion of political reform. Referring to the Polish crisis as a reflection of "internal ideological chaos" (*neibu sixiang hunluan*), Wang asserted that due to the worsening Polish situation, "Comrade Xiaoping's blueprint for 'reform of the party and state leadership system' must no longer be propagated." Chen Yun concurred, arguing that "if we're not careful . . . China may develop its own Polish-style situation."[60] In response to such expressions of alarm, Hu Yaobang formally requested relevant party and government organs to draw up recommendations for dealing with the contingency of a Polish-type crisis in China.[61]

Some conservatives sought to discredit the liberal wing of Deng's reform coalition. On November 12 Deng Liqun (who had been given the sobriquet "Little Deng" to distinguish him from Deng Xiaoping) gave a series of talks at the Central Party School in Beijing. Although his ostensible purpose was to publicize Chen Yun's newly compiled three-volume *Selected Works*, his lectures went well beyond the mere promotion of Chen's writings to include allegations concerning the existence of high-level intraparty opposition to the four cardinal principles. Equally significant, in coining the slogan "In economic work learn from Comrade Chen Yun" and in claiming that Chen Yun had been the principal architect of China's socialist economic construction, Little Deng implicitly discounted Deng Xiaoping's role as China's preeminent economic reform strategist.[62]

At a Central Committee work conference in mid-December, Chen Yun, visibly disturbed over recent political and economic trends, raised the slogan "oppose bourgeois liberalization" (*fandui zichanjieji ziyouhua*) as a counterweight to the Gengshen reformers' one-sided emphasis on combating feudal influences.[63] In the economic sphere, Chen proposed a new tightening up of central fiscal and administrative controls to reduce burgeoning budget deficits and sectoral imbalances, and to restore discipline on the construction, price, and wage fronts. Calling for sharp temporary reductions in capital spending to combat a deficit that had grown by an additional RMB ¥12.75 billion since the end of 1979, Chen defended his strong-medicine approach, arguing that "it is better to suffer [now] for one year than to suffer [later] for five years."

Neither Zhao Ziyang nor Deng Xiaoping raised significant objections to Chen's stringent readjustment proposal. Indeed, Zhao's speech to the CC work conference echoed Chen's warning that an economic crisis was likely if strong preventive measures were not taken.[64] To put teeth into Chen's proposal, new wage and price freezes were imposed, along with a 10 percent cut in the state budget and a cancellation (or indefinite postponement) of seventeen large-scale industrial turnkey projects purchased from the West and Japan, valued at more than U.S. $7 billion—including Li Xiannian's much maligned Baoshan iron and steel complex.[65] All of these measures were implemented with Zhao Ziyang's full concordance.

Thus, by late December 1980 a confluence of three factors—a seriously unbalanced national economy, mounting anxiety over Poland's political crisis, and a swelling conservative backlash against bourgeois liberalism on the political and ideological fronts—had created a mood of deepening concern for "ensuring stability and unity" (*baozheng anding tuanjie*). Responding to these concerns, Deng's December 25 speech ushered in a major phase change in the fang/shou cycle. As his central theme, he stressed that the tasks of readjusting the economy and safeguarding political stability and unity had to take precedence over all other goals, including structural reform. Accordingly, he ordained that the pace of political and economic reform should be slowed down so that reform could be "subordinated to readjustment, serve it, and not impede it." In line with Chen Yun's recommendations, Deng also stressed the temporary need for "a high degree of centralism and unification" in economic policy and administrative decision making, and he flatly declared that no new experiments in enterprise reform would be conducted in the coming year.[66]

Avoiding any direct reference to the worsening Polish crisis, Deng clearly had that situation in mind (along with China's recent local elections) when he urged state organizations to "adopt appropriate laws and decrees calling for mediation to avoid strikes by workers or students." Calling for an outright ban on all unauthorized protest marches and demonstrations, Deng stated that new government regulations should be adopted "to forbid different units and localities from banding together for harmful purposes, and to proscribe the activities of illegal organizations and the printing and distribution of illegal publications." Urging strong action in cases of serious civil disturbance or acts of sabotage, Deng allowed that where necessary, martial law could be declared, with public order in such cases to be ensured by "specially trained troops."[67]

Instead of encouraging free trade unions and student organizations to articulate their members' interests, as recommended by Liao Gailong and others, Deng now called for strengthening the party's organizational and propaganda work within trade unions, women's federations, the Youth League, and student associations. The purpose was to "see to it that our . . . young people are imbued with high ideals and moral integrity," and to encourage them to "cultivate good habits such as respecting discipline, observing good manners, and safeguarding the public interest."[68] Indeed, so far did Deng now depart from his original proposal for augmented industrial democracy that when the party center finally promulgated long-awaited provisional regulations governing the organization and functions of workers' congresses in the spring of 1981, the provisions were so restrictive as to represent little or no improvement over the standard, party-dominated labor unions encountered in orthodox Stalinist systems.[69]

Tying his concern for political stability and unity specifically to his renewed endorsement of the four cardinal principles, Deng now repeated his August 18 criticism of the harmful tendency to worship capitalism, adding to it a fresh injunction to oppose bourgeois liberalization, which he now lumped together with anarchism and extreme individualism.[70]

Rampant crime and corruption also received considerable attention in Deng's December 25 address. Noting that the frequency of serious crimes—including murder, arson, dynamiting, robbery, burglary, rape, smuggling, tax evasion, speculation, profiteering, bribery, and embezzlement—had increased significantly in the past year, Deng attributed the new crime wave to several factors, including sabotage by remnants of the "Lin Biao clique" and the Gang of Four; people who "want chaos in the country"; "surviving elements of the exploiting classes"; and "serious corrosion by feudal or capitalist ideas and . . . corresponding life-styles." To deal with the crime wave, which he now referred to as a form of class struggle, Deng called for strengthening the state apparatus of the people's democratic dictatorship.[71]

Allowing that some people might argue that by endorsing strong governmental action to deter and punish troublemakers of various kinds "we are trying to 'tighten up' (*shou*), . . . exercising dictatorship without democracy," Deng nonetheless insisted—as he had previously done in January—that such a view was completely wrong. Since there had never been a decision to "loosen up" with respect to the treatment of counterrevolutionaries or criminals, he argued, the question of tightening up simply could not arise.[72] Notwithstanding Deng's denial, his address of December 25 effectively spelled the end of the 1980 Gengshen reforms.

THE TRIAL OF THE GANG OF FOUR

With crime, counterrevolution, and class struggle very much on the minds of party leaders at the end of the year, the long-awaited trial of the Gang of Four began in late November. After four years of detention and many months of pretrial preparation, the Gang finally stood in the dock, along with Chen Boda and five surviving members of the "Lin Biao clique."[73] Originally scheduled for September, the twin trials had been repeatedly postponed while government prosecutors sought, in vain, to extract a confession of guilt from the recalcitrant ringleader of the Left, sixty-seven-year-old Jiang Qing.

The case against Jiang and her codefendants was painstakingly prepared. Several hundred government investigators collected and sifted through mountains of evidence. Twenty-four special prosecutors were assigned to argue the government's case in a special court presided over by thirty-five judges. When the formal indictments against the ten defendants were handed down in mid-November, they ran to a length of some twenty thousand words.[74]

Because the trial of the "Beijing ten" was the first significant test of the government's new commitment to the rule of law, strict observance of legal

Courtroom scene: Joint trial of the Gang of Four and "Lin Biao antiparty clique," December 1980.

norms—in particular the norm of due process—was deemed vital. Nevertheless, outside observers noted a number of apparent flaws in the government's handling of the case. For one thing, a provision of the 1979 code of criminal procedure setting a maximum three-month limit to the length of time a suspect could be detained without trial was suspended by special decree of the State Council, thereby denying the defendants—six of whom had been in jail for nine years or longer—an important legal safeguard. In addition, all of the defendants had been publicly reviled and pronounced guilty by party and government leaders (and by the state-controlled press) long before formal judicial verdicts were handed down. To make matters worse, many of the judges hearing the case had themselves been victims of Cultural Revolution persecution, thus raising serious questions about the court's impartiality.[75] Finally, despite an explicit provision in the new criminal procedure code calling for public access to all criminal trials, the trials of the Gang and the clique were closed to all but a small number of hand-picked observers on grounds that the anticipated exposure of important state secrets overrode the statutory principle of public access.[76]

Questions of due process aside, the case against members of the Gang of Four centered on allegations that they had masterminded massive numbers of fraudulent frame-ups and persecutions during the Cultural Revolution. Directly or indirectly, they were held responsible for causing the deaths of 34,800 people and the torture (or severe mistreatment) of 726,000 others during China's "decade of destruction." They were also formally charged with conspiring to carry out a coup d'état in the aftermath of Mao's death.

The Gang of Four in the dock, December 1980. From left: Zhang Chunqiao, Chen Boda, Wang Hongwen, Yao Wenyuan, Jiang Qing.

A partial listing in the indictment of the alleged victims of Gang-inspired persecutions and frame-ups read like a virtual "Who's Who" of top Chinese party and government leaders. Headed by Liu Shaoqi and Deng Xiaoping, the list contained the names of twenty past or present members of the Politburo (including Chen Yun, Li Xiannian, Ye Jianying, Hu Yaobang, Peng Zhen, Wang Zhen, Yao Yilin, Bo Yibo, and Song Renqiong); thirteen members of the Central Party Secretariat (including Hu Qiaomu, Yang Shangkun, Wan Li, and Wang Renzhong); eighty-eight full and alternate members of the Central Committee; twelve vice-premiers of the State Council; five vice-chairmen of the Military Affairs Commission; four first secretaries of regional party bureaus; sixty members of the Standing Committee of the National People's Congress, and at least eighty-three other high-ranking officials.[77]

Represented in court by ten defense attorneys, and carefully coached in advance by government prosecutors, most of the defendants, after being presented with graphic (and in some cases grisly) evidence of their crimes, in due course admitted guilt and begged for mercy from the court. Some were more unyielding than others, however; and at least one defendant steadfastly refused to bow to government pressures to confess. To the very end, Jiang Qing, acting as her own defense attorney, head held high in a studied gesture of defiance, denied her guilt. Denouncing prosecution witnesses as traitors, she derided the court and challenged the very legitimacy of the government. On two occasions, Jiang was ejected from the courtroom after engaging in shouting matches with witnesses, judges, and prosecutors.[78]

For all of Jiang Qing's dramatic defense gambits—including her ultimate claim that she had acted entirely at Mao's behest—the outcome of the trial was never seriously in doubt. The only real question concerned the severity of the sentences. After a post-trial delay of several weeks, during which time the thirty-five judges repeatedly consulted with party leaders in clear violation of the spirit, if not the letter, of the Gengshen reforms, the defiant Jiang Qing and her principal coconspirator, Zhang Chunqiao, were given suspended death sentences, with the possibility of commutation to life imprisonment after two years in the event of sincere repentance. Other Gang members, as well as the surviving leaders of the "Lin Biao clique," drew prison sentences ranging from sixteen years to life.[79]

The conviction and sentencing of the Gang cleared the way for enlarging the scope of judicial reprisals against other Cultural Revolution malefactors. At least sixty coconspirators had been publicly named at the trial, including Mao's nephew, Mao Yuanxin, and former Shanghai mayor Ma Tianshui. By the end of 1980, several hundred reputed followers of the Gang of Four were under arrest in Shanghai alone, with similar figures reported from other parts of the country.

With public anger and desire for revenge running strong as a result of the grim revelations made during the trial of the Gang of Four, party leaders took pains to discourage an indiscriminate flood tide of judicial vengeance. According to one official, the basic criterion to be followed in exposing erstwhile Leftists was to be "justice, not revenge." Even Deng Xiaoping came in for a subtle reminder about the virtues of forgiving one's enemies. At the end of December, *Red Flag* published a parable about an elderly Chinese general who, for the good of his country, swallowed his personal pride in order to collaborate with a younger minister toward whom he harbored deep personal antipathy. The commentary accompanying the parable praised the old general's forgiveness and drew the following moral lesson: "One must have a large heart and not hold grudges."[80]

PREPARING FOR HUA GUOFENG'S FINAL EXIT

Motives of revenge, along with admonitions to forgive one's enemies, also played a substantial part in the events leading to Hua Guofeng's final exit from the Chinese political stage in the winter of 1980–81. While Hua's power and influence had been steadily eroded in the two years since the Third Plenum, he remained the nominal chairman of both the party and the MAC. In pressing for Hua's final ouster, Deng Xiaoping now displayed only the mildest inclination to "have a large heart."

In late November 1980 Hua Guofeng's last remaining stronghold of political authority was breached. At a Politburo meeting that coincided with the first two weeks in the trial of the Gang of Four, Hua was required to issue a preliminary self-criticism. In it, he acknowledged committing a number of errors in the three years following Mao's death. These included pursuing a Leftist political line; persisting in the promotion of the "two whatevers"; opposing a reversal of verdicts on the Qingming incident; attempting to block, or at least delay, the rehabilitation of Deng Xiaoping and Chen Yun (among others); and promoting the "Leftist style of a new 'Great Leap'" in economic policy.[81]

After Hua dutifully renounced his past behavior, repented his mistakes, and expressed the opinion that he should no longer be entrusted to lead the party, the Politburo on December 5 adopted a resolution detailing Hua's shortcomings as a leader:

> Comrade Hua Guofeng eagerly produced and accepted a new cult of personality. He had himself called the wise leader, had his own pictures hung beside the pictures of Comrade Mao Zedong. . . .
>
> In 1977 and 1978, Comrade Hua Guofeng promoted some "Leftist" slogans in the realm of economic work . . . resulting in severe losses and calamities for the national economy. . . . Comrade Hua Guofeng is not alone responsible for this, but he has to assume an important part of the responsibility. . . .
>
> [Although] Comrade Hua Guofeng has also done some successful work, it is extremely clear that he lacks the political and organizational ability to be chairman of the party. That he should never have been appointed chairman of the Military Affairs Commission, everyone knows.[82]

After thus rebuking Hua, the Politburo stopped short of demanding his immediate resignation. Accepting Hua's own opinion that he should be relieved of responsibility for current party work, the December 5 resolution postponed his resignation so that the Sixth Plenum, originally scheduled to meet at the conclusion of the CC work conference that followed the November–December Politburo meeting, could render a "final decision" on his future status. Until then, the resolution declared, "he is still officially the chairman of the party Central Committee and he will have to receive foreign guests in [that] capacity." While refusing to preempt the Central Committee's formal authority to oust Hua and choose his successor, the Politburo nonetheless recommended that the Sixth Plenum appoint Hu Yaobang chairman of the Central Committee and Deng Xiaoping chairman of the Military Affairs Commission. (Originally, the Politburo had proposed that Deng should take both posts, but Deng had refused on the grounds that someone "young and vigorous" should chair the Central Committee—whereupon he personally nominated Hu Yaobang for the job.) In the meantime, until the Sixth Plenum could meet, the Politburo invited Hu and Deng to assume immediate responsibility for the work of the two offices on an informal basis.[83]

According to unofficial Chinese sources, there was more to Hua's agreement to resign his last remaining party posts than met the eye. Reportedly, Deng Xiaoping had revealed his intention to include in the indictment against the Gang of Four a series of criminal charges pertaining to their role in conspiring to suppress the 1976 Qingming incident. If pressed in court, these charges would have rendered Hua Guofeng vulnerable to possible prosecution as an accessory to, or coconspirator in, the Gang's criminal misdeeds. Facing the potential threat of criminal liability, Hua Guofeng consented to resign his party posts. In exchange, all references to the Qingming incident were expunged from the indictment, and the number of formal charges against the Gang was duly reduced from fifty to forty-eight. Shortly thereafter, Deng, in a somewhat gratuitous display of belated big-heartedness, declared that "Chairman Hua deserves protection."[84]

The Politburo's decision to accept Hua Guofeng's resignation, followed in short order by the conviction of the Gang of Four, brought to a close a half-decade of political conflict triggered by the 1976 deaths of Mao Zedong and Zhou Enlai. At long last, the crisis of succession was resolved. But even as old scores were being settled and old ghosts laid to rest, a fundamentally new set of problems and conflicts—centering on the direction, pace, and scope of systemic reform—conspired to undermine further the fragile stability and unity of the Chinese polity. As the year 1981 began, the forces of reaction grew louder and more insistent.

PART II

The Road to Tiananmen, 1981–1989

Polarization and Paralysis:
January 1981–April 1982

While we are continuing to develop democracy in the party and
among the people, we also need to strengthen discipline. . . .
We want stability and unity as well as vitality and anima-
tion. . . . How can this be called "reneging"? . . . As for the few
antagonistic elements who have engaged in counterrevolutionary activity . . . [or] who have made reactionary statements in
opposition to the "four cardinal principles," there has never
been any question of "condoning," let alone "reneging."

—People's Daily, *January 19, 1981*

THROUGHOUT most of 1980 the liberal wing of Deng's reform coalition managed to retain the policy initiative. By the beginning of 1981, however, the
balance had shifted perceptibly. One key indicator of the rising influence of
conservatives was their success in freezing political and economic reforms in
the early winter of 1980–81; another was Deng Xiaoping's decision to support
a generally positive, upbeat assessment of Mao's historical contributions; yet
a third indicator was the stiffening resistance to change displayed by the PLA,
whose leadership had yet to be reconciled either to ideological de-Maoization
or to structural reform.

In 1981 the army began to fight back. From the very beginning, the Chinese
military had been a reluctant partner in Deng Xiaoping's reform program.
When Deng first revealed his plan to transfer or retire a number of regional
commanders and commissars late in 1979, following this with a sharp cutback
in the 1980 military budget, reaction within the PLA had been highly negative. One of the newly displaced commanders, Xu Shiyou—Deng's erstwhile
ally—was reportedly so upset over Deng's treatment of the military (including the fact that Deng had passed him over for a promotion) that he angrily
accosted Deng at the conclusion of the Fifth Plenum in early March 1980,
accusing him of being ungrateful and disrespectful.[1]

Whether true or merely hyperbole, such reports may be taken as indirect
evidence of mounting antagonism between "old guard" regional PLA leaders
and members of Deng's reform coalition. Nor did the PLA's discontent stop

at the highest level of leadership. According to a document issued by the CCP Central Secretariat in October 1980, four of eight divisional commanders in the Nanking military region who were slated to be transferred to new posts under Deng's military reorganization plan initially disputed their reassignment orders.[2]

Morale and discipline problems were said to be even more severe among midlevel officers. With 45 percent of the PLA's officer corps having been recruited during the decade of the Cultural Revolution, Leftist influences were still very prominent; many officers were said to be "opposing all reform and everything new. . . . [They] do not understand fighting and they have no knowledge; but they do have their methods, such as special privilege, the use of relationships . . . , and the taking of revenge."[3] Discipline problems were said to be particularly serious in four of China's eleven greater military regions—Nanjing, Fuzhou, Wuhan, and Shenyang; in Nanjing, officers in one divisional command reportedly balked at obeying civilian party orders, saying: "What business does the Central Secretariat have controlling the military? Where does Hu Yaobang stand in the [military] hierarchy?"[4] And when the MAC promulgated a document calling for further extending the household production responsibility system in agriculture, reaction within the PLA was hostile. Among senior officers the new policy was denounced, among other things, for its alleged contribution to renewed class polarization in the countryside and for hastening a "capitalist restoration" in agriculture.[5]

Visibly upset with Deng's policies, senior PLA commanders had begun openly to embrace neo-Leftist rhetoric as early as the spring of 1980.[6] In doing so they had a natural ally in Hua Guofeng, who by this time had little left to lose. Thus, while Deng was busy building his anti-Hua majority in the Politburo and the State Council, several of China's ranking generals, with Hua's active support, launched an ideological counterattack against political and economic reform.

So serious and so sensitive were the problems of PLA morale and discipline that no consensus could be reached on naming a new defense minister to replace the outgoing minister, Xu Xiangqian, who had announced his retirement in September 1980. When a new minister was finally chosen in March 1981— survivor General Geng Biao—the long delay was attributed to differences of opinion among high-ranking commanders.[7]

At the Central Committee work conference of November–December 1980, which Ye Jianying failed to attend ostensibly because of illness (though it was also rumored that he may have boycotted the meeting), Deng and his colleagues discussed the military problem at length and issued the following warning:

> Within the army there has existed a problem of not paying sufficient attention to the spirit of the Third Plenum and not thoroughly grasping it. . . . Many people have not understood that the Third Plenum . . . represented a fundamental change in the party's political, organizational, and ideological lines, namely, a change from "Leftist" mistakes to a down-to-earth approach. The thinking of many peo-

ple has [consequently] been limited to those things they were familiar with, such as "continuing the revolution." . . . Because they had not yet freed themselves from "Leftist" shackles, various contradictory sentiments appeared.[8]

DEFENDING MAO: THE PLA FIGHTS BACK

With the conservative backlash of winter 1980–81 providing convenient cover for antireform propaganda, the PLA began stepping up its efforts to uphold Mao's legacy and challenge the policies of the reformers. At a January work conference held by the PLA General Political Department, GPD director Wei Guoqing spoke out bluntly against the "worship of capitalism" and "bourgeois liberal tendencies." This was accompanied by a demand for more political and ideological study among the army rank-and-file.[9] Also in January, the PLA newspaper *Liberation Army Daily* revived a slogan first popularized by Lin Biao in 1966, at the outset of the Cultural Revolution: "First, do not fear bitterness; second, do not fear death!"[10]

In February the PLA launched a well-publicized propaganda campaign to "emulate Lei Feng," the martyred army conscript who died in 1962 while allegedly devoting his energies to serving the Communist Party, socialism, and the Chinese people. Chairman Mao had lionized Lei Feng in 1963, and the revival of the emulation campaign early in 1981—a revival initiated by Wei Guoqing and supported by Propaganda Director Wang Renzhong—appeared to be part of a concerted attempt to blunt the thrust of de-Maoization.[11] At the same time, the national media began to publish a number of nostalgic articles by veteran army officers reminiscing about the "good old days" of austere communal life in the hills and caves of Yan'an in the 1930s and 1940s.[12]

In April and May PLA leaders stepped up their verbal assault on the "Right deviationist" view which held that the four cardinal principles were contrary to the spirit of the Third Plenum.[13] Taking issue with party liberals who claimed that Leftist deviations were more dangerous than Rightist ones, the *Liberation Army Daily* argued that both tendencies were equally pernicious.[14] At around the same time, the mass media published a speech by CDIC secretary Huang Kecheng, in which the eighty-two-year-old general strongly defended the Maoist legacy against its detractors. Arguing that some people had gone to extremes in criticizing Mao, to the point of denying him any merit whatsoever, General Huang brushed aside such negative opinions, calling them defamatory, distorted, and detrimental to the party and the people. Though he allowed that Mao's mistakes had caused many "misfortunes and wounds," Huang insisted that the Chairman had meant well. For this reason, the elderly general admonished, all true Chinese patriots should "understand and forgive him, with love and respect."[15]

Aside from the sensitive issue of Mao's legacy, another area of extreme PLA touchiness was the question of military privilege, corruption, and nepotism. Ever since the Third Plenum, reform leaders, including Deng himself, had been striking out at abuses of power and authority within the army. In a 1979 speech to the party committee of the Guangdong Military District, provincial party chief Xi Zhongxun, a close friend of Deng Xiaoping, upbraided leading cadres in the provincial military command for such things as showing favoritism in appointing friends to official positions and using their authority to pursue private gain.[16] In a lecture by the head of the Jilin Provincial Party Committee, army officers were similarly accused of

> caring little for the sufferings of the masses. Some have strong desire for position and fame and lack a sense of organization and discipline. When assignments are being made, some often complain that their "official titles" are not high enough. . . . Some always seek pleasure and comfort while fearing hardship. . . . They lack the kind of enthusiasm they displayed in making the revolution years ago. . . . They love to assume official airs in speech and action.[17]

Specific criticisms—sometimes naming the units and individuals involved—were directed at military commanders who had engaged in such activities as appropriating lavish housing for themselves and their families;[18] illegally occupying public facilities, including university campuses;[19] habitually soliciting back-door benefits, bribes, and kickbacks;[20] freely spending public funds on private automobiles and entertainment;[21] demanding reduced prices on "special orders" from factories;[22] bending the law for the benefit of relatives and friends;[23] and otherwise harming the army's work style, morale, and confidence.[24] In these and numerous other contemporaneous examples, the PLA officer corps was portrayed more as the privileged master of society than its humble servant.[25]

"General, You Cannot Do This"

One of the most notorious cases of military impropriety to emerge in this period involved General Yang Chengwu, a former acting PLA chief of staff who had been purged by Lin Biao in 1968. After having been restored to power as commander of the Fuzhou Military Region in 1978, General Yang had reportedly ordered the demolition of a kindergarten to make way for construction of a new villa for himself. The villa, equipped with every modern convenience, was reportedly built at a cost of tens of thousands of dollars in foreign currency.[26]

This incident, with General Yang's identity thinly disguised, was the subject of a biting, satirical poem entitled "Jiangjun, ni buneng zheyangzuo" (General, you cannot do this). Composed by a young PLA writer named Ye Wenfu, the poem was first published in a Chinese literary journal in August 1979. Its main theme was a bitter reproach to a "noble old warrior" gone bad:

> What can I say? How can I put it?
> You are a highly respected man of the older generation

And I am a Johnny-come-lately.

. . . .

To criticize you is a thought that has never
    occurred to me.

. . . . . .

My general whose body is riddled
    with bullet holes, . . .
Your voice that rang out like thunder
    is now eroded . . . to a thin, feeble whisper:
        "Give to me . . ."
            "give to me . . ."
If we gave you the moon
    you'd complain it's too cold.
If we gave you the sun
    you'd complain it's too hot. . . .
We offer you everything for your enjoyment. . . .
How is it you don't want the oath you took
    when you entered the party?

. . . .

Ah, my general, with your high rank and great power . . . .
old war horse, campaigning for decades,
    what, after all, was it for?

. . . .

To make way for your "modernization"
    a kindergarten has been torn down.
What do you care for the generations to come!
    . . . how many years will you live in comfort?

. . . .

The people must by no means keep silent. . . .
On the route of this new Long March
We can hear the voice of future generations
    . . . crying aloud with one voice:
        "General, you cannot do this."[27]

Not only did real PLA generals do such things; *fake* generals sometimes did them as well. One notorious case involved a confidence trickster in Liaoning Province who passed himself off as the son of a famous PLA general. Everywhere he went, the "general's son" was given VIP treatment and back-door access to a wide variety of goods and services. By simply invoking his father's famous name, he became the recipient of virtually unlimited privileges and perks—all without paying a cent, and all without ever having his identity checked. Eventually, the imposter was caught and arrested; the attendant publicity greatly embarrassed party and military authorities.

Cases like the Liaoning "general's son" struck a raw nerve in a society long accustomed to exaggerated fawning and favor-currying toward high officials.

In the summer of 1979 the Liaoning incident served as inspiration for a play by three young Shanghai writers, Sha Yexin, Li Shoucheng, and Yao Mingde. Their moral satire, *Jiaru woshi zhende?* (What if I were real?), was loosely modeled after Gogol's *The Inspector General*.[28] It detailed a swindle perpetrated by a young man who succeeded in defrauding numerous people merely by hinting that he was the son of a high-level hero of the revolution. He is eventually unmasked, arrested, and put on trial. The play ends in a dramatic scene where the imposter's purported father—a real revolutionary hero—sternly addresses a group of party cadres who have testified against the pretender:

> A society that still maintains special privileges . . . provides fertile soil for fraudulent activities. Some of our "swindlees," who are party cadres, handed the accused his opportunities and even helped him to carry out his fraud. One reason these comrades behaved this way is that they acted from habits rooted in a feudalistic, privilege-oriented mentality. But there is another reason—they wanted, through the accused, to satisfy their own individual selfish desires. . . . It is clear that they are not only victims but also collaborators. . . .
>
> [Turning toward party cadres in the witness box who have testified against the imposter:] In the past the masses gave us their unbounded sympathy and devotion. . . . They thought we could save the nation [and] benefit the people. . . . You [cadres] have told the people to make allowances for the difficulties of the nation, to show self-restraint and obedience . . . while there you are—grabbing your housing and calculating your own self-interest. You tell everybody else's children to "put down roots in the countryside," while you use every means at your disposal to have your own sons and daughters transferred back to the city. And you want the masses to suffer privation . . . while you yourselves crave a life of even greater luxury! . . .
>
> Beware, comrades, or else—though some of you may now be sitting in the witness box— . . . you will just as surely be standing in the dock of the accused![29]

After a few performances at the Shanghai People's Art Theater in the late summer of 1979, *What if I Were Real?* was banned by local authorities in the burgeoning backlash against the Democracy Movement. Its quintessential message about the morally degrading consequences of feudal privilege proved extremely irksome to party traditionalists, who criticized the play for reflecting "unreformed petit-bourgeois thinking."[30]

BOURGEOIS LIBERALISM AND *UNREQUITED LOVE*

Growing increasingly impatient with both the outpouring of negative media publicity and the rising popularity of literary and artistic works such as "General, You Cannot Do This" and *What if I Were Real?*, PLA conservatives struck back in the spring of 1981. The immediate target of their wrath was a screenplay entitled *Kulian* (Unrequited love). Authored by veteran PLA writer Bai Hua and first published in a Shanghai literary journal in September 1979, *Unrequited Love* tells the fictional tale of a young Chinese intellectual who goes to the United States in the 1940s to study painting. Returning to China after 1949 to participate in the cause of socialist construction, the man later finds himself under attack as a "bourgeois revisionist" during the Cultural Revolution. Shaken by the experience, and by the cruelty and injustice he has witnessed, the protagonist posts a dazibao in Tiananmen Square on April 4, 1976, criticizing the dictatorial behavior of the country's Leftist leaders. Thereafter, he becomes the target of a police manhunt.

On the run, the man begins openly to question his country's humanity—and his own faith in the Communist Party. At one point he laments, "My whole life has been an affair of unrequited love, of one-sided affection." When he contrives to arrange a final, furtive meeting with his daughter, she tells him: "Father, you love your country. Through bitter frustration you go on loving it. . . . But Father, does your country love you?" Unable to answer, he becomes a fugitive once again. Hunted down by a mob of radicals at the edge of an icy pond, he drags himself along the ground. His body inscribes a giant question mark in the snow; his own frozen form marks the final dot.[31]

On April 20, 1981, *Unrequited Love* was sharply attacked in a front-page commentary appearing in the *Liberation Army Daily*. According to the unsigned eight-thousand-word commentary, Bai Hua's screenplay had "impugned patriotism" and thereby violated the four cardinal principles. Arguing that the appearance of the work was not an isolated phenomenon, the article called *Unrequited Love* a reflection of "anarchistic, ultra-individualistic, bourgeois liberalistic, anti-four cardinal principles thinking" and warned that "if this erroneous type of thinking is allowed to spread freely, it will inevitably become a threat to our political stability and unity."[32]

The public attack on Bai Hua—the first major assault on an established writer/artist since Mao's death—was occasioned by the filming of Bai's screenplay, under the title *Sun and Man*. Prior to final editing, a rough cut of the film was screened for an audience of high-level party cadres and PLA general staff officers at the Central Party School in Beijing. Members of the general staff who attended the screening reacted strongly to the film's ostensibly anti-Maoist, antipatriotic message. After the army officers complained about the film to Wei Guoqing and Huang Kecheng, Wang Renzhong arranged a special screening of *Sun and Man* for Deng Xiaoping at Zhongnanhai. According to unofficial Chinese sources, after viewing the film Deng "went off in a huff. . . . He said the film had given up everything, even patriotism . . . [and that] criticism against the film . . . must be launched throughout the country." Since the film had never been exhibited to the public, however, the criticism was directed at Bai Hua's original screenplay, which had been published.[33]

At the end of March 1981, in a talk with leading comrades of the GPD, Deng Xiaoping suggested that it was necessary to criticize the film script of *Unrequited Love*. Urging the PLA to take the initiative in opposing Rightist ideology in literature and the arts, Deng admonished the editors of the *Libera-tion Army Daily* to write "more articles . . . to explain, ideologically and theo-retically, the importance of adhering to the four cardinal principles."[34] With Deng's explicit backing, in April the *Liberation Army Daily* commenced its attack on *Unrequited Love* and bourgeois liberalism.[35]

The campaign against bourgeois liberalism continued unabated throughout the late spring and summer of 1981, adding several new targets in the process. In addition to Bai Hua, other writers singled out for criticism included Ye Wenfu, author of "General, You Cannot Do This" (Ye was publicly attacked by Deng Xiaoping and General Chen Zaidao, among others);[36] Sha Yexin, coauthor of *What if I Were Real?* (Sha was attacked by Propaganda Director Wang Renzhong);[37] Shanghai literary figure Wang Ruowang (whose 1979 autobiographical novella, *Hunger Trilogy*, had documented the grim condi-tions of Chinese prison life during the Cultural Revolution);[38] and investiga-tive journalist Liu Binyan (whose 1979 exposé on bureaucratic corruption, "People or Monsters?," had greatly offended conservative party and military leaders).[39]

After initially abstaining from the campaign to criticize Bai Hua, several of the party's mainstream newspapers, including *People's Daily*, *Worker's Daily*, and *Wenhui Daily*, came under intense pressure from Wang Renzhong and other conservatives publicly to renounce bourgeois liberalism.[40] After Deng Xiaoping personally endorsed the anti–Bai Hua campaign at the Sixth Plenum in late June, the mass media capitulated, belatedly climbing on board the antibourgeois bandwagon. Shortly thereafter, several newspapers, along with a number of leading officials in Chinese literary, cultural, and journalistic circles, issued written self-criticisms dutifully finding fault with *Unrequited Love*, acknowledging the importance of the struggle against bourgeois liber-alism, and pledging to support the four cardinal principles.[41]

Some of the offending officials were members of the Chinese Writers' As-sociation, which, in a gesture of defiance, had awarded Bai Hua its highest poetry prize in late May, one month *after* Bai was initially attacked in the *Liberation Army Daily*. Also in May, the Writers' Association awarded its top nonfiction prize to muckraking journalist Liu Binyan.[42] Such blatant (if indi-rect) defiance of hard-line policies evidently angered the conservatives fur-ther, leading them to step up their demands for thoroughgoing literary and artistic criticism and self-criticism.[43]

In mid-July Deng Xiaoping joined the public chorus of criticism against Bai Hua and Ye Wenfu, chastising educational and cultural officials for their "weak ideological work" and suggesting that stepped-up criticism was needed to combat Rightism. Arguing that the main problem was not so much the existence of Rightism, but rather the party's lack of firmness in handling it, Deng opened the door to conservatives to step up their attack.[44] Responding to Deng's invitation, in early August Hu Qiaomu darkly suggested that many of the liberalizing trends of recent times had appeared in the guise of carrying out the policies of the Third Plenum. Placing the blame for lax discipline directly on the Central Party Secretariat under Hu Yaobang, Hu Qiaomu charged that "the Secretariat has not adopted . . . effective measures to solve existing problems in ideological work."[45]

Placed on the defensive, Hu Yaobang gave ground. Belatedly, he registered his support for the antiliberalism campaign.[46] At a September meeting commemorating the centenary of Lu Xun's birth, Hu denounced an unnamed group of intellectuals "who have a deeply ingrained hatred for the new China, for socialism, [and] for the party." Claiming that such people "disguise themselves and stick a knife in your back when you are unaware," the general secretary urged that "this sort of counterrevolutionary crime must be punished by law."[47]

Seeking to soften the impact of his uncharacteristically strident anti-Rightist rhetoric, Hu later met with a group of leading artists and writers to explain that the draft of his Lu Xun centenary speech had been rewritten by members of the party Central Committee and did not reflect his personal views.[48] And in a number of collateral statements, Hu called for exercising caution and restraint in implementing the campaign against bourgeois liberalism.

Although Hu Yaobang was thus forced to bend to conservative pressures, he did win one important skirmish in the summer of 1981: he secured the ouster of hard-line Propaganda Director Wang Renzhong. Wang had reportedly become angered over the lack of enthusiasm for the antiliberalism campaign displayed by his deputy, former Chinese culture czar Zhou Yang. In April and May 1981 Zhou had taken a neutral, noncommittal stance on the Bai Hua affair, refusing to criticize *Unrequited Love*. In response, Wang reportedly accused Zhou of "sitting on his rear end, in the wrong position."[49] Using Zhou's prolonged ill health as a pretext, Wang sought to pressure the seventy-four-year-old Zhou into retirement, offering him an advisory role with the propaganda department. When Hu Yaobang—a close friend of Zhou Yang—got wind of Wang's plan, he interceded to protect Zhou. As a condition of keeping his job, however, Zhou was required to issue a self-criticism in which he conceded that *Unrequited Love* was an example of an "erroneous trend" and suggested that its author "should be helped to recognize the problem."[50] While Zhou Yang thus got off rather lightly, Wang Renzhong was subsequently pressured to resign as director of party propaganda—after he launched a rather indiscreet attack on Deng's open policy.[51] While Hu Yaobang won this particular skirmish, the larger battle proved inconclusive, as Wang Renzhong's position was soon filled by fellow conservative Deng Liqun.[52]

While hard- and soft-liners thus struggled—with mixed results—to gain the upper hand, the thrust of the antiliberalism drive was effectively blunted in the late summer of 1981 when Deng Xiaoping softened his previous call for resoluteness in criticizing ideological laxity and weakness in the cultural field. Evidently concerned that conservatives were endangering the entire reform effort by pushing the anti-Rightist campaign too hard on too many fronts, Deng, in a statement to a national conference on ideological work in late August, leavened his attack on bourgeois liberalism, calling for moderation and restraint. "In dealing with the problems of the present," he said, "we must accept the lessons of the past; we must not travel old roads, carry out [mass] movements, or use 'surround and attack' tactics. Care must be taken . . . to keep criticism within proper bounds."[53] Chen Yun concurred with Deng, noting that "the people are tired of political movements. . . . We will be aiming at the wrong target if, in opposing 'bourgeois liberalization,' we criticize questionable works like *Unrequited Love*."[54]

Dutifully reflecting the new, softer line, Acting Minister of Culture Zhou Weizhi, speaking in early September, inveighed against employing the type of "improper and excessive criticism carried out in the past." "We must try," he said, "to set at ease the minds of those who have well-meaning concern about the development of our art and literature."[55] With the targets and methods of acceptable criticism now subject to clear limits, the campaign soon diminished in scope and intensity. With few exceptions, offending writers and literary cadres were rebuked for specific errors of judgment and standpoint—but not for more serious political crimes and misdemeanors; their self-criticisms were correspondingly mild.[56] The reform movement was thus protected against its hard-line detractors.

In October Bai Hua issued a written self-criticism, addressed to Hu Yaobang, in which he acknowledged a lack of balance and an "erroneous trend of thought" in his screenplay. Apologizing for his failure to appreciate the party's capacity to solve its internal problems, Bai profusely thanked the party and the people for helping him to overcome his initial lack of a humble attitude toward criticism of his work. On December 23 his self-criticism was published in *Liberation Army Daily*.[57] Thereafter, Bai was permitted to resume writing, albeit with a lowered profile; he was also allowed to retain his party membership. In December Hu Yaobang declared the Bai Hua affair to be over.[58]

Although most establishment intellectuals weathered the 1981 ideological storm with minimal damage to their careers and reputations, not everyone escaped so easily. Ye Wenfu, unwilling to bend to the rules and requirements of the antiliberalism campaign, refused to issue a self-criticism and was severely reprimanded and subjected to ongoing political harassment.[59] Faring even worse were a number of outspoken critics who had been involved in the 1978–79 Democracy Movement. As the campaign against Bai Hua unfolded in the spring of 1981, underground writers Wang Xizhe (the most outspoken member of the former "Li Yizhe" group), Xu Wenli (editor of *April 5th Forum* and author of a recent open letter in defense of Poland's Lech Walesa), and Chen Erjin (a coal mine worker whose critical essay on proletarian democracy had been published in *April 5th Forum*), among others, were quietly detained and sentenced without trial to terms of labor reeducation ranging from ten to fifteen years each.[60]

HUA GUOFENG'S LAST STAND

Concurrently with the onset of the neo-Leftist ideological offensive of spring 1981, supporters of Hua Guofeng mounted one last attempt to "reverse the verdict" on their fallen leader. With Ye Jianying remaining deeply distrustful of Hu Yaobang ("to hell with him" was one statement attributed to Ye), the old marshal, who was said to be seriously ailing and unable to move about, reportedly threw his support behind an eleventh-hour comeback attempt by the "little gang of four"—Wang Dongxing, Chen Xilian, Ji Deng-kui, and Wu De. According to unofficial Chinese sources, Ye now openly stated that he would "advance or retreat side by side with Chairman Hua Guofeng."[61]

Bolstered by Ye's support, Hua had strong second thoughts about his December request to step down from the CC chairmanship. Shortly after tendering his resignation offer, Hua began to display signs of passive resistance, refusing to cooperate with Hu Yaobang or Deng Xiaoping. On one occasion in early January, for example, Hua failed to show up to host an important reception at the Great Hall of the People, pleading illness despite being in perfect health.[62] Then, at a Politburo meeting in March, Hua reportedly displayed open hostility in the face of pressure for him to honor his commitment to resign from the chairmanship. When Deng Xiaoping offered him a compromise, under the terms of which Hua would be permitted to stay on as a vice-chairman of the CC, Hua allegedly refused. "If my leadership ability isn't good enough," he replied scornfully, "I couldn't function as a party vice-chairman either."[63] In the final run-up to the Sixth Plenum, Hua remained defiant. Toward Deng Xiaoping and Hu Yaobang, he reportedly declared: "I won't cooperate with them; they are conspirators."[64]

In the campaign to obstruct Hu Yaobang's rise to power, Hua Guofeng's remaining allies occasionally enlisted the support of disgruntled members of Deng's reform coalition. In the spring of 1981, for example, conservative ideologues sought to block the promotion of Hu's friend and colleague, CASS Vice-President Yu Guangyuan, to the presidency of the organization. Nominated to replace outgoing CASS chief Hu Qiaomu, who had expressed a desire to concentrate his energies on his work at the Central Secretariat, Yu Guangyuan was challenged by conservative CASS Vice-President Deng Liqun. Claiming that Yu had "certain problems" in his work style and in his personal behavior that required further investigation, Little Deng was able to block Yu's proposed promotion. In doing so, however, he stirred up a rather strong storm of protest. Previously slated for an appointment to the Central Secretariat, Deng Liqun was reportedly dropped from the list of approved candidates on the eve of the Sixth Plenum. When the plenum finally met, the only newcomer added to the Secretariat was Deng Xiaoping's old Guangdong associate, Xi Zhongxun.[65]

132 • CHAPTER 5 •

THE SIXTH PLENUM: HUA GOES DOWN

Although Ye Jianying and Hua Guofeng ultimately failed in their attempt to reverse the December 1980 Politburo decision, they did manage to soften the blow somewhat. When the Sixth Plenum finally met in late June, Hua's resignation as chairman of the party CC and MAC was officially confirmed, as was his replacement by Hu Yaobang in the former post and Deng Xiaoping in the latter. (The splitting of the two top party posts reflected the lingering distrust harbored by senior PLA commanders and General Staff officers toward Hu Yaobang and his associates.)

Despite Hua Guofeng's earlier refusal to consider a lesser position, he was now offered a post as CC vice-chairman, which he quietly accepted; he was also permitted to retain his membership on the Politburo Standing Committee, where his rank was downgraded from first to seventh (and last) place, behind Chairman Hu and the five other CC vice-chairmen: Ye Jianying, Deng Xiaoping, Zhao Ziyang, Li Xiannian, and Chen Yun.[66] This face-saving arrangement was said to have been the result of intense, often acrimonious negotiations. The final breakthrough in securing Hua's demotion reportedly occurred when Deng pointedly reminded his colleagues of Hua's vigorous attempts in 1976 and 1977 to obstruct the rehabilitation of a number of veteran cadres, including Chen Yun, Hu Yaobang, Deng himself, and several other members of the current Central Committee.[67] The reason publicly advanced for not dismissing Hua Guofeng outright was that "Party history shows that knocking out a comrade once he commits some mistakes would make people overcautious and prevent them from speaking their minds freely. This would damage democracy."[68]

When the long-awaited official reassessment of the Maoist era—"Resolution on Certain Questions in the History of Our Party since the Founding of the People's Republic of China"—was adopted by the Sixth Plenum on June 27, it dealt with Hua Guofeng in critical but measured terms. Detailing Hua's Leftist errors, the document noted that he had tried to suppress the criterion-of-truth debate in 1978; delayed the rehabilitation of veteran cadres in 1976–77; opposed the redress of past injustices such as the erroneous verdict on the 1976 Tiananmen incident; promoted a cult of personality; and blindly adhered to the "erroneous two whatevers." On the positive side, Hua was praised for having contributed to the struggle to overthrow the Jiang Qing clique and for doing certain useful work after that, of a type and quality unspecified.[69]

In explaining the resolution's relatively mild and measured criticism of Hua, Deng Xiaoping stated that it had been necessary to adopt moderate language because "the resolution is a document that will enter the historical record" and will thus be "more weighty" than previous internal Politburo declarations.[70] *Requiescat in pace publicae*, Hua Guofeng.

Signaling his concurrence with the final disposition of Hua's case, Ye Jianying—who attended only one session of the Sixth Plenum due to ad-

Old and new party leaders chat during a break at the Sixth Plenum, June 1981. From left: Chen Yun, Deng Xiaoping, Hu Yaobang, Li Xiannian, Zhao Ziyang.

vanced age and infirmity—stated in a letter to the Politburo Standing Committee: "I feel the Central Committee has properly handled Comrade Hua's criticism, assistance, and the reassignment of his position." Ye's only apparent point of disagreement was a mild (and perhaps pro forma) demurrer expressing the view that Deng Xiaoping should have been ranked higher than himself in the new Standing Committee lineup.[71]

In his speech to the Sixth Plenum, Li Xiannian also voiced approval of the way Hua's demotion was handled, although he put a rather different spin on it: "The purpose of putting Comrade Hu Yaobang first and moving Comrade Zhao Ziyang up a little," he said, "is to allow relatively young and energetic members . . . to preside over the work on the first line, and to show that the highest leaders of the party center are prepared to . . . take the lead in changing the custom of ranking by seniority." Noting that he himself, along with Ye Jianying, had initially proposed promoting Deng Xiaoping and Chen Yun to the two top spots on the Standing Committee, Li revealed that other members of the SC, including Deng and Chen, had rejected the idea, feeling that "it would be best to make no [further] changes in order to avoid unnecessary speculation at home and abroad."[72]

Li's assessment was echoed by Hu Yaobang, who acknowledged that "it was the original will of the vast majority of the comrades . . . that Comrade Deng Xiaoping should undertake the responsibilities of party chairman." Modestly averring that "there are quite a lot of other old comrades who are more suitable than I," Hu bowed deeply to the four venerable party elders on the Standing Committee, thanking them for their past support, reassuring them that their "usefulness has not changed," and earnestly requesting their continued guidance in the future.[73]

Acting out his assigned role as humble acolyte, Hu Yaobang took special pains to flatter Deng Xiaoping, whom he referred to as the "primary decision maker in the CCP today." To reassure those senior leaders who may have harbored reservations about his own fitness for the office of CC chairman, Hu twice pointed out that his classification and grade level within the *nomenkla-tura*—the party's official personnel system—remained unchanged. The implication was that despite his promotion to CC chairman, Hu continued to rank beneath the four Standing Committee elders in the formal hierarchy. To further dispel residual doubt and distrust, Hu dutifully asked "the entire party . . . and members of the Central Committee for supervision" so that "I might have a correct assessment of myself."[74] On the whole, it was a suitably modest and self-effacing performance. Even the ever-wary Deng Liqun was seemingly impressed, calling Hu's words "truly earnest and sincere . . . a complete change from some of the work-styles in our party in the past."[75]

EXORCISING MAO'S GHOST

Along with the delicate matter of securing Hua Guofeng's replacement, the most important piece of business transacted at the Sixth Plenum was the official adoption of the party's long-awaited postmortem on Mao. The process of drafting and revising the "Resolution on Certain Questions" had been a long and laborious one. "We have spent more than a year writing this document," explained Deng at a Politburo meeting in May 1981, "and it has gone through I don't know how many drafts." Noting that "people are watching China with some doubts about its stability and unity," Deng had urged rapid completion of the final document. "We can't take any longer," he said; "further delay will be unfavorable."[76]

Deng cited two key issues that lay at the heart of the impasse over the wording of the resolution: "First, with regard to Comrade Mao Zedong: Which were primary, his achievements or his mistakes? Second, in the last thirty-two years, and especially the ten years before the Cultural Revolution, were our achievements or our mistakes primary? Was the situation in those years all dark, or was the bright side dominant?"[77]

With Hu Yaobang formally presiding over the drafting committee and Hu Qiaomu in charge of directing the actual writing of the resolution, Deng Xiaoping found himself once again perched uncomfortably between two contending wings of the reform coalition, attempting to mediate a steady stream of historiographic disputes between the two Hus. On the question of Mao's mistakes, for example, Deng dismissed an early draft of the resolution as too negative and disparaging. "It is no good," said Deng impatiently in June 1980;

"the historical role of Mao Zedong must be affirmed . . . and [his] Thought adhered to and developed." Criticism of Mao's errors and shortcomings is necessary, Deng allowed, "but it must be appropriate. . . . What is most important is the question of systems and institutions. . . . Shouldn't the concluding section include a passage about our determination to go on developing Mao Zedong Thought?"[78]

Nine months later, in March 1981, Deng again chided members of the drafting committee, this time for dismissing the entire decade of the Cultural Revolution as an unmitigated disaster. "There were some healthy phenomena even in that decade," he noted, citing as three examples the "February adverse current" of 1967 (which he now defended as a "good current"),[79] the 1971 restoration of China's rightful seat in the United Nations, and the February 1972 U.S.-China Shanghai Communiqué. In raising these caveats, Deng's stated purpose was to insure proper balance in the final document. Otherwise, he said, people with ulterior motives would seize upon the CCP's admission of past mistakes to divert attention from their own destructive behavior.[80]

As successive drafts of the resolution were reviewed, revised, and resubmitted, criticism of Mao became progressively milder and more diffuse. What had been referred to early on as "serious mistakes" (*yanzhong cuowu*) or even "crimes" (*zuixing*) were now reduced to ordinary mistakes or errors of judgment. In part, this was due to Deng's stated desire for balance and restraint; but in part it was also due to the growing strength of the neo-Leftist backlash that had taken shape in the first half of 1981.

When the document was finally approved in June (after Deng had reportedly run out of patience), it was considerably kinder and gentler toward Mao than the earliest drafts had been. Nevertheless, it did not constitute a whitewash. Noting that Mao had become arrogant and "divorced from practice and from the masses" in his later years, the resolution detailed a number of Leftist errors committed by Mao after 1956. These included incorrectly broadening the scope of the 1957 anti-Rightist rectification movement, which led to "unjustifiable labeling of a number of intellectuals, patriotic people, and party cadres"; becoming "smug with success" and "impatient for quick results" during the Great Leap Forward, which resulted from Mao's "overestimating the role of man's subjective will"; and pursuing an "entirely erroneous" appraisal of class struggle in the mid-1960s, which led Mao to "confuse the people with the enemy" during the Cultural Revolution.[81]

The resolution also singled out for special criticism Mao's behavior at the time of the Qingming incident of 1976. In view of Deng Xiaoping's role in shaping the new document, this hardly came as a surprise. Noting that Mao had been unwilling to accept Deng's various proposals for "systematic correction" of the errors of the Cultural Revolution, the resolution charged Mao with personally triggering the 1976 movement to "criticize Deng and oppose the Right deviationist wind of reversing correct verdicts"—a movement that "once again plunged the nation into turmoil." Compounding the late Chairman's error, in April 1976 "Comrade Mao wrongly assessed the nature of the Tiananmen incident and dismissed Comrade Deng Xiaoping from all his posts."[82]

Although some of Mao's errors (along with others detailed in the resolution) were said to be serious, causing considerable damage to the party and to the people, they were nonetheless held to be the mistakes of "a great proletarian revolutionary" who had paid "constant attention to overcoming shortcomings."[83] And in the last analysis, Mao's successes were said to greatly outweigh his failures. Although no fixed ratio of pluses to minuses was given (the standard 70:30 formula was not used in the June 1981 resolution), the final verdict on Mao was, on balance, favorable. Even more favorable was the resolution's evaluation of "the system of Mao Zedong Thought," which was now held to be a collective achievement that represented "the integration of the universal principles of Marxism-Leninism with the concrete practice of the Chinese revolution"—a phrase lifted verbatim from the CCP's 1945 Constitution.[84]

Turning from the reassessment of Mao's historical contributions to a review of the party's development since the downfall of the Gang of Four, the resolution reaffirmed the correctness of various reform-oriented policies and principles adopted during and after the Third Plenum. At the same time, it strongly upheld the four cardinal principles, adding a new warning concerning the need to counter the decadent influences of bourgeois *and* feudal thinking. Echoing the conservative critique of Bai Hua's ostensibly unpatriotic screenplay, *Unrequited Love*, the resolution strongly exhorted the party and the people to "foster the patriotism which puts the interests of the motherland above everything else."[85]

One thing the resolution did *not* do was offend the PLA. An early draft of the document had reportedly contained a section highly critical of the army's "three supports and two militarys" campaign during the Cultural Revolution, under the aegis of which PLA forces had seized control of local and regional units of civil government and administration early in 1967.[86] Some of Deng's supporters, including Beijing Military Region Commander Qin Jiwei, argued that the campaign had been a disaster and had inflicted great damage upon the army.[87] Left-leaning military leaders, on the other hand, strongly praised the campaign. Deng himself took a middle-of-the-road stance, resisting military attempts to glorify the campaign, but also hedging his criticism of it. Two things needed to be said about the "three supports and two militarys," Deng stated in March 1981: first, it "did prove useful"; second, it "greatly detracted from the army's prestige."[88] In the final draft of the "Resolution on Certain Questions," nothing at all, positive or negative, was said about this highly controversial chapter in PLA history; nor was any reference made to other historical military errors or deficiencies—apart from the obligatory criticism of the PLA's "traitorous" former commander-in-chief, Lin Biao. In the face of strong military pressure, Deng was evidently persuaded to abstain from criticizing the PLA.[89]

By a show of hands, the Central Committee unanimously adopts the "Resolution on Certain Questions in the History of Our Party" at the Sixth Plenum, June 1981.

Putting his personal seal of approval on the final draft of the resolution on the eve of the Sixth Plenum, Deng made no mention of the myriad compromises and watered-down language that had gone into the finished document. Instead, he accentuated the positive, noting—with evident relief—that "On the whole, this is a good resolution and a good draft, . . . a balanced appraisal . . . based on facts. . . . I think we have been rather careful and conscientious."[90]

STREAMLINING ADMINISTRATION:
THE REJUVENATION OF LEADERSHIP

Having come to grips—after a fashion—with some of Mao's (and the party's) more egregious historical errors, Deng Xiaoping in the latter half of 1981 turned his attention to a pressing current issue: the need to "rejuvenate" (*nianqinghua*) ossified leadership. Immediately following the Sixth Plenum, Deng gave a speech to a forum of provincial and municipal party secretaries in which he predicted that if China did not solve the problem of intergenerational leadership succession on a nationwide scale within three to five years, "chaos may ensue." The heart of the problem, he argued, lay in the fact that many veteran cadres, though old and "unable to work," stubbornly refused to retire and invariably either obstructed the promotion of younger people or insisted on promoting only their own supporters. "To put it bluntly," Deng stated, "the question of whether people are appointed on merit or by favoritism has not been settled satisfactorily."[91]

To remedy the problem, Deng endorsed a proposal, first advanced by Chen Yun at the December 1980 CC working conference, to select tens of thousands of well-educated young and middle-aged cadres, generally between forty and fifty years old, for recruitment into leading bodies at the provincial, municipal, and ministerial levels within three to five years. To make room for these new third-generation leaders, Deng urged setting a mandatory retirement age for all veteran cadres. Pointing out that in most countries army officers retire at age sixty while civilian officials are expected to retire at sixty-five or even younger, he argued that "we too should have some age limits."[92]

Noting that the Central Committee had proposed establishing two new central agencies—an "advisory committee" and a "discipline inspection commission"—to help absorb displaced veteran cadres, Deng coupled his appeal for elderly and infirm comrades to step aside with the announcement of an impending administrative reform that would greatly reduce the number of leading cadres in state organs. "Why do we need more than a dozen vice-ministers for each ministry?" he asked rhetorically. "Aren't one minister and two to four vice-ministers enough?" Arguing that the problem of administrative overstaffing was inseparable from "our grave propensity to bureaucratism," Deng called for a thoroughgoing streamlining of administrative agencies and personnel.[93]

In his "Report on the Work of the Government" to the Fourth Session of the Fifth NPC, meeting in November 1981, Premier Zhao Ziyang elaborated upon Deng's rejuvenation theme and outlined a broad plan of attack for restructuring inefficient, overstaffed bureaucratic organs:

> The State Council is determined to adopt firm measures to alter the intolerably low efficiency resulting from overlapping and overstaffed administration with its multitiered departments crammed full of superfluous personnel and deputy and nominal chiefs who engage in endless haggling and shifting of responsibility. The State Council has therefore adopted a decision to restructure the administration, beginning with the departments under the State Council itself, and to ensure accomplishment within a specified time limit. . . . During the restructuring, there will be relatively important reductions in or merging of State Council departments, accompanied by all possible cuts in staff and fairly big changes in leadership.[94]

Five weeks later Deng Xiaoping spelled out in detail just what was meant by "all possible cuts." At a Politburo meeting in January 1982 he proposed eliminating more than one-third of all cadre and staff positions in party and government agencies within two years—a total of almost seven million jobs nationwide. Tying the problem of cadre retirement to the need to promote vigorous, talented younger people to positions of authority and responsibility, Deng warned that "If we let the old and ailing stand in the way . . . not only will the four modernizations fail but the party and state will face a mortal trial and perhaps perish."[95]

Anticipating resistance from cadres facing involuntary retirement or lay-offs, Deng noted that "we can expect some trouble, including demonstrations. . . . Don't be afraid of the possibility of marches and demonstrations and of the appearance of dazibao. . . . Come what may, we must stick to our guns." To those elderly comrades who balked at retirement in the belief that they were still capable of performing their jobs, Deng issued a challenge: Such people would have to prove that they were able to work eight hours a day. If they flunked the test, they would have to retire. There was, however, an implicit double standard in Deng's challenge: Acknowledging his own inability to endure the rigors of an eight-hour workday, Deng nonetheless refrained from volunteering to retire. (A few months earlier he had said, "Comrade Chen Yun [and I] frankly . . . would be very happy to retire now. But of course we can't do that.")[96] To sweeten somewhat the prospect of forced retirement for others, Deng once again held out the promise of honorary positions for those "ailing old comrades" who chose to step down voluntarily.[97]

In the aftermath of Deng's tough talk, a number of government organs participated in the campaign to streamline state administration. At a series of meetings of the NPC Standing Committee in the spring and summer of 1982, the first major administrative reorganizations and staff cuts were announced.[98] Among the positions eliminated were 11 of 13 vice-premiers of the State Council. In addition, 13 of the State Council's 52 ministries and commissions and 31 of 41 subordinate departments were slated for elimination or consolidation, bringing a net reduction in the number of ministers and vice-ministers from 505 to 167. Overall, the number of administrative cadres and staff personnel employed by central organs of government was to be reduced by more than one-third, from 49,000 to 32,000. A similar (if less dramatic) paring of cadres and staff also took place within the thirty organs directly controlled by the party Central Committee, where personnel reductions totaling 17.3 percent were announced.[99]

As promised, many of the high-level veteran cadres displaced in the reorganization drive were offered roles as "state councilors" or "special advisers." Few, if any, suffered reductions in income or fringe benefits, as they were permitted to retain their existing salaries, houses, chauffeured automobiles, and other cadre privileges and perks. Nevertheless, and despite such blandishments, a large majority of superannuated cadres displayed stubborn resistance in the face of repeated party and governmental efforts to coax them into retirement.[100]

ECONOMIC CRIME, CORRUPTION, AND THE "THREE CRISES OF FAITH"

The drive to streamline government operations and rejuvenate cadre leadership was one of two "great struggles" launched by party leaders after the Sixth Plenum. The second was a drive to halt the rising epidemic of economic crime and corruption on the part of party members and cadres, an epidemic that threatened to undermine further the public's already flagging confidence in party leadership.[101]

The "guiding principles on inner-party life" adopted by the Fifth Plenum in February 1980 had spoken gravely of "the special-privilege mentality" that was rampant among party cadres, leading them to "abuse their functions and powers in pursuit of their own selfish interests."[102] By the late fall of 1980, the situation of malfeasant cadre behavior had become serious enough to warrant an urgent warning by CDIC Chairman Chen Yun. Speaking in late November, Chen argued that problems of party discipline were a "life-and-death matter" affecting the very survival of the CCP.[103]

Notwithstanding such warnings, evidence of widespread and pervasive economic misbehavior by party cadres continued to mount throughout 1981. In Anhui, leading cadres were said to be "weak and ineffective . . . have dirty hands. . . . If they themselves are not straight, how can they straighten up others?"[104] In Fujian, 30,000 cases of "economic irregularity" involving cadres were reported in 1981.[105] Numerous examples of official corruption were detailed in the mass media in this period, ranging in severity from such common practices as cadres feasting at government expense at fine hotels and restaurants to embezzlement of hundreds of thousands of yuan.[106]

Responding to the mounting incidence of cadre malfeasance, the CDIC in early August 1981 issued a "Notice on Strengthening Party Discipline and Doing Away with the Improper Use of Special Relationships." Acknowledging that the "evil habit of special relationships" posed an immense threat both to the party and to society at large, the CDIC directive outlined a number of strict guidelines to be followed in the drive to eradicate cadre corruption.[107] Notwithstanding its high moral standards and good intentions, however, the newly created CDIC, charged with monitoring and enforcing party discipline, lacked the nationwide organizational personnel and resources needed to carry out its mandate. Under these circumstances, the principal weapons employed in the drive to "rectify unhealthy styles of work" were the old standbys, ideological education and moral suasion. Now, however, a new weapon was added to the anticorruption arsenal: public opinion. In the fall of 1981, mounting popular anger over improper cadre behavior fueled a sharp upsurge in the number of letters to the editor submitted by irate newspaper and magazine readers around the country, many of whom declared themselves to be fed up with dishonest, greedy cadres.[108]

Lamenting the dearth of effective enforcement mechanisms, party leaders declared war on economic crime in the late fall and winter of 1981–82. Deng Xiaoping, Zhao Ziyang, and Chen Yun took the early lead in the new campaign. At a Politburo meeting in mid-November, Deng pointed out that although almost two years had passed since the CC first adopted its "guiding principles" at the Fifth Plenum, many comrades continued to act "as if they have heard nothing." As a result, an unhealthy atmosphere had spread within the party. Offenses against party discipline and law had reached "intolerable proportions," giving rise to what Deng now referred to as "the so-called three crises of faith."[109]

Commenting on the adverse effects of an alleged "onslaught of bourgeois thinking from abroad," Deng argued that some cadres had become so corrupted by bourgeois life-styles and material comforts that they acted "without restraint or scruples . . . doing serious damage to the reputation of the party and country." Localities and departments most severely affected by such bourgeois corruption were said to be those "that have contact with foreigners, the special economic zones in Guangzhou and Fujian, and some other coastal areas." Pointing out that corruption in these areas was often linked to "degenerate children of high-ranking cadres" who "utilize their special connections to extort money from foreign businessmen . . . accept bribes . . . lower prices of goods at will, arbitrarily tear up . . . agreements made with foreign companies, and import unnecessary equipment as they see fit," Deng called for harsh punishment to be meted out to all offenders in such cases, regardless of cadre rank or status.[110]

Conceding that children of high-ranking cadres were often shielded from criminal prosecution by parental intervention, Deng called for the thorough elimination of such behavior. "A section of cadres," said Deng, "rely on connections and plead people's cases everywhere. Even more extreme are those who create scenes in law enforcement agencies, put on pressure, and influence the impartiality of legal organs, thereby destroying the prestige of the party and arousing tremendous resentment among the people." In dealing with such cases, Deng urged harsh treatment.[111]

Picking up where Deng left off, Premier Zhao Ziyang, in his Government Work Report to the Fourth Session of the Fifth NPC in early December, prescribed a system of graduated punishments for errant cadres. The proposed disciplinary measures ranged from conventional criticism and self-criticism (for cadres who committed "ordinary" ideological mistakes) to organizational discipline (for those making "serious mistakes" in violation of administrative regulations) to criminal prosecution (for those engaged in patently illegal activities). Currently, it was extremely difficult to punish corrupt cadres, Zhao conceded, because "some units are unwilling to submit criminal cases in the economic field to judicial organs." To remedy this defect, the premier called for "quick and resolute change" in the traditional practice of shielding cadres from criminal prosecution.[112]

A few weeks later, in early January 1982, Chen Yun signaled the CDIC's determination to add teeth to the party's call for a crackdown on cadre corruption: "I propose that we deal sternly with those who commit serious economic crimes," he said. "Let us send a number of them to prison, and even execute some. We should firmly implement this policy . . . and give it newspaper publicity."[113]

In April Deng Xiaoping addressed the Politburo on the subject of economic crime. Repeating earlier calls for a crackdown on lawbreakers, he emphasized that the recent, sharp increase in cadre corruption was at least partly a function of China's decision to pursue economic reform and opening up to the outside world:

A number of cadres have been corrupted in the brief year or two since we adopted the policy of opening up and stimulating the economy. . . . Their misdeeds are more serious than the crimes exposed in the days of the "three-anti" and "five-anti" movements. At that time, people who had embezzled ¥1,000 or more were rated as "small tigers," and those who had embezzled ¥10,000 or more as "big tigers." Today, we have many cases of very big tigers. . . .

A lot of money has gone to line the pockets of certain individuals and groups. The sum would be even larger if we counted theft of public property and the like. We must not underestimate the gravity of all this. It is an ill wind and a strong one. Indeed, unless we take it seriously and firmly stop it, the question of whether our party will change its nature may arise. This is not just alarmist talk.[114]

Noting that the prevalent trend in party discipline work was to avoid imposing severe penalties, Deng called for a sharp change in policy. "We have to take prompt, swift, and stern measures," he said, including use of "the ultimate penalty"—execution—in those cases judged to be particularly grave. "We cannot afford . . . to be too lenient," he concluded.[115]

In establishing a presumptive link between the rising incidence of cadre corruption and the Third Plenum's policy of opening up to the outside world, Deng Xiaoping inadvertently provided opponents of his reform program with new ammunition. Many conservatives harbored serious doubts about Deng's open policy. Some vocally complained about the role played by "decadent Western ideas and life styles" in leading China's young people toward a life of crime.[116] Others were highly critical of the permissive socioeconomic and ideological climate found in the special economic zones along China's southeastern coast, where foreign investors were offered special privileges and inducements to set up joint ventures.[117] By Deng's own admission, the SEZs had become deeply involved in contraband trade, smuggling, and other illegal activities. In February 1982 conservative Wang Renzhong referred to such activities as a "manifestation of class struggle." Asserting that "we are in the midst of a battle between erosion and counter-erosion," Wang called for all-out warfare against bourgeois influences spread by "foreign capitalists who do business with us" and by "residents of Hong Kong and Taiwan, and overseas Chinese who come to visit, sightsee, and travel."[118]

In making such extreme statements, Wang apparently overstepped the bounds of propriety. One month after his speech was published, he was ousted as director of party propaganda; a few months after that, at the Twelfth Party Congress, he was removed from the Central Secretariat. Despite his removal, however, Wang had made his point: bourgeois decadence was a by-product of the open policy. It was a point that would come back to haunt Chinese reformers in years to come.

Defining the Spirit of Socialism:
Summer 1982–December 1983

Don't imagine that a little spiritual pollution doesn't amount to
very much and is not worth making a fuss over. . . . If we do
not immediately . . . curb these phenomena, . . . the
consequences could be extremely serious.

—Deng Xiaoping, October 1983

BY THE second half of 1982 a number of cleavages—political, ideological,
and economic—had caused Deng's reform coalition to fragment into a plurality of semidistinct, semiantagonistic leadership clusters and opinion groups.
Doing his best to keep his shaky coalition—and the country—together, Deng
continued to occupy the middle ground on matters of ideology and policy,
balancing off the contending concerns of his principal coalition partners and
protagonists. However, as the fissures grew wider and the polarization of
opinion grew more intense, Deng's quest for balance became more elusive.
The strains and tensions inherent in his position became apparent when the
Twelfth Party Congress met in September 1982.

THE TWELFTH PARTY CONGRESS

In his opening address to the Congress, Deng made an appeal for ideological
harmony. Speaking like a politician on the stump, he artfully embraced a variety of disparate (and in some cases implicitly contradictory) goals and priorities. For example, after calling for the further expansion of China's opening to
the outside world, he added a firm injunction to avoid "corrosion by decadent
ideas from abroad," vowing "never to permit the bourgeois way of life to
spread in our country."[1] Embracing a second set of antinomies, Deng contin
ued to hedge his bets on the primacy of economic versus ideological priorities
in socialist modernization. After declaring that the party's major task domesti-
cally for the remainder of the decade was "to step up socialist modernization
. . . [with] economic construction at the core," he tacitly contradicted himself
by predicating China's economic development upon the prior establishment
of a "socialist spiritual civilization." Deeming the latter an "important guar-

antee" of the former, Deng implicitly reversed the arrow of developmental causality that underpinned his own "black cats, white cats" thesis.[2]

The term "spiritual civilization" had first been used publicly in Ye Jianying's National Day speech of September 1979, where it was proposed as an antidote to the country's "crisis of faith" and a corrective to the liberal reformers' one-sided emphasis on economic growth and productivity. Fifteen months later, Deng alluded to the need to "build a spiritual civilization" in his reform-freezing speech of December 25, 1980. In that address, Deng invoked the "precious revolutionary spirit" of the party's Yan'an days, arguing that to inculcate such a spirit "by no means requires very good material conditions . . . or a high level of education." In thus seeming to deny the developmental primacy of matter over spirit, Deng tacitly reversed the priorities established at the time of the Third Plenum in December 1978, when the development of society's productive forces had been elevated to the Communist Party's *summum bonum*. To justify his apparent volte-face, Deng raised a rhetorical question: "Without a spiritual civilization, without communist thought and morality, how could we build socialism?"[3]

At the Twelfth Party Congress, Deng openly embraced the goal of constructing a "socialist spiritual civilization" (*shehuizhuyi jingshen wenming*). In so doing, he tacitly sided with Hu Qiaomu and Deng Liqun, who had consistently stressed the importance of political and ideological education and indoctrination as counterweights to Hu Yaobang's insistence on the primacy of the productive forces. In many respects, Deng's delicate balancing act on the issue of material versus spiritual foundations of socialism was reminiscent of Premier Zhou Enlai's shifting stance in the highly charged "red and expert" debates of the late 1950s and early 1960s.

After ambivalently endorsing economic construction as the "core" and spiritual civilization as an "important guarantee" of China's socialist modernization, Deng went on to reiterate four additional key tasks for the CCP in the 1980s: restructuring the state administrative apparatus and the economy; rejuvenating China's aging cadre corps; combatting economic crime; and rectifying the party's work style.[4] Beyond laying out these broad goals, however, Deng's speech provided few operational elaborations or guidelines.

RETIRING THE OLD GUARD: THE CENTRAL ADVISORY COMMITTEE

In pursuit of the goal of cadre rejuvenation, the Twelfth Party Congress formally approved Deng's proposal to establish a Central Advisory Committee (CAC) to serve as a temporary way station en route to full retirement for senior party leaders with more than forty years of service. In the new party constitution, adopted at the Twelfth Congress, the CAC was described as "political assistant and consultant" to the Central Committee. Its 172 members would comprise, in effect, a council of elders. They would retain their full salaries, ranks, and perks and would be consulted regularly by party leaders on all matters of importance; but they would cease serving on the party's regular decision-making bodies, thus making room for younger, more vigorous and technically proficient cadres.[5]

On the eve of the Twelfth Congress it had been widely expected that with the creation of the CAC, a substantial number of party veterans would voluntarily retire from active duty.[6] In the event, such expectations proved overly optimistic, as fourteen veteran Politburo members—including Ye Jianying, Chen Yun, Li Xiannian, Peng Zhen, Wang Zhen, and Song Renqiong—pointedly chose not to exercise the retirement option.[7] Through an adroit parliamentary maneuver, Deng Xiaoping also managed to finesse the question of his own retirement: as newly elected chairman of the CAC, he was constitutionally mandated to serve, ex officio, as a voting member of the Politburo's Standing Committee.

Prior to the Twelfth Congress, in preliminary discussions of the proposal to establish the CAC, it had been the stated intent of the commission's designers (including Deng Xiaoping, who first proposed the idea in his August 1980 speech on leadership reform) to make the CAC independent of, and coequal with, the Central Committee in power and authority. A third leading party body, the CDIC, had also been slated to enjoy coequal status with the Central Committee and the CAC. The idea of three-way parity was rejected at the Twelfth Congress, however, and the two new party commissions were given a reduced role in policy making—a fact that may have contributed to the last-minute decision of several elderly Politburo members to delay their retirement.

Defending his personal decision not to retire, Chen Yun argued that "there aren't many young cadres qualified to take over leadership posts. . . . Some [of us] still have to stay on the front line." Chen's Standing Committee colleague, Ye Jianying, was even more blunt in his refusal to step down: "I'll [continue to] perform my duties with all my energy . . . and stop only when I die" which he finally did in 1986.[8]

As an added retirement sweetener for recalcitrant veteran cadres, the new party constitution, ratified by the Twelfth Congress, stipulated that all members of the CAC were entitled to attend plenary meetings of the Central Committee in a nonvoting capacity; at the same time, the several vice-chairmen of the CAC were granted the statutory right of nonvoting participation in plenary sessions of the Politburo.[9] Such provisions apparently helped take the sting out of retirement, as a group of sixty-five Central Committee members and alternates over the age of seventy relinquished their seats and accepted appointment to the new commission.

In addition to these voluntary retirees, another group of 131 incumbent members and alternate members of the Eleventh CC, elected in 1977, failed to gain reelection at the Twelfth Congress. The majority of the unseated CC members were erstwhile Leftists and "whateverists" who had risen to prominence during the Cultural Revolution and the Hua Guofeng interregnum, and who were now being systematically weeded out by Deng's followers.

Old comrades reminisce at the Twelfth Party Congress, September 1982.
From left: Song Renqiong, Yang Shangkun, Chen Yun, Lu Dingyi, Yao Yilin.

Despite the obvious reluctance of some of China's senior leaders to leave the political stage, in the end a rather substantial turnover in party leadership did take place—*below* the Politburo level. Thus, fully 60 percent of the 341 Central Committee members and alternates elected at the Twelfth Congress were newcomers. Two-thirds of the new members were under sixty years of age; the youngest was thirty-eight. A substantial minority had received at least some postsecondary education, and one-sixth were occupationally classified as "professional" or "technical" cadres (compared with less than 3 percent on the Eleventh CC).[10]

While applauding the overall rejuvenation of the party's leadership, official media accounts of the proceedings of the Twelfth Congress tended to ignore the fact that the twenty-five members of the new Politburo were actually *older* on average, at seventy-two, than their predecessors on the Eleventh CC. This somewhat paradoxical outcome was the result of two factors: first, apart from the removal of such "young" Politburo leaders as Hua Guofeng (sixty-one), Chen Yonggui (sixty-nine), and Peng Chong (sixty-seven), only two party elders over the age of seventy—Xu Shiyou and Geng Biao—were dropped from the Politburo at the Twelfth Congress, while a third, Wei Guoqing, was removed shortly after the Congress ended;[11] and second, all six of the new Politburo members elected at the Twelfth Congress were in their seventies: Yang Shangkun, Song Renqiong, Yang Dezhi, Hu Qiaomu, Xi Zhongxun, and Liao Chengzhi.[12] Older still, on average, was the new six-man Politburo Standing Committee, which had exactly the same composition as the old SC. Made up of Hu Yaobang, Ye Jianying, Deng Xiaoping, Zhao Ziyang, Li Xian-

Deng Xiaoping chairs the first plenary session of the Central Advisory Committee, September 1982. From left: Xu Shiyou, Deng Xiaoping, Bo Yibo, Tan Zhenlin.

nian, and Chen Yun, the committee's members had a median age of seventy-four—only one year younger than the median age of the 172 elderly retirees who comprised the new CAC (which outside observers sarcastically referred to as the party's "sitting committee").

Despite Xu Shiyou's bitter feud with Deng Xiaoping, Xu was named vice-chairman of the new CAC, along with conservative reformers Bo Yibo and Tan Zhenlin and the born-again liberal Li Weihan. General Wei Guoqing, who had refused to retire to the CAC, was dismissed from the Politburo in late September, following publication of a thinly veiled attack on Hu Yaobang in the *Liberation Army Daily*. The offending article, written by members of the Political Department of the Chinese Navy (which operated under the jurisdiction of Wei Guoqing and navy chief Ye Fei), alleged that certain central party leaders had failed to take timely corrective action when "some responsible comrades" in the fields of culture, ideology, and the mass media had "sup ported bourgeois liberal points of view."[13]

If inducing elderly cadres to retire voluntarily proved extremely difficult, so too did the task of reforming and institutionalizing the party's command structure. Pursuant to Deng's oft repeated call to combat the problem of autocratic, overconcentrated power and to strengthen the norm of collective leadership, the Twelfth Party Congress, after considerable debate, formally abolished the posts of CC chairman and vice-chairmen. In future, the general secretary of the Central Secretariat was to be the top-ranked party leader, though his power was limited by a new provision in the party constitution which held that "no party member, whatever his position, is allowed to . . . make decisions on major issues on his own."[14] It was widely conjectured that the primary reason Deng and other reformists favored a general secretary over a new chairman was that the former, as part of a duly constituted collective body, the Central Secretariat, would merely be first among equals, thus reducing the likelihood of the emergence of an overbearing or dictatorial leader. By contrast, the Politburo Standing Committee had no formal institutional standing and no binding rules of procedure; it could thus be convened or not—and its advice heeded or not—at the whim of the party chairman. For this reason, Deng Xiaoping and Hu Yaobang reportedly favored outright abolition of the Politburo Standing Committee in favor of a more broadly empowered Central Secretariat. The proposal met with resistance from several of Deng's more conservative colleagues, however, and was ultimately shelved.[15]

Unlike the Politburo, which continued to be dominated by elderly revolutionaries of the first (i.e., Long March) generation, the Central Secretariat, under the direction of Hu Yaobang, comprised a number of younger, well-educated leaders, including members of both the second (anti-Japanese war) and third (civil war) revolutionary generations. Among the veteran cadres who resigned from the Central Secretariat at the Twelfth Congress were newly designated Politburo members Hu Qiaomu, Song Renqiong, and Yang Dezhi; leaving the Central Secretariat under somewhat greater political duress were Wang Renzhong and Peng Chong, who were nonetheless reelected to the Central Committee. Chosen to replace the departing Secretariat members were the irrepressible Deng Liqun, age sixty-seven; Hu Yaobang's brother-in-law, PLA general Yang Yong, age seventy; former Shanghai party leader Chen Pixian, sixty-six; and longtime Hu Yaobang associate Hu Qili, fifty-three. Despite the relatively advanced years of three of the new appointees, the average age of the twelve full and alternate members of the Secretariat was lowered from sixty-eight to sixty-three—almost a full decade younger than their Politburo counterparts. Of the ten full members of the Central Secretariat, four—Hu Yaobang, Wan Li, Xi Zhongxun, and Yu Qiuli—held concurrent membership on the Politburo.[16]

Building "Socialist Spiritual Civilization"

In response to Deng Xiaoping's admonition to guard against the corrosive effects of bourgeois decadence, and in recognition of the potency of the recent backlash against liberalism, Hu Yaobang substantially modified his stance on the developmental relationship between matter and spirit. In his political report to the Twelfth Party Congress, Hu echoed Deng's assertion that the successful construction of a socialist material civilization in China ultimately depended on the prior attainment of a high level of spiritual civilization. The ostensible reason for Hu's about-face was his admission that the wind of bourgeois liberalization had encouraged "capitalist forces and other forces hostile to our socialist cause . . . to seek to corrupt us and harm our country." Facing such a challenge, he continued, "it will not be possible to prevent in all cases the degeneration of some members of our society and party or block the emergence of a few exploiting and hostile elements." To minimize the effects of such degeneration, CCP members were called upon to hold firmly to the party's established ideals, moral values, and organizational discipline.[17]

In thus raising the specter of renewed disturbances by Rightist forces, Hu Yaobang was clearly bowing to pressure applied by Chen Yun and other conservative party elders. They remained deeply skeptical of the strength of Hu's commitment to Marxist-Leninist principles, and hence they were unsure he could be trusted to pursue mainstream policies following their own retirement from active duty.

Nor was this the first time Hu Yaobang had been obliged to prove himself worthy as heir to the top party post. A year earlier, in July 1981, at the height of the anti–Bai Hua campaign, Hu had given a lengthy address on the occasion of the CCP's sixtieth anniversary. In it, he had demonstrated his command of the full repertory of orthodox ideological arguments in support of the four cardinal principles and against bourgeois liberalization.[18] Now, a year later, he once again trimmed his sails in an attempt to mollify elderly conservatives. In carefully measured language, Hu hedged his nominal endorsement of the traditionalists' claim that "class struggle still exists," pointing out that it existed only "within certain limits" and no longer constituted the "principal contradiction."[19] And in announcing the Central Committee's decision to launch a comprehensive three year party "consolidation" and "rectification" campaign in the latter half of 1983, Hu Yaobang went out of his way to stress that Maoist-style methods of mass mobilization and struggle would not be employed in the new campaign.[20]

In sum, then, the Twelfth Congress struck an ambivalent stance on China's most pressing political and ideological issues, seeking to minimize (or at least paper over) conflict among contending leadership factions and constituencies. While pragmatically stressing the need to deepen further the process of economic reform and opening up to the outside world, party leaders simultaneously intensified their warnings against spiritual degeneration; by the same token, while declaring class struggle "in the main" to be over, they held out the clear possibility (made explicit in the new CCP constitution) that class struggle could become "even sharper" in the future. While the Twelfth Congress thus compromised on a number of troublesome issues of ideological and political orientation, the resulting ambivalence left considerable room for future discord.

INSTITUTIONALIZING REFORM: THE 1982 PRC CONSTITUTION

In the aftermath of the Twelfth Congress, considerable attention was focused on the newly revised PRC State Constitution, approved by the National People's Congress on December 4. Two years in the making, the new constitution reflected a clear rejection of the ultra-Left political philosophy of the Cultural Revolution and a reversion to a more routinized form of socialist legality, akin to the system originally imported from the Soviet Union in 1954.[21]

Echoing a number of themes recurrently raised since the Third Plenum in December 1978, the new constitution emphasized the creation of orderly, accountable, legally regulated governmental institutions and procedures. Toward this end, the legislative functions and powers of the NPC and its Standing Committee were enhanced; tenure in office for government leaders was limited to two consecutive five-year terms; and new stipulations were added prohibiting certain officials from serving concurrently in two or more leadership posts. Such measures were explicitly intended to create a clear division of power and offices and to ensure a "strict system of responsibility" in implementing laws.[22]

The 1982 Constitution also sought to strike a careful balance between civil liberties and civic duties. A number of new citizens' rights and safeguards were incorporated into the document, including the right to "personal dignity" and to the sanctity of the home. As in the case of the 1979 criminal codes discussed earlier, however, the practical effects of such libertarian innovations were sharply reduced by a series of explicit caveats and qualifiers. For example, the right of citizens to enjoy "freedom and privacy of correspondence" was subject to the proviso, "except in cases involving state security or criminal investigation." Equally limiting was a clause stipulating that "The exercise by citizens . . . of their freedoms and rights may not infringe upon the interests of the state, of society, and of the collective, or upon the lawful freedoms and rights of other citizens."[23]

Although the 1982 Constitution reaffirmed the substance of the party's four cardinal principles, it did so in language that was relatively mild, and that appeared to give equal emphasis to the importance of strengthening China's socialist democracy and legal system:

> Under the leadership of the CCP and the guidance of Marxism–Leninism–Mao Zedong Thought, the Chinese people will . . . continue to adhere to the people's democratic dictatorship and follow the socialist road, steadily improve socialist institutions, develop socialist democracy, improve the socialist legal system, and work hard . . . to turn China into a socialist country with a high level of culture and democracy.[24]

On the whole, China's new constitution—like the Twelfth Party Congress itself—represented an attempt to balance the inherently conflicting imperatives of fang and shou. Relatively tolerant and permissive by comparison with previous charters, the document reflected a clear break from the political philosophy of the Cultural Revolution. At the same time, it fell well short of institutionalizing the principles of limited government and rule of law.[25]

THE RIFT BETWEEN HU AND ZHAO

The many political and ideological contradictions, contortions, and compromises on display at the Twelfth Party Congress and in the language of the new state constitution were highly symptomatic of the growing fissures within Deng's reform coalition. The divisions were not merely between liberals and conservatives, as before; now the liberal wing of Deng's coalition showed clear signs of internal cleavage, with Hu Yaobang and Zhao Ziyang openly vying for the support and approval of their senior colleagues. At issue were the direction, scope, and limits of economic reform; at stake was the succession to Deng Xiaoping.

Although conventional wisdom holds that in the early and mid-1980s a single, cohesive liberal faction headed by Zhao and Hu stood opposed to a monolithic conservative bloc headed by Chen Yun, the reality was considerably more complex. As nominal head of the State Council and a relative newcomer to Beijing's political wars, Zhao Ziyang, to be an effective prime minister, required the cooperation of key central planners, finance officials, and ministerial heads. In an effort to build a support base among these powerful Beijing bureaucrats, Zhao by 1982 had begun actively to promote a type of economic and fiscal reform that would permit central planners to retain substantial control over the nation's industrial and commercial activity.

Zhao's preference for uniform, centralized fiscal policies put him increasingly at odds with Hu Yaobang, who tended to identify more closely with the interests and aspirations of local government cadres and enterprise managers. Where Zhao sought fiscal and administrative uniformity, Hu sought enhanced operational autonomy and decentralized fiscal administration.[26]

Toward the end of 1982, the budding rivalry between Zhao and Hu (and their respective support networks) took the form of a rather arcane and esoteric debate over how best to apportion enterprise profits so as to maximize managerial efficiency and responsibility. For Zhao, the preferred method of revenue-sharing, one that was also favored by leading officials in the Ministry of Finance and the State Planning Commission, was *li gai shui* (exchanging profits for taxes). Under Zhao's plan, central authorities would exercise direct fiscal control over factories and firms through a system of uniform, progressive enterprise taxation; at the same time, factory managers would be given an incentive to improve enterprise performance by granting them discretionary control over a certain percentage of after-tax profits.

In contrast to Zhao, Hu Yaobang, backed by top officials in the State Economic Commission, preferred a system of contractually fixed profit remittances, similar to the household contract-based "production responsibility systems" widely introduced in Chinese agriculture after the Third Plenum. Allowing industrial enterprises to retain all residual profits after remitting a specified lump sum to the state, the system of fixed contracts provided a strong incentive for enterprise managers to pursue a strategy of short-term profit maximization. At the same time, the system of fixed remittances also reinforced the financial power of local governments by granting them the authority both to negotiate the amount of each enterprise's mandatory remittance and to specify the permissible uses of residual, self-retained enterprise profits.

Understandably, Hu's system of separately negotiated fixed remittances, which put a cap on revenues collected by the central government, was strongly preferred by managers of large, heavy industrial enterprises and by most local government industrial departments. By contrast, Zhao's proposal for direct, progressive enterprise taxation was supported by a majority of fiscally conservative central bureaucrats in Beijing as well as by managers of small and medium-sized, light industrial enterprises.[27]

Among those endorsing Zhao's plan was Chen Yun. Chen had become visibly distressed over Hu Yaobang's libertarian political impulses as well as his efforts radically to decentralize economic decision making. Since occupying the post of general secretary, Hu had become something of an economic gadfly. By temperament a populist, he had increasingly championed the cause of local autonomy. Advised and supported by a retinue of liberal economists at the CASS Institute of Industrial Economics, Hu had raised the ire of Chen Yun, who was strongly inclined to favor continued central planning and unified state fiscal policies within a framework of partially decentralized administration. In a 1983 conversation with the general secretary, Chen obliquely expressed his dissatisfaction with Hu's preference for radical decentralization: "Ziyang and I speak Pekingese," he said reproachfully, "while you speak local dialect."[28]

Chen's concern with retaining overall central control of the economy was clearly manifested in his famous bird cage analogy, first articulated in January 1982:

> One cannot hold a bird tightly in one's hand without killing it. It must be allowed to fly, but only within its cage. Without a cage, it would fly away and become lost. Of course, the cage must be of appropriate dimensions; it must have the necessary room. . . . That is to say, one may readjust the size of the cage . . . [but] regulation of economic activity by the market must not entail abandonment of the orientation provided by the plan.[29]

By the early winter of 1982-83, tension between Chen Yun and Hu Yaobang had begun to mount. In late December Zhao Ziyang departed on a four-week, eleven-nation goodwill tour of Africa. In Zhao's absence, Hu reportedly sought to further his own economic and political agenda, promoting the system of fixed enterprise remittances and calling, among other things, for a sharp acceleration in the country's economic growth rate. Upon learning of Hu's activities, Chen Yun reportedly became irate. At a Politburo meeting convened shortly after Zhao's return from Africa in mid-January 1983, Chen issued a ten-point critique charging Hu Yaobang with responsibility for "making a mess of the economy" (*gaoluan jingji*). For his part, Zhao, piqued over Hu's evident attempt to usurp the premier's authority in the realm of economic policy making, openly sided with Chen.[30]

At first, Deng Xiaoping refused to take sides in the dispute between his two protégés, remaining steadfastly silent at the January Politburo meeting as Chen and Zhao, by turns, castigated Hu. After the meeting was over, however, Deng reportedly took Hu Yaobang aside, privately reprimanding the general secretary and instructing him to "stick to politics" and leave economics to Zhao.

Shortly thereafter, Deng Liqun, seeking (as always) to capitalize on Hu Yaobang's political missteps, called a meeting of *Red Flag* staff members and associates. At the meeting, Little Deng spread the word of Hu's recent scrape with Chen and Zhao. Almost immediately, rumors began to circulate in Beijing about Hu's possible dismissal from office.

Concerned over the mounting talk of elite instability, Deng Xiaoping sought the advice of Ye Jianying. Counseling restraint, Marshal Ye reportedly advised against removing Hu Yaobang. Although his job was thus saved, Hu emerged from this minidrama with his prestige and political stature considerably diminished. Not only was his fixed profit-remittance plan finally rejected in 1983 in favor of Zhao's *li gai shui* system, but thereafter the freewheeling general secretary was placed on a tighter leash. Enjoined by Deng from becoming embroiled in disputes over economic policy, Hu dutifully narrowed his attention to issues of ideology and politics, though he continued periodically to speak his mind to journalists and other "outsiders"—a habit that got him in trouble with party elders.[31]

Notwithstanding Hu Yaobang's ostensible withdrawal from the economic arena, tension continued to mount between the general secretary and the premier. Although the two men were forced by dint of circumstance periodically to join forces—for example, to repel hard-line conservative attacks against spiritual pollution and the open policy—by the end of 1984 the rivalry between them had reached a point where Zhao reportedly wrote a letter to Chen Yun and Deng Xiaoping complaining that he could no longer work with Hu and urging the Central Committee to remove Hu from the post of general secretary.[32]

THE DEBATE OVER ALIENATION AND SOCIALIST HUMANISM

While internal stresses continued to build within the liberal wing of the reform coalition, China's critical intellectuals, silenced for almost two years in the wake of the 1981 Bai Hua affair, became markedly bolder in the winter of 1982–83. The first sign of renewed "blooming and contending" was the initiation of a vigorous academic debate on the question of the relevance and utility of such Western concepts as "alienation" (*yihua*) and "humanism" (*rendaozhuyi*) in socialist society. Among the more prominent participants in this debate were Wang Ruoshui, deputy editor-in-chief of the *People's Daily*, and Ru Xin, vice-president of the Chinese Academy of Social Sciences. Along with a handful of other liberal critics of dogmatic Marxism, Wang and Ru had begun writing essays on the relationship between socialism and humanism as early as 1980.[33]

The debate heated up in mid-January 1983 with the publication of Wang Ruoshui's controversial essay "In Defense of Humanism." In this essay Wang noted that certain "well-meaning comrades" in the party disapproved of humanist values, regarding them as anti-Marxist heresy. "They set Marxism and humanism in total opposition to one another," he wrote; hence they are unable to see any universal relevance in the idea of human worth. Rejecting this view on the grounds that it erroneously equated the concept of human worth with bourgeois humanism, Wang proposed an entirely different type of humanism:

Socialist humanism implies resolutely abandoning the "total dictatorship" and merciless struggle of the ten years of chaos, abandoning the deification of one individual . . . , upholding the equality of all before truth and the law, and seeing that the personal freedoms and human dignity of citizens are not infringed upon. . . . Why should this sort of socialist humanism be treated as a strange, alien, or evil thing?[34]

Academic advocacy of humanist values reached a high watermark in the spring of 1983. In March, at a Beijing symposium marking the centenary of Karl Marx's death, CCP Deputy Propaganda Director Zhou Yang presented a paper pointedly upholding the contemporary relevance and utility of socialist humanism. Defending the controversial notion that alienation could arise under socialism, Zhou suggested that China's previous lack of democracy and sound legal norms had given rise to a situation wherein the people's servants had become their masters. This, he said, was a relevant example of political alienation. Economic alienation also existed, averred Zhou, because of China's critical lack of experience in socialist construction. As a result, he charged, "we did many stupid things" and "ate our own bitter fruit." Arguing that economic and political alienation existed objectively, he concluded that it was pointless for people to be alarmed by such concepts.[35]

Adding another strong critical voice to the flourishing debate on socialist humanism and alienation, senior party theoretician Su Shaozhi, in a paper delivered at the aforementioned Beijing centenary symposium on Marxism, affirmed that a crisis of Marxism existed. Calling the crisis "our punishment for having treated Marxism in a dogmatic fashion," Su argued that the bitter reaction against Cultural Revolution dogmatism had led some people to deny completely the contemporary relevance of Marxism. While carefully avoiding personal endorsement of such a view, Su concluded that "only by creatively developing Marxism can we truly uphold [it]."[36]

For a brief period in the spring of 1983, even the conservative wing of the CCP's reform coalition appeared to accept the propriety (if not the validity) of such arguments. At a meeting on "Marx and Man" held in early April, for example, Deng Liqun, who had recently replaced Wang Renzhong as head of the CC propaganda department, conceded that the debate on socialist humanism and alienation contained many good points and would contribute to the vigorous development of the party's "double hundred" policy toward intellectuals.[37] Indicative of ideological tensions within the party's propaganda apparatus, Little Deng's guarded comments on socialist humanism were published in *People's Daily* under a provocative headline presumably supplied by liberal-leaning editors Hu Jiwei and Wang Ruoshui. The headline read, "To discuss humanism and the theory of human nature is an excellent thing."[38] Not coincidentally, Hu Jiwei and Wang Ruoshui were among those subsequently removed from office for promoting bourgeois liberalism.

After more than three months of relatively free-flowing blooming and contending, official tolerance for the ongoing debate over socialist norms and values began to diminish noticeably. Social critics like Wang Ruoshui and Su Shaozhi had come uncomfortably, if only elliptically, close to denying the party's doctrinal and political legitimacy, and such defenders of the faith as Deng Liqun were finding it increasingly difficult to refrain from calling them to account. By the end of May the party media had stopped reporting on the humanism/alienation debate altogether; and by early June Little Deng had coined a new term to describe the apostasy now being propagated by Wang, Su, and other members of the humanist school. He labeled them "spiritual pollution" (*jingshen wuran*).[39]

STRAWS IN THE WIND: THE SIXTH NPC

The first significant public hint of a shift in the prevailing political climate was contained in Zhao Ziyang's work report, delivered in early June at the First Session of the Sixth NPC. While defending the party's established policies of economic reform, opening up to the outside world, and intellectual blooming and contending, Zhao added a fresh warning against the growing danger of bourgeois liberalism in the ideological and cultural spheres. Examples were said to include writers and artists who "disregard the social consequences of their work" and who "view their work as a means to grab fame and fortune." Such behavior, said Zhao, was symptomatic of "decadent ideology" and was "incompatible with the policy of serving the people and socialism."[40] While no concrete measures were called for beyond a general exhortation to criticize such trends, Zhao's remarks—coming from an erstwhile champion of system reform—proved worrisome to China's oft-burned critical intellectuals.

Also of concern to liberal perusers of Zhao Ziyang's June 1983 NPC work report was the premier's unusually harsh language on the subject of law and order. Expressing concerns previously voiced mainly by Chen Yun and other left-of-center reformers, Zhao took note of the rising tide of economic crimes and crimes of violence. The former were linked to a wave of corruption on the part of cadres seeking personal gain through abuse of their position and power. Attributing the breakdown in social order to "intolerable political and ideological apathy" displayed by public security and law enforcement personnel, Zhao stressed that it was necessary to suppress counterrevolutionary activities and deal "powerful blows" to criminals in all spheres.[41]

In the wake of Zhao's call for enhanced law and order, a draconian crackdown on crime was launched in the summer of 1983.[42] Marked by the suspension of certain constitutional and statutory rights of criminal defendants, the campaign witnessed a flurry of mass trials, hasty verdicts, truncated appeals, and summary executions. A resolution adopted by the NPC Standing Committee in early September waived a number of statutory provisions governing the handling of criminal cases—including provisions setting time limits for delivery of indictments, issuance of subpoenas, and the right to appeal convictions. The stated purpose of the suspension was to "promptly punish criminals who seriously jeopardize social order." According to various sources, between six thousand and ten thousand convicted lawbreakers were executed in the second half of 1983.[43]

While not necessarily unpopular with China's crime-wary citizens, the anticrime campaign gave further impetus to the ideological chill that had begun to envelop China. Most important, it gave party traditionalists a potent issue (law and order) and a viable pretext (the need to combat crime at its putative source) for launching a new offensive against ideological corrosion.

The offensive took shape at the end of the summer. Beginning in mid-September there was a marked increase in the militancy of articles published in certain bellwether journals. The editors of *Red Flag*, for example, now pointedly criticized "some people in cultural circles" who had been "taken in" by the allure of abstract humanity and humanism, to the point where "social and class nature have been abandoned." Calling this a reflection of a "serious antagonistic struggle" in the political sphere, the article stressed that since class struggle still existed it was necessary to strengthen the organs of people's democratic dictatorship in order to combat harmful views.[44] In a subsequent article, *Red Flag*'s editors went even further, claiming a presumptive link between the influence of bourgeois mentality, on the one hand, and the severity of China's recent crime wave, on the other:

> Although our country has already abolished the system of exploitation and established a socialist society, . . . all kinds of elements hostile to the socialist system and to the people still exist. Various kinds of crime are bound to occur where the influence of bourgeois extreme individualism . . . is still present. We must see that these serious offenders are detestable in the extreme. . . . If we let them get away with [their] crimes . . . and fail to suppress them, if we speak of "mercy" and "humanism," it will be a grave dereliction of our duty . . . to the cause of socialism.[45]

As early as 1981 conservatives had begun to suggest that China's rising crime rate was at least indirectly linked to an influx of decadent bourgeois ideas under China's open policy. In the fall of 1983 an internal Chinese publication went a step further by making explicit such a presumptive link. "Five years have passed since the Gang of Four were overthrown," noted the journal. "Why hasn't the security situation taken a basic turn for the better? . . . Since the policy of opening up to the outside, encroachments by bourgeois ideology from abroad [and] infiltration by hostile foreign influences [have] directly or indirectly fostered criminal activity in society. This is the objective reason."[46]

COMBATING HUMANISM AND SPIRITUAL POLLUTION

Under mounting pressure from the conservative wing of the reform coalition, the uneasy truce forged by party leaders at the Twelfth Congress a year earlier now began to come undone. The fault lines within Deng's coalition were clearly evident at the Second Plenum of the Twelfth Party Congress, held on October 11–12, 1983. In his speech to the plenum, Deng once again sought to steer a middle course between the feuding factions of his coalition. First he addressed the principal concerns of the party's moderate-to-liberal wing. Speaking of the need to continue combating remnant Leftist influences from the Cultural Revolution, he noted that "three kinds of people" (*sanzhong ren*) were continuing to undermine party unity and discipline from the Left: those who had secured career advancement by following the ultra-Left line in the Cultural Revolution; those who had displayed serious factional tendencies or extreme partisanship; and those who had engaged in "beating, smashing, and looting" during China's decade of destruction. Such people, said Deng, should be firmly disciplined, including expulsion from the party where necessary. To accomplish this task, he said, the forthcoming party consolidation movement would concentrate on exposing and rectifying the "three kinds of people."[47]

After addressing the main concerns of his centrist and liberal constituencies, Deng shifted his focus almost 180 degrees to launch a sharp, three-pronged attack on abstract humanism, the theory of socialist alienation, and spiritual pollution. Sardonically observing that a considerable number of party theorists preferred to indulge in abstract contemplation of human nature rather than attempting to understand and resolve concrete problems encountered by real people, Deng tersely dismissed abstract humanism as "un-Marxist; it leads youth astray." On the related issue of the possibility of alienation occurring under socialism, Deng sharply rebutted the viewpoint advanced by Zhou Yang and others in the spring of 1983:

> A number of comrades . . . say that alienation exists in socialist society . . . in the spheres of economics, politics, and ideology. . . . Such talk cannot help people gain a correct understanding . . . of the many problems which have appeared in socialist society. . . . In fact, this can only lead people to criticize, mistrust, and negate socialism, to lose confidence in the future of socialism and communism.

Turning to questions of political orientation, Deng noted that a number of unhealthy ideas had become fashionable of late among party theoreticians, including "abstract concepts of democracy," advocacy of free speech for counterrevolutionaries, and doubts about the four cardinal principles.[48] Such ideas ran counter to Marxist common sense, averred Deng; in addition, they tended to discredit the party's proletarian character and to engender doubts about the future of socialism, thereby sowing confusion in the minds of party members. Displaying contempt for writers and artists who "dwell eagerly on the gloomy and the pessimistic," Deng called on party workers in literature and the arts to glorify the CCP's revolutionary traditions, the four cardinal principles, and the heroic achievements of the Chinese people under socialism.

Continuing in this vein, Deng next decried a growing attitude of "doing anything for money" among writers and performing artists, many of whom "run around everywhere, . . . indiscriminately giving performances . . . using low and vulgar form and content to turn an easy profit." Such people are guilty of "pandering to the low tastes of a section of their audiences," Deng continued; they "commercialize spiritual productions" and thus "occupy an unworthy place in the world of art." Pointedly labeling such phenomena "spiritual pollution," Deng called for a vigorous ideological struggle to "resolutely overcome weakness, laxity, and liberal attitudes."

Although the effects of spiritual pollution were said to have seriously affected only a minority of party theoreticians and ideological workers, Deng warned of dire consequences if firm steps were not taken to combat the problem. "Don't imagine," he warned, "that a little spiritual pollution doesn't amount to very much and is not worth making a fuss over. . . . If we do not immediately . . . curb these phenomena, . . . the consequences could be extremely serious."

Having thus addressed the principal concerns of his coalition's liberal and conservative wings, Deng instructed his comrades to avoid going to extremes to rectify ideological problems of the Right or the Left. In the forthcoming party consolidation movement, he urged, comrades must at all times "seek truth from facts" and resist the temptation to employ the "crude and extreme" methods of the past, characterized by "cruel struggle and merciless blows." It was essential, he concluded, to adopt a kindly attitude toward comrades who have committed mistakes, resisting the temptation to "take every bush and tree for an enemy."

At the conclusion of its brief two-day plenum, the Central Committee adopted twin resolutions on party consolidation and rectification. Responding to Deng Xiaoping's injunction to avoid crude and extreme methods, the resolutions hewed closely to the ideological midline, denouncing with equal vigor "three kinds of people" on the Left and spiritual polluters on the Right.[49] Under the guidance of the CCP's Central Discipline Inspection Commission, headed by Chen Yun and Bo Yibo, the consolidation drive was to be carried out in two stages over a period of three years. Although no specific targets or quotas were announced, diplomatic sources in Beijing reported that some three million party members, principally young Leftists who had been recruited during the ten years of chaos, were initially targeted for rectification.[50]

Although it has been conjectured that Deng's strong denunciation of spiritual pollution at the Second Plenum may have been a tactical ploy designed to mollify conservatives and dissuade them from attempting to sabotage the reformers' efforts to rid the party of remnant ultra-Leftists,[51] in light of Deng's well-established pattern of ideological oscillation and fluidity it would appear that he was being true to his role as a political balancer in denouncing spiritual pollution. "Deng Xiaoping knows quite well that the value of his existence does not lie in acting as 'the great standard bearer,'" wrote an observer in the semiofficial Hong Kong Communist newspaper *Wenwei po* some years later, "but is based on balancing the strength of all sides. Should one side win complete victory, and the other side suffer complete loss, the value of his existence would thereupon be lost."[52] By seeking to straddle the ideological fence, linking his attack on "liberal attitudes" (Rightism) with an equally sharp attack on the "three kinds of people" (Leftism), Deng avoided giving conservatives an excuse to attack his hard-won policies of economic reform and opening up.[53]

Whatever Deng's original intent, the 1983 party consolidation movement quickly veered off the tracks and out of control. No sooner had the Second Plenum ended than a barrage of Leftist newspaper articles appeared, canonizing the four cardinal principles, condemning spiritual pollution in all its manifold forms, and vigorously denouncing abstract humanism and the theory of socialist alienation.[54] In late October the Central Committee disseminated "Central Document No. 36 (1983)," which instructed party and youth league branches throughout the country to "seriously investigate the actual situation concerning problems in ideology and spiritual pollution in all organizations and units. . . . All kinds of pornographic video recordings, pornographic books, pamphlets, pictures, pieces of folk art [sic], and hand-copied manuscripts . . . must be decisively, quickly, and thoroughly cleaned up."[55] By early November a number of leading reform conservatives, including Deng Liqun, Wang Zhen, and Peng Zhen, joined belatedly by Chen Yun, weighed in on the dangers of bourgeois ideological corrosion, explicitly invoking Deng Xiaoping's remarks at the Second Plenum to support their arguments.

From the outset, Deng Liqun was the conservatives' point man. According to reports circulating in Hong Kong, Little Deng's leading role in the early attack on spiritual pollution was motivated by two main considerations: his deeply held traditional values and his intense personal antipathy toward Hu Yaobang. Little Deng's dislike of Hu (and his estrangement from Deng Xiaoping) was well known and was said to stem from envy kindled in 1978–79 when he was passed over for promotion to the inner circle of party leadership. Armed with the potent issue of spiritual pollution—an issue on which Hu Yaobang was believed to be vulnerable—Deng Liqun set out to undermine his rival's prestige and political authority.[56]

Attacking the concept of abstract humanism as a bourgeois contrivance, Little Deng urged resolute resistance to "corrupt and vulgar bourgeois things." Echoing Deng Xiaoping's criticism of the pursuit of money above everything else and "box office values" in literature and art, he urged a return to the party's tradition of socialist realism—that is, "propagating the advanced achievements of advanced people; encouraging the patriotic fervor of the people"—and a tightening of political censorship of the nation's cultural fare.[57]

At a symposium on scientific socialism held on October 23, 1983, Wang Zhen took up the anti–spiritual pollution baton. Assailing the concepts of universal humanism and socialist alienation as "totally inconsistent" with the Marxist idea of scientific socialism, "Big Cannon Wang"[58] noted that in certain quarters it had become fashionable to ridicule people who "seriously advocate the communist spirit of total devotion to others with no thought of self." Calling for a "resolute struggle" to be waged against bourgeois liberalization and various other "Right deviationist trends," General Wang exhorted his comrades to "earnestly purify the ranks of party theoreticians and educators."[59] In a somewhat less combative vein, Peng Zhen argued that if spiritual pollution were not cleaned out, it would be impossible to build a socialist civilization of any type, spiritual or material.[60]

Before Deng Liqun launched his initial attack on spiritual pollution, he reportedly sought—and received—Chen Yun's blessing. As Little Deng's newest patron, Chen had recently been the recipient of a great deal of flattering publicity in the mass media, much of it generated by the fawning, conservative propaganda specialist. By endorsing the anti–spiritual pollution campaign, Chen may have been repaying the favor.[61] Whatever his reasons, Chen's endorsement of the antipollution drive represented a clear turnabout for the senior reform strategist. Although Chen had firmly declared his opposition to bourgeois liberalization as early as December 1980, he had subsequently adopted a rather mild and tolerant position in the 1981 campaign to criticize Bai Hua and Ye Wenfu. Now he began visibly to toughen his stance.

Under Little Deng's guidance, the antipollution campaign was extremely broad and diffuse, covering a wide range of undesirable social and cultural behavior. Among the many phenomena singled out for intense public criticism in the fall of 1983 were the "worship of individualism"; the proliferation of pornographic films and videotapes; the attitude of "looking to make money in everything"; the wearing of Western-style hairdos and high-heeled shoes by female college students; the uncritical praise of Western thought and culture; the resurgence of feudal superstition; the appearance of misleading, "Hong Kong–style" sales promotions and advertisements to entice retail customers to buy trash; and the taste for "decadent music."[62]

In some areas, vigilantes harassed people whose hair was unusually long or who wore flared trousers. In other places, factory workers were organized to search for "yellow" (pornographic) audiotapes and books. In the city of Lanzhou, provincial police headquarters reportedly organized local gendarmes to "read good books and sing revolutionary songs" as an antidote to such putative evils as "wearing mustaches and whiskers, singing unhealthy songs, being undisciplined, and not keeping one's mind on work."[63] In Beijing, the following notice was posted on the front gate of the headquarters of the Beijing Municipal Party Committee: "No admittance to persons with hair too long, skirts too short, slacks too tight, or face powdered and rouged."[64]

As an adjunct to their crusade against bourgeois values and life-styles, China's antipollutionists directed strong criticism at China's special economic zones. Alleging that "nothing in Shenzhen is socialist except for its five-starred red flag," Deng Liqun accused the Guangdong SEZ of being "practically like Hong Kong."[65]

In addition to denouncing all manner of bourgeois decadence, China's cultural watchdogs also attacked a number of alleged high-level purveyors of ideological corrosion. Wang Ruoshui and Zhou Yang were singled out for particularly harsh criticism, as was Hu Jiwei, Wang Ruoshui's boss and chief editor of the *People's Daily*, who was a key supporter of Hu Yaobang. The attack on Zhou Yang was spearheaded by Hu Qiaomu. Arguing that Zhou's theory of alienation constituted a clear example of "counterrevolutionary agitation," Hu charged that

> Zhou Yang's sayings could be used by dissidents for their political program. According to his theory of alienation, there is no freedom in our country, and exploitation has not been abolished. He says that in our society workers are not masters of their own products, that they are oppressed, and that . . . creative work [is] impossible, and so on. This is counterrevolutionary agitation, reversing right and wrong.[66]

Under considerable pressure to recant, Zhou Yang made a series of self-criticisms in October and November 1983. In them, he retracted many of his earlier statements on the subject of humanism and socialist alienation and accepted personal blame for spreading spiritual pollution in the cultural arena.[67] At around the same time, Hu Jiwei reportedly got in trouble, among other reasons, for trying to suppress publication of Wang Zhen's October 23 speech attacking Wang Ruoshui's theory of humanism.[68]

Drawing the Line: Hu and Zhao Fight Back

In late October Hu Yaobang began to fight back. At a two-day meeting held to explore the concept of spiritual pollution, he questioned the factual basis of the theory of pollution proposed by Deng Liqun. Arguing that the seven years since Mao's death had been "one of the best periods since Liberation," Hu called the development of the post-Mao reform movement "smooth and proper," attributing its success to the party's adoption of "a correct line and direction and policy, a correct method and procedure and order."[69]

At an enlarged Politburo conference held in early November, Hu Yaobang joined forces with Zhao Ziyang to launch a counterattack against the conservatives, claiming that the antipollution campaign had gone too far and that Leftists were taking advantage of the ideological cover provided by the new campaign to sabotage the "correct line" of the Eleventh CC's Third Plenum, negating economic reform (particularly in rural areas) and opposing China's opening to the outside world. Calling the attack on spiritual pollution a "false show of force," Hu and Zhao argued that the main focus of party consolidation and rectification should be the elimination of the "three kinds of people."[70]

At a meeting of the Central Party Secretariat, Hu and Zhao were assailed by an unidentified speaker (reputed to be Deng Liqun) who "shouted at the top of his voice that 'spiritual pollution threatens the life of the party.'" At that point, Zhao Ziyang played his trump card. Noting that "Japanese capitalists are postponing agreements with us . . . because they are frightened by the . . . movement to eliminate spiritual pollution," Zhao threatened to resign: "If things go on like this," he warned, "I shall be prime minister no longer."[71]

In the end, fearing disruption of his hard-won economic reforms and open-door policies, Deng Xiaoping intervened on behalf of Hu and Zhao to bring the antipollution campaign to a screeching halt. It was later reported that

Deng's son, Deng Pufang, had warned his father that if the campaign were pursued too vigorously it would seriously undermine the entire reform program and thus erode Deng's own prestige.[72]

One indirect indicator that the antipollution campaign was being deemphasized was the public appearance of Hu Yaobang in a Western suit and tie (rather than the more austere Mao jacket favored by conservatives) during a trip to Japan in late November. A few weeks later, Zhao Ziyang echoed Hu's sartorial strategy, appearing in Western dress throughout his official visit to the United States. (Later, in 1984, Hu Yaobang would manage to offend conservative sensibilities further by recommending the replacement of China's traditional food-serving utensils with individual Western-style utensils, ostensibly for hygienic reasons.)[73]

While the antipollution campaign was never formally terminated, it was subjected to a series of sharp restraints and limitations in the late fall of 1983. At the end of November word filtered down from the top that the countryside was henceforth to be exempted from implementing the campaign. A week later the exemption was extended to cover the entire economy. A week after that, science and technology were added to the list. Having begun with a bang, the anti–spiritual pollution campaign ended with a whimper.[74]

Explaining the campaign's decline to a group of leading cadres from the PLA General Political Department in late December, Politburo member Yu Qiuli, the former leader of the petroleum clique who had been selected to replace Wei Guoqing as head of the GPD, delivered the epitaph for the antipollution campaign. While he generally affirmed that the struggle to overcome the "various poisons" of spiritual pollution was a long-term job that remained unfinished, Yu (who held the military rank of general) acknowledged that some people had carried the campaign altogether too far:

> For example, it is not right to speak of wearing high-heeled shoes, getting permanents, wearing sunglasses, wearing new styles of clothing, and smoking filtered cigarettes as manifestations of spiritual pollution. . . . There will be chaos in our thinking if everything is regarded as spiritual pollution.
>
> . . . Some people have arbitrarily expanded the scope of investigations and seizures. . . . They have confiscated [legitimate] magazines, artistic photographs and literary works, . . . [even] photographs of soldiers' families and friends. This is clearly mistaken.
>
> It is absolutely necessary to seek truth from facts . . . [and] draw clear limits. We must not . . . indiscriminately turn into spiritual pollution everything that one has not seen before, does not care for, or is unaccustomed to, as some comrades have done. . . . If we do not attend to . . . preventing the expansion and confusion of policy limits, the results will be extremely serious.[75]

Although Hu Yaobang and Zhao Ziyang ostensibly prevailed in their confrontation with Deng Liqun, they did not emerge wholly unscathed. In return for securing the agreement of senior conservatives narrowly to limit the scope and magnitude of the campaign, Hu was pressured into accepting the dismissal (technically labeled a "reassignment") of his two top supporters at *People's Daily*, Wang Ruoshui and Hu Jiwei.[76] With a political quid pro quo thus effected, the antipollution storm quickly abated; by the turn of the new year, 1984, all that remained were a few occasional squalls—and a good many hard feelings.

Although Deng Liqun succeeded in securing the dismissal of two leading liberal media critics, he nonetheless emerged from the clash over spiritual pollution as the biggest loser, narrowly averting the loss of his own job. According to knowledgeable sources, a decision to replace Little Deng as party propaganda director had been made at the highest levels. The decision was prematurely leaked to the Voice of America, however, which broadcast the news of his imminent ouster. Angry at the leak and not wanting to be upstaged by foreign media, Deng Xiaoping reportedly intervened at the last minute to save Little Deng's job.[77]

Though he thus managed to retain his post, Deng Liqun was subsequently placed in the extremely awkward position of having to defend in public various reform policies with which he clearly disagreed. In a series of press statements and interviews with visiting foreigners, the veteran propagandist now spoke approvingly (albeit reservedly) about the need to expand the scope of economic reforms and the open policy; he also toned down considerably his warnings against the dangers of ideological degeneracy. Though ostensibly humbled by the experience, Little Deng's bitter antagonism toward Hu Yaobang remained undiminished. Later he would have ample opportunity to exact his revenge; for now, however, he was seemingly content to nurse his wounds and bide his time: a new phase of fang was about to begin.[78]

The Rebirth of Liberal Reform:
January 1984–Summer 1985

To get rich is glorious.

—Chinese reform slogan, ca. 1984

IN THE WAKE of the abortive anti–spiritual pollution campaign, China's reformers found themselves faced with a new set of problems on the economic front. Although the conservative ideological offensive had been nipped in the bud, it had struck a raw nerve in many parts of the country, particularly in rural areas where economic reform had (at best) brought only mixed results. In some rural districts, village officials, resentful of the new-found prosperity of peasant-entrepreneurs, had taken advantage of the anti–spiritual pollution drive to restrict the legitimate market activities of peasants and to impose a variety of discriminatory taxes and fees on newly affluent "specialized households."[1] In China's less developed interior provinces, opposition to Deng Xiaoping's open policy, which gave preferential treatment to coastal provinces and special economic zones, also began to crystallize in this period. Throughout the country, those localities, groups, and individuals most highly disadvantaged by reform, or simply afflicted with envy of others more successful than themselves—a condition known as "red-eye disease" (*hongyan bing*)—took advantage of the antipollution campaign to decry the high costs and adverse side effects of economic reform. The result was a revival of antireform sentiment in several interior provinces, a tendency that was especially pronounced in poorer rural areas.[2]

Faced with a potentially serious antireform backlash, the liberal wing of the reform coalition displayed new concern with the strength and tenacity of the Leftist challenge. On the theory that the best defense is a good offense, reformers seized the initiative in 1984, pushing ahead on a variety of fronts. Leading the charge were Hu Yaobang and Zhao Ziyang, fresh from their successful encounter with the antipollutionists.

Operating on a somewhat longer leash than before, Hu Yaobang began to speak more bluntly about the need for further reform. No longer tightly constrained by the need to prove his mainstream mettle to elderly conservatives, Hu instructed the editorial department of *People's Daily* in late February 1984 to draft for publication a series of hard-hitting commentaries supporting a major expansion of economic reform. One of these articles contained an ironic echo of the ultra-Leftist Cultural Revolution slogan, "boldly smash the old and create the new." Such blatant mockery evidently aroused the ire of the conservatives. Soon after the articles were drafted, Deng Liqun reportedly tried to have them suppressed, but without success.[3]

Throughout the late winter and spring of 1984, a plethora of unsigned editorials and commentaries in party newspapers reinforced the impression that the liberal wing of the "practice" faction had regained the policy initiative. Five main themes were stressed in these articles: (1) the principal danger at the present time is Leftism; (2) market reforms and responsibility systems in rural areas must be further expanded and perfected; (3) a key objective of economic reform is to "enable people to get rich"; (4) intellectuals are a precious national resource to be nurtured and cherished; and (5) China's opening to the outside world is a long-term policy that will be further expanded and enriched in the future.[4]

In April 1984 a major expansion of the open policy was officially announced, as fourteen coastal cities, including Shanghai, Tianjin, and Guangzhou, joined the four existing SEZs (Shenzhen, Shantou, Xiamen, and Zhuhai) as approved sites for preferential foreign investment and technology transfer.[5] Deng Xiaoping himself provided the initial push behind the expansion of the open policy. In a late January/early February 1984 tour of three coastal development zones in Guangdong and Fujian provinces, Deng praised the SEZ experiment, stating that the guiding philosophy behind China's opening-up was "not shou but fang" (*bushi shou ershi fang*).[6] Accompanied on his inspection tour by Wang Zhen, Deng strongly upheld the "correctness of our policy" during a visit to Shenzhen; in She'kou, he endorsed the controversial slogan, "Time is money; efficiency is life"; in Zhuhai, he proclaimed the SEZ experiment to be a success; and in Xiamen, he urged local officials to "run the SEZs with [even] better and faster results."[7]

Prompted by Deng's enthusiastic endorsement, even the crusty Wang Zhen appeared to gain a new appreciation for SEZs. Only a few months earlier, the Big Cannon had reviled the special zones as breeding grounds for spiritual pollution and bourgeois liberalism. Now he changed his tune. In a speech to the Central Party School in Beijing, delivered shortly after the conclusion of his joint inspection tour with Deng Xiaoping, General Wang claimed that "When Comrade Xiaoping said Xiamen should become a free port, I applauded with both hands."[8]

Well, maybe; but not all conservatives were so ostensibly enamored with the SEZs. Deng Liqun and Hu Qiaomu, for example, were both openly skeptical of the experiment; for his part, Chen Yun registered his disapproval rather more subtly, refusing to inspect any of the SEZs.[9] (He was virtually the only senior party leader who failed to visit at least one of the special zones.) Perhaps not surprisingly, it was over the issue of whether or not to expand the SEZ experiments that Deng Xiaoping and Chen Yun first openly quarreled in 1984–85.

ZHAO ZIYANG AND THE "THIRD WAVE"

While Hu Yaobang labored in 1984 to fashion a more benign political and ideological environment for the expansion of economic reform and the open policy, Zhao Ziyang was busy promoting a different sort of reform. With Deng Xiaoping providing key political backing, Zhao and his supporters began to flog the notion of a Chinese information revolution. Based on the Third Wave theories of American futurologist Alvin Toffler, who lectured in China in January 1983, the idea of a technology-driven, microelectronic-based global information revolution attracted a great deal of favorable attention among technoeconomic reformers working in various think tanks and policy advisory groups affiliated with the State Council.[10]

For a number of reasons, the Third Wave concept proved particularly appealing to China's anti-Leftist reformers. For one thing, the information revolution lay at the farthest frontiers of global technological development. This made it attractive to all modernization-minded "scientific socialists" in China, regardless of ideological predisposition. Moreover, the information revolution had the advantage of being, on the face of it, class neutral, that is, untainted by putative spiritual pollutants. Finally, Third Wave technology was readily transferrable internationally; its acquisition would enable China rapidly to close the gap with the "four little dragons" of East Asia. For all these reasons, an epidemic of "Third Wave fever" broke out in Chinese reform circles in early 1984.[11]

Despite its evident appeal, Third Wave thinking was not embraced with enthusiasm by all Chinese leaders. When Alvin Toffler visited China in January 1983 at the invitation of reform economists Yu Guangyuan and Tong Dalin of the China Futures Society, Hu Qiaomu tried to limit attendance at Toffler's lectures. Hu reportedly objected to Toffler on the grounds that Third Wave theory was predicated on the notion that socialism was an obsolete economic system.[12]

Undeterred by Hu Qiaomu's reservations, Zhao Ziyang continued to argue in support of the "new technological revolution." Shortly after returning from a state visit to the United States in January 1984, Zhao made a well-publicized tour of a microelectronics exhibit in Shanghai. Almost immediately thereafter, the press was flooded with articles publicizing the computer revolution. Between March and October a number of workshops were held for members of the Politburo, Central Secretariat, and key military organs, with the purpose of popularizing the nature and implications of the new information revolution. According to Chinese sources, more than two thousand leading cadres attended these meetings.[13] Also in 1984, the first big wave of microcomputer imports hit China, facilitated by a U.S. $200 million loan from the World Bank and by the largesse of a score of Western computer companies, all eager to provide free demonstration machines to Chinese universities, research institutes, and government offices as a way of getting a foot in the door of the burgeoning China market.[14]

The renaissance of reform fever on the economic and technological fronts received a significant boost in the spring of 1984 with the publication, on April 1, of an important political commentary in *People's Daily*. Based on a talk by Hu Yaobang, the commentary flatly stated that Leftism, rather than bourgeois liberalism, was currently the principal source of ideological weakness and laxity. Reviewing past damage inflicted on the country by ultra-Leftist policies, the commentary called for the complete eradication of Cultural Revolution influences, which were said to have penetrated "very deeply."[15]

This shift in emphasis was highly significant. In the course of the antipollution campaign several months earlier, Deng Xiaoping had issued stern warnings against the pernicious effects of Rightist ideological weakness and laxity. By now redefining the principal problem as Leftist in origin, Hu Yaobang was ostensibly signaling that his mentor had undergone a change of heart. (In this connection, it should be noted that in a 1984 interview with a Hong Kong journalist, Hu stated that although he and Zhao Ziyang generally took the initiative in deciding routine matters of policy within their respective spheres of authority, decisions on important issues were always referred to Deng Xiaoping—and to Deng alone.[16] Since redefining the main source of ideological weakness and laxity was anything but a routine matter, it is assumed that Deng personally approved the change in emphasis.)

The new anti-Leftist tilt was rapidly incorporated into the CCP's ongoing consolidation/rectification campaign, which entered its second phase in March 1984. Party consolidation was designed to be carried out "from top to bottom" in two distinct stages, with each stage consisting of two or more phases.[17] In the initial stage, party committees and leading offices at the central, provincial, major municipal, and autonomous regional levels were to study relevant documents and directives for three months (phase one), then engage in "examining and comparing" standards of organizational and individual behavior (phase two). Reportedly, some 960,000 party cadres underwent examination during the latter phase of stage one.

In stage two, which commenced in the winter of 1984–85, the movement was extended to some 13.5 million cadres in party organs at the county, municipal, and local levels (including enterprises, research institutes, schools, and universities). In this second stage, the main tasks were said to be "unifying thought" (*tongyi sixiang*); "correcting work-styles" (*zhengdun zuofeng*); "strengthening discipline" (*jiaqiang jilu*); and "cleaning up organization" (*qingli zuzhi*). The final and most critical phase of the campaign's second stage involved reregistration of all party members and expulsion of those found guilty of serious attitudinal and behavioral impurities.

Although some three million party members had originally been slated for organizational discipline, official sources subsequently revealed that less than forty thousand people were expelled from the party in the first two-and-a-half years of the campaign; of these, roughly 25 percent belonged to the "three kinds of people." The remainder had committed various non–Cultural Revolution–related offenses, including bribery, extortion, and embezzlement.

Beginning in 1985, on the heels of the mass media's exposure of a rash of large-scale economic crimes (including a notorious U.S. $1 billion black-market import ring on Hainan island, organized by children of high-level cadres), there was a marked increase in the number of expulsions from the party. According to official statistics released in 1988, a total of 150,000 party members were expelled for corruption between 1983 and 1987, with the vast majority of expulsions occurring after the middle of 1985.

RECRUITING THE THIRD ECHELON

Throughout the spring and summer of 1984, two themes dominated media discussions of party rectification: admonitions to stamp out Leftist factionalism, and exhortations to promote young, technically competent members of the "third echelon" (*disan tidui*) to positions of responsibility in the party and government. Even such erstwhile conservatives as CAC Vice-Chairman Bo Yibo now hewed to the anti-Leftist line. In August Bo argued that the elimination of Leftist influences was an essential prerequisite for opening China to the outside world and for successfully adopting new technologies.[18]

It was hardly coincidental that the party consolidation drive should now focus on the search for talented younger leaders: many of the harshest attacks on spiritual pollution in the fall of 1983 had come from veteran cadres who were at or near—and in some cases well beyond—the age of retirement, including such Politburo holdouts as Chen Yun, Peng Zhen, and Wang Zhen. Nor was it entirely coincidental that the man placed in charge of the party's third-echelon executive headhunt, veteran CCP organizer and Mao biographer Li Rui, should use a literary review of Chen Yun's *Selected Works* as the vehicle for launching the new youth movement.[19] Whatever the ironic intent behind Li's choice of venues, the media now published a number of articles praising the talents of younger intellectuals, technocrats, and other well-educated third-echelon leaders who had made outstanding executive contributions, some of whom, it was duly noted, had received advanced training in the West. At the same time, veteran party bureaucrats were chastised for obstructing the proper employment, promotion, and utilization of younger talent.[20]

Addressing the issue of generational change (and resistance thereto), Hu Yaobang pointed out, in an interview with a Hong Kong journalist, that despite a concerted effort to encourage veteran cadres to retire, well over two-thirds of the members of the CCP Central Committee were over the age of sixty. "If a crisis exists," Hu argued, "this is it." Flatly declaring that it was a "natural law" for old cadres to retire, he vowed to fill the CC with younger people the following year. Citing examples of third-echelon cadres who had recently been elevated to responsible positions in central party and government organs, Hu singled out a number of individuals for special mention, including Hu Qili, secretary of the Central Party Secretariat; Wang Zhaoguo, director of the CCP General Office; Hu Jintao, head of the CYL; and Tian Jiyun and Li Peng, both vice-premiers of the State Council.[21]

SPEEDING UP REFORM: ECONOMICS TAKES COMMAND

In line with the revised focus of party consolidation, the mass media in the summer of 1984 stressed the need further to develop and expand economic reforms and the open policy. In June "Central Document No. 1 (1984)" was published, granting expanded rights of private economic activity and extended land-use contracts to individual peasant households.[22] In early July it was announced that urban economic reform would commence in the autumn of the year, centering on the restructuring of state-owned enterprises, with a view toward increasing the operational autonomy, managerial responsibility, and profit incentives of state firms.[23] Also in early July, Beijing's newest architectural monument, the glitzy chrome and-glass Great Wall Hotel, opened for business—a joint Sino-American venture that neatly symbolized Deng Xiaoping's commitment to modernization and the open door.

In September 1984 a group of liberal young economists affiliated with Premier Zhao Ziyang's reform network convened a four-day working conference at Moganshan, Zhejiang. Participants in the conference voiced strong support for a stepped-up program of aggressive structural reforms, including, inter alia, an end to the "iron rice bowl" of lifetime employment, enhanced operational autonomy for enterprise managers, and greater reliance on market mechanisms. Widely regarded as a watershed in the post-Mao reform movement, the Moganshan conference served to catalyze support for the fundamental restructuring of the Chinese economy.[24]

Throughout this period of accelerating relaxation and reform, the mass media played up China's efforts to attract and protect foreign investment; to refine and enforce China's newly enacted commercial laws and procedures; to encourage individual and collective entrepreneurship; to discourage "eating out of a common pot"; and to "smash the iron rice bowl." Occasionally, the examples selected for favorable publicity in the official media caused eyebrows to be raised. Under the headline "Prosperous Girls Attract Husbands," for example, a major Shanghai newspaper approvingly recounted the story of a group of peasant spinsters from a poor village in neighboring Jiangsu Province who suddenly become objects of intense matrimonial interest on the part of young men from a nearby factory after the women struck it rich as a result of adopting the new household responsibility system in agriculture.[25] Other articles sounded the praises of all manner of private enterprise—from short-order cooks and free-lance photographers to young girls who hired themselves out as personal maids and nannies.[26] Still other articles celebrated the achievements of such trail-blazing reformers as the director of a collectively owned shirt factory in Zhejiang Province, who composed a song to inspire pride among the workers in his plant, where variable piece rates, individualized bonuses, and other "common pot"–smashing productivity incentives had recently been introduced:

> Work hard, hard, hard.
> We are the glorious shirtmakers!
> With good workmanship and novel designs,
> We dedicate our youth
> To making life beautiful.[27]

In the face of such unbridled enthusiasm, the occasional voices of ideological dismay or uncertainty raised in the mass media were drowned out in a chorus of proreform affirmation. Although it was periodically acknowledged that "some people" entertained doubts about certain economic innovations that ostensibly "eliminated the superiority of socialism" or "slid back from socialism to capitalism," such reservations were generally dismissed as misplaced or ill-informed.[28]

Further reflective of China's new mood of permissiveness was the reappearance, with official approval, of high-fashion Western clothing, including short, slitted skirts for women,[29] and the proliferation of certain risqué art forms that less than a year earlier would have stood condemned as spiritual pollution. *Beijing Review*, for example, ran on its inside back cover photos of two seminude female sculptures,[30] while the new international lounge of the Beijing Airport featured a wall-length mural depicting bare-breasted ethnic minority women frolicking in their native habitat. In the high tide of socioeconomic experimentation and openness that swept through China in the summer of 1984, such things were possible.

URBAN REFORM: THE THIRD PLENUM OF OCTOBER 1984

While restrictions on private entrepreneurship were greatly relaxed in the summer of 1984, reform in state-owned enterprises lagged noticeably behind.[31] The growing disparity between a dynamic private and collective economy and a stagnant public sector was addressed in the Central Committee's long-awaited "Decision on Reform of the Economic Structure," adopted by the Third Plenum of the Twelfth Central Committee in late October. Among the many reforms called for in the new CC decision were a reduction in the scope of mandatory central planning for state enterprises (with a concurrent increase in flexible guidance planning); the introduction of the controversial *li gai shui* system of enterprise taxation (replacing the system of contractually fixed profit remittances); and an expansion of enterprise autonomy in such areas as supply and marketing, product mix, hiring and firing of staff, and allocation of retained profits. Also included was a call for coupling the gradual reform of China's irrational pricing system to the phasing out of costly and inefficient state subsidies in such areas as urban housing, energy supply, grain, and transportation. Finally, the Third Plenum's reform decision provided assurances that the state positively supported small-scale private business activity and would not seek to expropriate legitimate individual profits. In introducing its urban reform program, the Central Committee claimed that these various measures were essential to ensuring the overall success of the entire reform effort.[32]

Loosely patterned after the Hungarian model of market socialism, China's 1984 urban reforms envisioned creation of a "socialist planned commodity economy" (*shehuizhuyi youjihuade shangpin jingji*) that would incorporate elements of both central planning and market regulation. The state would continue to own the bulk of large and medium-sized enterprises and would continue to regulate production and pricing of a number of strategic commodities; but the market mechanism would now be permitted to play an increasingly important (albeit supplemental) role in the pricing and allocation of nonstrategic goods and services, as well as in the allocation and remuneration of labor. China's new "planned commodity economy" would, in other words, permit the bird of protocapitalist market forces to fly with considerably more freedom than before within the newly enlarged cage of central planning.[33]

Because of its potentially far-reaching implications, the Central Committee's urban reform decision was not approved without considerable debate and disagreement. At a leadership meeting held at the seaside resort of Beidaihe, near Tianjin, in August 1984, reform leaders reportedly navigated their way through a minefield of conservative ideological objections. Most highly controversial of all was the idea of a planned commodity economy. First systematically articulated by reform economist Xue Muqiao in 1981, the concept had initially prompted Chen Yun to formulate his famous bird cage analogy. Continuing to insist that market regulation of economic activity must remain secondary, at all times subordinate to central planning, Chen Yun and other party traditionalists pressed hard to insert language into the new CC decision emphasizing the primacy of planning and public ownership and the overall superiority of socialism.

For his part, Hu Yaobang was strongly inclined to resist compromising the liberal thrust of the urban reform decision. His secretary, Zheng Bijian, openly complained of "erroneous tendencies" displayed by those who "regard all reforms that run counter to the economic pattern formed under certain historical conditions as heresies or departures from socialism."[34] Zhao Ziyang, on the other hand, was more conciliatory. Seeking to smooth the ruffled feathers of party elders, Zhao agreed to modify certain passages in the text of the decision. As a result, the final language of the October 1984 CC document was oddly disjointed.[35]

Satisfied with his compromise handiwork, Zhao sent a letter to the Politburo Standing Committee on September 9, detailing his recommendations and explaining the text's altered language. The SC unanimously endorsed his views. Chen Yun applauded Zhao's efforts, and he took pains to point out that this was not the first time the CCP had found it necessary to modify Soviet economic institutions to suit Chinese conditions.[36] At a meeting of the CAC immediately following adjournment of the Third Plenum, Deng Xiaoping gave his stamp of approval, calling the October urban reform decision a "very good document." Notwithstanding his personal endorsement, however, Deng conceded that his more conservative colleagues were less than enthusiastic over the new plan. "Some of our comrades," he said, "are afraid of seeing capitalism suddenly looming up after having worked all their lives for socialism and communism, and they cannot stand such a sight."[37] It was a complaint that would be heard again and again, in various forms and permutations, in years to come.

CHINA UNCHAINED: THE URBAN ECONOMIC BOOM OF 1984–1985

Bold and innovative in design, the 1984 urban reforms were slow to get off the mark following the Third Plenum. For one thing, lack of elite consensus over the priorities, sequences, and pacing of reform led to repeated delays in implementation. For another, substantial resistance was encountered in many state-owned enterprises, where workers, staff, and cadres were reluctant to relinquish the traditional security of the "iron rice bowl" and the "common pot."[38] Equally damaging was a strong surge of provincial opposition to the proposed *li gai shui* system. If fully implemented, the new tax-for-profit scheme would have stripped local governments of the power to negotiate profit-retention contracts with the enterprises under their jurisdiction. Not wishing to relinquish their proprietary financial rights, provincial leaders resisted implementing the new system; consequently, a key fiscal component of the urban reform program was never put on firm footing.[39]

In the absence of a clear consensus on policy implementation, the October CC decision had an unsettling psychological effect on urban residents throughout the country. Fearful that imminent decontrol of prices and reductions in state subsidies might lead to a run-up in retail prices of vital consumer goods and services, anxious urbanites in many areas, including Shanghai, Beijing, and Guangzhou, rushed to withdraw money from the bank to stock up on essential commodities. With demand sharply up and retail inventories depleted, production units saw a golden opportunity to raise prices; with demand and prices both rising, output and profits increased, putting more money into circulation, which led to an even greater upsurge in consumer demand, which led to still further retail shortages. The result was the beginning of an inflationary spiral in which the fear of rising prices was mother to the fact—a classic self-fulfilling prophecy under capitalism.

Coincidental with the mounting economic insecurity of late 1984, there occurred a sudden, sharp spurt in urban private business activity. For various reasons, including local governmental encouragement and the demonstration effect of private entrepreneurs who had grown prosperous without suffering adverse political consequences, large numbers of urbanites now embarked on the road of private business.[40] Between 1983 and 1985, the number of officially registered private enterprises and *getihu*—individual households engaged in small-scale domestic trade—doubled, from 5.9 to 11.7 million; taking into account nonregistered households, the total was higher still.[41] Among those drawn into private business in this period were substantial numbers of unemployed youths, former Red Guards, ex-prisoners, laid-off workers from other enterprises, disabled people, moonlighting state employees, and pensioners seeking to supplement their incomes.

Alongside the burgeoning army of petit-bourgeois getihu, a wholly new category of upscale, quasi-private urban entrepreneurs now began to appear on the scene. These were the so-called *gaogan zidi*, children and other blood relatives of high-level cadres whose family connections gave them excellent financial and commercial contacts throughout the party and state bureaucracies. With the advent of a commodity economy, such people were ideally positioned to take full advantage of the government's liberalized commercial policies and credit controls to set up new trading companies, secure business loans, and establish supply and marketing networks.[42] Within a matter of months, China's overprivileged gaogan zidi began to wheel and deal on scale not seen since before the revolution. In Liaoning Province alone, more than nine hundred gaogan-affiliated companies were established between the summer of 1984 and the spring of 1985.[43]

The mid-1980s also witnessed dramatic growth in the rural collective industrial sector. Responding to strong fiscal incentives and pressures from the center to expand local revenue bases (in many cases irrespective of anticipated productivity gains), village and township governments throughout the country hastened to establish small-scale rural industries. Under the slogan "a factory for every village," collective village and township enterprises employed fifty-two million people in 1984–85, accounting for almost 40 percent of total rural output. With banks loans and credit readily available to finance construction and expansion of these enterprises (banks, too, were under considerable pressure to generate new sources of local revenue), many inefficient, redundant, or otherwise uneconomical enterprises were set up, contributing substantially to the country's fast-growing fiscal imbalance.[44]

As a result of the confluence of these various reform-induced developments, by the fall and winter of 1984–85 China's economy had begun seriously to overheat.[45] Money supply increased by almost 40 percent in the last quarter of 1984 (compared with the corresponding quarter of the previous year), while industrial wages and bonuses rose 19 percent over the same period. Bank loans were also up a steep 29 percent, while foreign exchange reserves plummeted, the result of a wave of big-ticket foreign imports. With the rate of inflation reaching double digits in some Chinese cities for the first time since the early 1950s, consumer unrest now became a cause for concern. The potential gravity of the problem was conveyed in a comment made by a Chinese housewife to a visiting journalist early in 1985: "My mother says that ten years ago China was in chaos, but Mao kept prices stable. She says now China is stable, but prices are in chaos."[46]

Zhao Ziyang acknowledged the seriousness of such concerns in his report to the Third Session of the Sixth NPC in March 1985. Noting that the "temporary difficulties" of an overheated, unbalanced economy could not be ignored, Zhao admitted that a major source of difficulty lay in the fact that "we lack experience in restructuring an entire economy." Notwithstanding such inexperience, Zhao announced the government's intention to stay the course with respect to the main components of structural reform.[47]

As it turned out, inflation, a runaway money supply, and an upsurge in unregulated business activity were only the tip of a rather ominous economic iceberg. Just beneath the surface another, potentially even more debilitating, side effect of China's hybrid structural reforms was beginning to make itself felt: an epidemic of brazen, high-stakes economic profiteering and corruption, much of it committed by gaogan zidi.

CADRE CRIME AND CORRUPTION: ACHILLES' HEEL OF REFORM

Leninist systems, because of their bloated administrative bureaucracies, chronic shortages of consumer goods, and informal networks of "back-door" clientelist ties, generally tend to spawn a high degree of corruption.[48] Although economic crime and corruption were hardly unknown in China during the Maoist era, their severity was limited by the relatively small financial rewards and relatively high social and political costs involved. Under Mao, the party's egalitarian, antibourgeois ethos made it extremely risky for anyone to engage in the conspicuous pursuit or consumption of wealth. Where corruption did exist, it tended to be localized, unorganized, nonmonetized, and limited in scale; much of it involved cadres extorting "donations" of various kinds—including money, consumer goods, and sexual favors—from members of their work units.[49] Now, however, in the more permissive, "to-get-rich-is-glorious" environment of postreform China, the cost/benefit calculus changed dramatically; now there was a manifold increase in both the incentive to engage in corruption (in the form of substantially greater economic payoffs and diminished ideological restraints) and the opportunity to do so (presented by the rapid proliferation of deregulated, contract-based commercial exchanges). With the stakes thus raised and the transaction costs lowered, corruption and economic crime flourished.

One important new source of corruption was the hybrid nature of China's partially restructured economy. Writing in December 1984, a dissident Chinese intellectual foresaw with uncanny accuracy how a series of emerging gaps—in productivity, in pricing, and in performance—between the new, market-regulated sectors of the economy and the old, centrally planned sectors would inevitably give rise to a plethora of illicit commercial transactions. With scattered islands of free-market autonomy floating in a sea of socialist planning, the inevitable result, he predicted, would be a tremendous upsurge in economic malfeasance and "back-doorism":

> Some of the reforms will have the effect of loosening the constraints on [smaller, nonstrategic] enterprises, leaving their management in the hands of workers and staff. The products of these enterprises will be regulated by the market mechanism. However, major enterprises such as . . . those dealing with steel, oil, and electricity will still fall under the centrally planned economy. It can be predicted that the pace of their development will fall behind that of the [market-regulated] enterprises. . . . Hence, energy resources and certain raw materials which were already in short supply before [the advent of reform] will tend to be in even shorter supply afterwards. When there is not enough to go around, the [market-regulated] enterprises will use all kinds of methods (including bribery) to get hold of energy resources and raw materials destined for large enterprises under the state plan. The income of the staff and workers in the large enterprises which are subject to guidance planning will not be as high as those working in [market-regulated] enterprises. It will be difficult to avoid a situation wherein certain staff members receive a "secondary salary" distributed in private by the [market-regulated] enterprises, in order to bribe the units to open wide their "back doors." This kind of unhealthy practice will increase and, if it does not attract notice, will become ever more prevalent. . . . Economic crime will increase by leaps and bounds.[50]

In addition to structurally induced corruption, economic crime of a different sort began to flourish in China's special economic zones and open coastal cities in the winter and spring of 1984–85. In these hyperactive enclaves of commercial laissez-faire, a wave of speculation, smuggling, profiteering, and currency manipulation by gaogan zidi and other quasi-private entrepreneurs resulted in a series of major financial losses to the state. In one well-publicized scandal, a group of high-ranking cadres and gaogan zidi were dismissed from their posts in the duty-free port of Hainan after it was revealed that they had floated hard-currency bank loans and credits in the amount of RMB ¥4.2 billion for the purpose of importing 89,000 Toyota automobiles, 16,000 vans, 2.9 million television sets, 252,000 videocassette recorders, and 122,000 motorcycles, all destined for resale at a high profit on the domestic market. As a result of these and other unauthorized transactions, China's foreign exchange reserves plummeted by more than one-third—almost U.S. $6 billion—in the first six months of 1985.[51]

Responding to such developments, CAC Vice-Chairman Bo Yibo sounded a series of stern warnings in the spring and summer of 1985 against party members and cadres engaging in improper commercial activities. Among the common practices cited were: establishment and operation of dummy companies (*pibao gongsi*: lit., "briefcase companies") for private profit; black-market buying and selling of foreign exchange certificates; unauthorized sale of lottery tickets and "bonus coupons"; distribution of money and goods under false pretexts; squandering of public funds on lavish feasts and gift-giving; and the practice of nepotism and cronyism in personnel appointments and promotions. Bo Yibo attributed the rising incidence of such practices to a general decline in "party spirit" among CCP members, many of whom allegedly "put money above everything else" and "use their authority to secure personal gain" (*yiquan mousi*).[52]

"What merits our grave concern," said Bo Yibo in October, "is that the principle of commodity exchange has permeated the political life of some party organs." Noting that indiscipline had become very serious in some places, he argued that a substantial number of CCP members and cadres were unqualified for membership. Calling such people "black sheep who have the appearance of party members," Bo stated that their corrupt, arrogant behavior had so infuriated the people that widespread demands were being raised for criminal courts to take resolute action to punish the offenders.[53]

Bo Yibo's demand for the judicial system to play a stronger role in punishing corrupt party members and gaogan zidi represented a major shift away from the CCP's traditional emphasis on punishment via internal party discipline. Indeed, Bo's reference to mounting public fury over the lack of legal accountability of party members struck a highly sensitive nerve within the party.

Beginning in 1984–85 the investigation of cases involving corrupt gaogan zidi became a significant issue in intraparty politics. On more than one occasion, disputes among senior leaders were transferred or displaced onto their children. In one widely discussed incident, Hu Yaobang raised the ire of Hu Qiaomu by proposing formally to charge the latter's son, Hu Shiying, with criminal corruption. The young man reportedly had been involved in a number of illicit activities, including providing pornographic videotapes for PLA sex parties and skimming off ¥3 million in tuition fees paid to his privately operated correspondence law school. When Hu Shiying was placed under arrest in 1986 as an example to others that corruption so egregious must be exposed "no matter whose son was involved" (as Politburo security expert Qiao Shi put it), the incident provoked an immediate reaction among powerful party elders. Spearheaded by Hu Qiaomu, who affected great outrage over the handling of his son's case, a campaign to oust Hu Yaobang quickly took shape. At the same time, Hu Qiaomu reportedly threw himself at Deng Xiaoping's mercy, tearfully imploring the paramount leader to show mercy toward his errant offspring. Although no "smoking gun" ever surfaced to connect the Hu Shiying affair directly to events that followed, it is interesting to note that whereas Hu Yaobang was unceremoniously ousted from his party leadership post a few months later, Hu Shiying was given a mild rebuke and quietly released from custody, with all formal charges against him dropped.[54]

Although a small number of corrupt municipal, county, and provincial cadres and their children were tried and convicted in courts of law, such cases generally involved extraordinarily blatant or heinous crimes. The vast majority of ordinary cases of official corruption—along with virtually all cases involving high-ranking cadres and their offspring—continued to be dealt with behind closed doors.

The highest-level gaogan zidi to be judicially punished in this period was the daughter of General Ye Fei, former commander of the Chinese Navy. In 1986 Ye Zhefeng was tried and sentenced to seventeen years in prison for selling confidential economic information to foreign business interests. The singling out of General Ye's daughter for prosecution may not have been entirely coincidental. In 1982 the general, together with Wei Guoqing, had sharply criticized Hu Yaobang for failing to halt the spread of bourgeois liberalization.[55]

Other gaogan zidi who came under criminal investigation in this period included the prodigal offspring of conservative party elders Peng Zhen and Wang Zhen. Like Ye Fei and Hu Qiaomu, Peng and Wang had been vocal critics of bourgeois liberalization, and the raising of allegations of corruption against their children thus carried a strong hint of political retaliation. Despite all the anticorruption sound and fury, however, very few children of top-level cadres were ever prosecuted. Most were let off with a lecture and a warning (in some cases accompanied by a demand for the repayment of ill-gotten wealth), thus sparing their powerful families the humiliation of criminal proceedings.[56]

In an interesting footnote to the Hu Shiying and Ye Zhefang affairs, at the height of the Tiananmen crisis in the spring of 1989, Zhao Ziyang startled his colleagues by offering to turn over two of his own free-wheeling entrepreneurial sons, Zhao Dajun and Zhao Erjun, to a special tribunal for investigation of possible corruption. Flabbergasted, senior party leaders hastily declined Zhao's offer—opting instead to remove him from power.[57]

Responding to strong social demand for action to eliminate the spreading cancer of economic crime and corruption, the CDIC in 1985 shifted the main focus of its second-stage rectification drive. The first stage had stressed rooting out remnant Maoists, "whateverists," and other assorted "three kinds of people." Now, several months into the second stage (which had begun in the winter of 1984–85), the emphasis shifted to the elimination of a series of "new unhealthy tendencies"—tendencies that sprang not from remnant Cultural Revolution ultra-Leftism, but from economic indiscipline, opportunism, and the pervasive "get rich quick" mentality that had begun to infect the country—

and the party—since the introduction of economic reform. With that shift, the sensitive directional indicators of the fang/shou cycle began to oscillate once more, moving back toward the reaffirmation of traditional ideological principles and values.

THE BATTLE OVER MARXISM AND CAPITALISM

As in each previous phase of ideological tightening, the conservative revival of early 1985 brought with it renewed expressions of concern for preserving the doctrinal integrity of Marxism. During the heyday of entrepreneurial liberalism in the fall of 1984, the position of orthodox Marxism had ostensibly been attenuated, among other things, by Deng Xiaoping's widely quoted statement to the effect that "a little capitalism isn't necessarily harmful."[58] By autumn's end, a small storm had erupted over the issue of whether (and how) Marxism could be creatively developed and enriched to prevent it from becoming totally anachronistic and irrelevant to China's current needs.

The controversy began when *People's Daily* declared, in a front-page commentary published on December 7, that "since Marx has already been dead for 101 years . . . some of his assumptions are not necessarily appropriate." Calling the worship of individual words and sentences from Marxist texts "childish ignorance," the commentary said it was unrealistic to expect the works of Marx and Lenin, written in the nineteenth century, to "solve today's problems." A few days later, a Chinese government official went a bit further, asserting that "most people today don't care whether something is capitalist or socialist. They just want their lives to improve. The details are a matter for the theoreticians."[59] At this point a leading liberal reform theoretician, Su Shaozhi, entered the fray and proclaimed bluntly: "There are no Marxist quotations for what we are doing now."[60] Reacting to such developments, a few foreign journalists were moved to speculate, somewhat hyperbolically, that Marxism had been officially abandoned in China.[61]

In the event, such obituaries proved premature. In a rare editorial retraction, *People's Daily* informed its readers that a mistake had been made in a key sentence of its December 7 commentary, and that the sentence in question should have stated that Marxist-Leninist works could not "solve *all of* today's problems."[62] In discussing the source of the error, Chinese officials informed a group of foreign journalists that the original commentary had been flawed because it "did not sufficiently stress the continuing importance of Marxist principles."[63] Notwithstanding such disclaimers, it was widely rumored that the offending sentence in the original commentary had been drawn directly from a talk given by Hu Yaobang in late November.[64]

Mounting conservative pressures soon caused Deng Xiaoping to back off a bit from his October assessment of the harmlessness of "a little capitalism." In a 1985 New Year's message to the Chinese people, Deng continued to defend his tolerance of a small amount of private enterprise on the grounds that without it, China would not be able to catch up with the level of the developed countries "within fifty years." But he tempered his endorsement with a candid admission that some of his old comrades were concerned that capitalism was beginning to make deep inroads in China. To mollify these comrades, Deng ruled out the possibility of a wholesale departure from socialism, insisting that in the twenty-first century, "the basic things will still be state-owned."[65]

Deng's attempt to reassure nervous old-timers failed to stem the swelling ideological backlash, which was now being fueled by fresh reports of corruption, black-marketeering, smuggling, and economic mismanagement. Such reports prompted party conservatives to issue new allegations of moral degeneration.[66] Ever sensitive to such criticism, Deng continued to give ground. Speaking at a national science conference in March, he acknowledged that "Some people are worried that China will turn capitalist . . . We cannot say that they are worried for nothing."[67]

RENEWING THE STRUGGLE AGAINST BOURGEOIS LIBERALISM

With the second stage of party consolidation now focusing on the rectification of cadres afflicted with spiritual disorders of the get-rich-quick variety, conservatives soon broadened their ideological offensive. As on previous occasions, a principal target of attack was bourgeois liberalism in the mass media. Also as on previous occasions, the lead role in the new offensive was played by Deng Liqun.

Little Deng had reportedly been irritated by recent comments on the subject of press freedom by Hu Yaobang and two of his principal supporters, Hu Qili and Hu Jiwei. At the end of December 1984, at the Fourth Congress of the Chinese Writers' Association, Hu Qili stressed that literary creation must be free and that journalists and writers must not be subject to political litmus tests or discrimination.[68] At the same meeting, Hu Yaobang stated that people should no longer talk about eliminating spiritual pollution and combating bourgeois liberalization.[69] A similar plea for creative freedom was made by Hu Jiwei (who had been reassigned to the Educational and Cultural Committee of the NPC following his ouster from *People's Daily*) at a gathering of journalists and scholars held in Shanghai early in 1985.[70]

Addressing a meeting of the Central Party Secretariat in early February, Deng Liqun pressed Hu Yaobang to reaffirm the party's traditional norms concerning adherence of the mass media to the line, principles, and policies of the CCP. Bowing to pressure (some of it reportedly applied by Deng Xiaoping), Hu Yaobang conceded that the proper role of the official media was to serve as "mouthpiece of the party," although he hastened to add that the media should also faithfully reflect the views of the people.[71] At the same meeting, Hu gave additional ground to Deng Liqun and the conservatives, calling on the mass media to stop being so gloomy in their coverage of China's domestic situation. In general, he said, "newspapers should devote 80 percent of their space to achievements and the positive side, and only 20 percent to shortcomings and criticism." Continuing his tactical retreat, Hu conceded that a recent proliferation of unauthorized liberal tabloids (*xiaobao*) in several Chinese cities represented a harmful tendency that should be boycotted and opposed.[72]

At this point in Hu's remarks, Deng Liqun reportedly interrupted with a sharp dig at the general secretary's liberal friends in the official media, pointing out that some of the underground tabloids in question had actually been set up, financed, and controlled by the party's own newspapers. Presumably, Little Deng had in mind such underground journals as *Yecao* (Weeds), published in Guangzhou, which had run two articles highly critical of him, calling him, among other things, a "sycophantic yes-man" who was out to "curry favor with Deng Xiaoping."[73]

Deng Liqun's hard-line literary policies resulted in renewed political pressure being brought to bear on China's critical intellectuals. In March 1985 a serialized essay written by investigative journalist Liu Binyan, entitled "Dierzhong zhongcheng" (A second kind of loyalty), was banned from publication, as was the tabloid that had featured it.[74] In this controversial essay, Liu argued that the party Central Committee lacked the courage to acknowledge that it had committed a number of grave mistakes in the past. Decrying the leadership's proclivity to deny categorically (or cover up) its errors, Liu disparaged the type of loyalty displayed by "obedient tools" of the party, such as Lei Feng, who always agreed with their superiors and compulsively glorified the party's line and policies. In place of such mindless obeisance, Liu proposed a higher standard of fealty: individual moral conscience—and the courage to follow it. Acknowledging that this second kind of loyalty was extremely rare in modern-day China, he attributed its scarcity to the fact that its practitioners "have often had to pay the price of freedom, happiness, or even life itself for their kind of loyalty." Under such unfavorable conditions, he argued, "the fact that it has survived at all is a miracle."[75]

The first installment of "A Second Kind of Loyalty" appeared in the inaugural issue of the magazine *Kaituo* (Pioneer) in January 1985. The issue was quickly withdrawn from circulation, and Beijing authorities banned subsequent installments. Somewhat disingenuously, party leaders gave two reasons for banning Liu's essay: first, the author had belittled the campaign to learn from Lei Feng; second, he had touched on "sensitive issues" involving relations between the Communist parties of China and the Soviet Union.[76]

Liu Binyan's call to oppose blind obedience to higher authority was anathema to party traditionalists. Equally unacceptable were the ideas of writer Wang Ruowang, who, like Liu, had repeatedly asserted the primacy of the demands of individual conscience over the mandates of the state. Wang's works, too, were now banned from publication.[77]

Guerrilla warfare between Deng Liqun and Hu Yaobang continued for several months. In mid-April 1985 Little Deng, with the help of his patron Hu Qiaomu, succeeded in embarrassing Hu Yaobang by arranging to have the full text of the general secretary's February remarks concerning restrictions on press freedom published in *People's Daily*—without Hu's prior approval—while the general secretary was away on a visit to Australia and New Zealand.[78]

Seeking to even the score upon his return to China, Hu Yaobang held a lengthy (and at times seemingly indiscreet) interview with a friendly Hong Kong journalist named Lu Keng. Responding to the interviewer's query about his adversarial relationship with Deng Liqun, Hu obliquely damned Little Deng with faint praise, claiming that he was a man of great talent who should not be held solely responsible for all the shortcomings and mistakes in the party's ideological work.[79]

Not to be outdone, Deng Liqun launched a broadside of his own, zeroing in once again on liberals in the mass media and their supporters in the party hierarchy. In one statement, he noted with deep alarm that "some people" in the party and the media treat as outmoded ideas such hallowed CCP traditions as plain living, sacrifice, and hard struggle. In another statement, he observed ruefully that under the onslaught of monetary transactions, China's "spiritual pillar" had been seriously eroded, to the point where "it has now become inadvisable to advocate . . . communist morality."[80]

Little Deng's tactics apparently had a certain effect. At the end of spring, third-echelon liberal Hu Qili, who only a few months earlier had championed total creative freedom for writers and artists, spoke out on the need to "criticize, educate, and help" those misguided party members who, "having lost their socialist and communist convictions and ideals, have even advocated Western 'democracy' and 'freedom' and advertised the bourgeoisie's liberal thinking."[81]

Notwithstanding Deng Liqun's heavy-handedness and Hu Qili's softening spine, Hu Yaobang got the last laugh, at least for the time being. Early in the summer, without comment or explanation, Deng Liqun was removed from his position as director of the CC's propaganda department; named to replace him was Zhu Houze, Hu's ally and a strong supporter of creative freedom for artists and writers. At the time, it was widely rumored (though never confirmed) that Deng Liqun's dismissal was related to his indiscreet criticism of Deng Xiaoping's open policy.[82]

THE STRUGGLE OVER SEZs AND THE OPEN POLICY

Central to the bubbling furor over bourgeois liberalism was mounting conservative discomfort with the free-wheeling economic and social environment of China's fourteen open coastal cities and SEZs, in particular the thriving South China township of Shenzhen, just across the border from Hong Kong. Shenzhen's close proximity to, and increasingly intimate financial and social contacts with, the largest capitalist entrepôt in East Asia made it an especially tempting target for those who had serious questions about the nature and implications of China's wide-ranging reforms.

In the winter of 1984–85 the Chinese press had been filled with favorable publicity concerning Shenzhen's remarkable progress as a model development zone.[83] But in early spring, new concerns were voiced over a rising tide of illicit commercial activities, including foreign exchange laundering, fraudulent bank loans, excessive wage and bonus payments to workers and managers, smuggling, gambling, prostitution, and pornography.[84] As spring turned to summer, the attack grew sharper. Speaking during a tour of the Xiamen SEZ in late June, Hu Qiaomu warned against giving preferential treatment to foreign investors in the SEZs. Citing the disastrous experience of the Qing dynasty in granting economic privileges and concessions to foreign powers in the late nineteenth century, Hu cautioned against giving up Chinese rights to outside interests, and he insisted that "foreign investment enterprises are not concessions; their inordinate demands cannot be given tacit consent."[85] Later in the summer, the irrepressible Deng Liqun joined the chorus, stating that all patriotic Chinese should "oppose the trend of worshipping things foreign and fawning on foreigners."[86]

The critics may have hoped to derail China's economic reforms by attacking them at their point of greatest vulnerability. Other major elements of the reform program, most notably the rural agricultural responsibility system, were less susceptible to challenge because of their visible contribution to the nation's economic growth, and to the rising family incomes of the majority of China's eight hundred million rural dwellers. But the open policy was vulnerable to criticism on the highly sensitive issues of national sovereignty and bourgeois corrosion. By pointing out the twin dangers of selling out the nation's independence to foreigners and breathing too closely the toxic fumes of capitalism, conservatives could hope to cast dark shadows on the propriety of liberal reform.

Confronted with mounting economic difficulties and a rising conservative backlash, the reformers gave additional ground. Backing away from his earlier defense of the economic freedom and autonomy of the SEZs, Deng Xiaoping in early July allowed that the SEZs were merely an experiment whose correctness had yet to be demonstrated.[87] Concurrently, the Chinese government announced that ten of the fourteen coastal cities opened to foreign investors in the spring of 1984 would slow down the signing of new contracts with foreigners.[88]

But if Deng Xiaoping was willing to retreat a bit on the SEZs and open cities, he was clearly not prepared to backtrack on the general principles of his open policy. In October 1984 he had argued that the open policy was needed to overcome three hundred years of impoverishment, backwardness, and ignorance caused by China's self-imposed isolation from the outside world.[89] Six months later, in the face of a mounting furor over the spread of bourgeois corrosion along China's exposed eastern seaboard, Deng dug in his heels: "To open to the world is a fundamental policy for China," he insisted. "If there is to be any change in the policy, it will be that China's doors will be opened even wider."[90] Although the details of the SEZ and open-city experiments might be subject to negotiation and compromise, the open policy itself was not.

REFORM OF THE PLA

In the midst of the swirling ideological currents of 1984–85, an important series of structural reforms was carried out, affecting China's military establishment. Long a bastion of neo-Maoist thinking, the PLA high command had stubbornly resisted implementing Deng Xiaoping's reform policies. Each time reformers had attempted to make inroads, military pressure had forced them to back off.[91] Frustrated by such intransigence, Deng Xiaoping had on more than one occasion since 1981 referred to members of the PLA's senior officer corps as "undisciplined, arrogant, extravagant, and lazy."[92]

Following the exposure of serious corruption in a PLA tank division under the command of "survivor" General Li Desheng late in 1983, the mass media began to criticize the persistence of Leftist tendencies within the army.[93] When the party consolidation drive entered its second stage in the early winter of 1984–85, pressure on the PLA began to increase noticeably. Reformers now brought two main weapons to bear on the army: retirement and reorganization.[94] In late December it was announced that forty senior general staff officers had opted to retire—the largest top-level group retirement in PLA history. In an interview that accompanied the announcement, Deng Xiaoping said he "hoped to see more open-minded people in the army." Most of the retiring officers were over the age of sixty; several had served as section chiefs, equivalent to the rank of lieutenant general and above.[95]

This pruning of the general staff was followed, in early January 1985, by an announcement of substantial cutbacks in military budgets and manpower. PLA Chief of Staff Yang Dezhi, a Deng Xiaoping appointee, explained the cuts as being vital to the success of the nation's overall modernization drive. To reduce military outlays and pave the way for a much-needed technological upgrading of the armed forces, Yang argued, it was necessary to streamline the PLA and reduce noncombatant personnel.[96]

In a bold reorganization measure, several hundred thousand PLA security troops were demobilized and reassigned to a state security force known as the People's Armed Police (PAP). In a related move, the PLA Railway Corps, long reputed to be a haven for unreconstructed Maoists, was placed under civilian jurisdiction. Finally, thousands of factories engaged in defense production were turned over to the manufacture of nonmilitary consumer goods, such as motorcycles and electrical appliances.[97]

Predictably, many aging veterans of the PLA's early guerrilla struggles, who continued to staff the upper levels of the military hierarchy, were unmoved by the logic of such reforms. In their speeches they now began to refer defensively to the importance of giving "careful consideration" to any changes that might undermine the nation's military preparedness. Ignoring such precautionary pleas, the reformers pushed on, with Deng Xiaoping's clear blessing. In a highly symbolic gesture laced with deep political overtones, it was announced that the streamlined PLA would soon be outfitted with new uniforms, complete with insignias of rank, which had been abolished at Mao Zedong's behest in 1965, on the eve of the Cultural Revolution.[98]

Shortly after the 1985 Lunar New Year, a number of additional military reorganization measures were introduced. In early March it was announced that forty-seven thousand officers, approximately 10 percent of the entire officer corps, would be retired before the end of 1986, with twenty to thirty thousand additional officers slated for retirement by 1990. In disclosing this decision, the official Xinhua News Agency said the officers to be demobilized had joined the PLA during the anti-Japanese and civil wars of the 1930s and 1940s. Most were said to have attained junior rank up to regimental level—the equivalent of major—or lower. To help mollify the new retirees, a program of improved military pensions and welfare benefits, including new housing, was instituted.[99]

In April, while on a visit to New Zealand, Hu Yaobang announced that within the next year the Chinese Army would be subject to conventional force reductions totaling one million men, amounting to approximately 25 percent of the current force level. The money saved was to be earmarked for the technological modernization of China's antiquated weapons systems and for upgrading the professional qualifications of the officer corps.[100]

In May a Hong Kong journalist asked Hu Yaobang whether disgruntled military critics of reform, including controversial regional commander Li Desheng (whom the interviewer characterized as "a nail that can't be pulled out") might use troops under their command to resist further military cutbacks, including their own forced retirement. Hu responded that such a thing would be "absolutely impossible" and could "never occur in our party." Responding to a question about whether General Li Desheng was untouchable, Hu answered cryptically: "Outsiders *think* he cannot be removed."[101]

In early June the other shoe dropped. At a meeting of the party MAC, chaired by Deng Xiaoping, it was decided to "readjust" once more the regional command structure of the PLA, consolidating the eleven existing military regions into seven, and pensioning off several superannuated regional commanders—including the untouchable General Li Desheng, who was offered a postretirement sinecure as political commissar of the National Defense University. The Xinhua dispatch that announced the shake-up pointedly noted that younger, better educated, and professionally more competent officers had been selected to succeed the retiring commanders. By the end of summer, the readjustment had resulted in a full 50 percent reduction in the number of senior officers in the seven newly consolidated regional commands, and a 24 percent cut in the number of ranking officers at the PLA general staff headquarters, the GPD, and the General Logistics Department.[102] Interestingly, a disproportionate number of the regional commanders and field officers who managed to survive the "readjustment" of 1985 had strong pre-1949 ties to Deng Xiaoping through their prior affiliation with Deng's Second Field Army.[103]

The influence of the PLA was further reduced by a series of top-level CCP leadership changes carried out at the end of summer 1985. At the Twelfth CC's Fourth Plenum, held in mid-September, six of China's highest-ranking veteran military leaders—Ye Jianying, Nie Rongzhen, Xu Xiangqian, Wang Zhen, Song Renqiong, and Li Desheng—retired en masse from the Politburo.[104] Their resignations left only a token contingent of professional soldiers sitting on the party's highest decision-making body. To help ease the pain of retirement, all outgoing Politburo members were appointed to the CAC. Among the small handful of military figures who remained on the Politburo were longtime Deng Xiaoping associates Yang Shangkun and Yang Dezhi. To all outward appearances, the reformers had succeeded in taming the PLA.[105]

THE THIRD ECHELON ARRIVES

The retirement of the six Politburo military veterans represented only a small fraction of a much larger turnover in party leadership that took place in September 1985. After three years of alternately persuading, cajoling, and demanding that elderly cadres step down in favor of younger blood, Deng Xiaoping's youth movement finally reached fruition.[106] Altogether, sixty-four full and alternate members of the Central Committee announced their retirement at the Fourth Plenum. With three exceptions, all were over the age of sixty-seven, including forty-four septuagenarians and seven octogenarians. Included among the outgoing leaders were one member of the Politburo Standing Committee (Ye Jianying), nine ordinary Politburo members, and twenty-six senior army officers In addition to the six retiring PLA marshals and generals mentioned above, the civilian Politburo retirees were Deng Yingchao (age eighty-one), Ulanfu (seventy-nine), and Zhang Tingfa (sixty-seven).[107] It was widely reported that among the many inducements offered to elderly Politburo members to ease their retirement was the appointment of their offspring or other relatives to high-level administrative or commercial positions.[108]

Seven members of the Politburo old guard succeeded in avoiding retirement at the September plenum: Deng Xiaoping, Chen Yun, Li Xiannian, Peng Zhen, Yang Shangkun, Hu Qiaomu, and Yang Dezhi. With Ye Jianying's resignation, the Politburo's Standing Committee was now reduced from six members to five, creating a virtual deadlock between the committee's first-echelon conservatives, Chen Yun and Li Xiannian, and its second-echelon liberals, Hu Yaobang and Zhao Ziyang. In this situation, Deng Xiaoping—as usual—occupied the pivotal swing position.

At the time of the Fourth Plenum it was rumored that the conservatives had wanted to promote Peng Zhen to the SC to replace Ye Jianying, while the liberals preferred to add third-echelon newcomer Hu Qili.[109] With neither side willing to budge, and with Deng refusing to commit himself one way or the other, no one was selected. According to reports circulating in Beijing toward the end of 1985, Peng Zhen's popularity and prestige were badly damaged— and along with them his hopes for advancement to the Standing Committee— when the local citizenry angrily opposed his grandiose scheme to tear down a large residential neighborhood near the Great Hall of the People to make room for an expensive new municipal government complex.[110]

To replace the retiring Central Committee members, a special "national party conference" was convened on September 18, immediately following adjournment of the Fourth Plenum. The convening of this special conference was another of Deng Xiaoping's many ad hoc organizational improvisations. Although the 1982 party constitution stipulated that the National Party Congress elects members of the Central Committee, the Thirteenth Party Congress was not scheduled to meet for another two years. Not wanting to wait that long to select new leaders, Deng resorted to creative institution-making. When asked why the task of replacing elderly Central Committee members could not be put off until the Thirteenth Congress, Deng's spokesperson Zhu Muzhi said, "We cannot wait two years. . . . By then some comrades' state of health might have changed. . . . It is better to make gradual changes now."[111]

Of the sixty-four new CC members and alternates selected at the September 1985 party conference, the overwhelming majority belonged to the third echelon. Seventy-six percent were college educated; their average age was just over fifty.[112]

At the Fifth Plenum of the Twelfth CC, held immediately following the national party conference, six newcomers were named to the Politburo, including two men tabbed by informed sources as likely successors to Premier Zhao and General Secretary Hu, respectively. The first, Vice-Premier Li Peng (age fifty-six), was a Soviet-trained, Russian-speaking engineer with experience primarily in the hydroelectric power industry. He was the adopted son of outgoing Politburo member Deng Yingchao and the late Premier Zhou Enlai. The second major Politburo newcomer, Central Secretariat member Hu Qili (fifty-six), was a protégé of Hu Yaobang, under whose leadership he had previously toiled as a cadre in the CYL.

Other new faces in the Politburo included fifty-six-year-old Vice-Premier Tian Jiyun, a reform economist; former CCP Organization Department Director Qiao Shi (sixty-one), who reputedly had ties to Peng Zhen; and Foreign Minister Wu Xueqian, sixty-four. A sixth newcomer, sixty-eight-year-old Vice-Premier Yao Yilin, a conservative economic planner with strong ties to Chen Yun, was promoted from alternate to full Politburo status. Members of the third echelon also gained five seats on the party's Central Secretariat. In addition to Politburo appointees Li, Tian, and Qiao, the other newcomers were Wang Zhaoguo (forty-four), director of the party's General Office, and

Deng Xiaoping and Hu Yaobang review PLA units. Hu's civilian clothes underscore his lack of military experience and credibility.

Hao Jianxu (fifty), a former cotton mill worker who had served briefly as textile minister (and who was the only female promoted to a top party post at the September party meeting).

The drive to promote talented, energetic younger people to party leadership roles was also mirrored in the CCP's shifting recruitment policies and priorities at the grass-roots level. Between 1984 and 1987 the proportion of party members with at least a senior high school education rose from 17.8 percent to 28.5 percent of the total; in the same period, almost a million college graduates were added to the roster of the CCP—the largest influx of intellectuals in party history.[113]

For all the younger generation's highly acclaimed advances, however, party traditionalists managed to avoid a clean sweep in the leadership changes of September 1985. In addition to the carryover of certain members of the Politburo old guard, conservatives also won two other skirmishes: first, despite intense opposition from the party's liberal wing, Deng Liqun was permitted to retain his seat on the Central Secretariat; second, the PLA high command flatly refused to ratify Deng Xiaoping's choice of Hu Yaobang to succeed him as chairman of the party's MAC.[114]

Hu's problems with the PLA leadership were legendary. In a 1986 incident, Deng Xiaoping sent a memo to Hu concerning the political situation in Taiwan, requesting a contingency plan for dealing with a possible Taiwanese declaration of independence following President Chiang Ching-kuo's death.

Hu wrote on the memo, "Attack Taiwan with 50,000 or 500,000 troops." Hu Qili, also asked for his opinion, wrote "Use missiles. Conquer Taiwan in three days." Apprised of their responses, a high-ranking PLA official laughed: "Pundits! How bookish. How do we send troops in if we don't have control of the air? How could such persons control our armed forces?"[115]

For Hu Yaobang, who had long been a thorn in the side of PLA hard-liners, the army's adamant refusal to accept his leadership eventually proved to be a fatal blow, forcing Deng Xiaoping, reluctantly, to resume his search for an acceptable successor.

Reflecting the mixed outcome of the leadership changes of September 1985, Deng Xiaoping's closing address to the national party conference contained a strong, measured appeal to all factions to close ranks in pursuit of the twin objectives of reform and "socialist spiritual civilization." Calling on his old comrades to overcome ossified thinking and his new comrades to resist the temptations of bourgeois liberalization—which he now ominously equated with "taking the capitalist road"—China's paramount leader sought once more to chart a middle course between the Scylla of dogmatism and the Charybdis of spiritual pollution.[116]

Social Origins of Student Protest:
Summer 1985–December 1986

I am here to tell you that the socialist movement, from Marx
and Lenin to Stalin and Mao Zedong, has been a failure. I think
that complete Westernization is the only way to modernize.

Fang Lizhi, November 1986

FOR A variety of reasons, Deng's middle course became progressively harder to steer. Despite the paramount leader's periodic pleas for stability and unity, a series of reform-related stresses now began to tear seriously at the social fabric of urban China. Three emergent social trends contributed to this overall effect, commingling and ultimately synergizing to produce the beginnings of a serious urban crisis. The first was a new wave of free expression in literature and the arts; the second was a mounting mood of urban socioeconomic malaise and alienation; the third was a sharp rise in the urban crime rate.

Partly inspired by China's rapidly expanding cultural contacts with the outside world, and facilitated by the July 1985 removal of Deng Liqun from his post as party propaganda chief, Chinese art and literature received a liberal boost in the summer of 1985. Encouraged by Little Deng's reformist successor, Zhu Houze, and by the renowned writer and newly appointed minister of culture Wang Meng, Chinese intellectuals enjoyed a period of enhanced creative expression. The new era, which lasted approximately sixteen months, witnessed a strong revival of pre–spiritual pollution–era philosophical debates—over socialist alienation, humanism, the current relevance of Marxist economic theory, and so forth.

In mid-1985 Wang Ruoshui launched the liberal revival with a pointed refutation of Hu Qiaomu's January 1984 critique of Zhou Yang's theory of "alienation under socialism." Shortly thereafter, "Ma Ding," a pseudonymous academic economist, wrote a controversial article questioning the contemporary relevance of nineteenth-century Marxist economic theories. At around the same time, a third liberal critic, Liu Zaifu, launched a bold philosophical defense of the concept of universal humanism.[1]

The period 1985–86 also witnessed a number of collateral innovations on the cultural front. These included the proliferation of professional societies in a variety of academic and technical fields; the production of bold new theatrical, cinematic, artistic, and literary works;[2] the birth of several proreform newspapers and magazines;[3] and an outpouring of hard-hitting sociopolitical commentaries by such respected liberal critics as Liu Binyan, Su Shaozhi, Wang Ruowang, and Fang Lizhi. In many respects it seemed that an incipient "civil society" might be emerging in China, one in which the opinions and attitudes of the creative and critical intelligentsia would play an expanded role in charting the country's future course of development.[4]

THE MOBILIZATION OF URBAN DISCONTENT

The second major trend that emerged in 1985 was an increase in social mobilization and protest among various urban social groups and strata. Increasingly since the early 1980s, the fabric of urban life in China had been strained by the manifold contradictions and adverse by-products of partial, discontinuous reform. Frequent policy oscillations within the fang/shou cycle, combined with serious inflation, rampant official corruption, and a host of other reform-related inequities in the social distribution of the costs and benefits of reform, had resulted in a pronounced rise in the level of urban frustration, alienation, envy, and anger. For the first time since the reforms were introduced in the winter of 1978–79, Chinese cities now began to witness significant social unrest.[5]

On the surface, the various urban disturbances that broke out in 1985 seemed random, spontaneous, and almost wholly unrelated. In May a riot occurred at a Beijing soccer match, touched off when a team of Hong Kong Chinese unexpectedly defeated the local club. Shortly thereafter, a group of three hundred former Beijing residents who had been "sent down" to rural areas in Shanxi Province in the last years of the Maoist era held a sit-in at the headquarters of the Beijing municipal government, demanding the right to return to their homes in the Chinese capital. In late May a new round of price decontrols in Beijing triggered inflationary fears, giving rise to a fresh wave of vocal complaints and letters to newspapers from anxious, angry consumers.[6]

Chinese students, too, grew more restive in 1985. Their unhappiness stemmed from multiple sources, including poor food and unhealthy dormitory conditions on college campuses, low monthly stipends (averaging around RMB ¥22), rising living costs, and flagrant profiteering by gaogan zidi.[7] Toward the end of summer, students began to show signs of social activism. On September 18, on the occasion of the fifty-fourth anniversary of Japan's invasion of Manchuria, one thousand college students in Beijing took to the streets to protest Japanese Prime Minister Nakasone's visit to a Shinto shrine honoring the militarists who had launched Japan's World War II invasion of China.

Posters wielded by student protesters in Tiananmen Square alluded to mounting popular resentment over a "new economic invasion" from Japan and called for a boycott of Japanese products; others criticized Chinese university authorities for trying to intimidate students by threatening to withhold job assignments after graduation; still others took a dim view of all authority, calling on the masses to rise up against "bureaucrats [who] make up rules and regulations whenever they please . . . [telling] us we can't march, . . . can't go to Tiananmen Square because they tell us not to."[8] In response to what was said to be the largest Chinese student protest in over a decade, Beijing police arrested several demonstrators. In November a fresh wave of student disturbances occurred, in open protest over the recent Japanese "economic invasion."[9]

China's top leaders were said to be deeply concerned about the latent antigovernment, antireform overtones of the new demonstrations. On November 16 a Reuters dispatch reported that a Central Committee directive, seen in Hong Kong, had referred to the student protests as potentially posing "the gravest challenge since the downfall of the Gang of Four."[10] This rather startling revelation lent credence to unconfirmed reports that the student demonstrations had been secretly orchestrated and encouraged by offspring of CCP conservatives, who had suffered something of a setback at the hands of liberal reformers at the September national party conference. According to this theory, the predominant anti-Japanese theme of the student protests reflected the conservatives' attempt to convert growing popular concern over urban economic conditions into a movement to oppose Deng's open policy.[11] While there may have been an element of truth to this hypothesis (insofar as conservatives seldom wasted an opportunity to point out the corrupting effects of economic reform), it is unlikely that the primary source of campus unrest in 1985 was backstage agitprop by disaffected gaogan zidi. Had it not been for the existence of widespread popular concern over perceived gaps and inequities in the reform program, any attempt to manufacture or covertly manipulate student protest would most likely have failed to produce significant results.[12]

Mounting urban unrest also expressed itself in a resurgence of antiforeign chauvinism and racial intolerance on Chinese college campuses. On the occasion of "Sino-African Friendship Day" in the autumn of 1985, several hundred Chinese students at Tianjin University blockaded the school's canteen, shouting insults at African students gathered there and making angry allegations of social and sexual misconduct. In a similar incident in the spring of 1986, eighteen African students in Beijing were besieged by approximately five hundred male Chinese students at a dance, resulting in several injuries. Two weeks later, a group of two hundred African students demonstrated in Beijing against racial discrimination on campus.[13] Among the accusations leveled against African students in this period were complaints that they had engaged in sexual relations —sometimes forcibly—with Chinese coeds, and that they habitually played their stereo equipment at maximum volume in campus dormitories, thereby interfering with the studies of Chinese students.[14]

Other campus disturbances were unrelated to racial tensions. In late December 1985, fifteen hundred students at the Beijing Agricultural University occupied campus dormitories and staged a march in protest over the continued presence of military personnel on campus.[15] At around the same time, a group of approximately one hundred Uighur students demonstrated in Beijing in a protest against continued Chinese nuclear weapons testing in Lop Nor, Xinjiang.[16]

In the relatively permissive urban political climate of 1985–86, students and others could give vent to their frustrations and anxieties more openly than at any time since the winter of 1978–79. In one incident, reported in the Hong Kong press, a high-ranking Chinese military officer, whose son had been arrested during the September 18 anti-Japanese demonstration at Tiananmen Square, managed to gain the youth's release from custody when Deng Xiaoping personally intervened on his behalf. Thereafter, students throughout Beijing reportedly felt free to express their feelings of alienation and discontent, perceiving themselves to be relatively safe from the threat of arbitrary arrest and detention.[17]

AMPLIFYING DISCONTENT: THE URBAN BACKLASH

Despite bringing enhanced freedom of expression, China's increasingly permissive urban milieu was a distinctly mixed blessing: while containing the embryo of an emergent civil society, marked by incipient socioeconomic pluralism and the first stirrings of autonomous behavior on the part of newly emerging social forces, it also served to amplify all the various social cleavages and contradictions engendered in the process of discontinuous, incomplete reform. The result was a situation that was both highly stressful and increasingly volatile.

As early as mid-1985, public opinion polls began registering a slight downturn in popular enthusiasm for reform. In one eleven-city, sixteen-county survey taken in February, over 80 percent of the 2,400 urban respondents queried reported a rise in their standard of living since the advent of reform; by July of the same year, however, a follow-up survey revealed that the number had declined to 70 percent, with a threefold increase in the number of people who indicated that their living standard had actually declined overall. Not surprisingly, those who experienced a decline in living standards were noticeably less enthusiastic about reform than those who felt themselves to be doing well. By early 1986, public enthusiasm for economic reform had further dwindled: now, only 29 percent of urban residents surveyed felt that the reforms provided equal opportunity for all; by November of the same year, almost 75 percent of the people queried expressed dissatisfaction with rising inflation.[18]

Young people were especially sensitive to the mounting pressures and stresses of reform. Surveys in 1986 revealed a youth culture that was becoming significantly more cynical, materialistic, and hedonistic—and considerably less idealistic—than that of preceding generations. For many urbanites, young and old alike, perceptions of unequal opportunity fueled a mounting sense of resentment. As revealed in various opinion surveys of this period, urban residents were becoming more and more convinced that the costs and benefits of reform had been inequitably distributed. For example, pollsters frequently encountered the view that whereas private entrepreneurs and getihu could pass rising costs on to consumers, and whereas government cadres could use their authority and/or commercial contacts to profit handsomely from buying and selling goods and materials acquired in the state sector, "ordinary folks" (including industrial workers, lower-level administrative staff, students, housewives, and intellectuals, inter alia) had no such options or opportunities available to them.[19] Partly reflecting the prevalence of such views, there were increasing reports of reform-related labor disturbances in the summer of 1986, including strikes, work slowdowns, and even occasional riots.[20]

The rising sense of popular malaise was also affected by the third major social trend of the mid-1980s—a new urban crime wave. After dropping sharply toward the end of 1983, the nation's crime rate began to creep upward again in 1984. By 1985, crime and corruption were said to be increasing almost geometrically.[21] In response to the rising tide of lawlessness, one million new public security personnel were added in 1985;[22] the following year a nationwide crackdown on crime was initiated, with a reversion to earlier techniques of mass trials, heavy sentences, perfunctory appeals, and, in the most severe cases, immediate executions. It was widely rumored (but never officially confirmed) that the new crackdown had been precipitated by two incidents in the summer of 1986: the rape of a high-level official's daughter in Beijing, and the armed robbery of a high cadre on the road from Beijing to the seaside resort of Beidaihe, near Tianjin. As in previous anticrime campaigns, the objective of the new crackdown was to intimidate and deter potential lawbreakers through the demonstration effect of harsh, immediate punishment.[23]

Although these three emerging urban trends of 1985–86 —creative freedom for intellectuals, social mobilization of urban unrest, and rising crime—were not formally interconnected, their effects tended to reinforce each other. With rising freedom of expression accompanied by rising crime rates, and with higher food prices commingling with higher frustrations, the resulting social chemistry was becoming quite volatile, and more than a little worrisome to China's leaders.

POLITICAL REFORM REDIVIVUS: THE SUMMER OF 1986

In part because of the perceived worsening of urban unrest, and in part because of the growing political influence of the third echelon, pressures for political reform began to build again in the winter of 1985–86. In January CASS published in its official journal a lengthy critique of China's system of government administration. Reporting on a National Conference on Administrative Reform held in November 1985, the journal claimed that previous efforts to rationalize China's administrative structure had failed because they lacked a systemic viewpoint and paid inadequate attention to political reform as an essential prerequisite for successful economic reform. To remedy these failings, CASS analysts argued, it was necessary to do two main things: (1)

completely separate the party from economic decision making and adminis-tration; and (2) institute a civil-service system for the recruitment, promotion, and dismissal of cadres.[24]

The CASS recommendations were prepared at the initiative of third-eche-lon reformers, whose political influence had increased significantly in the af-termath of the September 1985 national party conference. Supported by Zhao Ziyang and Hu Yaobang, the third echelon's rising stature was confirmed in January 1986 when a new party rectification "leading group" was set up under third-echelon cadres Qiao Shi and Wang Zhaoguo for the purpose of monitor-ing improvements in the party's work style. Henceforth, elderly CDIC/CAC watchdogs such as Chen Yun and Bo Yibo would share the rectification spot-light with these technocratic newcomers.[25]

The new rectification leading group was created at a meeting attended by eight thousand party cadres. Significantly, none of the CCP's three top senior leaders—Deng Xiaoping, Chen Yun, and Li Xiannian—was in attendance. While not replacing the conservative-dominated CDIC, the new body was given a broad mandate to make recommendations on a variety of issues affect-ing party organization, discipline, and spirit.[26]

The divergence in outlook between the revolutionary cadres of the first two echelons and the technocratic reformers of the third echelon was striking. In analyzing problems of economic crime and corruption, for example, the younger leaders tended to stress the systemic, structural sources of aberrant conduct, arguing that institutional reform was a prerequisite to improved party discipline and work style; by contrast, old-guard conservatives tended to stress the moral and spiritual sources of behavioral malfeasance, arguing that it was individuals, not institutions, that required remolding.

In the spring of 1986, progressive reformers of the third echelon gained Deng Xiaoping's sympathetic ear. Under their influence, Deng revived his August 1980 call to reform China's ossified, overbureaucratized leadership system at an April meeting of provincial governors.[27] At another meeting held in the same month, Deng pointed to the inseparability of economic and politi-cal reform, posing the rhetorical question, "What good is it to decentralize power [to enterprise managers] . . . if it is always being taken back again [by party committees]?" Two months later, at a party meeting on June 20, Deng suggested that much of the official racketeering recently uncovered in China was not merely coincidental or occasional, but was the product of basic flaws in the political system. Without taking action to reform the system, he argued, it would be impossible to root out unhealthy tendencies in the party. "All comrades," he instructed, "should consider the problem of reform of the po-litical structure." At the same meeting, Deng made the provocative suggestion that China's ruling Communist Party should be "subject to restrictions."[28]

With Deng once again receptive to the idea of political reform, something like a bandwagon effect took shape. First to fall into line were the mass media. Taking their lead—and much of their language—from Deng's 1980 treatise on leadership reform, the media, under the overall direction of newly installed

CCP propaganda chief Zhu Houze, now began to publish frequent articles criticizing such feudal remnants as patriarchal authority, bureaucratic work styles, corrupt personal networks based on kinship, special cadre privileges, and a host of other serious abuses in the political system.[29] Increasingly, newspapers and journals treated political reform as a vital guarantee against future abuses of power and an essential prerequisite for successful economic reform.

Many of the key theoretical articles on political reform were written by CASS scholars. Among the most active reform theorists in this period were Yan Jiaqi, director of the CASS Institute of Political Science; Su Shaozhi, director of the CASS Institute of Marxism–Leninism–Mao Zedong Thought; and Li Honglin, director of the Fujian provincial Social Science Academy. Party leaders prominent in the political reform revival included Hu Qili, Tian Jiyun, Wang Zhaoguo, Zhu Houze, and Yan Mingfu, director of the CC's united front work department.

In June CASS political scientist Yan Jiaqi published a broad critique of the Chinese political system. In Yan's analysis, which closely paralleled Deng's 1980 report, the Chinese polity suffered from four main defects, all of which were traceable to the "overconcentration of power":

> (1) We have never defined the scope of functions, powers, and responsibilities of party organizations, as distinct from governmental organizations. . . . Party organizations at all levels have, in practice, taken on matters which should have been handled by [executive] organs of state power. . . . (2) Not only does the party function in place of executive agencies, but the system of people's congresses has never functioned effectively. . . . (3) Powers are overcentralized, so that the initiative of local authorities cannot be brought fully into play. . . . (4) We have never defined the scope of functions, powers, and responsibilities of governmental bodies as distinct from those of economic enterprises and social institutions. [Hence,] enterprises and institutions became, in effect, subsidiary bodies of executive agencies.[30]

Although Yan Jiaqi did not directly address the sensitive issue of political democratization, a handful of other liberal scholars did, albeit circumspectly. This was uncharted territory, insofar as advocacy of anything other than "socialist democracy" (i.e., democracy under party leadership) could be construed as contravening the four cardinal principles. Those writers who did broach the subject of democracy generally limited themselves to attacking safe, preapproved targets, such as the (conveniently unnamed) "some feudal patriarchs," who purportedly "never consult with subordinates" and "always arbitrarily impose their will on others." Such people, wrote social scientist Li Honglin in June, "tremble with fear whenever they hear the word 'democracy.'" They treat democracy as a "weapon used by subordinates and the masses against higher-ups and cadres, a force to weaken and shatter stability and unity, even something tantamount to anarchy." Worse yet, wrote Li, they "take any expression of different opinions as a sign of rebellion, and put any convenient political label upon those who voice them."[31]

The issue of the detrimental effects of political labeling and intimidation was taken up by Vice-Premier Wan Li in an address to a national conference on "soft sciences" in late July. Arguing that such feudal practices had caused great damage in the past, Wan proposed the adoption of legislation to protect people engaged in policy-oriented research from the threat of political pressure, intimidation, or recrimination. Along similar lines, he presented a strong defense of the principle of independence and political insulation for social science think tanks.[32]

With few exceptions, the great majority of voices calling for political reform in the spring and summer of 1986 were moderate, technocratic, and non-provocative. Advocating such limited measures as enhanced administrative rationalization, expanded freedom of expression, and legislative supervision within the existing framework of Leninist party leadership, they stopped well short of proposing radical innovations such as limited government, separation of powers, or multiparty competition. Though a few theoretical articles spoke approvingly of such Western concepts as checks and balances (*zhiheng*), they did so only to the extent that such devices might be applied within the Communist Party, not between the party and other institutions. Similarly, the American doctrine of three separate, coequal branches of government, while occasionally praised, for example, for having "prevented the restoration of feudal dictatorship" in the West,[33] was generally rejected as inappropriate for a socialist country such as China, since the doctrine had allegedly been invented "to protect the secure rule of the bourgeoisie."[34]

As reform expectations heightened in the summer of 1986, a flurry of organizational activity took place. In July a conference on reform of the political structure was held at the Central Party School in Beijing. Attended by several hundred younger cadres from various party organs who had been sent by their senior leaders, the conference was addressed by party propaganda chief Zhu Houze. According to those in attendance, Zhu urged the young cadres to study, clarify, and absorb relevant Western, non-Marxist political ideas and institutions. Later, Deng Liqun would allege that "it was this conference that started a new upsurge in liberalism."[35]

Responding to Zhu Houze's call, a few reform theorists began to speak with bolder voices in the late summer of 1986. Yan Jiaqi, for example, now suggested that China should seriously study parliamentary forms of government, while Su Shaozhi recommended the introduction of political pluralism and multiparty competition.[36] Also in this period, Liu Binyan, Fang Lizhi, Wang Ruowang, and Yu Haocheng all began to intensify their ongoing criticisms of the party's prevailing ideological ethos, characterized by blind obedience to authority, monistic interests, "forbidden zones," and intolerance toward creative intellectuals.[37]

Toward the end of summer, the Standing Committee of the Politburo established a five-person "central discussion group for reform of the political structure." Comprising three middle-aged technocratic reformers (Zhao Ziyang, Hu Qili, and Tian Jiyun) and two septuagenarian neotraditionalists (Bo Yibo

Deng Xiaoping cools off during a break at the Beidaihe summer leadership conference.

and Peng Chong), the "five-person group" represented a cross section of China's three echelons of leadership. Though liberals enjoyed a numerical advantage, party seniority favored the elders. The group's mandate, articulated by Deng Xiaoping, was to "clarify the content of political restructuring, and work out the details."[38]

THE QUESTION OF GUIDING PRINCIPLES

Against this background of renewed organizational activity, party leaders gathered in August for their annual midsummer conference at the Bohai Gulf resort of Beidaihe. The main topic on the agenda was how to understand the party's "guiding principles" in an age of societal transformation. While Politburo reformers wanted to push ahead with new definitions and new theoretical guidelines concerning questions of political and ideological orientation, conservatives balked at anything that might undermine the four cardinal principles, preferring instead to stress the struggle against bourgeois liberalization. In the estimation of people like Chen Yun, Li Xiannian, and Peng Zhen, pushing political reform too rapidly could easily undermine social stability; they remained largely unmoved by the argument that political reform was an essential precondition for successful economic reform.[39]

With the two principal factions deeply divided, no new ideological ground could be broken at the summer 1986 Beidaihe meeting. When the Twelfth CC's Sixth Plenum met in late September, China's leaders publicly papered over their differences, passing a highly ambivalent, middle-of-the-road reso-

lution on "building a socialist society with an advanced culture and ideology."
It was a convoluted document, filled with lofty—frequently self-contradictory—moral imperatives. For example, while exalting the four cardinal principles and condemning bourgeois liberalization, the resolution also stressed
the importance of promoting intellectual freedom, democracy, socialist humanism, and learning from advanced capitalist countries.[40] Thus deadlocked,
the Sixth Plenum postponed serious consideration of political reform for another year, until the Thirteenth Party Congress, scheduled to be held in 1987.

Despite the superficial blandness of the CC's resolution on guiding principles, a tense drama reportedly took place behind the scenes at the Sixth Plenum. Originally, Deng Xiaoping had decided not to raise the divisive issue of
bourgeois liberalization at the plenum, for fear of alienating the party's proreform wing. In the course of the meeting, however, he changed his mind.

The event that precipitated Deng's about-face was a speech delivered by Hu
Yaobang. During the debate over the party's guiding principles at the Sixth
Plenum, Hu Yaobang drafted a speech questioning the appropriateness of the
four cardinal principles and proposing as an alternative theory the concept of
"one center and three unshakables." The essence of Hu's draft proposal was to
regard economic construction as the central core of all work, while "unshak-
ably" carrying out structural reform of the economic and political systems and
building a spiritual civilization. Also emphasized in Hu's speech were the
importance of expanding creative freedom for intellectuals and pursuing a
high degree of political democratization as a goal, and not merely an instru-
ment, of reform.[41]

Led by Wang Zhen, conservatives took strong exception to Hu's proposed
draft, directing a flurry of protest toward Deng Xiaoping. Hu Qiaomu and
Deng Liqun reportedly sought to have Hu's speech revised. To placate the
conservatives, Hu belatedly added a section affirming the need to oppose
bourgeois liberalization. An argument ensued, with proreform CAC veteran
Lu Dingyi accusing Hu Yaobang of capitulating to Stalinism. At this point,
Deng Xiaoping stepped in. In a highly emotional speech the patriarch sternly
denounced bourgeois liberalization, warning that if the recent ultraliberal
trend were not opposed, it would "lead our present policies onto the capitalist
road." He reminded reformers that it was not just a few diehard conservatives
who opposed bourgeois liberalization: "I am the one," he claimed, "who has
talked about it most often and most insistently." Immediately after Deng's
impassioned outburst, Wang Zhen eagerly publicized Deng's remarks in a
speech to the Central Party School.[42]

The ostensible reason for Deng's sudden intervention lay in his allegation
that certain party leaders had failed to pay adequate attention to his periodic
warnings against bourgeois liberalization. "Apparently my remarks had no
effect," said Deng. "I understand they were never disseminated. . . . I haven't
changed my mind about opposing spiritual pollution. . . . The struggle against
bourgeois liberalization will last for at least twenty years."[43] Pausing for effect, Deng then added: "If some people don't like hearing this, we will add

another fifty years, so it will last until the middle of the next century."[44] Deng's allusion to his past statements having had no effect suggests that he was aiming his barb at Hu Yaobang, who had instructed party cadres in December 1984 to cease speaking out about spiritual pollution and bourgeois liberalization. Ironically, Deng's complaint about the lack of attention to his views was reminiscent of a sarcastic comment once made by Mao Zedong about Deng himself. At a CC work conference in October 1966, the Chairman observed that whenever he and Deng attended meetings together, "though he was hard of hearing, Deng always took a seat farthest away from me."

With the Central Committee increasingly paralyzed by factional divisions, with political reform shelved for another year, and with Deng Xiaoping growing visibly impatient with party liberals, the momentum of the reformers, built up over a period of several months, was now partially lost. Distancing himself from Hu Yaobang at a crucial point in the debate over political reform and bourgeois liberalism, Deng rendered Hu vulnerable to renewed conservative attack.[45]

Although the activities of the Standing Committee's "five-person group" on reform of the political structure continued following the Sixth Plenum, the prevailing atmosphere in Beijing began to change.[46] The optimism of summer now gave way to pessimism, as rumors began to spread to the effect that liberal ideas and values were about to be criticized once again. Some newspapers began to display visible apprehension over this perceived change in the political climate. On November 1, for example, *Guangming Daily* ran an editorial arguing that just because some people in China no longer saw communism as the ultimate goal, this was no cause for alarm.[47]

The evidence of a new shift in the political wind was fragmentary but palpable: in early November, a second young cadres' conference on reform of the political structure, scheduled to be held at the Beijing Central Party School, found its venue suddenly changed, as the school's two top officials, generals Li Desheng and Wang Zhen, refused permission for the convocation to be held on school premises. In similar fashion, the Chinese Air Force now withdrew its sponsorship from a reform-oriented journal, *Lilun xinxi bao* (Theoretical information news). Shortly thereafter, a nationwide academic conference on political reform, scheduled to be held in Shanghai, was abruptly canceled a few days before its scheduled opening, with no explanation given.[48]

In mid-November conservatives mounted an ideological counterattack against liberalism. Point man for the assault this time was Peng Zhen. Peng indirectly criticized a key economic premise of reform, namely, that it was perfectly all right for some people to get rich before others. Under socialism, he admonished, "people [must] get rich together."[49] Addressing a session of the NPC Standing Committee in late November, Peng turned his attention to politics, noting sarcastically that "Some people cherish bourgeois democracy. To these people, it seems that even the moon in the capitalist world is brighter than the sun in our society."[50] In a pointed rejoinder to liberals who had complained about the undemocratic nature of party discipline, Peng gave the following definition of intraparty democracy: "We follow whatever ideas are correct. If there is no unanimity of views, then the minority submits to the majority, the individual submits to the organization, the lower level submits to the higher level, and the entire country submits to the central government. . . . This is the essential content of our system of collective democracy."[51]

Thus did the conservatives sharpen their polemical swords. With ideological battle-lines drawn, the battle itself was not long in coming.

FANG LIZHI AND THE STUDENTS

During the student demonstrations of autumn 1985, astrophysicist Fang Lizhi had made a series of controversial speeches on Chinese college campuses, including Beijing University (Beida) and Zhejiang University. One of Fang's main themes had been to challenge Chinese students boldly to "break all barriers" that served to impede intellectual awareness and creativity. At Beida he had urged young people to take their future into their own hands, speaking passionately about the continued prevalence of corruption and patronage within the party organization. Unlike most establishment critics, however, Fang Lizhi named names. He cited, for example, the case of Beijing Vice-Mayor Zhang Baifa, who had recently traveled to the United States as a member of an academic delegation attending a seminar on high-energy physics. "What was he doing there?" asked Fang. "This kind of free-loading is corrupt. . . . I don't care if it is Zhang Baifa, I'm going to stand here and say it."[52]

Almost a year after delivering the above remarks, Fang Lizhi went on another multicampus speaking tour. By all accounts, his November 1986 talks were even more provocative than the earlier ones. Speaking at Shanghai's Jiaotong University on November 6, Fang elaborated on the theme of breaking barriers. He now urged students to challenge authority and to demand democratic rights and freedoms, rather than waiting for them to be bestowed from above:

> I really feel that now we should not be afraid of anybody. Some people do not dare to challenge our leaders; but I have found that if you challenge them, they dare not do anything against you. . . . For instance, last year I criticized Zhang Baifa by name. . . . Later he began to find fault with me. But he can no longer pick on anyone now. (Laughter from the audience) In August, I criticized Hu Qiaomu by name at a press conference, and he did not do anything against me. (Laughter from the audience). . . . This year I criticized leaders of the Politburo. (Laughter) . . . I insist on expressing my own opinion. . . .
>
> The core problem is: If China's reforms depend completely on the moves of our top leaders, China will not become a developed nation. . . . Democracy granted by leaders is not true democracy. (Applause) What is the meaning of democracy? Democracy means that each human being has his own rights and that human

beings, each exercising his own rights, form our society. Therefore, rights are in the hands of every citizen. They are not given by top leaders of the nation.[53]

Fang Lizhi reiterated these themes on other college campuses in the Shanghai area. Speaking to students at Tongji University on November 18, he delivered perhaps his most controversial statement: "I am here to tell you that the socialist movement, from Marx and Lenin to Stalin and Mao Zedong, has been a failure. I think that complete Westernization is the only way to modernize." Everywhere Fang went, students were reportedly moved by his words; he rapidly became a campus hero.[54]

Party leaders, including some who had actively supported political reform, were not nearly so enthralled by Fang's provocative rhetoric. On November 30 Vice-Premier Wan Li paid a visit to Fang's home campus, the Chinese University of Science and Technology (CUST) in Hefei, where he delivered a thinly veiled warning from his comrades in Beijing, reminding Fang (who was vice-president of CUST) that university leaders had an obligation to implement the line, principles, and policies of the Communist Party.[55] In an impromptu debate with Fang Lizhi, the vice-premier failed to make any headway, either with the astrophysicist or with an informal audience of students. At one point, a visibly frustrated Wan Li reportedly said to Fang, "I have already granted you enough freedom and democracy." Thereupon Fang shot back, "What do you mean, 'enough democracy'? It was the people who made you vice-premier. It's not up to any single person to hand out democracy."[56]

Perhaps coincidentally, when Chinese college students began to demonstrate in early December, the arc of political contagion followed rather closely (though not precisely) the itinerary of Fang's 1985–86 lecture tours. Beginning at CUST in Hefei, student protest quickly spread to Jiaotong and Tongji in Shanghai, before moving northward to Beida. All along the arc of contagion, Chinese students began to break barriers.

BREAKING BARRIERS: DECEMBER 1986

The movement began on December 5, when several hundred students at CUST gathered to protest their exclusion both from the process of selecting the head of the campus student union and from nominating candidates for the provincial People's Congress. Just a few days earlier, China's 1979 election law had been amended to make selection procedures for people's congresses at the provincial level more democratic.[57] The day before the first student protest, on December 4, Fang Lizhi had told his students, "democracy is not granted from the top down; it is won by individuals."[58] Stirred by Fang's rhetoric, students began taking to the streets.

Four days after the first protest, on the occasion of the fifty-first anniversary of the anti-Japanese student movement of December 9, 1935, between two and three thousand CUST students marched through the streets of Hefei, criticizing the provincial government for reneging on its promise of expanded electoral democracy. Embarrassed by the protest, provincial authorities gave in to student demands and postponed the People's Congress election. Smaller demonstrations occurred on the same day at a handful of college campuses in other cities, including Wuhan and Xian. According to eyewitnesses in these cities, the complaints of the student demonstrators varied widely and lacked coherent focus. Some clamored for electoral democracy; others complained about the poor quality of campus food and living conditions (including the presence of rats in student dormitories); still others protested against inflation, corruption, rising tuition fees, and the elimination of automatic student aid.[59]

When word of the Hefei students' victory reached other college campuses, it served as a catalyst, amplifying local protest and creating a contagion effect. This effect was reportedly given added, if unintended, impetus by Deng Xiaoping himself. On December 7 *People's Daily* published an article containing a quotation from Deng that appeared to lend support to student demands: "In carrying out political reform," it said, "daring and determination should come first; prudence second." Taking Deng at his word, students stepped up their protests. On December 10 wall posters calling for democracy appeared at Jiaotong and Beida. Small demonstrations also broke out on college campuses in Jilin, Shenzhen, and Kunming.

At Jiaotong and Beida, university authorities issued orders to remove the posters. Students at Jiaotong planned a march to protest the removal order. When Shanghai Mayor Jiang Zemin visited the campus on December 18 to try to cool down the students, pleading for stability and unity, he was repeatedly interrupted by hecklers. At one point, a student provocatively asked Jiang Zemin whether he had been elected mayor by the people of Shanghai. Momentarily taken aback, the mayor asked for the student's name and major department. Offended by what appeared to be a clumsy attempt at intimidation, a number of students in the audience verbally leapt to their classmate's defense.[60]

News of the Jiaotong confrontation spread rapidly, and students at nearby Tongji and Fudan universities took to the streets on December 19, angrily denouncing bureaucratism and demanding liberty and democracy. Congregating at Shanghai's People's Square, several thousand students demanded a meeting with Mayor Jiang. After a delay of several hours, during which time the movement began to dissipate, students marched to city hall, singing the "Internationale" en route. Eventually Jiang Zemin sent a vice-mayor to meet with student representatives. The students presented four demands: (1) Mayor Jiang should address them personally; (2) their demonstration should be treated as legal and patriotic; (3) they must have assurances against future government recrimination; and (4) newspapers should carry fair and accurate reports of the demonstration. These demands bore a striking resemblance to the demands that would be raised by Beijing students more than two years later, in the Tiananmen demonstrations of 1989.

The vice-mayor tried to convince the Shanghai students to return to their campuses, offering buses to escort them. Undaunted, hundreds of protesters remained at city hall. At around 5:45 A.M. the next morning, police marched in and forceably removed the students, putting them in buses to be driven back to their campuses. A handful of students who refused to leave were briefly detained; a few were roughed up; one reportedly suffered a broken leg. Over the next few days, the protests at People's Square grew larger, now involving more than ten thousand people, including substantial numbers of nonstudents. According to eyewitnesses, the level of emotional excitation now surpassed anything seen in China since the Cultural Revolution.

In Nanjing, Tianjin, and Beijing, thousands of students demonstrated during the week of December 22–26, 1986. Some voiced their support for the Shanghai students; others were merely responding to the heightened emotional excitement and stimulation of the moment. Altogether, several tens of thousands of people, students and nonstudents alike, from more than 150 colleges and universities in 17 cities, participated in demonstrations in the last half of December 1986. Estimates of total participation varied widely, from a low of around 20,000 (roughly 2 percent of China's total college population), as reported in the official *People's Daily* on December 31, 1986, to a high of over 75,000, representing compilations made by various unofficial Chinese and foreign media sources. The largest individual demonstrations were those in Shanghai and Beijing, where crowds as large as 30,000 people (including both demonstrators and spectators) were reported.

The official media, which had previously ignored the demonstrations altogether, now sought to cool things down by publishing commentaries urging moderation and restraint. On December 22, Xinhua publicized a statement by Tianjin's proreform mayor, Li Ruihuan, exhorting the people of his city not to be unduly alarmed by the disturbances. "There is nothing extraordinary about such incidents," he said; "there is no reason for us to lose our composure." At the same time, the mayor cautioned students against being led astray by people like Fang Lizhi who claimed that China's future lay in "complete Westernization." Such notions were entirely inappropriate, said Mayor Li, and must be resolutely opposed.[61] A few days later *People's Daily* ran an editorial urging Chinese students to have patience, arguing that democratization was a lengthy process that could not be achieved overnight.[62] Meanwhile, municipal authorities in Beijing employed more direct, straightforward means of discouraging protest: On December 26 they enacted new regulations restricting the issuance of parade permits; this was followed by the arrest of a handful of demonstrators on charges ranging from disturbing the peace to incitement to riot.

Despite scattered arrests and sporadic use of intimidation tactics by public security forces, local authorities generally refrained from using excessive force to quell student protest. In the absence of inflammatory government behavior, popular passions gradually subsided, and the movement began to lose momentum. By early January a combination of chill winter weather and the natural dissipation of student energies served to dampen the protestors' fervor. Before returning to their classes, however, students in Beijing engaged in one final act of symbolic political defiance. On January 5, 1987, they made a public bonfire out of purloined copies of the *Beijing Daily*, the official organ of the municipal government, which the students claimed had presented a grossly distorted view of their movement.

THE EMPIRE STRIKES BACK

Throughout most of December, party leaders maintained their outward composure. Inwardly, however, many were seething. Beijing Mayor Chen Xitong and municipal party chief Li Ximing were said to be particularly enraged over the students' burning of the *Beijing Daily*. Shanghai Mayor Jiang Zemin, at a meeting of municipal cadres, roundly denounced the students at Jiaotong University for opposing the party. Afterward, he reportedly ordered that "not one word" of his remarks should be repeated outside of the meeting.[63]

On December 28, party hard-liners spoke out: Bo Yibo, Hu Qiaomu, and Deng Liqun all issued statements denouncing bourgeois democracy, which they claimed would destabilize the country and retard modernization.[64] Two days later, Wang Zhen raised the temperature of the controversy. In a fiery speech at the Central Party School, addressed to those students who had expressed sympathy for the demonstrators, the Big Cannon exploded. "You have three million college students," he said, "but I have three million soldiers; and I will cut your freakin' heads off!" He then asked rhetorically, "Do you know who I am? I'm Zhou Cang, guardian of the Temple of Guan Di [god of martial arts]. If you don't believe it, come and try me!" In the midst of his tirade, Wang reportedly became so agitated that he broke his microphone.[65] Later, the outspoken General Wang was criticized for his intemperate remarks and was forced to resign his post as president of the Central Party School.[66]

Silent until now, Deng Xiaoping entered the fray on December 30. In a meeting with Hu Yaobang, Zhao Ziyang, Wan Li, Hu Qili, Li Peng, and State Education Commission Vice-Chairman He Dongchang, Deng delivered a talk "On the Problem of the Present Student Disturbances." In his statement, Deng leveled what was by far his most vitriolic attack to date against bourgeois liberalism. Placing the blame for escalating student disturbances (*naoshi*) squarely on the shoulders of "leaders in [various] places who failed to take a firm attitude . . . toward bourgeois liberalization," Deng asserted that this was "not just a matter of one or two places, or one or two years' duration"; rather, he said, it was a question of "failing to take a clear stand . . . over a period of several years."[67]

Lashing out at members of the liberal intelligentsia, whom he blamed for instigating student turmoil, Deng named names and demanded punishment: "I have seen statements by Fang Lizhi," he said. "They are absolutely unlike anything a party member ought to say. What point is there in allowing him to remain in the party?" Of Wang Ruowang, Deng said: "[He] is a cunning ras- cal. I said a long time ago that we ought to expel him. Why haven't we done it?" Next, Deng denounced bourgeois democracy: "When we speak of de- mocracy, we must not mean bourgeois democracy. We cannot set up such gimmicks as the separation of powers between three branches of government. This causes great trouble."

Alluding to the way dissidents were handled during the short-lived Democ- racy Movement of 1978–79, Deng asserted that "We cannot allow people who turn right and wrong around . . . to do as they please. Didn't we arrest Wei Jingsheng? . . . We arrested him and haven't let him go, yet China's image has not suffered the slightest damage." Praising the Polish government's handling of the Solidarnosç crisis in 1981, Deng said that the Polish leaders had showed "cool and level-headed judgment. Their attitude was firm. . . . They resorted to martial law to bring the situation under control." For Deng, the lesson to be drawn was clear: "This proves," he said, "that you cannot succeed without recourse to methods of dictatorship."

Arguing that it was generally advisable to "arrest as few as possible," Deng nevertheless insisted that a show of force was an indispensable tactic in deal- ing with unruly demonstrators. In a passage that ominously foreshadowed events of May and June 1989, Deng raised the question of how to deal with people who are determined to provoke a confrontation:

[I]f they want to create a bloody incident, what can we do about it? . . . We do all we can to avoid bloodshed. If not even one person dies, that is best. It is even preferable for our own people to be injured. But the most important thing is to grasp the object of struggle. . . . If we do not take appropriate steps and measures, we will be unable to control this type of incident; if we pull back, we will encoun- ter even more trouble later on. . . . Don't worry that foreigners will say we have ruined our reputation . . . We must show foreigners that the political situation in China is stable.[68]

Such was paramount leader Deng Xiaoping's prescription for dealing with the fire next time. For the moment, however, the situation gradually returned to relative quiescence following the arrest of thirty-three Beida students in Tiananmen Square on January 1. Sobered by this experience and chilled by Beijing's wintry winds, the students backed off, returning to their college campuses to complete their studies and prepare for the Lunar New Year holi- day ahead. With that, the crisis went into remission and Deng's darker side, momentarily exposed, was once more hidden from view.

Combating Bourgeois Liberalization:
January 1987–Spring 1988

Some of our comrades detest 'Leftist' thinking. . . . This is
understandable and should be appreciated. . . . But these
comrades turn a blind eye to bourgeois liberalization. Now it is
time for them to sober up. Bourgeois liberalization is a
tendency which poisons our youth, is harmful to socialist
stability and unity, [and] disrupts our reform and
"open policy." . . . How can we ignore it?

—People's Daily, *January 6, 1987*

THE STUDENT demonstrations of December 1986 were the leading edge of a
wider pattern of urban unrest that began to affect China in the mid-1980s.
Although calls for greater democracy comprised the lowest common denominator of campus protest, student demands tended to be vague and unfocused,
often masking a wide variety of underlying social stresses, grievances, and
tensions. Some of these were preexisting, while others were reform-induced;
all were subject to intensification in the swirling vortex of heightened expectations, loosened behavioral controls, and accelerated social mobilization that
characterized China in the mid-1980s.

If the students themselves were somewhat diffuse and unfocused in their
demands and objectives, China's rebounding conservatives were not. They
knew exactly what they wanted: the removal of Hu Yaobang. This was nothing new; conservatives had been visibly unhappy with Hu since the early
1980s. Now, however, they had a powerful new weapon at their disposal—the
wrath of Deng Xiaoping—and they used it to maximum effect, bringing to a
jarring halt the short-lived liberal opening of 1986.

THE RESIGNATION OF HU YAOBANG

On December 27, 1986, a delegation of party elders, including five vocal conservatives—Wang Zhen, Peng Zhen, Hu Qiaomu, Bo Yibo, and Deng
Liqun—paid a visit to Deng Xiaoping. Raising numerous allegations of mis-

conduct against Hu Yaobang, they requested the latter's immediate dismissal.[1] At first, Deng temporized; though he had already made up his mind that Hu would have to step down eventually, Deng preferred to wait until the Thirteenth Party Congress, scheduled for the fall of 1987. Now, however, he was being pressured to act immediately.[2]

Meanwhile, the backlash against the December student turmoil was intensifying. On January 6, following the public burning of copies of the *Beijing Daily*, the Politburo promulgated "Central Document No. 1 (1987)." It called on leading cadres in all organizations and at all levels to take an "unwavering stand" on the "front lines of the battle" to quell student unrest. Those who violated the party's injunction against supporting student turmoil would be dealt with "in accordance with party rules and regulations"; where circumstances were serious, severe punishment would be meted out.[3] Three days later it was reported that Fang Lizhi, Liu Binyan, and Wang Ruowang had been ordered expelled from the CCP.[4]

In the aftermath of the *Beijing Daily* incident, Deng Xiaoping made up his mind: Hu Yaobang had to go. According to unofficial reports, Deng ultimately decided to sack Hu because Chen Yun persuaded him that Hu's "lax" leadership style risked splitting the party and provoking the formation of autonomous labor unions (and strikes) among urban workers—a sort of "Chinese Gdansk."[5] On January 16, at an enlarged meeting of the Politburo that was also attended by seventeen leading members of the CAC, Hu was relieved of his duties as general secretary—after having repeatedly been rebuffed in the attempt to submit his resignation. More than twenty people spoke out against Hu at the meeting, including some of his erstwhile supporters.[6] According to knowledgeable Chinese sources, Zhao Ziyang was among Hu's detractors — though his criticism was relatively low key and restrained.[7] Evidently, the only senior party leader openly to object to the condemnation of Hu Yaobang at the January 16 Politburo meeting was Xi Zhongxun, who reportedly rose to his feet at the outset to challenge his comrades: "What are you guys doing here? Don't repeat what Mao did to us."[8]

The next day, January 17, the Politburo promulgated "Central Document No. 3 (1987)," cataloguing Hu's alleged misdeeds. Six separate charges were set out in the document: (1) Hu Yaobang had for several years resisted the party's "entirely correct" efforts to combat spiritual pollution and bourgeois liberalization in the ideological sphere, thus contributing to an upsurge in liberal demands for "total Westernization," culminating in the student turmoil of December 1986;[9] (2) he had failed to provide correct leadership in the party rectification/consolidation campaign, virtually ignoring the four cardinal principles and "only opposing the 'Left'" while "never opposing the Right"; (3) in economic work, he had overemphasized the need to stimulate and satisfy consumer demand, leading to undue acceleration in the rate of planned economic growth and making it impossible adequately to "lay the ideological groundwork" for rapid growth, thus causing the economy to go "out of control"; (4) in political work, he frequently violated legal procedures and "repeatedly spoke out about government legislative work in a way that was not serious"; (5) in foreign affairs, he "said many things he should not have said"; and (6) he often disobeyed party resolutions and frequently took the initiative in expressing his own ideas "without authorization from the Central Committee."[10]

The charges contained in Central Document No. 3 were based on a report delivered by Bo Yibo, summarizing the proceedings of a top-level leadership meeting held in Beijing from January 10 to 15. Of the six charges raised against Hu, the first two were considered the most serious; by contrast, the last three were extremely vague and skeletal. Later, Peng Zhen would boast of the key role he and other "old comrades" had played in engineering Hu Yaobang's ouster at this meeting.[11]

In addition to outlining a wide range of conservative grievances against Hu Yaobang, Central Document No. 3 also contained a summary of Hu's self-criticism, delivered to members of the Politburo. In it, he apologized for over-stepping the bounds of his authority as general secretary, acknowledging that because he had occupied a leading position his errors had caused "very grave damage" to the party, the nation, and the people. He also conceded that his errors "were not isolated mistakes but a whole series of major errors involving political principles." At the same time, however, Hu refused to admit to the most damaging charge, namely, that his own ideological laxity had helped make the country more susceptible to spiritual pollution and bourgeois liberalization, thereby fostering student turmoil.[12]

Despite Hu's reluctance to acknowledge some of the most serious charges against him, those present at his self-criticism expressed satisfaction with his "feelings and attitude" of contrition. Consequently, it was decided that he should not be expelled from the party. For the sake of maintaining stability and unity, Hu was permitted to retain his seat on the Politburo—at least for the time being. Although he accepted the judgment against him gracefully, Hu later expressed his regrets for having capitulated to the conservatives so readily, without putting up a fight.

Toward the end of Central Document No. 3, a brief passage was devoted to the question of how to prevent future occurrences of reckless or irresponsible behavior by top-level party leaders. Though it received scant attention at the time, this passage subsequently provided the rationale for allowing retired party elders to override younger leaders in time of crisis: "The comrades who took part in the session all felt that, for the long-term peace and order of our country, it would be a good idea if, while such older generation revolutionaries as Deng Xiaoping, Chen Yun, and Li Xiannian are still in good health, a system might be devised to control and supervise leaders at the highest levels in party and government."[13] Such a system was, in fact, put in place later in the year, at the time of the Thirteenth Party Congress; some eighteen months later it was invoked to override the authority of Zhao Ziyang during the student "turmoil" of May 1989.

THE ANTILIBERALIZATION CAMPAIGN

Notwithstanding the vehemence of the party leadership's denunciation of bourgeois liberalization, the ensuing propaganda campaign was neither as sweeping in its scope nor as indiscriminate in its selection of targets as its predecessor, the antipollution campaign of 1983. The reason was clear: negative backlash from the earlier campaign had threatened to scare off foreign investors and undermine Deng's reform program. To avoid repetition, the 1987 campaign was narrowly circumscribed from the outset. It was not to be a mass movement, but was to be confined within the ranks of the party apparatus; expulsions from the party were to be relatively few, as were removals from office. Indeed, aside from Hu Yaobang, the only other high-level party officials actually sacked in the aftermath of the December 1986 student demonstrations were Zhu Houze and Public Security Minister Ruan Chongwu. Zhu, who was permitted to retain his party membership, was replaced as party propaganda chief by Wang Renzhi, the hard-line former deputy editor-in-chief of *Red Flag*.

Among prominent liberal intellectuals, only Fang Lizhi, Wang Ruowang, and Liu Binyan were expelled from the party in the immediate aftermath of the student disturbances of December 1986, although five other liberal intellectuals—Su Shaozhi, Wang Ruoshui, Sun Changjiang, Zhang Xianyang, and Wu Zuguang—were formally requested to resign from the CCP in the summer of 1987. Two of the five (Zhang and Wu) ultimately complied, while the other three were spared the loss of their party membership when Marshal Nie Rongzhen — who had been Sun Changjiang's patron — intervened on their behalf.[14]

Apart from CUST Vice-President Fang Lizhi, a handful of other academic administrators, including Fang's boss, CUST President Guan Weiyan, were also dismissed from their posts early in 1987. Several others, including the president and vice-president of the Chinese Academy of Sciences, Lu Jiaxi and Yan Dongsheng, were criticized but retained their positions. After being expelled from the party, Fang Lizhi and Liu Binyan were permitted to continue to attend professional meetings in China; a year later, Liu, Wang Ruowang, Su Shaozhi, and other blacklisted intellectuals were granted permission to travel abroad.

Although tight press censorship and a ban on certain liberal magazines (and writers) were imposed in the late winter and spring of 1987, no large-scale police crackdown was launched against people who had supported the student demonstrations. A small number of alleged troublemakers, most of them non-students, were quietly jailed for instigating the December turmoil, however. In late January a student at Tianjin University was arrested on a charge of supplying classified information to a French journalist during the student demonstrations—a charge strikingly similar to one leveled against Wei Jingsheng in 1979. In March two nonstudents were convicted of inciting riots on college campuses and were sentenced to prison terms of three and five years, respectively.[15] And in May there was a report that another individual arrested during the December disturbances had been sent to prison for three years.[16] There may have been other criminal convictions as well, but reliable documentation was sparse.

Although arrests were few, blacklisting and press censorship were heavy. "Central Document No. 4 (1987)," released in March, called for removing people with persistent bourgeois liberal tendencies from leading posts on newspapers and periodicals. The document also said that "we have decided to suppress further publication of those newspapers and periodicals that have committed political mistakes or which contain material not on a high level."[17] Most of the periodicals affected by this decision were smaller, lesser-known journals, such as *Society News* (Shanghai), *Special Economic Zone Workers' News* (Shenzhen), *Youth Forum* (Hubei), and *Science, Technology and Financial Report* (Anhui). The more notorious *World Economic Herald* of Shanghai was criticized, but not shut down in this period. Among the liberal editors and journalists suspended from their posts in the winter and spring of 1987 were Liu Zaifu of *Literary Criticism* and Liu Xinwu of *People's Literature*, both of whom had actively participated in the 1986 critical debates on Marxist theory. Other prominent liberal intellectuals criticized or blacklisted in this period included Wang Ruoshui, Hu Jiwei, Su Shaozhi, Yu Guangyuan, Li Honglin, Wu Zuguang, Wen Yuankai, Zhang Xianyang, Xu Liangying, Guo Luoji, and Ge Yang.[18]

In an attempt to provide an incentive to stimulate production of newspaper and magazine articles denouncing Liu Binyan, Wang Ruowang, and Fang Lizhi, Hu Qiaomu and Deng Liqun reportedly offered writers who were willing to sign their real names to accusatory articles a fee of RMB ¥90 for each thousand words of criticism—more than four times the going rate of ¥20 per thousand—plus a daily allowance of ¥15 for living expenses. Among reputable members of the literary community, there were reportedly no takers.[19]

Undeterred by this setback, conservatives stepped up their assault against bourgeois liberalization. In a behind-the-scenes drama that went unreported at the time, an early draft of Central Document No. 4, prepared by the Central Secretariat under Deng Liqun's direction, called for extending the campaign into all sectors of China's economy and society. Alarmed, Zhao Ziyang asked his political secretary, Bao Tong, to prepare a revised draft, which Zhao submitted directly to Deng Xiaoping, bypassing the Secretariat. Alarmed that the antiliberalization drive might be used as a pretext by opponents of reform and the open policy to sabotage the entire reform effort, Deng approved Zhao's draft. When the directive was released in March, it contained an explicit injunction against "using the Left to criticize the Right." Calling for stricter control over the mass media, Document No. 4 added the important caveat that "no general housekeeping will be carried out," further stipulating that there should be "no sudden switching from Right to Left, no requiring permission for everything, and no interfering with the normal development of literature and art."[20]

ZHAO ZIYANG'S POLITICAL ASCENT

Although both Hu Yaobang's resignation and the subsequent antiliberalization campaign were a boon to party conservatives, Deng Xiaoping was anxious to minimize the fallout from these events, lest they endanger his reform program. In a move designed to ensure a modicum of continuity in party leadership and policy, Deng nominated another erstwhile liberal reformer, Premier Zhao Ziyang, to succeed Hu Yaobang as acting CCP general secretary. Endorsed by key members of the CAC, including Chen Yun, Zhao's nomination was unanimously approved by the Politburo.[21]

One of Zhao Ziyang's first acts in his new role as party leader was to reassure the country, and the world at large, that Hu Yaobang's removal would not affect the policies of reform and opening up:

> China will not launch a political movement to oppose bourgeois liberalization. . . . The current work of opposing bourgeois liberalization will be strictly limited within the CCP and will be mainly carried out in the political and ideological fields. Nothing of the sort will be conducted in rural areas, while in enterprises and institutions the task will be handled in the form of study and self-education.[22]

Throughout the late winter and spring of 1987, reform leaders took great pains to calm popular fears, both domestic and foreign, of an imminent ideological witch-hunt. Toward this end, the same issue of *Beijing Review* that carried Zhao's reassuring message about "no political movement" also carried, on its inside front cover, a full-page color photo of a relaxed and smiling Deng Xiaoping, casually attired in a Western-style sweater and open-necked sportshirt—playing bridge.

Even Deng Liqun showed new and rather uncharacteristic self-restraint. In a February article aimed at a youthful audience, the erstwhile firebrand gently admonished China's young people to consider the harmful impact of recent student disturbances. Questioning the appropriateness of letting young people "do their own thing," Deng advocated stepping up political and ideological study in schools and universities.[23] But his tone was now schoolmasterly rather than strident, didactic rather than dogmatic. Indeed, Little Deng could afford to be calm and avuncular. He had finally rid himself of his nemesis. At long last, Hu Yaobang was gone.

Notwithstanding Deng Liqun's patronizing tone, Chinese students and educators soon found themselves subject to tightened security measures, strengthened political loyalty tests, and intensified ideological indoctrination. Vice-

A relaxed and casual Deng Xiaoping pauses for a photo
opportunity after Hu Yaobang's dismissal.

Premier Li Peng set the tone for these changes in a February speech to a
national conference on educational work. While urging educators to "do our
best to win the understanding and support of students," Li announced that all
schools and universities in China would soon undergo a tightening of control
in order to rigorously enforce rules and regulations.[24] The vice-premier also
called for changes in the focus of the educational curriculum, centering on the
need to readjust the content of liberal arts courses to promote the goal of
"graduating young people with high ideals, moral character, culture, and discipline." Finally, Li announced that henceforth, political character and "attitude toward the four cardinal principles and bourgeois liberalization" would
be taken into consideration as major qualifications for students taking high
school and college entrance examinations.[25]

Also in February 1987, in a proposal designed to enable the old comrades
of the CAC to remain active in leadership roles and thus retain a modicum of

control over the actions of their successors, Bo Yibo called for a revival of the previously discarded "three-in-one" (*san jiehe*) leadership formula, combining old, middle-aged, and young leaders. Bo's call was echoed a month later by Vice-Premier Yao Yilin in a press conference for foreign journalists.[26]

With Hu Yaobang in disgrace, with liberalism in disrepute, and with elderly conservatives once again balking at the prospect of total retirement, Zhao Ziyang found himself operating on a very short leash. Although he remained an important symbol of reform continuity and moderation, Zhao was forced to accommodate to the party's prevailing antiliberal mood. In March his political report to the NPC reflected a delicate balance between continued strong support for "total overall reform" of the economy and equally firm denunciation of bourgeois liberalization. Blaming the December student demonstrations on "ideological confusion" sown as a result of the "erroneous trend" of bourgeois liberalization, Zhao now faithfully repeated Deng Xiaoping's warning of the previous December: "If bourgeois liberalization were allowed to spread unchecked . . . it would plunge our country into turmoil and make it impossible for us to proceed with our normal construction and reform programs."[27] Arguing that China must resolutely adhere to the four cardinal principles, Zhao flatly rejected the notions of "total Westernization" and "Americanized bourgeois liberal democracy," which were said to have exerted a pernicious influence on China's socialist modernization. President Li Xiannian stressed a similar theme in a meeting with visiting Japanese politicians on March 3. On that occasion, Li stated that it was "wishful thinking" for foreigners to expect China to go in for a market economy, capitalism, and total Westernization.[28]

Stretching to bridge the deep chasm that divided the contending wings of the party, Zhao Ziyang argued that there was no necessary antagonism between the four cardinal principles and the policies of structural reform and opening up to the outside world. "They are not mutually exclusive," he asserted; "they complement and penetrate each other, forming an integral whole."[29] It was an assertion Zhao would later have ample cause to reconsider.

In the event, however, Zhao's ideological concession to the party's orthodox old-timers proved short-lived. In April the conservatives badly overplayed their hand. At a seminar held in Zhuo County, Hebei, a group of hard-line conservatives charged that bourgeois liberalism in the economic sphere was even more dangerous and more insidious than bourgeois liberalism in the ideological sphere. When Zhao Ziyang apprised Deng Xiaoping of this attack, Deng instructed him to terminate the antiliberalization campaign forthwith. According to reform economist Chen Yizi, Deng was particularly upset—as he had also been in November 1983—over the threat to his economic reform and open policies posed by overzealous conservatives. As on that earlier occasion, Deng's decision to terminate the antiliberalization campaign was reportedly influenced by his son, Deng Pufang.[30]

The Re-revival of Liberal Reform

As the attack on bourgeois liberalization subsided, talk of leadership rejuvenation and reform of the political structure increased. As early as mid-March, Deng Xiaoping told the visiting governor general of Canada that "at the Thirteenth Congress this year we shall discuss plans for reform of the political system." At around the same time a new volume of Deng's collected writings was issued, containing several of the senior leader's pre-December 1986 statements stressing the need for political reform.[31]

Signaling this latest shift in the political winds, Peng Zhen granted a rare interview to a group of foreign journalists in April. At his press conference Peng revealed that he and the other remaining members of the CCP's "eight immortals"—with the notable exception of Deng Xiaoping—would announce their forthcoming retirement at the Thirteenth Party Congress. As for Deng, Peng said that "We should keep just him on the Standing Committee as an old-timer, and let all the rest be relatively young."[32] Reform of China's political and administrative structures would resume, Peng predicted, but only within the framework of the four cardinal principles; in the reform process, emphasis would henceforth be placed on enhancing the administrative autonomy of urban enterprises and rural villages and increasing the supervisory functions (though not the political independence) of people's congresses at all levels. It was a formula that strongly suggested accommodation and compromise, if not long-term political viability.

Having gained an added measure of leverage vis-à-vis the party's conservative wing, Zhao Ziyang was able to resist pressures from the Left severely to discipline progressive political reformers such as Yan Jiaqi and Su Shaozhi. On the recommendation of his political secretary, Bao Tong—who claimed that Deng Liqun had fabricated evidence against Yan Jiaqi—Zhao now exonerated Yan of the charge of bourgeois liberalism.[33]

Meanwhile, Zhao and his "five-person group" (which by this time had been expanded to nineteen members) resumed work on their blueprint for reform of the political structure. In March 1987 the group transmitted a letter to Deng Xiaoping outlining some preliminary thoughts on the problem of reform. After a few days, Deng returned the letter with the annotation, "The design is good."[34] In May the first working draft of a plan was submitted for Deng's approval. At its core was a proposal completely to separate party and governmental authority—one of Deng's principal reform recommendations of August 1980.

Notwithstanding Deng's earlier encouragement, Zhao and his colleagues apparently went farther toward circumscribing and balancing the power of the Communist Party than Deng had intended. The paramount leader now balked at Zhao's draft, pointing out sharply that the bourgeois system of checks and balances was "still being dished up in new form." The political structure reform group thereupon went back to the drawing board.

In addition to the five original members of Zhao's reform group, three other individuals played prominent roles in drafting political reform proposals in this period. They were Zhao's political secretary, Bao Tong, who was also vice-minister of the State Commission on Economic Restructuring; CASS political scientist Yan Jiaqi; and Gengshen reform advocate Liao Gailong, who was responsible for coordinating the theoretical recommendations made by the group's various study panels.[35]

At least four additional drafts were prepared between May and September, some of which were disseminated for debate and discussion. The final version—draft number seven—was approved at the Seventh Plenum of the Twelfth CC, meeting in mid-October on the eve of the Thirteenth Party Congress.[36]

Throughout the summer there was a great deal of speculation about the upcoming Party Congress. In June Deng had confounded party old-timers, who wished to retain a share of power at the top, by announcing his personal decision to retire.[37] In August, at the annual leadership meeting at Beidaihe, there were reports that Deng had agreed, after intense lobbying by Chen Yun and others, to approve the promotion of two of Chen's second-echelon allies, Song Ping and Yao Yilin, to the Politburo and its Standing Committee, respectively, in partial compensation for the voluntary retirement of elderly veterans.[38] Later in the summer, Deng Liqun was also put forward as a possible conservative candidate for a Politburo seat.

In late August Xinhua revealed that the guiding document for political reform at the Thirteenth Congress would be Deng Xiaoping's recently reissued August 1980 speech, "On the Reform of the System of Party and State Leadership."[39] Also at the end of August, Hu Qili listed seven members of the Politburo who intended to retire at the Congress; contrary to expectations, Deng Xiaoping was not among them.[40] At around the same time, it was reported that Vice-Premier Li Peng would be named to succeed Zhao Ziyang as premier, enabling Zhao to concentrate on his party leadership duties.[41]

Reform and Renewal: The Thirteenth Party Congress

The Thirteenth Party Congress met from October 25 to November 1. As expected, two items dominated the agenda: leadership changes and Zhao Ziyang's reform blueprint. In both of these aspects, the Congress appeared to represent a victory for reformers.[42]

Almost half the members of the old Politburo, nine out of twenty, announced their retirement at the Congress. Heading the list, surprisingly, was Deng Xiaoping himself; the others were Chen Yun, Li Xiannian, Peng Zhen, Hu Qiaomu, Xi Zhongxun, Yu Qiuli, Yang Dezhi, and Fang Yi. Although both Peng Zhen and Hu Qili had previously indicated that Deng would not step down at the Thirteenth Congress, Deng's last-minute decision to retire was rumored to be part of a quid pro quo, arranged at the insistence of Chen

Yun, who steadfastly refused to resign from the Standing Committee unless Deng joined him.[43]

Among the party's top leaders, only four Politburo members remained from the twenty elected at the Twelfth Party Congress in 1982: Yang Shangkun, Wan Li, Zhao Ziyang, and—surprisingly—Hu Yaobang, who easily gained reelection despite his recent disgrace. At age eighty, Yang Shangkun was by far the oldest member of the new Politburo; no one else was over seventy-three. Yang was reportedly retained as the result of an agreement between Deng and Chen Yun that would permit both men to retire while giving party old-timers a reliable proxy on the Politburo.

The new Politburo Standing Committee, headed by General Secretary (no longer "acting") Zhao Ziyang, included Hu Qili, Li Peng, Qiao Shi, and Yao Yilin. Politburo newcomers included CCP Organization Department Director Song Ping (age seventy), Shanghai Mayor Jiang Zemin (sixty-one), Beijing Municipal Party First Secretary Li Ximing (sixty-one), Tianjin Mayor Li Ruihuan (fifty-three), and the head of the State Commission for Economic Restructuring, Li Tieying (fifty-one). Former alternate Qin Jiwei (seventy-three) was now elevated to full Politburo membership, thereby becoming the lone career military figure on the new ruling body. As a result of these changes, the average age of Politburo members was reduced from seventy to sixty-four.

Arguably the most significant of all the Politburo selections was one that was not made—Deng Liqun. Most of the personnel changes announced at the Thirteenth Congress had been agreed to in advance by party leaders. Little Deng's exclusion came as a surprise, however. It was the result of new election procedures instituted at the Thirteenth Congress. To insure a modicum of democratic competition, the new rules, introduced by Zhao Ziyang, required that there be ten more nominees for the Central Committee than the total number of seats to be filled; the ten candidates receiving the least electoral support in the first round of voting (which was to be conducted by secret ballot) were to be dropped, but would automatically have their names added to a list of nominees for alternate CC membership. A second ballot would then be taken, after which the sixteen lowest vote-getters would be excluded altogether.[44]

When this system was used to elect the Thirteenth Central Committee, it produced a major surprise: on the first ballot, Deng Liqun polled fewer votes than all but a handful of nominees. Deng's electoral rebuff was doubly embarrassing insofar as the seventy-two-year-old ideologue had previously been tabbed by party leaders (reportedly as a result of some heavy arm-twisting by Chen Yun) to replace Little Deng's retiring mentor, Hu Qiaomu, on the Politburo. After having been flatly rejected for CC election on the first ballot, however, Deng Liqun apparently chose not to risk further humiliation, for he withdrew his name from the second ballot, thereby forfeiting his eligibility for selection to the Politburo.[45]

In the wake of this rebuff, Chen Yun lobbied hard to have Deng Liqun's name belatedly added to the ballot for election to the Standing Committee of the Central Advisory Committee. Once again, however, Little Deng failed to gain acceptance, as he reportedly received less than half the votes cast by CAC members. Deng Liqun's humiliating rejection by his peers at the Thirteenth Party Congress must have come as sweet revenge for Hu Yaobang, who, despite his recent fall from grace, received sufficient delegate support to be handily reelected to both the CC and the Politburo. Also receiving substantial delegate support in the CC elections at the Thirteenth Congress was Hu Yaobang's disgraced predecessor, Hua Guofeng.

As a result of revamped rules and procedures adopted at the Thirteenth Congress, the new CC was considerably smaller, younger, and better educated than its predecessor. Its size was reduced from 385 full and alternate members to 285, a drop of more than 25 percent. Forty-two percent of the CC members and alternates were first-timers, while more than 70 percent were college educated; 57 members were employed in high technology fields. Only 20 percent of the members were over the age of sixty-one; almost half were fifty-five years of age or younger; slightly more than half—50.4 percent—had joined the party after 1949. Finally, the Thirteenth Central Committee was noteworthy for its strengthened provincial and local representation: the largest single bloc of CC members elected at the October 1987 Party Congress—122 (43 percent of the total)—came from the ranks of provincial, municipal, and local party secretaries and government officials (compared to only 31 percent from central party and government organs). Although military representation on the new Politburo remained low, the picture was somewhat more ambiguous on the full CC, where almost 20 percent of the members were PLA officers.[46]

Even more ambiguous was the relationship between the party and the army. Prior to the Thirteenth Congress, Deng Xiaoping had made it clear that he wanted to resign from his post as chairman of the party MAC, and that he wished to have Zhao Ziyang installed as his successor. PLA leaders were apparently unmoved by Deng's appeal, for they refused to ratify Zhao's selection; consequently, Deng was forced to retain the MAC chairmanship—the only party post he did not relinquish at the congress.[47] In deference to Deng's wishes, senior military leaders consented to name Zhao as first vice-chairman of the MAC; at the same time, however, they insisted on installing Yang Shangkun as "permanent" vice-chairman and Yang's younger half-brother, General Yang Baibing, as chief of the PLA's General Political Department. Through such arrangements, China's conservative senior military leaders hoped to insure against the possibility of a "hostile takeover" of the MAC by liberal elements in the event of Deng Xiaoping's early death or disability. In this respect, as with respect to his continued presence on the Politburo, Yang Shangkun's designated role was to serve as a proxy for CAC old-timers.

Yet another important safeguard against a possible liberal takeover of the party was put into place at the Thirteenth Congress, though it went unreported for almost two years afterward. In response to the concerns of certain old comrades over possible future recurrences of reckless party leadership, voiced initially at the time of Hu Yaobang's ouster, it was now stipulated that henceforth the Politburo Standing Committee would consult with Deng Xiaoping on all important political matters, and with Chen Yun on all important economic matters, before making any major decisions. In this way, China's outgoing elder statesmen would retain effective veto power over vital policy initiatives even after retiring from office.

The irony of such an arrangement was considerable: to help effect a smooth transition to a more highly developed structure of formal, institutionalized political power, China's leaders were opening a back door to the reassertion of informal, highly personalized authority. The existence of such an arrangement, which had been foreshadowed in "Central Document No. 1 (1987)," was first indirectly confirmed in November 1987 in a speech by Zhao Ziyang to a plenary session of the Central Committee. In the speech, Zhao said: "Comrade Xiaoping still has the power to convene our standing committees whenever he feels it is necessary. When we have any major problems it is still to him that we should turn to seek instruction."[48] The arrangement was not made public, however, until Zhao Ziyang's fateful meeting with Mikhail Gorbachev on May 16, 1989—less than three weeks before the Beijing massacre.[49]

STRUCTURAL REFORM IN THE PRIMARY STAGE OF SOCIALISM

If leadership change was one of the big stories of the Thirteenth Congress, a potentially even bigger story was the unveiling of Zhao Ziyang's long-awaited blueprint for reform of the political structure. Zhao's report to the congress contained a number of significant doctrinal departures. These included a new basic party line, identified as "one center and two basic points" (*yige zhongxin, liangge jibendian*) and a novel Marxist ideological rationale for undertaking bold economic experiments: the theory of the "primary stage of socialism" (*shehuizhuyide chuji jieduan*).[50]

As spelled out in Zhao's report, economic development was the central task of the present era, to be pursued by grasping simultaneously two basic points: adherence to the four cardinal principles and persistence in the policy of reform and opening up to the outside world. What made this somewhat stylized formulation noteworthy was its explicit subordination of the four cardinal principles to the strategic requirements of economic development. "Whatever is conducive to the growth [of the productive forces]," said Zhao, "is in keeping with the fundamental interests of the people and is therefore needed by socialism and allowed to exist." Conversely, Zhao continued, "whatever is detrimental to this growth goes against scientific socialism and is therefore not allowed to exist."[51] Following the conclusion of the Thirteenth Congress, Zhao combined the "two whatevers" of this formulation into one single, complex "whatever," thereby avoiding invidious comparison with the Leftist "two whatevers" promulgated by former party chairman Hua Guofeng. The upshot was that the "theory of the productive forces" was now back in, while the concept of the primacy of "socialist spiritual civilization" was out.[52]

If Zhao's ethos of "whatever works" did not explicitly give Chinese reformers carte blanche to try out anything they thought might spur economic growth and then call it socialism, it certainly came very close. In support of this pragmatic ethos, Zhao invoked China's developmental backwardness. Harking back to the New Democratic era of the early 1950s, Zhao stated that "because our socialism has emerged from the womb of a semicolonial, semi-feudal society, with the productive forces lagging far behind those of the developed capitalist countries, we are destined to go through a very long primary stage." In this stage, said Zhao, China must use whatever means are available to catch up with the advanced capitalist countries. It would be "naive and utopian," he argued, to believe that China could skip over this primary stage and proceed directly to mature socialism; indeed, such a utopian belief comprised "the major cognitive root of Leftist mistakes."[53]

The phrase "primary stage of socialism" had first appeared in the Central Committee's June 1981 "Resolution on Certain Questions." An earlier version of this concept, known as "undeveloped socialism" (*bufadade shehuizhuyi*), had been introduced at the CCP's theory conference in the spring of 1979. Credit for popularizing the idea of a "primary stage of socialism" is widely given to Su Shaozhi.[54]

In the realm of economic policy, Zhao's report to the Thirteenth Congress went well beyond the party's cautious October 1984 "bigger bird cage" proposals for urban reform, calling now for substantially stepped-up use of the free-market mechanism and for rapid expansion of the collective and privately owned sectors of the economy. In an interview on October 29, Zhao predicted that within two or three years only 30 percent of China's economy would be subject to central planning.[55]

Under the slogan "the state regulates the market; the market guides the enterprise," Zhao urged the creation of private markets for "essential factors . . . such as funds, labor services, technology, information, and real estate." In another break from Marxist tradition, Zhao further indicated that "in the future, buyers of bonds will earn interest, and shareholders dividends; enterprise managers will receive additional income to compensate for bearing risks." New price reforms were also called for, to be introduced gradually and in conjunction with rising incomes, "so that actual living standards do not decline." The report further recommended the introduction of "new types of institutions for commodity circulation, foreign trade, and banking, as well as networks of [autonomous] agencies to provide technology, information, and service." In an effort to deflect conservative objections that such radical economic innovations smacked strongly of capitalism, Zhao tersely asserted that none of the measures called for in his report were peculiar to capitalism.[56] Notwithstanding such liberal ideological legerdemain, Zhao did make two notable concessions to party conservatives: First, he backed away from advocating rapid, comprehensive price reform; second, he stressed the vital importance of increasing the nation's output of staple foodgrains, which had declined significantly since the mid-1980s due to the relatively higher profits available to farmers specializing in cash crops.[57] Both issues had been sources of major concern to Chen Yun and other party conservatives at least since 1985.

POLITICAL REFORM: TOWARD "NEO-AUTHORITARIANISM"

Turning next to the realm of politics, Zhao called political reform an urgent matter, noting that the Central Committee "believes it is high time to put reform of the political structure on the agenda for the whole party." Otherwise, he asserted, economic reform would be doomed to failure. Henceforth, the two were to be considered inseparable.

Zhao's proposals for political reform were more skeletal and suggestive than concrete or substantive. Reiterating basic themes initially raised in August 1980 by Deng Xiaoping and subsequently elaborated by Hu Yaobang, Liao Gailong, and Yan Jiaqi, among others, Zhao argued that China's feudal heritage had created severe problems of overconcentrated power, bureaucratism, and feudalization of the political structure. To remedy these defects, Zhao called for reform in seven broad areas: (1) separating party and government; (2) delegating state power and authority to lower levels; (3) reforming government bureaucracy; (4) reforming the personnel (cadre) system; (5) establishing a system of political dialogue and consultation between the party and the people; (6) enhancing the supervisory roles of representative assemblies and mass organizations; and (7) strengthening the socialist legal system.[58]

Although Zhao's report contained few specific proposals for implementing these reforms, some potentially far-reaching structural changes were suggested. For example, in calling for the gradual elimination of "leading party members' groups" (*dangzu*) in governmental organs at all levels, Zhao sought to neutralize a major obstacle to the achievement of the reformers' oft-stated goal of separating party from government. In a similar vein, Zhao announced his intention to halt the traditional practice whereby each provincial and local party committee that paralleled a governmental department would routinely appoint a Standing Committee member (generally a full-time deputy secretary) to oversee the work of the government department concerned. Henceforth, only Standing Committee members holding formal government appointments were to be permitted to take charge of government work at the provincial and local levels. Finally, Zhao recommended that those CCP organs responsible for enforcing party discipline—the Discipline Inspection Committees at various levels—should no longer exercise exclusive jurisdiction over breaches of law by party members. This represented a major departure from existing policy, insofar as it strongly implied that henceforth party members would cease being routinely shielded from criminal prosecution for their misdeeds.[59]

New also was Zhao Ziyang's call for a major overhaul of the cadre personnel management system, the nomenklatura, and its replacement by a civil service system of impersonal, professionalized cadre recruitment and evaluation. Although campaigns to eliminate excessive bureaucratism had been frequent occurrences in China under both Mao and Deng, never before had a top Chinese leader called for such broad, sweeping civil service reform. If implemented, Zhao's proposal could have spelled the end of the CCP's traditional monopoly of control over the government's personnel staffing and review procedures.[60]

In a section of his report detailing suggestions for improving the quality of "mutual consultation and dialogue" between the government and the people, Zhao made yet another noteworthy departure from China's established political tradition. He implicitly rejected the conventional notion of "unified public opinion" under socialism, arguing that the government should be concerned with listening to and reflecting the divergent opinions and interests of its citizens. "Different groups of people may have different interests and views," he said; "they too need opportunities and channels for the exchange of ideas."[61] Zhao had made a similar point on the eve of the Thirteenth Congress, arguing that "Socialist society is not a monolith. . . . [S]pecial interests should not be overlooked. Conflicting interests should be reconciled."[62]

In each of these respects, Zhao Ziyang's report to the Thirteenth Congress broke significant new ground, albeit only in preliminary fashion, and only on paper. Painfully short on programmatic details, the report nonetheless offered some tantalizing glimpses into the political philosophy and strategy of Deng Xiaoping's latest heir apparent. Perhaps most importantly, the report revealed Zhao to be an advocate not of Western-style liberalism but of Chinese-style "neo-authoritarianism" (*xin quanweizhuyi*), a doctrine that stressed the need for strong, centralized technocratic leadership throughout the "primary stage of socialism."

Insofar as modernization and structural reform were inherently turbulent and stressful processes, Zhao argued, there were inevitably "many factors making for instability." For this reason, he averred, the transition to democracy had to be undertaken step by step, in an orderly way.[63] Explicitly rejecting bourgeois democracy—with its separation of powers, multiparty competition, and freedom of political expression—as unsuited to China's current conditions, Zhao invoked the memory of Cultural Revolution chaos (and, by implicit extension, the more recent memory of student turmoil) to bolster his argument for limiting popular political participation and free expression. "We shall never again," he warned, "allow the kind of 'great democracy' that undermines state law and social stability." In lieu of competitive political parties and free elections, Zhao proposed further to refine and perfect the party's existing institutions and mechanisms of "democratic consultation and mutual supervision."[64]

While Zhao's composite vision for China's future political development thus had a decidedly illiberal edge to it, it nonetheless represented a significant break with the past. Falling well short of a blueprint for bourgeois democracy, it offered the first broad, tentative sketches of a nontotalitarian future, one that contained at least the seeds, if not the sprouts, of incipient political pluralism. Viewed in this light, as a transitional neo-authoritarian manifesto, Zhao Ziyang's report to the Thirteenth Party Congress was a most important—if not an obviously revolutionary—document.

CONSOLIDATING THE GAINS

In the aftermath of the October 1987 Party Congress, Zhao moved to consolidate his political gains. He first sought to reassert control over the party's propaganda apparatus. Commenting that he "never read" the Central Committee's in-house ideological organ, *Red Flag*, Zhao indicated his intention to disband the journal, which had long been a thorn in the side of reformers. During the 1983 anti–spiritual pollution campaign, for example, the editors of *Red Flag* had been outspoken critics of bourgeois liberalization. Perturbed, Zhao's predecessor Hu Yaobang had returned the favor, claiming at one point that he found the journal "boring."[65]

Alarmed by Zhao's expression of contempt, a group of CAC old-timers, led by Bo Yibo and the party's current propaganda chief, Wang Renzhi, recommended that the journal should be placed on probation, rather than shut down. Undeterred, Zhao initiated a shake-up in the party's propaganda apparatus. In December 1987 *Red Flag*'s editor and deputy editor were quietly retired, as was the conservative deputy director of the CC propaganda department. In May 1988 it was officially announced that *Red Flag* would cease publication, to be replaced by a new journal with a significantly altered title: *Qiushi* (Seeking truth).[66] The new journal was placed under the jurisdiction of the Central Party School, rather than the CC's propaganda department as before, thereby implicitly lowering its political profile.[67]

Meanwhile, it was decided that the traditional ceremonial portraits of Marx, Engels, Lenin, and Stalin would no longer grace Tiananmen Square after the PRC's fortieth anniversary celebration in October 1989. As if for emphasis, two oversized statues of Mao Zedong were quietly hauled away from the Beijing University campus in the dark of night, following at least one unsuccessful attempt at on-the-spot demolition.

With the party's pragmatic reform wing seemingly in control, a mood approaching elation prevailed among China's intellectuals. In November 1987 a symposium was convened in Beijing to discuss the outcome of the Thirteenth Party Congress. At the meeting, a number of prominent Chinese political scientists expressed their deep satisfaction with the results of the congress:

[Zhao Ziyang's] report directly or indirectly contains all the proposals we have advocated.[68]

The theory [of] the primary stage of socialism is a great breakthrough. . . . Stepping off the path is not running away from the road; differing with those at the top is not rebellion; esteeming things foreign is not toadying to alien ways.[69]

This session of the party congress produced great results. . . . [It] went far beyond what was expected. , , , For the first time [it] elevated reform to the position of a major societal activity under socialism.[70]

The most wonderful accomplishment of this session . . . was holding elections in which the number of candidates exceeded the number of positions.[71]

Not everyone shared the enthusiasm of these reform-oriented political scientists, however; indeed, some liberal critics of the regime were openly skeptical. Fang Lizhi, for example, reminded a Hong Kong interviewer that while Zhao Ziyang's report to the Thirteenth Congress was "very moving to listen to," in his own time "Mao Zedong made speeches that were even better to listen to than this one. It's not enough just to read the speeches. . . . You also have to keep your eye on the concrete indicators."[72]

SIGNS OF STRESS: THE ECONOMY OVERHEATS

Not long after the Thirteenth Congress adjourned, the concrete indicators began to go sour. As during the previous reform-induced growth spurt of 1984–85, it was China's overheated, unbalanced economy that produced the early warning signs. Freed from some, but not all, of its traditional central planning constraints, the Chinese economy began to lurch out of control toward the end of 1987. The main problems were familiar enough: spiraling wage-price inflation, a runaway money supply, surging consumer demand, overinvestment in capital construction, rampant commercial speculation, and official profiteering. In a rather gloomy 1988 New Year's economic message, the government broke the bad news:

Inflation has become a problem. . . . People worry that unless price rises are checked, the benefit from the reform will be canceled out. . . . Price rises point to economic instability, resulting mainly from excessive demand. Inordinate investment in capital construction, consumption outstripping production, and excessive money supply have remained uncorrected for a number of years. . . .

Many enterprises have failed to comply with the state's rule that enterprises should spend 60 percent of their operating funds on production . . . and have instead spent most of the money on welfare and bonuses, resulting in a further expansion of consumption funds.

Taking advantage of relaxed controls, some enterprises raised prices without authorization. Some . . . joined lawless retailers in speculation to disrupt the market and harm the consumers' interests.[73]

With many enterprises granting unauthorized wage and bonus increases to workers, large quantities of money were being pumped into an already overheated economy. As consumer demand rose, output and prices also soared for certain luxury goods, such as automatic washing machines, color televisions, refrigerators, and stereo sets.[74] By contrast, output of vital capital goods for the national economy remained relatively static.

In Guangzhou municipality, the purchasing power of urban residents rose 55.4 percent in the first quarter of 1988, compared to the same quarter in 1987. The highest spending growth was in the areas of appliance purchases and "treating friends to meals."[75] In the electronics industry, over 70 percent of total national output in the early winter of 1987–88 was accounted for by luxury goods such as television sets, radios, and stereos.[76]

Aggregate economic data confirmed the worsening situation of imbalance. Despite the central government's repeated efforts to limit wasteful, redundant, or nonessential new investment and construction, a rapid expansion of commercial credits and bank loans at the provincial and local levels, made possible by the fiscal decentralization measures of the early 1980s and spurred on by expansion-minded, revenue-hungry local governments, caused the nation's money supply to grow at twice the rate of economic output. Food prices on urban markets, which had increased more than 10 percent in 1987, continued their upward march: In the first quarter of 1988, prices for nonstaple foods rose by 24.2 percent, while fresh vegetable prices soared 48.7 percent. To deal with surging demand (and surging prices), the government reintroduced rationing for pork, eggs, and sugar.[77]

For the first time since the reforms began, there was a real drop in the purchasing power of substantial numbers of urban wage earners. In a 1987 survey of more than 2,300 households in 33 Chinese cities, more than two-thirds indicated that their real income was falling. Rising prices were the number one source of worry for more than 70 percent of those sampled.[78] Reflecting such concerns, early in 1988 Xinhua reported that a married couple, each earning an average wage of 70–80 yuan per month, could not afford to raise a child in Beijing. Throughout the winter and early spring of 1988, a swelling flow of letters to the editors of China's major newspapers testified to the painful effects of inflation. With so many leading indicators of the nation's economic health flagging so badly, the stage was set for yet another round of conflict over priorities, strategies, and limits of structural reform.

Bittersweet Fruits of Reform:
March 1988–April 1989

We need to create a new civilization; this time it cannot pour

forth from the Yellow River. Like the silt accumulated on the

bed of the Yellow River, the old civilization has left a sediment

in the veins of our nation. Only deluge can purge us of its dregs.

Such a flood is industrial civilization, and it beckons us.

—"River Elegy" (1988)

AGAINST a background of declining urban economic health, the Seventh NPC convened in late March 1988. The meeting was dominated by reformers of various stripes. The party's conservative wing, dealt a major blow at the Thirteenth Party Congress, was little in evidence, save for some largely ceremonial appointments and functions. Indeed, the demographic composition of the NPC suggested the extent of the third echelon's dramatic ascent to political maturity: more than 70 percent of the almost three thousand delegates were first-timers; the average age of all delegates was only fifty-two; 56 percent had received postsecondary education. Generational change was equally striking on the NPC Standing Committee, where 64 percent of the 135 ordinary members were elected for the first time. Only at the very top of the NPC hierarchy was there substantial leadership continuity, as eleven of the nineteen previous SC vice-chairmen were reelected. At the apex of the organization stood the newly elected chairman of the Standing Committee, Wan Li. The choice of Wan, an ally of Zhao Ziyang, to replace the retiring Peng Zhen augured the likely development of a more open and democratic NPC work style.[1]

The delegates to the Seventh NPC did, in fact, display a considerably stronger inclination toward independence, spontaneity, and critical scrutiny of the government than did their predecessors. In a secret ballot to elect a successor to retiring PRC President Li Xiannian, Deng Xiaoping's hand-picked candidate, Yang Shangkun, received an unprecedented 124 negative votes and an additional 34 abstentions. In the contest for vice-president there were even more nay-sayers, as Wang Zhen, the senior leadership's choice, received 212 "no" votes and 77 abstentions—more than 10 percent of the total ballots cast.

The most frequent dissenting votes at the NPC were cast by delegates from Hong Kong, Macao, and China's coastal cities and provinces. One noncandidate for office, Hu Yaobang, received twenty-six write-in votes for the PRC presidency and twenty-three more for the vice-presidency. Aside from the Big Cannon, Wang Zhen, the only other leaders to draw more than a 10 percent negative vote at the Seventh NPC were Standing Committee candidate Chen Muhua—a woman—who had unsuccessfully sought a Politburo seat at the Thirteenth Party Congress, and eighty-nine-year-old NPC Vice-Chairman Zhou Gucheng, a close friend of the late Chairman Mao who was believed by many delegates to be too old to serve in an official capacity.[2]

In addition to showing signs of incipient independence in the election of state leaders, NPC delegates also engaged in a good deal of lively debate over government policies. Members held numerous small-group meetings, where they openly protested various social ills such as inflation, low pay for teachers, inequitable distribution of benefits from the coastal development strategy, and the forcible imposition of central policies in minority nationality areas such as Tibet.[3] An opinion poll conducted among several hundred NPC delegates at the conclusion of the March 1988 NPC meeting revealed that a large number of the people's deputies took seriously the notions of democratic supervision and consultation, which had been the catchwords of Zhao Ziyang's neo-authoritarian proposals for political reform at the Thirteenth Party Congress.[4]

While the Seventh NPC thus displayed a new degree of openness and a new diversity of opinions, arguably its most critical function was to serve as a sounding board for the government's emerging strategy for the next stage of economic reform. Generally speaking, policymakers opted for one of two competing approaches: speed or caution. Zhao Ziyang favored the former; newly installed Premier Li Peng strongly preferred the latter. Li, who had been named acting premier by the NPC Standing Committee shortly after the Thirteenth Party Congress, was formally confirmed in his new post at the Seventh NPC.

On the eve of the NPC Zhao outlined a bold, optimistic plan for further structural reform. At the Second Plenum of the Thirteenth CC, meeting in mid-March 1988, he spelled out his three main concerns: to further emancipate thinking, to deepen reform, and to stabilize the economy—in that order. Central to Zhao's plan was the further extension of decentralized responsibility systems in state-owned industrial enterprises, breaking once and for all the industrial workers' "iron rice bowl" and eliminating the "common pot" of assured budgets and benefits for enterprise managers. Zhao also stressed the need gradually to enlarge the scope of price reforms and to expand further the coastal development strategy in order to give preferential incentives to export-oriented areas and enterprises that could succeed in attracting foreign investment and technology.[5]

The priorities outlined in Zhao's plan stood in marked, albeit subtle, contrast to Li Peng's priorities, adumbrated earlier in the year. Where Zhao stressed emancipating the mind, Li stressed cultivating socialist ethics; where Zhao called for a deepening of reforms to be followed by efforts to stabilize the economy, Li called for stability first, then—and only then—deepened reform. The word order was crucial, since the term "stabilize the economy" had become a conservative euphemism for limiting the scope and pace of structural reform.[6]

Li Peng's government work report to the Seventh NPC represented an effort to downplay his differences with Zhao Ziyang. Revised and rewritten at least four times, the final version was a consensus-seeking document, designed to minimize conflict and contention. Once again, however, Li's primary emphasis was on stabilization rather than emancipation, caution rather than boldness. Addressing himself to some of the key concerns of party conservatives, Li stressed the need to increase grain production while simultaneously developing the country's basic industries and infrastructure—issues that were of perennial concern to central planners in command economies. On price reform, by contrast, the premier's report remained largely silent.[7]

In terms of new legislation, the most significant action taken at the Seventh NPC was final approval of a long-delayed law on enterprise reform. The new law, which had been bottled up for two years by outgoing NPC-SC Chairman Peng Zhen, had as its key provisions the separation of ownership from management (allowing state-owned enterprises to exercise greater autonomy in management, contracts, and leasing arrangements) and the director responsibility system (giving enterprise managers legal authority to hire and fire workers, plan production, and allocate retained profits without interference by local party secretaries). With the enterprise reform law enacted, the PRC's long-dormant bankruptcy law, approved in December 1986 but never implemented, was scheduled to take effect in three months. Despite a certain amount of ambiguity in its provisions, the bankruptcy law provided both a legal basis and a procedural framework for shutting down chronically unprofitable state-owned enterprises.[8]

The Seventh NPC also enacted constitutional changes guaranteeing the legal status of private enterprises and delegating additional powers over rural land contracting to local governments. The latter provision, which established a legal basis for the long-term lease and transfer of property rights, gave Chinese farmers greater control over land-use decisions, thus encouraging them to invest in land improvement. Finally, the NPC also approved creation of a new provincial-level administrative unit, Hainan Island, which was granted the autonomous commercial status of a special economic zone.

Toward Urban Socioeconomic Meltdown: The Crisis of 1988

In the months following the Seventh NPC, China's urban malaise, which had been deepening quietly throughout the winter, took a turn for the worse. As on previous occasions, students were the bellwether. In early April, students at Beida began to demonstrate again, first on campus and then moving to Tiananmen Square; the targets this time were rising living costs, meager student stipends, and an inadequate government education budget. Significantly, their first protest took place on April 5, the twelfth anniversary of the Qingming incident. After Beida administrators pleaded unsuccessfully with the students to halt their demonstration, the protest ended peacefully when an NPC delegate agreed to deliver student petitions to the Presidium of the People's Congress.[9]

Reflecting a marked rise in urban stress, the first six months of 1988 witnessed protest demonstrations on seventy-seven college and university campuses in twenty-five Chinese cities. In response to rising student activism, the central government now set up public security branch offices on many university campuses.[10]

In addition to issues directly affecting students, another focal point of rising urban discontent was the government's plan to privatize housing and decontrol rents for urban dwellers, moves that would force families to pay a larger share of their household income for rent at a time when food prices were already rising rapidly. Fearful of consumer backlash, government officials in many areas began to provide temporary cost-of-living subsidies to renters, in the form of redeemable housing certificates, to offset the costs of decontrol. Like so many other stop-gap measures of the 1980s, however, the housing subsidies, once they were in place, tended to become permanent.[11]

As worries over inflation deepened, labor problems also began to increase. Following enactment of the enterprise reform law, managers of state enterprises for the first time became seriously concerned with the need to increase profits and cut production costs. Given enhanced authority over enterprise operations, factories now began to reduce wages and lay off redundant workers, of whom there were said to be between twenty and thirty million in state-owned enterprises.[12]

First to be laid off were recently hired contract workers, who lacked job security. State enterprises had started hiring new workers on fixed-term contracts in 1986 as a means of breaking the iron rice bowl, reducing labor costs, and strengthening productivity incentives. However, by 1988 only about 4 percent of the work force in state enterprises were employed under such contracts.[13]

In the spring and early summer of 1988, 400,000 workers were laid off from 700 factories in Shenyang municipality; additional tens of thousands of contract workers were also reportedly laid off in Shanghai, Hunan, Hubei, and Shandong.[14] By August, Chinese officials had almost doubled their previous estimates of the 1988 urban unemployment rate, from 2 to 3.5 percent, representing over four million people. At around the same time, many enterprises were reported to be unable (or unwilling) to pay taxes. According to government estimates, more than 50 percent of all state and collectively owned enterprises failed to remit their full taxes in the first half of 1988; among private entrepreneurs the figure was even higher, officially put at 80 percent.[15] Enterprise failures were also up sharply, particularly in small towns and villages, with the majority of affected firms being collective and cooperatively owned ventures.[16]

Despite enactment of a bankruptcy law, in the absence of a national system of unemployment benefits or adequate job retraining programs there was a clear reluctance on the part of government officials to force closure of state-owned enterprises. Consequently, in the first two years of the law's operation, only a handful of state enterprises formally declared bankruptcy. However, beginning in 1988 a number of chronically unprofitable firms were either consolidated or sold off to collective and individual buyers.[17]

With rural and small-town unemployment up, labor migration increased, as did urban vagrancy; in Beijing, 1.1 million "floaters" (*liudong renkou*) lived an illegal and for the most part squalid existence; the number was even higher in Shanghai. Forming a broad urban underclass, floaters commonly took low-wage jobs eschewed by ordinary workers. Many became street vendors, hawkers, or prostitutes; others panhandled. For the first time since 1949, beggary was widely observed in many Chinese cities, accompanied by a dramatic rise in the incidence of street crime, particularly petty larceny.[18]

With the threat of layoffs and/or bankruptcy now looming over chronically unprofitable firms (which reportedly accounted for approximately 20 percent of China's six thousand largest state-owned enterprises), there was a rise in the incidence of labor unrest. Forty-nine industrial work stoppages were reported in the first half of 1988; by the end of the year the total had risen to more than one hundred.[19]

Given the size of the Chinese labor force and the magnitude of the economic dislocations faced by workers, the number of reported work stoppages was relatively low. The most commonly cited reason was that tight party control of the trade unions made organized protest difficult at best. In the absence of autonomous labor organizations, economic difficulties associated with rising inflation and unemployment were presumably not serious enough, in isolation from other reinforcing factors, to lead to extensive political mobilization among industrial workers. In this connection, it has been widely observed that workers were among the last urban strata to join the Tiananmen protest of spring 1989.[20]

The nation's crime rate also continued to register a sharp increase in 1988. According to Chinese government statistics, over two million people had been prosecuted for various criminal offenses in China in the preceding five years. After going up 21 percent in 1987, "serious crime" rose by 34.8 percent in the first half of 1988. By year's end, public security organs had handled a total of 820,000 criminal cases.[21] Profiteering and corruption by party members and cadres were said to be particularly rampant. In 1987 people's courts heard over 77,000 cases of serious economic crime, the majority of which involved cadres.[22]

THE GROWING CREDIBILITY GAP

With the incidence of official misconduct reported to be at an all-time high, one Communist-sponsored newspaper acknowledged a precipitous decline in public confidence in the integrity of the Communist Party:

The decay of party discipline, bribery and corruption, covering up for friends and relatives, deceiving and taking advantage of good cadres and party members, open violations of the law . . . being covered up through "special connections" of various kinds . . . —all these types of flagrant misconduct have produced such harmful social results and led to such a deterioration of the party's image that the damage done is inestimable.[23]

It may or may not have helped the party's tarnished image when it was revealed, in the summer of 1988, that between 1983 and 1987 the CCP had expelled more than 150,000 members, mostly for corruption, with an additional half million members receiving lesser punishment for assorted varieties of misconduct.[24] Notwithstanding this internal housecleaning, *People's Daily* in May 1988 conceded that official corruption still had not been punished severely enough. Many in China would have agreed, since only 97 of the more than 650,000 party members disciplined from 1983 to 1987—a minuscule 0.01 percent of the total—were cadres at or above the provincial level. Those near the top clearly remained substantially immune from punishment.[25]

The CCP, which once prided itself on the integrity, spirit, and devotion of its members, now suffered greatly diminished popular prestige. In one nationwide survey involving more than 600,000 Chinese workers, taken after three years of party rectification, only 7 percent of the respondents believed that there had been a "clear change for the better" in party spirit. Among more than twenty occupations rank-ordered according to their public image by 1,700 respondents in another 1988 survey, basic-level cadres, government cadres, and party cadres all ranked in the bottom third—a notch below railroad workers and a notch above tax collectors. In a third survey involving 2,000 educated rural youths in Gansu Province, only 6.1 percent of the young people polled expressed any interest in joining the party.[26]

Students were among the most pessimistic of all groups polled about the Communist Party. After the 1986 student demonstrations, 92 percent of graduate students and 62 percent of undergraduates interviewed in a survey commissioned by the Beijing Municipal Party Committee saw the root causes of student unrest to be corrupt party work styles and/or lack of democracy. Fewer than 10 percent of the undergraduates surveyed said they were "very confident" that party members' work styles would improve within the next few years.[27]

As public cynicism mounted, open defiance of party authority also increased. In a widely publicized incident that occurred in the town of She'kou, near the Hong Kong border, three veteran party propaganda cadres addressed a meeting of young workers organized in January 1988 by the local branch of the Communist Youth League. When one of the cadres finished his talk (in which he praised the virtues and successes of the party's current line and policies), a young worker stood up and asked the propagandist to "stop delivering empty sermons and speak about substantial questions." Referring to the propagandist's criticism of people who think only about reaping profits and driving foreign cars, the young worker asked, "What's wrong with that? . . . What is illegal about making money in modern China?" When one of the cadres pointedly asked the young man for his name, members of the audience rallied around the worker, subjecting the cadre to verbal abuse for his intimidation tactics. Such open disrespect for the party and its cadres had been virtually unknown in China before the 1980s.[28]

With public confidence in the party, the government, and the economy sagging badly in the late spring and summer of 1988, there was a significant rise in anomic crimes of violence. In May, 131 people were injured in a soccer riot in Sichuan. Most of the rioters were youths; half were peasants; many were unemployed.[29] According to Chinese legal sources, cases of first-degree murder, assault with injury, gang violence, armed robbery, and even dynamiting had all dramatically increased. In one province, almost three hundred enterprise managers were physically assaulted in the first six months of 1988, most for reasons of personal revenge. Organized gangs operating along roads, highways, and railway lines in several areas reportedly hijacked dozens of buses and trains, robbing passengers and stealing cargo. In some areas things got so bad that foreign researchers were issued travel advisories by their work units warning them to avoid using interior roads and highways because of the increasing threat of banditry.[30]

The rising incidence of lawlessness triggered a backlash of social protest. In December 1987 more than one thousand students from Beijing's University of Foreign Relations and Trade marched in protest over the murder of a student in a campus store; six months later, in early June 1988, in what was said to be the most serious threat to public order since the student disturbances of December 1986, two thousand Beida students gathered outside their campus to demand action from the government following the murder of a student by a gang of local hoodlums. Some of the protesters put up posters criticizing party and government leaders; others called for mass demonstrations against corruption and in support of human rights.[31] In July the governor of Guangdong Province, Ye Xuanping, strongly condemned a rising tide of juvenile crime after vandals defiled the memorial stele of his father, Ye Jianying, at a cemetery for revolutionary heroes.[32]

In this situation of mounting social anxiety and unrest, a television documentary broadcast in China in the summer of 1988 provided a focal point for questioning the nation's fundamental goals and values. The documentary, "Heshang" (River elegy), used the slow-moving, heavily silted waters of the Yellow River—long known as "China's Sorrow"—as a metaphor to represent the unbroken cultural continuity and conservatism of Chinese civilization. The image of a stagnant, meandering Yellow River, unwashed by the dynamic, vibrant blue waters of the oceanic littoral, neatly symbolized the traditional isolationism and xenophobia of the Middle Kingdom. Painting a grim picture of the enervating long-term effects of China's insular traditions and atavistic values, the authors of "River Elegy" were openly and severely critical of the dogmatic chauvinism inherent in classical Confucianism and revolutionary Maoism alike; by the same token, they were lavish in their praise of modern Western technology, institutions, and values.[33]

The six-part documentary was initially aired over Beijing's Central Television Station in mid-June, with several other provinces and municipalities rebroadcasting the series in quick succession. The Beijing telecast evoked a storm of excitement, as the station reportedly received more than a thousand letters requesting that the series be rerun. It was reported that a number of PLA generals and their wives took videotaped copies of "River Elegy" to Beidaihe for their summer vacation viewing.

Within the party leadership response was mixed. Zhao Ziyang approved and reportedly gave a copy of the controversial documentary to visiting Singapore statesman Lee Kuan Yew. Wang Zhen, on the other hand, was livid. An informal discussion meeting was held at the Beijing Central Television Station, at which a number of conservative officials blasted the series for being antiparty and antisocialist, and for ostensibly advocating "total Westernization." Liberal reformers defended the series as forthright and honest. After initially equivocating, the party's central propaganda department issued a notification that no further showings of "River Elegy" would be permitted, either at home or abroad.[34] It was later reported that Hu Qili, the Politburo Standing Committee member in charge of ideological work, had solicited various leaders' opinions about "River Elegy" before deciding to ban it, delaying his decision just long enough to permit the complete series to be aired.[35]

CONFLICT AT THE SUMMIT: BEIDAIHE, SUMMER 1988

As China's urban malaise worsened in the first half of 1988, a debate took place involving a number of leading reform economists and their high-level political patrons. At issue was whether to place primary stress on enterprise reform, on price decontrol, or on privatization of the economy. Each of the three approaches had its advocates. A prominent spokesman for the primacy of enterprise reform was Beida economics professor Li Yining, an adviser to Zhao Ziyang. Price reform was the preferred priority of economist Wu Jinglian of the State Council's Research Center for Economic, Social, and Technological Development. The leading figure in the privatization school was Chen Yizi, director of the State Council's Institute for Economic Structure Reform.[36]

Although Zhao Ziyang was an early advocate of price reform, the inflationary spiral of 1984–85 had convinced him of the need to give priority to enterprise reform; Deng Xiaoping, on the other hand, was a belated convert to the camp of the price reformers, apparently becoming convinced in the spring of 1988 that China could withstand the anticipated transitional shock of a "big bang" in price deregulation. Deng signaled his preference in a meeting with a visiting Korean leader in late May, stating that "We now have the requirements to risk comprehensive wage and price reforms"; he went on to assert that "I have told my comrades to be brave and not be afraid of taking risks."[37]

At a June 1988 Politburo meeting, Deng pushed through a proposal for accelerated deregulation of prices; immediately thereafter, Zhao Ziyang dutifully instructed the Central Committee's economic reform think tank to prepare plans for a multiyear program of wage and price reforms. Zhao reportedly asked for three different plans to be studied, with three different timetables for price reform: three years, five years, and eight years. He subsequently combined elements of the three- and five-year plans into a four-year "preliminary price rationalization program."[38]

In the late spring of 1988 retail prices in urban markets were deregulated for four types of nonstaple foods: meat, sugar, eggs, and vegetables. In July cigarettes and alcoholic beverages were added to the list of deregulated commodities. With each new step toward deregulation, real or only rumored, consumer anxiety mounted and retail demand surged, as heightened fears of inflation fueled the beginnings of a new urban spending spree.[39]

Against this background of renewed market volatility, China's party leaders congregated at Beidaihe for their annual summer meeting. Discussions began on July 20 amid unconfirmed rumors of intense top-level disagreement over economic strategy. The rumors centered around Zhao Ziyang, who had shifted his position since the resignation of Hu Yaobang to favor more radical economic decentralization and structural reform of state enterprises, and Li Peng, who favored a gradual policy of balanced reform, slow growth, and centralized economic authority. The disagreements between the two were reputed to be so serious that several top party leaders, including Zhao himself, went out of their way to deny them.

Persisting reports of elite conflict were matched by new rumors of imminent, sweeping price decontrol. Fueled by reports out of Beidaihe that Deng Xiaoping remained committed to rapid price reform, a fresh wave of panic buying broke out in several cities at the end of July, as nervous consumers rushed to stockpile everything from blankets and sewing machines to color television sets and refrigerators. In Harbin, the largest department store sold over RMB ¥1.1 million worth of electrical appliances in the month of July—two hundred times its normal monthly average. To pay for these purchases, consumers drew down their savings. In one three-day period, from July 25 to 27, Harbin residents withdrew more than RMB ¥12 million from local banks.[40] A similar run occurred in Guangzhou, where panicky consumers drained their bank accounts to buy whatever they could in anticipation of imminent price hikes. To stem the outflow of savings, China's banks announced substantial hikes in interest rates on long term deposits; but even at the new rates of 10 to 13 percent, bank interest was considerably lower than the current rate of inflation, which unofficially exceeded 20 percent at midsummer.[41]

Sensitive to the new signals of alarm emanating from the urban economy, Deng began to back away from supporting a big push in price reform. According to reports out of Hong Kong, the unprecedented urban buying spree and bank run of late July and early August convinced China's paramount leader of the need to tighten the nation's money supply and delay further price deregulation. According to these reports, Deng personally decided to abort price reform after reading two studies prepared by Zhao's think tank on the subject of China's foreign debt and the reform experience in Eastern Europe.[42] Whether the reports were accurate or not, a number of alarming economic signals were readily available to Deng at this time. For example, in the first half of 1988 the nation's aggregate demand grew by a whopping 31.4 percent, almost doubling the 17.2 percent increase in supply; also by midyear 1988, urban subsidies were 59 percent higher than the corresponding figure for the previous year. In the same period, bonuses for urban staff and workers registered a 36 percent increase.

With Deng Xiaoping suddenly changing his mind about price reform, Zhao Ziyang was left holding the bag of responsibility for China's mounting economic difficulties. When Deng was pressed by senior conservatives to clarify the extent of his confidence in Zhao's economic leadership, he carefully backed away from his previous expression of unqualified support. "I won't vouch for anyone," he reportedly demurred; "if the situation continues to deteriorate, let the general secretary be responsible." Shaken by Deng's apparent withdrawal of support, Zhao reportedly fought back, attacking the rationale for the conservatives' emphasis on slow growth and economic stability. Taking aim at Li Peng, he challenged the premier's tight-money policy. "You always stress tightening money [supply]," he said. "Who will be responsible if production declines?" To this Li Peng allegedly responded, "There is nothing wrong with slowing down development. It's time to pour cold water on an overheated economy." With Deng standing aloof, Zhao reportedly threatened to resign: "All of you say that I have failed to do my work well. You come and do it. I don't want to do it any more."[43]

Lost amid all the commotion and recrimination over price deregulation was a rather dramatic irony: the consumer panic that served to precipitate Deng's sudden decision to reverse his position on price reform was initially sparked by rumors emanating directly from top party leaders themselves. By all accounts, the 1988 Beidaihe meetings were unusually well-publicized, being punctuated periodically by media interviews, policy briefings, and receptions for Chinese and foreign visitors. Such unprecedented elite openness and accessibility—reflections of an emergent Chinese *glasnost*—provided much of the grist for the PRC's hyperexcitable rumor mill. In this sense the party's own top leaders, including Deng Xiaoping himself, arguably bore much of the responsibility for precipitating the consumer panic of 1988.[44]

ZHAO DESCENDS; LI PENG RISES

Having at least indirectly triggered the panic, party leaders now moved to end it. After weeks of discord, the Politburo in mid-August passed favorably on a "tentative plan for price and wage reforms." The plan represented a tactical victory for Li Peng's economic stabilization line insofar as it effectively delayed implementation of new price reforms while vaguely upholding, at least in principle and in the long run, the ultimate goal of further decontrol. It was subsequently reported that Li Peng's victory at Beidaihe had been facilitated by several old comrades of the CAC, who backed the premier in his confrontation with Zhao Ziyang.[45]

Having lost the policy initiative to Li Peng, and having lost Deng's personal endorsement as well, Zhao quickly fell from grace. In an interview with a foreign visitor in early September, the general secretary acknowledged that he no longer played a major role in economic policy making. Asked how much time he spent each day handling his various duties, he responded: "I do not directly deal with economic affairs but concentrate my efforts on research and investigation so that I can discuss major policy issues with my colleagues at party meetings." With Zhao's economic star deeply descending, Li Peng's correspondingly rose. Primary responsibility for economic policy making now shifted from the party CC, where Zhao was in charge, to the State Council, where Premier Li and his top economic adviser, Vice-Premier Yao Yilin, were able to dominate discussions of economic strategy.[46]

Despite having lost confidence in Zhao's economic policies, Deng did not completely abandon his former protégé, as he had abandoned Zhao's predecessor, Hu Yaobang. In political and diplomatic affairs Zhao continued to be highly visible, presiding over important party meetings, attending to public ceremonies, and meeting foreign heads of state. On one occasion, Deng obliquely defended Zhao's economic thinking, venturing the opinion that China's inflation was primarily due not to price reform but to lax economic management.[47] Still, the damage had been done, and Zhao never recovered his lost prestige.

With Li Peng seizing the initiative, a joint work conference of the Politburo and the State Council was held in mid-September; there, Zhao came under heavy fire for his economic policies. Forced to make a self-criticism, he accepted partial responsibility for China's economic difficulties. A week later, the Third Plenum of the Thirteenth CC was convened. Once again Zhao faced criticism; reportedly, it was only the intervention of Deng Xiaoping that saved him from being dismissed.[48] The major action taken at the Third Plenum was a decision to freeze consumer prices for two years. This and other related measures to tighten up the economy were said to be necessary to help restrain aggregate societal demand, curb excessive capital construction, and check runaway inflation.[49]

In addition to favoring price and monetary controls, Li Peng and Yao Yilin were decidedly cool toward Zhao Ziyang's coastal development strategy. Since Deng had personally endorsed the strategy, however, they did not move to reverse existing policy in this area. Indeed, with Deng's apparent blessing Zhao Ziyang continued to speak out on behalf of the coastal strategy long after the conclusion of the Third Plenum.

Throughout the autumn of 1988, as Li Peng and Yao Yilin moved farther away from Zhao's accelerated reform agenda toward restabilization and a partial recentralization of economic decision-making, what had initially been presented as a temporary respite from economic overheating took on the appearance of a more fundamental, long-range readjustment. To some observers, it appeared that Chen Yun's bigger bird cage theory had finally triumphed over Zhao Ziyang's new laissez-faire approach. As if to confirm this view, in early December price controls were reimposed in Beijing on thirty-six categories of previously decontrolled goods, from beef and eggs to shoes, towels, television sets, and washing machines. Fines of up to RMB ¥10,000 were authorized to be assessed against violators.

When local and provincial leaders balked at giving back some of their recently gained economic autonomy, Deng Xiaoping pointedly reminded them of their dependent status: "Since we can delegate power, we can also take it back any time we like."[50] In the event, however, Deng's boast proved at least partially hollow. Long after the Third Plenum had adjourned, provincial and local governments continued to issue their own commercial rules and regulations, collect their own taxes, and provide their own incentive packages to lure business and investment away from other regions—all in defiance of central authority, and all further contributing to China's emerging macroeconomic incoherence. In the view of an increasing number of observers, inside and outside China alike, Beijing had, by the autumn of 1988, lost the ability to regulate and control a considerable portion of the country's provincial and local economic activity.[51]

As part of the attempt to bring China's runaway economy back under control, a new get-tough policy toward cadre-centered speculation and profiteering was announced in the fall of 1988. Put in charge of the anticorruption drive was Politburo Standing Committee member Qiao Shi, a specialist in party organization and security affairs. Qiao was reportedly the swing voter in the five-person Politburo SC elected at the Thirteenth Party Congress, with Zhao Ziyang and Hu Qili forming the SC's liberal wing and Li Peng and Yao Yilin on the conservative side.[52]

Targeted for special attention in the new campaign was the phenomenon of "official racketeering" (*guandao*), the practice of high-level cadres and gaogan zidi using official connections to bestow commercial favors on private trading companies with which they (or their family members) were affiliated. In his report to the Third Plenum of the Thirteenth CC, Zhao Ziyang had made a special plea to attack this problem: "It is necessary . . . severely to punish 'official racketeers.' All [private] companies . . . must sever their links with party and government organizations. . . . Otherwise, their licenses will be revoked."[53] To help put teeth into this injunction, the State Council in October 1988 issued new regulations stipulating that retired cadres above the county level were forbidden from either setting up or accepting employment in commercial enterprises.

More than 360,000 trading companies had been set up in China between 1986 and 1988; although the majority of these were small in size and modest in scale (e.g., the so-called briefcase companies), a few had vast dimensions and resources, including the "Big Four Companies": CITIC, Kanghua, Everbright, and China Economic Development Corporation.[54] Among the senior staff of these giant corporations were many former ministers, vice-mayors, and party secretaries. Although nominally private, these companies all enjoyed high-level political patronage, and hence protection. As China's officially approved "windows to the world," they also enjoyed quasi-monopolistic access to foreign businesspeople, commodity markets, and hard currency reserves.[55]

It was this system of official patronage and protected market access that gave rise to the epidemic of guandao that beset China in the late 1980s. As observed in the party's new theoretical journal, *Seeking Truth*, official racketeering was an "ulcer" feeding on the "sick system" of cadre corruption:

> With the deepening of reforms, we have been trying to separate the party from the government, the functions of the government from those of the enterprise, and administrative power from managerial power. Those who use their official posts to obtain profits for their own ends . . . lose no time in taking advantage of the transition between the old and new systems. They truly feel that if they miss the opportunity while they still have power, it will be too late. To transform power into currency is the card trick [performed by] guandao.
>
> If our old system breeds and covers up the corruption of some officials, the emergence of guandao is the ulcer that feeds on this sick system. Unless guandao is eliminated, there will not be any peace in China. . . .
>
> . . . What is peddled in the guandao [market] is the party spirit of the members of the Communist Party and the conscience of society's public servants. If such commerce is not abolished, what will depreciate is not only the [money] in the hands of ordinary people, but their confidence in and support of the ruling party and government.[56]

Although the new antiracketeering drive was nominally directed at all firms engaged in speculation, profiteering, and currency manipulation, it was generally the smaller, less well-connected companies that bore the brunt of the government's get-tough policy. Only one of the major trading corporations, Kanghua, was directly affected by the crackdown of autumn 1988; the vast majority of firms that got caught were much smaller in scale.

Because Deng Xiaoping's son, Deng Pufang, had close connections with Kanghua, this case was carefully watched as a possible bellwether of government intentions with respect to cleaning up racketeering among gaogan zidi. Under pressure, Deng Pufang eventually severed his connections with Kanghua; he was never formally accused of wrongdoing.[57]

Despite an announcement by the CDIC in November that 330,000 party cadres had been charged with racketeering-related offenses since 1983, there was a widespread perception that the really big fish had, as usual, been allowed to slip away. In those relatively few cases where criminal charges were filed against party cadres, trials were often postponed or indefinitely delayed. Aware of this problem, the Supreme People's Court issued a notice on No-

vember 3, 1988, requiring all courts to enforce the law vis-à-vis cadre profiteers "in the strictest possible fashion" and to "bring all [pending] cases to
trial."[58] Despite such admonitions, the continued exemption of high-level
malefactors from prosecution was a major source of public outrage when
China's restive students took to the streets once more in the spring of 1989.

ZHAO'S NEO-AUTHORITARIAN COUNTEROFFENSIVE

In the autumn of 1988 Zhao Ziyang's supporters, seeking to restore their
leader's tarnished image and reverse his slide from power, began openly to
promote the theory of neo-authoritarianism. Spearheaded by economists Chen
Yizi, Wu Jiaxiang, and other intellectuals affiliated with reform-oriented think
tanks, and backed behind the scenes by Zhao Ziyang's political adviser Bao
Tong, the neo-authoritarians raised a number of general proposals. Arguing
that market forces alone could provide the dynamism necessary to successfully reform the Chinese economy, they proposed a wholesale dismantling of
the bureaucratic apparatus of the command economy and a privatization of
state-owned industrial and commercial property. This put them squarely at
odds with the cautious conservatism of the "stability" faction, represented by
Li Peng and Yao Yilin, who continued to assert the need for unified political
and economic command under the people's democratic dictatorship. The conservatives' gradual, incremental approach to reform was doomed to failure,
averred the neo-authoritarians, because the persistence of powerful bureaucratic vested interests served to block fundamental structural change. To overcome this obstacle, and to get China started down the road toward genuine
market reform, a clear separation between politics and economics was necessary. To effect such a clean break with China's Maoist-Stalinist past, strong
political leadership was necessary, à la Mikhail Gorbachev. This was precisely the role the neo-authoritarians sought to carve out for their patron, Zhao
Ziyang. For the sake of reform, they argued, "there must be sufficient authori-
tative power to remove the obstacles formed by forces such as the vested
interests in the old system." This, in turn, "requires a strong centralization of
power in the political sphere. . . . What neo-authoritarianism emphasizes is
not the political *system* but the *leader*."[59]

Throughout the late fall and winter of 1988–89, reform-oriented journals
such as the *Guangming Daily* and the *World Economic Herald* published a
number of articles promoting neo-authoritarian theories and concepts. The
common denominator of these articles was their call for strong political leadership to effect a withdrawal of the instruments of proletarian dictatorship
from the economic sphere.[60]

In their new emphasis on the need for a powerful central leader to impose
structural reforms from above, the neo-authoritarians diverged philosophically from their liberal-democratic counterparts, including Fang Lizhi, Yu
Haocheng, Su Shaozhi, and Liu Binyan, who, throughout this period, contin-

ued to stress the urgent necessity of democratic political reforms. While both groups shared a deep concern over the implications of Zhao Ziyang's recent loss of stature vis-à-vis Li Peng, the evident political Bonapartism of the neo-authoritarians put them increasingly at odds with China's liberal democrats. However, the growing schism between these two groups was not clearly manifested until May 1989, when a series of internecine disputes began to erode the unity of the student movement at a critical juncture in the Tiananmen demonstrations.[61]

The Gathering Storm: Winter 1988–1989

In the face of the neo-authoritarians' attempt to reverse Zhao Ziyang's political decline, conservatives in the autumn of 1988 stepped up their efforts to oust the general secretary. In November Chen Yun issued the first of eight opinions on the subject of Zhao Ziyang's leadership. The rift between the two had grown steadily wider in the eighteen months since Zhao replaced Hu Yaobang as general secretary. Chen was said to be particularly unhappy over Zhao's lack of firmness in dealing with bourgeois ideology. Complaining, among other things, that under Zhao "almost all proletarian ideological bridgeheads have been occupied by bourgeois ideologies," Chen reportedly claimed that "it is time for us to counterattack."[62]

Chen's anxieties could hardly have been allayed when, the following month, at a conference of reform-oriented intellectuals jointly sponsored by the CCP propaganda department and CASS to commemorate the tenth anniversary of the historic Third Plenum of the Eleventh CC, Su Shaozhi gave a bold speech attacking the campaigns against spiritual pollution and bourgeois liberalization. With several members of the Politburo's Standing Committee in attendance, Su called for a reevaluation of two prominent victims of the earlier campaigns, Wang Ruoshui and Yu Guangyuan. Although he refrained from actually naming those responsible for persecuting Wang and Yu, Su tacitly pointed the finger of accusation at Hu Qiaomu as the individual most responsible for appropriating Marxist theory as his "own private preserve."[63]

Visibly disturbed by the combative tone of Su Shaozhi's remarks, the party's top propaganda officials, Hu Qili and Wang Renzhi (who, ironically, had helped organize the decennial conference), now sought to bar publication of his speech; their efforts were foiled when the text of Su's talk was printed on December 26 in the Shanghai *World Economic Herald*, whose publisher, Qin Benli, was an outspoken proponent of accelerated structural reform. Two days later, the *Guangming Daily* ran the first of two provocative editorials arguing, among other things, that China needed to "courageously draw lessons" from the modern democratic forms that had evolved under Western capitalism.[64]

In late December and early January, a new series of racially motivated campus disturbances revealed the existence of intensified urban stresses. On

Christmas Eve, 1988, a riot broke out at Hehai University in Nanjing when a group of male African students reportedly brought Chinese women to their dormitory, refusing to register them in accordance with school regulations. The Africans were accosted by a crowd of angry Chinese males who hurled sexual epithets and other verbal abuse at them. In the ensuing melee, two Africans and eleven university employees were injured. For several days thereafter, the situation in Nanjing remained tense, as armed security troops were called in to maintain order among the more than five thousand Chinese students who took part in anti-African demonstrations. On New Year's Eve, Chinese security police, using clubs, forcibly dispersed a group of over one hundred African students who had barricaded themselves in a guest house in suburban Nanjing.[65]

The next day, January 1, 1989, a similar incident occurred at the Beijing Language Institute, several hundred miles to the north. There, an African student who had allegedly abused a Chinese woman was the object of an angry protest by several hundred Chinese students who put up wall posters and demanded punishment for the African. Two weeks later, African students at Zhejiang Agricultural University went on strike in protest against Chinese officials who charged the Africans with transmitting the deadly HIV virus.[66]

Although these incidents clearly involved elements of racism, there were other, nonracial undercurrents and overtones as well. The anti-African protests served to rekindle many of the chauvinistic, antiforeign sentiments that had previously risen to the surface during the 1985 and 1986 campus demonstrations. Such sentiments tended to be symptomatic of the intensified, reform-induced social tensions and emotional stresses that characterized urban China in the mid and late 1980s. From this perspective, it did not matter so much that the targets of student hostility in the winter of 1988–89 were Africans rather than Japanese (or even corrupt Chinese officials); what mattered was that many Chinese—not just students—were feeling threatened by forces beyond their control; stressed and confused, they lashed out at convenient, culturally preselected targets.[67]

In this situation of rising social volatility, the renewed activism of China's liberal intellectuals further stirred things up. In early December, on the occasion of the tenth anniversary of the opening of Xidan Wall, a former activist in China's short-lived Democracy Movement of 1978–79, Ren Wanding, publicly released a four-page letter addressed to the United Nations Commission on Human Rights, Amnesty International, and the Hong Kong Commission for Human Rights, requesting inquiries into the condition of democracy activists imprisoned in 1979–80. Ren himself had been released from prison in 1983; others, however, including Wei Jingsheng, remained in confinement.[68]

On January 6, 1989, Fang Lizhi carried Ren Wanding's request for an investigation into the condition of China's political prisoners a step further. In an open letter to Deng Xiaoping, copies of which were made available to the foreign press, Fang called for the release of all political prisoners in China, specifically including Wei Jingsheng. Fang argued that May 4, 1989—the seventieth anniversary of China's historic May Fourth incident—would provide a suitable symbolic occasion for a general amnesty.

In mid-February two young Chinese writers, Bei Dao and Chen Jun, collected the signatures of thirty-three Chinese scholars and writers supporting Fang Lizhi's open letter and calling for an acceleration of political structure reform. A similar letter of opinion, signed in early March by forty-two prominent scholars and scientists, was sent to CCP leaders and to the Standing Committee of the NPC.[69] These incidents marked the first time since 1957 that substantial numbers of establishment intellectuals had joined together collectively to oppose party policy on a sensitive political issue.

REENTER THE GERONTOCRATS

As political agitation by liberal intellectuals increased, so too did political counterpressure from party elders. After Chen Yun had delivered the first of his eight opinions about Zhao Ziyang's leadership, Bo Yibo circulated a letter of appeal protesting the December conference at which Su Shaozhi had launched his attack on the anti–spiritual pollution and bourgeois liberalization campaigns. Bo charged that a number of "middle-aged intellectuals" were whipping up public opinion, undermining the four cardinal principles, and encouraging bourgeois liberalism; and he characterized the tenth anniversary conference as an "attack on the party CC." Several old-timers from the CAC, including Bo, Chen Yun, Li Xiannian, and Wang Zhen, now began pressuring Deng Xiaoping to sack Zhao Ziyang for his "failure to do public opinion, ideological, and theoretical work properly." At one point during this process, Li Xiannian reportedly flew to Shanghai to consult secretly with Deng about possible scenarios for Zhao's resignation.[70]

According to one scenario outlined by Li, Zhao would be required to make a self-criticism for his errors and resign at the CC's upcoming Fourth Plenum, scheduled for March 1989. Deng is said to have refused, arguing that (a) one of his closest deputies (Hu Yaobang) had already been deposed; and (b) there was no one suitable to replace Zhao. China's paramount leader then decided to put off the question of whether to replace Zhao until summer, after Deng's anticipated summit meeting with Mikhail Gorbachev.[71]

Although conservatives thus failed to secure Zhao's immediate ouster, they did manage to block him from exercising effective leadership over the party's MAC. According to Hong Kong sources, Deng ordained that Yang Shangkun, though nominally ranked below Zhao on the MAC, was to be the principal military decision maker, with Zhao given access to Yang's decisions only after the fact.[72]

Under pressure, and in danger of losing the last remaining shred of Deng Xiaoping's confidence, Zhao Ziyang backpedaled. Though he refused to bow to hard-line demands either to submit his resignation or to undergo self-criticism, he nonetheless began to take a firmer stance toward liberal intellectuals. Together with Hu Qili, Zhao summoned the outspoken publisher of the *World Economic Herald*, Qin Benli, to Beijing, where the journalist was reprimanded for printing Su Shaozhi's incendiary decennial speech; thereafter, Qin Benli agreed to accept a six-month moratorium on publishing articles submitted by any of the thirty-three signatories to the petition demanding amnesty for Wei Jingsheng.[73] At around the same time, the party's propaganda department also issued an order for the *People's Daily* not to publish any articles written by Yan Jiaqi (who had signed the petition of thirty-three) without prior approval from the Central Committee.[74] Seeking to justify such censorship, Zhao Ziyang, speaking at a seminar for party cadres, explained that the improvement of ideological and political work within the party was an urgent concern that would henceforth occupy 50 percent of the party's attention.

For all his evident equivocation, Zhao managed to retain at least some freedom of maneuver. He did not, for example, move to have Su Shaozhi expelled from the party, as demanded by certain old-timers. Instead, Su was informally advised by his boss, CASS President Hu Sheng, to "go abroad for a while." Nor did Zhao agree to transmit around the country Chen Yun's eight opinions of November–December 1988, as Chen's supporters had insisted. And finally, in response to Bo Yibo's criticism, Zhao defended China's critical intellectuals by saying "Intellectuals have their own understanding of problems. What is there to be surprised at?"[75]

In late February Fang Lizhi inadvertently reentered the political arena. Newly elected U.S. President George Bush, paying a brief visit to Beijing en route to Tokyo for the state funeral of the recently deceased Japanese Emperor Hirohito, issued an invitation to Fang to attend a presidential banquet at Beijing's Great Wall Sheraton Hotel. Intended as a sign of strong American support for human rights in China, President Bush's gesture provoked an equally strong negative response from China's leaders. On the night of the banquet, February 26, Fang Lizhi's car was followed and repeatedly stopped by Chinese police, who harassed the astrophysicist and his wife, Li Shuxian, preventing them from reaching the hotel. Having missed the banquet, Fang later gave a press conference at which he sardonically quipped that the incident revealed the weakness of a Chinese leadership that "had to go to all this trouble" just to prevent one scholar from attending a banquet.[76]

Deng Xiaoping reportedly was not amused by Fang Lizhi's remarks. Even Zhao Ziyang reacted with dismay, pointedly cautioning President Bush that any American interference in China's internal politics could undermine the country's stability and thereby play into the hands of the opponents of reform. A week after the Fang Lizhi incident, Zhao gave a speech at an enlarged Politburo meeting in which he denounced recent Western criticism of alleged Chinese human rights abuses.[77]

With political tension mounting in Beijing, Hu Yaobang suddenly reentered the Beijing political picture. Returning to the capital in early April from a sojourn in southern China, Hu attended an enlarged Politburo meeting, convened to discuss problems of reform in education. Forty minutes into the April 8 meeting, at 9:40 A.M., during a speech by Li Tieying, people seated near Hu noticed that he was looking pale. Feeling dizzy, Hu raised his hand to request permission to leave the hall. In mid-sentence he suddenly slumped down in his chair, eyes closed, stricken by a heart attack. Revived by nitroglycerin tablets administered by Shanghai party chief Jiang Zemin, Hu was transported to Beijing Hospital, where his condition gradually stabilized. Precisely one week later, at 7:30 A.M. on Saturday, April 15, Hu Yaobang suffered a second, massive heart attack while visiting with family members in his hospital room. Efforts to revive him failed. He was pronounced dead at 7:53 A.M. Within hours, the Beijing Spring began.[78]

PART III

The Beijing Spring, 1989

CHAPTER 11

The Beijing Spring: April–May 1989

Some people crave nothing short of national chaos. . . .
We must take a clear-cut stand and forceful measures to oppose
and stop the turmoil. Don't be afraid of students, because
we still have several million troops.

— *Deng Xiaoping, April 25, 1989*

EVEN before Hu Yaobang died, a rumor began circulating in Beijing to the effect that he had suffered his initial heart attack while engaged in a heated debate with Bo Yibo.[1] Though later denied, the rumor added to the already powerful sense of frustration and alienation shared by many Chinese students, providing the catalytic spark that reignited the smoldering fuse of campus unrest.

MOURNING BECOMES ELECTRIC

One day after Hu's death, on Sunday, April 16, several hundred students from various Beijing universities marched to Tiananmen Square to place memorial wreaths at the foot of the Heroes' Monument. Over the next several days, the ranks of the mourners swelled to tens of thousands.[2] The first prodemocracy rallies also took place in this period, accompanied by demonstrations in front of the Zhongnanhai state residential compound. At this stage, the movement was composed almost entirely of university students.[3]

Between April 18 and April 20, the first autonomous, nonofficial student organization was set up at Beida. Not coincidentally, the first set of student demands, addressed to the NPC Standing Committee, also appeared at this time. Among the seven points raised by the students, the most important were those calling for a "correct evaluation" of the merits and demerits of Hu Yaobang; rehabilitation of all people wrongly persecuted in the campaigns against spiritual pollution and bourgeois liberalization; publication of the salaries and income sources of all top party and government leaders and their offspring; new legislation promoting freedom of the press and public expression; and substantially increased stipends, salaries, and budgets for students, teachers, and educational programs.[4] With the exception of the relatively new demands for making public the incomes of top leaders and their children (a product of rising popular anger over guandao) and for reversing verdicts on bourgeois liberalization, the demands were virtually identical to those raised at the time of the student demonstrations of 1985 and 1986.[5]

On the night of April 18–19, student demonstrators, numbering more than ten thousand, repeatedly attempted to gain entry into Zhongnanhai, demanding to see Premier Li Peng. The students eventually clashed with soldiers guarding the compound, and several students were injured when police charged into their ranks. When the official police report failed to mention student casualties and referred to demonstration leaders as "troublemakers" who had incited students to injure police officers, the students were handed a potentially potent new weapon: martyrdom.[6] It was a weapon they would use against the government with great effect in succeeding weeks.

On Friday night, April 21, crowds of people began arriving at Tiananmen Square for the official memorial service for Hu Yaobang, scheduled for the following morning. In anticipation of possible disorder, approximately two thousand uniformed soldiers and security police were mobilized for duty in and around the square. At the same time, up to twenty thousand troops from the PLA's 38th Army, stationed in Baoding, north of Beijing, were given orders to proceed to the capital.[7]

Despite official warnings to clear the square, in the early morning hours of Saturday, April 22, as many as 100,000 people gathered quietly for the funeral ceremony. At 10:00 A.M. the service began inside the Great Hall, accompanied by the broadcast of somber music throughout the square. Although Zhao Ziyang in his eulogy praised Hu Yaobang as "a great Marxist," the general tone of the service was reserved and low-key. When party and government leaders left the hall at the conclusion of the service around 11:30 A.M., students chanted, "Dialogue, dialogue, we demand dialogue" and "Li Peng, come out." After having reportedly been told that the government would grant their request for an audience with high-level officials, the students waited for a government spokesman to appear. By 1:30 P.M., when no government official had shown up, student leaders conducted a mock ceremonial remonstrance on the steps of the Great Hall, presenting their scrolled-up demands on hands and knees in the stylized, obsequious manner of an imperial petition.

Believing they had been fooled by government leaders, students angrily surged forward toward the Great Hall, only to be pushed back by police; a few students were reportedly hit with police batons; many students broke down in tears. The drama of the moment was powerful; the feelings intense.[8] Later, Chinese officials would claim that no government spokesperson had ever been requested to meet with students on the afternoon of April 22, and that student leaders had invented the promise of a meeting to whip up sentiments of betrayal and martyrdom among the students. While the evidence on this point is inconclusive, such a scenario is not entirely implausible.

Responding to the escalating threat of student protest and martyrdom, the Politburo on April 22 held an urgent meeting at which it was decided (a) to terminate the official period of mourning for Hu Yaobang; (b) not to capitulate

Students attempt to present a scrolled-up petition to the government in a ceremonial
remonstrance following Hu Yaobang's funeral, April 22, 1989.

to student demands to reverse the verdict on Hu; and (c) to reaffirm the correctness of the 1987 campaign against bourgeois liberalization. Among those
present at the meeting, only Zhao Ziyang, Wan Li, and a small handful of
others reportedly opposed the Politburo's decision. The next day, Zhao left for
a scheduled week-long visit to Pyongyang, North Korea.

With Zhao Ziyang out of the country, Li Peng convened an emergency
session of the remaining members of the Politburo Standing Committee (Li,
Qiao Shi, Yao Yilin, and Hu Qili) plus Yang Shangkun, who served as Deng
Xiaoping's proxy. At the meeting, the student protest was described, for the
first time, as "turmoil" (*dongluan*), a more serious category of offense than
"disturbance" (*naoshi*), the term Deng had used to characterize the student
demonstrations of December 1986.

On April 25 Li Peng and Yang Shangkun briefed Deng Xiaoping on the
Standing Committee meeting and on the developing student protest situation.
An unofficial transcript of Deng's response, which included a sharp jab at
Zhao Ziyang's memorial characterization of Hu Yaobang as "a great Marx-
ist," subsequently circulated among party cadres:

> Some people want to build up [Hu Yaobang] as "a great Marxist." . . . Even when
> I die they will not call me a great Marxist. Who do they think that turtle egg
> Yaobang was? . . . Hu Yaobang was irresolute and made concessions in combat-

ing bourgeois liberalism. The drive against spiritual pollution lasted only a little over twenty days. If we had vigorously launched the drive, the ideological field would not have been . . . so tumultuous [as it is today]. . . . Some people crave nothing short of national chaos. . . . We must take a clear-cut stand and forceful measures to oppose and stop the turmoil. Don't be afraid of students, because we still have several million troops.[9]

Claiming that the demonstrations had been organized and led by trouble-makers with ulterior motives who were engaged in a premeditated plot to overthrow China's socialist system, Deng once again warned (as he had done in December 1986) of the dangers of a Polish-style uprising: "Events in Poland prove that making concessions provides no solutions. The greater the concessions made by the government, the greater the opposition forces became."

Deng had reason to be concerned, for a new and potentially troublesome element was now being added to the equation of student protest: working class involvement. On April 20 a newly formed Beijing Workers' Autonomous Federation (Gongzilian) issued a public manifesto blaming "dictatorial bureaucrats" for social ills ranging from soaring inflation and a sharp drop in urban living standards to "expropriating the minimal income of the people for their own use." The manifesto further exhorted the citizens of Beijing, specifically including police and fire fighters, to "stand on the side of the people and justice" and not become "tools of the people's enemies." "We the working class of Beijing," the manifesto concluded, "support the just struggle of the college students across the nation!"[10] Notwithstanding such extravagant claims, relatively few industrial workers actually joined the protest movement until the latter part of May, after the government's declaration of martial law.[11]

Between April 22 and 25, students in several Chinese cities, organizing themselves into autonomous unions, launched protests of various types. In Shanghai, Tianjin, Nanjing, and Wuhan, as well as in Beijing, citywide boycotts of classes were initiated. In Beijing, a Students' Autonomous Federation (BSAF), known as Gaozilian, was established on April 26 at a meeting attended by two thousand students from ten universities.[12]

For the most part, student protest in this period was relatively calm and orderly. In a few places, however, most notably the cities of Changsha and Xian, peaceful demonstration degenerated into vandalism and rioting as non-student elements, including unemployed workers, floaters, and juvenile gang members, took advantage of student protest to fish in troubled waters, resulting in declarations of martial law in both cities.[13]

Faced with a seemingly contagious situation of expanding student protest, mounting citizen unrest, and escalating anomic violence on the part of urban marginals, party leaders now toughened their stance. Basing themselves on Deng Xiaoping's uncompromising statement of April 25, they drafted a hard-line editorial for publication in *People's Daily*. The editorial, published on

April 26, appeared under the page-one headline, "It Is Necessary to Take a Clear-cut Stand to Oppose Turmoil." The editorial echoed Deng's allegations about the unpatriotic motives of student leaders, claiming that the student demonstrations constituted a "planned conspiracy" incited by "a small number of people with ulterior motives" whose intention was "to sow dissension among the people, plunge the entire country into chaos, and sabotage the political situation of stability and unity."

The editorial had reportedly been assigned to Hu Qili to draft. When Hu attempted to soften the thrust of the commentary by describing the students' actions as "demonstrations," Deng reportedly crossed out the milder phrase and inserted the word "turmoil."[14] Although Zhao Ziyang was out of the country on April 26, and although he subsequently disavowed the hard-line thrust of the April 26 editorial, it was later claimed (by Yang Shangkun) that Zhao had cabled his "complete support" of the editorial's contents from North Korea.[15]

On April 24, two days before the *People's Daily* editorial appeared, the Shanghai *World Economic Herald* published a plea by Yan Jiaqi for a posthumous reevaluation (and validation) of Hu Yaobang's contributions. "The people's wish is very simple," asserted Yan. "Comrade Yaobang was treated unjustly. . . . If the party center selflessly recognizes its error, I feel China has prospects. If not, the old disastrous road lies ahead."[16] On April 26 Shanghai Party Secretary Jiang Zemin announced the party's decision to reorganize the *Herald* and fire its editor, Qin Benli. At the time of his firing, Qin was preparing to publish a full, candid account of Hu's 1987 dismissal.[17]

THE AFTERMATH OF APRIL 26: PUBLIC RESENTMENT DEEPENS

If the *People's Daily* allegations were calculated to have a sobering, intimidating effect on student demonstrators and their nonstudent sympathizers, the calculation clearly misfired. As soon as the editorial was published, BSAF seized the moral initiative, calling for immediate "patriotic" mass marches on Tiananmen in support of "socialist order" and in opposition to "bureaucracy, corruption, and special privilege."

The counterproductivity of the government's approach became evident almost immediately. On April 27, the day following publication of the controversial editorial, the number of protesters marching to Tiananmen Square from Beijing's university quarter doubled over the previous day's total, involving over 100,000 people; it was said to be the largest spontaneous demonstration to occur in the PRC since 1949. For the first time, significant numbers of nonstudents now began to march alongside students; in addition, more than half a million Beijing residents lined the streets of the demonstration route, offering encouragement, food, and drink to the protesters. Arriving at Tiananmen to the accompaniment of approving crowds, the demonstrators broke

A massive student march to Tiananmen Square follows publication of the hard-line
People's Daily editorial on April 26, 1989.

through police lines positioned to obstruct their entrance to the square; the
police backed off without serious incident. Cognizant of government warnings concerning the possible use of the military to quell disorder, student or-
ganizers dispatched squads of monitors to maintain order and discipline
within the ranks of the demonstrators.[18]

After years of mounting socioeconomic stress, the cumulative pressures of
a decade of spasmodic, uneven reform now began to break through the re-
straining bonds of party and government authority. Galvanized by the government's ineffectual attempt to intimidate them into submission, the students
seized the initiative. Occupying the moral high ground, they made effective
use of the weapons of irony, shame, and martyrdom. During their marches, for
example, they regularly chanted orthodox socialist slogans, sang the "Internationale," and carried ironic banners urging citizens to support the party's
"correct" leadership. By the end of April, such devices had become part and
parcel of the students' attempt to reverse the roles of hero and villain, patriot
and provocateur, and thereby shame and humiliate party hard-liners in the
eyes of the citizenry.[19] Apart from its ironic intent, the students' tactic also
served to reduce the likelihood of a police crackdown, insofar as it would have
been extremely awkward for the authorities to justify arresting students who

were demonstrating peacefully while singing the "Internationale" and chanting officially approved Marxist slogans.

Popular opposition to the government's heavy-handedness spread rapidly: A public opinion poll conducted by the psychology department of Beijing Normal University at the end of April indicated that a majority of inflation-fearing, corruption-weary citizens in the nation's capital now supported the students.[20] Concerned over their tarnished image and reduced credibility, party and government leaders sought ways to disarm a perilous situation. Their preferred responses varied considerably. For Beijing Party First Secretary Li Ximing, the optimal solution was to get even tougher. He repeatedly threatened students with harsh reprisals and warned of the serious unforeseen consequences of a failure to terminate student demonstrations. At a high-level strategy session on April 28, a group of younger, more reform-oriented party leaders, including Zhao Ziyang's associates Bao Tong and Yan Mingfu, opposed Li Ximing's views, counseling against a government crackdown.

In a two-pronged attempt to deflect mounting public criticism and drive a wedge between various different groups of Beijing students, government leaders now agreed to hold televised talks with representatives of official, government-approved student unions, but not with the Students' Autonomous Federation. Having been refused the right to participate, the BSAF's newly elected president, Wu'er Kaixi, angrily withdrew his group from the talks.

When the meeting was held on April 29, State Council spokesman Yuan Mu pointed out that the target of the April 26 *People's Daily* editorial had not been the broad masses of patriotic student demonstrators, but rather a small group of "behind-the-scenes conspirators."[21] At the same meeting, State Education Commission Deputy Director He Dongchang reiterated the government's refusal to recognize the legality of the BSAF. Three days later, BSAF leaders delivered a twenty-four-hour ultimatum demanding government approval of their conditions for dialogue. The government rejected the ultimatum on May 3. The following day, protest demonstrations reached a peak, as a crowd estimated at 150,000 people filled Tiananmen Square to mark the seventieth anniversary of the 1919 May Fourth movement.

Similar (albeit smaller) demonstrations occurred on May 4 in Shanghai, Changsha, Nanjing, Wuhan, Xian, Changchun, and Dalian. In Harbin and Shenyang, campus gates were locked to prevent students from marching. Altogether, demonstrations were reported in more than twenty cities, involving upwards of one million people. According to an official survey, between May 4 and May 19 (the day martial law was declared) over 1.5 million students and staff from five hundred Chinese institutions of higher education in eighty cities joined demonstrations in support of the Beijing students. By the end of the month that figure almost doubled again.[22]

Returning from North Korea at the end of April, Zhao Ziyang traveled hurriedly to Beidaihe to confer with Deng Xiaoping and to convey his misgivings about the government's choice of tactics in dealing with rebellious students. Apparently taken by surprise by the strength of the popular backlash against the April 26 editorial, Deng agreed to allow Zhao to try a softer approach with the students, telling the general secretary: "The most important thing is to stabilize the situation. . . . [Once] the situation is stabilized, you may carry out your plans; if they prove feasible [you may] disregard what I said [before]."[23]

In line with Deng's instructions, Zhao Ziyang outlined a more conciliatory government response in remarks delivered on May 4 to representatives of the Asian Development Bank, meeting in Beijing. Claiming that most of the protesters "are in no way opposed to our basic system; they only demand that we correct malpractice in our work," the general secretary declared that "the reasonable demands of the students must be met through democratic and legal means." "We must remain calm," he said; "we must employ reason and restraint."[24]

Although clearly intended to dampen political passions, Zhao's conciliatory remarks had the paradoxical effect of polarizing the student movement, undermining its unity and cohesion in a way that the government's previous hard-line rhetoric had failed to do. For one thing, it prompted radical elements within the movement's leadership, whose sense of moral indignation was strong to begin with, to adopt an even more intransigent posture vis-à-vis the government; at the same time, by revealing the existence of a clear split among top party leaders, Zhao's talk emboldened many previously inert social forces, including workers and journalists, to join in the movement and press for their own particular demands and interests, thereby both enlarging the arena of protest and diffusing its content. As a result, the movement's previous unity of purpose and outlook became increasingly strained.

By the beginning of May, the core student demands had been reduced to three: (1) retraction of the April 26 editorial (with apologies to the students); (2) reevaluation of Hu Yaobang; and (3) government recognition of BSAF. Following Zhao's May 4 remarks, however, these basic student concerns were quickly conflated with a number of other demands raised by nonstudent groups, including demands to reassess bourgeois liberalization (raised by a group of nonstudent intellectuals); to make public the salaries and benefits of top party and government leaders and their offspring (raised by the newly organized Beijing Workers' Autonomous Federation, among others); and to grant enhanced freedom of the press (raised by a group of five hundred journalists employed in state-controlled newspapers).[25]

With students and nonstudents alike pursuing a multiplicity of diverse, often shifting agendas, some of which were rather murky, it became increasingly difficult to formulate a coherent strategy within the movement, and more difficult still for concerned party leaders like Zhao Ziyang to respond effectively. Perhaps most damaging to the movement was the widening rift between radical student leaders such as Chai Ling and Lu Li, who sought to escalate the students' moral confrontation with the regime, and more moderate elements in the democracy movement, including student leaders Wang Dan and Wu'er Kaixi and veteran nonstudent activists Chen Ziming and Wang Juntao, who sought a negotiated settlement. With both government and students internally divided between hard-liners and soft-liners, the result was a standoff marked by increasing immobility and intransigence.[26]

Under these circumstances, the enthusiasm of many students began to ebb, and in the second week of May the number of demonstrators at the square dwindled noticeably. Faced with the prospect of an imminent loss of critical mass, student leaders were hard-pressed to sustain the momentum of their movement. At this critical juncture, a golden opportunity presented itself: the approaching visit of Soviet leader Mikhail Gorbachev, scheduled for May 15–18. As the date of Gorbachev's arrival approached, the eyes of the entire world would focus on Beijing. It was manna from Moscow, a situation made to order for the students and their increasingly media-conscious leaders.

WAGING MORAL WARFARE: GORBACHEV, THE MEDIA, AND THE HUNGER STRIKE

On May 13, with scores of international journalists and television cameras converging on Beijing to record the long-awaited Sino-Soviet summit, protest leaders dramatically escalated their confrontation with Chinese authorities. Declaring their moral abhorrence of a government that callously labeled the patriotic actions of loyal citizens as turmoil, several hundred students from Beida and Beijing Normal University began a sit-in and hunger strike in Tiananmen Square.[27] With the government unable to take effective countermeasures because of the imminent arrival of Gorbachev and the presence of the global mass media, the ranks of the hunger strikers quickly swelled to over three thousand; large crowds of sympathetic onlookers also began to flock to the square, forcing the Chinese authorities to reroute Gorbachev's motorcade and change the venue of the Soviet leader's scheduled press conference.

Originally conceived as a limited symbolic protest, the hunger strike was so stunningly successful in generating favorable publicity for the students that movement leaders soon decided to fast "to the bitter end," or until the government capitulated to their demands. By this time, the core demands of the students were down to only two: (1) the government must enter into a dialogue "on the basis of equality" with a "dialogue delegation" (*duihua daibiaotuan*) made up of student representatives from various universities in Beijing; and (2) the government must "stop its name-calling" and confirm the patriotic nature of the democracy movement.[28]

With an important foreign head of state in the Chinese capital, with a plethora of international television crews on hand to record the proceedings, with the Chinese news media taking a strongly sympathetic view of the hunger strike, and with public opinion swinging sharply over to their side, the students felt relatively safe from the threat of a government crackdown. The safer they felt, the more audacious and intransigent some of them became. On the eve of Gorbachev's visit, one group of students in Tiananmen Square rejected overtures from Zhao Ziyang designed to bring about a settlement, contemptuously referring to Zhao's emissaries, including Bao Tong, as "neo-authoritarians." Other attempts to mediate a settlement, undertaken by well-meaning sympathizers such as the noted writer Dai Qing, were similarly rebuffed.[29]

With the onset of the hunger strike, the rhetoric of moral outrage also became inflated. In one of the more dramatic student manifestos of this period, a group of hunger strikers waxed eloquent about their chosen path of martyrdom: "Farewell, fellow students, take care! Remember, though we may be dead, our loyal hearts remain among the living. Farewell, sweethearts, take care! We hate to leave you but we must. . . . Our pledge, written at the cost of our lives, will surely illuminate the skies of our Republic."[30] Such dramatic moral covenants—some written in blood for heightened effect—served further to polarize the conflict.

By this time, the striking students and their supporters, now including people of all ages and from all walks of life, had taken effective control of Tiananmen Square and its immediate environs. Using sophisticated broadcast equipment hooked up to loudspeakers in the square, strike leaders could counteract government propaganda broadcasts and spread their own messages among the milling throngs. Mimeograph machines poured out a steady stream of handbills, policy statements, and other printed materials. (Some time later, after the crackdown, the student communication network would be dubbed "seeking truth from fax.") Posters now went up in the square—some written in English to attract foreign media attention—calling for the resignations of Li Peng and Deng Xiaoping. Unflattering cartoon caricatures of Chinese leaders were also in evidence.

In the face of rapidly polarizing attitudes on both sides, Zhao Ziyang persisted in trying to bring about a peaceful resolution. On May 15 he (along with Hu Qili) agreed to meet the demands of several hundred petitioning journalists to allow the mass media to report on the student demonstrations objectively, free from official censorship. The next day, at a meeting of the Politburo Standing Committee, Zhao proposed, among other things, to retract the April 26 editorial, publish the incomes and emoluments of top party and government leaders, and set up an organization under the auspices of the NPC to investigate allegations of guandao among high officials and their offspring. The proposal was voted down, four to one; even Hu Qili, Zhao's erstwhile strongest supporter on the SC, now reportedly voted against him.[31]

Some weeks later, Yang Shangkun would allege that the Standing Committee had not rejected all of Zhao Ziyang's proposals outright, and that "everyone agreed" with at least two of his early suggestions, namely, that problems should be solved "on the basis of democracy and law," and that an official audit should be made of all private business companies. Evidently Yang's allegation was intended to shift the onus for continued intransigence off of party hard-liners and onto Zhao and the students.[32]

The primary reason for Zhao's increasing isolation among his peers was a rather simple one: Deng Xiaoping had already made up his mind to get tough with the students. The growing popular support and self-assurance of the pro-

Student leader Wu'er Kaixi appeals to hunger strikers at Tiananmen Square, May 1989.

test movement had confirmed the patriarch's worst-case scenario, namely, that further government concessions would bring not peace but an incessant escalation of demands, leading ultimately to Polish-style chaos. Under these circumstances, the hunger strike proved to be the final straw. On May 16 Yang Shangkun, relaying Deng's views, instructed an enlarged meeting of the party's MAC to make preparations for assembling troops to impose military control in Beijing.[33]

Deng's loss of confidence in Zhao, and Zhao's consequent loss of influence over decisions affecting the handling of the student movement, were signaled to the world during a meeting between Zhao and Mikhail Gorbachev on May 16. In this remarkable meeting, Zhao confirmed the existence of the secret protocol enacted at the Thirteenth Party Congress, granting Deng Xiaoping (and, to a lesser extent, Chen Yun) final say on all important matters of policy. When he learned of Zhao's revelation, Deng reportedly became livid.[34]

The next day, May 17, Zhao, clearly on the defensive in his struggle against the hard-line gerontocrats of the CAC (who by this time had begun regularly to attend and speak out at all important leadership meetings), made one last attempt to bring about a peaceful resolution of the crisis. Sending a message via Yan Mingfu to the hunger strikers in Tiananmen Square on behalf of the Central Committee and the State Council, Zhao personally acknowledged the patriotic spirit of the student movement and promised no reprisals if the students would terminate their strike. Although a clear majority of the young strikers reportedly favored accepting Zhao's offer, acceptance was blocked by a minority coalition of hard-line Beijing students and students from out of town. The hard-line Beijing faction was led by Chai Ling, who later gained notoriety by her harrowing escape from China in the aftermath of the June 4 crackdown.[35]

According to eyewitness accounts, Yan Mingfu worked hard throughout the period of Gorbachev's visit to convince student leaders that they should narrow their demands to only two: retraction of the April 26 editorial and governmental recognition of the BSAF. However, Yan's efforts to achieve a compromise settlement were reportedly rejected by Deng Xiaoping as well as by Chai Ling. As one participant subsequently noted, "There was no majority opinion in Tiananmen Square at that time. Everybody had his own ideas. Even if Deng had accepted those two points, it was still useless."[36]

On the evening of May 17 Zhao attended an expanded meeting of the Politburo Standing Committee, held in Deng Xiaoping's Broadway Street home behind the Forbidden City. At the meeting, which was also attended by Yang Shangkun and several old comrades of the CAC, including Chen Yun, Li Xiannian, Peng Zhen, and Wang Zhen, Zhao once again appealed for a retraction of the April 26 editorial. Deng refused, arguing that "We cannot retreat. One retreat will lead to another." He added, "Comrade Ziyang, your speech to the Asian Development Bank officials on May 4 became a turning point, because after that the students created more serious disturbances." Deng next proposed to implement martial law. The old comrades present agreed, noting that things had "gone far enough."

In response to Zhao's plea to refrain from imposing martial law, Deng played his high card. "I have the army behind me," declared the patriarch. "But I have the people behind me," countered Zhao. "Then you have nothing," trumped Deng, the consummate bridge player. Defeated, Zhao informed the Standing Committee that under the circumstances he could no longer serve as general secretary. His attempt to resign was rejected out of hand, and the SC proceeded to approve Deng's proposal to implement martial law at the conclusion of Gorbachev's visit. Presented with a fait accompli, Zhao sought to wash his hands of responsibility for the consequences that might follow: "Let Comrade Xiaoping make the final decision," he said.[37]

Although China's senior leaders had thus decided by May 17 to crack down on the student movement, there was considerable anxiety among the leadership (shared by hard-liners and moderates alike) that some of the hunger strikers, weakened by exhaustion and lack of nourishment, might die in front of the world's television cameras. If that were to occur, they argued, it would provide the student movement with instant martyrs and would probably touch off massive new demonstrations.

Such concerns were hardly idle. By this time, approximately 2,500 hunger strikers had already been treated for dehydration and heat exhaustion at local hospitals and makeshift health stations around Tiananmen Square. Under such circumstances, the authorities made a number of improvised, last-ditch efforts to coax the students into calling off their strike and peacefully evacuating the square.

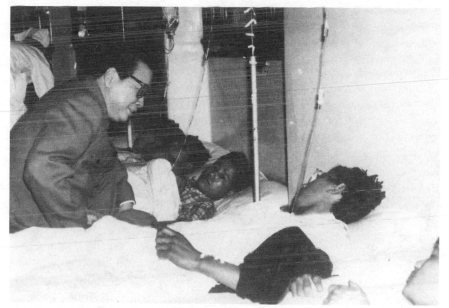

Li Peng visits hospitalized hunger strikers on May 18, 1989, seeking to persuade students to call off their strike.

THE FINAL STRAW

In the early morning hours of Thursday, May 18, four members of the Politburo Standing Committee paid a well-publicized, predawn "comfort visit" to a group of hospitalized hunger strikers. In televised film footage of this visit, Zhao Ziyang, Li Peng, Qiao Shi, and Hu Qili (Yao Yilin was not present) displayed visible concern for the health and well-being of the frail, weakened students, shaking hands with them and stopping to chat at their bedsides. The dominant image conveyed by the television cameras was one of benevolent paternalism. During the visit, Zhao Ziyang told one of the students: "The goal of the party and government is identical with that of the students; there is no fundamental conflict of interests. A variety of methods can be adopted to exchange views and resolve problems; don't adopt the method of a hunger strike. . . . You should look after your health." Talking with another bedridden student, Hu Qili counseled patience, saying that "Some problems cannot be solved immediately." When the student indicated that the party needed to reestablish its credibility in order to restore people's confidence, Hu Qili responded, "We fully agree with you." The student continued: "If you want to have prestige, I think that those who practice guandao and those high-ranking officials involved should start taking action against their own sons." After several minutes, the Chinese leaders left the hospital without having secured an agreement to end the strike.[38]

A second government initiative came later the same day, May 18, in a televised address by State Counselor Li Tieying. Again adopting a paternalistic stance, Li sought to reassure the striking students. "Your country loves you," he said; and he implored the protesters to end their hunger strike: "Come back, students; come back!"

Noting that both the Standing Committee's hospital visit and Li Tieying's impassioned plea came after the decision to impose martial law had already been taken, some observers have treated the government's show of concern for the welfare of the hunger strikers at this point as a cynical charade, designed to shift the burden of responsibility for the coming crackdown from the party to the student leaders. Alternatively, however, it is also quite plausible that many Chinese leaders were sincere in their desire to engineer an eleventh-hour settlement of the hunger strike—although they undoubtedly had their own reasons for doing so, ranging from genuine concern for the students' welfare to fear of a massive popular uprising in the event of deaths among the hunger strikers.

By far the most important official initiative to break the deadlock was a televised meeting that took place at the Great Hall of the People on the afternoon of May 18 between party and government officials, including Li Peng, Li Tieying, Chen Xitong, and Yan Mingfu, and leaders of the student hunger strike, represented by Wu'er Kaixi, Wang Dan, and others. Wu'er, who had been rushed from hospital to attend the meeting, was clothed in pajamas and bathrobe; looking pale and weak, he had an oxygen tube attached to his nose. At this remarkable meeting, excerpts of which were broadcast on national television later in the evening, Li Peng began by calmly striking a concerned, paternalistic posture; shortly thereafter, things began to deteriorate:

Li Peng: Today we will discuss one issue: how to relieve the hunger strikers of their present plight. The party and government are most concerned about the health of the students. You are all young, the oldest among you is only twenty-two or twenty-three, younger than my youngest child. None of my children are engaged in guandao—

Wu'er Kaixi: Excuse me for interrupting you, Premier Li, but time is running short. We are sitting here comfortably while students outside are suffering from hunger. You just said that we should discuss only one issue. [Wu'er points his index finger at Premier Li.] But the truth is, it was not you who invited us to talk, but we, all of us on Tiananmen Square, who invited you to talk. So we should be the ones to name the issues to be discussed. . . .

Wang Dan: . . . For the students to leave the square and call off the hunger strike, our conditions must be met in full. . . . First, a positive affirmation of the current student movement as a democratic and patriotic movement, not a "turmoil." Second, a dialogue to be held as soon as possible. . . .

Yan Mingfu: . . . We are very worried about how events will continue to develop. The only influence you can now exert is to decide to evacuate all hunger strikers. . . . The major issue concerning people now is the lives of the young hunger strikers; we must treasure their lives and take responsibility for them. . . .

Li Peng: . . . Neither the government nor the party Central Committee has ever said that the students are causing a turmoil.[39] We have consistently acknowledged your patriotic fervor. . . . However, events are not developing in conformity with your good intentions. . . . The fact is, social disorder has occurred in Beijing and is spreading to the whole country. The current situation . . . is out of control. . . . Anarchy has reigned in Beijing for the past several days. I have absolutely no intention of putting the blame on [individual student leaders], but the anarchy I have just described is a reality. The government of the People's Republic of China . . . cannot disregard such phenomena. . . .

Wu'er Kaixi: . . . I want to repeat what I have just said: We don't want to be bogged down in discussions. Give an immediate response to our conditions, because the students in the square are starving. If this is overruled, and we remain bogged down on this one question, then we will conclude that the government is not at all sincere in solving this problem. Then there will be no need for us representatives to stay here any longer.

Wang Dan: If Premier Li thinks that turmoil will ensue that will cause a bad impact on society, then I can declare on behalf of all the students that the government will be entirely to blame.[40]

At the conclusion of this remarkable exchange, Wu'er Kaixi collapsed on the floor in a faint.[41] As the meeting adjourned, Li Peng rose and awkwardly extended his hand toward the students in a gesture of apparent conciliation. When his outstretched hand was brushed aside, the premier was heard to remark: "You've gone too far." Visibly angered and struggling to maintain his composure, Li walked stiffly out of the room.[42]

With Gorbachev departing from China on May 18, and with student leaders refusing to terminate their hunger strike without prior government concessions, a break in the student ranks occurred. Perceiving the imminence of a governmental show of force, a substantial majority of fasting students favored evacuating Tiananmen Square. However, because the hunger strikers had previously agreed to abide by the rule of "decision by consensus," a small, vocal minority could—and did—continue to block settlement of the strike.

At a Politburo meeting that lasted well into the early morning hours of Friday, May 19, Zhao Ziyang made one last attempt to forestall a declaration of martial law. Offering to take full responsibility for the student disturbance, Zhao repeated his offer, initially made a week earlier, to empower a special anti-guandao panel to investigate his own sons, Zhao Dajun and Zhao Erjun, for possible corruption in connection with their business activities in Hainan and Shenzhen. His offer was rejected out of hand.[43] An argument reportedly ensued between Zhao and Deng Xiaoping, during the course of which Zhao once again offered to resign. As before, Zhao's resignation was rejected on the

Zhao Ziyang tearfully bids farewell to students in Tiananmen Square, May 19, 1989.

grounds that it would reveal a deep split within the leadership and would thus encourage the students to continue their strike.

At this point Zhao left the meeting, ordered up a car, and asked to be driven to Tiananmen Square. Accompanied by a visibly nervous Li Peng, Zhao arrived at the square shortly before 5:00 on Friday morning. Addressing student hunger strikers through a borrowed, hand-held amplifier, he plaintively apologized to them: "We've come too late," he said, his voice heavy with emotion, his eyes filled with tears. "I'm sorry. You should criticize us and blame us. It is reasonable that you should do so." This was to be Zhao's last public act as general secretary. Thereafter, he returned home and refused all requests to see visitors, pleading illness.

Within hours of Zhao's visit to the square, the first contingents of PLA troops began arriving at the outskirts of Beijing. Soldiers were also moved into position to take over radio, television, and newspaper facilities throughout the capital.

MARTIAL LAW: THE CRACKDOWN THAT FAILED

Shortly before midnight on Friday evening, May 19, Li Peng addressed an emergency meeting of several thousand party leaders, military officers, and Beijing municipal officials who had gathered at the auditorium of the PLA General Logistics Department in southwest Beijing. With public loudspeakers

Li Peng declares a state of emergency in Beijing, May 19, 1989. Note the empty chair on the dais at left, belonging to the absent Zhao Ziyang.

throughout Beijing and other major cities broadcasting the proceedings, Premier Li stated that the government had decided to take "resolute and powerful measures" to quell the turmoil in Beijing. He was followed to the podium by President Yang Shangkun, who solemnly declared that under the circumstances there was "no choice" but to move PLA units into the capital. Four of the five remaining members of the Politburo Standing Committee were on stage during the speeches by Li Peng and Yang Shangkun; the lone absentee was Zhao Ziyang, whose chair remained conspicuously empty. Later, President Yang would allege that Zhao's nonattendance at the meeting gave striking students a feeling of hope that they had a high-level supporter, thus encouraging them to "stir up greater trouble."[44]

At 9:30 A.M. on Saturday, May 20, Li Peng signed the order imposing martial law in eight administrative districts of the nation's capital. Shortly afterward, he defended his actions: "There was no way out. You go back a step, they advance a step; you go back two steps, they advance two steps. It got to the point where there was nowhere left to go. Any further retreat, and we might just as well have handed the country over to them."[45]

By the time Li Peng declared martial law, some seven or eight full divisions of PLA troops, numbering approximately 100,000 soldiers, supported by armored personnel carriers (APCs), were already in Beijing, having entered the capital the previous night. Making use of six main access routes and several

Citizens block a convoy of army vehicles attempting to enter
central Beijing, May 20, 1989.

minor ones, the troops had advanced under cover of darkness toward the center of the city. Before they could reach their destination, however, their separate paths had been blocked by an army of aroused citizens.

Alerted to the incoming troops by student pickets, the people of Beijing
took to the streets throughout the night of May 19, erecting makeshift barricades along key motor routes and placing themselves squarely in the path of
the military convoys. By 4:30 A.M.—a full five hours before martial law formally commenced—most incoming army units had been immobilized, their
paths effectively blocked by solid masses of citizens. Unarmed and apparently
unprepared for such overwhelming popular resistance on the part of the
shimin (urban residents) of Beijing, the soldiers were engulfed in a virtual sea
of nay-saying humanity. With that, the leadership's worst fears of a catalytic

fusion of hitherto fragmented, atomized pockets of urban alienation and discontent into a single, coherent rebellion began to come true.

Eyewitnesses variously estimate the total number of shimin who took part in the May 19–20 effort to stop the PLA from entering the city at between one and two million people.[46] The scene, though intensely emotional, was generally nonviolent. No shots were fired, and relatively few physical scuffles took place. Indignant residents, offended by the government's attempt to impose martial law, heatedly lectured soldiers about the peaceful, patriotic aims of the movement. A few soldiers were seen flashing the "V for Victory" sign to the crowds that surrounded their vehicles; some even held handwritten placards attesting to their support for human rights and democracy; most simply appeared bored or bewildered, as they awaited further instructions from their equally bewildered officers.[47]

Because nothing quite like this had happened before in the PRC, neither the students nor the shimin knew what to make of the situation, or how to react. For almost two days, reports of government ultimatums and rumors of an imminent military crackdown circulated in Beijing and other cities, creating a tense, anxious situation. A near-total government blackout on news concerning conditions in Beijing, imposed following the martial law declaration, made it difficult to obtain accurate information.

Despite the news blackout, urban residents along China's eastern seaboard were able to keep abreast of at least some of the latest developments in Beijing through Voice of America (VOA) short-wave radio broadcasts, television satellite transmissions, and telephone/fax contacts. In Nanjing, young men with portable stereo "boom boxes," perched high in the branches of trees in the town square, played recorded tapes of hourly VOA news summaries throughout the weekend of May 20–21, for the benefit of large crowds of listeners gathered below. In Shanghai, guests at major tourist hotels throughout the city were able to view the latest developments in and around Tiananmen Square on television via a mysteriously unbroken satellite downlink.[48]

Notwithstanding either the paucity of reliable news, the wave of unsubstantiated rumors, or the palpably heightened anxieties of the urban populace, on May 21 approximately one million Beijing residents demonstrated against the imposition of martial law.[49] The same day, the hunger strikers at Tiananmen Square ended their nine-day fast in order to join forces with other urban groups and strata in support of the rapidly burgeoning movement of popular resistance to martial law.

Movement leaders now made active preparations to deal with a possible military assault on Tiananmen Square. The hunger strike was officially ended. Makeshift roadblocks, set up the previous night to prevent entry of army vehicles into the city, were now hardened and reinforced; checkpoints were established by students along key thoroughfares, with coded identification required to pass in or out. "Flying Tiger" brigades, composed of newly affluent young urban getihu on motorcycles, recruited their members to ride picket along the

Demonstrators carry banners in English, appealing to a global media audience.

outer perimeter and to serve as messengers. Gifts of money, supplies, and equipment began to pour in to Tiananmen from various places, including Hong Kong and Taiwan, as a semipermanent encampment was erected in the square. Among the benefactors was the Stone Computer Company, a quasi-private Chinese enterprise whose president, Wan Runnan, reportedly donated U.S. $25,000 in cash plus a considerable amount of electronic broadcasting equipment to the antigovernment forces. By May 22 the student encampment at Tiananmen had become, in effect, a state within a state, complete with its own communications center, security apparatus, and housing and sanitation departments.

As the first tense days under martial law passed with no sign of government response, the ranks of the demonstrators continued to swell. Now whole factories and government work units openly displayed their solidarity with the students; banner-waving contingents representing Communist youth groups, government ministries, official media agencies, CASS research institutes, university departments, hotels, even public security agencies and law courts marched together in open support of what had become, by this time, an extremely broad-based urban coalition.

Significantly, the one major occupational group not represented in the demonstrations in any substantial number was the peasantry. By and large, China's farmers, particularly those living in the fertile deltas near urban centers along China's eastern seaboard, had done relatively well under Deng Xiaoping's agricultural and marketing reforms; consequently, most appeared relatively indifferent to (and ignorant of) the events unfolding in Beijing.

While urban popular support for the movement continued to swell, opposition to the government's hard-line tactics increased among a number of respected active and retired leaders of the Chinese army and government. On Sunday, May 21, the only two living PLA marshals, Nie Rongzhen and Xu Xiangqian, issued statements praising the patriotism of the students and assuring them that the PLA would not be used to quell their movement; the following day it was reported that seven senior PLA generals had drafted a letter to Deng Xiaoping protesting the imposition of martial law and affirming the view that the People's Liberation Army "belongs to the people. . . . it should never spill the blood of the people." One hundred senior army officers reportedly endorsed the letter.[50]

Notwithstanding such reassurances, by Sunday night rumors began to spread of an impending PLA assault on Tiananmen Square. Lending credibility to the rumors was the fact that warnings of an imminent crackdown were being issued to students in the square by people with high-level political connections, including a representative from the China Handicapped Association, headed by Deng Pufang. In the face of such dire warnings, student leaders were divided among themselves on how to deal with the contingency of armed attack. Some, including Wu'er Kaixi, counseled immediate withdrawal from the square, lest the Democracy Movement end in a bloodbath. Others argued that the rumor of an imminent attack was a piece of government disinformation, designed to trick the students into abandoning their stronghold.[51]

In the event, the rumors proved false; no assault was forthcoming, either in Beijing or elsewhere. At 7:00 A.M. on Monday, May 22, orders were passed down to PLA unit commanders throughout Beijing to withdraw to the outskirts of the city. Shortly after the orders came down, Wu'er Kaixi was ousted as president of the BSAF, his reputation sullied as a result of his having believed the rumors of an imminent attack.

The decision to have the army pull out proved highly controversial within the Politburo. At least one member of the Politburo Standing Committee, security expert Qiao Shi, reportedly argued against such a move, warning that a troop pullback would have the effect of making the students "think they had won" the struggle.[52]

Despite such reservations, the order to evacuate was generally carried out calmly and peacefully. One major exception occurred at Liuliqiao, on the main road leading to Beijing's southwestern Fengtai District. There, violence erupted on Monday evening when a motorized convoy of retreating soldiers found its path blocked by a barricade of disabled trucks and buses. Frustrated and fatigued, the soldiers found themselves surrounded by citizens. Some bricks were thrown from the crowd, and a melee ensued. Official sources later claimed that twenty-nine soldiers, suffering from various minor injuries, were admitted to a local hospital. Unofficial sources put the total number of casualties from the Liuliqiao incident at forty, including roughly equal numbers of soldiers and civilians.[53]

The following day, Tuesday, May 23, the first military fatality was reported, also in Beijing's Fengtai District, when a PLA political instructor died of head injuries reportedly suffered when he fell off a truck that had accelerated suddenly in the course of the army's retreat. Later, on May 29, the Central People's Broadcasting Station would claim that the soldier's injury had been sustained when he was shoved under a moving truck by a rioter.

In the first, tension-filled week following the declaration of martial law, a number of political initiatives were undertaken with a view to bringing about a peaceful resolution of the conflict. On the government side, three petitions were circulated among members of the NPC Standing Committee calling for a special session of the SC to be convened immediately to deal with the crisis. The petitions were drawn up and circulated at the initiative of Hu Jiwei, assisted by Cao Siyuan of the Stone Company.[54] On May 24 the three petitions, bearing the signatures of 57 members of the Standing Committee (out of a total of 156), were delivered to the General Office of the NPC along with a cover letter from Hu Jiwei, addressed to Standing Committee Chairman Wan Li and First Vice-Chairman Xi Zhongxun. Hu and other leaders of the petition drive intended to resolve the crisis by using the constitutional authority of the NPC to challenge—and annul—Li Peng's martial law declaration. However, the 57 signatures (6 of which were later alleged to be unauthorized) fell well short of the absolute majority of 78 needed to call a special session of the committee; consequently, the petition drive failed.[55]

Two days before the petitions were delivered, on Monday, May 22, Wan Li, in the course of an official visit to Canada and the United States, publicly criticized the decision to invoke martial law and declared his intention to "firmly protect the patriotic enthusiasm of the young people in China." The following day, Wan cut short his visit to North America and returned to China, citing health problems as the reason.

Wan Li's return was eagerly awaited. In lieu of a written request from an absolute majority of NPC SC members requesting an emergency meeting of that body, leading members of the committee, including its chairman and vice-chairmen, were authorized to convene a special session on their own initiative. On May 22, two days before Hu Jiwei's petitions were filed with the NPC General Office, Wan Li's predecessor, Peng Zhen, convened a vice-chairman's meeting. At the meeting, Peng explained to the eighteen NPC vice-chairmen that a declaration of martial law had been necessary because some of the students in Tiananmen had failed to follow "the orbit of law" in expressing their opinions and raising demands. In its official report on this meeting, Beijing Radio claimed that the vice-chairmen had collectively expressed their gratitude to Peng for providing necessary clarification.[56]

Two days later, on May 24, while Wan Li was en route to China from the United States, a majority of those in attendance at the NPC SC vice-chairmen's meeting defied Peng Zhen and registered their support for the appeal by Hu Jiwei and the 57 petitioners to convene a special session of the Standing

Committee. All that remained was to secure Chairman Wan's endorsement of the appeal—which helps to explain why the students and their supporters so eagerly awaited Wan's return from North America.[57]

CIRCLING THE WAGONS: DENG PREPARES HIS RESPONSE

Following the army's withdrawal from central Beijing on May 22–23, the students and their allies were left effectively in control of the heart of the city. To all outward appearances, the protesters had won. Behind the scenes, however, the situation was quite otherwise. Shortly after ordering the imposition of martial law, Deng Xiaoping reportedly traveled to Shijiazhuang, southwest of Beijing, to line up the support of PLA regional forces.[58] By May 26, commanders of all seven greater military regions had publicly declared their support, with the Beijing regional commander the last—and apparently the most hesitant—to do so.

The reluctant commander of the Beijing Military Region, General Zhou Yibing, was subsequently transferred to another post. His deputy commander, General Yan Tongmao, was also relieved of his duties shortly after the June 3–4 crackdown.[59] Also disciplined for insubordination in this period was the commander of China's elite 38th Group Army, General Xu Qinxian, who had reportedly feigned recurrence of an old leg injury in order to avoid ordering his troops to enforce martial law in Beijing. General Xu was arrested in late May; he was later court-martialed and sent to prison.[60]

Meanwhile, on May 22 the Politburo Standing Committee, minus Zhao Ziyang, convened an enlarged meeting of the Politburo. At the meeting, Yang Shangkun, Li Peng, and Qiao Shi all spoke in support of the decision to impose martial law and to criticize Zhao Ziyang's handling of the situation between April 29 and May 19. Yang and Li were restrained in their critique of Zhao's behavior, accusing him of making "mistakes" but avoiding the type of inflammatory rhetoric previously used in the attack against Hu Yaobang in 1987. By contrast, Qiao Shi's assessment of the current situation was more foreboding. "At present," said the party's top security expert, "we will on the one hand use troops as a deterrent, and on the other find [a suitable] occasion to clear the square. . . . The reason we have procrastinated [until now] is that we . . . are trying to avoid bloodshed. But it won't do to [let things] drag on like this."

Two days later, on May 24, at yet another enlarged session of the Politburo, Zhao Ziyang's dismissal from the Politburo SC was approved. The stated reason for Zhao's ouster was his post facto withdrawal of support for the April 26 *People's Daily* editorial, an act that, according to Deng Xiaoping, had sown confusion within the party and split the party leadership into "two headquarters." At the May 24 meeting, Hu Qili defended Zhao and registered his opposition to the May 20 martial law declaration.

With the general secretary now officially in disgrace, Yang Shangkun stepped up his criticism of Zhao's behavior. At an enlarged meeting of the MAC on May 24, Yang endorsed the opinion of "Chairman Deng"[61] that Zhao's actions after returning from North Korea on April 29 had served to split the party into two competing camps. Acting as Deng Xiaoping's stand-in, a role that he faithfully enacted throughout the May-June crisis, Yang Shangkun revealed the thinking of China's paramount leader. At one point in his statement to the MAC, Yang compared the behavior of the Zhao-inspired Beijing students with the anarchistic behavior of Red Guards during the Cultural Revolution.[62] This was a serious charge, one that could, if upheld, result in Zhao's expulsion from the party, or even worse. At another point in his remarks, Yang Shangkun spoke ominously about necessary preparations for undertaking military action against student demonstrators: "We can no longer retreat, but must launch an offensive. I want to tell you about this today so that you can prepare yourselves mentally. In particular, the army must be consolidated; this is of vital importance. . . . If any troops do not obey orders, I will punish those responsible according to military law."[63] At the conclusion of his remarks Yang reportedly instructed army commanders to move their troops into preassigned positions, then "take a rest" in preparation for action.[64]

WAN LI RETURNS

While Yang Shangkun was addressing the MAC on May 24, Wan Li was in flight back to China from the United States. His return, eagerly awaited by the students in Tiananmen Square, proved to be a major disappointment to them. Landing in Shanghai in the early morning hours of May 25, Wan was immediately whisked into seclusion by Shanghai party chief Jiang Zemin. When he reemerged two days later, having been fully briefed on the latest political developments in Beijing, Wan not only failed to endorse the objectives of the Democracy Movement, including the demand to convene a special session of the NPC SC, he also publicly announced his support for martial law.

Wan Li's last-minute about-face apparently resulted from a wholly pragmatic calculation: since the hard-liners had clearly carried the day both in the Politburo and in the MAC, there was little to be gained by belatedly resisting a fait accompli, however unpleasant.[65] Notwithstanding Wan's tactical retreat, however, the NPC SC chairman continued, in his public statements, to refer to the student movement in Beijing as "patriotic."

Taking a decidedly more sinister view of the situation in Beijing, Chen Yun, in a televised address on May 26, indirectly implicated Zhao Ziyang in the conspiratorial activities of a "treacherous antiparty clique." The same day, six of Zhao's supporters, including Hu Qili, Defense Minister Qin Jiwei, and political reform adviser Bao Tong, were singled out for criticism by CAC hard-liners at a leadership meeting.

Meanwhile, in Tiananmen Square there was noticeable attrition in the ranks of the encamped students. While massive public demonstrations continued to be held almost daily, dwindling numbers of students living and sleeping on the square bespoke the growing physical and emotional exhaustion of the movement. On May 27 —the same day Wan Li emerged from seclusion in Shanghai to endorse Li Peng's declaration of martial law—Wang Dan and Wu'er Kaixi proposed to end the occupation of Tiananmen Square. Their proposal called for holding one final, massive demonstration on May 30, followed by a triumphal procession to evacuate the square. As before, however, a minority coalition composed of out-of-towners and radical confrontationists objected to the evacuation proposal, blocking its adoption and binding the students to remain in the square until June 20, the date of the next regularly scheduled meeting of the NPC Standing Committee.[66]

ENTER THE WORKING CLASS

With student interest and enthusiasm dwindling noticeably in the last week of May, industrial workers for the first time began to play a significant role in the Tiananmen protests. Latecomers to the movement, Beijing workers had generally refrained from openly supporting the students in April and early May. Somewhat disdainful of the snobbish, elitist college students, and fearful of possible government (or work unit) reprisals, workers generally held back, maintaining a low profile. By May 2, only about two thousand workers had reportedly registered to join Gongzilian, the newly formed Beijing Workers' Autonomous Federation.[67]

Two events served to galvanize Beijing's industrial workers: the hunger strike of mid May and, more importantly, the successful display of massive citizen resistance to the martial law declaration of May 20. Thereafter, the ranks of working class protesters swelled appreciably. By the beginning of June, Gongzilian had increased its membership tenfold, to around twenty thousand.[68] Spokespersons for the dissident workers included a soft-spoken young railway electrician, Han Dongfang, age twenty-five, and thirty-four-year-old Li Jinjin, a law student turned labor organizer.

From the outset, worker interests and demands were relatively distinct from those of students. Abstract democracy and human rights were of only limited, instrumental importance to workers, who tended to be more deeply concerned with bread-and-butter economic issues and with gaining government recognition of their right to protect and promote their own interests. Secondarily, workers were motivated by anger at the manifest corruption and profligacy of high-level party and government officials and their offspring.

By and large, workers in state-owned enterprises tended to be less supportive of China's urban economic reforms than were students; to such workers, the prospect of a broken "iron rice bowl" was a source of considerable anxiety and insecurity.[69] Nor were they particularly enamored of either Deng Xiaoping or Zhao Ziyang, whom workers saw as being largely impervious to the pain and suffering of common people: "Where are you taking us?" asked a Gongzilian handbill dated May 29. "You bureaucrats have made a mess of China. . . . It's not enough to say that you are 'feeling for stones as you cross the river'; what about those of us who fall in and drown? We've had ten years of reform and we don't know where we're going. The bureaucratic cats get fat, while the people starve."[70]

In the last half of May, while the rebel Gongzilian was increasing its following among alienated members of Beijing's working class, China's official labor union, the All-China Federation of Trade Unions (ACFTU), remained in the background. Although informally supportive of the students in the square, ACFTU leaders, apparently fearing government recrimination, refused to assist Gongzilian in the latter's efforts to achieve official recognition as a legal trade union. Unable to gain organizational aid from the ACFTU, Gongzilian leaders, acting on their own initiative, established informal ties with sympathetic workers in several large industrial enterprises in Beijing, including the Capital Iron and Steel Corporation and the Beijing Coking Coal Plant. Workers from these and other enterprises took part in the massive daily marches that commenced on May 17. Worker participation increased once again after the government's May 20 martial law declaration. By that time, the acting head of the ACFTU, Zhu Houze, had clearly signaled the organization's prodemocratic sympathies by writing out a check to the students in the amount of RMB ¥100,000.[71]

After keeping the workers' organization at arm's length for several weeks, by the end of May student leaders, recognizing that their own ranks were thinning rapidly, finally allowed Gongzilian to move its operations into Tiananmen Square. Although workers were thus belatedly welcomed as participants in the movement, they were not given equal standing. They were not, for example, permitted to use student facilities to publicize their call for a general strike; and they were repeatedly reminded that the protest movement was under the control of students, not workers. For the most part, Workers' Federation members were assigned the task of providing security for demonstrators in the square.[72] By the end of May, a "workers' picket corps" (*gongren jiuchadui*) and four "dare-to-die brigades" (*gansidui*) had been set up to help defend the square in the event of hostile action by police or military personnel.

In response to increased worker participation in the protest movement in the last week in May, the government began to organize counterdemonstrations among workers, students, and ordinary citizens. One progovernment rally, held in suburban Daxing County, drew as many as four thousand participants—many of whom claimed they had been ordered to attend by their work-unit leaders. In Beijing, railway workers and government employees were reportedly offered a cash bonus of RMB ¥100 to stay away from student rallies; in some places, workers who abandoned their posts to attend prodemocracy demonstrations were threatened with fines.[73] By the end of May, workers in Beijing were under heavy pressure to choose sides.

THE GODDESS AND THE CHAIRMAN

At dusk on May 29, with less than ten thousand protesters remaining in Tiananmen Square, a group of students from Beijing's Central Arts Academy began to construct a bamboo scaffolding at the northern end of the square, between the Heroes' Monument and the Forbidden City, squarely in front of the portrait of Mao Zedong that hangs atop the Gate of Heavenly Peace. With the scaffolding completed, the students next assembled, from prefabricated sections brought to the square on bicycle carts, a thirty-five-foot-high statue of a woman grasping a torch in her upstretched arms. Variously known as the "goddess of democracy" (*minzhu nushen*), the "spirit of democracy" (*minzhu zhishen*), the "goddess of the nation" (*minzu nushen*), and the "goddess of liberty" (*ziyou nushen*), the statue was completed in the early morning hours of May 30.

The original working model for the statue—a four-foot-high male figure with one arm upraised—had been hand-carried by train from Shanghai several days earlier. During the construction process at the Central Arts Academy, the statue had been modified into a two-handed female figure. The statue's final appellation—Goddess of Democracy—appears to have emerged as an unplanned afterthought. According to one participant in the project, the name was blurted out spontaneously by a student craftsman on May 30, in response to a television interviewer's question. The name stuck.[74]

Construction of the statue, like Mikhail Gorbachev's visit to Beijing two weeks earlier, served to inject new life and energy into the dwindling student movement. As many as 300,000 spectators flocked to Tiananmen Square on May 30-31 to see the white plaster, wire, and styrofoam Goddess standing eyeball-to-eyeball with Chairman Mao Zedong, torch defiantly upraised. Whether or not mockery had been the conscious intent of the art students, it surely was the effect, as dozens of television cameras expertly framed the ironic, silent confrontation between the Goddess and the Chairman, the Democrat and the Dictator. The students, their flagging spirits revived, announced their determination to remain in the square.

Two days later, four prominent prodemocracy activists initiated a second hunger strike, led by the popular Taiwanese-born folk singer, Hou Dejian.[75] The four strikers raised but one demand in their manifesto: the government should cooperate in constructing a civil society of "legal autonomous organizations" to balance the monopolistic powers of the Communist Party-dominated state. The strike was intended to be of limited duration—seventy-two hours—after which the four activists and their supporters would leave the square. To celebrate the beginning of the hunger strike, Hou Dejian led the assembled crowd in an impromptu sing-along.

In the event, the new hunger strike had little impact. Several days earlier, a high-level contact had unofficially warned student leaders that they might soon be subject to arrest as agents of Zhao Ziyang. Confirming their worst

Unveiling the Goddess of Democracy, May 30, 1989.

fears, on May 28 Bao Tong—the man who issued the warning—was himself secretly detained by police. Two days later, the arrests began in earnest.

Significantly, student leaders were not included in the initial group of police detainees; their allies, the newly radicalized shimin of Beijing, were. Among the first to be rounded up shortly after midnight on May 30 were three members of Gongzilian and eleven members of the Flying Tigers motorcycle brigade.[76] Under these circumstances, Hou Dejian's June 2 hunger strike and hootenanny were largely irrelevant. The crackdown had begun.

Cracking Down: June 1989–February 1990

The crux of the current incident is basically a
confrontation between the four cardinal principles and
bourgeois liberalization.

—*Deng Xiaoping, June 9, 1989*

I⊤ IS tempting to pinpoint the appearance of the Goddess of Democracy on
May 30 as the final straw, the catalyst that brought the full militarized wrath
of Deng Xiaoping and the old comrades of the CAC down upon the heads of
the audacious, libertarian students of Beijing and their newfound allies, the
shimin of urban China. Almost certainly, however, the decision to crack down
had been made a week earlier. Moreover, the catalyst that triggered the debacle that followed was not so much the audacity of the students themselves as
the rising groundswell of popular sympathy and support evoked by the students' defiance. Clearly, a raw nerve had been touched.

Two developments were of particular concern to party leaders. One was the
rapid rise of a militant, autonomous workers' movement that proclaimed its
solidarity with the students, thereby bringing ever closer to reality Deng Xiaoping's recurrent Polish nightmare; the other was the progressive defection of
substantial numbers of party, government, and army leaders to the side of the
students, lending critical weight and legitimacy to the antiregime fervor that
was sweeping through China's major urban centers.

In light of Deng's overriding concern with avoiding a Polish-type situation,
it is hardly accidental that the first to be arrested in the June crackdown were
dissident industrial workers rather than students. Historically, students comprised an elite substratum within China's paternalistic political order; even in
contemporary times they have been shielded from severe state reprisals in all
but the most extreme circumstances. Similar latitude has seldom been granted
other occupational groups, however—especially not workers, and most especially not after the Polish crisis of 1980–81. As one Beijing worker put it,
"You know, with students it's nothing; they arrest you for a couple of days
and let you go. But when we workers get arrested, they shoot us. . . . The
government is ruthless toward us workers."[1]

Mindful of the potential for spontaneous self-organization among urban
workers, China's leaders in April and May 1989 nervously monitored the
growing impact of the student movement upon the industrial labor force. By

arresting leaders of Gongzilian before they could effectively mobilize mass popular support, the authorities hoped to nip working class protest in the bud.

Alongside mounting fear of working class rebellion there was another, equally powerful reason for the government to crack down sooner rather than later: a rising tide of defections from, and disarray within, the ranks of the Communist Party itself. According to an internal party audit conducted shortly after the crackdown of June 3–4, more than ten thousand cadres from central party and government departments had taken part in the May demonstrations in Beijing.[2] Nationwide, the figures were even more disturbing, as Communist Party sources subsequently confirmed that at least 800,000 CCP members (out of a total of more than 45 million) participated in prodemocracy rallies in 123 cities during the Beijing Spring of 1989. Within the Ministry of Culture, some 2,800 employees, including at least 500 department-level and 50 bureau-level cadres, representing 15 percent of the total, participated in the demonstrations.[3] A report by the CDIC later revealed that 90,000 party members requested to resign from the party in the first eight weeks after martial law was declared on May 20, 1989.[4]

In short, China's leaders acted in early June to preempt what they viewed, not without reason, as a rapidly deteriorating, deeply threatening situation. In light of events that subsequently unfolded in East and Central Europe in the latter part of 1989, Chinese leaders' fears of being swept away in a burgeoning, out-of-control antigovernment rebellion may not have been so far off the mark.

Preparing for the Crackdown

Many things remain unclear about just what happened and why in the first week of June 1989. At least two things are quite clear, however. First, a substantial number of civilians died in the course of a massive assault by heavily armed, armor-backed PLA infantry units in central Beijing on the evening of June 3–4, as well as in subsequent mopping-up operations. Best available estimates (which remain inconclusive) place the total number of dead at between 1,000 and 2,600, including at least 36 students and several dozen soldiers and PAP personnel. In addition, 6,000 military and public security personnel reportedly suffered nonfatal injuries, with an unknown (but almost certainly substantially larger) number of civilians wounded.[5] Second, despite persistent rumors to the contrary, no cold-blooded massacre of students took place in Tiananmen Square itself.[6]

The military crackdown was ominously, if obliquely, foreshadowed on Wednesday, May 31, when Beijing Mayor Chen Xitong told a group of local schoolchildren, assembled to celebrate the occasion of Children's Day, "I think you will soon be able to pay tribute to the revolutionary martyrs at the Monument to the People's Heroes."[7] On the same day, as if to add emphasis to Mayor Chen's remark, the government stepped up its efforts, under way since the previous weekend, quietly to infiltrate PLA combat troops directly into the center of Beijing.

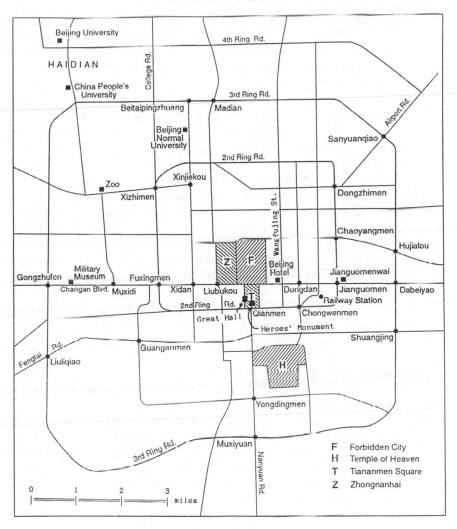

Central Beijing.

Under orders to maintain a low profile and avoid attracting attention, the incoming soldiers for the most part were neither armed nor outfitted in combat dress. Some came by truck, their telltale military license plates removed; some were ferried into the city in unmarked buses, minivans, jeeps, and even ambulances, arriving a few—or a few dozen—at a time; others advanced casually on foot, in small groups, outfitted in civilian clothes.[8] Weapons were transported into the city separately, also in unmarked trucks, buses, and vans. In addition, as many as ten thousand fully equipped soldiers were infiltrated into the heart of Beijing through underground tunnels, ultimately being disgorged inside the Great Hall of the People, along the western edge of Tiananmen Square (see map).

By Friday, June 2, the government's effort to achieve a large-scale, low-profile military infiltration of Beijing had aroused considerable citizen attention and concern. In midevening, concern turned to outright anger when a jeep belonging to the People's Armed Police, traveling at high speed without license plates, careened out of control near Muxidi, west of Tiananmen, striking and killing two bicyclists and a pedestrian. When the driver of the vehicle refused to take responsibility for the injuries, claiming immunity under martial law, a group of angry bystanders converged on the jeep, smashing its windshield, pulling the driver out, and slapping him in the face. The driver was rescued by his passengers—three soldiers out of uniform—who whisked him away from the angry throng.

Word of the jeep incident spread quickly through the city. Alerted to the accelerated movement of incoming troops, and anticipating a possible military assault, citizens took to the streets in large numbers, determined to thwart the government's plans once again. Throughout the evening of June 2–3, numerous contingents of soldiers, some traveling in motorized convoys, some on foot, were discovered, isolated, encircled, and in some cases assailed by the aroused shimin of Beijing. Under orders to avoid conflict with civilians, soldiers generally remained passive when confronted by hostile citizens. Some were visibly frightened and confused. Others broke away from their captors, disappearing into the crowds. In some cases, buses and vans carrying PLA weapons and/or ammunition were stopped and seized by civilians, their cargoes exhibited as booty. To avoid provoking a strong military reaction, student leaders urged citizens to put all captured rifles and ammunition back inside the vehicles from which they had been seized.

One of the most curious incidents in this unfolding drama took place in the predawn hours of June 3. At around 2:00 Saturday morning a column of approximately six thousand unarmed, ill-seasoned young PLA soldiers, dressed in short-sleeved white shirts, olive pants, and running shoes, was spotted on East Chang'an Boulevard, approximately three miles from Tiananmen, jogging doubletime toward the square. By around 2:30 A.M. the head of the military column reached the intersection of Wangfujing Street near the Peking Hotel, a few hundred yards from the square. At that point the unit's progress was halted by a makeshift traffic barricade and a solid wall of citizens, who had been alerted to the imminent arrival of the troops by a squad of civilian bicycle riders.

By 3:00 A.M. the soldiers at Wangfujing had been enveloped in a vast sea of hostile shimin. The six thousand infantry—unarmed, weary, visibly confused, and for the most part leaderless—were easily immobilized. Broken up into clusters, the hapless young conscripts were subjected to verbal (and occasional physical) harrassment for several hours, receiving heated lectures on subjects ranging from democracy and human rights to civil-military harmony. After a while, one group of soldiers broke through the encircling crowd and fled in disarray. Eventually, the remaining troops were permitted to retreat—minus shoes, rations, and rucksacks—in the direction of the Peking

Railway Station. As they fled, they were repeatedly jostled and subjected to continuing verbal abuse. Once again, as on May 19–20, it seemed that the people of Beijing had won a stunning victory over an inept Chinese government.

There remains considerable controversy over the underlying purpose of the rather artless military maneuvers carried out by the government in the first three days of June. So unsuccessful were the government's attempts to disguise the PLA's entry into Beijing that some observers have speculated that this may have been a deliberate provocation, designed to achieve one of two possible objectives: either to highlight the army's patient endurance of intolerable abuse and humiliation at the hands of student-led mobs, or to provoke a physical attack upon unarmed soldiers by "ruffians" and "thugs"—or perhaps both. Either way, the government would be provided with a convenient pretext for launching its intended crackdown.[9]

On the other hand, it has also been observed, with equal persuasiveness, that had the six thousand unarmed troops trapped on East Chang'an Boulevard managed to make it past the Wangfujing barricade to Tiananmen, they would have been united both with their own weapons (which had been separately transported into the city) and with other combat units that had already begun converging on the square. With this in mind, an alternative scenario gains added credibility. This view, which takes at face value the government's clumsy attempt to move combat units quietly into position in the heart of the city, postulates that the purpose of the operation was not to provoke but to *prevent* premature confrontations with civilians—confrontations of the type that had foiled the government's initial attempt to enforce martial law on May 20. According to this scenario, the failure of incoming military units to avoid arousing suspicion was the result of accidental exposure compounded by ineptness, rather than design.

Irrespective of government motivations or intentions, the triumph of the Beijing *shimin* proved short-lived. With the enveloping darkness of a new moon due to arrive on the evening of June 3, preparations for the crackdown were nearing completion. According to unofficial tabulations, between 150,000 and 200,000 troops from at least twelve group armies, representing three greater military regions, had converged upon the Beijing area and were now in position.[10]

THE "TIANANMEN MASSACRE"

The first serious confrontation between government forces and citizens occurred early Saturday afternoon, June 3, when a large contingent of riot police attempted forcibly to "liberate" a busload of automatic rifles and machine guns that had been seized by civilians the previous night at Liubukou, west of Tiananmen near Zhongnanhai. Earlier in the day, around 10:00 A.M., a team of soldiers had tried to negotiate the release of the bus and its cargo, but the

Beijing citizens display military hardware taken from a
captured arms bus at Liubukou, June 3, 1989.

attempt had been thwarted when student leaders balked at the prospect of
turning captured weapons directly over to PLA combat forces.

At around 2:00 P.M. government loudspeakers at Liubukou blared out a
directive from the martial law command headquarters, ordering the crowd—
which by this time had swelled to around two thousand people—to release the
imprisoned bus and immediately disperse. When the shimin failed to comply,
government forces fired a round of tear gas at the crowd. A gust of wind blew
the gas cloud back toward the soldiers, and the now-angry crowd began to
surge forward. Hurling rocks and bottles, the people soon encountered a solid
wall of three thousand helmeted, baton-wielding riot police who had emerged
from the main entrance of Zhongnanhai. Firing tear-gas shells and clubbing
anyone unfortunate enough to get in their way, the police eventually succeeded in cordoning off the street and reclaiming the arms-laden bus. According to one eyewitness, more than forty demonstrators were injured in the hour-

Demonstrators confront riot police at Liubukou, June 3, 1989.

long melee, which provided a grim, if nonlethal, preview of the cataclysm to come.[11]

Shortly after the fighting broke out at Liubukou, a force of several thousand soldiers, unarmed but in full battle dress, emerged from the western entrance of the Great Hall of the People. Sent on a mission to help the embattled riot police at Liubukou reclaim the busload of captured rifles, the troops never reached their destination. As soon as they left the protective shelter of the Great Hall, they were surrounded by shimin. Scuffles broke out, and several civilian demonstrators were dragged to the ground, beaten and clubbed by the soldiers. Enraged, an angry crowd of several hundred workers began hurling stones and bricks at the Great Hall of the People, smashing a number of ornately decorated light posts. Some twenty to thirty civilians and a handful of soldiers were injured in the fighting.

Student monitors and Red Cross representatives, urging restraint and non-violence, eventually succeeded in separating the two groups of combatants. A human cordon was thrown around the troops, insulating them from the angry shimin and preventing them from moving. Though tempers were frayed and incidents of shouting, jostling, and physical assault flared episodically throughout the remainder of the afternoon, the situation at the west end of the Great Hall of the People was gradually brought under control. Forced to sit passively on the ground enveloped in a sea of hostile humanity for several hours, the soldiers were eventually permitted to beat an undignified retreat back into the Great Hall from whence they came.[12]

Meanwhile, at around 4:00 Saturday afternoon, the commanders of the various group armies that had been brought to Beijing assembled at the headquarters of the Beijing Military Region to receive their final instructions. The "liberation" of Tiananmen was scheduled to commence with several divisions of motorized infantry entering the city separately, from different directions, in three successive waves starting at around 5:00 P.M. The initial assault waves were to be followed, around 10:30 P.M., by two additional waves spearheaded by armored divisions. A deadline was set: Tiananmen Square was to be cleared no later than daybreak Sunday morning.

At around 6:30 P.M. the Beijing municipal government and martial law headquarters issued an emergency notice warning Beijing residents not to go out onto the streets or into the square; violators would be "responsible for their own fate." The message was rebroadcast repeatedly from 7:00 to 9:00 P.M. on government radio and television stations.

Escorted by armored personnel carriers (APCs), the initial wave of motorized infantry units made their way into Beijing from suburban staging areas between 5:00 and 6:00 P.M. By the time the first convoys reached Beijing's Third Ring Road, a major beltway encircling the central city some four to five miles outside of Tiananmen, they encountered a series of dilatory obstacles. As on May 19–20, citizens blockaded a number of key thoroughfares, bridges, and intersections. Forcing numerous army vehicles—and sometimes even entire convoys—to stop, the people lectured their captive military audiences once again on the immorality of using the PLA to quell the people.[13]

While civilians blocked traffic in many areas of the city, it was on the main western approach to Tiananmen, along a three-mile stretch of West Chang'an Boulevard between the Third (outer) and Second (inner) Ring Roads, that citizen resistance was heaviest. It was there that the Chinese Army first fired upon the Chinese people.

Shortly before 9:00 P.M., advancing infantry units from the 38th Group Army, supported by armor and artillery, and escorted by an elite vanguard of six hundred well-armed riot-control forces from the PAP, encountered a mass of several thousand angry civilians just east of the Third Ring Road. Blocking the path of the oncoming convoy, the shimin began shouting at the soldiers, imploring them to "get the f—— out of here." Some young men in the crowd began throwing rocks, bricks, and bottles at the convoy, shattering truck windows. Ignoring the hail of stones and bottles, the soldiers pushed on. Ahead of them a human wall, comprising approximately fifteen thousand citizens, arrayed fifteen rows deep, retreated slowly, separated from the head of the advancing military column by a no-man's land approximately one hundred meters wide.

The first shots were fired shortly after 10:00 P.M., when several short bursts of automatic rifle fire—evidently intended as a warning—were discharged into the air, above the heads of the angry demonstrators. Surprised but not intimidated, the people held their ground, refusing to disperse. "Put down your weapons!" they shouted to the troops. The PAP antiriot forces escorting the army convoy responded by hurling several dozen stun grenades at the demonstrators. No injuries were inflicted, as the grenades exploded twenty meters or so in front of the massed protesters. At this point, frightened by the noise and smoke from the grenade attack, some people in the crowd began to flee.

As the convoy resumed its eastward march, passing the Military Museum some four miles from Tiananmen, the retreating protesters regrouped behind a barricade of disabled buses and traffic dividers. Encountering the barricade, the army column halted its advance, whereupon it was greeted with a new fusillade of rocks and projectiles hurled from the crowd. At around 10:45 P.M., as the soldiers broke through the barricade, a second barrage of automatic rifle fire rang out. This time, the troops aimed their rifles lower.[14]

Under orders to clear Tiananmen Square by dawn Sunday or face military discipline (which under martial law meant the near certainty of a firing squad), the soldiers now discharged their AK-47s directly into the crowd. At first paralyzed by dismay and disbelief, the people quickly dispersed. Some fled in panic; others stayed behind to care for the dead and wounded. Bullets flew in random, stray patterns, felling fleeing protesters and bystanders alike. Several apartment buildings facing Chang'an Boulevard were strafed as the armored convoy approached the canal bridge at Muxidi, three miles from Tiananmen Square.

Most of the killing in Beijing took place between 10:45 P.M. and 3:00 A.M., as the scene near Muxidi was replayed, with minor variations, at several locations throughout the city. With fast-moving APCs running interference for motorized infantry units, driving armored wedges through the makeshift barricades and crowds of people that blocked the paths of oncoming troops, PLA units continued their relentless drive toward the square, shooting as they went. Enraged, the people now fought back with whatever weapons they could find (or make), including Molotov cocktails, steel construction rods, and an assortment of makeshift knives and clubs. Jamming iron rods into the exposed treads of APCs, they succeeded in disabling a number of the armored vehicles, many of which were then set afire; when the frightened APC crews tried to escape, some were set upon by the angry crowds and savagely beaten; a few were immolated, hanged, dismembered, or even disemboweled. Many others were escorted to safety by student and Red Cross monitors.

Though acts of deadly violence occurred throughout the city, the killing was most concentrated and intense along a two-mile stretch of West Chang'an Boulevard between Muxidi and Xidan, later dubbed "Blood Road." There, according to government statistics, 65 PLA trucks and 47 APCs belonging to the 38th Group Army were totally destroyed, and 485 other military vehicles were damaged.[15] The government's official casualty count from this single "battle" totaled 6 soldiers killed and 1,114 wounded. There are no reliable figures for the number of civilian casualties suffered along this particular

Armored personnel carriers set afire on Chang'an Boulevard,
June 4, 1989.

stretch of Chang'an Boulevard, though it is believed that the civilian death toll
was in the hundreds. In any event, numerous eyewitnesses have testified to the
carnage that took place there.

Although the Chinese government would later allege that "counterrevolutionary conspirators," "hooligans," and "rioters" initiated the bloodbath of
June 3–4 by committing a series of unprovoked atrocities against martial law
forces, it is reasonably clear that most acts of citizen violence against soldiers
were a consequence, rather than a cause, of the army's deadly assault on the
shimin of Beijing. Even the government's vaunted "smoking gun," a crudely
edited videotape purporting to show "thugs" savagely attacking and torching
disabled army vehicles, turns out to have been recorded some hours *after* the
initial killing of civilians had commenced near Muxidi.[16]

Charred corpse of a PLA soldier, June 4, 1989.

THE EYE OF THE HURRICANE

As the PLA armored pincer movement approached Tiananmen shortly after midnight, the mood among students in the square became increasingly tense. All around, tracer bullets could be seen cutting a path through the night sky, and staccato bursts of automatic rifle fire could be heard in all directions. But in Tiananmen Square itself, where an estimated three to five thousand students sat huddled close together on the tiers and steps surrounding the base of the Heroes' Monument, no shots were fired.

Beginning around 1:30 A.M., an "emergency notice" was broadcast repeatedly over government loudspeakers around the square, reporting that a "serious counterrevolutionary rebellion" had broken out, and that "ruffians" were "savagely attacking" PLA units, setting military vehicles afire, kidnapping soldiers, and seizing army weapons. After having previously acted with "great restraint," the PLA would now have to "resolutely counterattack the counter-revolutionary rebellion," the notice proclaimed.

Closing in from three directions, soldiers sealed off the square between 2:00 and 3:00 A.M. Almost all nonstudents, including foreign journalists, had left the square by this time.[17] The students who remained at the Heroes' Monument had in their possession two rifles and at least one machine gun, manned by a team of Gongzilian workers' pickets and pointed in the general direction of PLA troops arrayed in front of the Great Hall of the People. According to one eyewitness account, the soldiers facing the students shouted, "We will not attack the people unless they attack us first" (*renbufanwo, wobufanren*).[18]

At this point a dispute reportedly arose between Chai Ling, who was in favor of allowing students in the square to stay there "to the end," and another group of strike leaders who sought to persuade the remaining few thousand students to evacuate peacefully before it was too late. The Chai Ling group, which controlled access to the loudspeaker system mounted high up on the Heroes' Monument, announced its intention to lead the students in singing one final, defiant rendition of the "Internationale" as their moment of truth approached.

After considerable heated debate, the pro-evacuation group, led by the four activists who had initiated the second Tiananmen hunger strike two days earlier—Taiwanese folksinger Hou Dejian, Beijing Normal University lecturers Liu Xiaobo and Gao Xin, and sociologist Zhou Duo—managed to take control of the machine gun at the base of the Heroes' Monument, which they proceeded to dismantle, thereby averting a potentially disastrous clash with the troops arrayed opposite. Their attempt to persuade the students to leave the square suffered a setback, however, when the Chai Ling–controlled loudspeaker system suddenly went dead.

Some time after 3:00 A.M., Chai Ling left Tiananmen Square. At 4:00 A.M., all lights in the square suddenly went out; for the few thousand students who remained huddled around the base of the Heroes' Monument, the moment of truth was at hand. According to eyewitness observers, a curious calm now descended upon the Heroes' Monument, which had become the eye of the hurricane.

Meanwhile, the four pro-evacuation leaders, Hou Dejian, Liu Xiaobo, Gao Xin, and Zhou Duo, redoubled their efforts to avoid a holocaust. Hoping to negotiate a last-minute student withdrawal from the square, they descended from the Heroes' Monument and hitched a ride with a passing ambulance, seeking out the local commander of the PLA forces in Tiananmen Square. After some initial confusion, they managed to locate the political commissar of the 27th Group Army, who listened to their evacuation proposal. A few minutes later, the local troop commander arrived and approved the plan, which called for the students to file out of the square toward the southeast. The students were promised safe conduct and a period of grace in which to leave.

Just after 4:30 A.M. the lights in the square went back on. Clearly visible along the western perimeter of the square were two lines of troops, several thousand strong, arrayed in front of the Great Hall of the People. On the eastern side of the square, three thousand soldiers lined the steps of the Museum of Revolutionary History. At 4:40 A.M. the troops proceeded to shoot out the student loudspeakers atop the Heroes' Monument.[19]

At this point a representative of Gongzilian urged the students to evacuate the square immediately, before a bloodbath took place; his advice was seconded by Hou Dejian, who had hurriedly rejoined the students after completing his negotiations. Hou's pleas were countered, however, by another speaker who urged the students to stand firm. After a brief period of uncertainty, punctuated by the sound of tank engines coming to life at the northern end of the square, without a vote being taken, Hou Dejian declared that a "democratic decision" had been made to leave the square.

The evacuation, which was calm and orderly, began shortly before 5:00 A.M. and lasted just over half an hour. Cordoned on either side by a column of soldiers, the students marched in rows toward the southeast corner of the square, singing the "Internationale." By 5:30 A.M. only a small handful of people remained at the monument. By the time the first line of bayonet-wielding soldiers climbed the steps to reclaim the monument a few minutes later, most of the stragglers had also left.

One eyewitness to these final moments at the Heroes' Monument, a Chinese scholar named Yu Shuo, later recounted her experience:

> As I was talking to an [army] officer I suddenly realized that I was the last person left at the monument. As I walked down the terrace . . . I saw that a soldier was about to pierce a bed with his bayonet. I saw two feet sticking out from it. . . . I rushed forward and dragged the feet. A boy fell down from the bed; he was not completely awake yet. He was the last student to leave the square.[20]

A second eyewitness account differs only marginally from this one, over the question of who was the last to leave the monument:

> Chen Zheng might be the last one to leave. She and a friend from Hong Kong refused to leave, sat on a step of the Monument to the People's Heroes, and kept crying. A soldier stood on a higher step, ordered them to leave immediately, cursing and threatening. I ran to them and pushed them away.[21]

Although there was evidently no wanton killing of students in Tiananmen Square during the evacuation, a few students among the final group to leave the square reportedly were beaten by soldiers wielding rifle butts; other groups reportedly encountered deadly gunfire shortly after leaving. In one incident witnessed by foreign journalists, a column of exiting students, circling clockwise around the outside perimeter of the square from the southeast to the northwest, encountered a tank column near Liubukou. Eleven students were reportedly crushed to death when one of the tanks ploughed straight into their ranks.

PLA infantry units reoccupy Tiananmen Square at daybreak,
June 4, 1989.

The first infantry units to reoccupy the square—including elements from the 27th and 38th Group Armies—reportedly had instructions to inspect the more than two hundred tents that had been erected on the square to make sure no students remained inside when APCs and tanks arrived on the scene. While it is now widely accepted that most of the tents were, in fact, empty when the first APCs arrived, there is grim photographic evidence that at least one person was crushed under an APC as he/she lay wrapped in a quilt inside one of the tents.

Just before dawn broke at 5:23 A.M. on Sunday, June 4, a Chinese armored unit at the northern end of Tiananmen Square crushed the Goddess of Democracy—but not before first removing the statue's severed torch as a memento.

AFTER THE STORM: THE CRACKDOWN CONTINUES

Sporadic, apparently random shootings of civilians, including innocent by-standers and apartment dwellers, by martial law troops continued at various points around Beijing for several days after June 4. On Monday, June 5, a lone civilian, nineteen-year-old Wang Weilin, dressed in a white shirt and trousers and carrying a jacket, calmly stepped in front of a column of tanks on East Chang'an Boulevard, near the Peking Hotel. Forcing the column to halt, he climbed atop the lead vehicle and conversed briefly with the tank commander. After resuming his position directly in front of the tank column, refusing to give ground as the lead tank gunned its engine, Wang was whisked to safety by a group of onlookers.[22]

On June 7 Chinese troops fired on the foreign diplomatic residential compound at Jianguomen, east of Tiananmen Square, in an apparent attempt at intimidation. Although there were frequent rumors in this period of an impending civil war involving allegedly rebellious armored units of the PLA, no organized military mutiny occurred; there were, however, numerous reported cases of intra-PLA dissension and failure to carry out orders.[23]

On June 6 Beijing Mayor Chen Xitong publicly congratulated the martial law forces on winning "initial victory" in the struggle to quell counterrevolutionary rebellion; at the same time, he cautioned that final victory would require a "long and complicated struggle." Also on June 6, State Council spokesman Yuan Mu held a press conference at which he presented the government's first official account of the events of June 3–4.[24]

Later that same day, Fang Lizhi and his wife, Li Shuxian, whose names were about to appear on a government arrest warrant, sought and received sanctuary inside the U.S. Embassy compound in Beijing. Also on June 6, antigovernment demonstrations broke out in at least a dozen Chinese cities. The most serious incidents took place in Chengdu, where rioting by angry crowds led to a declaration of martial law, culminating in the shooting of scores of people, and in Shanghai, where antigovernment workers set fire to a train that had previously hurtled into a crowd of protesters, killing six and wounding at least six others. It was subsequently reported that between thirty and three hundred people had been killed and more than a thousand others injured (including security forces) in the Chengdu violence, which continued for three days after June 4.[25]

The mass arrests began on June 6; among the first group of prodemocracy dissidents to be detained by security forces were human rights activist Ren Wanding and hunger strike organizer Liu Xiaobo. On June 11 arrest warrants were issued for a number of other fugitive activists, including student leaders, prominent Chinese intellectuals, and other outspoken supporters of human rights who stood accused of instigating or supporting the counterrevolutionary rebellion. Among the names appearing on government "most wanted" lists in this period were Fang Lizhi, Li Shuxian, Wu'er Kaixi, Wang Dan, Chai Ling, Han Dongfang, Yu Haocheng, Yan Jiaqi, and Wan Runnan; arrest warrants were also issued for the outspoken co-author and director of "River Elegy," Su Xiaokang, as well as for veteran democracy activists Chen Ziming and Wang Juntao.

On June 7 China's highest prosecuting authority, the Supreme People's Procuratorate, issued an emergency notice to public security bureaus around the country, advising them not to be "hamstrung by details" in the detention and prosecution of hooligans and rebels. Over the next several days, large-scale detentions of suspected counterrevolutionaries were carried out in Beijing and elsewhere. Within two weeks, the number of officially reported arrests throughout the country reached 1,600, with unofficial estimates running many times higher. By the spring of 1991 the Chinese government had confirmed a total of 2,578 arrests in connection with the May–June disturbances. Hong Kong sources put the figure at more than 4,000, of whom 1,730 were convicted and sent to prison.[26]

The government's arrest figures generally included only people formally charged with committing rebellion-related crimes; unofficial figures, compiled by foreign human rights groups, tended to include along with those formally arrested a much larger number of people, generally reckoned in the tens of thousands, who were picked up by police and detained for questioning (often for twenty-four to forty-eight hours) before being released.[27]

Not all "most wanted" Tiananmen activists were successfully apprehended by government security forces. In the weeks following the June 4 crackdown at least forty fugitive student leaders and dissident intellectuals managed to evade the government's dragnet.[28] Escapees included Wu'er Kaixi, Chai Ling, Yan Jiaqi, Gao Gao, Chen Yizi, Wan Runnan, and Su Xiaokang. Many were able to elude police and leave the country with the assistance of an underground network organized and financed by a Hong Kong–based group known as the Alliance in Support of the Patriotic Movement in China.[29] Once out of China, the exiled dissidents took up residence in such places as Paris and Princeton, New Jersey, where they and their supporters established a number of organizations for the promotion of Chinese democracy and human rights.

Some fugitive activists, including Gongzilian leader Han Dongfang, turned themselves in to the authorities. Others, including Wang Dan, Yu Haocheng, and historian Bao Zunxin, were hunted down and arrested by police in the weeks following the June 4 crackdown. After avoiding capture for several months, Chen Ziming and Wang Juntao were taken into custody in 1990.

Singer Hou Dejian spent the first ten weeks of the crackdown hiding in the Australian Embassy, returning to his Beijing residence in August. After initially agreeing publicly to corroborate the government's claim that no students had been massacred in Tiananmen Square on June 4, Hou later declared himself in opposition to the regime. At the end of May 1990 he, Zhou Duo, and Gao Xin announced their intention to hold a press conference on the first anniversary of the Tiananmen crackdown in order to read an open letter to Chinese leaders demanding the release of all political prisoners, including the fourth member of their Tiananmen negotiating team, Liu Xiaobo. When the three dissidents were detained by security police before they could hold their press conference, Hou Dejian, a celebrity whose international fame made it difficult for the government to crack down on him with impunity, negotiated his second evacuation agreement with the authorities: in exchange for a government pledge not to arrest him or his two collaborators, Hou agreed to accept deportation to his native Taiwan. He was escorted out of the country toward the end of June.

Following the initial round of post-Tiananmen arrests and executions, a flood of international protest caused Chinese authorities to adopt a lower profile and a less ruthless demeanor in dealing with the perpetrators and participants of the Beijing Spring. In January 1990, with anti-Chinese sentiment mounting in the U.S. Congress, the Chinese government terminated martial law in Beijing and released from custody the first batch of 573 political prisoners.[30] Two additional groups of post-Tiananmen detainees were freed in May and June 1990, respectively, bringing the total to 881. Toward the end of June, fugitive dissident Fang Lizhi was permitted to leave his sanctuary inside the U.S. Embassy in Beijing for safe passage abroad to England. These latter measures were evidently timed to coincide with the start of U.S. congressional debate over renewal of the PRC's most favored nation (MFN) trade status—a debate whose outcome was of considerable importance to China's economic health and well-being.

Early in 1991, at the height of the Persian Gulf crisis, while the world's attention was focused on the Middle East, thirty-one imprisoned Chinese intellectuals were tried, convicted, and sentenced to prison terms ranging from two to thirteen years for assorted counterrevolutionary crimes committed during the Tiananmen disturbances. Formal charges against eighteen other dissidents were dropped, while an additional forty-five detainees were released from custody in the absence of criminal indictments. Among the thirty-one convicted dissidents, some, including Liu Xiaobo, were credited for time already served and were released from custody after reportedly showing "sincere repentance" for their actions. Wang Dan, whose alleged crimes included "counterrevolutionary propaganda and incitement," reportedly showed repentance at his trial and was sentenced to four years in prison. Ren Wanding, remaining unrepentant throughout, was sentenced to seven years; Chen Ziming and Wang Juntao, displaying continued defiance in protesting their innocence, were given the harshest sentences of all, thirteen years each, on charges of sedition. According to reports circulating in Beijing, the defense lawyers who represented Chen and Wang at their trials were subjected to considerable governmental harassment following the conclusion of the courtroom proceedings, including the suspension of two attorneys' licenses to practice law and the revocation of another's municipal residence permit.[31]

CONTROLLING DAMAGE: THE CENTER TIGHTENS ITS GRIP

As a deterrent to would-be counterrevolutionaries, in the last two weeks of June 1989 at least thirty-five people in five cities—mostly workers, unemployed youths, and members of the urban floating population—were hastily tried, sentenced, and executed for various acts of violence committed during the uprising of early June. Contrary to persistent rumors, no students or intellectuals were among those sentenced to death for their role in the June disturbances. Among those executed were the three young Shanghai workers who set fire to the train that plowed into a crowd of demonstrators on June 6.[32]

While the public security apparatus mobilized for a crackdown on "ruffians" (*liumang*), "thugs" (*baotu*), and other assorted counterrevolutionaries, party and government leaders turned their attention to the delicate task of fashioning an intra-elite consensus in support of the June 3–4 crackdown. With the leadership deeply divided by the events of the previous two months, this proved no mean feat.

First came an orgy of self-congratulations; then came the denials. On June 6 the government officially complimented the martial law forces for their bravery, restraint, and self-discipline in the face of counterrevolutionary rebellion. A day later the political commissar of the PLA's 27th Group Army appeared on Chinese television to assert that not a single student had been killed by troops during the operation to clear Tiananmen Square. The distinction here was a rather fine one. Although the 27th Army had been responsible for much of the bloodshed that occurred in the western part of Beijing between Muxidi and Tiananmen Square on the night of June 3–4, neither it nor any other main force units of the PLA had shot down students in the square. And though there were early reports of Chinese tanks crushing students in sleeping bags and tents, only one such fatality has been reliably documented.

Seeking to shift the focus of attention from the PLA's bloody assault on the shimin of Beijing to acts of violence committed against the army by "ruffians" and "rioters," the commissar of the 27th Group Army described in detail a series of antimilitary atrocities that occurred on June 3–4. This was to become the pattern for government self-justification in the weeks and months to follow, namely, that the PLA's use of deadly force was a defensive reaction forced upon the martial law forces by the violent provocations of counterrevolutionary conspirators.[33]

On June 8 Premier Li Peng, accompanied by a somber and restrained Wan Li, appeared on television to reaffirm the government's gratitude to the martial law forces for their heroic role in restoring order in Beijing. The appearance of Wan Li, who did not speak, alongside Li Peng on this occasion was clearly intended to show to the Chinese people (and more particularly to restive party, government, and army cadres throughout the country) that the party's top leaders had closed ranks, and that even those leaders who had

Gerontocrats dominate the leadership meeting of June 9, 1989. From left: Wang Zhen, Li Peng, Deng Xiaoping, Li Xiannian, Yang Shangkun, Peng Zhen.

previously sympathized with student protest had now gone over to the side of the hard-liners.

The next day, June 9, virtually the entire Chinese civilian and military high commands, minus only Zhao Ziyang, Hu Qili, and Chen Yun (who was reportedly recuperating from illness), assembled for a meeting, cum photo opportunity session, designed to demonstrate once again the unity and stability of China's top leadership. President Yang Shangkun presided over the meeting; the seating arrangement, assigned by protocol rank, had elder statesmen Deng Xiaoping, Li Xiannian, and Yang Shangkun occupying the top three positions, followed by Li Peng, Peng Zhen, Wang Zhen, and Bo Yibo. Significantly, the six octogenarians were seated at the head of the table, where they appeared to outrank current members of the Politburo Standing Committee, all of whom (with the sole exception of Premier Li) were seated further down.[34] From this seating arrangement, it was abundantly clear that real power in China lay with the octogenarians of the CAC.

For full effect, extensive film clips from the June 9 leadership meeting were shown on national television. At the meeting, Deng Xiaoping, appearing publicly for the first time in several weeks, gave a speech in which he effusively praised the martial law forces for their bravery in nipping counterrevolutionary rebellion in the bud. Reflecting on the sources of China's crisis, Deng defended his reform policies and argued that the rebellion had been the inevitable result of party leaders permitting the global climate of bourgeois liberalization to spread unchecked within China:

> In recent days I have pondered these points. . . . Is there anything wrong with the basic concept of reform and openness? No. Without reform and openness how could we have what we have today? . . . [Nor is] there anything wrong with the four cardinal principles. If there is anything amiss, it's that these principles haven't been thoroughly implemented; they haven't been used as the basic

Deng Xiaoping congratulates military leaders on suppressing the
"counterrevolutionary rebellion," June 9, 1989.

concept to educate the people, educate the students, and educate all the cadres and
party members. The crux of the current incident is basically a confrontation between the four cardinal principles and bourgeois liberalization.[35]

Notwithstanding the elaborately staged display of elite unity and stability at
the leadership meeting of June 9, the outward appearance of harmony masked
a great deal of underlying tension. According to a semi-official Chinese press
report issued in 1992, more than three years after the fact, for several days
prior to the June 9 meeting certain unnamed senior party leaders had tried to
use the Tiananmen debacle as a pretext for derailing China's economic reforms. Labeling Deng's program of economic marketization (*jingji shichang-
hua*) as one of "three pillars of capitalist freedom"—the other two being political democratization (*zhengzhi minzhuhua*) and ideological pluralization
(*sixiang duoyuanhua*)—conservatives had reportedly sought to mobilize elite
opinion to halt the reform process dead in its tracks.[36]

Facing a strong challenge to his reform program, Deng met privately with
top military officials in advance of the June 9 leadership meeting. Arguing
that "We must stick with a combination of planned economy and market economy," Deng sought to convince army leaders that China must not change
course. Although no contemporaneous account of Deng's session with the
PLA top brass is available, by early July, when Deng's remarks were leaked

to the public, the term "market economy" (*shichang jingji*) had been watered down to read "market-regulated economy" (*shichang tiaojie jingji*), thus downgrading the role of the market vis-à-vis the state plan. The latter term was then standardized in party and government documents, marking a clear, conservative departure from Deng's original intent. According to subsequent press reports, the change in terminology had been engineered by "certain theoreticians and politicians." While no names were mentioned, from the language and context of the reports it was evident that Chen Yun, Hu Qiaomu, and Deng Liqun were the probable perpetrators.[37]

SCAPEGOATING ZHAO ZIYANG: THE FOURTH PLENUM

With Deng on the defensive, party leaders convened an enlarged CC plenum near the end of June. Attended by almost two hundred old-timers of the CAC, the Fourth Plenum formally removed Zhao Ziyang and Hu Qili from the Politburo and the Central Secretariat.[38] Zhao stood accused of a series of grave errors and mistakes, including "splitting the party." Though he was not expelled from the party, he was stripped of all formal powers and posts; his request to address the plenum in his own defense was turned down.

At an earlier meeting of the Politburo, held on June 14, Zhao had steadfastly refused to acknowledge his culpability. At that time, he had insisted: "First, I did not make a mistake; second, I still hold that the starting point of the student movement was good. They were patriotic."[39] Despite such fervent disclaimers, Zhao's role as prime scapegoat for the debacle of May-June was secure.

Hu Qili, in turn, was reprimanded at the Fourth Plenum for having supported the wrong side at the critical moment, but he was spared further disciplinary action. Two other erstwhile Zhao loyalists, Yan Mingfu and Rui Xingwen, were also dismissed from the Central Party Secretariat. Other key liberals removed from party posts at this time included Zhao's political adviser, Bao Tong (who had already been arrested); An Zhiwen, vice-minister of the State Commission for Economic Structural Reform; and Du Runsheng, director of the Rural Policy Research Center. On June 23 the pro-Zhao director of *People's Daily* was removed from his post along with the paper's chief editor, ostensibly for reasons of health. Shortly afterward, Minister of Culture Wang Meng and his deputy, Ying Ruocheng, were also forced to resign.[40]

After securing the dismissal of Zhao and his key liberal allies, the Fourth Plenum turned to the business of selecting a new general secretary, an exercise that should have been largely pro forma, given the fact that Deng Xiaoping had already made known his personal choice for the post: Shanghai Party Secretary (and former mayor) Jiang Zemin.

As early as May 31, Deng had indicated that Jiang Zemin should be the "core" (*hexin*) of the new party leadership.[41] Taking issue with Deng's recommendation, however, Wang Zhen urged his comrades to pledge their support to "the third-echelon leadership with Jiang Zemin *and Li Peng* as the core."[42] Chen Yun also balked at Deng's endorsement of Jiang, preferring to have Yao Yilin named to replace Zhao Ziyang as general secretary. Not to be left out, Peng Zhen reportedly urged the promotion of Qiao Shi. With the old comrades thus divided among themselves, Jiang Zemin barely mustered a majority of votes. Despite having obtained Wang Zhen's enthusiastic endorsement, Li Peng received little or no support for the top party post, having been badly tainted in the view of many because of his highly visible role in imposing, and later enforcing, martial law.

A compromise candidate, Jiang Zemin had originally been singled out for praise by Li Xiannian, whose recommendation of Jiang was based on four main criteria: first, Jiang occupied a centrist position on the reform spectrum, that is, he was committed to both economic reform and the four cardinal principles; second, like Hua Guofeng before him, Jiang was an outsider who was not beholden to any of Beijing's entrenched factions; third, Jiang had taken a firm stand against bourgeois liberalism in Shanghai during student demonstrations in December 1986 and again in May 1989; and fourth, he had on both of these occasions succeeded in defusing student protest in Shanghai without recourse to either martial law or organized violence.[43]

To round out the party's new leadership, two other newcomers were promoted from the ranks of the Politburo at the Fourth Plenum to join Jiang Zemin, Li Peng, Qiao Shi, and Yao Yilin on the revamped Standing Committee: seventy-two-year-old Song Ping, conservative head of the party's organization department, and fifty-five-year-old Li Ruihuan, the progressive, reform-oriented former mayor of Tianjin. With the addition of Jiang, Song, and Li to the SC, replacing Zhao and Hu Qili, the committee was expanded to six members. To replace the three dismissed members of the Central Party Secretariat (Zhao, Yan Mingfu, and Rui Xingwen), two new members—Li Ruihuan and Party General Office Director Ding Guan'gen, age sixty—were now added to that body.

Concurrent with the Fourth Plenum, a meeting of the NPC Standing Committee was held in late June. At this meeting, a number of SC vice-chairmen severely criticized fellow committee member Hu Jiwei for having sponsored the ill-fated petition drive of late May that urged the Standing Committee to hold an emergency meeting to rescind martial law. Hu himself was now accused of complicity in a plot to further the sinister aims of the "turmoil conspiracy," including the aim of securing Li Peng's dismissal. In his defense, Hu insisted that the petition drive had been wholly "reasonable and legal," and he denied that his real motive had been to oust Premier Li. Hu's arguments were dismissed as "flawed" and "lacking in justification."[44] On July 3 Li Peng sent the NPC SC a draft law on demonstrations, stipulating, among other things, that henceforth demonstrators would not be allowed to question the leadership of the Communist Party or undermine the nation's stability and unity in any way.

New Politburo Standing Committee selected at Fourth Plenum, June 24, 1989.
From left: Song Ping, Qiao Shi, Jiang Zemin, Li Peng, Yao Yilin, Li Ruihan.

THE OLD COMRADES TAKE CENTER STAGE

In the aftermath of the Fourth Plenum, China's elderly hard-liners sought to consolidate their gains. Calling Zhao Ziyang the "'root of evil' . . . who intended to reach his required goals through turmoil," Li Xiannian urged initiation of a new rectification drive to eliminate remnant pockets of Zhaoist influence within the party. Wang Zhen charged Zhao with "surrendering to the bourgeoisie." Along similar lines, Peng Zhen accused Zhao of "working with hostile forces at home and abroad to overthrow the CCP and disrupt the socialist system." Official media sources now began to hold the former general secretary personally responsible for a wide variety of societal ills, including hyperinflation, social instability, and rampant official profiteering.[45]

Aside from venting their anger upon Zhao Ziyang, elderly hard-liners also recommended harsh treatment for "bourgeois intellectuals" who had supported the student demonstrations. Wang Zhen, for example, proposed sending four thousand dissident intellectuals from Beijing and Shanghai to China's remote northwestern province of Xinjiang for military "reeducation."[46]

In the face of strong pressures to prosecute Zhao Ziyang for alleged criminal behavior, spearheaded by CAC hard-liners and backed by Li Peng and Yao Yilin, Deng Xiaoping refused to be drawn into an anti-Zhao vendetta. Counseling caution and restraint in the handling of Zhao's case, China's paramount leader once again revealed his underlying concern for counterbalancing fang and shou. "Let us not get tangled up in who is responsible for what right now," he said on June 16; "Let those questions be raised two or three years from now."[47] Deng prevailed, and no formal charges were filed against Zhao; however, for the next several months the former general secretary remained confined to quarters, living in relative comfort in a small house at No. 6 Fuqiang Lane, on a quiet, tree-lined street near Wangfujing, behind the Peking Hotel.[48]

Although Deng's personal intervention enabled Zhao to avoid criminal prosecution, several old comrades from the CAC nonetheless continued in their effort to root out remnant Zhaoists within the party apparatus. At the end of June 1989 the CDIC, now under the leadership of Peng Zhen's protégé Qiao Shi, launched a rectification drive. In the course of the new campaign, all party members in Beijing and other cities were required to undergo investigation and reregistration in connection with their attitudes and behavior during the critical six weeks of turmoil.

DEALING WITH URBAN OUTRAGE

Even as party and government leaders circled their wagons in support of the June crackdown, they came under intense pressure to confront the underlying problems that had given rise to the massive urban protests of April and May. As early as June 6, State Council spokesman Yuan Mu acknowledged the need to open a dialogue between government and citizens on a wide range of socioeconomic and political issues. "Once the whole situation is stabilized," he said, "the government will give much thought to proposals and suggestions raised by the people of various circles, including the students, on punishing official profiteering, uprooting corruption, and promoting democracy, and will earnestly accept suggestions from various quarters."[49]

In a similar vein, Deng Xiaoping, in a speech on June 16, explicitly linked the restoration of public confidence in the party and government with the continuation of reforms and with the need to deal forthrightly with the problem of official corruption: "We must perform certain acts to inspire satisfaction among the people. There are two aspects to this: one is to pursue the reform and openness policies more aggressively, and the other is to catch and punish those who engage in corruption. . . . If we fail to catch and punish corrupt people, particularly those inside the party, we run the risk of failure."[50] To put teeth into his anticorruption proposal, Deng recommended setting a public example by severely punishing "one or two dozen" of the most flagrant, high-status profiteers.

In line with Deng's recommendation, the party launched a high-profile antiracketeering drive in the summer of 1989. On July 10 *People's Daily* announced the expulsion of hundreds of corrupt party members; two weeks later the Politburo decreed that henceforth all gaogan zidi were to be banned from engaging in private business, and that top party officials would no longer have access to imported cars and private supplies of food.[51] At the same time, the Politburo ordered the breakup of the notorious Kanghua Development Corporation, whose far-flung operations reportedly included ownership of a publishing house specializing in erotic books. Other large investment companies with major gaogan connections—including CITIC, Everbright, China Economic Development Corporation, and China Rural Trust and Development Corporation—were also investigated by government auditors and fined sums totaling more than RMB ¥50 million for engaging in activities of dubious legality. Significantly, however, no criminal charges were filed in any of these cases.

THE UNQUIET SUMMER OF 1989

With popular emotions continuing to run high, armed assaults by angry civilians against martial law troops, including occasional sniper attacks, were reported in Beijing throughout the summer of 1989. In late July a government newspaper disclosed an attempt by a Beijing resident to kill martial law troops by offering them a bucket of drinking water laced with poison.[52] In a highly unusual display of civil-military rancor, the commander of the 27th Group Army, who was widely believed to have given the initial order for troops to open fire on civilians near Muxidi on the night of June 3, was reportedly hissed by an audience composed primarily of civilian cadres when he rose to address a propaganda conference in Beijing in August; obviously flustered, the general angrily denied that his troops had slaughtered innocent civilians.

On Beijing's college campuses, the situation remained tense throughout the summer of 1989. In an attempt to treat the problem of student unrest at its putative source, the government on July 21 announced a decision to cut back on new college enrollments in the humanities and social sciences for 1989–90 by a total of thirty thousand students. Two days later, several hundred Beida students registered their disapproval by spontaneously marching through the campus late at night, protesting both the cutbacks and the crackdown. As the students marched, they sang a well-known revolutionary song, adding to its lyrics a strong hint of irony and sarcasm: "Without the Communist Party, there would be no new China." When the song was finished, the students began to chant, with gleeful double entendre, the lyrics to a popular animated television commercial for pesticide spray: "We are the mighty pests! We are the mighty pests! Uh oh, here come the dreaded pest-killers; let's get out of here!"[53]

No disciplinary action was taken against the students who participated in the July 23 night march. Three weeks later, however, the tolerant, reform-minded president of Peking University, Ding Shisun, was dismissed; named to replace him was a conservative Marxist economist, Wu Shuqing. Concurrently, it was announced that the entire 1989 Beida freshman class, whose numbers had been cut back from two thousand to only eight hundred, would be required to undergo a year of military training before being permitted to attend regular classes.

In mid-August Beijing Mayor Chen Xitong disclosed that previously announced plans to hold a military parade in Beijing on October 1—the fortieth anniversary of the founding of the PRC—were being scrapped. At the same time, it was announced that Tiananmen Square, closed to the public since June 4, would soon be reopened to selected tour groups, "in an organized manner." Although the government now routinely asserted that everything was back to normal in the nation's capital, the continued presence of large numbers of uniformed, fully armed martial law troops in the heart of Beijing bespoke a different condition: *neijin, waisong* (internally tense, externally calm). As if to underscore that condition, at summer's end the authorities in Beijing intervened at the last minute to cancel a performance of Verdi's "Requiem," which was to have been performed on the grounds of the Beida campus to commemorate the passing of the first hundred days since the PLA's assault on Tiananmen. In place of the canceled performance, Beida students held a silent candlelight vigil.

When the PRC marked its fortieth anniversary on October 1, 1989, there were few congratulations and still fewer smiles. Though legions of gaily outfitted dancers and multicolored fireworks brightened the appearance of Tiananmen Square, the still-visible imprint of tank treads on crushed paving stones belied the artificial gaiety of the occasion.

It was a far cry from October 1, 1949, when Mao Zedong had ascended the rostrum at Tiananmen to the accompaniment of thunderous cheers, proclaiming triumphantly, "The Chinese people have stood up!" On that earlier occasion there had been genuine popular elation and high hopes for China's future. Now, forty years later, hope seemed strangely out of place, and elation wholly absent, as the nation's shoulders sagged visibly under the weight of the Tiananmen tragedy.

SIDESTEPPING CONFLICT: THE FIFTH PLENUM

With underlying stress levels continuing to run high and popular confidence in the CCP running perilously low, party leaders nervously convened the Fifth Plenum of the Thirteenth Central Committee in early November. In the run-up to the plenum, rumors were rife concerning an imminent CC verdict on the crimes and misdemeanors of Zhao Ziyang. Such a verdict, eagerly sought by elderly hard-liners, never came, as Deng Xiaoping, eager to prevent an open split between the party's moderate and conservative wings, intervened personally to secure indefinite postponement of a final decision on Zhao's case. Speaking on October 1, Deng instructed newly installed Party General Secretary Jiang Zemin not to "throw mud at Zhao Ziyang any more. . . . [D]o not bring up old scores again."[54] Though hard-liners reportedly balked at Deng's injunction, in the interest of stability and unity they dutifully refrained from raising the issue at the Fifth Plenum.

In a dramatic if not unexpected gesture at the conclusion of the plenum on November 9, Deng Xiaoping announced his decision to resign from his last official post, chairman of the Military Affairs Commission. Commenting on his decision to retire, Deng noted that as men get old, their judgment is not always clear. Calling his decision final, China's paramount leader politely urged his colleagues not to consult with him in the future.

Making a well-publicized final official appearance on November 13, Deng welcomed a delegation of Japanese trade representatives to Beijing's Great Hall of the People. At this meeting, Deng affirmed his intention to refrain from meddling in the affairs of party, government, and army leaders. At the same time, however, China's patriarch allowed that "if I have any useful ideas and suggestions, I will gladly convey them to the new leadership."[55]

True to his word, Deng conveyed at least one useful idea to the Fifth Plenum: he nominated Jiang Zemin to succeed him as MAC chairman. A man with no prior military experience, Jiang's nomination did not sit well with Yang Shangkun, who reportedly harbored MAC chairmanship ambitions of his own. During the enlarged CC work conference that preceded the Fifth Plenum, Yang sought to table the question of the MAC chairmanship, urging his comrades to refrain from discussing all top-level personnel matters at the plenum. By framing the issue in these terms, Yang evidently sought to finesse Deng, tieing postponement of Jiang Zemin's promotion to Deng's own desire to avoid rendering a verdict on Zhao Ziyang.[56] Refusing to go along with Yang's dilatory gambit, however, Deng insisted on keeping the cases of Zhao and Jiang separate and distinct, and he pushed for a vote on the latter. Acceding to Deng's wishes, the Central Committee formally approved the appointment of Jiang Zemin to chair the MAC. In accepting the appointment, Jiang acknowledged that because he had no prior experience in military work, he was not fully prepared to assume the duties of MAC chairman; and he humbly pledged to "make every effort to learn about military affairs and familiarize myself as soon as possible with the armed forces."[57]

Although Yang Shangkun lost the battle to prevent Jiang's ascent, he indirectly strengthened his own hand in the process: in exchange for agreeing not to openly contest Jiang's promotion, Yang was named to the position of MAC first vice-chairman, replacing Zhao Ziyang; in addition, Yang's half-brother, Yang Baibing, age sixty-nine, was appointed to the Central Party Secretariat and was concurrently named to fill the newly created position of MAC general secretary. In this latter post, he was responsible for overseeing the day-to-day operations of the commission. Occupying two of the top four posts on the MAC, the "Yang family generals" thus greatly increased the weight of their influence over military policy.[58] Partially to offset the increased potency of the Yang clan, Deng picked General Liu Huaqing, seventy-three, a former Second Field Army associate, to be second vice-chairman of the MAC.

Speaking at the Fifth Plenum in his capacity as CCP general secretary, Jiang Zemin carefully balanced his firm condemnation of bourgeois liberalization and peaceful evolution with an attitude of benign tolerance and forgiveness toward those of his comrades who might have been "confused" or "misled" into siding with the rioters during the counterrevolutionary rebellion in May and June.[59] Reinforcing the general impression of a post-Tiananmen reversion to traditional CCP ideological symbols and values, Jiang Zemin, Wan Li, and other erstwhile party moderates conspicuously donned old-style Mao jackets for an official photograph at the Fifth Plenum. At the same time, however, in an ironic reversal of role imagery, Yang Shangkun, Li Peng, and Yao Yilin all appeared in the same photograph wearing Western-style suits and ties.[60] Presumably, their intent was to convince the outside world that they were not die-hard reactionaries, as generally portrayed in the Western media. A similar attempt to reassure nervous international opinion may have underlain Li Peng's well-publicized tour of several coastal SEZs following the Fifth Plenum, in the course of which Li praised the SEZs for successfully merging capitalist management techniques with socialist values.

CHEN'S BIGGER BIRD CAGE MEETS DENG'S OPEN DOOR

The last major piece of business transacted at the Fifth Plenum was approval of a thirty-nine-point economic retrenchment program. Eschewing the type of overheated, unbalanced economic growth produced by Zhao Ziyang's liberal reforms in the mid-1980s, party leaders now endorsed a return to the more cautious, bigger bird cage approach to economic reform first popularized by Chen Yun during the readjustment of 1981–83.

Upholding a series of austerity measures imposed in the second half of 1988, the new program was long on general principles but rather short on policy specifics. Calling for "sustained, stable, and harmonious" development of the national economy, the CC document mandated a general economic slowdown. Specific targets included reducing the rate of real economic growth to between 5 and 6 percent annually (from a 1988 high of around 14 percent); lowering the inflation rate to less than 10 percent (from a high of 27 percent in the first quarter of 1989); sharply limiting the growth of the country's money supply; and balancing the national budget. To attain these goals, a number of "important links" were stressed: (1) reduction of aggregate consumer demand, to be achieved by holding the line on wage and bonus increases; (2) close examination and "rectification" of the financial dealings of China's free-wheeling private and semiprivate trading companies; (3) strengthening macroeconomic controls over industrial and fiscal administration; and (4) promotion of an industrial policy that accorded preferential treatment to large, state-owned factories producing energy or other industrial inputs over smaller, export-oriented firms producing light-industrial consumer goods.[61]

Although the thirty-nine-point program prescribed a strong dose of fiscal and administrative conservatism to overcome "serious confusion" in the country's economic life, it did not envision a wholesale abandonment of economic reform. On the contrary, the Central Committee's new manifesto contained a strong defense of Deng's open policy and a promise of renewed efforts to "reform and perfect" existing production responsibility systems and economic contract systems. Although prices remained frozen (out of concern for relieving inflationary pressures), the new document explicitly urged the gradual elimination of China's two-tiered price system. Also emphasized was the need to "boldly absorb foreign investment and import advanced technology." To facilitate foreign trade and international technical cooperation, the document called for "further perfecting" existing policies governing the operation of China's SEZs and open coastal cities.[62] With demands for economic austerity and retrenchment thus counterbalanced by commitments to resume economic reform and to open up still further, the Central Committee's 1989 stabilization program sought to steer a middle course between the two extremes of rigidly centralized command and freewheeling laissez-faire.[63]

A TALE OF TWO CITIES: BUCHAREST AND BEIJING

While the Central Committee grappled with issues of political and economic stabilization, party leaders were confronted with a new cause for concern. Throughout East and Central Europe, from Belgrade to Budapest, a rising tide of glasnost-induced citizen unrest had left in its wake a succession of teetering Marxist-Leninist regimes. In the course of this cascading popular upheaval, some Communist governments were swept away altogether; others survived only by renouncing their past histories, replacing their leaders, or redesigning their institutions. Coming so close on the heels of the Tiananmen rebellion, the "gentle revolution" of 1989 had an unsettling effect on China's already nervous leaders. To ascertain the seriousness of the situation in Eastern Europe, and to help formulate plans for "coordinated action" to deal with the situation, the Politburo SC dispatched its top security expert, Qiao Shi, along with Yao Yilin to visit East Germany, Bulgaria, and Romania in the autumn of 1989.[64]

In December the Politburo's anxiety turned to outright alarm. In Bucharest, officers of the Romanian Army, refusing to obey orders to fire on an assembly of peaceful demonstrators, ignited a massive popular revolt against the Communist regime of paramount leader Nicolae Ceausescu. Within a matter of days the government fell, and the dictator and his wife were executed.

Visibly shaken by Ceausescu's violent demise, Chinese leaders quickly erected a wall of rigid defiance. Dismissing out of hand all hints of similarity between conditions in Bucharest and Beijing, they quietly beefed up security forces in the nation's capital, placing them on standby alert.[65] At the same time, government spokesmen were dispatched to college campuses in Beijing to propagate the official party line on Romania.

That line was both complex and self-contradictory. Publicly, Beijing's response to the demise of Ceausescu was to congratulate the new Romanian government headed by reform-oriented ex-Communist Ion Iliescu, and to pledge continued bilateral friendship and cooperation.[66] Privately, however, Chinese leaders disseminated among party cadres a fundamentally darker, more pessimistic view of the Romanian upheaval, one that blamed Mikhail Gorbachev for stirring up political unrest in East and Central Europe through his "new thinking" and his reckless display of tolerance toward bourgeois liberalization.

At a series of Politburo meetings held shortly after the Romanian uprising, Chinese leaders severely criticized the Soviet leader. At one meeting, Deng Xiaoping faulted Gorbachev for having "pulled the wrong strings" in attempting to bring about structural reform in Eastern Europe. Chen Yun was more blunt, stating that "the weakness of Gorbachev's ideological line is that it is pointing in the direction of surrender and retreat. Our party cannot afford to stand idly by and watch this happen." Jiang Zemin went further still, arguing that Gorbachev was "basically of the same ilk" as the "traitor" Leon Trotsky, and insisting that the Soviet leader must be held fully responsible for the worsening state of affairs in Eastern Europe. Wang Zhen echoed this assessment, accusing the Soviet leader of "deviating from the socialist path" and calling for open criticism of Gorbachev's apostate "revisionism."[67]

Within days of the Romanian revolution, banners and wall posters alluding to events in Bucharest appeared on university buildings in Beijing. One banner, written shortly before Ceausescu's execution and draped across the wall of a student dormitory, called the Romanian dictator a "lost dog" and suggested that he might soon be on his way to the PRC to join four other "dogs"—a thinly veiled reference to Beijing's ruling quartet of Deng Xiaoping, Yang Shangkun, Li Peng, and Jiang Zemin.[68] Another banner, posted at the Beida student canteen, proclaimed that "Dictators are doomed to die."[69] On December 29, State Council spokesman Yuan Mu, dispatched to the Beida campus to explain the government's policy on Romania to an assembly of students, was jeered derisively and subjected to hostile questioning by members of the audience of seven hundred who packed the conference hall.[70]

FALLOUT FROM ROMANIA: RECTIFYING THE PLA

In addition to reviving government fears of public unrest, the Romanian revolution also underscored the vital importance of military loyalty and discipline in periods of political upheaval. Yang Shangkun put the matter succinctly at a meeting with high-level military officers. "Why did Romania collapse?" he asked; "the fundamental problem was that the army was divided." Calling the army the "pillar of our country," Yang went on to compare the state to a ship at sea. "If the ship turns turtle," he warned, "all of us will drown."[71]

Yang Shangkun's warning was more than mere rhetoric. According to his half-brother Yang Baibing, during the critical phase of martial law enforcement in Beijing from May 19 through June 6, 1989, there had been at least 111 serious breaches of military discipline by PLA officers at or above the level of company commander. In some cases, divisional and regimental commanders had refused to bring their troops into the city; in other cases, unit commanders had balked at carrying out orders to discharge their weapons against civilians. In addition, some 1,400 ordinary soldiers had reportedly "shed their weapons and run away" during the crackdown.[72] While these figures represented an extremely small fraction of the more than 200,000 troops who took part in the enforcement of martial law in Beijing, the problem of declining military discipline and morale was sufficient to arouse serious concern among party and government leaders. Among the more tangible signs of elite concern was the provision of a 15.2 percent boost in the military budget for 1990. Approved by the NPC in March, it was the first significant boost in the PLA's budget in over a decade.[73]

With the Romanian uprising providing a strong reminder of what can happen when a regime's armed forces fail to obey orders, China's nervous leaders launched a major shake-up in the country's military command structure in the winter of 1990. In the course of the rectification, a few high-ranking PLA officers were court-martialed and imprisoned; several others were demoted and/or transferred to new areas of assignment, including six of China's seven regional military commanders and five top regional political commissars.[74] Altogether, between 1,500 and 3,000 officers were investigated for possible breaches of discipline in connection with their behavior during the period of martial law.[75]

In addition to problems of troop morale and discipline, deep divisions were reported within the PLA high command. According to one rumor that swept through Beijing in the summer of 1989, Yang Shangkun, in an attempted putsch, had placed four high-level PLA officials, including Defense Minister Qin Jiwei and three regional commanders—Beijing's Zhou Yibing, Guangzhou's Zhang Wannian, and Nanjing's Xiang Shouzhi—under house arrest for alleged acts of insubordination. Another widespread rumor had warned of an impending tank battle between armored divisions of the 27th and 38th group armies.[76] While neither rumor proved true in their particulars, they nonetheless underlined the existence of a very real schism within the Chinese military between officers loyal to the "Yang family generals," who supported the June crackdown, and a group of veteran PLA commanders, who did not.[77] Among the elderly military leaders who reportedly expressed dissatisfaction with the Yang brothers were generals Zhang Aiping, Yang Dezhi, Chen Zaidao and Li Desheng, and marshals Nie Rongzhen and Xu Xiangqian.[78]

Pursuant to the shake-up of China's regional military leadership, renewed emphasis was placed on propaganda and political indoctrination within the armed forces. Under the watchful eye of the PLA's chief political commissar, Yang Baibing, the new campaign took as its centerpiece a stern injunction calling for the unconditional subordination of the army to party leadership. In conjunction with this call for absolute loyalty and discipline, soldiers were given stepped-up indoctrination against the twin evils of bourgeois liberalization and peaceful evolution. A relatively recent addition to the roster of dangerous ideological tendencies, "peaceful evolution" (*heping yanbian*) was a code phrase connoting alleged Western attempts to undermine socialism and promote the growth of capitalism and bourgeois democracy in China through the exertion of economic, cultural, political, and ideological influences and pressures from abroad.[79]

To insure the success of the new propaganda campaign, military units were now required to spend as much as half of their time in political study.[80] For new recruits, the requirements were even stricter. The majority of their time was now to be devoted to studying materials prepared in connection with the newly revived campaign to emulate Lei Feng, the martyred PLA conscript who died in 1962 while devoting his energies unselfishly to serving the party, socialism, and the Chinese people.[81] To ensure further the political reliability of PLA conscripts, military recruitment was henceforth to be concentrated in rural areas, away from urban centers of political alienation and unrest.

Among the most active boosters of the Lei Feng campaign (and other related PLA propaganda/indoctrination initiatives) was Yang Baibing. Yang's neo-Maoist propaganda techniques were not uniformly popular within the army, however, and were openly opposed by a number of high-ranking professional officers, including Deputy MAC General Secretary Hong Xuezhi. In a heated exchange with Yang Baibing at a working session of the MAC in the winter of 1990, the seventy-seven-year-old General Hong strenuously objected to Yang's repeated emphasis on implementation of the Lei Feng campaign. "I am afraid," he said, "Director Yang cannot lead the troops properly merely by paying lip service to the drive to learn from Lei Feng. . . . We are holding a Military Affairs Commission work meeting, not a discussion on emulating Lei Feng."[82] Shortly after this outburst, Hong Xuezhi retired from his post as deputy MAC general secretary; he was subsequently appointed to the significantly less important position of vice-chairman of the Chinese People's Political Consultative Conference.

. Alongside the PLA reorganization of winter 1990, a political rectification drive was also carried out within the PLA's paramilitary adjunct, the 600,000-member People's Armed Police. Many members of the PAP in Beijing had abandoned their posts prior to and during the June 3–4 crackdown. Some had showed open sympathy with student demonstrators; a few had even joined the Tiananmen demonstrations in full uniform. In February 1990 a major reshuffle of PAP leadership was announced. The senior commander and political commissar were both replaced, and the entire organization was placed under the operational control of the party's Military Affairs Commission, rather than the Ministry of Public Security, as before.[83]

With Deng Xiaoping at least nominally in retirement and Jiang Zemin essentially a figurehead as MAC chairman, the military reorganization of 1990 served greatly to enhance the power and authority of the "Yang family generals." Given the opportunity to move out from under Deng's shadow, the Yang brothers were now a potent political force in their own right, and one to be reckoned with.[84]

AFTER THE FLOOD: THE DAM HOLDS

Although China hovered on the brink of political chaos throughout the late spring and early summer of 1989, the regime eventually righted itself, avoiding a political meltdown and achieving a measure of restabilization. In retrospect, a number of factors can be seen to have contributed to this outcome. These included (1) a full decade of rapid—if spasmodic—economic growth preceding the Beijing Spring, which served to mollify Chinese consumers and mitigate economic hardship; (2) the CCP leadership's remarkable display of political solidarity after June 4, which strengthened the appearance of unity at the top and thereby diminished popular enthusiasm for revolt; (3) the PLA's high level of discipline and responsiveness to civilian command, which, despite problems of low military morale, gave a strong impression of party-army harmony; (4) the absence of autonomous institutions of civil society, making organized resistance to the regime extremely problematical after June 4; (5) strategic and tactical divisions within the student movement, which diminished the movement's cohesion and rendered unified action difficult; (6) the students' unwillingness to forge an alliance with industrial workers and other urban strata during the formative stages of the Tiananmen protests; and (7) a deep-seated fear of *luan* (chaos), heightened by vivid memories of Cultural Revolution anarchy. In combination, these several factors helped ensure that the 1989 Beijing Spring would follow a path fundamentally different from that of the "gentle revolution" that subsequently engulfed major portions of the communist world.[85]

Decade of Economic Reform

Throughout much of East Europe and the Soviet Union, grinding poverty and consumer despair contributed heavily to the cascading anti-Communist insurgency of 1989–91. In China, by contrast, a full decade of economic reform in the 1980s served to provide an expanding, if uneven, flow of consumer goods onto urban markets and to raise the living standards and expectations of most citizens. Although these gains were partially offset by periodic overheating of the urban economy, by rapidly rising retail prices, and by perceived inequities in the social distribution of the costs and benefits of reform, the introduction of a tight governmental austerity program in the last half of 1988 succeeded, within about a year, in slowing the inflationary spiral and restoring a measure of economic stability and consumer confidence.

Because of the growth-enhancing effects of earlier reforms, the country could tolerate the austerity measures of 1988–89 without experiencing massive consumer despair. With a strong assist from China's booming private and small-collective enterprises, the economy was successfully jump-started again in 1990. A growing economy, in turn, provided little incentive for renewed popular political agitation and mobilization. Indeed, in the southern coastal provinces of Guangdong and Fujian—where market reforms were farthest advanced and the people's standard of living most dramatically improved as a result of the reforms—popular support for the student movement was slow to develop, limited in scope, and relatively mild in intensity, even at the height of the Beijing Spring. In the largest cities in each of these provinces, observers noted that the nonstudent populations appeared to be "more interested in making money than in politics."[86] In this respect, Deng Xiaoping's ultimate gamble—that successful economic reform would dampen the people's demand for fundamental political change—proved prescient.

Also noteworthy in this connection was the near-total lack of involvement by peasants (and other rural groups and strata) in China's 1989 democracy demonstrations. Scattered observations and interviews conducted by the author in a number of small towns and villages in southern Jiangsu and Anhui provinces at the height of the Tiananmen protests indicated that rural dwellers along China's eastern seaboard, unlike their urban counterparts, tended to be (a) relatively more satisfied with Deng's economic reforms, and (b) overwhelmingly unconcerned about what was taking place in Beijing.[87] In a country where three-fourths of the population live in nonurban areas, rural apathy posed a formidable obstacle to effective mass political mobilization.

Communist Party Discipline

In April and May 1989, popular perceptions of factional cleavage within the CCP contributed heavily to the escalation of student unrest. When Zhao Ziyang sent a signal to demonstrators in Tiananmen Square that he was sympathetic to their demands, it emboldened student leaders to intensify their opposition to government hard-liners. However, Zhao's actions greatly irritated Deng Xiaoping, who quickly moved to sack Zhao and restore the appearance of party unity. In the aftermath of the June crackdown, party discipline was ruthlessly and rigidly reimposed. All CCP members and cadres were required to denounce the "counterrevolutionary rebellion" and reaffirm their support of a conservative party line. The public's perception of absolute, unwavering party unity in support of the crackdown, in turn, played an important role in discouraging renewed protest.

Military Loyalty

The dampening effects of a robust economy and a seemingly unified Communist Party were further reinforced by the generally high degree of military loyalty displayed by the PLA throughout the Tiananmen crisis. Despite numerous reports of flagging army morale and of officers hesitating to carry out orders, the PLA came through the crisis with its reputation for loyalty to civilian command largely in tact. Party leaders were thus able to avoid the type of massive military defections that later sealed the fates of the Romanian regime of Nicolae Ceausescu and the conservative plotters of the abortive Soviet coup of August 1991. In this connection, Yang Shangkun was undoubtedly correct when he pinpointed military loyalty as the key to regime survival: "If the ship turns turtle, all of us will drown."[88]

Absence of Civil Society

Further reducing the mobilizational capacities of antigovernment forces was the virtual lack of any viable Chinese institutional framework of civil society. The presence of a powerful state coercive apparatus, coupled with the near-total absence of autonomous, self-confident social forces—such as independent trade unions, churches, newspapers, student unions, or commercial associations—clearly contributed to the dearth of organized resistance to the June crackdown. In Eastern Europe, by contrast, quasi-autonomous civic groups such as Charter '77, Civic Forum, Solidarity, and the Catholic Church, though periodically forced to operate underground in the years preceding the "gentle revolution" of 1989, nonetheless remained alive as focal points for the in-gathering of social protest during the darkest days of regime repression.[89]

In view of the important role played by civic associations in Eastern Europe, it is hardly accidental that the Chinese government attached highest priority during the June crackdown to arresting the leaders of newborn independent labor organizations, student unions, and newspapers. By moving quickly to crush the incipient structures of civil society, the government effectively broke the back of the democracy movement. Once the widespread initial shock and indignation occasioned by the sheer brutality of the June 4 massacre wore off, the most common behavior displayed by ordinary Chinese citizens was passive resignation and political withdrawal—highly symptomatic of an atomized, powerless populace.

Schisms within the Student Movement

Almost from the outset, students and others participating in the Tiananmen demonstrations were divided over the movement's aims and tactics. Some sought total moral victory (and wholesale government capitulation), while others preferred reaching a negotiated settlement that would allow both sides to save face. Employing traditional moral devices such as ritualized imperial remonstrance alongside more modern techniques like the hunger strike, confrontationists assumed that superior moral virtue (and broad public sympathy) would carry the day against unjust government authority. They were wrong.[90]

Student Disdain for the Working Class

Closely related to the confrontationists' penchant for stylized moral theater was their pronounced elitism. Socialized in the Confucian ethos of the superiority of the literati class, and generally disdainful (despite four decades of

proletarian propaganda) of manual laborers, student leaders sought to maintain the purity of their protest, eschewing joint action with the Gongzilian and
other organized workers' groups, and even refusing to share Tiananmen
Square with such groups until after the May 20 martial law declaration.[91] Such
moral exclusivity served to alienate an important segment of the working
class, further contributing to the movement's lack of organizational staying-
power in the wake of the crackdown.

Fear of Chaos

Finally, the potential for sustained democratic protest was visibly diminished
by a pervasive popular fear of *luan*, or chaos. This phobia, deeply ingrained in
China's political history and culture, and reinforced by the recent anarchism
of the Cultural Revolution, was played upon incessantly by regime propagandists in the months following the Tiananmen debacle. As Deng Xiaoping put
it in June 1990, "If China is unstable, the world will be unstable. If civil war
were to break out in China, nobody would have the means to stop it."[92]

Reinforced by mounting public anxiety over the deep economic and political shocks experienced in East and Central Europe in the aftermath of the
1989 "gentle revolution," the regime's post-Tiananmen propaganda campaign
clearly produced its intended effect, as large numbers of ordinary Chinese
citizens—including many erstwhile supporters of the Tiananmen democracy
movement—began to cite fear of chaos as a primary reason for their lack of
enthusiasm for renewed political protest.[93]

In a similar vein the sudden, unexpected collapse of the Soviet Union in
1991, far from accelerating the process of political reform and transformation
in China, had the paradoxical effect of lending credence to Deng Xiaoping's
dire warning of the disastrous consequences of uncontrolled political mobilization: "Après moi le déluge." Fearful of flooding, the Chinese people backed
away from the brink, giving the regime an opportunity to patch the cracks in
its political facade. Though the party and government suffered a profound loss
of popular legitimacy and credibility as a result of the Beijing massacre, the
dam held.

PART IV

The Old Order Changes, 1990–1995

Picking Up the Pieces:
Winter 1990–Autumn 1991

If we fail to wage a resolute struggle against liberalization,

or [against] capitalistic reform and opening up,

our socialist cause will be ruined.

— *Deng Liqun, October 1991*

WITH the regime at least temporarily restabilized, a new scare was thrown into China's elderly helmsmen when, in early February 1990, Mikhail Gorbachev announced his intention to revise the Soviet constitution to create a competitive, multiparty electoral system and thus end the Soviet Communist Party's seventy-two-year monopoly on political power. Although the official Chinese media discreetly refrained from commenting directly on the Soviet president's stunning proposal, citing the principle of "noninterference in the internal affairs of another country" as their reason,[1] a spate of articles obliquely attacking "bourgeois multiparty democracy" soon appeared in the state-run press. Belying the ostensible nonchalance of party leaders, the articles sharply criticized the inherent inequities of Western-style "class-based democracy" and asserted that the Chinese system of "one-party leadership with multiparty cooperation and consultation" was far superior, enjoying the "overwhelming support" of the Chinese people.[2]

On February 7, 1990—less than forty-eight hours after Gorbachev dropped his constitutional bombshell—the Chinese media released the text of a twenty-four-point CCP Central Committee opinion on the subject of multiparty cooperation and political consultation. Prepared several weeks earlier, in the anxious aftermath of the overthrow and execution of Nicolae Ceausescu, the document acknowledged that the CCP "greatly needs to hear various kinds of opinion and criticism and accept supervision by the masses of the people." Rejecting out of hand the idea of Western-style political pluralism, however, it asserted that popular criticism and supervision of the party and government could best be secured by strengthening the consultative role of existing nongovernmental bodies such as the Chinese People's Political Consultative Conference (CPPCC) and China's eight officially approved "democratic parties."[3] By granting these non-Communist groups and individuals expanded—albeit only informal and advisory—access to government policymakers, China's leaders evidently hoped to preempt demands for more fundamental, systemic political reform. Unlike their Soviet counterparts, China's rulers had no intention of sharing power.

WHAT'S IN A NAME? RECLASSIFYING THE TIANANMEN TURMOIL

Another issue that helped keep political temperatures high in Beijing in the aftermath of Gorbachev's repudiation of Leninism was the nagging question of how to characterize China's 1989 national trauma. For their part, party hard-liners continued to insist that the Tiananmen upheaval had been a "counterrevolutionary rebellion" (*fan'geming baoluan*), and that Zhao Ziyang and his associates should be dealt with accordingly, as criminal conspirators. Those on the now-truncated liberal end of the reform spectrum, meanwhile, tried to blunt the thrust of the hard-liners' rhetorical assault by describing the turbulence of spring 1989 either as a "student movement" (*xuechao*), an "incident" (*shibian*), or merely an "event" (*shijian*)—relatively benign terms devoid of serious pejorative connotation. In between these two terminological extremes, Deng Xiaoping and Yang Shangkun continued to refer to the upheaval either as "turmoil" (*dongluan*) or "chaos" (*hunluan*), intermediate categories that, while politically onerous, neatly skirted the issue of criminality.

Seeking to forestall renewed conflict over the nature and definition of the Tiananmen crisis, Deng Xiaoping, speaking on the occasion of his eighty-sixth birthday in August 1990, urged his comrades to refrain from reassessing the events surrounding the June 4 crackdown until after his death.[4] Notwithstanding such avuncular advice, by the late spring of 1991 a new centrist coalition within the Politburo, with Deng's apparent blessing, reached preliminary agreement on the need to begin salving the wounds of 1989. One measure reportedly recommended by the Politburo at this time was a formal CC resolution downgrading the upheaval from the category of *baoluan* (rebellion) to that of *dongluan* (turmoil). As the summer of 1991 approached, it appeared that China's leaders might soon attempt to put the Tiananmen crisis behind them.

It never happened. Following the bungled Soviet coup attempt of August 1991, China's hard-liners dug in their heels. Using the Soviet Union's sudden, deep descent into political turmoil to support their contention that the Tiananmen crackdown had been fully warranted, they strongly opposed adoption of a softer line toward domestic dissent—much as they had done a decade earlier during the escalating Polish crisis of 1980–81. Consequently, the proposed Politburo recommendation on downgrading the 1989 disturbance was never adopted.

In the wake of the disintegration of the Soviet Union, Bo Yibo, in a speech to the CAC, referred to Mikhail Gorbachev as a "degenerate" Marxist and a "double-crosser" whose liberal political line had "caused chaos and regression in the state machinery, in social order, and in people's thinking, . . . creating a state of anarchy."[5] Under the weight of such virulent assessments of the sources of the Soviet collapse, any further movement toward healing the wounds of 1989 became all but impossible. Instead, the Politburo circled its political wagons ever more tightly, reaffirming the designation of the May-June upheaval as a *fan'geming baoluan*—counterrevolutionary rebellion.[6]

Closely linked to the issue of how to characterize the events of spring 1989 was the question of Zhao Ziyang's fate. With the dispute over the nature of the Tiananmen crisis still unresolved, Zhao's political status remained in limbo. Throughout 1990 and 1991, rumors periodically circulated concerning the state of Zhao's health, personal and political, and future prospects for rehabilitation. Reportedly living under guard in a modest dwelling formerly occupied by Hu Yaobang,[7] the seventy-year-old Zhao was variously rumored to have been (1) admitted to a Beijing hospital in critical condition;[8] (2) released from house arrest;[9] (3) never placed under house arrest;[10] (4) steadfast in his refusal to admit guilt;[11] (5) accused of collaborating with agents of the U.S. Central Intelligence Agency;[12] (6) cleared of all charges of criminal wrongdoing;[13] (7) observed playing golf by Japanese businessmen;[14] and (8) instructed by Deng Xiaoping to resume administrative duties after a year of "investigation and research" in the provinces.[15] Not since Mao's final months had rumors flown so fast and furious in Hong Kong.

With Zhao's fate continuing to hang in the balance, three of his closest associates within the CCP hierarchy, ex–Central Secretariat members Hu Qili, Rui Xingwen, and Yan Mingfu, all of whom had been sacked in the wake of the Tiananmen crackdown, were quietly rehabilitated and given vice-ministerial posts in June 1991, reportedly at the initiative of Jiang Zemin and with the backing of both Deng Xiaoping and Chen Yun.[16] Although reinstatement of the three liberal reformers appeared to represent a victory for the party's moderate wing, it was at best a limited triumph, since all three were assigned to positions substantially less powerful and prestigious than those they had previously held.[17]

CONSPIRACY OF SILENCE: THE PURGE THAT FAILED

While Deng continued to shield Zhao from the wrath of the hard-liners, a different type of political protection was extended to rank-and-file party members who had displayed liberal tendencies during the Beijing Spring. In the aftermath of the June crackdown, a large number of party members and cadres had come under CDIC investigation for their activities in support of the Beijing students. In the summer of 1989, party branches in all government offices and work units in Beijing and other cities were ordered to rectify and reregister their membership. In the course of this campaign, party members and cadres were required to give detailed accounts of their actions—and the actions of their coworkers—throughout the period of the spring disorders.

According to Communist Party sources, the initial stage of the campaign focused on isolating and criticizing approximately 250 liberal-minded leading cadres at and above the bureau and department levels in central party organs who had played an active role in supporting the student disturbances. These officials were required to account for their mistakes during four stages of the 1989 upheaval: (1) from the death of Hu Yaobang (April 15) to the fall of Zhao Ziyang (May 19); (2) from the announcement of martial law (May 20) to the military crackdown (June 3–4); (3) the weekend of June 3–4; and (4) from June 4 onward. As part of the self-examination process, all cadres under investigation were required to reveal their "original thinking" (*yuanshi sixiang*) upon first hearing the news that shots had been fired on the evening of June 3–4.[18]

Party rectification campaigns, in which targeted individuals are required to "lay down burdens" and redeem themselves through painstaking ideological study, criticism, and self-criticism, had often in the past proved effective in promoting uniformity of thought and eliciting information about deviant behavior in party organs. This time, however, the campaign reportedly fizzled. According to numerous Chinese sources, the hard-liners' repeated attempts to identify and punish active supporters of the democracy movement were at least partially thwarted by two things. First was the fact that large numbers of party members and cadres had displayed open sympathy toward the student movement in April and May 1989, making it extremely difficult for hard-liners to isolate and weed out a putative "small handful" of liberal miscreants; second was the existence of a tacit conspiracy of silence among leading cadres and their deputies in administrative offices and work units throughout Beijing and other Chinese cities. Under considerable pressure from higher levels to elicit the names of cadres and staff personnel who had participated in protest-related activities, work-unit leaders in many government organs and offices responded to the new rectification drive with perfunctory, pro forma compliance, refusing to implicate others and thereby diminishing the impact of the probe.[19] In some cases, unit heads—up to and including some central party and government leaders—publicly denounced the student disturbances while privately working behind the scenes to protect vulnerable colleagues and subordinates from recrimination. Hard-liners were said to be so upset by such subterfuge that Li Peng was forced to issue an urgent order to redo the entire campaign.[20]

When the final results of the post-Tiananmen party rectification and reregistration campaign were announced by the CDIC at the Fourteenth Party Congress in October 1992, the numbers were surprisingly small. A total of 13,254 party cadres were required to undergo party discipline for various political offenses, including both Right and Left errors; of this total, only 1,179 cadres (out of over 800,000 party members and cadres who had supported the student movement) were punished for participating in mass demonstrations and related "disturbances."[21] Among the more prominent party members denied permission to reregister in 1990 were Zhu Houze and Bai Hua.[22]

REDUCING THE CREDIBILITY GAP: THE ANTICORRUPTION DRIVE

According to an opinion poll conducted among students in eight Chinese universities and made public in the spring of 1990, popular resentment over the rising incidence of economic crime, corruption, and inequality of opportunity had been the leading cause of antigovernment protest during the Beijing Spring.[23] Many party leaders, including Deng Xiaoping and Chen Yun, had acknowledged this to be the case. To help reduce the level of popular cynicism and distrust, the party in 1990 stepped up its drive to clamp down on economic crime and corruption.

Within the CCP, the anticorruption drive reportedly netted more than 325,000 offenders in its first eighteen months of operation. In 1990, 79,000 party members were expelled; by the spring of 1991, an additional 256,000 members had received lesser degrees of party discipline.[24] By October 1992 the cumulative total had risen to 733,543 party cadres disciplined for economic corruption, of whom 154,289 were expelled from the party.[25] Although these aggregate data are difficult to interpret in the absence of further categorical refinement, it is instructive to note that in a 1990 survey of international businesspeople conducted by a Hong Kong–based political and economic risk-consultancy firm, the PRC had the highest perceived rate of official corruption among the ten Asian countries studied. (Lowest in perceived frequency of official corruption was Singapore.)[26] Reinforcing this widespread impression of cadre malfeasance, *People's Daily* reported the results of a 1992 public opinion poll, which revealed that more than 78 percent of the Chinese people surveyed agreed that in the current socioeconomic climate "you can't get anything done without giving gifts."[27]

Corruption appeared to be particularly rampant among Chinese police. Although hard data on this highly sensitive subject were lacking, as early as 1983 then-premier Zhao Ziyang placed much of the blame for China's steeply rising crime rate on a severe decline in the ethics and integrity of the nation's public security forces.[28] In a similar vein, a December 1990 circular issued by the Ministry of Public Security noted a sharp upsurge in public complaints about police misconduct and ordered security organs throughout the country to undergo rigorous self-examination and self-correction in order to halt an alarming rise in three types of police corruption, known as the "three disorders" (*san luan*): acceptance of bribes, unauthorized imposition of fines, and unauthorized sharing of official fees. In addition, the December 1990 circular instructed all public security bureaus to launch a campaign to "love the people" in order to help overcome the widespread public impression that police were "cold and callous."[29]

Noting that graft and corruption were on the upswing among the country's police forces, China's minister of public security in July 1992 banned police departments from setting up private businesses to "earn money by making use of privileges granted by the state." The minister decried the widespread practice of policemen accepting petty bribes such as cigarettes or other gifts in exchange for favors, and he announced a ban against police personnel moonlighting in private business or owning shares of stock in private companies.[30]

Judges, procurators, and other legal professionals were also said to be widely tainted by corruption. With nearly three million cases of economic crime and corruption being handled by Chinese prosecutors and courts annually, opportunities for bribery and gift-giving were plentiful. Early in 1992 Politburo SC security expert Qiao Shi acknowledged that a substantial number of judicial personnel had accepted bribes in exchange for lenient sentencing or outright dismissal of criminal charges. Decrying the behavior of judges and procurators who "trade power for money" and "seek personal gain in violation of law," Qiao called for strict enforcement of legal standards in order to deal "quick, heavy blows" to criminals.[31]

Although substantial numbers of public employees were accused of bribery, graft, and other economic crimes during the anticorruption drive of 1989–92, as usual only a small handful of high-level officials were indicted or brought to trial. Among the most visible offenders netted during the campaign were the ex-governor of Hainan Province and two ministers of the State Council (for communications and construction, respectively), all of whom were dismissed from their posts. Despite the reported involvement of all three in serious economic irregularities, political motives appeared to underlie their selection as anticorruption targets: all three men had been associates of Zhao Ziyang, and all had reportedly opposed the use of force against students in May–June 1989.[32] Significantly, after being dismissed from their posts, none of the three was formally indicted or brought to trial. The governor of Hainan, Liang Xiang, was spared from criminal prosecution after he reportedly returned more than RMB ¥500,000 in ill-gotten gains pocketed from the sale of houses and motor vehicles.[33]

Among the relatively few high-ranking cadres to face criminal prosecution in this period were the mayor of Luoyang municipality, who was jailed briefly in 1990 for accepting RMB ¥25,000 in bribes;[34] the former director of the Railway Ministry's Transportation Bureau, who received a suspended death sentence for embezzling ¥102,000 in public funds and accepting ¥31,700 in bribes;[35] and the former president of the Zhengzhou Municipal District Court, who was sentenced to eighteen years in prison for taking bribes.[36]

By the end of 1991, a total of 24,176 party cadres had been prosecuted on criminal charges since the onset of the 1989 anticorruption campaign, including 889 cadres at the county level and 34 at the provincial level—but only 1 at the ministerial level.[37] In the first nine months of 1992, criminal proceedings were initiated against an additional 17,240 cadres, bringing the three-year total of officials prosecuted for economic crimes to over 42,000. Of this total, only 110—a mere quarter of 1 percent—were cadres at or above the province level (or equivalent military rank).[38]

CHEN YUN'S CHALLENGE

One interesting facet of the anticorruption drive was the role it played in the growing schism between Deng Xiaoping and Chen Yun. At an informal meeting of party leaders in the summer of 1990, Chen implicitly placed the blame for the deteriorating honesty and integrity of party members squarely on Deng's shoulders. Allowing that corruption within the party had reached an all-time high, Chen claimed that the primary source of corruption was the spirit of bourgeois liberalization that had been permitted to flourish under the leadership of Deng's two hand-picked protégés, Hu Yaobang and Zhao Ziyang. Arguing that public anger over official corruption had been the principal cause of the 1989 student demonstrations, Chen charged Hu and Zhao with "unshakable responsibility" for the spread of corrupt practices; he further suggested that certain unnamed senior party leaders "must also accept some blame," thereby tacitly implicating Hu and Zhao's principal patron, Deng Xiaoping.[39]

In addition to directing attention to Deng's role in the genesis of the Tiananmen crisis, Chen Yun—who had supported the government's display of force against protesting students—also sought to highlight the paramount leader's personal responsibility for the bloody events of June 3–4. Arguing that Deng had shifted his position from support of Rightist economic policies before the Beijing Spring to advocacy of Leftist political and military measures at the time of the crackdown, Chen implied that Deng bore responsibility not only for the April–May crisis itself, but for the June debacle as well.[40] Rallying to Deng's defense, PLA Chief of Staff Chi Haotian, who headed the Beijing martial law command in 1989, flatly asserted that whoever ordered troops to open fire on civilian demonstrators on the evening of June 3 had failed to consult in advance either with himself or with Deng.[41]

Notwithstanding such denials, Chen Yun continued to chip away at Deng Xiaoping's exalted status and prestige. In the summer of 1990 Chen succeeded in embarrassing his rival by pointedly defending four senior party intellectuals—CASS Vice-President Yu Guangyuan, Mao's former biographer Li Rui, former State Science and Technology Commission deputy director Li Chang, and CC agricultural policy specialist Du Runsheng—against a recommendation of the CDIC to expel them from the party for having actively supported the student disorders of spring 1989. Chen's seemingly uncharacteristic defense of the four aging liberal intellectuals (all of whom were well over seventy) was widely interpreted as a calculated slap at Deng Xiaoping, designed to boost Chen's own image as a compassionate leader who was capable of healing the wounds of June 3–4.[42]

Chen's well-documented animus toward Deng stemmed from a variety of sources. For one thing, Chen was said to be resentful over Deng's tendency to claim exclusive, personal credit for launching China's post-Mao economic

320   • *C H A P T E R 1 3 •*

reforms; for another, Chen's economic instincts were inherently more cautious and conservative than Deng's. But Chen's irritation was also due in part to the style of Deng's leadership, in particular his habit of acting as a "one-man decision maker" (*yiyan tang*: lit., a "one-voice hall") in important matters of policy.[43] Chen was said to be highly vexed, for example, over Deng's unilateral decision of late May 1989 to summon China's seven military region commanders to an emergency meeting for the purpose of rallying support behind his proposal to use armed force against students. Deng's decision to convene this meeting (taken in his capacity as MAC chairman) was reportedly made without consulting his senior colleagues—a procedure Chen Yun regarded as a clear breach of the party's norm of collective leadership.[44]

One of Chen's underlying grievances against Deng—his feeling of having been slighted as coauthor of the economic reform policies introduced after the Third Plenum in December 1978—was brought into the open at a theoretical symposium held in Beijing in the autumn of 1990. At the symposium, Chen's supporters, including Peng Zhen, Deng Liqun, and CASS Vice-President Liu Guoguang, sought to reclaim a share of the spotlight for their patron. To highlight Chen's putative contributions to the theory and practice of socialist reform, they introduced the term "Chen Yun Thought" and proclaimed Chen's written works to be the "summation of . . . our experience in socialist construction over several decades."[45]

Notwithstanding the evident hyperbole of such claims, there is at least some validity to the notion that the economic reform and readjustment policies of 1979–81 initially bore Chen Yun's imprint at least as clearly as they bore Deng Xiaoping's. Indeed, Deng's fingerprints had been readily visible on major portions of Hua Guofeng's ill-fated ten-year economic program, unveiled in February 1978 and supplanted a year later by Chen's "eight-character charter."

COUNTDOWN TO CONFLICT: THE SEVENTH PLENUM

The deepening rift between the CCP's two senior statesmen was highlighted in the run-up to the CC's Seventh Plenum. Originally scheduled for mid-autumn 1990, the plenum was delayed when a serious dispute surfaced over the general economic orientation of China's Eighth Five-Year Plan (1991–95). During the summer, the State Council had prepared a draft of the plan under the supervision of Li Peng and Yao Yilin. Discussing the draft report at a high-level meeting in early October, Premier Li strongly endorsed Chen Yun's views on the importance of continued central planning and slow, balanced growth. More significant, he directly contradicted Deng Xiaoping's injunction to treat further economic reform and opening up as China's highest priorities. "Reform and opening up should not be taken as the guiding principle," said Li; "instead, sustained, steady, and coordinated development should be taken as the guiding principle."[46]

Reacting to Li Peng's challenge, Deng Xiaoping rejected the premier's proposed draft of the Eighth Five-Year Plan, criticizing it for overemphasizing state control at the expense of renewed reform. "The decade of the 1990s is the best time to continue the opening-up and reform policies," said Deng; "We should try to make an even bigger step forward."[47] Deng had reportedly become annoyed at Premier Li earlier in the year, when Li and Vice-Premier Yao Yilin had sought to annul two important reform policies adopted by the Thirteenth Party Congress: the theory of "one center and two basic points" (which openly restated Deng's theory of the productive forces) and the concept that "the state regulates the market; the market guides the enterprise" (which greatly expanded the scope of enterprise autonomy). Making it clear that he saw no problem with these two policies, Deng advised Premier Li not to challenge lightly the formulations of the Thirteenth Congress; and he flatly rejected the idea of reopening debate on these subjects.[48]

In October 1990 Deng went farther still, as he began to stress the need to resume reform of the political structure, interrupted by the Tiananmen crisis. "Now is the time to consider taking this step," he said. "Last year's disturbance delayed the progress of reform. We can no longer afford a wait-and-see attitude."[49]

Unwilling to accept defeat, conservatives redoubled their efforts to undermine proreform leaders and policies. While Deng Liqun and other theorists actively promoted "Chen Yun Thought" as a counterweight to Deng Xiaoping's leadership on the economic front, hard-liners mounted a parallel attack on the political front. Taking the lead in this effort was Vice-President Wang Zhen, with support from Peng Zhen.

At Beidaihe in the late summer of 1990, General Wang paid a visit to Deng Xiaoping. During their meeting, the Big Cannon complained about the behavior of proreform politicians Wan Li and Li Ruihuan and suggested that Jiang Zemin, too, was lacking in leadership ability. Deng reportedly became annoyed with the general's carping and admonished him to stop minding other people's business.[50] Giving vent to his rising frustration with Wang and other old comrades who continued to obstruct his policies, Deng signaled his intention to dissolve the CAC at the upcoming Seventh Plenum: "The 'leading core' of the third echelon has taken shape," he said; "our historical mission is over." Wang Zhen reportedly became so angry at this that a short time later, in an agitated encounter with fellow octogenarian Peng Zhen, he accidentally fell and broke his pelvis, requiring a hospital stay of several months.[51]

Wang Zhen's fragile physical condition underlined a serious source of concern among party conservatives, namely, the declining health and vitality of three of their key senior spokesmen: Wang, Chen Yun, and Li Xiannian. In November 1990 the three ailing veterans reportedly sought to ensure continuity in leadership by nominating their own successors. Chen Yun, ostensibly disregarding Deng's threat to abolish the Central Advisory Commission, endorsed Bo Yibo as his choice to become the next chairman of the CAC; Li Xiannian backed Wang Renzhong as chairman of the CPPCC; and Wang

Zhen recommended Deng Liqun for the vice-presidency.[52] At the same time, to counteract attempts by party moderates to regain a dominant position in the ideological field, a group of five leading conservative theorists and propagandists—Deng Liqun, Acting Minister of Culture He Jingzhi (Ye Jianying's adoptive son-in-law), CC Propaganda Department Director Wang Renzhi, *People's Daily* editor Gao Di, and Beijing Municipal Propaganda Director Xu Weicheng, who were sometimes sarcastically referred to as the "gang of five"—stepped up their criticism of Wan Li and Li Ruihuan. According to unofficial party sources, the five conservatives sought to erect "blockades" against the moderate reformers, "surrounding them layer by layer," and thereby making it difficult for them to maneuver.[53]

When the Seventh Plenum finally met in late December 1990, a standoff was in evidence. Acknowledging the lack of leadership consensus, Qiao Shi commented: "At present, it is difficult to establish a clear direction. . . . Our problems are many."[54] The proceedings of the Seventh Plenum reflected the lack of clear direction. On the one hand, pursuant to Deng's instructions, the plenum avoided criticizing the economic formulations of the Thirteenth Party Congress; on the other hand, however, Deng failed to follow through on his promise to abolish the CAC. Indeed, no organizational or personnel matters of any significance were decided at the plenum—including the case of Zhao Ziyang, consideration of which was postponed yet again.[55]

Having aroused Deng Xiaoping's ire with their original draft proposals for China's Eighth Five-Year Plan, Li Peng and Yao Yilin backed away from provoking an open split with more liberal-minded reformers at the Seventh Plenum. The proposals they finally submitted to the plenum were much more even-handed and ideologically balanced than their original draft. Reflecting an obvious attempt to bridge the gap between the ideas of Deng and those of Chen Yun, the new five-year proposals called for renewed reform and opening up, but within the framework of cautious, prudent growth and continued emphasis on state-sector dominance.[56]

Like the thirty-nine-point program adopted at the Fifth Plenum a year earlier, the Seventh Plenum's economic proposals contained a substantial number of familiar, ritualized exhortations (e.g., "firmly follow the road of building socialism with Chinese characteristics . . . handle properly the relations between central and local authorities . . . [and] firmly implement the principle of promoting both material civilization and socialist culture and ethics") along with a series of ambivalent and at times self-contradictory injunctions (e.g., "China must base economic construction on its own efforts . . . and run special economic zones still better"). Long on hortatory rhetoric, the document was extremely short on concrete programmatic guidelines or initiatives. Reflecting the dissatisfaction felt by some participants in the plenum over the abstraction and generality of Li Peng's proposals, one Central Committee staff member privately characterized the document, which ran to some twenty-eight thousand characters in length, as a "soporific" that put everyone reading it to sleep.[57]

Unrest at the Periphery: Tibet and Xinjiang

With personal and political rivalries continuing to simmer and occasionally to boil over in Beijing, another major political problem was taking shape far from the Chinese capital, in the remote western Chinese territories of Tibet and Xinjiang. In Lhasa, Tibet, ethnic unrest had been intensifying since 1987. Beginning in February 1989, a series of anti-Chinese street demonstrations triggered a violent crackdown by the PAP, in which several hundred Tibetans were killed and hundreds more injured.[58] Following the imposition of martial law, tensions between Tibetan Buddhists and Chinese security forces remained extremely high, with periodic clashes resulting in several hundred additional Tibetan casualties.[59]

When martial law was lifted in the spring of 1990, on the eve of the resumption of U.S. congressional debate over renewal of China's most-favored-nation trade status, ethnic unrest broke into the open once more, taking the form of periodic street demonstrations and protests. In April 1990 two hundred Tibetan monks walked out of their monasteries in protest over the forcible expulsion of one of their brethren by Chinese security forces.[60] In June, ten Tibetan students and thirteen Buddhist monks were arrested in Lhasa for participating in a pro-independence demonstration.[61] A few months later, a group of Buddhist monks led a demonstration in protest over the forced expulsion of several dozen of their colleagues from local monasteries and to denounce alleged police harassment of hundreds of Tibetan youths who had recently been released from custody after serving time in jail for participating in anti-Chinese demonstrations in 1989. Amid widespread reports of mounting police brutality and judicial reprisals, fifty-eight Tibetan monks and nuns fled their monasteries in the fall of 1990, intending to seek sanctuary in neighboring Nepal. Only fifteen made it safely; the rest were halted at the Nepalese border, where they were turned over to Chinese authorities. Those who reached safety told of worsening conditions of police repression and torture in Lhasa.[62] This, in turn, prompted the self-exiled god-king of Tibetan Buddhism, the Dalai Lama, to denounce Chinese brutality and retract his previous, conditional acceptance of the principle of Tibetan self-governance under Chinese sovereignty. Thereafter, the Dalai Lama increasingly lent his support to the movement for full Tibetan autonomy and self-determination.[63]

Stung by the Dalai Lama's apparent turnabout, by a February 1991 U.S. State Department report sharply criticizing Chinese human rights abuses in Tibet, and by President George Bush's well-publicized April 1991 meeting with the Dalai Lama, Beijing angrily denounced Western accounts of political repression in Tibet as biased and unjustified.[64] To emphasize their unhappiness with foreign media coverage, Chinese leaders tightened the existing ban on travel to Tibet by "unfriendly" foreign journalists. As the fortieth anniversary of Tibet's May 1951 Liberation approached, a fresh outbreak of violence was reported in Lhasa, where nine Tibetans stormed a military arsenal in an attempt to seize weapons and ammunition. Thereafter, PAP forces reportedly made a series of preemptive sweeps, arresting dozens of people in an effort to prevent new protests from breaking out during the May 23 anniversary celebrations.[65] In mid-September a street demonstration by Buddhist monks resulted in the beating and arrest of eight monks, one of whom subsequently died in police custody, reportedly as a result of bayonet wounds.[66]

The ethnic situation was no less strained in China's northwest border region of Xinjiang, where deep tensions between Chinese authorities and indigenous minority groups had been evident for decades. In April 1990 an armed clash broke out in the town of Baren, near the former Silk Road trading center of Kashi (Kashkar), when units of the Chinese PAP attempted to break up an anti-Chinese rally by two thousand militant Uighur separatists. The Uighurs—Turkic Muslims—had reportedly stockpiled weapons smuggled from nearby Afghanistan in preparation for launching a Jihad (holy war) to liberate Xinjiang. In the ensuing siege, which lasted two days, at least twenty-two people were killed and more than two hundred arrested.[67] It was the most serious outbreak of ethnic violence in Xinjiang since 1981, when Chinese troops opened fire on a column of Uighur partisans who had stormed a PLA armory near Kashi in an attempt to procure weapons with which to support an anti-Chinese uprising.[68]

In the aftermath of the April clash, China's official *Liberation Army Daily* warned of the strong possibility of local wars and military conflicts in China's volatile Central Asian border regions.[69] At around the same time, the Xinjiang Provincial People's Congress issued a televised statement warning that "a very small number of hostile elements in our society . . . may stir up new trouble."[70] To prepare for such a contingency, security forces in the capital city of Urumqi, in Kashi, and elsewhere were substantially reinforced. Overseeing the buildup was Politburo security chief Qiao Shi, who visited the area in the summer of 1990. At the conclusion of his visit, Qiao called for stern measures to combat secessionist elements, who were said to be demanding creation of an independent, transnational East Turkestani Republic.[71]

Disregarding such hard-line warnings, a group of Uighur taxi drivers demonstrated peacefully for independence on October 1, 1991—China's National Day. They were promptly arrested and placed under extrajudicial "administrative detention" for terms ranging from one to three years.[72]

ETHNIC FALLOUT FROM THE COLLAPSE OF THE USSR

With the rejection of Marxism-Leninism by the Mongolian People's Republic in 1990, followed by the sudden disintegration of the Soviet Union the following year, the rising tide of ethnic separatism in Central Asia became even more worrisome to Beijing's leaders. In Mongolia, the collapse of communism served to trigger popular demonstrations on both sides of the border in support of Greater Mongolian nationalism. In one incident reported in 1991, twenty-eight Inner Mongolian activists were arrested by Chinese security agents for taking part in pro-independence demonstrations in the provincial capital of Huhehot.[73] Across the border, in the newly de-Stalinized Mongolian Republic, a sit-in was staged in October 1991 by a group of students at the Chinese Embassy in Ulan Bator. The students had gathered thirty thousand signatures on a petition demanding an end to Chinese human rights abuses in Inner Mongolia and the immediate release of six Inner Mongolian political activists arrested during the Tiananmen crackdown.[74] Although the incident ended peacefully, it served to underscore the extreme volatility of resurgent nationalism in the region.

In Tibet, the Soviet collapse brought with it a rare acknowledgment by the head of the province's internal security apparatus that many Communist Party cadres stationed in Tibet, including a substantial number of leading cadres, had become excessively enamored of the local culture and customs of the Tibetan people. No longer upholding the four cardinal principles, these cadres were said to be insufficiently alerted to serious "splittist" tendencies displayed by "a small number of hostile forces and counterrevolutionary hooligans." Insisting that no mercy must be shown to splittists, the security chief called for firmness in suppressing local nationalism.[75]

Despite such warnings, the protests continued. In March 1992 a group of five hundred Buddhist demonstrators marched in Lhasa in support of independence. Police fired shots to disperse the crowd and arrested four dissident monks.[76] In mid-May, in the weeks preceding the forty-first anniversary of Tibet's Liberation, sixty-nine people were reportedly arrested in a series of street demonstrations led by monks and nuns carrying Tibetan flags.[77] Responding to such incidents, Chinese authorities in Lhasa accused the West of capitalizing on the Soviet collapse to foment separatism in Tibet and ordered security forces to "put down fiercely" any new pro-independence manifestations.[78]

In Xinjiang, Chinese fears of resurgent ethnic and religious nationalism also rose sharply in the wake of the Soviet Union's disintegration. Shortly after the failed Soviet coup attempt of August 1991, Vice-President Wang Zhen paid a nine-day visit to Xinjiang, in the course of which he expressed his determination firmly to crush secessionist forces in the province.[79]

As in Tibet, however, dire Chinese warnings produced only limited results. During the Chinese Lunar New Year celebrations in February 1992, Muslim separatists in Urumqi blew up a Chinese bus, killing six and wounding more than twenty.[80] A month later, the *Xinjiang Daily* openly acknowledged that there had been a substantial increase in ethnic unrest following the Soviet collapse. Adopting a hard-line stance toward such disturbances, the newspaper urged party members to strengthen their grip over hostile forces, warning that "dictatorship must be firmly exercised over those ethnic separatists who link up with hostile foreign powers to split the motherland or who use religion to complicate relations between ethnic groups."[81]

CENTER VERSUS PROVINCES: THE ECONOMIC
STRUGGLE INTENSIFIES

If the centrifugal forces of ethnic and religious nationalism were not worrisome enough, Beijing faced the added difficulty in the early 1990s of struggling to hold the line against a rising tide of provincial economic assertiveness. Since the advent of administrative decentralization a decade earlier, provincial and local governments had become increasingly bold in circumventing (and in some cases utterly disregarding) many of Beijing's directives and policy guidelines. By 1989, after almost a full decade of fiscal and administrative reform, China's national economy had become effectively "cellularized" into a plethora of semi-autarkic regional enclaves. To protect local markets and revenue sources, provincial and local authorities had erected a series of regulatory barriers against the importation of various commodities, ranging from alcohol and tobacco to clothing, washing machines and automobiles, from other provinces. These protectionist measures, which were often in violation of central directives, were enforced through a patchwork system of roadblocks, cargo seizures, ad hoc taxes, commercial surcharges and licensing fees, and, in a number of well-publicized cases, outright highway robbery.[82]

As early as the summer of 1988 Deng Xiaoping had tried to bring freewheeling provincial authorities to heel, arguing that "Since we delegate power, we can take it back any time we like."[83] In the event, however, Deng's threat proved partly hollow. Despite the imposition of rigorous austerity measures by the central government in 1988–89, regional and local authorities continued to go their own way, issuing commercial regulations, assessing and collecting local taxes and incidental fees, printing local specie, and providing discretionary incentive packages to lure business and investment away from other regions—all more or less in defiance of central authority. Faced with such regional recalcitrance, by 1989 Beijing appeared to have lost effective regulatory control over a substantial portion of the nation's economic activity, resources, and revenues.[84]

At a Central Committee work conference held on the eve of the Fifth Plenum in early November 1989, regional party secretaries, primarily representing China's southeastern coastal provinces, including Guangdong, Fujian, and Hainan, staged a minor revolt against the central government's attempt to collect more taxes and financial contributions from the provinces. Reacting strongly against the restrictions on local economic initiative mandated under the government's austerity program of 1988, the provincial secretaries lobbied intensely for an expanded money supply and relaxed credit restrictions. Under pressure, Li Peng and Yao Yilin grudgingly relented, agreeing selectively to loosen monetary controls exercised by the Bank of China.[85]

By the spring of 1990, Chinese economists were using terms like "feudal prince economy" (*zhuhou jingji*) and "independent kingdom" (*duli wangguo*) to describe the alarming trend toward semi-autonomous provincial, sub-provincial, and local divisions of administrative and fiscal authority. As one Beijing economics journal put it, under the impact of reform,

> regional governments went from being managers of economic activity to independent economic entities with their own interests. To augment their financial revenues, these regions began to use any means at their disposal to develop regional enterprise. With total disregard for principles of national planning and regional division of labor, they blindly threw themselves into production and redundant construction, effectively turning themselves into mutually opposed "independent kingdoms." Furthermore, some regions with higher revenues . . . began gradually to neglect [the delivery of] funds to the state. . . .
>
> Regional governments naturally shy away from enforcing any regulatory measures that touch upon their role as [corporate] bodies with special economic interests of their own. When the judge is also the accused, the verdict cannot possibly be impartial—this is the underlying reason for "feudal prince economies."[86]

In the autumn of 1990, at a series of working conferences held in preparation for the CC's Seventh Plenum, local authorities once again displayed their financial muscle, refusing to bend to Beijing's dictates in such areas as revenue sharing and capital investment. In one well-publicized September confrontation, Premier Li Peng lectured a group of provincial leaders on the dangers of excessive decentralization, asserting that such excesses had given rise to economic separatism and chaos. A long, awkward silence reportedly followed, broken only when the princeling governor of Guangdong Province, Ye Xuanping, took the floor to challenge the premier's assertion.[87] At a meeting two months later, in November 1990, regional leaders reportedly presented Beijing with a stark, unpleasant choice: either institute a degree of economic federalism or face a further decline in central control and possible economic disintegration.[88]

Responding to what appeared, on the face of it, to be a clear case of provincial blackmail, central government leaders backed down, agreeing to reduce the scope of direct taxation and extend the system of contract-based profit sharing favored by regional and local officials. Under the latter system, local governments retained control over the allocation of profits from enterprises under their jurisdiction after remitting a contractually fixed amount to Beijing. The alternative favored by central government planners—uniform adoption of the *li gai shui* (tax-for-profit) system previously championed by Zhao Ziyang—would have given Beijing added macroeconomic leverage by substituting mandatory taxes for negotiated remittances. After drawing heavy criticism from provincial leaders, Li Peng withdrew the government's proposal to universalize the *li gai shui*.[89]

This retreat by Beijing in the face of provincial resistance was almost without precedent. In the past, the regime had been able to rely on its tight control over provincial appointments and purse-strings to secure local compliance with central directives.[90] After a decade of administrative and fiscal decentralization, however, central leaders could no longer overwhelm or intimidate fractious provincial authorities. With the center controlling a steadily diminishing share of the nation's material and fiscal resources, Beijing's relations with the provinces had come to resemble a semi-anarchic game of mutual bargaining, backscratching, and bickering, rather than a hierarchical game of centralized command and control.

The provinces' ostensible victory over the center was not totally one-sided, however. In April 1991 Guangdong Governor Ye Xuanping, son of Ye Jianying and a principal player in the 1990 provincial economic rebellion, was peremptorily promoted by the central government—reportedly against his wishes—to the highly visible but essentially powerless post of vice-chairman of the CPPCC. By kicking him upstairs, central authorities effectively separated Ye from his power base in Guangdong, demonstrating in the process that they still retained a modicum of political and administrative clout.[91]

Although Ye Xuanping's power was ultimately curtailed, the problem posed by incipient regional "independent kingdoms" remained unresolved. Writing in January 1991, Chen Yuan, deputy director of the Bank of China and son of Chen Yun, argued for a recentralization of the country's economic and political controls to counteract the dangerous centrifugal tendencies of recent years. If the trend toward economic fragmentation continued unchecked, warned Chen, China might soon confront the prospect of social and political disintegration.[92]

Reacting to such perceived dangers, and galvanized into action by the Soviet coup attempt of August 1991, Chen Yuan and other middle-aged *gaogan zidi*, irreverently known as the *taizidang* (princelings party), formulated a new strategic agenda for China's post–cold war political and economic development. Their program was labeled "neoconservatism" (*xin baoshouzhuyi*).

THE NEOCONSERVATIVE AGENDA

Neoconservatism had its origins in a conference on "traditional Chinese culture and socialist modernization," held under the auspices of the ideological and theoretical section of the newspaper *China Youth Daily* in early December 1990.[93] Once a bastion of support for Zhao Ziyang's neo-authoritarian ideas and methods, the newspaper's theoretical brain trust had abandoned neo-authoritarianism following Zhao's dismissal and were now searching for a viable developmental alternative, one that would shed the stale, shopworn dogmas of orthodox Marxism-Leninism while at the same time eschewing the dangerous toxins of bourgeois liberalism. Participants in the December 1990 conference included such establishment conservatives as State Council spokesman Yuan Mu and propaganda specialist Xu Weicheng, as well as CASS left-wing philosopher-gadfly He Xin.[94]

A highly centralized, repressive variant of neo-authoritarianism, neoconservatism took as its starting point a deep aversion to peaceful evolution and

bourgeois liberalism and a strong determination to prevent an East European-
(and later Soviet-) style political meltdown in China. Placing substantially
greater emphasis than the neo-authoritarians on the need for gradualism and
caution in economic reform, on the importance of Communist Party control of
the economy, and on the stabilizing effects of cultural nationalism, China's
neoconservatives premised their call for political stability and unity not on a
revival of the discredited dogmas of the Maoist era, but rather on a renaissance
of traditional Chinese culture and values.[95]

To counteract the perceived threat of internal disorder stemming from
Western efforts to promote peaceful evolution in China, the neoconservatives
sought to cultivate such Confucian virtues as corporate loyalty and discipline,
hierarchy, and social harmony. By the same token, they offered little legitimate scope for individual self-expression, autonomous socioeconomic activity, or the political articulation and representation of group interests. Although
neoconservatives sometimes alluded to democracy as an ideal form of political rationality, it was said to be impractical because of China's "national condition" (*guoqing*).[96]

Shortly after the failed Soviet coup attempt of August 1991, the theoretical
section of *China Youth Daily* sponsored publication of a series of articles
outlining the neoconservative agenda. A key article in the series, entitled "Realistic Responses and Strategic Choices for China after the Soviet Coup,"
published on September 9, constituted a virtual manifesto of neoconservative
goals and priorities:

> In struggling against peaceful evolution, we must conspicuously strengthen con-
> cepts of national and state interest; in reforming and "opening up" we must force-
> fully promote realism and rationality; in economics we must prevent and criticize
> radical reformism. . . .
>
> We must realistically accept that among a certain section of the masses, the
> appeal of the ideology of the past has declined [to the point where] the only thing
> stimulated by promoting the old-style ideological education is popular rebellious-
> ness. . . . [Under such circumstances] it is inappropriate to stress class strug-
> gle. . . . It is the unique appeal of Chinese patriotism . . . [and] the lofty and noble
> cultural traditions of the Chinese people that can provide the broad masses with
> a rebirth of ultimate values in the moral and spiritual domains. . . . It follows that
> we must create a brand new culture that relies on Chinese tradition and is ade-
> quately inclusive. . . .
>
> The CCP must grasp not only the gun barrel, but property [ownership] as well.
> If the party owned property, this would provide a vehicle for political stabil-
> ity. . . . The party would become a huge corporate interest . . . exerting all manner
> of influence over the National Peoples Congress, and [thereby] securing a broader
> political domain in which to operate. . . . History proves that without an advanced
> corps holding definite assets and empowered to use them, it is impossible to main-
> tain stability. . . .
>
> In party building, the urgent task is to complete the transition from a revolu-
> tionary party to a ruling party. . . . We must seize the initiative on the premise of

stability, replace anarchy with stability, and overcome agitation with quiescence. . . . Our basic point of departure . . . must be promotion of such deeply appealing slogans as "stability above everything else."[97]

In addition to placing primary emphasis on the revival of Confucian values and the symbols and sentiments of cultural nationalism, neoconservatives also differed from traditional party conservatives in their desire to downplay the ideological and political significance of the 1989 Tiananmen crisis. Avoiding inflammatory terms like "counterrevolutionary rebellion" and "turmoil," neoconservatives generally opted for more neutral phrases such as "June Fourth event" in their discussions of the Beijing Spring. In this connection, Chen Yuan, a major supporter of the neoconservative movement and son of patriarch Chen Yun, was one of the first important Chinese political figures openly to call for healing the wounds of June 4.

According to one Hong Kong source, Chen Yun reacted favorably to publication of the "Realistic Responses" article, approving its contents for reproduction and distribution to leading cadres in Beijing.[98] Another source, with reputed close ties to the *taizidang*, claims that Chen Yun and other old-timers went so far as to request the Politburo to give advice on the possibility of revising the article for incorporation into the general secretary's political report to the Fourteenth National Party Congress in 1992.[99]

To its proponents, including such prominent princelings as Chen Yuan, Deng Yingtao, and Chen Haosu,[100] the neoconservative manifesto embodied a revival of the progressive, patriotic spirit of such revered late-nineteenth-century Chinese modernizers as Kang Youwei, Liang Qichao, and Yan Fu. To its detractors, who saw in its platform and principles a highly elitist, chauvinistic ethos of state patrimonialism, the neoconservative agenda contained clear and ominous overtones of incipient fascism.[101]

THE POST-SOVIET TRAUMATIC STRESS SYNDROME

With old-timers and princelings alike stepping up their critique of peaceful evolution and bourgeois liberalism in the summer and fall of 1991, Deng Xiaoping faced his most serious political challenge since the Tiananmen crisis. Even before the Soviet collapse, party conservatives had taken the initiative, rushing new editions of Mao's writings into print, stepping up political and ideological study in China's schools and universities, and pushing through a series of neo-Maoist policies in such areas as party organization, recruitment, and personnel assignment.[102]

One issue of particular concern to conservatives in the spring of 1991 was the party's sharply diminished prestige and popularity among young people. According to an opinion poll conducted in 1988, on the eve of the Tiananmen disturbances, only 6.1 percent of educated youths in China's Gansu Province were seriously interested in joining the Communist Party. A clear majority of the young people surveyed were either hostile or indifferent to the CCP.[103] Another poll, published two years later, showed that among the minority of Beijing college students who expressed some interest in joining the party, only one in six was motivated primarily by political or ideological convictions. The vast majority were concerned mainly with paving the way for their future careers.[104]

Alongside the precipitous decline in youth support for the political ideals of the Communist Party, there had also occurred a serious erosion of Communist morality and ethics in China's rural villages. In a remarkably candid speech by Wang Zhen, disseminated among senior cadres in the winter of 1991, the octogenarian vice-president noted with alarm that China's rural areas were being overrun by "feudalistic forces" and that "fewer and fewer people want to enroll in the party . . . [while] more and more people want to join religious groups." Even more alarming, in Wang's view, was the fact that in many villages "new capitalists are buying power with money," creating local patronage networks by donating generously to village and clan charities, dispensing loans, and creating jobs. Some of these nouveaux riches entrepreneurs had hired party cadres as business consultants; others had become village administrators; still others had used their financial resources to campaign for election to local people's congresses. As a result, Wang noted, corruption and influence-peddling were everywhere on the rise, while the morale and esprit of party members and cadres were subject to continuous erosion.[105]

In an effort to counter such problems, party conservatives pushed through a number of important policy changes in the areas of party-building and personnel. In June 1991, on the eve of the seventieth anniversary of the founding of the CCP, *People's Daily* announced ten new guidelines to be followed in party organization work. The guidelines, which had strong neo-Maoist overtones, called, among other things, for leading cadres to be rotated periodically in their job assignments and sent down to grass-roots units to "learn from the masses." It was also stipulated that CCP recruitment efforts would henceforth be concentrated primarily in rural areas, away from urban centers of alienation and social unrest. To further ensure that the party remained free from the pernicious influences of peaceful evolution and bourgeois liberalism, intellectuals and private entrepreneurs would no longer be given priority in party recruitment. Finally, in an implicit reversal of Deng Xiaoping's ten-year drive to reduce political interference by party secretaries in the day-to-day management of administrative organs and enterprises, the institution of the "party cell"—a branch organization comprising all party members within a basic-level economic, educational, or administrative work unit—was slated for strengthening. Henceforth, party cells were to serve as the "political core" (*zhengzhi hexin*) of party leadership in villages, state enterprises, schools, and universities throughout the country.[106]

Pushing their conservative agenda, Wang Zhen, Deng Liqun, and Li Xiannian went so far as to attempt tacitly to reverse the verdict on the Cultural Revolution. Upholding the wisdom of Mao's 1966 decision to launch a mass campaign of criticism against the bourgeoisie, the three conservatives explicitly praised the late Chairman's directives concerning the severity of class struggle and the need to study Marxism-Leninism. In response, Jiang Zemin pointedly reaffirmed the CCP CC's previous (negative) verdict on the Cultural Revolution. "The Cultural Revolution was a catastrophe and a tragedy," said Jiang, speaking at a Politburo meeting in June 1991; "this is a conclusion that no one can alter or reverse."[107] Not coincidentally, Jiang's remarks were delivered on the tenth anniversary of the CC's June 1981 "Resolution on Certain Questions"—a historic document that pronounced the Cultural Revolution an unmitigated disaster.

Notwithstanding his dutiful denunciation of the Cultural Revolution, throughout the spring and summer of 1991 Jiang Zemin edged closer to positions taken by Chen Yun and the conservatives (and farther from those of Deng Xiaoping). At the same Politburo meeting where he reaffirmed the party's 1981 verdict on the Cultural Revolution, for example, Jiang conveyed to his comrades a recent speech made by Chen Yun concerning the need to study Marxism-Leninism and to retain centralized planning and unified control over the economy. He also passed along Chen's demand that the party should take forthright action to clean up corruption and to make public the financial situation of all leading cadres—demands that were widely interpreted as an attempt to embarrass Deng by obliquely pointing to his children's suspected illegal financial dealings and other abuses of power.[108]

On July 1, following a short trip to the Soviet Union, Jiang Zemin gave a particularly hard-line speech on the occasion of the CCP's seventieth anniversary. Reportedly drafted by a writing group under the supervision of Hu Qiaomu and Deng Liqun, Jiang's speech praised the brilliance of Mao Zedong's Thought and called for an intensification of class struggle against bourgeois liberalization, peaceful evolution, and infiltration and subversion by "hostile foreign forces." Jiang also strongly affirmed the need to persist in centralized economic planning and socialist ownership, as well as the four cardinal principles. Both in tone and in content, Jiang's July 1 speech was remarkably rigid and strident. After reading it, Deng Xiaoping was reportedly moved to call it "one-sided."[109]

Following closely upon the party's organizational and ideological tightening, the rapid deterioration of the Soviet political situation in the late summer of 1991 further emboldened CCP conservatives to step up their criticism of Deng Xiaoping's economic reform and open policies. In late August, Wang Zhen, in the course of a visit to trouble-plagued Xinjiang Province, pointedly suggested that if peaceful evolution was to be prevented from undermining the cause of socialism in China, "senior leaders in particular" had an urgent need to arm themselves with Marxism–Leninism–Mao Zedong Thought.[110] In early September Chen Yun attacked Boris Yeltsin by name, warning that China too could fall prey to bourgeois-liberal politicians like Yeltsin if the CCP failed to draw the proper lessons from the crumbling of communism in the Soviet Union.[111]

At around the same time, rumors began to circulate concerning the poor state of Deng Xiaoping's health. Deng had dropped out of sight in mid-February, after conveying his Lunar New Year greetings to the citizens of Shanghai, causing speculation to mount that he was seriously ill. One persistent rumor held that Deng had prostate cancer, a rumor that family members and government spokespersons subsequently denied.[112] Notwithstanding such denials, Deng's poor health prevented him from making his usual journey to Beidaihe in the summer of 1991, forcing cancellation of the party's annual leadership conference—a cancellation without precedent in recent party history.[113]

With Deng in failing health, with conservatives on the warpath, and with vast areas of East China inundated by floodwaters from torrential rains that struck in the early summer of 1991, there was ample reason for party reformers to be concerned for their own—and their country's—future tranquility. The 1991 summer floods, which killed more than two thousand people and left eighty million homeless, evoked vivid memories of the catastrophic Tangshan earthquake of 1976. In the wake of that earlier disaster, it had been widely whispered that the killer quake, which struck as Mao Zedong lay near death, was an omen, a sign that the Mandate of Heaven was about to pass to a new dynastic founder. After Mao's death, there ensued two years of political turbulence. Coincidence or not, the juxtaposition of Deng's reputed illness and the occurrence of a devastating flood in the summer of 1991 was sufficient to trigger a fresh wave of nervous rumors concerning imminent dynastic disorder and change.[114] (One interesting anecdote that made the rounds in Beijing in this period involved a homophonic play on Jiang Zemin's name, with the middle character altered to produce the meaning "River Inundates People.")

WHILE THE CAT'S AWAY . . .

With Deng absent and said to be in failing health, conservatives redoubled their attack on bourgeois liberalism and peaceful evolution in the autumn of 1991. Shortly after the failed Soviet coup attempt of late August, Chen Yun warned that the CCP must do everything in its power to prevent a "Yeltsin-like figure" from emerging in China. Though he mentioned no names, Chen's warning was ostensibly aimed at Zhu Rongji, the reform-minded vice-premier and ex-mayor of Shanghai whom Deng Xiaoping had hand-picked in April 1991 to take charge of the country's economic restructuring program.[115] To counter the putative trend toward economic and ideological liberalism among third-echelon reformers such as Zhu Rongji, Chen recommended that veteran theoreticians Hu Qiaomu and Deng Liqun—both of whom, he claimed, had been unjustly reviled and cold-shouldered in the past—should be given leading positions in central party organs, in recognition of their unwavering adherence to Communist ideology and values.[116]

Continuing the conservative campaign against peaceful evolution, *People's Daily* in early September published a controversial article on leadership recruitment. The article, written by a reputed follower of Chen Yun, argued that given the very real danger of peaceful evolution in China, political integrity rather than ability should be the main criterion employed in selecting the next generation of party leaders.[117]

Alarmed by the conservatives' newfound boldness and militancy, Deng Xiaoping on September 25 relayed instructions to Jiang Zemin and Yang Shangkun concerning the importance of resolutely persevering on the road of reform and opening up. Stressing the need to guard against a resurgence of Leftist thinking, Deng downplayed the threat of peaceful evolution. "So long as the leadership groups adhere to Marxism and the party's basic line," he said, "we do not fear peaceful evolution. We must speak about it less to the lower levels."[118] Two weeks later, in a speech marking the occasion of the eightieth anniversary of the first Chinese revolution of October 10, 1911, Yang Shangkun reaffirmed the party's primary commitment to economic reform and opening up. Invoking Zhao Ziyang's controversial "theory of one center," Yang affirmed that the core task in all party work was the drive to promote economic construction.[119]

Undeterred, conservatives continued their attack. In October Bo Yibo, addressing the CAC, denounced Mikhail Gorbachev as a degenerate Marxist whose rampant liberalism had created a state of anarchy in the Soviet Union.[120] In late October *Guangming Daily* published a commentary claiming that reformers' attempts to put "economics first" in China were fraught with danger and had to be tempered by renewed ideological vigilance, including increased attentiveness to class struggle.[121] At around the same time, *People's Daily* ran a signed article by Deng Liqun warning of an imminent threat to the survival of socialism. "If we fail to wage a resolute struggle against liberalization or [against] capitalistic reform and opening up," cautioned the conservative firebrand, "our socialist cause will be ruined."[122] In his most blunt and direct challenge yet to Deng Xiaoping's reform program, Little Deng boldly asserted that " 'reform and opening up' is itself a banner for peaceful evolution in China."[123]

As a prime example of "capitalistic reform and opening up," party conservatives began openly to criticize one of China's boldest and most controversial economic experiments, the "Wenzhou model" of private enterprise in Zhejiang Province. Famous for having some of China's richest entrepreneurs, the city of Wenzhou had achieved a sevenfold increase in industrial and agricultural output value in the decade of the 1980s. With the private sector accounting for fully 35 percent of local economic activity, Wenzhou was an obvious target for antibourgeois propaganda.[124]

Shortly after the June 4 incident, Wang Zhen took the lead in criticizing Wenzhou, remarking that "I have long heard that Wenzhou's political power is not in the hands of the Communist Party."[125] Taking their cue from the Big Cannon, conservative propagandists labeled Wenzhou a "quasi-capitalistic enclave" and a "boat floating toward the capitalist shore." To support their claims of bourgeois endangerment, they cited an upsurge of prostitution and drug abuse in the city. "Wanna know what capitalism is?" asked conservatives rhetorically. "Go to Wenzhou and have a look."[126]

Deng Liqun's use of the term "capitalistic reform and opening up" to describe Wenzhou-type economic experiments constituted a calculated slap at Deng Xiaoping. Other, equally provocative statements attributed to Little Deng were directed against Li Ruihuan, Politburo SC member in charge of ideological work. Following the Soviet collapse, Li had continued to speak out against the dangers of Leftism and in favor of the further emancipation of thinking, thus putting him squarely at odds with the "gang of five" in the propaganda and media apparatus.[127]

On National Day, October 1, Li Ruihuan reportedly foiled an attempt by the "gang of five" to publish in *People's Daily* a left-wing editorial that deemphasized reform and stressed instead the need to intensify the struggle against liberalism. Alarmed by the wording of the proposed editorial, which included a demand to "clarify the question of whether reform and opening up are surnamed socialism or capitalism?" Li Ruihuan hastily submitted a draft of the editorial for Deng Xiaoping's personal comments. Alarmed, the patriarch instructed Li to undertake a thorough revision of the piece. In its rewritten form, the editorial included the phrase, reportedly authored by Deng himself, "Empty talk undermines the country."[128]

In November Deng Liqun took a strong, if oblique, swipe at Li Ruihuan, charging that "liberal thoughts have again surfaced within the party and in newspapers." Alleging that liberalism was being promoted by certain (unnamed) high-level party officials, Little Deng characterized the situation as "extremely dangerous."[129] His militant remarks were ostensibly a response to Li's rewritten National Day *People's Daily* editorial as well as to a series of strikingly liberal commentaries that had recently appeared in the *Beijing Youth News* and the Shanghai *Liberation Daily* (not to be confused with the *Liberation Army Daily*). These commentaries, some of which had been written under the pseudonym Huang Fuping ("Huangpu River criticism"), called upon the party and the Chinese people to be more daring in emancipating their thinking; modifying rigid, outmoded ideas; discarding habits of "self-seclusion, dogmatism, complacency, and conservatism"; and further opening up the economy to the outside world. According to press reports, conservative propagandists had sought—unsuccessfully—to censor or suppress several of the offending commentaries, some of which allegedly bore a family resemblance to the controversial 1988 "River Elegy" narratives. These same reports indicated that Li Ruihuan had taken the lead in blocking the censorship effort.[130]

In addition to Deng Liqun, various other conservative leaders also spoke out with increasing stridency in the fall of 1991. At the end of October, hardline Peking University President Wu Shuqing accused the Voice of America and the British Broadcasting Corporation of "poisoning young minds and polluting society." Complaining that there existed a "realistic danger of producing democratic individualists who are full of capitalistic ideologies," Wu threatened to fire liberal-minded teachers who were overly enamored of the West and who lacked faith and enthusiasm for Marxism and socialism.[131]

In late November, on the eve of the CC's Eighth Plenum, Wang Zhen allegedly flew into a rage when Deng Xiaoping instructed senior party leaders, at an enlarged Politburo SC session convened at Deng's home, to downplay China's struggle against peaceful evolution and to compromise with the United States on the question of human rights. "We should not repeatedly mention the peaceful evolution plot by the West," said Deng, because "we need the United States to promote our reforms and opening up. If we always confront the United States, we'll leave ourselves no room to maneuver."[132] Livid, Wang Zhen reportedly challenged Deng's commitment to Marxism, accusing him of fostering peaceful evolution in China.[133] In a conversation with fellow conservatives, Wang charged that Deng's policies were leading the country down the capitalist road. Shortly after his tirade against Deng, the frail, elderly Big Cannon, now said to be suffering from cancer, took a sudden turn for the worse, which forced him to cancel several scheduled public appearances.[134]

To blunt the thrust of the conservative offensive, Deng Xiaoping, recuperating from an undisclosed illness, gave Li Ruihuan a strong vote of confidence in early November. In a message reportedly relayed to Li by Yang Shangkun and Jiang Zemin, Deng instructed Li to ignore ideological interference from the Left, reminding him that "you are in charge of ideological work" and assuring him that "the Central Committee has not made a decision to allow others to do the job." In an oblique reference to die-hard conservatives, Deng said, "I know some [people] are disobedient. But you have to speak up regardless." Bolstered by Deng's vote of confidence, Li Ruihuan told a meeting of party officials in Shanghai that the Central Committee was well aware of Leftist attempts to interfere in propaganda and media affairs. "The party center will not turn a blind eye to [such] practices," he said.[135]

Bracing for a showdown, Li Ruihuan made known his intention to overhaul the party's propaganda machinery. Citing a series of articles in the *People's Daily* and *Guangming Daily* that had recklessly equated market reforms with capitalism, emancipation of the mind with bourgeois liberalism, and foreign investment with imperialist domination, Li prepared to seek the ouster of four members of the troublesome "gang of five"—Wang Renzhi, He Jingzhi, Gao Di, and Xu Weicheng. Scene of the showdown would be the CC's Eighth Plenum, which had twice been postponed due to intense factional infighting in the aftermath of the Soviet collapse.[136]

In the run-up to the Eighth Plenum, elderly CAC conservatives attempted to pack central party organs with their orthodox followers, hoping thereby to forestall a political comeback by the party's resurgent liberals. Recommending several of his old comrades for top-level positions, Chen Yun singled out Hu Qiaomu, Deng Liqun, Yao Yilin, Song Ping, Bo Yibo, and Wang Renzhong as individuals worthy of high-level appointment despite their relatively advanced age. In similar fashion, Wang Zhen nominated nine veteran political conservatives for positions on the Politburo and Central Secretariat, including Deng Liqun, Wang Renzhi, He Jingzhi, and Yuan Mu. Deng Xiaoping countered by encouraging proreform members of the Politburo Standing Committee to have the courage to select "proper leaders" and successors who could satisfy three main criteria: they should possess a strong party spirit; they should resolutely support the policies of the Third Plenum of December 1978; and they should have made outstanding contributions to national construction and modernization in the period since June 4. Few, if any, of the candidates nominated by Chen Yun or Wang Zhen met all three of Deng's criteria. Indeed, Deng was particularly adamant on the subject of Hu Qiaomu and Deng Liqun. Categorically rejecting Chen Yun's proposal to appoint the two veteran theoreticians to central leadership posts, Deng issued a terse response: "Hu Qiaomu and Deng Liqun should not be allowed into the leadership group."[137]

Ironically, Deng's outburst against Hu Qiaomu came just as the latter was undergoing a change of heart about the dangers of Rightism and reform. According to a knowledgeable senior member of the Communist Party, Hu Qiaomu's two-month visit to the United States in the winter of 1989—shortly before Tiananmen—had left him more tolerant of bourgeois society and culture than before.[138] Thereafter, the elderly theoretician began to tone down his opposition to Deng's reform program. And with the exception of his rather pro forma role in overseeing the drafting of Jiang Zemin's hard-line seventieth-anniversary speech of July 1991, Hu Qiaomu did not play a leading part in the anti–bourgeois liberalization initiatives of the early 1990s.

Although Hu Qiaomu had softened somewhat, Chen Yun clearly had not. On the eve of the Eighth Plenum, Chen weighed in with a strong appeal to slow down the movement toward market reform in the economy and peaceful evolution in the ideological sphere. Despite his poor health, Chen put in a rare personal appearance at a top-level leadership meeting early in November 1991. Pointing out that peaceful evolution had already become a serious problem in some parts of China, Chen claimed that "Western ideologies are rapidly spreading [from the coast] to the interior. If our direction is not correct . . . a huge price will have to be paid."[139] A week later, in talks with leading members of the State Council, Chen further complained that economic reformers had become so enamored of market mechanisms and special economic zones that "not even cold water can cool [them] down." Complaining that reformers were too quick to dismiss the socialist planned economy as outmoded, Chen called for a "proper ratio" of 8:2 between the planned economy and market regulation. He also warned against indiscriminate establishment of special economic zones and other "development zones" that were intended to hasten the influx of foreign capital. Cautioning against pinning China's hopes for modernization on foreign capitalists, Chen noted that foreigners were only interested in maximizing their own profits.[140] Echoing Chen's warning, Beijing Party Secretary Li Ximing pointedly referred to foreign-owned joint ventures in China as a "tail of capitalism" that had to be cut off.[141]

Back from the Brink: The "Mediocre" Eighth Plenum

When the Eighth Plenum finally met at the end of November, the anticipated fireworks failed to materialize. In an effort to avoid protracted internecine conflict, party leaders decided to postpone action on the most controversial agenda items. Included among the measures deferred for future debate were proposals to promote neoconservative princeling Chen Yuan to the Central Committee, to reorganize the CC propaganda department, and to adopt policy guidelines governing enterprise reform and the handling of cadre corruption. Deng Xiaoping himself reportedly made the decision to sidestep these contentious issues.

Although Deng did not attend the November plenum, on the eve of the meeting he advised party leaders to refrain from engaging in bitter, divisive struggles. "Issues that cannot be handled with assurance," he said, "can be set aside for the moment."[142] Heeding Deng's advice, after four days of debate that was sometimes tense, sometimes tepid, the plenum took action on three relatively noncontroversial items: (1) ratification of a Politburo decision (previously announced in April 1991) to appoint Zhu Rongji and Zou Jiahua as vice-premiers of the State Council; (2) adoption of a set of general policy guidelines to be followed in rural work; and (3) approval of a recommendation, supported by Deng Xiaoping, to appoint Yang Baibing to fill the Politburo seat currently occupied by his brother, Yang Shangkun, whose retirement was due to be announced shortly. Of these three measures, only the Politburo nomination of Yang Baibing reportedly evoked more than mere token criticism among rank-and-file members of the Central Committee.[143]

When the communiqué of the Eighth Plenum was released, it clearly reflected Deng's decision to minimize conflict. Totally devoid of references to the most contentious issues of ideology, economic policy, and personnel changes, the communiqué concentrated almost exclusively on articulating a series of rather bland, consensual guidelines to be followed in the party's agricultural work. Reiterating the CCP's perennial concerns with "promoting all-around growth of the rural economy," "doing a good job of helping poor areas," and "enhancing the party's leadership over rural work," the communiqué was decidedly insipid and noncontroversial. Indeed, one Hong Kong source characterized the plenum itself as "unexpectedly mediocre."[144] With reformers and conservatives alike backing away from open confrontation, decision on the most critical issues facing the party was put off until the Fourteenth Party Congress, scheduled for the autumn of 1992.

The Gathering Storm

Though an open breach had been averted for the time being, partisan political maneuvering quickly intensified. Immediately following adjournment of the Eighth Plenum, the CAC held its own plenary session, attended by 167 leading old-timers. At the meeting, Bo Yibo put forward a provocative list of six opinions that had been written by Chen Yun, who was unable to attend the session due to poor health. First, Chen subtly altered Deng's initial criterion for the recruitment of Politburo successors—"strong party spirit"—by pointedly stressing that the Politburo's new leaders must all be "*Marxists* with strong party spirit." Second, Chen rejected Deng's recommendation to compromise with the United States on human rights issues, roundly denouncing the United States for waging a campaign of peaceful evolution that was designed to sabotage and subvert socialism. Third, he reaffirmed Mao Zedong's definition of "line struggles" within the party, arguing that such struggles constituted a normal part of party life. Fourth, Chen suggested that the party must be purified in order to preserve its vanguard role in society and thereby guarantee the consolidation of China's socialist system. Fifth, he suggested that overzealousness, impatience, and utopianism on the part of liberal reformers had caused the party to pay a heavy price. And finally, in contradistinction to Deng's increasing emphasis on opposing Leftist tendencies, Chen said that the party's main ideological task was to "oppose the Right while guarding against the Left" (*fanyou, fangzuo*), a formula that gave clear priority to the struggle against bourgeois liberalism. On at least five of these six points, Chen Yun's views ran counter to positions previously articulated by Deng Xiaoping.[145] Moreover, Chen now boldly rejected Deng's reform-oriented "theory of one center," calling instead for "another center," namely, "to strengthen the party's ideological construction."[146]

While Chen sought to mobilize resistance to Deng's line and policies, Deng Liqun now concentrated on undermining Deng Xiaoping's putative claim to ideological and theoretical preeminence. In personal appearances at a series of academic, cultural, and propaganda forums between mid-November 1991 and early January 1992, Little Deng preached a revival of Mao Zedong Thought. Seeking to capitalize upon a recent wave of popular Maoist nostalgia, Deng Liqun hailed the "Mao Zedong craze" as a powerful antidote to the spread of bourgeois liberalization, reminding his audiences that "Comrade Mao Zedong was the first one to warn us of 'peaceful evolution' . . . and the only one to have ever prophesied what is currently happening in East Europe and the Soviet Union."[147] Drawing an invidious comparison between Mao's "brilliant" (*jingpi*) theoretical insights and the lesser contributions made by Deng Xiaoping, Little Deng pointedly objected to the recently coined phrase "Deng Xiaoping Thought," which he derided as unscientific and inappropriate.[148]

In December Deng Liqun reportedly met with fellow hard liners Wang Zhen, Li Ximing, Wang Renzhi, and Song Renqiong to discuss drafting an emergency report to the Central Committee warning of the danger of a capitalist restoration in China. Among the key points raised at this meeting were allegations concerning the existence of a dangerous anti-Marxist ideological trend within the party and a claim that the "reformist road" was in reality the "capitalist road."[149]

Not to be upstaged by his adversaries, Li Ruihuan fought back. In December he lashed out at the left-wing editors of the journal *Zhenlide zhuiqiu*

(Search for truth), an internal organ published by the CC propaganda department. In its November issue, the magazine had carried an article criticizing certain unnamed "reformists taking the capitalist road within China." Challenging the journal's editors to put up or shut up, Li Ruihuan demanded that they "explain clearly just who on earth are these 'reformists taking the capitalist road.'"[150] A short time later, in response to Wang Renzhi's call for a tightening of ideological controls to prevent peaceful evolution, Li Ruihuan told a conference of senior party propaganda cadres that it was high time to "stop delivering dry and empty sermons and stop conveying formalistic propaganda."[151]

Disturbed by the intemperate statements of Wang Zhen, Deng Liqun, and other veteran hard-liners, Deng Xiaoping grew increasingly irritated. On one occasion, he said angrily: "Old Wang has been abnormal when giving many of his speeches. . . . Why has he made such irresponsible remarks? Who does he represent?" To help restrain the outspoken general, the Central Party Secretariat issued instructions to relevant departments not to disseminate or publicize any of Wang's recent statements, stating that "some of his remarks and views . . . are incorrect."[152]

With the temperature of factional conflict rising precipitously, it was only a matter of time before something had to give. The proverbial last straw came in late December, when a group of CAC veterans reportedly drafted a joint letter to the Central Committee proposing severely to restructure and restrict China's coastal SEZs. In their letter, the elderly conservatives charged that the SEZs were capitalist in nature and had become hotbeds of peaceful evolution.[153]

Galvanized into action by the old-timers' frontal challenge, Deng Xiaoping marshalled his remaining physical energies and made a dramatic gesture designed to recapture the policy initiative on behalf of his reform program. Laying down the gauntlet, Deng challenged Chen Yun to accompany him on an inspection tour of China's southern SEZs, to see for himself the fruits of a dozen years of economic reform and opening up. Though he now experienced noticeable difficulty walking and talking, and though he lacked sufficient strength to play bridge for more than an hour at a time during his customary twice-weekly card game,[154] China's paramount leader threw caution to the wind. Heading south in the middle of winter, Deng launched his last major political campaign.

Deng's Final Offensive:
January–October 1992

A great deal of verbal gymnastics goes on about
whether reform and opening up are surnamed capitalism or
socialism. . . . Some people say that with each dose of foreign
capital we become more capitalist. . . . These people lack even
the most basic common sense about developing capitalism. . . .
China must watch out for the Right, but mainly
defend against the Left.

—Deng Xiaoping, January 1992

CONVINCED that failure to push ahead boldly with reform would invite the type of disaster that had befallen other Communist regimes since 1989, Deng Xiaoping launched his final offensive on the eve of the 1992 Lunar New Year. Amid a tight veil of security, the patriarch began his tour of Southeast China's bustling coastal development regions and SEZs on January 15, 1992.[1]

Deng's reasons for making this dramatic *nanxun* (southern tour) were complex. On the one hand, by calling attention to the rapid economic progress achieved in the special zones and open cities since the Third Plenum of December 1978, Deng hoped to bolster his claim that reform and the open policy were all that stood between China and a Soviet-style political meltdown. On the other hand, he badly needed to shore up his own increasingly precarious historical legacy. According to Hong Kong sources, two of the patriarch's children, Deng Pufang and Deng Nan, were deeply concerned that the dark shadows cast by June 4 might forever stain their father's reputation as a reformer and statesman. Given the strong expectation that the original verdict on the Beijing massacre would eventually be reversed, his children greatly feared that in the absence of any dramatic new evidence confirming the brilliance of their father's economic theories and strategies, his reputation might suffer grievous, possibly irreparable, posthumous damage—as Mao's reputation had done.

Deng's decision to make the southern trip on his own was finalized after Chen Yun declined Deng's invitation to accompany him. In turning down the invitation, Chen, who was convalescing in the scenic West Lake district of Hangzhou, pointedly commented on the unhealthful environment of the southern coastal zones.[2]

DENG'S SOUTHERN STRATEGY

Deng's month-long nanxun, which began in Wuhan, was undertaken at a leisurely pace in the relative comfort of his private railroad car. The trip included stopovers in Shenzhen, Zhuhai, and Shanghai. En route, he gave a number of speeches and impromptu talks, the common denominator of which was the call for an immediate, rapid acceleration of market reforms and the open policy.[3] Taking aim squarely at his conservative critics, Deng borrowed one of Mao Zedong's favorite metaphors. Reform and opening up "must not be like a woman with bound feet," he said, but must "stride boldly forward" for thirty or forty more years. Flatly rejecting the Leftist argument that "with each dose of foreign capital we become more capitalistic," Deng characterized such arguments (and the people who made them) as lacking in "basic common sense" about capitalism. Pressing his point, he drew a direct connection between the success of China's reforms and the prospects for future political stability. "If it hadn't been for the achievements of reform and opening up," he said, "we would not have made it beyond June 4. . . . [We] would have had chaos and . . . civil war."[4]

Deng went on to deny the existence of a vital link between market economics and capitalism, on the one hand, or between economic planning and socialism, on the other. "Market economies need not be surnamed capitalism," he asserted. "Socialism has markets, too. Plans and markets are simply economic stepping stones . . . to universal prosperity and richness." Reiterating a point he had first raised in 1984, Deng conceded that while inequalities in personal income and regional growth rates would probably widen in the early stages of reform and opening up, this was acceptable because over time advanced areas would "pull along" more backward regions.[5]

As a model of a rapidly developing regional economy, Deng cited Guangdong Province, and he expressed hope that Guangdong might, before too long, catch up with the "four little dragons" of East Asia—Taiwan, South Korea, Singapore, and Hong Kong. Shanghai might make even faster progress, Deng suggested, because of its superior human resources and infrastructure. Seeking to counter conservative claims that a rapid influx of foreign capital into China's coastal regions would hasten bourgeois liberalization, Deng said that so long as people were "sober-minded" they need not be overly concerned about the introduction of capitalist funds and techniques.

Deng even had nice things to say about Shenzhen's fledgling stock exchange, long an object of ideological disdain to conservative critics of bourgeois liberalization. Denying that stock markets were necessarily an exclusive preserve of capitalism, Deng argued that they were fully compatible with so-

Deng Xiaoping, supported by daughter Deng Rong, pauses for a
photo opportunity in Shenzhen during his "southern tour,"
January 1992. At left, in the wheelchair, is Deng's
handicapped son, Deng Pufang.

cialism; along similar lines, he suggested that China should quickly strive to
create "several Hong Kongs" within its borders.[6] Eager to accept Deng's challenge, local cadres in Hainan boasted that their province would be the first to
be rebuilt into a Chinese Hong Kong.[7] In response to those who warned that
Hong Kong—style economic reform would hasten the process of peaceful
evolution, Deng drew a line between economics and politics. "Don't be afraid
that the forces of imperialism will stage peaceful evolution," he said. "The
crucial thing is that nothing happens within the party."[8]

Throughout his southern tour, Deng's sociopolitical message was distinctly
more conservative than his economic message. Citing "historical experience,"
Deng argued that authoritarian measures had to be taken in order to consolidate political power, and that in the course of economic reform dictatorship
must continually be exercised over enemies of the socialist state. It was also
necessary, he said, to clamp down vigorously on such social evils as drug use,

prostitution, and economic crime, which he acknowledged to be flourishing in Guangdong's major cities and special economic zones. Unless such contemptible practices were resolutely stamped out, he argued, Guangdong would be unable to catch up with the four dragons.[9]

Notwithstanding his accent on law and order, Deng's overall message represented a clear ideological gain for the renascent liberal wing of the party and an equally serious setback for Deng Liqun, Chen Yun, and their fellow conservatives. Avoiding emphasis on the four cardinal principles, which were invoked only indirectly within the context of the slogan "one center and two main points," Deng Xiaoping aimed his criticism almost entirely at the Left. In the most widely quoted (and most highly controversial) statement of his entire southern journey, the patriarch exhorted his compatriots to "watch out for the Right, but mainly defend against the Left" (*yao jingti you, dan zhuyao shi fangzhi zuo*). In this one simple phrase, Deng completely reversed the thrust of Chen Yun's December injunction calling on party members mainly to "oppose the Right while guarding against the Left" (*fanyou, fangzuo*). In transposing Chen's Left-Right priorities, Deng offered the following rationale: "The Left is more dangerous than the Right, because the former have more power."[10] In an apparent reference to Deng Liqun, Li Ximing, and Song Ping, the patriarch noted that "Some theorists and politicians have used serious charges to intimidate people. . . . To them, it seems that being Leftist is equal to being revolutionary. . . . [They] denounce reform and openness for introducing and developing capitalism, and hold that the main danger of peaceful evolution comes from the economic field. This is Leftism."[11]

Toward the end of his southern journey, in the second week of February, Deng issued a stern reminder to his elderly colleagues that old age tends to make people stubborn, rendering them afraid to make mistakes. If such people cannot display greater tolerance and flexibility in their thinking, admonished Deng, they had better "go to sleep."[12]

Deng's remark about age making people stubborn was evidently aimed at Chen Yun, who agreed to hold a brief meeting with Deng in Shanghai at the conclusion of Deng's southern tour. Deng's purpose in seeking the meeting was to persuade his rival to endorse the "theory of one center." Chen balked at Deng's proposal, however, and reportedly countered with his own variant—the "theory of another center"—which stressed not economic construction but ideological construction as the party's core task.[13]

THE STRUGGLE ON THE PROPAGANDA FRONT

Reflecting the severity of the ongoing contest for control of the party's propaganda apparatus, Deng's whirlwind southern tour went unreported in the official media for several weeks—no film footage, no news stories, no quotations.[14] Despite the lack of formal publicity, however, word of Deng's sojourn—along with unofficial excerpts from his speeches—spread very quickly from Shenzhen to Hong Kong and thence to Shanghai and beyond.

On February 14 President Yang Shangkun, who had accompanied Deng on the final leg of his nanxun, echoed the patriarch's call for bold steps to be taken in borrowing advanced Western technology and management techniques to accelerate China's economic development.[15] Three days later, NPC SC Chairman Wan Li echoed Yang's appeal from Yunnan Province, where he was making an inspection tour of his own.[16] On February 17, the semiofficial Hong Kong Communist newspaper *Wenwei po* revealed that a compilation of Deng's southern speeches was being circulated by Jiang Zemin among top party officials in Beijing.[17]

At a Politburo meeting convened on February 12, near the conclusion of Deng's journey, a majority of Standing Committee members, including Jiang Zemin, Qiao Shi, Li Peng, and Li Ruihuan, endorsed Deng's "important remarks" and went on record expressing their support for the new reform speed-up.[18] Immediately thereafter, a spate of pro-reform, anti-Leftist articles and editorials began to appear in the Shanghai newspapers *Liberation Daily* and *Wenhui Daily*. Toward the end of February, a few Beijing newspapers and magazines followed suit. "Why do we say that in the overall process of reform and opening up the Left is the principal danger?" inquired a *Workers' Daily* editorial of February 20. It is because "past experience tells us that it is much more difficult to oppose interference from the Left than to correct errors of the Right. . . . The ingrained power of the Left must not be underestimated."[19] Paraphrasing one of Deng's key southern statements, the editors of the Beijing *Economic Information Daily* said "there are hazards that accompany deepening reform. But if we do not reform, the risks are even greater." While acknowledging that resistance to reform was still strong in certain quarters, the newspaper claimed that "reform's opponents have less and less of a market . . . [they] have less and less ground to stand on."[20] In a similar vein, the magazine *Youth Reference*, paraphrasing the paramount leader's latest remarks, which it characterized as unprecedentedly strong, bluntly admonished, "Reform and opening up are the only way out for China. . . . Whoever does not support reform must leave office."[21]

By the end of February the conservative editors of *People's Daily* had come under intense pressure to endorse Deng's southern initiative. Acting on instructions from Li Ruihuan, the newspaper on February 23–24 printed two articles calling for accelerated economic reform and opening up. In one of the articles, a pseudonymous commentator lauded the policy of borrowing from capitalism's useful aspects to promote rapid development of the Chinese economy. Asserting that China's past refusal to make use of capitalism's strong points had been the result of Leftist deviation, the article claimed that such refusal had "nothing to do with socialism."[22]

Not all conservatives bent with the wind. Toward the end of February, a group of thirty-five CAC and CDIC members, including Chen Yun, Li Xiannian, Wang Zhen, Wang Renzhong, Deng Liqun, and He Jingzhi, signed their names to a letter addressed to Deng Xiaoping requesting Deng to take prompt, forthright action to alter the party's direction of development, which had allegedly departed from the socialist path. Urging Deng vigorously to oppose peaceful evolution, to promote communist ideology and morality, and to launch only those reforms and open policies that were surnamed socialism, the letter represented a major challenge by supporters of Chen Yun's "theory of another center." In response to the letter, Deng reportedly urged those of his old comrades "who listen to biased opinions and hold fast to the book" to test the correctness of his line by conducting their own investigations at the grassroots level.

Seeking to blunt the thrust of the reform offensive, Deputy Propaganda Director Xu Weicheng ordered the *People's Daily* to run a series of articles on the subject of "socialist spiritual civilization." The order was quickly countermanded by Li Ruihuan, who was now clashing regularly with Leftists in the propaganda apparatus.[23]

Experiencing increasing difficulty getting their views aired in the mass media, diehard Leftists turned increasingly to internal (*neibu*) publications and political forums. Writing in the February 1992 issue of *Dangdai sichao* (Contemporary trends), a house organ of the CC propaganda department, a pseudonymous commentator claimed that some people were using opposition to Leftism as a convenient pretext for opposing the four cardinal principles and promoting bourgeois liberalism. If this type of deceptive anti-Leftism were not dealt a decisive blow, the author warned, the results would be catastrophic.[24]

At Peking University, the Leftist-dominated party committee initially downplayed the importance of Deng's southern speeches, issuing a series of comments in which it was claimed, inter alia, that "Xiaoping's speeches are just a rumor. . . . We shouldn't believe all rumors that come floating to our ears." When the abridged contents of Deng's speeches were first published in "Central Document No. 2 (1992)" in early March, Beida party leaders sought to minimize the impact by proclaiming that "there was nothing new in comrade Xiaoping's speeches. . . . We are to carry out opening up and reform while continuing to oppose bourgeois liberalization."[25] In thus discounting the importance of Deng's southern journey, Beida officials were taking their cue from Chen Yun, who had reacted to the publication of Central Document No. 2 by stating that "the document on Comrade Xiaoping's southern tour only reflects his own opinion and local opinion."[26]

Though they displayed outward disinterest toward Deng's newest statements, Peking University officials were privately alarmed. In a series of closed-door cadre meetings on the Beida campus, Deputy Party Secretary Lin Yanzhi called for political work cadres to dig in their heels. "You don't want to be sold out again!" he admonished. "We've [already] been sold out again," replied one embittered cadre; "our work in the previous stage was all in vain." Another cadre predicted that if socialism were to be abandoned in China, the country would quickly plunge into chaos "worse than that seen in the USSR."[27]

Hard-line Beida President Wu Shuqing joined the anti-Deng chorus. The conservative Marxist economist, who had reportedly refused to walk unescorted on his own university campus after dark in the fall of 1989 for fear of being assaulted by angry students, warned an assembly of university cadres of the dire consequences that would quickly follow if Deng's recent reform proposals were to be accepted:

> You'd better prepare yourselves, because this year reform and opening up will be accelerated. The housing system will be revised, rents will go way up, . . . you will have to pay for your own medicine. Prices will certainly rise sky-high, and wages will be unstable as well. A system to retain only efficient workers will be put into effect, and many people will find themselves out of work. You'd better get ready for all this.[28]

Having induced heightened anxiety among his listeners, President Wu went on to urge university cadres to strengthen their resolve in preparation for the coming struggle. "We shall not waver," he said; "we shall not falter; our ideology shall not be moved."[29] In his declaration of defiance, Wu Shuqing echoed Deng Liqun, who, following publication of Central Document No. 2, vowed to continue fighting for the socialist cause "until the last man."[30]

THE ANTI-LEFTIST SPRING OFFENSIVE

In the face of such determined resistance, the forces promoting accelerated reform scored a major victory in early March, when the Politburo formally endorsed Deng Xiaoping's "theory of one center" and identified Leftism as the principal current danger.[31] Leading the proreform forces at the Politburo meeting were Yang Shangkun and Jiang Zemin. Speaking on Deng's behalf, Yang strongly admonished his colleagues to rally around the CC's core leadership under Jiang Zemin, warning potential dissidents that "it is normal to have differences of opinion, but opposition in action is not allowed. . . . Anyone who fails to realize this point is no communist!"[32] For his part, Jiang Zemin issued a self-criticism acknowledging that in recent years he had not promoted reform and opening up with sufficient vigor; and he went on to offer some avuncular advice to those conservative politicians who had been slow to embrace Deng's reform initiative, urging them to "take criticism and self criticism as the key."[33] After hearing the admonitions (and implied threats) of Yang and Jiang, a group of Politburo conservatives, including Yao Yilin, Song Ping, and Li Ximing, fell grudgingly into line, issuing self-criticisms and —outwardly at least—embracing Deng's program. Influenced by their example, several other erstwhile hard-liners, including Chen Xitong, Wang Renzhi, and Gao Di, followed suit.[34] In a stunning display of subtle political pressure mixed in with some not-so-subtle arm-twisting, Deng's supporters thus overwhelmed conservative opponents of the patriarch's "theory of one center." Even some of the CAC's perennial nay-sayers now joined the ranks of the born-again reformers, as Peng Zhen, Song Renqiong, and Bo Yibo openly endorsed Deng's policies.[35]

In yet another indication that reformers had gained the upper hand, the National People's Congress, meeting in late March, made more than 150 changes in the proposed text of Premier Li Peng's government work report, incorporating, among other things, a new emphasis on the positive virtues of private enterprise and stock markets, and a repetition of Deng's admonition to guard principally against the Left. The amended report also explicitly called for the general line adopted at the Thirteenth Party Congress—"one center and two basic points"—to remain in effect for one hundred years. In a vote many observers interpreted as a tacit rebuke to Chen Yun, as well as to Premier Li and the party's conservative wing, legislators approved the much-amended work report by a margin of 2,583 to 10.[36] Shortly afterward, a number of provincial leaders openly criticized Premier Li's reluctance to oppose Leftism and his failure to embrace bolder targets for economic growth and opening up.[37] Making the best of what was clearly a bad situation for him, at the end of the NPC session Li cut his losses, promising to give earnest consideration to provincial leaders' requests to speed up the pace of economic construction and urging legislators from Yunnan, Shanxi, Hunan, and Inner Mongolia to "seize the opportunity and quicken the pace of reform."[38]

Li Peng also had rough going on another front at the March NPC meeting, as one-third of China's legislators withheld support from a government motion, enthusiastically supported by Premier Li, to move ahead with construction of the controversial San Xia (Three Gorges) Dam. The proposed 600-foot-high concrete gravity dam was to be sited on the middle reaches of the Yangzi River, near Yichang. It would create an artificial lake over 300 miles long, take 18 years to complete, and cost between U.S. $11 billion (the government's official estimate) and $30 billion (an unofficial estimate by project engineers). Its hydropower capacity—listed at between 13,000 and 17,680 megawatts, depending on final design and budgetary decisions—would be the largest in the world. Approximately 60,000 acres of prime agricultural land would be inundated once the dam was operational, and upwards of 1.1 million people residing in 140 towns and 13 county seats along the banks of the Yangzi would have to be relocated, along with 657 factories.[39]

NOT BY A DAM SITE

First proposed by Sun Yat-sen around 1920, the San Xia Dam was given serious consideration by the Chinese government in the mid-1950s. In 1958 Mao Zedong and Zhou Enlai tentatively endorsed the project. However, action was postponed indefinitely as a result of severe economic and political disruptions encountered during the Great Leap and the Cultural Revolution.[40]

When China initiated its post-Mao reform and open policies in 1978–79, the government expressed renewed interest in the San Xia project. Feasibility studies were prepared in the early 1980s, and a massive lobbying campaign was launched on behalf of the proposed dam. Li Peng, then minister of China's electric power industry, took the lead in promoting construction of the dam, hailing it as a major developmental breakthrough. In their enthusiasm, Li and other government leaders neatly dodged a number of potentially troublesome issues, including questions of cost effectiveness, potential damage to the environment, questionable earthquake safety, inadequate precautions against flooding, vulnerability to aerial bombardment in time of war, and excessive reservoir sedimentation, inter alia.[41]

Due to strenuous objections by a number of respected Chinese scientists, engineers, and environmentalists, including Mao Zedong's one-time secretary and former vice-minister of water conservation and electric power, Li Rui, and the popular author-journalist Dai Qing, the controversy remained alive, resulting in a series of additional postponements in the mid- and late 1980s. The last such postponement occurred in April 1989, on the eve of the Tiananmen student demonstrations.

The Tiananmen crisis dramatically altered the political character and calculus of the San Xia debate. Among those incurring the wrath of party and government hard-liners for supporting student protests in April and May 1989 were Li Rui and Dai Qing, the two staunchest critics of the Three Gorges Dam. Shortly after the June crackdown, distribution of Dai's 1989 book on the San Xia controversy was banned in China, while Li Rui was targeted for expulsion from the CCP.[42] With the dispute thus having taken on serious new political and ideological overtones, the government all but abandoned its previous effort to encourage open dialogue, debate, and consensus-building. Instead, Li Peng signaled his intention to push ahead with the project at full speed, ostensibly without regard for continuing technical and environmental objections.

At the March 1992 NPC session, the Three Gorges Dam was put to a formal vote. Although a clear majority of legislators approved the project, an unprecedented number—fully one-third of the 2,633 deputies in attendance—either voted in the negative (177), abstained (664), or cast no ballots at all (25). With the announcement of the final vote tally, the die was cast, though it remained for the Fourteenth Party Congress to put the party's final seal of approval on the project.[43]

Following the 1992 NPC meeting, the controversy surrounding the Three Gorges decision was dutifully downplayed by the Chinese press, as the nation's news media turned their attention to the new anti-Leftist campaign. Beginning in late March, film footage and photographs from Deng Xiaoping's southern journey were widely displayed on Chinese television and in official newspapers; Deng's speeches were also publicly disseminated and praised at this time. The media blitz was accompanied by a series of well-publicized endorsements of accelerated reform by a number of provincial leaders, noted economists, and other important public figures.[44]

CLIMBING ABOARD THE BANDWAGON

In the aftermath of the March 1992 NPC meeting, Vice-Premier Zhu Rongji served as principal spokesman for Deng's economic program. A former economics professor, institute director, and ex-mayor of Shanghai, Zhu had been a colleague of Jiang Zemin prior to the latter's promotion to general secretary in June 1989. Zhu had come to Deng Xiaoping's attention in the early 1980s and had subsequently worked for Deng as an economic consultant. In the spring of 1991 Deng picked Zhu Rongji to take charge of the work of restructuring China's stagnant, money-losing state enterprises.

Although Zhu had previously been skeptical of such radical innovations as privatized factory ownership and stock markets ("No way; that's capitalist!" he reportedly exclaimed in 1988), he now assumed the role of point man for Deng's reform drive. In April 1992 the polished, English-speaking vice-premier (Zhu was once dubbed "China's Gorbachev" by the Western media—before the Soviet collapse) had words of praise for Shanghai's new stock exchange and words of warning for China's inefficient, money-losing socialist state enterprises.[45] A month later, Deng Xiaoping singled out Zhu Rongji for special praise as "one of the few cadres who really understands how the economy works." Shortly thereafter, in early June, Zhu was placed in charge of the State Council's newly created Economic and Trade Office. The new agency was given a broad mandate to design macroeconomic policies governing the operation of state enterprises, joint ventures, stock companies, and foreign trade, assuming in the process many of the functions previously performed by the State Planning Commission under Zhu's more conservative colleague and budding rival, Vice-Premier Zou Jiahua.[46]

With the reform bandwagon steadily picking up momentum, the *People's Daily* in early May ran an unsigned commentary—consigned to page five by Gao Di—urging all bystanders who had previously adopted a wait-and-see attitude toward accelerated reform to "boldly step forward" and enthusiastically participate in the new campaign. The commentary called the acceleration of reform and opening up an inevitable historical trend and argued that if people were unwilling to abandon their risk-aversive, "fear-this-fear-that; wait-here-wait-there" mentality, the prognosis for successful reform would be poor.[47]

Among the many erstwhile bystanders who belatedly endorsed Deng's radical reform proposals were Jiang Zemin, Qiao Shi, and Li Peng. In the aftermath of the patriarch's southern journey all three men, sensing that a potent proreform bandwagon was rapidly taking shape, redoubled their public commitment to reform and the open policy.[48]

On the heels of his Politburo self-criticism of early March, Jiang Zemin, who had gained a reputation for shifting with the wind since his appointment as general secretary in June 1989, threw himself fervidly into the Deng camp. Addressing a group of college students in Beijing in May, he urged his audience not to get bogged down in abstract definitional disputes over the question, "Is it surnamed socialism or capitalism?" Eschewing the party's (and his own) previous anticapitalist rhetoric, Jiang stated that in the drive to accelerate economic development, China should make use of "all the social productive forces and all the excellent cultural achievements made in capitalist society." According to one official media commentary, Jiang's open embrace of capitalism's positive aspects was the first such endorsement ever made by a top-ranking party leader.[49]

Jiang Zemin's belated conversion to the cause of accelerated reform was evidently intended to assuage Deng's mounting displeasure with the general secretary's performance since 1989. Deng was said to be particularly irritated over Jiang's tendency to endorse Leftist positions in various speeches and policy statements made in 1990–91. The most controversial of these was the general secretary's July 1, 1991, address commemorating the seventieth anniversary of the CCP, which contained strong neo-Maoist ideological overtones.[50]

Seeking to overcome the burdens of the past, Jiang Zemin now eagerly embraced the rhetoric of radical reform.[51] In early June 1992 he addressed a group of provincial- and ministerial-level officials at the Central Party School. In his speech he enthusiastically endorsed Deng Xiaoping's views concerning the need to guard against the Left, describing China's reform effort as a high-speed "revolution to liberate the productive forces." In such a revolution, said Jiang, it is necessary to seize upon all favorable opportunities to promote accelerated growth.[52]

Not to be outdone, another erstwhile high-level fence-straddler, Qiao Shi, also lined up squarely behind Deng's reform offensive. In late March Qiao addressed an informal meeting of the Shanghai delegation to the NPC. Gushing praise for Deng Xiaoping's theories, Qiao claimed that it was necessary to undertake prolonged, repeated study of Deng's various statements in order to appreciate the profundity of his thinking. To achieve deeper understanding, Qiao asserted, mere repetition of the patriarch's words would not suffice; his ideas had to be put directly into practice.[53]

Even Li Peng hopped deftly—if gingerly—onto Deng's bandwagon. With his five-year term as premier due to expire in 1993, and with Deng Xiaoping now openly praising the virtues of Zhu Rongji, Li was said to be growing nervous over his diminished prospects for long-term job security.[54] Sensing the need to position himself a bit more flexibly near the center of the policy spectrum, Li commenced reshaping his image as a moderate reformer in the winter of 1991–92, even before Jiang Zemin did so.

Addressing a meeting of senior central and provincial government officials in early January, on the eve of Deng's southern tour, Li cautiously endorsed the idea of accelerated reform, stating that the conditions were now ripe for China to take an "appropriately bigger stride" in restructuring its economy.[55] In the aftermath of Deng's triumphant journey, Li became more effusive in his praise of reform and opening up. Addressing the State Council in March, Li urged government departments to "grasp the current favorable opportunity to step up economic and political reforms," going so far as to tentatively support the Shanghai stock market experiment.[56] However, he stopped short of personally endorsing Deng's thesis concerning Leftism as the principal danger.

Taking his cues directly from such born-again reformers as Li Peng, Jiang Zemin, and Qiao Shi, Vice-Premier Zou Jiahua, who was a member of Ye Jianying's extended family and a former Moscow classmate of Li Peng, also jumped on the bandwagon in late March. Normally a staid, sober voice of caution and restraint, Zou now claimed that an economic growth rate as high as 20 percent might be acceptable so long as it was based on real gains in efficiency and productivity.[57]

Joining the parade of erstwhile conservatives who decided to switch rather than fight, hard-line CASS publicist He Xin swallowed his pride and ceased railing against peaceful evolution in the spring of 1992, downplaying the importance of the Tiananmen crisis ("What's the big fuss?") while half-heartedly endorsing the government's new economic policies.[58] In an even more stunning reversal of form (albeit one that proved to be more cosmetic than real), *People's Daily* editor Gao Di, in a clear bid to save his job, instructed the newspaper's staff to oppose Leftists with as much vigor as they had hounded Rightists in the past.[59] Around the same time, a veritable avalanche of strongly worded pro-Deng, proreform newspaper and magazine articles and editorials appeared in Beijing and the provinces.[60]

As the reform bandwagon gathered momentum, more and more pieces fell into place. Even Chen Yun was forced to backpedal. In early May, Chen half-heartedly endorsed Deng's spring initiative in a brief but well-publicized meeting with Shanghai municipal officials. Under the improbable headline "Chen Yun Backs Bolder Reform Drive," Chen was cited as having urged Shanghai's party and government leaders to emancipate their minds still further and to "take bold steps" to ensure the success of the city's new Pudong development zone.[61] In response to Chen's ostensible words of encouragement, Shanghai's city fathers proudly informed the eighty-seven-year-old patriarch that "the Shanghai people are studying and implementing Deng Xiaoping's speeches made during his inspection tour in South China."[62] Under the circumstances, Chen could hardly have derived much comfort from such reassurances. Indeed, the official photograph accompanying the story of Chen's visit to Shanghai revealed a visibly pale and pasty-faced Chen Yun slumped awkwardly in an overstuffed chair, grinning feebly at his hosts.[63]

CHEN HEDGES HIS BETS

In the aftermath of his Shanghai interview, Chen Yun clarified his putative endorsement of Deng's spring initiative, making it clear that his support for accelerated reform and opening up was highly contingent and conditional.

With preparations now under way for the Fourteenth Party Congress, Chen raised three specific conditions for his continued support and cooperation: first, the "Jiang-Li axis" should remain undisturbed, that is, neither Jiang Zemin nor Li Peng should be ousted at the upcoming Party Congress; second, neither Yao Yilin nor Song Ping should be forced to retire; and third, the controversial Shenzhen reforms should not be popularized as a model for nationwide emulation.[64] Also at Chen Yun's urging, the party's organization department circulated a directive stating that only those "politically meritorious" party members who had compiled a good record in opposing bourgeois liberalization should be chosen as delegates to the upcoming party congress.[65]

Notwithstanding Chen's attempt to apply the brakes to Deng's juggernaut, proponents of radical reform continued to press their advantage. In the boldest and most provocative anti-Leftist statement yet made by a top party leader, Vice Premier Tian Jiyun in late April disdainfully urged creation of a "special Leftist zone" to which China's hard-line Marxists could be banished. Speaking to senior cadres at the Central Party School in Beijing, Tian complained that "Some Leftists have derived immense material benefit from the policy of reform and opening up, yet they still denounce the policy." His voice dripping with sarcasm, the vice-premier then offered a mock proposal for dealing with conservative opponents of reform and opening up:

> Let us carve out a piece of land where policies favored by the Leftists will be practiced. For example, no foreign investment will be allowed there, and all foreigners will be kept out. Inhabitants of the zone can neither go abroad nor send their children overseas. There will be total state planning. Essential supplies will be rationed and citizens of the zone will have to queue up for food and other consumer products.[66]

After inquiring rhetorically whether Leftists would be so faithful to their ideological principles as to volunteer to live in such an austere, isolated environment, Tian Jiyun went on to belittle certain unnamed party leaders—collectively referred to as the "wind faction" (*fengpai*)—who had the habit of opportunistically altering their allegiances and policy positions with each new shift in the political winds. According to Chinese sources, Tian's barb was directed specifically at Jiang Zemin and Li Peng; indirectly, it may also have been aimed at Qiao Shi and Yang Baibing.[67]

In late May 1992 Deng Xiaoping, unwilling to be upstaged by Chen Yun's Shanghai photo opportunity, paid a brief visit to Beijing's Capital Iron and Steel Works, a large state-owned industrial complex that had been a pioneer in the field of enterprise reform.[68] Accompanying Deng was daughter Deng Rong, who had become her ailing father's constant nursemaid-interpreter— and who, it was rumored, had recently become a paid consultant to Capital Iron and Steel.

In the course of his inspection visit, Deng Xiaoping praised the entrepreneurial spirit of Capital's top managers and renewed his call for accelerated

Supported by his daughter, Deng Rong, Deng Xiaoping greets workers at the
Capital Iron and Steel Plant, May 1992.

market reform. More pointedly, he warned that a substantial number of conservative cadres were in danger of losing their jobs in the coming economic
transformation. Specially targeted for dismissal were "those who have ruled
for many years unchanged as the mountains and rivers, and those who are lazy
and conservative, living off the gains of their forefathers." Claiming that a
little chaos was an acceptable price to pay for such a sweeping economic
transformation, Deng said that "we should use the market economy [as a yard-
stick] to measure our cadres. . . . We should permit failure in market competition, but we cannot permit failure to act, to break new ground, or to
compete."[69]

Deng's remarks, issued on May 22, were not publicized in the party press
until early July, when they were first quoted by the proreform editors of the
Shanghai *Liberation Daily*. In the official photograph that accompanied the
story of Deng's visit to the steel mill, the patriarch appeared surprisingly animated and healthy, in contrast to Chen Yun's recent pasty-faced appearance
in Shanghai. Belying Gao Di's ostensible conversion to the cause of accelerated reform and anti-Leftism, the *People's Daily* remained conspicuously silent on Deng's visit to Capital Iron and Steel, failing to publish either his
comments or his photograph.[70]

Loath to allow Deng Xiaoping to have the last word on the subject of economic reform, Chen Yun met with his old rival again in Shanghai in early

Chen Yun greets local party and government officials in Shanghai, May 1992.

June. Accompanied by Peng Zhen, Chen bemoaned the dominant tendency toward Rightism in the party, criticizing the "non-Marxist ideological trend" and "degenerate capitalist ideology" that were allegedly corroding the country's socialist spirit. Countering Deng's glowing praise for market-oriented reform at the Capital Iron and Steel Works, Chen argued that the giant steel mill's economic success was primarily due to sober-minded, scientific state planning, and not the vagaries and caprices of the free market.[71]

Undaunted by Chen's lack of cooperation, the reformers pushed on. In July the deputy head of the State Commission for Restructuring the Economy directly rebutted Premier Li Peng's March NPC call for a modest economic growth rate of 6 percent, claiming that a rate of 10 percent or more was fully sustainable. He also warmly endorsed the social-Darwinian concept of the "survival of the fittest" in the realm of economic competition.[72] Early in July, a one-day conference on "strengthening development of the socialist market economy" was held in Beijing. Encouraged by NPC SC chairman Wan Li's open call to "discard centralized planned economics in favor of socialist market economics," the conference was attended by many of China's leading reform economists, including several who had previously been criticized for supporting bourgeois liberalization.[73]

On July 24 the State Council publicized a new fifty-four-point decree designed to free state-owned enterprises from central planning authority and to subject them to the discipline of the marketplace. Drafted under the supervision of Zhu Rongji, the new regulations gave enterprises expanded freedom in such areas as imports and exports, investments, employment (including the right to reject state-appointed workers), pricing, and marketing. The decree also stipulated conditions under which debt-ridden firms would be ordered to stop production and be merged, dissolved, or declared bankrupt.[74]

LIBERALIZATION ON THE PROPAGANDA AND CULTURAL FRONTS

By the midsummer of 1992, Li Ruihuan's year-long effort to cleanse the party's propaganda apparatus of Leftist influences had begun to bear fruit. In August Communist Party sources reported that hard-line Propaganda Director Wang Renzhi had tendered his resignation, while Acting Minister of Culture He Jingzhi and *People's Daily* editor Gao Di had been notified that they would soon be replaced.[75]

Reflecting the increased self-confidence of liberal reformers, Li Ruihuan now declared that art and literature need not be weapons of political indoctrination. Decrying the "biased views" promoted by Leftists, Li argued that literature and art had a number of proper functions, including pure entertainment and aesthetics. More provocatively, he urged that artistic and literary works that did not explicitly violate the PRC's constitution or state laws should not be subject to censorship.[76] It was the boldest call for cultural freedom to emanate from a member of the Politburo Standing Committee since Hu Yaobang's short-lived advocacy of total press freedom in 1984.

One week later it was announced that two of new-wave film director Zhang Yimou's more controversial theatrical movies, *Raise the Red Lantern* and *Ju Dou*, both previously banned from exhibition in China for "exposing too much darkness," had been approved for domestic distribution. The announcement conveying the decision said that the release of the two films was "a sign of more flexible and practical policy toward the arts in China, which implies bolder reforms in this field."[77]

The growing mood of political and ideological tolerance reached its zenith a short time later, when a former deputy head of the CC propaganda department, Gong Yuzhi, who had helped draft Zhao Ziyang's report to the Thirteenth Party Congress, boldly questioned the sanctity of the four cardinal principles. Going well beyond Li Ruihuan's challenge to the policy of applying political litmus tests to all creative works, Gong Yuzhi turned the CCP's "sole criterion of truth" argument around, aiming it squarely at the four cardinal principles. Claiming that the validity of the four principles could only be established by submitting them to the test of practice, Gong asked, "Do they benefit the development of the productive forces? . . . Do they benefit raising the living standards of the people? If a thing conforms in practice to these benefits but not to our stubborn concepts," he continued, "should we resist the thing, or should we change our concepts?"[78] Because the implications of Gong's final question were so potentially far-reaching, no one in a position of authority responded—or even acknowledged that the question had been raised.

Stock Market Fever

With the fang/shou cycle undergoing a pronounced phase change in the direction of greater economic and cultural liberalization in the summer of 1992, little official notice was paid to some new and potentially unsettling trends in the domestic economy. Beginning in the spring of the year, the Shanghai and Shenzhen stock exchanges, recent recipients of Deng Xiaoping's personal blessing, started to overheat badly.[79] Holding an estimated RMB ¥1.3 trillion in private savings, Chinese citizens had rushed to purchase shares on the newly legitimated "noncapitalist" stock market. An estimated two million Shanghai residents—one-sixth of the city's population—reportedly waited, cash at the ready, for the opportunity to invest.

With demand virtually unlimited, share prices soared. In the first six months of 1992 the Shanghai index rose 1,200 percent, with the volume of transactions topping RMB ¥5 billion. Between March and June the Shenzhen stock index jumped 171 percent. To calm down mobs of unruly people who began to fight over places in line at the Shanghai and Shenzhen exchanges, a system of selling numbered tickets, called "share purchase certificates," was introduced. When the ticket-holder's number was called, each share purchase certificate (which had a face value of ¥30) entitled the bearer not to purchase his or her stocks of choice, but merely to enter a lottery whose winners were given the opportunity to buy a limited number of shares of whatever stock happened to be available.

Notwithstanding this rather crude rationing system, the popular hunger for stocks remained unabated, leading to the creation of secondary markets in which the lottery certificates themselves were sold at prices much higher than face value. Like ticket scalpers at a popular entertainment or sporting event, speculators and petty criminals moved in quickly to capitalize on these secondary markets, for example, by paying people to wait in line to secure the prized certificates, then bidding up the price. In Shenzhen, certificates that originally sold for ¥30 were being openly peddled on the black market for as much as ¥1,400.[80]

With the paper value of listed stocks rising steadily, a sense of euphoria pervaded the country's financial markets. Because share prices kept rising, it was assumed that cash-strapped firms could help themselves (and their employees) to become rich simply by converting into shareholding companies. Once a company's stock was listed, its price-to-earnings ratio typically skyrocketed, commonly reaching levels as high as 100, 200, or even 300:1. In such a situation, share prices bore little or no relation to a company's actual performance or profitability.

Lacking a basic understanding of the principles and mechanics of a stock market, including the concept of risk, many Chinese investors simply assumed that prices always went up, never down. Based on such assumptions, investors quickly bought up whatever stocks were available, at whatever price was asked; holding on for what was assumed would be an uninterrupted upward ride, they refrained from selling. With demand greatly outstripping supply, prices spiraled up even more rapidly. As one Chinese observer put it:

> As soon as new stocks have been put on sale, residents have rushed to buy but have seldom sold them, feeling free from any worry of risk or crisis. . . . Many people do not understand what stock is all about. One Shanghai resident who bought some stocks said, "The price of stocks is rising every day. Buying stocks can make money, I don't care how things will stand in the future. I'll just wait and see."[81]

When a temporary market correction caused a brief downward slide in prices on the Shanghai stock exchange in May 1992, the Chinese press reported the country's first market-induced suicide. This was followed by the first market-related homicide, occasioned by gang members fighting over places in line at the Shenzhen exchange.

The crunch came in midsummer. On Saturday, August 8, rioting broke out in Shenzhen when thousands of would-be investors, many of whom had been standing in line since the previous day to secure application forms for a forthcoming stock lottery, began jostling for position at more than three hundred distribution points set up by the municipal government. Demand for the lottery application forms was so high that some people reportedly paid as much as RMB ¥2,000 merely for a place in line. Members of local street gangs, seeking to capitalize on the opportunity for windfall profits, shoved their way into line and began fighting with impatient crowds.

With the sale of application forms not scheduled to take place until Sunday, August 9, shortened tempers, added to oppressive midsummer heat and humidity, created an explosive situation. By noon on Sunday, more than a half million people had joined the lines. Trouble began when a rumor spread to the effect that police had made off with thousands of application forms and were selling them on the black market. When it was announced shortly afterward that the entire supply of five million forms had sold out, the crowd spontaneously erupted in anger, directed mainly at the Shenzhen municipal authorities. Riot police were called in to restore order. With Hong Kong television crews recording the scene, a number of protesters were beaten.

The following day, August 10, angry crowds at the Shenzhen municipal government headquarters accused police of criminal behavior in the black-market sale of lottery application forms. Waving banners and placards protesting police corruption and violence, protestors broke windows and overturned and burned a number of vehicles. Nervous police retaliated with water hoses, tear gas, and shots fired into the air. A dozen or more people were injured. The riot ended only when the Shenzhen government promised to distribute more application forms the following day.

In the immediate aftermath of the August 8–10 disturbances, the mayor of Shenzhen, Zheng Liangyu, characterized the incident as the work of "a small number of hooligans who exploited the lack of supply of stock application forms and some of our shortcomings in the operation [of the lottery] to incite the public and cause trouble." Employing language reminiscent of the Tiananmen crackdown of 1989, the mayor pledged to deal harshly with "those who have taken advantage of public sentiment to stir up turmoil."[82]

Beijing was not nearly so eager to take a hard-line stance. Mindful of the disastrous consequences of the government's inflammatory language during the Tiananmen crisis, and equally mindful that Deng Xiaoping had personally approved the Shenzhen stock market experiment during his southern tour, central authorities sought to downplay the significance of the August riot. Under pressure from Beijing, Mayor Zheng backed down, acknowledging that the rioting had been due, in large measure, to "inexperience" and "imperfections" in the system of selling lottery applications. Paying a well-publicized visit to injured demonstrators in a local hospital, the mayor was extraordinarily contrite. "We have made you go through all this," he said, "because we did not do well in our work. We are sorry about you, and express our apology." Finally, the government promised fully to investigate reports of police corruption in the distribution of lottery application forms.[83] Sincere though Mayor Zheng might have been, his contrition was evidently insufficient to compensate for the embarrassment he had caused central authorities. In November, the mayor was quietly sacked.[84]

With investor confidence shaken by the August riot, the Shenzhen and Shanghai stock markets plunged to new lows. By the time the Fourteenth Party Congress met in October, the Shenzhen index had fallen by almost two-thirds from its spring 1992 high, while the Shanghai index was off almost 60 percent.

Armed with fresh ammunition and feeling vindicated in their opposition to the reformers' headlong rush to open new markets for stocks and other securities, party conservatives sought once more to blunt Deng's reform initiatives. Pointedly referring to the August stock market riot as "turmoil," Chen Yun placed primary responsibility for the violence squarely on the shoulders of local party and government officials. In a written instruction dated August 12, Chen suggested that cadre malfeasance had been at least partly to blame for the incident. Demanding a "clear explanation" of the Shenzhen affair, Chen specifically ordered an examination of the role played by "special privileges" and the "pursuit of personal gain" in the genesis of the August turmoil.[85]

Elaborating upon the nature of his concerns at a CAC meeting in late August, Chen Yun issued a ten-point critique of Deng's reform program. Warning his comrades against the adverse effects of pursuing excessively high economic growth rates, chasing after foreign capital, and making a "headlong rush" into opening new stock markets, Chen argued that too-rapid market reforms and an overreliance on foreign capital would only serve to exacerbate problems such as inflation, corruption, and stock-market fever. Adding a mischievous anti-Rightist twist to his warning, Chen compared such problems to the type of Leftist-induced chaos that had periodically plagued China in the past.[86]

Seeking to deflect Chen's criticism, the liberal *Beijing Youth News* in September defended the institution of stock markets, informing its readers that Karl Marx himself had dabbled in stocks on the London exchange in 1864, clearing a net profit of £400 in his various transactions.[87]

Sensitive to conservative criticism of the causes of the Shenzhen stock market riot, Deng's supporters began to softpedal the issue. In his work report to the Fourteenth Party Congress, Jiang Zemin bowed to pressures from Chen Yun and the CAC. While calling for "continued efforts . . . to build up financial markets, including markets for bonds, stocks, and other negotiable securities," Jiang urged his comrades to "proceed from actual conditions" and not "rush headlong" into new reforms without considering their economic and social impact.[88] In line with Jiang's appeal for prudence, the central government, citing fear of market chaos, announced in November a three-year moratorium on the opening of new stock and securities markets throughout the country, pending a thorough review and strengthening of existing laws and regulations governing transactions on the Shanghai and Shenzhen exchanges.[89]

In addition to grappling with fallout from the "Shenzhen shock," Deng's supporters were also placed on the defensive by China's rapidly overheating economy. Fueled by the relaxation of government austerity measures and by Deng's new full-speed-ahead approach to reform and opening up, fixed capital investments in the first half of 1992 rose by 32 percent over the corresponding level a year earlier. Similarly, year-on-year industrial output rose almost 19 percent in the first six months of 1992, while overall economic growth jumped 16 percent in the same period—more than double the rate recommended by Li Peng at the March NPC meeting. By the end of summer, even such proreform stalwarts as Zhu Rongji were displaying serious concern over the trend toward unrestrained, unbalanced economic growth. Commenting on the fact that some poorly run state enterprises were managing to get rich by engaging in a frenzy of stock-market transactions, while other, well-run enterprises were missing out, Zhu noted cryptically that "enterprises that should be hot are not, while test points that should not be hot are getting hotter and hotter." To cool off China's superheated economy, Zhu in September called for the application of "appropriate controls."[90]

THE FOURTEENTH PARTY CONGRESS: ECONOMICS IN COMMAND

With conservative backlash from the Shenzhen disturbance and from economic overheating building steadily, Deng Xiaoping pressed his colleagues to convene the Fourteenth Party Congress ahead of schedule. Originally planned for late in the fall, the Congress was moved up, at Deng's insistence, to the second week in October.[91] At the Congress, reform leaders pushed ahead boldly on a variety of economic fronts. Most importantly, they ratified Deng's "brilliant thesis" (*jingpi lunduan*) concerning the need to shift China from a "socialist planned commodity economy" (*shehuizhuyi jihua shangpin jingji*) to a "socialist market economy" (*shehuizhuyi shichang jingji*).[92]

This change in terminology was extremely important insofar as it legitimated the abolition of traditional mechanisms of central planning in favor of the introduction of macroeconomically regulated market competition. In the absence of direct state planning, the "socialist" component of the socialist market economy would henceforth be limited almost exclusively to public ownership of productive property, which was slated to remain the predominant form of ownership "for a long time to come."[93]

To make a claim for the continued prevalence of public ownership in the face of rapid increases in the number and size of private and collectively owned enterprises in China, some linguistic legerdemain was necessary. Accordingly, in his work report to the Party Congress Jiang Zemin lumped the collective sector (which by 1992 accounted for approximately one-third of the country's total industrial output) together with the state sector under the category of "public ownership," thereby adding substantially to the nominal bulk of the latter. In practice, however, the vast majority of China's mushrooming collective enterprises were semiprivate firms set up by village and township governments and run by local entrepreneurs who relied on inside connections with state agencies for their supplies, markets, and investment funds. The increasing prevalence of such hybrid firms, which were quite different from China's traditional (prereform) state-owned, state-run enterprises, raised doubts about the accuracy of Jiang Zemin's classification scheme and suggested that China's reformers were attempting, once again, to cover their handiwork with a veil of conventional socialist respectability.[94]

In addition to its economic breakthrough, Jiang Zemin's work report contained a significant ideological innovation. In the most liberal appeal for emancipated thinking to be formally issued by any top party leader since 1986, Jiang called upon all party members and cadres to

> break the shackles of traditional conceptions and subjective prejudices and overcome our habit of following the beaten track and rejecting new things. We must not simply cling to certain Marxist principles, to a dogmatic interpretation of certain theories, to an unscientific or distorted understanding of socialism, or to ideas that are wrong because in the primary stage of socialism they are premature.[95]

Although Jiang appealed for boldness in ideological innovation, he had little to say that was new—or encouraging—on the subject of political reform. While repeating reformers' perennial pleas for a separation of party and government functions, for simplification of state administration, and for "scientific" reform of the nomenklatura system, he also (somewhat contradictorily) echoed the call of party conservatives for a revitalization of party cells at the primary levels to serve as the "political core" of economic enterprises, government departments, schools, research institutes, and urban neighborhoods. In a clear departure from the neo-authoritarian orientation of Zhao Ziyang's report to the Thirteenth Party Congress, Jiang failed to acknowledge the need to allow a plurality of divergent individual and group interests to find political expression, either within the party or in society at large.[96]

While echoing Deng Xiaoping's recent admonition to "watch out for the Right, but mainly defend against the Left," Jiang carefully stressed the need to strengthen the people's democratic dictatorship in order to deal more effectively with "hostile forces" in society. Referring to the 1989 student disturbances as a "counterrevolutionary rebellion" (*fan'geming baoluan*), Jiang reaffirmed the correctness of the government's crackdown. He did not, however, discuss the role of Zhao Ziyang in that affair.

THE VERDICT ON ZHAO ZIYANG

He did not need to. At the Ninth Plenum of the Thirteenth CC, held just prior to the opening of the Fourteenth Congress, the Central Committee announced its decision to terminate the investigation of Zhao Ziyang's case. Leaving stand the Fourth Plenum's June 1989 decision that stripped Zhao of all party posts for his role in "supporting turmoil (*dongluan*) and splitting the party," the Ninth Plenum spared Zhao from further humiliation and punishment, permitting him to retain his party membership. Significantly, the official notice conveying the Central Committee decision referred to the events of April–May 1989 in relatively mild terms, as a "political disturbance" (*zhengzhi dongluan*) rather than a "counterrevolutionary rebellion."[97]

Although the resolution of Zhao's case was presumably final, it was not secured without a struggle. According to Hong Kong sources, a motion to expel Zhao from the party was introduced at the Ninth Plenum, receiving substantial conservative support both within the CC itself and from members of the CAC, who were also in attendance. To derail the motion, Jiang Zemin temporarily halted the plenum and convened an expanded meeting of the Politburo, which rejected the proposal to expel Zhao, endorsing instead the Fourth Plenum's decision merely to remove him from all official posts.[98]

Though Zhao ultimately managed to retain his party membership and avoid criminal prosecution, not all of his associates were so fortunate. A few months before the opening of the Fourteenth Congress, in July 1992, Zhao's former chief of staff, fifty-nine-year-old Bao Tong, was tried and convicted of "leaking state secrets, inciting rebellion (*baoluan*), and opposing and sabotaging the implementation of state laws and decrees" during the 1989 upheaval.[99] Following a closed-door trial that lasted less than a day, Bao was sentenced to seven years in prison, minus three years' credit for time already served. As Zhao Ziyang's designated surrogate, Bao was the highest-ranking Tiananmen defendant to face criminal prosecution. In the aftermath of Bao's trial, one somewhat cynical Communist Party member referred to Bao as the victim of an elaborate sacrificial ritual whose sole purpose was to save face for party hard-liners. "Bao is the sacrifice," he observed; "this trial is about [upholding] the prestige of the party."[100] With Bao Tong taking the rap for his boss, Zhao Ziyang's case was quickly brought to closure, and the question of Zhao's role in the Tiananmen crisis never arose at the Fourteenth Congress.[101]

Although Jiang's work report explicitly endorsed the four cardinal principles, it did so in a way that left the door open for possible future challenges to the sanctity of those principles. By explicitly stating that the purpose of adhering to the four principles was "to liberate and develop the productive forces to an even greater extent" (a caveat that had merely been implicit in Zhao's 1987 formulation of "one center and two basic points"), Jiang hinted that in future the four principles might be viewed instrumentally, rather than absolutely, that is, in light of their practical contributions to China's modernization and economic development.[102]

Paying effusive homage to Deng Xiaoping's life and works, Jiang Zemin's work report went well beyond previous official encomiums. Calling Deng the "principal architect" of reform and opening up (a designation that doubtless rankled Chen Yun who, like Deng, failed to attend the congress), Jiang also gave Deng exclusive credit for conceiving the idea of building "socialism with Chinese characteristics."[103] In a similar vein, he heaped praise on Deng's "brilliant thesis" concerning the adoption of a socialist market economy. In thus lionizing China's patriarch, Jiang Zemin ostensibly violated the Central Committee's 1981 decision to stress collective authorship of the party's major theoretical canons and concepts. It was, by all odds, the most exaggerated official display of idolatry toward a living Chinese leader since the "whateverists" launched their abortive drive to fashion a personality cult for Hua Guofeng in 1977–78.[104]

Although Deng did not attend the Fourteenth Congress, he nonetheless remained a dominant, if shadowy, presence throughout the proceedings. On the eve of the congress, Deng reportedly spent two and one-half days reviewing and revising the text of Jiang Zemin's work report, the first draft of which had been prepared by a writing team that included at least one staunch ally of Li Peng (Yuan Mu).[105] At the conclusion of the congress, to dispel doubts about the paramount leader's physical and mental capacities, Deng held a well-publicized meeting with a group of delegates. The official photograph marking the occasion showed a jaunty, ambulatory (and air-blown, wrinkle-free) Deng Xiaoping exchanging pleasantries with provincial representatives.[106]

Inasmuch as Deng personally vetted and revised Jiang Zemin's speech, he evidently did not object to the general secretary's attempts at idolatrization. Nor did Deng appear to object when, a few months later, the newly reshuffled leadership of the CCP propaganda department issued instructions to party and government offices to include Deng Xiaoping's theories as required discussion material in future ideological study sessions. The document conveying the instruction praised Deng's ideas as a "synthesis of the basic theories of Marxism and the reality and present-day characteristics of contemporary China. [It is] a continuation and development of Mao Zedong Thought and represents modern Chinese Marxism." To facilitate the dissemination and study of Deng's thoughts, the Central Committee in the early winter of 1993 published a new volume of *Selections of Comrade Deng Xiaoping's Theories of Building Socialism with Chinese Characteristics*, making it required reading for cadres and students in party schools.[107]

ORGANIZATIONAL AND PERSONNEL CHANGES AT THE FOURTEENTH CONGRESS

In line with Deng Xiaoping's oft-stated goal of rejuvenating party leadership, 46 percent of the members of the new Central Committee elected at the 1992 Party Congress were first-timers. Average age of the 189 full members of the Fourteenth CC was 56; more than 5 in 6 (84 percent) were college-educated, up from 70 percent in the Thirteenth CC. Significantly, military representation on the new CC was also up, from 16 percent to 22 percent.[108]

Although young technocrats registered significant gains at the October 1992 Party Congress, liberal supporters of ousted general secretary Zhao Ziyang did not fare so well. Rui Xingwen, Yan Mingfu, and Wang Meng were all dropped from the Central Committee, while Sichuan's proreform party leader, Yang Rudai, was removed from the Politburo. On a somewhat more encouraging note, Vice-Premier Tian Jiyun retained his Politburo seat while Hu Qili was reelected to the CC. Contrary to previous expectations, however, neither man received a promotion at the Fourteenth Congress. Reportedly, Chen Yun personally blocked Hu Qili's bid to return to the Politburo.[109]

While liberals thus scored relatively few gains at the Fourteenth Congress, hard-line conservatives fared even worse. Having failed to be selected as a delegate to the congress, Deng Liqun did not stand for election to the Central Committee. With the death of his eighty-one-year-old mentor, Hu Qiaomu, just days before the opening of the Fourteenth Party Congress, Little Deng's star appeared to be on the wane.

In a clear victory for Li Ruihuan, three members of the erstwhile "gang of five"—Wang Renzhi, He Jingzhi, and Gao Di—were dropped from the new Central Committee. Also failing to gain reelection to the CC was the conservative vice-minister of education, He Dongchang, who, along with Li Peng and Beijing party leaders Li Ximing and Chen Xitong, had adopted a harsh, uncompromising stance toward student demonstrators in the spring of 1989. The removal of the four third-echelon hard-liners left the voices of political and ideological orthodoxy significantly weakened at the party center.[110]

Despite heightened expectations concerning the possible political enthronement of the princelings, new conservatives and other gaogan zidi generally fared poorly at the Fourteenth Party Congress. Aside from such veteran cadres as Li Tieying (son of Li Weihan), Ye Xuanping, and Zou Jiahua (son and son-in-law, respectively, of Ye Jianying), no newcomers from the ranks of the *taizidang* were elected to the Central Committee. Indeed, a number of prominent gaogan zidi—including Deng Pufang, Chen Yuan, Deng Yingtao,

Wang Jun, Liu Yuan (son of Liu Shaoqi), and Bo Xicheng (son of Bo Yibo) failed even to be selected as delegates to the Party Congress. (Though one of Deng Xiaoping's daughters, Deng Nan, was a congress delegate, she was not elected to the CC.) According to Hong Kong press reports, the combination of a strong public opinion backlash against the profligacy of the princelings plus chronic bickering among the princelings' illustrious parents over the distribution of high level posts had resulted in an agreement between Deng Xiaoping and Chen Yun to refrain from supporting any gaogan zidi for CC membership.

In composition, the new Politburo reflected mixed gains for Deng's policies of accelerated reform and opening up. Of the fourteen full members of the old Politburo, eight either retired or were pressed to resign at the Fourteenth Congress. The most celebrated retiree was eighty-five-year-old Yang Shangkun, whose slot was filled, per prior agreement, by his younger sibling, Yang Baibing, age seventy-two. Other prominent retirees included erstwhile hard-liners Yao Yilin (seventy-five), Song Ping (seventy-five), and Li Ximing (sixty-six), along with reformists Wan Li (seventy-six) and Qin Jiwei (seventy-eight).[111]

To replace the outgoing eight, fourteen new members were chosen, increasing the size of the Politburo from fourteen to twenty members. At least seven of the newcomers were considered firm supporters of Deng's reform and open policies: Vice-Premier Zhu Rongji (sixty-four), Foreign Minister Qian Qichen (sixty-four), Minister of External Trade Li Lanqing (sixty), Guangdong Party Secretary Xie Fei (sixty), Shandong Party Secretary Jiang Chunyun (sixty-two), Shanghai Party Secretary Wu Bangguo (fifty-one), and Tianjin Party Secretary Tan Shaowen (sixty-three). Of the other new Politburo members, two—Zou Jiahua (sixty-six) and Ding Guan'gen (sixty-three)—were centrists, while two others—Yang Baibing and Chen Xitong (sixty-two)—were erstwhile ideological hard-liners with wind-blown reformist economic leanings.

The new Politburo was noteworthy, among other things, for its predominantly technocratic composition. Over half of the twenty members elected at the Fourteenth Congress—eleven full members and one alternate—had received college training in engineering and related scientific fields; of the twelve Politburo engineer/scientists, eight had been trained in the Soviet Union or other former Soviet-bloc countries,[112] In addition to the Politburo's strong technocratic component, four members of the reconstituted body were leading cadres in China's political-military security apparatus.[113]

Like its parent body, the Politburo, the new Standing Committee was also balanced between reformers and centrists. To compensate for the retirement of SC conservatives Yao Yilin and Song Ping, who were pressured to step down at the Fourteenth Congress despite Chen Yun's earlier demand that they be retained, three new members were added: General Liu Huaqing (seventy-six), Zhu Rongji, and Hu Jintao (forty-nine), increasing the size of the SC from six to seven. Of the new members, Zhu was a strong supporter of reform and Hu a middle-of-the-roader, while Liu, an old army crony of Deng, was

Jiang Zemin introduces members of new Politburo Standing Committee at the conclusion of the Fourteenth Party Congress, October 1992. Left to right: Jiang Zemin, Li Peng, Qiao Shi, Li Ruihuan, Zhu Rongji, Liu Huaqing, Hu Jintao.

regarded as a caretaker whose main function was to liaise with the MAC.[114] As a result of these personnel changes, the new SC contained two activist reformers (Li Ruihuan and Zhu Rongji), three wind-blown centrists (Jiang Zemin, Qiao Shi, and Hu Jintao), one born-again hard-liner (Li Peng), and one ostensibly apolitical representative of the professional military establishment (Liu Huaqing). According to Hong Kong sources, Premier Li Peng received the lowest vote total of all the SC members who stood for election to the new CC, while the highest vote total was garnered by Li's emerging rival for the premiership, Zhu Rongji.[115]

On the new Central Party Secretariat, Jiang Zemin and Ding Guan'gen were the lone holdovers, as three members of the five-person body resigned their posts at the Fourteenth Congress: Li Ruihuan, Qiao Shi, and Yang Baibing. Replacing the three were Hu Jintao, Supreme People's Court President Ren Jianxin (sixty-seven), and the newly appointed CDIC head and minister of supervision, Wei Jianxing (sixty-one).[116] Wen Jiabao (fifty), director of the CC General Office and, along with Ding Guan'gen and Wan Li, a regular member of Deng Xiaoping's bridge club, was elevated from alternate to full membership on the new secretariat, increasing its size from five members to six. Reflecting party leaders' deep concern with the problem of combating crime and corruption, the presence of Ren Jianxin and Wei Jianxing on the Central Secretariat brought together in one leading organ, for the first time, the heads of China's public security, judicial, and party discipline bureaucracies.

The most surprising of all the personnel changes announced at the conclusion of the Fourteenth Congress was the exclusion of the "Yang family generals" from the MAC. Prior to the congress it had been widely assumed that Yang Baibing would succeed his retiring half-brother as permanent vice-chairman of the military commission. The younger Yang's firm (if belated) pledge of support for Deng's accelerated economic reforms had paved the way for his elevation to the Politburo, and his promotion within the MAC was expected to follow as a matter of course. Contrary to expectations, however,

Yang Baibing not only did not receive the expected MAC promotion, he was dropped from the commission altogether, losing his post as MAC general secretary and, for good measure, his job as head of the PLA's General Political Department as well.

Although Yang Baibing had previously received Deng's personal blessing for the MAC post, his candidacy had stirred up such strong opposition among the PLA's professional officer corps, as well as among civilian politicians alarmed over reports of Yang's factional activities within the army, that he garnered the fewest votes of any candidate elected to the Central Committee at the Fourteenth Party Congress.[117] One particularly damaging charge against Yang Baibing was that he had organized an unauthorized meeting of Chinese military leaders in September 1992 for the specific purpose of planning for the post-Deng transition. At a "Party Life Meeting" held after the close of the Fourteenth Congress, Yang Baibing reportedly made a self-criticism in which he indirectly confessed to having engaged in "faction-building" activities within the army.[118]

With the Yang family generals out of the picture, a new troika was placed in charge of the MAC at the conclusion of the Fourteenth Congress. Jiang Zemin was retained as commission chairman, his authority clearly enhanced by the departure of the Yang brothers. Jiang was now assisted by two aging vice-chairmen, Liu Huaqing (former PLA navy commander, generally regarded as a political lightweight) and General Zhang Zhen, seventy-eight, honorary president of the National Defense University, and a former deputy PLA chief of staff. According to unofficial Chinese sources, Liu Huaqing was already suffering from the effects of old age, having become somewhat "unclear in his brain and slow in his responses." The same sources claim that General Zhang had drafted a letter to Deng Xiaoping in the late summer of 1992, signed by fourteen retired senior officers, describing Yang Baibing's factional activities within the army. As a reward for his loyalty to Deng, Zhang was called out of retirement to serve on the reorganized military commission.[119]

Filling the remaining slots on the new MAC were four younger professional officers, only one of whom, PLA Chief of Staff Chi Haotian (sixty-three), concurrently appointed minister of defense, was a holdover from the previous commission. The other three MAC members, all newcomers, were concurrently appointed to head the PLA's three general headquarters: Zhang Wannian (sixty-four) replaced Chi Haotian as chief of general staff; Fu Quanyou (sixty-two) was appointed head of the General Logistics Department; and Yu Yongbo (sixty-one), Yang Baibing's deputy, succeeded his former boss as acting head of the GPD. All three had previously been regional military commanders, and all were considered strong advocates of military modernization. Of the three, only Yu Yongbo had personally participated in the Tiananmen crackdown. They replaced two outgoing MAC members, retiring Defense Minister Qin Jiwei, seventy-eight, and General Logistics Department Director Zhao Nanqi (Cho Nam Gi), sixty-six.[120]

Aside from these key personnel changes, the most striking organizational change enacted at the Fourteenth Party Congress was the final abolition of the CAC, whose long-awaited demise was ostensibly self-recommended.[121] The extinction of the CAC, viewed in conjunction with the unseating of four hard-line CC propagandists and the closely clustered deaths of four leading conservative CAC old-timers in the spring and summer of 1992—Wang Renzhong (March 16), Li Xiannian (June 21), Deng Yingchao (July 11), and Hu Qiaomu (September 28)—had the effect of further diminishing the potency of the party's senescent Left. While abolition of the CAC did not in itself guarantee final withdrawal of CCP octogenarians from the political arena, especially the arena of informal power, it permanently revoked the ex officio right of party elders to attend meetings of the CC and Politburo. With that, and with the deaths of the four elderly conservatives, the era of gerontocratic power appeared to be nearing an end.

The Last Cycle: October 1992–Summer 1993

East Wind urges plum tree to flourish its petals, soft as **DOWN**;

The hawk unfurls its wings, soars far away **WITH** the wind.

The moon shines, sheds tears on the **LI**-ward sea,

And a sojourner in the **PENG**-hu islands thinks of home.

I'll strive to the **END** to realize our hopes for the motherland.

The **PEOPLE'S** gift to me is worth more than millions.

RAGE, impetuous rage, invigorates the good earth,

As we wait for spring to spread across the land.

—"Lantern Festival," Zhu Haihong,
People's Daily, *March 20, 1991*

ALTHOUGH the conservative cause had been dealt a series of stunning blows in 1992, it was not yet finished. In the aftermath of the Fourteenth Congress, the Left's flagging spirits were briefly revived as stories began to circulate concerning a widening rift between Deng Xiaoping and his old friend Yang Shangkun.

The split first emerged during the run-up to the Fourteenth Congress, when Yang proposed to reconsider the verdicts on the Tiananmen disturbance and on Zhao Ziyang. According to unofficial party sources, Yang hinted that by reversing the two verdicts the party could greatly improve its public image and help restore the sagging morale of its own rank-and-file. Although Deng Xiaoping had previously voiced support for Zhao's return to work, the patriarch was said to be greatly alarmed over Yang's proposal to link Zhao's rehabilitation to an overall reassessment of the 1989 crisis—a reassessment that Deng flatly opposed.[1]

At the 1992 Beidaihe summer leadership conference, Yang Shangkun reportedly told senior party leaders that he was in possession of information that could help to heal the festering wounds of Tiananmen. Claiming that "I have documents to show [who made] the decisions in 1989," Yang implied that he had clear proof of Deng's personal responsibility for initiating the deadly conflagration of June 3–4. Evidently, Deng feared that Yang might use such documents to further his own bid for power following the patriarch's death.[2]

Deng's concern was further heightened when several other top party leaders, including Wan Li, voiced agreement at Beidaihe with Yang's assessment that popular confidence in the party had been seriously undermined by the "June 4 complex." Deng was also said to be upset over a suggestion made by Yang early in 1992 to the effect that either Li Ruihuan or Qiao Shi would make a suitable replacement for Jiang Zemin as CCP general secretary. Both Li and Qiao had evidently questioned Jiang's leadership qualities, and Li had expressed doubts about the strength of Jiang's wind-blown commitment to opposing Leftism. Qiao Shi had, moreover, indicated his support for a declaration of limited amnesty for dissidents involved in the Tiananmen disturbances—a move strongly opposed by Deng.[3]

The appearance of an emerging anti-Jiang, pro-amnesty united front among a number of Deng Xiaoping's erstwhile allies added fuel to the paramount leader's mounting—and highly ironic—fears of a posthumous betrayal. Almost a quarter-century earlier, in the autumn of 1978, a strong challenge to the credentials of a Chinese patriarch's designated successor, coupled with the granting of amnesty to a group of demonstrators arrested for taking part in a "counterrevolutionary incident" at Tiananmen Square, had foreshadowed Deng's rise to power; now similar developments threatened to debase his legacy. Deng's rising apprehension over such an ironic outcome, in turn, goes far toward explaining the curious fact, noted earlier, that despite the Fourteenth Congress's overwhelming endorsement of Deng's reform initiatives, both the Yang family generals and the party's liberal wing suffered unexpected positional losses at the congress. What should have been Deng's victory celebration had turned instead into a display of patriarchal pique.

Shortly after the Fourteenth Congress, in a move apparently designed to neutralize the Yang brothers' remaining influence within the PLA and to firm up support for Jiang Zemin, Liu Huaqing, at Deng's behest, engineered a major reshuffle of military leadership. Within two months, 190 senior army officers were removed or reassigned to new posts—the largest single shake-up in the history of the PLA. At the same time, new emphasis was placed on rapid modernization and development of China's military capabilities. To help pay for such upgrading—and to gain much-needed political support from China's military leaders—Jiang Zemin in January 1993 approved a plan to permit the PLA greatly to expand its own independent business operations, known generically as *bingshang* (military commerce).[4]

DENG HALTS THE ANTI-LEFTIST CAMPAIGN

By opening a potentially serious rift within the reform camp, Deng's falling out with the Yang brothers gave conservatives new room for political maneuver. Backing away from his previous attack on hard-line opponents of reform and opening up, Deng now sent a letter to Central Committee members enjoining them to call off the party's year-long campaign against Leftism and to heighten their vigilance against peaceful evolution. The letter also stated, in no uncertain terms, that the official verdict on the June 4 incident "must never be overturned."[5] When the contents of Deng's letter were mysteriously leaked to the press and to the public, it was a signal for Deng's foes, largely silent since the spring of 1992, to step up their oppositional activities.[6]

In mid-January 1993, on the first anniversary of Deng's epoch-making southern tour, Chen Yun and Wang Zhen came out of seclusion to make their first public appearances in many months, conveying Lunar New Year's greetings to Chinese citizens at a series of official receptions. The mass media prominently featured photos of the two elderly conservatives. Not to be outdone, Deng Xiaoping followed suit a few days later, making a well-publicized appearance at a Shanghai reception, where he was photographed in the company of Jiang Zemin and a number of local officials and workers. In a brief but pointed New Year's greeting, Deng attempted to rally support for Jiang, calling him a "good leader" and a "trustworthy core of the party."[7]

Unwilling to be upstaged by Deng, Yang Shangkun paid a hasty, impromptu visit to Shenzhen, where he made an inspection tour of towns and facilities near the Hong Kong border. His official reception in his old Guangdong bailiwick was markedly low-key and unenthusiastic, however. Arriving at the Shenzhen airport, he was reportedly snubbed by the provincial party establishment. His welcoming committee was made up of a group of second-tier local officials; and his visit to the SEZ went wholly unreported in the mass media—presumably a reflection of his recent fall from grace.[8]

Meanwhile, Deng Liqun, who had maintained a relatively low profile since the spring of 1992, also began to step up his activities. Fishing in troubled waters, as usual, he sought to exploit the growing rift between Deng and the Yang brothers by forging a new relationship with conservative senior army officers. Using his editorial influence with the party's propaganda journal, *Search for Truth,* Little Deng issued a call in January 1993 to "raise the combativeness" of the PLA.[9] His ostensible aim was to appeal to disgruntled military leaders who were unhappy with Jiang Zemin as their commander-in-chief, and who were stepping up their demands for a substantially larger share of the government budget. Little Deng's efforts evidently had an effect on party and government leaders, for when the 1993 national budget was unveiled at the Eighth NPC two months later, the PLA received a hefty 12.5 percent increase in its allocation, up from RMB ¥37.8 billion to ¥42.5 billion.[10]

As part of his campaign to stir up disaffection within the PLA, Deng Liqun reportedly invited Wang Zhen to help him recruit retired senior military commanders into a new organization, the "National Historical Institute," which Chinese sources described as a virtual clone of the now-defunct CAC — and a new home for the senescent, die-hard opponents of reform.[11]

STUMPING FOR VOTES: LI PENG HEADS SOUTH

While Yang Shangkun and Deng Liqun sought new constituency support, Li Peng set out to increase the value of his own political stock. With the encouragement of Chen Yun, Premier Li made a sudden, whirlwind tour of the

372   • *CHAPTER 15* •

Shenzhen and Zhuhai SEZs in early January 1993. Taking a page from Deng Xiaoping's book, the premier's purpose was twofold: on the one hand, he sought to reassure nervous local officials of the State Council's continuing support for Guangdong's unique brand of economic entrepreneurship; on the other hand, he sought to shed his public image as a dour, stuffy bureaucrat. With the Eighth NPC scheduled to meet in March, with Vice-Premier Zhu Rongji continuing to pick up solid support as China's new economic czar, with his own quest for a second five-year term as premier by no means assured, and with memories of his rebuff at the 1992 NPC still fresh in mind, Li was engaged in a fight for political survival.[12]

Visiting the Shenzhen Securities Exchange in the company of the Chinese press corps, Li Peng paused for a series of interviews and photo opportunities, in the course of which he expressed great interest in such technical matters as the determination of share prices and the mechanics of computerized stock trading. Although he carefully withheld praise for the stock market as an institution, he adopted a posture of benevolent concern for the welfare of the *gumin*, China's new breed of stock traders. "We must," declared the premier beneficently, "pay attention to protecting the interests of investors." In Zhuhai, Li visited construction sites for a new deep-water port and international airport, pronouncing his support for these controversial, costly ventures.[13] At every stop along the route of his three-day journey, Premier Li acted the part of a candidate stumping for votes.

Li Peng's concern with improving his image was well-founded. As principal lightning rod for the continued expression of popular hostility over the brutal Tiananmen crackdown, Li had, since 1989, suffered repeated public indignities. Two months before he was rebuffed by legislators at China's 1992 NPC meeting, for example, Li had been snubbed diplomatically and heckled by hostile crowds during a five-nation European-American tour; and several months before that, in March 1991, he had been the butt of a cleverly disguised diagonal acrostic appearing in the *People's Daily*: "Down with Li Peng, end people's rage" (*Li Peng xia tai, ping min fen*).[14]

Li's lack of personal popularity tended to resonate with and reinforce a growing mood of grass-roots resentment toward central authority in general. People's congresses in a number of provinces and municipalities, meeting in the early winter of 1993 to choose local government leaders and to select delegates for the upcoming NPC, had voted to oust incumbent officials who were backed by the party establishment. In both Zhejiang and Guizhou, provincial governors were unseated in legislative revolts intended to send a message of grass-roots discontent to party leaders in Beijing. In Guizhou the adoption of an open nomination process (similar to the system first introduced in China's 1980 local elections) led to the election of an outsider as governor, a man who had been attacked by hard-liners for sympathizing with student demonstrators in 1989. Similar displays of local legislative resistance to party-endorsed candidates were reported in Beijing, Sichuan, Guangdong, and Anhui.[15]

With regional resentment on the rise, several top-level party and government leaders, taking their cues from Li Peng, set out from Beijing in the late winter of 1993 to tour China's southeast coast, where they, too, lobbied for the support of provincial and local officials. From mid-January to early February, Politburo members Zhu Rongji, Zou Jiahua, Tian Jiyun, and Li Tieying all paid inspection visits to southern coastal areas, offering support for high growth rates and encouraging local cadres to pursue bold reforms.[16] To all outward appearances, China had entered its first real election campaign, with the southern SEZs serving as key precincts.

Recognizing the potential for a legislative revolt at the First Session of the Eighth National People's Congress, scheduled to open in Beijing on March 15, party leaders moved to tighten up the NPC's electoral rules, placing the power to nominate candidates for the NPC Standing Committee exclusively in the hands of the legislature's party-dominated Presidium. Although required to "consult and deliberate" (*yunniang*) with small subgroups of legislators on the nomination of candidates, the Presidium alone was given the final say in the preparation of candidate lists for the Standing Committee, with no accountability to the NPC as a whole.[17]

THE EIGHTH NPC

Carefully stage-managed to preclude delegate revolts or other unseemly occurrences, the First Session of the Eighth NPC went off without a hitch. As anticipated, Yang Shangkun retired from the PRC presidency, while Wan Li retired as chairman of the NPC Standing Committee. They were replaced by Jiang Zemin and Qiao Shi, respectively. With Li Ruihuan assuming the chairmanship of the CPPCC, replacing the deceased Li Xiannian, the three top-ranking nonparty positions in the Chinese political system were now, for the first time, occupied by members of the Politburo Standing Committee, all of whom were well below retirement age. The one major exception to this trend of inserting younger, active Communist Party leaders into top positions in nonparty organs was the post of PRC vice-president, which went to China's fabled "red capitalist," seventy-seven-year-old Rong Yiren.[18]

In economic policy, the Eighth NPC heartily endorsed the acceleration of reform and opening up initiated by Deng in 1992. In his work report to the congress, Premier Li Peng adopted a moderate, scholarly tone, recommending a revised annual growth rate of 8–9 percent, up from his 6 percent recommendation of the previous year but still considerably lower than China's actual 1992 growth rate of 12.8 percent. In recommending upward revision of his earlier growth estimates, Li for the first time explicitly endorsed Deng Xiaoping's "theory of one center." Arguing that "we should never lose sight of the central task of economic development," the premier embraced the core concept of Deng's modernization drive. In so doing, he may also have saved his job, as no attempt was made to unseat him at the Eighth NPC.

Aside from top-level personnel changes, the most significant action taken by the Eighth NPC was the adoption of a series of reform-related constitutional revisions. The most controversial of these codified Deng Xiaoping's definition of the Chinese economic system as a "socialist market economy" and reiterated Deng's view that the country's basic task in the primary stage of socialism was to "concentrate all effort on socialist modernization in accordance with the theory of building socialism with Chinese characteristics." In another key constitutional revision, the Preamble was amended to incorporate language calling for long-term continuation and perfection of the system of multiparty cooperation and political consultation under the leadership of the Communist Party. Seen as an acceptable alternative to the bourgeois concept of multiparty competition, the new constitution's emphasis on multiparty cooperation and consultation represented an attempt by the government to disarm democratic criticism while broadening somewhat its own base of popular legitimacy.[19]

One group of twenty NPC deputies, representing Hong Kong, was apparently unimpressed with the government's modest proposals for enhanced political consultation. Reacting against the NPC's newly adopted *yunniang* electoral rules, which placed the power to nominate candidates for top legislative posts exclusively in the hands of the NPC Presidium, the Hong Kong lawmakers urged the congress to adopt a statute requiring key officers of the NPC, including its vice-chairmen and Standing Committee members, to be democratically elected through a process in which the number of candidates would be greater than the number of seats to be filled. Not surprisingly, the proposal died without reaching the floor of the congress.[20]

Although significant democratic reform was not forthcoming at the Eighth NPC, the government used the occasion to introduce its plan to reduce by 20 percent the number of administrative personnel in China's bloated, chronically overstaffed state bureaucracy. Most of the planned reductions were to be accomplished by converting existing government agencies into semi-autonomous corporations. As a result of such conversion, tens of thousands of newly demobilized cadres were induced to *xiahai*—"take the plunge"—in the risky but potentially highly lucrative world of quasi-private trade and investment.[21]

In line with the Eighth NPC's accent on marketization, officials from several provinces held a joint press conference at the March 1993 legislative session announcing their intention to invite foreign investors to purchase shares in a number of chronically unprofitable state enterprises in their provinces. To help prepare Communist Party members to deal with the ideological and economic implications of such divestiture, the Central Party School in Beijing announced its intention to offer a series of new courses on finance, real estate, and securities markets.[22]

THE LAST GASP OF THE LEFT

Notwithstanding their successful midwinter minioffensive, conservatives had little cause for celebration in the aftermath of the NPC. At the March legislative session they decisively lost their decade-long struggle to retard the progress of marketization. More damaging still, on the very eve of the NPC, Wang Zhen, the feisty Big Cannon of the Left, succumbed to illness and old age, bringing to five the number of conservative leaders who had died within the most recent twelve-month period.

With Wang's demise and Yang Shangkun's retirement, for the first time in more than a decade no one over the age of eighty (and very few over seventy) held formal office at the top ranks of the party, government, and army hierarchies. With the majority of China's revolutionary immortals dead and the remainder afflicted with varying diseases and disabilities of old age, the intense ideological antinomies that had fueled the oscillations of the fang/shou cycle for a decade and a half now lost much of their capacity to inflame.

Among those most directly affected by the declining potency of the Left was Li Peng. Though he was reelected to the premiership in tightly controlled voting at the Eighth NPC, Li's political viability continued to decline in direct proportion to the deteriorating health of his key conservative patrons. With Wang Zhen dead and Chen Yun ailing and unable to appear in public, Li's stock dipped precipitously following the March 1993 NPC meeting.

Toward the end of April, Li was hospitalized with what was at first rumored to be a bad cold, subsequently upgraded to a mild case of pneumonia, and finally officially diagnosed as a heart attack. After spending several weeks recuperating in hospital, Li resumed a light work load in mid-June. A short time later, however, it was reported that the premier's recovery had not been going smoothly, and in early July the Politburo quietly relieved him of responsibility for overseeing China's economy. His duties were reassigned—"for the time being"— to Zhu Rongji. Within days, Communist Party cadres in Beijing began to speak of a new "Jiang-Zhu axis" to supplant the old Jiang-Li axis. Also in Beijing, it was rumored, with a wink and a nod, that the prescription for Li Peng to take an indefinite recuperative leave of absence had come from a certain "Deng Daifu"—Dr. Deng.[23]

Li Peng was not the only one adversely affected by the death of Wang Zhen. Hit equally hard was Deng Liqun. In the past, Little Deng had been able to play the role of conservative "spoiler" with great success because he had enjoyed the backing of Hu Qiaomu, Wang Zhen, and Chen Yun. With two of his principal patrons now dead (one of whom, Hu Qiaomu, had renounced his past Leftist excesses) and the third in failing health, Deng's capacity to obstruct reform was significantly reduced. In the view of party reformers in Beijing, Deng Liqun was the "software" (ruanjian) of the conservative movement, while Wang Zhen was the essential "hardware" (yingjian). When the hardware crashed, the software was silenced.[24]

Under the circumstances, party liberals appeared more optimistic than at any time since early 1988. In the course of a summer 1993 tour of the United States, the former chief editor of the People's Daily, Hu Jiwei, suggested that after years of bitter struggle Leftists had finally lost the capacity to derail, or even seriously to obstruct, the policies of economic reform and opening up. Claiming victory on behalf of the forces of modernization and change, Hu seemed barely able to contain his glee.[25] Meanwhile, six thousand miles away in Beijing, a senior reform economist offered a semiserious, tongue-in-cheek explanation for the remarkable progress of China's market reforms. "In the old days," he said, "we had a slogan: 'Use the countryside to surround the cities' (*yi nongcun baowei chengshi*). Today we have a different slogan: 'Use the corporation to surround the party center' (*yi gongsi baowei zhongyang*)."[26] It was a fitting, if ironic, epitaph for Mao Zedong's theory of people's war.

CHAPTER 16

The Mandate of Heaven: Summer 1993–Summer 1995

If there are problems in the villages, no one in the present

regime can hold on to power.

—Tian Jiyun (1993)

Corruption is a virus that has infected the party's healthy body.

If we ignore this phenomenon, it will bring down

our party and our system.

—Jiang Zemin (1993)

EVEN as reformers celebrated their hard-won victory, there were new and unsettling signs of socioeconomic malaise in the Middle Kingdom. Despite a greatly enlivened domestic economy (GDP grew almost 14 percent in 1993, while industrial production rose 25 percent and retail sales increased 21 percent), many of the reform-related stresses that had initially beset China in the mid-1980s were starting to reappear. In the aftermath of Deng's *nanxun*, for example, the nation's inflation rate, under control since the economic contraction of 1988–89, turned sharply upward. In the first quarter of 1993, the annualized rate of increase in consumer prices in thirty-five major Chinese cities rose to a post-1988 peak of 15.7 percent; a year later it hit 24.8 percent.[1]

Reflecting a dramatic easing of credit restrictions in the provinces, the first half of 1993 also witnessed a 50 percent year-on-year increase in the nation's money supply and an even greater jump in new investment. Among other things, the investment binge was fueled by the practice, widespread in rural areas, of local officials taking government revenues earmarked for payment to farmers (for state-procured agricultural products) and diverting the funds for investment in local construction projects, stock market transactions, and real estate speculation. According to a report in the official *Farmers' Daily*, only about one-third of the RMB ¥80 billion allocated by the central government for agricultural procurements in 1992 actually reached the hands of farmers. Most of the remainder was reportedly diverted by investment-minded local officials.[2] In lieu of cash, farmers in many provinces were being paid for their crops in IOUs or "white slips" (*baitiaozi*) issued by local governments, redeemable for cash at some (unspecified) time in the future.

BEGGARING THE PEASANTS

Official statistics confirmed the worsening plight of China's farmers. In the three years from 1988 to 1991, farm incomes in at least ten inland provinces suffered an absolute decline. While grain prices increased modestly over this period, the cost of fertilizer, equipment, and other agricultural inputs more than doubled. Overall, from 1985 to 1994 the urban-rural income differential in China rose by almost 40 percent—from 1.9:1 to 2.65:1. Between coast and interior, the gap grew larger still.[3]

With farm incomes reportedly stagnant or declining throughout much of the country, and with the urban-rural income gap growing, farmers in several provinces vigorously protested—and in some instances rioted—against the unauthorized diversion of funds by local officials. Also under protest were a wide variety of local taxes, licensing fees, and ad hoc levies imposed upon farmers by predatory rural cadres. One of the worst outbreaks of violence took place in Renshou County, Sichuan, where 15,000 farmers rioted in the spring of 1993, assaulting cadres and burning police vehicles in protest over a series of exorbitant local fiscal exactions.[4]

The Renshou eruption was just the tip of a larger iceberg. According to government statistics, in the sixteen months from January 1993 to April 1994 there were a total of 1,200 "large" rural disturbances (each involving more than 500 people and encompassing more than one village), 100 "very large" disturbances (involving at least 1,000 people), and 30 "especially large" ones (involving 5,000 people). Total casualties in these incidents surpassed 13,200, with property damage exceeding ¥20 billion.[5]

Describing mounting rural unrest as a threat to the nation's stability, Chinese leaders at the First Session of the Eighth NPC issued a series of stern warnings to village and township officials, prohibiting them from imposing local taxes in excess of 5 percent of farmers' incomes, enjoining them from siphoning off state funds intended to pay farmers, and ordering them to redeem all outstanding IOUs. "If there are problems in the villages," warned Vice-Premier Tian Jiyun, "no one in the present regime can hold on to power."[6] In an attempt to stem the rising tide of peasant discontent, the Ministry of Agriculture in May 1993 announced the cancellation of forty-three different levies on farmers. To halt the diversion of funds intended to pay farmers, the CDIC in August formally banned party officials at all levels from trading in securities.

In the face of declining farm incomes, large numbers of farmers opted to leave the land. In March 1993 a government spokesman revealed that unemployment, primarily rural in concentration and seasonal in nature, currently affected "not less than two hundred million people," or almost 35 percent of China's total workforce of 567 million.[7] Almost half of these—approximately one in eight adult Chinese—were members of China's vast "floating population" (*liudong renkou*), made up of underemployed farmers seeking work in urban areas. In Guangzhou alone, an estimated daily average of 190,000 rural floaters drifted in and out of the city in search of employment,[8]

Seeking to restore a semblance of stability to the nation's troubled agricultural sector—officially acknowledged to be the "weakest link" in the Chinese economy[9]—the government in 1994 announced its intention partially to re centralize agriculture. The declared goal was to bring the distribution of 70–80 percent of social commodity grains and edible oils back under state guidance. To ensure that grain production would be sufficient to meet rising demand, the State Council revived a number of previously discarded administrative measures, including mandatory provincial grain quotas and compulsory grain procurement. In addition, grain rationing was reintroduced in some cities and price controls were reinstated on more than two dozen staple foodstuffs and other essential farm products.[10]

Alongside renewed fears of spiraling inflation, economic overheating, and agrarian discontent, there was evidence of other worsening problems, including urban labor unrest. In 1992 some 540 illegal labor demonstrations and 480 serious work stoppages were reported, including 75 instances in which angry workers attacked party and government offices.[11] The following year the number of large-scale labor disputes reportedly exceeded 12,000. Many of these centered around allegations of abusive treatment of workers by enterprise managers and local officials. Others were the result of forced layoffs and furloughs, as workers in state enterprises protested the consequences of the broken iron rice bowl.[12]

THE DECLINE OF SOCIAL ORDER

An increase in violent crime—70 percent of it committed by young people under twenty-five, and much of it gang-related—was also acknowledged by the Chinese government, as was the fact that since the 1980s there had been a tenfold increase in the number of youthful criminal offenders. In 1992 Chinese police confiscated 200,000 illegal firearms. Evidently this had little effect on the crime problem: offenses involving the use of firearms increased by 50 percent the following year.[13] Also on the rise were crimes of violence against the guardians of social order. In the three years from 1990 to July 1993, over 4,700 public security personnel and local police were killed or wounded in the line of duty.[14] According to China's chief government prosecutor, Liu Fuzhi, the new epidemic of crime was linked to activities of mafia-like triad gangs that were said to be on a rampage throughout the country.[15]

Cadre corruption also continued to flourish. According to a report issued by Liu Fuzhi in July 1993, the number of government officials involved in bribery, embezzlement, and other forms of corruption was "increasing nonstop" despite a substantial rise in the apprehension of wrongdoers.[16] While growing numbers of cadres faced criminal probes, relatively few were prosecuted. In the first half of 1992, for example, criminal charges were filed in less than one-third of the 48,000 cases of cadre corruption that came under investigation.[17] As in the past, it was the small-fry who were pursued most vigorously, while officials at the top rungs of the political ladder were generally able to avoid prosecution: from 1988 to the spring of 1993, a grand total of five provincial- and ministerial-level cadres were convicted of economic crimes—an average of exactly one per year.[18]

Economic crime and corruption grew not merely in frequency but also in magnitude. In 1993, 265 cases of bribery, graft, and embezzlement involving amounts in excess of RMB ¥1 million each were investigated, along with 955 cases involving ¥500,000 or more—representing a 700 percent increase over the previous year.[19] To make matters worse, some of the most flagrant offenders were responsible officials of the Bank of China.[20] By the summer of 1993 Jiang Zemin was forced to acknowledge openly that "Corruption is a virus that has infected the party's healthy body. If we just ignore this phenomenon, it will bring down our party and our system." And in a rare public statement, Deng Xiaoping was quoted in *People's Daily* warning against "a world dominated by corruption, embezzlement, and bribery."[21]

Corruption, speculation, and profiteering were also on the rise at the upper reaches of China's military establishment. With the PLA actively involved in a variety of large-scale profit-making activities (*bingshang*), there were plentiful opportunities for private commercial gain by well-connected staff officers. According to foreign intelligence estimates, extrabudgetary sources generated approximately ¥30 billion in military income in 1992—accounting for almost half of the PLA's total outlays.[22] Because most *bingshang* operations lay beyond the scrutiny of the Ministry of Justice, the CDIC, or any other civilian watchdog agency, there was minimal oversight of military commerce—a situation that readily lent itself to burgeoning corruption. The several hundred posh Mercedes and Lexus automobiles imported (or smuggled) into China from Hong Kong and South Korea by high-ranking PLA officers in the early 1990s bore witness to the profits being generated by *bingshang*. Equally unsettling was the fact that much of the military commerce was being organized and run by the offspring of party elders.[23] So serious was the problem of unregulated military entrepreneurship that two leading members of the MAC, generals Liu Huaqing and Zhang Zhen, writing in July 1993 on the eve of the sixty-sixth anniversary of the founding of the PLA, warned that the "growing tide of corruption, money worshiping, and hedonism" in the PLA constituted a "threat to the development of the army."[24] Evidently the warning had little effect. Ten months later a report published in *The Times* of London suggested that as many as 10,000 PLA-owned business enterprises were currently operating without official authorization. Many of the offending firms were said to be major players in the freewheeling Hong Kong real estate and securities markets.[25]

A major epidemic of kidnapping, prostitution, and drug abuse was another source of growing concern. At the Eighth NPC it was conservatively reported that more than 100,000 offenders had been convicted since 1988 for crimes of inducing or forcing women into prostitution, abducting and selling women or children for gain, trafficking drugs, and producing or distributing pornographic materials.[26] This was just the tip of a much larger iceberg, however. In 1992 alone, police apprehended 50,000 purveyors of pornography along with more than 75,000 pimps and assorted "sex-traders." In Guangzhou, an estimated 30,000 prostitutes worked the city's tourist hotels, streets, and karaoke bars. From 1991 to 1994 Chinese authorities arrested over 50,000 kidnappers and freed more than 70,000 women and children from captivity.[27]

The figures on drug abuse (primarily opium and heroin addiction) were also alarming, with the number of registered addicts doubling annually, from approximately 70,000 in 1990 to over 250,000 in 1992. In 1993 Chinese drug enforcement officials conceded that only a small proportion of China's addicts had registered with the government.[28] Reports from Yunnan and Guangdong suggested that the total number of drug users was probably manyfold higher than the government's official estimates. In a 1987 survey involving 65,000 respondents in Yunnan Province—a major Chinese drug trafficking center on the opium trail from Southeast Asia's "Golden Triangle" to Hong Kong and beyond—almost 3.5 percent of those questioned admitted to being addicted to narcotics; and this was two years *before* the onset of the country's most serious drug epidemic in 1989.[29] In Guangdong, more than 10,000 addicts were arrested in the first five months of 1993. According to one estimate, the total number of drug users in Guangdong (including marijuana and hashish smokers as well as opium and heroin addicts) was between 500,000 and 600,000.[30] In Nanning, capital of Guangxi Province, police reported that 78 percent of all addicts were involved in some form of criminal activity, including burglary, theft, and prostitution.[31] In Yunnan province, a 1992 crackdown on a gang of drug traffickers in a remote town near the Vietnamese border erupted into a protracted, pitched military battle involving 2,000 government troops supported by field artillery and armored personnel carriers.[32]

Such fragmentary, anecdotal evidence bore testimony to a significantly strained social fabric. Among Chinese youths, a new crisis of faith was also in evidence. Up and down the bustling, densely populated east coast of China, from Harbin to Hainan, observers noted a deepening mood of alienation and anomie among young people, large numbers of whom were turning to "get-rich-quick" schemes, religion, the martial arts, or sex, drugs, and rock-and-roll as quick-fix antidotes to decaying belief systems, declining moral standards, and disintegrating social controls.[33]

On the whole, by the end of 1993 most social indicators had turned strikingly negative, necessitating a cautious assessment of the country's outward appearance of economic dynamism and prosperity. The coexistence of high industrial and commercial growth rates alongside swelling armies of impoverished rural floaters descending on crime-plagued cities gave the country an unsettled, schizophrenic appearance that lent added poignancy to the fading cries of alarm sounded by China's few remaining elderly conservatives. Since 1979, party old-timers had warned anyone who would listen of capitalism's boom-and-bust nature and polarizing tendencies, bitterly decrying the noxious sociocultural by-products of bourgeois liberalization. Now that their prophecy appeared in some measure to be coming true, their voices were no longer audible.

ZHU RONGJI'S ECONOMIC GAME PLAN

By the mid-1990s China thus appeared to be perched precariously on a developmental bubble. To prevent a rupture and achieve a "soft landing," Zhu Rongji—China's new economic czar—unveiled in July 1993 a sixteen-point austerity program designed to sharply curtail credit, limit new investment, reduce inflation, and generally cool down China's overheated economy.[34]

Zhu energetically pressed his attack on China's economic ills on a number of fronts. To eliminate rampant cronyism within the nation's banking system—which had resulted in a wave of unauthorized interbank transfers and inflationary binge-lending by branches of the People's Bank of China—Zhu removed the bank's governor, Li Guixian, and personally took over the job himself, bringing in several young protégés to assist him in overhauling the banks's operations and management. In a collateral move designed to control rampant speculation within China's booming real estate and securities markets, Zhu threatened to "chop off the head" of any government employee caught diverting public funds for speculative purposes.[35]

To increase the central government's dwindling share of total fiscal revenues, Zhu presided over the implementation of a new uniform national tax system. The system had two key features: a revival of Zhao Ziyang's controversial *li gai shui* and a new 17 percent value-added tax on manufactures. To reduce the 33 percent gap between China's official foreign exchange rate and the black (or gray) market rate—a gap that invited rampant currency speculation—Zhu overhauled China's dual currency system, abolishing the Foreign Exchange Certificate (FEC) and devaluing the RMB from its official exchange rate of ¥5.7:US$1 to the prevailing swap-market rate of 8.7:1.[36]

Notwithstanding Zhu Rongji's energetic efforts, which helped bring the country's economic growth rate down from 14 percent in 1993 to 12 percent in 1994, the obstacles to success were daunting. For one thing, Zhu's sharp tongue, abrasive manner, and reputation for political cunning had earned him a fair number of personal detractors. For another, there was the very magnitude—and the inherent intractability—of many of the problems he sought to solve, such as the inflation rate, which exceeded 21 percent in 1994, and the chronic "triangular debt" dilemma that was suffocating China's inefficient, cash-starved state enterprises. After making a brief, high-profile assault on the debt problem, Zhu eventually backed away, declaring victory after clearing up only about one-third of the reported ¥600 billion debt backlog. By 1995 the backlog had grown once again to approximately ¥700 billion.[37] And finally, in seeking to force upon the country the bitter medicine of fiscal and financial austerity, Zhu Rongji ran afoul of a number of his erst-while supporters, including free-spending provincial and local government officials, liberal reform economists, and jealous, turf-guarding central bureaucrats. Thus, when Zhu finally stepped down from his bank governor's job in 1995—after pushing a controversial central-bank law through a wary NPC—it was unclear whether his supporters were claiming victory or conceding defeat.[38]

COUNTDOWN TO SUCCESSION

With China's economy continuing to overheat, fresh reports of Deng Xiao-ping's declining health raised the level of political anxiety in the nation's capital. In the summer of 1993 it was rumored—and quickly denied—that Deng suffered from testicular cancer. Other reports, more highly credible, referred to the worsening Parkinsonian palsy in Deng's left arm, his inability to walk or talk without assistance, and his near-total deafness. For the second time in three years, Deng's doctors strongly advised against making the annual summer trip to Beidaihe.[39]

Rumors of the patriarch's worsening condition were further fueled during the 1994 Lunar New Year holiday, when Chinese state television aired a brief film clip showing a pallid and palsied-looking Deng Xiaoping, supported on either side by aides, taking a few slow, tentative steps forward. As the camera tracked his progress, Deng's eyes appeared blank and unfocused. He did not speak.[40] Though there was disagreement among veteran Deng-watchers as to whether he suffered from a specific terminal illness or merely from the effects of old age, the general consensus was that Deng Xiaoping was no longer capable of significant physical—or political—activity. With the deathwatch now beginning in earnest, China's succession drama was about to enter a new and critical phase.[41]

Ironically, it was not Deng Xiaoping but his old nemesis, Chen Yun, who "met Marx" first. After years of failing health, the eighty-nine-year-old Chen finally expired on April 10, 1995, of complications from chronic pneumonia.[42] His death, following by a few months the demise of fellow conservative Yao Yilin, served further to muffle the muted voices of the gerontocratic Left. In a departure from previous tradition, no public ceremony was held to honor Chen Yun, and no official mourning period was declared. An official obituary, printed in major Chinese newspapers and read aloud on state television two days after his death, praised Chen's many contributions but also hinted darkly at the existence of a split within the current Chinese leadership: "We must turn our pain to strength," the obituary exhorted, "and closely unite around the Central Committee with Jiang Zemin at the core." A small, low-key memorial service for Chen was held in the hospital where he died, attended by all members of the Politburo Standing Committee save for Qiao Shi, who was out of the country. At Chen's own behest, his body was cremated.[43]

Chen's passing, together with Deng Xiaoping's physical decline, underscored the fragility of existing arrangements for China's succession. Although Jiang Zemin now occupied all three "core" positions at the apex of China's interlocking party, army, and government bureaucracies, his inheritance rested on a thin foundation. Like Hua Guofeng before him, Jiang's principal claim to fame was the personal bequest of a senescent autocrat. Like Hua, he lacked an independent power base of his own.

JIANG ZEMIN'S SURVIVAL STRATEGY

Beginning in mid-1993, Jiang took a series of steps calculated to improve his prospects for political survival. One of his first priorities was to build a base of support inside the PLA. Lack of strong military backing had severely—perhaps fatally—weakened Deng Xiaoping's two previous heirs-apparent, Hu Yaobang and Zhao Ziyang; cognizant of his own weakness in this regard, Jiang set out to establish a personal patronage network within the PLA.[44]

In the winter of 1993–94, in the wake of Deng's decision to oust the "Yang family generals," Jiang, in his role as chairman of the MAC, presided over an overhaul of the country's top military leadership—the third substantial shakeup since 1989. Acting on the advice of four key Deng military loyalists—MAC vice chairmen Liu Huaqing and Zhang Zhen, and GPD director and deputy director Yu Yongbo and Wang Ruilin—Jiang ordered the retirement, transfer, or demotion of one thousand army officers, including some of the senior troop commanders who had participated in the 1989 Beijing massacre. To fill top-level vacancies, Jiang personally promoted nineteen senior officers to the rank of full general, including all seven of China's military region commanders and four regional political commissars.[45] At around the same time, Jiang presided over a partial reorganization of the PLA's command structure, bringing certain regional military units under the control of the MAC, rather than under local commanders, as before.

In addition to dispensing military patronage and enhancing the MAC's control over local forces, Jiang Zemin also took pains to promote the PLA's corporate interests. Throughout the early and mid-1990s he endorsed hefty, double-digit annual increases in China's military budget and lent his strong personal support to the PLA's quest for accelerated technological modernization.[46] Beginning in January 1993 Jiang also permitted the army to expand substantially its non-defense-related, profit-making commercial ventures. His stated reason for allowing the proliferation of *bingshang* was fiscal necessity: "If somebody could find me [another] ¥30 billion," he said, "I could stop the army from going into business."[47]

Second on Jiang's list of succession priorities, after improvement of his relations with the military, was the recruitment of key political associates to positions of leadership in the central party apparatus. Toward this end, in the fall of 1994 Jiang sponsored the promotion of Shanghai party secretary Huang

Ju to the Politburo, bringing to four the number of former Shanghai municipal leaders serving on the CCP's highest decision-making body: Jiang, Zhu Rongji, Wu Bangguo, and Huang Ju. In addition, Jiang secured promotions for a number of other ex-Shanghai associates, including Zeng Qinghong (director of the CC General Office), Zeng Peiyan (vice minister of planning), Gong Xinhan (deputy director of party propaganda), Liu Ji (vice president of CASS), and Wang Huning (CCP Central Research Office). Not since the heyday of the Gang of Four had a "Shanghai clique" enjoyed such high political visibility.[48]

Jiang's third major political initiative was his attempt to get out in front of the mounting wave of popular resentment over official corruption and profiteering. In a calculated bid to boost his own—and the CCP's—flagging credibility, in the summer of 1993 Jiang pledged to intensify the crackdown on economic crime and corruption, particularly at the upper levels of the party, government, and army. Solemnly promising that no wrongdoer, regardless of position or rank, would be immune from criminal prosecution, Jiang's message was clear and forthright.[49]

While 1994 witnessed only modest, gradual gains in the struggle against corruption,[50] a sharp change occurred early in 1995. Shortly after the New Year, the party boss of Guizhou Province, Liu Zhengwei, was sacked and his wife, Yan Jianhong, and the director of the Guizhou Public Security Department, Guo Jianmin, were sentenced to death after being convicted of "serious embezzlement."[51] Then, in mid-February, amid rumors of a brewing financial scandal in the nation's capital, the chairman of the board of Beijing's giant Shougang (Capital Iron and Steel) Corporation—Deng Xiaoping's long-time friend, seventy-seven-year-old Zhou Guanwu—suddenly announced his decision to retire. Just one day earlier Zhou's high-rolling son, Zhou Beifang, head of the Shougang Concord, Ltd.—a Hong Kong-based subsidiary of Capital Iron and Steel—had been detained for questioning by Beijing municipal authorities in connection with allegations of "serious financial impropriety." When the younger Zhou's arrest was officially confirmed a few days later, Hong Kong sources were quick to point out that two of Zhou Beifang's closest business associates had been Deng Zhifang, younger son of the Chinese patriarch, and Li Ka-shing, Hong Kong billionaire and Deng family intimate. Also reportedly under investigation was Deng Xiaoping's niece, Ding Peng, who was suspected of involvement in the embezzlement of funds from a Shenzhen corporation of which she was president.[52]

"TOUCHING THE TIGER'S ARSE"

Shortly after the Shougang case broke open, a second major scandal erupted in the nation's capital, involving allegations of widespread graft and corruption within the Beijing municipal government. By early April the trail of suspicion had led straight to Beijing Deputy Mayor Wang Baosen. Apprised that he was under criminal investigation for embezzling approximately U.S. $35 million in public funds, Wang allegedly drove out to a deserted spot near the Beijing suburb of Huairou and took his own life with a single bullet to the head.[53]

Following closely on the heels of the deputy mayor's violent death, a third bombshell exploded. In late April Chen Xitong, the unpopular, hard-line head of the Beijing Party Committee, was removed from his post after having been assigned "inescapable responsibility" for Wang Baosen's suicide—and for a host of related improprieties recently uncovered in the city's construction industry.[54]

In the wake of Chen Xitong's removal, State Council Research Office Director Yuan Mu—a hard-line ally of both Chen and Premier Li Peng—was removed from his post with no official explanation.[55] Chen's job as Beijing party secretary was taken over by an outsider, Politburo security specialist (and Central Secretariat member) Wei Jianxing, a protégé of Qiao Shi and the latter's successor as head of the CDIC.[56] Under Wei's guidance, the probe widened further in early May, netting at least one former top aide to Chen Xitong and a senior public security official, who were each held on charges stemming from their alleged participation in a U.S. $380 million loan-pyramid scheme. In addition, both Chen Xitong's wife and their princeling son, Chen Xiaotong, manager of Beijing's fashionable New Century Hotel, were arrested on suspicion of corruption, as were approximately forty assorted Beijing city officials, some of whom were reportedly involved in a scheme to sell off choice parcels of municipally owned real estate at bargain prices in exchange for huge kickbacks. Also caught uncomfortably in the crackdown were Beijing Mayor Li Qiyan and Deputy Mayor Zhang Baifa, who were reportedly offered lenient treatment (including temporary retention of their jobs) in exchange for their agreement to cooperate with government investigators.[57]

Chinese sources generally credited Jiang Zemin with initiating the Beijing anticorruption probe, with an active assist from Zhu Rongji and Qiao Shi. For Qiao, former head of the CDIC with a reputation as China's "Mr. Clean," blowing the whistle on high-level corruption in the nation's capital offered two obvious advantages: it furthered his reputation as a vigorous, no-nonsense crime-buster, and it enabled him to undermine the "capital clique" of Li Peng and Chen Xitong. For Zhu Rongji, the probe was more a matter of the CCP's long-term survival. "We should tell the people throughout the country that we will first hunt tigers, and then hunt wolves," he said. To those comrades who feared that a tiger hunt might bring ruination to the party, Zhu countered that a little "common ruin" was a small price to pay for "a long period of stability and peace."[58]

For Jiang Zemin, launching the crackdown represented a delicate political calculus. On the one hand, public outrage over the ubiquity—and increasing brazenness—of official corruption had reached a point where China's top leaders could ignore it only at their own peril.[59] On the other hand, however, by reaching into Deng Xiaoping's inner circle of family and friends to expose gross financial improprieties, Jiang was ostensibly biting the hand that fed him; further, he risked provoking a backlash among senior party and government officials, many of whom clearly lacked the general secretary's enthusiasm for "touching the tiger's arse." For these reasons, Jiang's course of action was inherently problematic.[60]

Despite the obvious downside risks, however, Jiang's strategy had a clear preponderance of upside merit. Two decades earlier, Hua Guofeng had hewed closely to his dying mentor's instructions, dutifully deferring to Mao Zedong's every idiosyncratic whim. Yet in the end Hua's abject, obsequious "whateverism" had not saved him; indeed, in the backlash from the 1976 Tiananmen incident it helped ensure his downfall. Now, by deliberately distancing himself from Deng Xiaoping's family (if not from Deng himself, who by this time was functionally incapacitated), Jiang could hope to achieve three important objectives: first, he could get out from under Deng's confining shadow by demonstrating his capacity for independent political judgment and leadership—not an insignificant consideration for a man with a reputation as a weak and windblown sycophant; second, by putting his weight behind the campaign to rectify corruption at the top, he could posture himself as a compassionate "man of the people," responsive to the concerns of ordinary citizens; and finally, by joining the assault against Chen Xitong et al., Jiang could hope to benefit from the declining prestige and influence of Li Peng.[61] For all these reasons, "touching the tiger's arse" had much to recommend it as Jiang's stratagem of choice.

Notwithstanding his newfound temerity, however, Jiang Zemin was evidently risk averse when it came to incurring his benefactor's wrath. According to unofficial Chinese sources, before zeroing in on the Shougang clique and Chen Xitong, Jiang summoned sixty of China's most distinguished medical specialists to Deng Xiaoping's bedside, where the physicians were asked to sign a sworn affidavit stating that their illustrious patient was no longer mentally competent. Armed with this important insurance policy—and with Deng's purported February 1994 instruction to "remove all hindrances" and "remove large stones" in the fight against corruption—Jiang was free to take action against some of the first family's high-flying associates.[62] Thereafter, Deng's wife, Zhuo Lin, reportedly became so upset over the probe of her son's business connections, and over Jiang Zemin's refusal to discuss the matter with her in person, that toward the end of April she suffered a minor stroke, requiring her to be hospitalized for several days.[63]

THE BEIJING SPRING OF '95

With one hard-line gerontocrat (Chen Yun) newly deceased, another (Deng Xiaoping) approaching death, a third key figure in the June 4 crackdown (Chen Xitong) under a deep cloud of criminal suspicion, a fourth (Yuan Mu) abruptly removed from office, and a fifth (Li Peng) increasingly isolated polit-ically, a wave of speculation swept through the Chinese capital in the spring of 1995 concerning a possible reversal of the 1989 Tiananmen verdict. Such speculation was fueled, among other things, by the revelation that in late March Jiang Zemin had unveiled a memorial plaque at the Jiangxi grave-site of Hu Yaobang, deceased hero of the 1989 student movement—and by Zhao Ziyang's attendance at a funeral service for a deceased comrade, Zhou Jiannan.[64]

Adding to the atmosphere of heightened political expectation, China's crit-ical intellectuals, after a self-imposed silence of almost six years, began to express themselves openly in the spring of 1995. Starting in late February, on the eve of the NPC's annual legislative session, a number of letters and peti-tions were delivered to the NPC Standing Committee. Signed by several dozen liberal activists, including recently paroled political prisoners Wang Dan and Chen Ziming, the petitions called, inter alia, for an immediate re-sumption of democratic reform, an end to corruption, and the abolition of extrajudicial labor reform.[65]

A newly revived democratic spirit was also in evidence at the March 1995 NPC meeting. Setting the tone were NPC Standing Committee Chairman Qiao Shi and his principal lieutenant, Vice-Chairman Tian Jiyun. In a speech to a group of congressional deputies from Guangdong, Tian strongly sup-ported an acceleration of political reform. Specifically, he advocated the adop-tion of multicandidate elections (*cha'er xuanju*) to fill cabinet-level positions and urged deputies to exercise their mandate to supervise the government by engaging in bold, freewheeling policy debate and interpellation on the floor of parliament.[66] Taking Tian at his word, NPC deputies displayed a greater mea-sure of political independence than usual, as an unprecedented 36 percent voted against Jiang Zemin's personal choice for vice-premier, Jiang Chunyun (no relation), and 33 percent voted against Zhu Rongji's proposed legislation establishing a semi-independent central bank. Speaking at the concluding ses-sion of the NPC, Qiao Shi congratulated the deputies on their "democratic development" and exhorted them to redouble their efforts to "reflect the will of the people." According to Chinese sources, the NPC's results tended to confirm the existence of a growing split between a "rule by law" faction, centering around Qiao Shi, Tian Jiyun, and Li Ruihuan (with behind-the-scenes backing from elder statesmen Wan Li and Yang Shangkun), and a "rule by core" faction centering around Jiang Zemin, Li Peng, and Zhu Rongji (with backstage support from Song Ping).[67]

Taking their show on the road after the NPC adjourned, Qiao and Tian separately toured a number of southern coastal areas, making appearances in Fujian, Guangdong, and Shenzhen. At successive stops they urged provincial and local officials "not to be afraid to take risks." In Guangzhou and else-where, Qiao Shi emphasized the importance of the NPC's "frontline" legisla-tive and governmental oversight functions, arguing that the people's congress was the institutional embodiment of constitutional government. Significantly,

Qiao was accompanied on his tour by former Zhao Ziyang economic brain-truster Tong Dalin. For his part, Tian Jiyun spoke out against recent conservative initiatives designed to recollectivize agriculture. Strongly defending the family-based contract responsibility system, Tian derided Chen Yun's pet theory of "taking grain as the key link" and opposed the reimposition of mandatory grain quotas and compulsory purchase.[68]

Meanwhile, back in Beijing, the petition movement continued to gather momentum. In mid-May a letter drafted by the noted historian of science Xu Liangying and signed by forty-five prominent Chinese intellectuals, including eighty-eight-year-old nuclear scientist Wang Ganchang and veteran Communist Party critics Wang Ruoshui and Wu Zuguang, strongly urged the government to rescind the 1989 Tiananmen verdict, release all political prisoners, and put an end to the "repressive attacks, surveillance, house arrest, and even detention" of people holding dissenting views. Another letter, dated May 19 and initiated by veteran democracy activists Wang Dan, Bao Zunxin, Liu Xiaobo, Huang Xiang, and Zhou Duo, among others, called for a "declaration of human rights and freedoms" enumerating the constitutional guarantees enjoyed by all Chinese citizens. A third petition, signed by twenty-six relatives of victims of the June 4 massacre, called on the NPC to establish a special commission to undertake an "independent and fair inquiry into the entire incident" and to "provide a full accounting . . . in accordance with legal procedure."[69] Altogether nine such epistles, signed by almost two hundred prominent individuals, were circulated in Beijing in the spring of 1995, representing the most significant upsurge in liberal political activism since the winter of 1988–89.

Chinese government spokesmen at first responded calmly to the spate of letters and petitions, pointing out that all Chinese citizens enjoyed a constitutional right to express their opinions. However, shortly after the contents of Xu Liangying's letter were published in the *New York Times* in late May, the other shoe dropped, as Beijing police detained Wang Dan and several other veteran activists, including Liu Xiaobo, Huang Xiang, and Wang Xizhe. By early June the number of activists arrested in Beijing reached twenty-two, with forty-five others detained for questioning.[70]

Coming on the eve of the sixth anniversary of the PLA's assault on Tiananmen Square, the detention of prominent political activists served effectively to shut off debate on both political reform and the reversal of verdicts. Reportedly, members of the "rule by core" faction had become alarmed over the possibility that the raising of fresh demands for political reform and liberalization, coming at a time of intense "anticorruption fever," might lead to new street demonstrations—and then to more serious political disorders. Reflecting a reported rise in the level of political anxiety behind the walls of Zhongnanhai, the anticorruption campaign slowed down noticeably toward the end of May, with no further financial scandals uncovered and no new high-level perpetrators unmasked. Also reportedly instrumental in causing the campaign's slowdown was Jiang Zemin's desire to mollify Zhuo Lin. According to Hong Kong sources, after Zhuo suffered her stroke Jiang visited her in the hospital, where he promised to drop the criminal investigation of her son, Deng Zhifang.[71]

In late May the CC issued a decree instructing provincial and local party leaders to seek permission from higher levels before launching corruption probes involving senior officials; at the same time, journalists and party propagandists were instructed to "exercise restraint" in reporting corruption cases in the mass media. Henceforth, it appeared, the tiger's arse would be given wider berth.

As June 4 approached, public security was visibly tightened in and around Tiananmen Square and Beijing's Haidian university district. Although beefed-up police precautions had become something of an annual rite of spring since 1989, observers generally agreed it was the tightest security seen in the nation's capital since the first anniversary of the Tiananmen debacle.[72]

When June 4 came—and went—without incident, the newly muted anticorruption probe appeared to regain some of its lost momentum. In the early summer, discipline inspection teams, which had fanned out across the country during the spring, netted a number of second-tier "wolves," including the deputy governor of Hubei Province, the president of the Hebei Provincial People's Court, four county- and municipal-level cadres from "capitalist" Wenzhou, the deputy mayor of Shandong's Jining municipality, and the party boss and fourteen city officials from Jilin's Tonghua municipality.[73] Despite being under instruction to exercise restraint in reporting such cases, the official media took the lead in publicizing these developments.

The frequent atmospheric shifts and disjunctions that characterized Beijing's response to issues of corruption, dissent, the Tiananmen verdict, and agricultural recentralization, inter alia, suggested that latent tensions between the "rule by law" and "rule by core" factions were becoming more pronounced. As if to confirm this perception, a new aphorism made the rounds in Beijing in the spring of 1995. Based on a traditional Chinese proverb, *shuiluo, shichu* ("when the water recedes, the stones appear"), the new version, slightly altered, read *Jiangluo, Shichu*—"when the river [Jiang] recedes, [Qiao] Shi appears." With the Mandate of Heaven up for grabs, the competition showed signs of heating up.

For the superstitious, there were ominous portents of trouble ahead. In the early summer of 1995, hundred-year floods wracked the lower regions of the Yangzi River, killing 1,200 people, injuring 26,000, rendering 550,000 homeless, and stranding 1.4 million others.[74] Fortune-tellers were quick to point out that 1995 was a rare *renbayue*—"double August"—the lunar calendar's equivalent of a leap year.[75] Occurring only once each nineteen years, *renbayue* is believed to bring with it bad fortune. The last such double August was in 1976, the year of the great Tangshan earthquake—and Mao Zedong's death.

Burying Deng

After I die you'll raise trouble. You'll criticize my errors,

want to promote another program, want to overturn the

existing central work of the party, want to overturn

the situation of reform and openness.

—Deng Xiaoping

WITH the paramount leader incapacitated, with members of his family caught up in the fallout from a series of major corruption scandals, and with the country facing a number of daunting socioeconomic and political difficulties, Deng Xiaoping's legacy appeared at risk. It was a legacy laced with contradiction and paradox. Deng's truth-from-facts willingness to discard outmoded dogmas and his black-cats–white-cats readiness to tinker with China's basic economic institutions had led him boldly to venture where no Chinese leader—no leader anywhere in the communist world—had previously dared to go. Early on, Deng decoupled the engine of market competition (good) from the stigma of capitalist exploitation (bad) and threw open China's doors to the outside world, setting in motion a process of accelerated socioeconomic development and modernization. But while pressing hard with one foot on the developmental accelerator, Deng kept the other foot firmly on the political brake. The resulting disjunctive stress— marked by periodic overheating, episodic repression, and spasmodic forward progress —brought the system perilously close to the point of breakdown in 1989.

Notwithstanding the high frictional costs of a jerky, start-and-stop reform process and a massive, costly military crackdown, China's aggregate achievements in the age of Deng Xiaoping were impressive by any standard: From 1978 to 1994 China's GDP quadrupled to U.S. $2.9 trillion, making it the world's second largest economy, exceeding Japan; in the same period per capita income rose threefold to exceed $1,500, while annual exports increased from under $10 billion to over $120 billion.[1] By the mid-1990s China had become the world's third largest producer of crude steel, third largest shipbuilder, and number one manufacturer of shoes, sweaters, toys, and sporting goods. In terms of regional economic growth, by the mid-1990s China's booming southeastern coastal provinces had become so highly capitalized and so closely interlinked with the economies of neighboring Hong Kong and

Taiwan that the resulting regional configuration—referred to as "Greater China"—easily surpassed the resource base of the other East Asian "dragon" economies.[2]

But if burying Mao brought certain obvious benefits to China, it also entailed substantial costs. Rapid but uneven economic growth, accompanied by a deep erosion of traditional ideological norms and social controls, produced a situation high in raw entrepreneurial energy but low in institutionalized immunity to a wide variety of potential systemic disorders, ranging from rising regional inequality and uncontrolled rural emigration to a nationwide epidemic of crime, corruption, and popular cynicism. All this arguably rendered China more volatile politically than at any time since the late 1940s.

Writing in 1993, two Chinese social scientists, Wang Shaoguang and Hu An'gang, concluded that unless sharply rising trends toward regional economic polarization and fiscal and administrative decentralization were quickly and decisively reversed, Deng Xiaoping's death could trigger a crisis of disintegration similar to the one that occurred in Yugoslavia after Tito. Noting that disparities in wealth between China's coastal and interior regions had reached levels equal to or greater than those existing in Yugoslavia prior to its disintegration, the social scientists issued a serious warning: "If a 'political strongman' dies," they wrote, "it is possible that a situation like that in post-Tito Yugoslavia will emerge. . . . In a few years, or at most between ten and twenty, the country will move from economic collapse to political breakup, ending with disintegration." To prevent such a collapse, the scholars urged the central government immediately to reclaim fiscal and financial powers previously relinquished (or delegated) to the provinces.[3]

Solemn and sober-minded in their diagnosis of China's ills, Wang Shaoguang and Hu An'gang were by no means isolated academic outliers. Less than a year after they issued their warning, in March 1994 a stunningly frank and candid analysis of China's deepening sociopolitical malaise was published in Shanxi Province. Entitled *Viewing China through a Third Eye* (Disanzhi yanjing kan Zhongguo), the book raised the alarming specter of rampant rural lawlessness leading to a possible collapse of the regime. In the view of the book's pseudonymous author, "Dr. Leninger" (reputed to be a neoconservative CCP literary cadre named Wang Shan), Deng Xiaoping's decision to lift previous restraints on peasant mobility, marketing, and emigration had turned the Chinese countryside into an "active volcano" of tens of millions of aimless, crime-prone rural itinerants—the floating population. "Whenever millions of people move about blindly," wrote the author, "the resonance of their interacting emotions . . . can produce a powerful destructive force that can explode at any time."[4]

Holding Deng Xiaoping's reforms responsible for unwittingly undermining the ideological and moral authority of the CCP, the author of *Viewing China through a Third Eye*, who reportedly enjoyed the patronage of neoconservative princeling Chen Yuan, portrayed a country lurching dangerously out of control—a situation deemed "much more ominous than Russia's." Under China's current, unstable social conditions, he argued, events such as the 1989

Tiananmen incident "are bound to recur in the future, and will be extremely muddled and chaotic." To avoid a debilitating collapse of the social order, it would be necessary to stem forcibly the flow of rural emigration and vigorously combat the rising tide of lawlessness. To achieve this, an "appropriate strengthening of political controls" would be needed—supplemented by military force, since it was "a fact of life" that "in the absence of ideological authority . . . order is . . . the result of timid submission."[5]

While *Viewing China through a Third Eye* could perhaps be discounted as an overly alarmist, self-serving neoconservative polemic, it was difficult to dismiss a number of other warning signals simultaneously being sounded in other quarters. Writing in 1994, a political scientist in the Jiangsu provincial public security apparatus predicted that instability was very likely to rise after Deng's death, since "political authority [cannot] be maintained for very long based on personal charisma." The author went on implicitly to dispute Deng Xiaoping's claim that rapid economic growth would disarm and deflect popular demand for political change. "We cannot," he said, "arrive at the conclusion that politics will be stable when the economy is developed."[6] Also in 1994, the official *China Youth News* published a commentary by a prominent Chinese scholar, Lu Jianhua, suggesting that because of ambient societal stresses the process of transferring power from Deng to his successors would be inherently destabilizing. "The issue of unity during the transference of power," wrote Lu, "is the most difficult to tackle. Once an obstacle to unity arises, it will elicit massive personnel changes or policy reversals, leading to turbulence in the social situation."[7] Deliberately oblique and imprecise in his language, Lu's conclusion—that China was perched uncomfortably close to the edge of disorder—differed only by degrees from the dark, disturbing premonitions of *Third Eye*.

The principal difference among these worrisome assessments lay not in their marginally disparate diagnoses of the nature and severity of China's predicament, but in their sharply divergent prescriptions for what to do about it. Where neoconservatives (such as Wang Shan) saw the need for strong, centralized political power backed by military force to stem the rising tide of rural emigration and lawlessness, neo-authoritarians (such as Wang Shaoguang and Hu An'gang) preferred economic solutions, urging the central government firmly to apply fiscal levers and macroeconomic pressures to counteract growing regional disparities and fissiparous tendencies. Still others advocated more pluralistic political remedies to treat China's ills. Lu Jianhua, for example, urged the establishment of a "new form of control" involving institutionalized "checking and balancing mechanisms" to give legitimacy to the political system. "Stability must rely on a more flexible form of control," wrote Lu, one that can "effectively mediate various acute social contradictions" and deal with political conflicts "in a timely manner."[8]

Regardless of the particular prescriptive spin—neoconservative, neo-authoritarian, or democratic—being put on China's post-Deng predicament, one common denominator that linked these various assessments was their concern with the possibility of future turbulence. Such concern was further mirrored in

Chinese opinion polls. In December 1994 a survey commissioned by the Research Center of the CCP Central Committee confirmed the existence of widespread elite anxiety about China's future. Among 4,650 people surveyed in six Chinese cities (including 3,340 Communist Party members and 2,155 active or retired cadres), 88 percent expressed "some concern" over the possible outbreak of disturbances or instability after Deng's death; more than one-third (34 percent) indicated they had "much concern." In a second opinion poll, conducted by economist Hu An'gang among middle-ranking cadres studying at the Central Party School in Beijing, 84 percent of the respondents agreed that "an excessive disparity in regional economic development will affect China's social stability."[9]

As Deng Xiaoping approached his rendezvous with Marx, he appeared to display an awareness of the fragility of China's current situation—and of his own posterity. In a bedside meeting with his old comrade Bo Yibo he noted that "there are many people who [believe] that the political situation will change after I die." Predicting that "local disturbances" would arise, and that his opponents would try to "raise trouble . . . criticize my errors . . . [and] want to overturn the situation of reform and openness," Deng told his old friend to "uphold the line" and guard against disunity within the party.[10]

In his last known series of "instructions," issued in the summer of 1994— shortly before a team of eminent physicians reportedly certified him as incompetent—Deng expressed his concern for preserving the CCP's monopoly of political power. In July he adjured his comrades to eschew multiparty pluralism and to "properly draw the lesson from the former Soviet Union. . . . The CCP's status as the ruling party must never be challenged." In mid-August, on the eve of his ninetieth birthday, Deng issued a similar admonition. "The leadership of the Chinese Communist Party is unshakable," he avowed. Belying the firmness of his dictum, however, Deng alluded to two serious problems that needed to be "handled well" if China's stability was to be safeguarded: powerful centrifugal forces in the provinces and a growing contradiction between "rule by law" and "rule by personality" at the center.[11] In a subsequent statement, reportedly distributed to top party officials across the country toward the end of 1994, the paramount leader revised his menu of primary concerns: "Instability in the new era," he warned, "may come from three areas: the army, regionalism, and minority peoples." Regardless of which of Deng's worry lists was considered definitive, the fading patriarch had cause for concern.[12]

So, too, did his successors, designated and otherwise. For almost two decades, burying Mao had proved to be a highly delicate, deeply divisive undertaking, one that required strong leadership and superb balancing skills on Deng's part—and more than a modicum of good fortune as well. Now, as the age of Deng Xiaoping drew to a close and China began looking—and lurching—uncertainly toward the future, the task of burying Deng promised to be no less daunting.

• *A B B R E V I A T I O N S   U S E D   I N   T H E   N O T E S* •

AFP	Agence France Presse
AP	Associated Press
AW	Asiaweek
AWSJ	Asian Wall Street Journal
BR	Beijing Review
BX	Baixing
CD	China Daily
CKJP	Chung-kuo jih-pao
CKYC	Chung-kung yen-chiu
CLG	Chinese Law and Government
CLYK	Chaoliu yuekan
CNA	China News Analysis
CND	China News Digest (Global News)
CNS	China News Service
CQ	The China Quarterly
CR	China Review
CSM	Christian Science Monitor
CT	Chicago Tribune
DD	Dangdai
DGB	Dagong bao
DX	Dongxiang
DXF	Dongxifang
FBIS	Foreign Broadcast Information Service—China: Daily Report
FEER	Far Eastern Economic Review
FXYJ	Faxue yanjiu
GMRB	Guangming ribao
GRRB	Gongren ribao
HQ	Hongqi
HW	Hsinhua Weekly
I&S	Issues & Studies
ICM	Inside China Mainland
JB	Jing bao
JEN	Japan Economic Newswire
JFJB	Jiefangjun bao
JJRB	Jingji ribao
JJYJ	Jingji yanjiu
JPRS	Joint Publications Research Service
JSND	Jiushi niandai
LAT	Los Angeles Times
LHP	Lien-ho pao
LW	Liaowang
MB	Ming bao
NFRB	Nanfang ribao
NYT	The New York Times

PR	*Peking Review*
QS	*Qiushi*
QSND	*Qishi niandai*
RMRB	*Renmin ribao*
SCMP	*South China Morning Post*
SCMPW	*South China Morning Post Weekly*
SHKX	*Shehui kexue*
SJJJDB	*Shijie jingji daobao*
SWB/FE	*BBC Survey of World Broadcasts—Far East*
TGM	*Toronto Globe and Mail*
UPI	United Press International
WHB	*Wenhui bao*
WSJ	*Wall Street Journal*
WWP	*Wenwei po*
XB	*Xin bao*
XH	Xinhua
XZRB	*Xizang ribao*
ZB	*Zhong bao*
ZBYK	*Zhongbao yuekan*
ZGQNB	*Zhongguo qingnian bao*
ZGZC	*Zhongguo zhichun*
ZM	*Zhengming*
ZMRB	*Zhengming ribao*
ZW	*Zhanwang*

PREFACE

1. See Richard Baum, "The Road to Tiananmen: Chinese Politics in the 1980s," in Roderick MacFarquhar, ed., *The Politics of China, 1949–1989*.

NOTE ON SOURCES

1. Recent scholarly works in these genres include Kenneth Lieberthal and Michel Oksenberg, *Policy Making in China: Leaders, Structures, and Processes*; Kenneth Lieberthal and David M. Lampton, eds., *Bureaucracy, Politics, and Decision Making in Post-Mao China*; and Melanie Manion, *Retirement of Revolutionaries in China: Public Policies, Social Norms, Private Interests*.

2. Several excellent studies of this type have recently appeared in print. These include Dorothy Solinger, *China's Transition from Socialism: Statist Legacies and Market Reforms, 1980–1990*, Joseph Fewsmith, *Dilemmas of Reform in China: Political Conflict and Economic Debate*; Susan L. Shirk, *The Political Logic of Economic Reform in China*; and Gordon White, *Riding the Tiger: The Politics of Economic Reform in Post-Mao China*.

3. Frederick C. Teiwes, "Politics, Purges, and Rectification since the Third Plenum," 11–12.

INTRODUCTION
THE AGE OF DENG XIAOPING

1. The circumstances surrounding the deaths of Mao and Zhou are clarified by Mao's personal physician, Li Zhisui, *The Private Life of Chairman Mao*, chaps. 1, 89–91. See also Harrison Salisbury, *The New Emperors: China in the Era of Mao and Deng*, chap. 40; and Cao Weidong, *Hongbing li* (Red medical record), 326–80.

2. For variations on the theme of reform cycles in post-Mao China, see Tang Tsou, "Political Change and Reform: The Middle Course," 219–58; Harry Harding, *China's Second Revolution: Reform after Mao*, chap. 4; Lowell Dittmer, "Patterns of Elite Strife and Succession in Chinese Politics"; Carol Lee Hamrin, *China and the Challenge of the Future*, 4–7; and Susan L. Shirk, "Cycles in the Process of Reform: The Economic Consequences of Chinese-Style Economic Reforms." The existence of reform cycles in Soviet-style command economies was suggested by Gertrude Schroeder, "The Soviet Economy on a Treadmill of 'Reforms.'" The locus classicus for analysis of cyclical phenomena in modern Chinese politics remains G. William Skinner and Edwin A. Winckler, "Compliance Succession in Rural Communist China: A Cyclical Theory."

3. *Caiwu yu kuaiji* (Property and accounting), January 20, 1982, cited in Susan L. Shirk, "The Political Economy of Chinese Industrial Reform," 331.

4. Susan L. Shirk, "The Political Price of Reform Cycles: Elite Politics in Chinese-Style Economic Reforms."

5. This Dengist tactic has been referred to as "criticizing the Right to control the

Left." See, for example, Jeremy Paltiel, "The Interaction of Party Rectification and Economic Reform in the CCP, 1984."

6. Shirk, "The Political Price," 26. Lowell Dittmer and Yu-shan Wu, "The Modernization of Factionalism in Chinese Politics," 483–92, sketch out four synchronous cycles of politico-economic expansion and contraction from 1980 to 1987. A similar pattern, involving somewhat longer cycles, is posited by the pseudonymous author of *Viewing China through a Third Eye*, 10–13. In this controversial critique of China's economic and social development under Deng Xiaoping, variations in political cycles are seen as a direct consequence of boom-and-bust economic oscillations: "The rhythm with which the economy rises and falls directs the pace of political reform. During periods of freeze or readjustment of economic development . . . political retrenchment and thought control seem especially severe" (12).

7. Another cogent illustration of asynchronous turbulence within the reform cycle is provided by the swirling political and ideological crosscurrents of 1982–83. In the aftermath of the Twelfth Party Congress, held in the fall of 1982, CCP liberals and conservatives each launched major ideological initiatives designed to undercut their opponents' credibility and authority. The result was a vortex of political volatility, culminating in the intense but short-lived anti–spiritual pollution campaign of October–November 1983. The fluid properties of China's post-Mao reform cycles were first elaborated by Hamrin, *China and the Challenge*, 3, 9n.

8. Nina Halpern, "Economic Reform, Social Mobilization, and Democratization in Post-Mao China," has explored the role played by the post-Mao power struggle in creating momentum for China's reforms.

9. Debate over the reversibility of reform, and the plausibility of a Leftist restoration, has raged for well over a decade, both inside and outside China. Only after Deng Xiaoping's powerful proreform "spring offensive" of 1992, however, did China's liberal intellectuals begin to speak with any confidence of the long-term irreversibility of the reform process.

10. In its general outlines, the concept of factional politics employed here is consistent with the behavioral and cultural models elaborated by Andrew J. Nathan, "A Factionalism Model for CCP Politics," and Lucian W. Pye, *The Dynamics of Chinese Politics*, respectively. Where the present analysis tends to differ from both Nathan and Pye is in its delineation of the fluid metastructures and fluctuations of factional composition, competition, and conflict.

11. The structural logic of balance-of-power politics in the post-Mao period is examined by Avery Goldstein, *From Bandwagon to Balance-of-Power Politics: Structural Constraints and Politics in China, 1949–1978*, 211–24; and Pye, *The Dynamics of Chinese Politics*, 22–27.

12. Nathan, "A Factionalism Model," 44, notes that "Internal cleavages tend to be increased by the fruits of victory. . . . If [a] faction . . . achieves victory in a conflict arena as a whole, the unifying factor of a common enemy ceases to exist, while divisive factors such as struggle over spoils and efforts by smaller . . . factions to buy over component units increase in salience."

13. On the complex relationship between Chen Yun and Deng Xiaoping, see Teiwes, "Politics, Purges, and Rectification," 28–33.

14. The checkered relationship between Zhao and Hu in the early and mid-1980s, and the subsequent abandonment of both men by their erstwhile patron, Deng Xiaoping, lends support to Nathan's insight ("A Factionalism Model," 44) into a key source of factional cleavage and instability in China: "There is a tendency for vertical cleav-

ages to develop within the complex faction, running up to the level directly under the highest leader. . . . Even if loyalty prevents an open revolt against the leader, it permits political clashes and struggles among his subordinates."

15. See chapter 12.

16. Teiwes, "Politics, Purges, and Rectification," 11, suggests that the difficulties involved in analyzing the personal and factional ties that bind senior Chinese leaders to each other, to their clients, and to their protégés are a function of "the elusive nature of the political questions involved. . . . [R]elationships both within the ranks of party elders and between individual veterans and active administrators can only be grasped imperfectly if at all."

17. See Pye, *The Dynamics of Chinese Politics*, chap. 1 and passim. The opaqueness of factions also helps explain why it is so difficult empirically to describe their activities and operations.

18. In this connection, Dorothy Solinger notes that "members of the elite are . . . extremely careful about the various shades of meaning they are communicating by the use of particular phrases, listings of priorities, qualifications, and omissions. . . . [L]eaders have a purpose in selecting their particular wording." See Solinger, "The Fifth National People's Congress and the Process of Policy Making: Reform, Readjustment, and the Opposition," 1241. With respect to intellectuals and ordinary citizens, Perry Link notes that the propensity toward stereotyped terminological homogeneity in China is a result of "linguistic engineering" employed by the party to preserve its monopolistic power to define (and thereby exert control over) human behavior. See Link, *Evening Chats in Beijing: Probing China's Predicament*, 175–91, and *Stubborn Weeds: Popular and Controversial Chinese Literature after the Cultural Revolution*, 1–28.

19. Nathan, "A Factionalism Model," 47, 49, takes a rather different approach to this question. He argues that insofar as Chinese factions tend to compete within a "broad ideological consensus," they are likely to "exaggerate small differences" among themselves. Throughout most of the 1980s, I would argue, the obverse was more often the case, wherein subtle linguistic differences tended to mask increasingly pronounced (albeit fluid) ideological cleavages.

20. On the structural dynamics of bandwagoning in Chinese politics, see Goldstein, *From Bandwagon to Balance*, chap. 4.

21. Throughout this book I have capitalized the words Left and Right (Leftism and Rightism) when referring to specific Chinese ideological labels; in all other (i.e., generic) situations and usages of these terms I have employed the lowercase.

22. Barry Naughton, "Deng Xiaoping: The Economist," analyzes Deng's lack of a guiding theory of reform.

23. Stuart R. Schram, "China after the 13th Congress," explores this theme at greater length.

24. The CAC was finally abolished at the Fourteenth Party Congress in the autumn of 1992.

25. The paradoxical consequences of partial, stop-and-start reforms are examined in Shirk, "Cycles in the Process"; and David Zweig, "Dilemmas of Partial Reform."

26. On the new authoritarian agenda, see Stanley Rosen, "The Debate on the New Authoritarianism"; Mark Petracca and Mong Xiong, "The Concept of Chinese Neo-Authoritarianism: An Exploration and Democratic Critique"; and Ma Shu Yun, "The Rise and Fall of Neo-Authoritarianism in China."

27. The term is borrowed from Lowell Dittmer, "China in 1989: The Crisis of In-

complete Reform." On the hybrid nature of the Chinese economy, see Solinger, *China's Transition from Socialism*, esp. chaps. 5, 6, and 11.

28. On the failure of the student movement effectively to challenge the power of the Chinese Communist regime in 1989, see Elizabeth J. Perry, "Casting a Chinese 'Democracy' Movement: The Roles of Students, Workers, and Entrepreneurs."

CHAPTER 1
BURYING MAO

1. On the maltreatment of party leaders during the Cultural Revolution, see Salisbury, *The New Emperors*, chaps. 26–31.

2. Two other key members of the survivors group, Premier Zhou Enlai and Marshal Zhu De, had died earlier in the year. A handful of other veteran party and military leaders, including the legendary one-eyed Marshal Liu Bocheng, were too ill or infirm to participate in the September memorial service.

3. Although Chen Yun had not been formally purged during the Cultural Revolution, he was removed from the Politburo due to a series of long-standing policy disputes with Mao, dating back to the late 1950s. Chen passed the most tumultuous parts of the Cultural Revolution safely in hospital, where he had gone for treatment of an undisclosed—and reportedly not very serious—ailment. See Salisbury, *The New Emperors*, 211.

4. Liu Shaoqi died while still in disgrace in November 1969. The origins of Mao's dispute with Deng and Liu are examined in Lowell Dittmer, *Liu Shaoqi and the Chinese Cultural Revolution*; and Richard Baum, *Prelude to Revolution: Mao, the Party, and the Peasant Question, 1962–66*. On Mao's relationship with Chen Yun, see David Bachman, *Chen Yun and the Chinese Political System*.

5. In September 1971 Defense Minister Lin Biao allegedly attempted to assassinate Mao and seize power in a military coup. The attempt went awry and several key conspirators, including Lin, his wife Ye Qun, Army Chief of Staff Huang Yongsheng, and the commanders of the Chinese Navy and Air Force, inter alia, were killed or imprisoned. The incident reportedly had a severely depressing effect on military morale in China. See Michael Y. M. Kau, *The Lin Biao Affair*, introduction and passim; Salisbury, *The New Emperors*, chap. 32; and Roderick MacFarquhar, "The Succession to Mao and the End of Maoism, 1969–82," 268–75.

6. Deng's association with China's top military leaders included a childhood friendship with Nie Rongzhen, who later became one of ten PLA generals to be honored with the title of marshal. On the eve of the Long March in 1934, Deng was named general secretary of the General Political Department of the First Front Army. After the Japanese invasion, he served as political commissar of the 129th Division of the Eighth Route Army (later reorganized as part of the Second Field Army), under the command of Marshal Liu Bocheng. In this latter post Deng worked closely with generals Peng Dehuai, deputy commander of the Eighth Route Army, and Xu Xiangqian, deputy commander of the 129th Division. After moving to Beijing in 1952, Deng was named vice-chairman of the National Defense Council. For details on Deng's military career, see David S. G. Goodman, *Deng Xiaoping and the Chinese Revolution*, chap. 3.

7. The "four modernizations" (*sihua*) called for accelerated development in the fields of industry, agriculture, national defense, and science and technology. First articulated by Zhou Enlai in December 1964, the concept was shelved during the Cultural Revolution. It was then revived in Zhou's "Report on the Work of the Government" at

the first session of the Fourth NPC in January 1975. In 1979 Deng Xiaoping reversed the rank order of the last two modernizations, implying a diminution in the PLA's prestige.

8. Fan Shuo, *Ye Jianying zai 1976*, analyzes these events. Mao's personal decision to promote Deng to succeed Zhou Enlai is confirmed in *Peking Review* (hereafter *PR*) 20, 35 (August 26, 1977): 27.

9. For complete texts of the three documents, along with selected Leftist criticisms thereof, see Chi Hsin, *The Case of the Gang of Four—With First Translation of Teng Hsiao-ping's "Three Poisonous Weeds,"* 201ff. Several of Deng's 1975 speeches and commentaries appear in Deng Xiaoping, *Selected Works of Deng Xiaoping (1975–1982)*, 11–50.

10. Jürgen Domes, *The Government and Politics of the PRC: A Time of Transition*, 131, has calculated that in January 1976 Deng had only five or six active supporters on the Politburo, including members of the survivors faction and a few of his former PLA comrades; by contrast, the combined opposition reportedly numbered as many as fifteen.

11. See Salisbury, *The New Mandarins*, 343–44; Li Jian, *Deng Xiaoping sanjin sanchu Zhongnanhai* (Deng Xiaoping's three entrances and three exits from Zhongnanhai), 271–86; and *Zhongkan: Kang Sheng pingzhuan* (Pleasing to look at, bitter to taste: A critical biography of Kang Sheng), 320.

12. Cited in Hua Guofeng, "Political Report to the 11th National Congress of the Communist Party of China," 26–28. Although Mao reportedly coined the term Gang of Four (*siren bang*) in July 1974, it was not used publicly until two weeks after the arrest of the four radicals in October 1976. See Xinhua (hereafter *XH*), October 21, 1976.

13. Salisbury, *The New Emperors*, 340. Li, *The Private Life*, 480–81, 576–79, 600–601, and passim, describes the growing strain in Mao's relationship with Jiang Qing.

14. Hua, "Political Report," 28.

15. In the absence of any formal mechanism of majoritarian voting within the Politburo, Mao often resolved important policy and personnel debates by making unilateral decisions. Li Jian, *Deng Xiaoping sanjin*, 278–93, examines the events surrounding the death of Zhou Enlai and the promotion of Hua Guofeng.

16. Mao's physician, Li Zhisui, *The Private Life*, 610, confirms that Mao alone made the decision to elevate Hua, and that in doing so surprised his colleagues, most of whom had been anticipating the selection of Wang Hongwen. For biographical information on Hua Guofeng, see Ting Wang, *Chairman Hua: Leader of the Chinese Communists*; Dorothy Grouse Fontana, "Background to the Fall of Hua Guofeng"; and Michel Oksenberg and Cheung-yeung Sai, "Hua Guofeng's Pre-Cultural Revolution Hunan Years, 1949–66: The Making of a Political Generalist."

17. See, inter alia, *Renmin ribao* (People's daily; hereafter *RMRB*), March 10 and 28, 1976; *PR* 19, 11 (March 12, 1976); and *Hsinhua Weekly* (hereafter *HW*) 12 (March 22, 1976).

18. Principal sources for the following discussion include George Black and Robin Munro, *Black Hands of Beijing*, chap. 2; Li, *Deng Xiaoping sanjin*, 293–305; Qing Ye and Fang Lei, *Deng Xiaoping zai 1976, shangce: Tiananmen shijian* (Deng Xiaoping in 1976, vol. 1: The Tiananmen incident), 160–232; Jin Chunming, "Guanyu Tiananmen shijian" (Concerning the Tiananmen incident); Yan Jiaqi, *Siwu yundong jishi* (A true record of the April 5 movement); Roger Garside, *Coming Alive: China after Mao*, 101–30; Li, *The Private Life*, 611–13; and *Liangci Tiananmen shijian*.

19. The allusion to the empress dowager was a thinly masked jab at Jiang Qing,

while the references to Qinshihuang—brutal unifier of the first Chinese empire—were directed at Mao Zedong.

20. For a selection of slogans, poems, and eulogies that appeared on the Heroes' Monument, see Xiao Lan, ed., *The Tiananmen Poems*; Garside, *Coming Alive*, 108–18; *Renminde daonian* (The people's grief); and *HW*, April 12, 1976.

21. According to Deng Liqun, "Answers to Questions Concerning the 'Resolution on Certain Questions in the History of the Party since the Founding of the PRC,' " 47, both Ye Jianying and Li Xiannian missed the meeting due to illness. However, Qing and Fang, *Deng Xioaping zai 1976, shangce*, 171, claim that Li attended the meeting. Li Jian, *Deng Xiaoping sanjin*, 297, suggests that Mao may have personally ordered Ye Jianying's name excluded from the invitation list. This claim is supported by Marshal Ye's biographer, who notes that Ye had visited Tiananmen Square in his car on April 4 and was "deeply moved" by what he saw there. Indeed, one of the marshal's sons reportedly wrote a poem and affixed it to the Heroes' Monument. See Fan, *Ye Jianying*, 89–93.

22. The proceedings of the April 4 Politburo meeting are discussed in Qing and Fang, *Deng Xiaoping zai 1976, shangce*, 170–83.

23. "Crewcut shorty" was later identified as Chen Ziming, age twenty-four, a labor reform inmate who was in Beijing on a weekend pass at the time of the Qingming demonstration. Chen was originally incarcerated for making derogatory statements about the Gang of Four. Along with political activist Wang Juntao, Chen Ziming gained notoriety several years later when he was sentenced to thirteen years in prison for his role in the 1989 Tiananmen disturbance. See Black and Munro, *Black Hands*, 16–18, 28–29, 301–6.

24. The workers' militias were paramilitary mass organizations created by Leftist leaders during the Cultural Revolution. There were approximately 50,000 militia members in Beijing in 1976.

25. Qing and Fang, *Deng Xiaoping zai 1976*, 193–97.

26. Li, *The Private Life*, 440, 443, 450, and passim, implies that Mao's lack of mental acuity in his later years was due to a long-time addiction to barbiturates, which he consumed in large quantities to alleviate chronic insomnia.

27. Ibid., 213–20; also *HW*, April 12, 1976.

28. The two *RMRB* editorials are translated in *HW* 11 and 13 (March 15 and 29, 1976), respectively.

29. Qing and Fang, *Deng Xiaoping zai 1976, shangce*, 223–24.

30. Li Jian (*Deng Xiaoping sanjin*, 293) claims that as many as thirty thousand militia members were mobilized to participate in the crackdown. The arrest and casualty figures were reported by China's deputy minister of public security in an address delivered several weeks after the fact. See *Wenhui bao* (hereafter *WHB*), November 21, 1978. There are conflicting reports concerning whether any protesters died from injuries suffered during the April 5 crackdown. In January 1978 a wall poster placed at the foot of the Heroes' Monument demanded to know, "Why are we still being trifled with and told that nobody died in this square during the 'Tiananmen incident' when everyone knows that this is false?" See *Foreign Broadcast Information Service—China: Daily Report* (hereafter *FBIS*), January 12, 1978, E1. Despite such claims, reports of fatalities have never been substantiated by reliable eyewitnesses or official retrospectives (see, e.g., *Liangci Tiananmen shijian*). In the course of a subsequent official inquiry into the Qingming affair, General Wu Zhong, Beijing garrison commander at the time of the April disturbance, swore that no one had been killed. See Jin, "Guanyu

Tiananmen shijian," 282. This conclusion is supported by Chinese political scientist Yan Jiaqi, who conducted an exhaustive personal inquiry and found no evidence of Qingming fatalities—though he did note that there were some associated suicides. See Yan, *Siwu yundong*; and Salisbury, *The New Emperors*, 355, 516n.

31. Qing and Fang, *Deng Xiaoping zai 1976, shangce*, 231–32; Li, *Deng Xiaoping sanjin*, 295. Li, *The Private Life*, 612–13, reports that Jiang Qing visited Mao at 11:00 pm on April 5 to report on the successful suppression of "counterrevolutionaries." According to Dr. Li, after leaving her husband's quarters Mme. Mao invited him to join her in a *maotai* toast: "We are victorious," she said. "Bottoms up. I will become a bludgeon, ready to strike."

32. At Mao's suggestion, Deng was permitted to retain his party membership. See Li, *Deng Xiaoping sanjin*, 295–97. The text of the two Politburo resolutions appears in *HW* 15 (April 12, 1976): 3.

33. Deng and Xu had served together in the PLA's 129th Division during the anti-Japanese war.

34. See *Chung-kuo jih-bao* (*China daily*; hereafter *CKJP*), December 20, 1977, in *FBIS*, December 20, 1977, E17; *Inside China Mainland* (hereafter *ICM*) 2, 7 (July 1980): 15; and Salisbury, *The New Emperors*, 355–56.

35. Quan Yanchi, *Canzhuo shangde Zhonggong lingxiu* (Chinese Communist leaders at the dinner table), 1–13.

36. Ibid.; also Li, *Deng Xiaoping sanjin*, 300–312; and Cao, *Hongbing li*, 417–22.

37. *RMRB*, November 21, 1978; and *Chung-kung yen-chiu* (Studies in Chinese communism; hereafter *CKYC*) 10, 5 (1976): 20–25.

38. According to a memorandum written by Wang Zhen, under duress Hu Qiaomu cooperated with the Leftists' investigation of Deng's "counterrevolutionary" behavior, providing damaging testimony concerning the origins of Deng's "three poisonous weeds." Later, however, Deng Xiaoping would forgive Hu, calling him "spineless, but not a betrayer." Unlike Hu Qiaomu, Deng Liqun refused to cooperate with the Leftists, remaining steadfastly loyal to Deng Xiaoping throughout the latter's period in the political wilderness. See Fewsmith, *Dilemmas of Reform*, 81, n. 13; and Liu Binyan, *"Tell the World": What Happened in China and Why*, 76–77.

39. On this point, see *FBIS*, July 10, 1981, W2–3; also Andres D. Onate, "Hua Kuo-feng and the Arrest of the 'Gang of Four.'" Party theorist Deng Liqun, "Answers to Questions," 14, concedes that Mao actually penned the six characters but argues that they were written to show the Chairman's support for the way Hua handled a particular problem, not to bestow supreme party leadership on him. "It meant," wrote Deng, "'I am comfortable with the way you handled this.' . . . It definitely did not touch upon . . . the question of whether Hua should become his successor."

40. Early in 1975 Mao had reportedly warned his colleagues that "Jiang Qing has wild ambitions. She wants . . . to be chairman of the Party Central Committee." Quoted in Chi, *The Case of the Gang of Four*, 27. See also *PR* 20, 35 (August 26, 1977): 27.

41. Note, for example, the headline that appeared over a Xinhua news release of August 4, 1976: "Premier Hua Guofeng Leads Central Delegation to Earth-quake-Stricken Area to Convey Loving Care of Chairman Mao and Party Central Committee."

42. *RMRB*, August 11, 1976.

43. According to subsequent accounts, what Mao actually said was "act according to *past* principles" (*an guoqu fangzhen ban*). The difference between the two terms, though subtle, was highly significant, insofar as "established principles" suggests con-

tinuity between past and present (i.e., preservation of the post–Cultural Revolution status quo) while "past principles" carries a more discontinuous, restorative meaning (i.e., implying the need to return to discarded pre–Cultural Revolution policies). On this point see Onate, "Hua Guofeng," 548–49; and Deng Liqun, "Answers to Questions," 15.

44. The text of Hua's eulogy appears in *RMRB*, September 19, 1976.

45. In the following account of the events surrounding Mao's death, I have drawn principally upon material presented in Fan, *Ye Jianying*, 120–308; Qing Ye and Fang Lei, *Deng Xiaoping zai 1976, xiace: Huairentang shibian* (Deng Xiaoping in 1976, vol. 2: The incident at Huairen hall); Onate, "Hua Guofeng"; and Keith Forster, "China's Coup of October 1976."

46. Deng Liqun, "Answers to Questions," 48. According to Ye Jianying's biographer, Chen Yun initially demurred from a proposal to arrest the four radical leaders, questioning the legality of such action. See Fan, *Ye Jianying*, 209–10.

47. The Maoist adjuration to "act according to established principles" first appeared in a September 16, 1976, editorial jointly published in *People's Daily, Hongqi* (Red flag; hereafter *HQ*), and *Jiefangjun bao* (Liberation Army daily; hereafter *JFJB*).

48. *History of the Chinese Communist Party: A Chronology of Events (1919–1990)*, 377. Forster, "China's Coup," 282–83, evaluates evidence supporting these allegations.

49. Forster, "China's Coup," 277–78, 282–83. After reviewing available evidence of Leftist mobilization, Forster suggests that the radicals may well have been expecting Hua Guofeng's supporters to launch a coup; hence, their preparations for struggle may have been more defensive than offensive in character.

50. There is some confusion over just how and where the four were arrested. According to Li, *The Private Life*, 634–35, Zhang Chunqiao and Wang Hongwen were seized by officers from Wang Dongxing's Central Garrison Corps as the two radicals arrived at the Huairen conference hall in Zhongnanhai, where they had been summoned by Hua Guofeng and Ye Jianying on the pretext of attending a Politburo meeting. Yao Wenyuan and Jiang Qing were late for the meeting, and were arrested at their respective living quarters a short time later. This version of events is generally supported by Fan, *Ye Jianying*, 293–300, and by Qing and Fang, *Deng Xiaoping zai 1976, xiace*. A colorful and perhaps somewhat apocryphal version of the capture of Jiang Qing holds that when Jiang was placed under arrest by Admiral Su Zhenhua, she cursed him and blurted out, "Before Chairman Mao's bones are even cold you are already doing this. What is this but a counterrevolutionary coup?" To which Admiral Su reportedly replied, "I don't care who's afraid of you; I'm not!" Thereupon, Su allegedly pulled the wig off Mme. Mao's head, leaving her bald and cursing. See *Zhengming* (hereafter *ZM*) 37 (November 1980), in *ICM* 2, 12 (December 1980): 12–14.

51. During the 1980 trial of the Gang of Four it was alleged that just prior to Mao's death, followers of the four Leftists in the Shanghai municipal committee distributed 74,000 rifles and ten million rounds of ammunition to workers' militias througout the city. Two days after the arrest of the Gang, on October 8, 1976, Shanghai party leaders deployed 33,500 armed militia in preparation for a coup attempt. See *Beijing Review* (hereafter *BR*) 23, 47 (November 24, 1980): 16-17. For analysis of the situation in Shanghai at the time of the arrest of the Gang, see Salisbury, *The New Emperors*, 375–76.

52. XH, October 8, 1976, emphasis added. Fan Shuo (*Ye Jianying*, 288) claims that immediately after the coup, Hua offered to forfeit his claim to the post of party chairman in favor of Ye, but that Ye refused on the grounds that Chairman Mao had person-

ally chosen Hua as his successor. Notwithstanding Ye's close friendship with Deng Xiaoping, to the end of his life the old marshal stubbornly supported Hua Guofeng's leadership claim—presumably out of his deep sense of personal loyalty to Mao Zedong.

53. XH, October 9, 1976 (emphasis in original). Although this was not the first published appearance of Mao's warning against splitting and conspiring, on previous occasions it had been coupled with the Chairman's alleged adjuration to "act according to established principles" (see, e.g., *RMRB*, October 1, 1976). The appearance of the former injunction without the latter proviso in the period after October 6 indicated an important shift in the direction of the accusatory arrow, which now pointed sharply toward the Left.

54. *RMRB*, *HQ*, and *JFJB*, October 10, 1976; XH, October 10, 1976.

55. *History of the Chinese Communist Party*, 379.

56. I am indebted to Tony Saich for providing an eyewitness account of these events.

57. XH, October 24, 1976.

58. Tan Zongji, "Shiyiju sanzhong quanhui shi jianguo yilai dangde lishide weida zhuanzhe" (The third plenum of the 11th Central Committee is a great turning point in the party's history since 1949), 329.

59. Hand-copied facsimiles of this letter, together with a second missive written by Deng in April 1977, circulated informally among party members in Beijing. The former editor of *RMRB*, Hu Jiwei, first publicly revealed their existence in a speech to the Central Party School in September 1979. See *ZM* 34 (August 1980): 51. I am indebted to Richard Siao for making available to me the texts of the two letters.

60. *RMRB*, October 25, 1976.

61. *History of the Chinese Communist Party*, 379.

62. The "two whatevers" were first spelled out in a proloyalist *RMRB* editorial of February 7, 1977: "Whatever decisions Chairman Mao made we will resolutely support. Whatever instructions Chairman Mao issued we will steadfastly obey."

63. The first hint of He Long's rehabilitation appeared in an article in the Guangzhou party newspaper, *Nanfang ribao* (Southern daily; hereafter *NFRB*), on December 26, 1976. In it, the deceased revolutionary hero was referred to as "Comrade He Long." See Domes, *The Government and Politics*, 145.

64. Certain provincial leaders—most notably in Hua's home province of Hunan—continued to refer periodically to Deng's "Right deviationist wind" up until February 1977.

65. See *Issues & Studies* (hereafter *I&S*) 13, 8 (August 1977): 63.

66. Garside, *Coming Alive*, 162; Domes, *The Government and Politics*, 146.

67. *HQ* 2 (February 1977): 17.

68. The text of the generals' letter, made available in Taiwan, appears in *Der Spiegel* 31, 17 (April 1977): 161–64. Its most critical passages, translated by Domes, *The Government and Politics*, 146–47, read as follows: "Everybody has, in his heart, taken account of all merits and mistakes of Chairman Mao. If the party center continues to hush up his shortcomings and mistakes . . . the authority of the party among the masses must suffer. . . . During his lifetime, Chairman Mao branded all comrades in the party who dared to air opinions disagreeing with him as class enemies. . . . [W]e cannot deny that there have been cases where such an evaluation was incorrect . . . and this category includes the problems of Comrade Peng Dehuai and Comrade Deng Xiaoping. . . . We do not need to emphasize that the basis for Comrade Hua Guofeng's

appointment as chairman of the Central Committee are the words of Chairman Mao: 'With you in charge, I'm at ease!' No matter how these golden words may shine, they can only represent Chairman Mao's personal opinion, and cannot express the will of the party, the army, and the people."

Despite its evident verisimilitude, the authenticity of this letter has been called into question on the grounds that its criticism of Mao was far too blunt and direct for the time period in which it was purportedly written. I am indebted to Richard Siao for bringing this to my attention.

69. Sources for the following discussion include Ruan Ming, *Deng Xiaoping diguo* (The empire of Deng Xiaoping), 41–43; Tan, "Shiyiju sanzhong quanhui," 323–58; *Ming bao* (hereafter *MB*), May 26 and 27, 1977; Garside, *Coming Alive*, 165–67; and MacFarquhar, "The Succession to Mao," 311–16.

70. Tan, "Shiyiju sanzhong quanhui," 331.

71. Although the full text of Deng's April 10 letter has never been officially released, I have obtained a hand-copied facsimile. Its contents conform closely to a paraphrased report that appeared as "Central Committee Document No. 15 (1977)." See *MB*, May 27, 1978, and Garside, *Coming Alive*, 167. A partial text of Deng's April 10 letter also appears in *BR* 24, 44 (November 2, 1981): 24.

72. "The 'Two Whatevers' Do Not Accord with Marxism" (May 24, 1977), in Deng, *Selected Works*, 51.

73. Garside, *Coming Alive*, 166–67.

74. "Mao Zedong Thought Must Be Correctly Understood as an Integral Whole" (July 21, 1977), in Deng, *Selected Works*, 55–60.

75. Ibid., 58–59.

CHAPTER 2
DENG TAKES COMMAND

1. See *PR* 20, 35 (August 26, 1977): 6–13; also *I&S* 13, 11 (November 1977): 21–34.

2. The text of the 1977 Party Constitution appears in *PR* 20, 36 (September 2, 1977): 16–23.

3. Ye's speech appears in ibid., 23–38. The old marshal's strong show of support for Hua's leadership was reportedly due to two factors: his personal respect for Mao's choice of Hua as his successor, and his concern that serious political instability might ensue if Hua were to be deposed.

4. Hua Guofeng, "Political Report," 26–28.

5. Ibid., 27–28.

6. After the Eleventh Party Congress the four imprisoned radicals were referred to generically as a "counterrevolutionary clique" (*fan'geming jituan*), a term that avoided the delicate issue of directionality. By the time of the Third Plenum of the Eleventh CC, held in December 1978, the policies of the Cultural Revolution era were openly termed "Leftist." See *History of the Chinese Communist Party*, 394–95. At the Fourth Plenum of the Eleventh CC, in September 1979, the political orientation of the Gang was officially labeled "ultra-Leftist."

7. Hua, "Political Report," 29.

8. In his closing statement, Deng did refer to Hua as chairman of the Congress Presidium, but not as chairman of the Central Committee.

9. Deng's speech appears in *PR* 20, 36 (September 2, 1977): 38–40.

10. The importance of subtle terminological distinctions as indicators of serious disagreement among rival CCP factions and leaders is examined in Dorothy Solinger, "The Fifth National People's Congress and the Process of Policy Making: Reform, Readjustment, and the Opposition," 1240–42. For further analysis of mounting tensions in the Deng-Hua relationship in 1977, see *I&S* 13, 12 (December 1977): 10–27.

11. Along with Deng, Hu was criticized in the spring of 1976 for his role in drafting the 1975 report "On Some Problems Concerning the Work of Science and Technology"—one of Deng's notorious "three poisonous weeds." Although Deng has generally been regarded as Hu Yaobang's main patron, Frederick Teiwes, "Politics, Purges, and Rectification," 7, suggests that Chen Yun may have been Hu's prime backer. For details of Hu's life and career, see Wang Shu-hsin, "Hu Yaobang: New Chairman of the Chinese Communist Party," and Yang Zhongmei, *Hu Yaobang: A Chinese Biography*.

12. *PR* 20, 47 (November 18, 1977): 4–9.

13. *FBIS*, December 15, 1977, E1, and January 27, 1978, E1–2.

14. The text of Hua's report appears in *PR* 21, 10 (March 10, 1978): 7–40.

15. Solinger, "The Fifth National People's Congress," 1247, notes Hua's appropriation of Deng's 1975 proposals.

16. In view of the manifest ambivalence of Hua's report, it is almost certain that the speech was collectively written. Important speeches are often drafted by a writing group and frequently go through several successive drafts. The speaker may shape the principal thrust of his or her message, but there is substantial opportunity for input and emendation by others, including people holding opposing viewpoints.

17. *PR* 21, 10 (March 10, 1978): 22, 24–26.

18. Ibid., 30.

19. Hua's role in China's post-Mao intellectual renaissance may help explain why he continued to receive substantial delegate support for Central Committee (and even Politburo) membership at party congresses long after he had been effectively removed from power by Deng Xiaoping in 1980–81.

20. The text of the 1978 State Constitution appears in *PR* 21, 11 (March 17, 1978): 5–14.

21. Liu Shaoqi had been the last incumbent to hold the office of state chairman; after his death in 1969, the office remained unfilled until its elimination by constitutional revision in 1975.

22. For further analysis, see *I&S* 14, 4 (April 1978): 8–9.

23. Ye's report appears in *PR* 21, 11 (March 17, 1978): 15–28.

24. *PR* 21, 10 (March 10, 1978): 31.

25. Li's early opposition to Hua's plan is reported in Tan, "Shiyiju sanzhong quanhui," 343–44.

26. For further analyses of factional alignments in this period, see Solinger, "The Fifth National People's Congress"; Parris Chang, "Chinese Politics: Deng's Turbulent Quest"; and Dorothy Grouse Fontana, "Background to the Fall of Hua Guofeng."

27. On the Bohai gulf disaster, see *ICM* 2, 9 (September 1980): 19–20; and 2, 10 (October 1980): 17–19. On the Baoshan steel mill, see Martin Weil, "The Baoshan Steel Mill."

28. See Willy Kraus, *Economic Development and Social Change in the People's Republic of China*, 284–89; and Domes, *The Government and Politics*, 197–200.

29. See Fontana, "Background to the Fall," 241–49.

30. This may help to explain why there is remarkably little discussion of economic

affairs in those sections of Deng's *Selected Works* covering the early years of reform. See David Bachman, "Differing Visions of China's Post-Mao Economy: The Ideas of Chen Yun, Deng Xiaoping, and Zhao Ziyang."

31. Deng's speech appears in *PR* 21, 12 (March 24, 1978): 9–18. It is interesting to note that in this speech Deng refers at least three times to the leadership of "Chairman Hua" rather than "Comrade Hua," as before.

32. For more on this comparison, see Richard Baum, *Scientism and Bureaucratism in Post-Mao China: Cultural Limits of the "Four Modernizations."*

33. *PR* 21, 12 (March 24, 1978): 12.

34. Ibid., 11, 14–16.

35. *PR* 21, 18 (May 5, 1978): 7.

36. Ibid., 8, 11–12.

37. These latter proposals were revealed to the author in the course of interviews with faculty members at Nanjing University in September 1978.

38. Deng Liqun, *FangRi huilai de sisu* (Thoughts upon returning from Japan), 2, cited in Joseph Fewsmith, *Dilemmas of Reform*, 36.

39. *Guangming ribao* (hereafter *GMRB*), May 11, 1978. For a history of the intra-party debate over the "criterion of truth," see Ruan Ming, *Lishi zhuanzhedianshangde Hu Yaobang* (Hu Yaobang at the turning point in history); also Michael Schoenhals, "The 1978 Truth Criterion Controversy," 243–48.

40. The article's author was reported to be Hu Fuming, a philosophy instructor at Nanjing University. Hu Yaobang's role in the publication of the article is discussed in Tan, "Shiyiju sanzhong quanhui," 334–35, and Schoenhals, "The 1978 Truth Criterion Controversy." In an interview with Stuart Schram ("'Economics in Command'? Ideology and Politics since the Third Plenum," 419) some years after the fact, Hu Fuming stated that he wrote the article on his own initiative. More recently, however, a number of Chinese intellectuals, including the eminent writer Dai Qing, have claimed that others—principally Sun Changjiang—played a key role in drafting the article. See Merle Goldman, "Hu Yaobang's Intellectual Network and the Theory Conference of 1979."

41. "Speech at the All-Army Conference on Political Work" (June 2, 1978), in Deng, *Selected Works*, 128.

42. Ibid., 128–31.

43. *RMRB*, June 4 and 5, 1978. Although Ye Jianying had been highly instrumental in securing Deng Xiaoping's rehabilitation, both he and Li Xiannian remained decidedly cool toward Deng's subsequent efforts to depose Hua Guofeng and discredit "whateverism," fearing that this would foster political instability. On this point, cf. Fontana, "Background to the Fall," 238–41, and MacFarquhar, "The Succession to Mao," 313–14.

44. *ZM* 34 (August 1980): 51.

45. See *FBIS*, April 4, 5, 6, 10, 11, and 14, 1978.

46. *RMRB*, June 24, 1978. The article in question was reportedly written jointly by Wu Jiang and Sun Changjiang for publication in the theoretical journal of the Central Party School in Beijing; however, pressure exerted on Party School Vice-President Hu Yaobang by Wang Dongxing and Hu Qiaomu, among others, led to the article being shelved. Thereafter, General Luo Ruiqing—a longtime friend of Deng Xiaoping—made some personal revisions in the article and secured its publication in *People's Daily*. See Ruan, *Lishi zhuanzhedian*, 14.

47. *RMRB*, July 1, 1978.

48. Hu Qiaomu's proposals appear in *FBIS*, October 11, 1978, E1–22. For further analysis, see Fewsmith, *Dilemmas of Reform*, 60–62.

49. *Qishi niandai* (The seventies; hereafter *QSND*) 106 (November 1978): 6–13, in *FBIS*, November 9, 1978, N2–5. On Hu Yaobang's recommendation, Hua Guofeng later approved for distribution the offending issue of *China Youth.*

50. Two other unrelated reform-oriented Hus—Hu Qiaomu and Hu Keshi, the latter a longtime CYL associate of Hu Yaobang—were also part of the inner circle of reform politicians in this period, thus giving rise to the term *wu Hu luan Hua* (the five Hus bring turmoil to China), a classical allusion to a particularly chaotic period in the history of the Tang dynasty. A sixth proreform Hu—a young Gansu construction cadre named Hu Jintao—was promoted to the post of second secretary of the CYL in 1982.

51. See *FBIS*, November 15, 1978, E3.

52. *RMRB*, November 24, 1978, in *FBIS*, December 5, 1978, E6.

53. *FBIS*, November 9, 1978, N2–5.

54. *ZM* 13 (November 1978): 51–52, in *FBIS*, November 9, 1978, N6–9.

55. *China Record*, November 1978, 4; cf. June Teufel Dreyer, "Deng Xiaoping: The Soldier."

56. Roger Garside records these events in *Coming Alive*, 183–86.

57. *FBIS*, December 1, 1978, E8.

58. Peng Zhen, Yang Shangkun, and Tao Zhu had been closely associated with Deng Xiaoping at least since the 1950s, when all three worked under Deng's command in the Central Party Secretariat.

59. *MB*, January 12, 1979, 3, in *FBIS*, January 17, 1979, N2–3. Chen's speech appears in Chen Yun, *Chen Yun wenxuan, 1956–1985* (Selected works of Chen Yun), vol. 3. For further analysis, see Wang Hongmo, *Gaige kaifang de licheng* (The course of reform and opening up), 122–23; and MacFarquhar, "The Succession to Mao," 319–21.

60. *FBIS*, January 17, 1979, N4.

61. Xiao Lan, *The Tiananmen Poems.*

62. According to knowledgeable Chinese sources, Hu Yaobang had initially argued strongly for blanket amnesty for all "Rightists" who had been labeled in 1957; he eventually agreed to settle for something less than an all-inclusive amnesty because his mentor, Deng Xiaoping, had been deeply involved in implementing the 1957 anti-Rightist campaign. Indeed, it was Deng who had reportedly conceived the idea of sending errant intellectuals down to the countryside for reeducation. See Goodman, *Deng Xiaoping*, 57–58.

63. Tan, "Shiyiju sanzhong quanhui," 349–51.

64. *FBIS*, January 23, 1979, N4. Deng's sardonic references to Engels and Stalin were omitted from the official transcript of his speech, which appears in Deng, *Selected Works*, 151–65.

65. Two notable exceptions were Peng Zhen and Liu Shaoqi, whose cases were held over for further investigation. Peng was rehabilitated early in 1979, Liu was cleared of wrongdoing a year later.

66. The official communiqué of the Third Plenum appears in *PR* 21, 52 (December 29, 1978): 6–16.

67. Other Deng supporters appointed to the CC at the Third Plenum were generals Huang Kecheng and Chen Zaidao, Huang Huoqing, Han Guang, and Zhou Hui. All had been purged during the Cultural Revolution.

68. Deng Xiaoping had occupied the post of general secretary prior to the Cultural Revolution. With the formal abolition of the Central Party Secretariat in 1969, day-to-

day control over party personnel and administration gravitated toward the CC General Office under Wang Dongxing. It was to help reverse this trend that Hu Yaobang was appointed "chief secretary" at the Third Plenum. Although Hu's new post was less imposing (and less powerful) than the previous office of general secretary, once the Central Secretariat was formally revived in February 1980, the earlier title was restored. Thereafter, Hu Yaobang became titular head of the CCP, and the CC General Office declined substantially in political importance.

69. See *QSND* 109 (February 1979): 8; *ZM* 15 (January 1979): 18; Chang, "Chinese Politics," 10. The General Office of the Central Committee is responsible, among other things, for overseeing the personnel files (*dang'an*) of party officials; through his control over these highly sensitive files, Wang Dongxing had been able to delay the rehabilitation of several prominent Cultural Revolution purge victims.

70. Chen Yonggui had been party secretary of the notorious Dazhai brigade in Shanxi Province. Under Mao Zedong's patronage Chen became a national model cadre in the 1960s. The Dazhai model came under increasingly critical scrutiny after Mao's death, culminating in Chen's fall from grace in 1980.

71. On the organization, personnel, and operations of the CDIC, see Jean-Pierre Cabestan, *L'Administration Chinoise après Mao: Les Réformes de l'ère Deng Xiaoping et Leurs Limite* (Chinese administration after Mao: The reforms of the Deng Xiaoping era and their limits), 345–67; and Graham Young, "Control and Style: Discipline Inspection Commissions since the 11th Congress."

72. Merle Goldman, "Hu Yaobang's Intellectual Network," 231, notes that the task of drafting the Third Plenum's communiqué had originally been given to a group associated with Hua Guofeng and Wang Dongxing, but that in the wake of strong criticism directed at the "whateverists" at the November 1978 CC work conference, Deng managed to have the task reassigned to Hu Yaobang.

CHAPTER 3
THE FIRST FANG/SHOU CYCLE

1. Early in 1978 proreform party leaders acknowledged that the Chinese economy had registered little or no improvement in per capita production and consumption of food for over twenty years, and that the government had "by no means solved the problem of feeding hundreds of millions of people" (*GMRB*, May 22, 1978).

2. Hamrin, *China and the Challenge*, chap. 3, and Harding, *China's Second Revolution*, chaps. 5–7, examine these developments.

3. On the rules governing decision making by consensus, see Shirk, *The Political Logic*, chap. 7.

4. Chen Yun's speech to the April CC work conference appears in *ICM* 2, 4 (April 1980): 1–7.

5. Quoted in Hamrin, *China and the Challenge*, 54, n. 4.

6. On the origins and early development of the SEZs, see Thomas Chan et al., "China's Special Economic Zones: Ideology, Policy, and Practice."

7. Both Ye Jianying and Li Xiannian nominally endorsed Chen's plan, while Hua Guofeng reportedly remained noncommittal. See Tan, "Shiyiju sanzhong quanhui," 344, and Fewsmith, *Dilemmas of Reform*, 90–91.

8. On Chen Yun's readjustment policy, and his mounting conflict with the petroleum group in 1979, see ibid. 87–92.

9. This helps to explain subsequent efforts by Chen Yun's supporters to reclaim for

him a fair share of credit for having designed China's post-Mao reforms (see chapter 4). On Sun Yefang's contribution to the theory of economic reform, see Barry Naughton, "Sun Yefang: Toward a Reconstruction of Socialist Economics." For a comparison of the economic reform proposals of Chen Yun and Xue Muqiao, see Dorothy Solinger, "Economic Reform via Reformulation in China: Where Do Rightist Ideas Come From?," 948–50. For comparison of the economic thinking of Chen Yun, Zhao Ziyang, and Deng Xiaoping, see Bachman, "Differing Visions."

10. See Greg O'Leary and Andrew Watson, "The Production Responsibility System and the Future of Collective Farming," and David Zweig, "The System of Responsibility: National Policy and Local Implementation."

11. Fewsmith, *Dilemmas of Chinese Reform*, 34–41. Hu Qiaomu's opposition to the household responsibility system is reported in Ruan, *Deng Xiaoping diguo*, chap. 5. In the early 1980s Chen Yizi's rural development group became a major source of ideas and inspiration for Deng Xiaoping's economic reforms. After the Tiananmen debacle of 1989 many of the group's former leaders, including Chen Yizi, were placed on the Chinese government's "most wanted" list for their alleged activities in support of "counterrevolutionary turmoil."

12. Prior to the Cultural Revolution, Zhao Ziyang had been first secretary of the Guangdong Provincial Party Committee. Wan Li had served with Deng in the Southwest Military-Administrative Command after the revolution. Later he became deputy mayor of Beijing under Peng Zhen. After the Cultural Revolution Wan served as minister of urban planning and minister of railroads. While in the latter post, Wan intervened decisively to end a series of Leftist-inspired railway strikes in 1975.

13. Under Wan Li's leadership, Anhui became the first province to renounce the Hua Guofeng-backed "Dazhai model" of rural egalitarianism and self-reliance in the winter of 1977–78. See Fewsmith, *Dilemmas of Reform*, chap. 1; also Salisbury, *The New Emperors*, 384–86. A popular piece of rural doggerel at the time held that "If you want rice, Wan Li's nice; if you want food, [Zhao] Ziyang's good." (*Yao chimi, zhao Wan Li; yao chifan, zhao Ziyang*). See *Viewing China*, 26.

14. On the Sichuan and Anhui experiments, see David Shambaugh, *The Making of a Premier: Zhao Ziyang's Provincial Career*, chap. 6; Fewsmith, *Dilemmas of Reform*, chaps. 1–2; *HQ* 3 (March 1978): 92–97; and *BR* 24, 34 and 24, 35 (August 24 and August 31, 1981): 21–26, 14–18.

15. On the composition and functions of these four research groups, see Nina Halpern, "Making Economic Policy: The Influence of Economists."

16. Hamrin, *China and the Challenge*, chap. 3, examines these developments.

17. For a map of central Beijing, see p. 277.

18. On the role of dazibao in modern Chinese politics, see Goran Leijonhufvud, *Going against the Tide: On Dissent and Big-Character Posters in China.*

19. The Chinese government later published the book. See Xiao, *The Tiananmen Poems.*

20. In the discussion that follows, I have relied extensively on Garside, *Coming Alive*, 195–243; John Fraser, *The Chinese: Portrait of a People*, 203–71; Kjeld Erik Brodsgaard, "The Democracy Movement in China, 1978–79: Opposition Movements, Wall Poster Campaigns, and Underground Journals"; Andrew J. Nathan, *Chinese Democracy*, 3–44; James D. Seymour, *The Fifth Modernization: China's Human Rights Movement*; and James Tong, "Underground Journals in China." Unless otherwise noted, passages quoted from wall posters and underground journals have been drawn from these sources.

21. The policy of sending senior middle school graduates to rural or urban work units for two years of manual labor prior to admission to college had been introduced in the late 1960s as a means of screening out politically unacceptable applicants. The policy was discontinued shortly after Mao's death, and nationwide unified college entrance examinations were resumed in 1977. However, by that time the backlog of college applicants was so great that the vast majority of "sent-down" middle school graduates of the Cultural Revolution era (most of whom were rather poorly educated due to the Leftists' stress on political and ideological indoctrination rather than academic study) were unable to compete successfully for college entrance. This huge cohort of semi-educated youths has been referred to as China's "lost generation."

22. The lack of widespread participation by students and professional intellectuals has been attributed to two factors: first, an elitist sense of self-importance, which in the heady atmosphere of late 1978 included a strong expectation that intellectuals would soon be called upon to play an important role in the country's modernization drive and hence had best "keep their noses clean"; and second, the Chinese intelligentsia's deeply ingrained fear of political retribution, born of two decades of recurrent, bitter experience.

23. *ZM* 22 (August 1979): 44. Two rather more benign versions of Deng's comment to his Japanese visitors were published in the official *RMRB* and the semi-official Hong Kong *Dagong bao* (hereafter *DGB*), respectively. In the former version, Deng was quoted as saying that "The masses' putting up big-character posters is a normal phenomenon, and is permitted by the Chinese constitution." See *FBIS*, December 19, 1978, N4–5; and *New York Times* (hereafter *NYT*), November 27, 1978, A1. In the latter version, it was claimed that Deng had informed his Japanese guests that "the whole party consented to the dazibao being displayed at Tiananmen" (*FBIS*, November 30, 1978, N1–2).

24. Fraser, *The Chinese*, 244–47.

25. *FBIS*, December 19, 1978, N2.

26. The U.S.-China normalization agreement was signed on December 15.

27. "Emancipate the Mind, Seek Truth from Facts and Unite as One in Looking to the Future" (December 13, 1978), in Deng, *Selected Works*, 155–56.

28. *South China Morning Post Weekly* (hereafter *SCMPW*), February 27–28, 1993.

29. See *BR* 22, 9 (March 2, 1979): 16. On the Li Yizhe affair, see *Chinese Law and Government* (hereafter *CLG*) 10, 3 (Fall 1977), and 14, 2 (Summer 1981).

30. Nathan (*Chinese Democracy*, 23) has estimated that at least fifty-five different "people's periodicals" were published in Beijing in the winter and early spring of 1978–79. Some of these journals were staffed by dissidents who had participated in previous prodemocracy demonstrations. For example, *Beijing Spring* counted among its editorial staff Wang Juntao and Chen Ziming, both of whom had played prominent roles in the Qingming disturbance of April 1976. See Black and Munro, *Black Hands*, 43–51.

31. For example, after visiting Xidan Wall with Deng Xiaoping on November 16, Hu Yaobang invited *Beijing Spring* deputy editor Wang Juntao to his home for a four-hour discussion. See Black and Munro, *Black Hands*, 55.

32. The petitioners' movement is discussed in Nathan, *Chinese Democracy*, 26–30, and Garside, *Coming Alive*, 230–36.

33. *FBIS*, January 15, 1979, E2–3.

34. *BR* 22, 38 (September 21, 1979): 7. According to incomplete statistics, almost six million "verdicts" and "labels"—including those of 300,000 erstwhile "rightists"—were reversed or removed between 1978 and 1980. See Deng, *Selected Works*, 228.

35. Fu was reportedly arrested without a formal warrant having been issued. This ostensibly violated Article 47 of the 1978 Chinese State Constitution, which stated, in part, "No citizen may be arrested without the ruling of a people's court or the recommendation of a people's procurator."

36. Ruan, *Lishi zhuanzhedian*, 35–36.

37. See Nathan, *Chinese Democracy*, 32.

38. From Taiwan sources, quoted in *FBIS*, March 21, 1979, L1–2; *NYT*, March 23, 1979, A7; and *Far Eastern Economic Review* (hereafter *FEER*), October 19, 1979, 38.

39. *Joint Publications Research Service* (hereafter *JPRS*) 073421, 29–30.

40. For documentation of collective violence involving petitioners in this period, see *ICM* 2, 2 (February 1980): 2 and passim.

41. Chen Yun, speech to the April 1979 Central Committee Work Conference, quoted in *ICM* 2, 4 (April 1980): 2–3.

42. Tan Zhenlin, speech to the Standing Committee of the NPC (no date), quoted in *ICM* 2, 5 (May 1980): 2.

43. Similar restrictions on free speech and assembly were enacted in Shanghai on March 6. See *BR* 22, 14 (April 6, 1979): 6.

44. *FBIS*, April 2, 1979, R1–2.

45. The following discussion draws on Goldman, "Hu Yaobang's Intellectual Network," 227–37, and Ruan, *Lishi zhuanzhedian*, 33–38, 105–19.

46. The meeting was originally proposed by Ye Jianying, who also recommended that Hu Yaobang should preside. Among those in attendance were a sizable number of Communist Party intellectuals who later ran afoul of the conservative wing of Deng's reform coalition: Hu Yaobang, Bao Tong, Hu Jiwei, Wang Ruoshui, Yu Guangyuan, Su Shaozhi, Yan Jiaqi, Li Honglin, Yu Haocheng, Liao Gailong, Ruan Ming, Wen Yuankai, Yang Xiguang, Zhang Xianyang, and Feng Lanrui, inter alia. Many of these people later got into serious political difficulty for supporting student demands for democratic reform in the late 1980s. A complete list of participants in the 1979 theory conference appears in Ruan, *Lishi zhuanzhedian*, 109–19.

47. Deng signaled China's intention to "teach Vietnam a lesson" in a speech delivered toward the end of his postnormalization goodwill visit to the United States.

48. See Daniel Tretiak, "China's Vietnam War and Its Consequences." The casualty figure is taken from a report by PLA Marshal Nie Rongzhen, cited in *ICM* 2, 7 (July 1980): 11.

49. See Ruan, *Lishi zhuanzhedian*, 36–37.

50. Cited in Tretiak, "China's Vietnam War," 752–53, n. 29, from *South China Morning Post* (hereafter *SCMP*), Aug. 4, 1979, 5. Also Richard D. Nethercut, "Deng and the Gun: Party-Military Relations in the People's Republic of China," 695–97.

51. Nie Rongzhen, report to the Central Military Affairs Commission (February 1980), cited in *ICM* 2, 7 (July 1980): 11.

52. "Uphold the Four Cardinal Principles" (March 30, 1979), in Deng, *Selected Works*, 166–85. Goldman, "Hu Yaobang's Intellectual Network," 235, reports that a sentence in Deng's original text (as drafted under the direction of Hu Qiaomu) arguing that "Rightism is currently the major danger" was deleted from the final version of the speech at the insistence of Hu Yaobang and others.

53. At several points in his text, Deng referred to the Central Committee as the source of his analysis of the situation. Indeed, his speech began with a disclaimer: "The Central Committee has asked me to set forth a few views." Such disavowals were out of character for Deng, whose forty-six other speeches and essays published in his 1984 *Selected Works* contained no similar demurrers.

54. Garside, *Coming Alive*, 237, has estimated that by the end of May 1979 thirty movement activists had been arrested in Beijing.

55. *BR* 22, 15 (April 13, 1979): 9–13.

56. *ICM* 2, 4 (April 1980): 3.

57. For a transcript of Wei Jingsheng's trial, see *ICM* 2, 1 (January 1980): 1–12. Wei's conviction on the seemingly incidental charge of endangering national security by leaking military secrets to a Reuter's correspondent may be taken as an indirect measure of Deng Xiaoping's anger over Wei's public criticism of China's February 1979 Vietnam offensive.

58. See, for example, *WHB*, April 13, 1979; *GMRB*, May 11, 1979; and *ZM* 21 (July 1979): 5–6.

59. Cited in Schram, "Economics in Command?," 421.

60. *Dongxiang* (hereafter *DX*) 9 (June 16, 1979): 4–7, in *FBIS*, June 28, 1979, U4–5.

61. Solinger, "The Fifth National People's Congress," 1253. Hua's address to the Second Session of the Fifth NPC was actually drafted by Hu Qiaomu; it differed substantially, in both tone and content, from the premier's report to the First Session a year earlier. See Deng Liqun, "Answers to Questions," 17–18.

62. "Implement the Policy of Readjustment, Ensure Stability and Unity" (December 25, 1980), in Deng, *Selected Works*, 335.

63. "There must be laws for people to follow; these laws must be observed; their enforcement must be strict. . . . Procuratorial and judicial organizations must maintain their independence as is appropriate; they must faithfully abide by the laws, . . . guarantee the equality of all people before the people's laws, and deny anyone the privilege of being above the law" (*PR* 21, 52 [December 29, 1978]: 6–16).

64. See *BR* 22, 27 (July 6, 1979): 32–36.

65. See *BR* 22, 28 (July 13, 1979): 8–16. In the mid-1950s Peng Zhen had been number two in command in the Central Party Secretariat under Deng Xiaoping. The two men had been bridge partners and had made frequent inspection tours together. However, their friendship was strained in the spring of 1966 when Deng, under duress, voted with the Maoist majority to censure his old friend for allegedly opposing Chairman Mao. Notwithstanding this temporary breach in their relationship, Deng, along with Chen Yun, was highly instrumental in securing Peng's rehabilitation in December 1978; thereafter, the three senior leaders worked together to oust Hua Guofeng. See David L. Shambaugh, "Deng Xiaoping: The Politician," 469–70 and passim.

66. The following discussion is based on Richard Baum, "Modernization and Legal Reform in Post-Mao China: The Rebirth of Socialist Legality."

67. Among other things, the new criminal law annulled a State Council decree of January 1967 that defined as counterrevolutionary any "malicious attack" against a party leader—including acts of verbal disrespect, however harmless or unintentional. This decree had been invoked during the Cultural Revolution to incarcerate a man who had unknowingly "maligned" Mao Zedong by wrapping an oily piece of fresh fish in a newspaper bearing a photo of the Chairman. Major features of the new criminal law are analyzed in *BR* 22, 33 (August 17, 1979): 16–22.

68. Among the more problematic features of the criminal laws were a stipulation permitting the government to grant exemptions from the procedure code "in special cases"; a provision that actions not explicitly defined as illegal in the criminal code could nonetheless be treated as crimes "in light of the most analogous provisions" of the code; the absence of any provision permitting criminal defendants (or their lawyers) to subpoena witnesses or to cross-examine government witnesses; an instruction to judges in criminal cases to show "leniency toward those who confess," with the clear

understanding that heavy sentences were to be imposed on those who refused to cooperate; and a delay in the implementation of the new statutes until 1980, by which time the trials (and convictions) of Wei Jingsheng, Fu Yuehua, and other Democracy Movement activists were already faits accomplis.

69. For more detailed analysis of the 1979 criminal laws, see *Criminal Code of the People's Republic of China*, 3–20; and Hungdah Chiu, "China's New Criminal and Criminal Procedure Codes," 14–23.

70. *BR* 23, 8 (February 25, 1980): 15.

71. See *BR* 22, 37 (September 14, 1979): 15–18.

72. The 1979 electoral reform is examined in *CLG* 14, 3–4 (Fall–Winter 1982–1983): 7–13, 60–99; see also Nathan, *Chinese Democracy*, 195–203.

73. Domes, *The Government and Politics*, 169, estimates that Deng now counted thirteen to fourteen supporters on the Politburo, while Hua Guofeng had only seven, with the remaining seven or eight members clustered around Ye Jianying and Li Xiannian.

74. The communiqué of the Fourth Plenum appears in *BR* 22, 40 (October 5, 1979): 32–34.

75. According to Hong Kong sources, Hu Yaobang originally drafted Ye's speech for presentation at the Fourth Plenum. It was then circulated for comments, with Deng and Ye making final revisions. See *ZM* 25 (November 1979): 5–6; and Chang, "Chinese Politics," 13.

76. *BR* 22, 40 (October 5, 1979): 14.

77. At the Tenth Plenum of the Eighth Central Committee in September 1962, Mao had called for intensified class struggle to combat dangerous "capitalist tendencies" at home and abroad. Thereafter, Mao incorporated this thesis into his polemical critique of Nikita Khrushchev's "modern revisionism."

78. *BR* 22, 40 (October 5, 1979): 15.

79. Quoted in Shirk, *The Political Logic*, 164.

80. General Xu had worked under Deng in the Second Field Army during the Sino-Japanese War. In 1979 he commanded Chinese forces in the war against Vietnam. When the war effort sputtered, Deng reportedly blamed Xu. Later, when Xu sought a top-level military post in Beijing, he was passed over by Deng. See Domes, *The Government and Politics*, 170–71.

81. "Senior Cadres Should Take the Lead in Maintaining and Enriching the Party's Fine Traditions" (November 2, 1979), in Deng, *Selected Works*, 216.

82. On the reshuffling of military commanders, see *I&S* 16, 3 (March 1980): 1–4; *The China Quarterly* (hereafter *CQ*) 82 (June 1980): 381–82; and *ICM* 3, 9 (September 1981): 9–12.

83. "The Present Situation and the Tasks Before Us" (January 16, 1980), in Deng, *Selected Works*, 224–58.

84. Ibid., 236–39.

85. Ibid., 238–39. Although no one was mentioned by name, Deng's warning was apparently directed at certain liberal associates of Hu Yaobang and Yu Guangyuan, including political theorist Yan Jiaqi, who had maintained informal liaison with prodemocracy activists and had even published articles in their journals.

86. Ibid., 239.

87. The text of the communiqué of the Fifth Plenum appears in *BR* 23, 10 (March 10, 1980): 7–10.

88. Domes, *The Government and Politics*, 171, calculates that out of the twenty-four remaining Politburo members, thirteen or fourteen supported Deng, seven or eight

were loosely affiliated with the Ye-Li faction, and only three marginally supported Hua.

89. The eight Dengists were Hu Yaobang, Hu Qiaomu, Wan Li, Wang Renzhong, Song Renqiong, Yao Yilin, Yang Dezhi, and Fang Yi; the remaining members of the Central Secretariat were petroleum clique member Yu Qiuli, survivor Peng Chong, and Vice-Premier Gu Mu.

90. *BR* 23, 10 (March 10, 1980): 9.

91. Citing a Guangdong provincial radio broadcast, Domes, *The Government and Politics*, 172, claims that Ye spent the afternoon of Liu's memorial service, May 17, refereeing a high school basketball game near his hometown in Guangdong.

92. Addressing a screenwriter's conference in February 1980, Hu stated: "These days, some people speak of 'crises' in our country. They mention 'crises' of faith, belief, and trust. When the revolution is frustrated, some people's thinking goes astray, even to the point of agitation. . . . There is nothing unusual about this." Quoted in *ZM* 33 (July 1980), in *ICM* 3, 9 (September 1980): 14.

93. "Guiding Principles for Inner-Party Political Life," *BR* 23, 14 (April 7, 1980): 12–19. All passages cited in the following section are from this document.

94. *BR* 23, 10 (March 10, 1980): 10.

95. *NYT*, April 25, 1980, A5.

96. Ruan, *Lishi zhuanzhedian*, 41.

97. Nethercut, "Deng and the Gun," 697; *BR* 23, 20 (May 19, 1980): 7–8.

98. Ruan, *Lishi zhuanzhedian*, 42. In repudiating this slogan, Deng allowed that he had initially "seen nothing wrong with it." Only later, he said, had he come to appreciate its antireform implications.

99. By likening Hua to a palace eunuch, his critics evidently sought to portray him as a politically impotent sycophant who had no legitimate right to rule. The campaign to undercut Hua's authority is discussed in Richard Baum, "From Feudal Patriarchy to the Rule of Law: Chinese Politics in 1980," 30–32.

100. Cited in Pye, *The Dynamics of Chinese Politics*, 253.

101. *GMRB*, August 19, 1980, cited in ibid.

102. "Answers to the Italian Journalist Oriana Fallaci" (August 21 and 30, 1980), in Deng, *Selected Works*, 328.

CHAPTER 4
HIGH TIDE OF REFORM

1. Fewsmith, *Dilemmas of Reform*, 63–70, traces many of Xue Muqiao's reform ideas to a conference of economic theorists held in Wuxi in April 1979. Serialized excerpts from Xue's book, *A Study on the Problems of China's Socialist Economy*, appear in *BR* 23, 5; 23, 12; and 23, 14 (February 4, March 24, and April 7, 1980).

2. *BR* 23, 12 (March 24, 1980): 21–26 (emphasis added). The idea that market regulation should serve as a supplement to state planning was originally proposed by Sun Yefang (née Xue Eguo), Xue Muqiao's cousin, who had worked under Xue's direction at the State Statistical Bureau in the mid-1950s.

3. *BR* 23, 5 (February 4, 1980): 20–21.

4. *BR* 23, 19 (May 12, 1980): 18.

5. Quoted in *BR* 23, 49 (December 8, 1980): 13.

6. By July 1980 there were some 400,000 privately owned commercial establish-

ments in China's cities, a fourfold increase over 1979. On average, each of these private "firms" employed only two people. See *BR* 23, 45 (November 10, 1980): 20; and Thomas Gold, "Urban Private Business and China's Reforms," 90.

7. *BR* 23, 22 (June 2, 1980): 20.

8. *BR* 23, 17 (April 28, 1980): 24–26.

9. *BR* 23, 41 (October 13, 1980): 15–21.

10. *BR* 23, 24 (June 16, 1980): 17.

11. For analysis of the nature and severity of the party's internal problems in this period, see Hsi-sheng Ch'i, *Politics of Disillusionment: The Chinese Communist Party under Deng Xiaoping, 1978–89*, chap. 2.

12. The following discussion draws from Ruan, *Lishi zhuanzhedian*, 42–46.

13. It is interesting that Deng should accept Li Weihan's advice on this issue. Deng and Li had reputedly been on bad terms since the 1930s, when Deng's wife had divorced him to marry Li. The child of that latter marriage, Li Tieying, later became China's education minister and a Politburo member. Periodically there have been rumors that Li Tieying may have been Deng's child, rather than Li Weihan's. See, for example, Teiwes, "Politics, Purges, and Rectification," 37, n. 111.

14. Ruan, *Lishi zhuanzhedian*, 42–43.

15. According to a former member of Hu Yaobang's entourage, gaining Ye Jianying's assent was a very important step. When Hu asked for Ye's support in the struggle to combat feudalism, Ye reportedly told him: "Eliminating feudalism is extremely important; Marx's early writings were antifeudal" (ibid., 43).

16. Ibid., 44.

17. Ibid., 45.

18. "On the Reform of the System of Party and State Leadership" (August 18, 1980), in Deng, *Selected Works*, 302–25. In the discussion below, all cited passages are from this document.

19. Three years later, in 1983, Deng's scathing denunciation of bourgeois decadence would be invoked by conservative theoreticians Hu Qiaomu and Deng Liqun to justify launching a major new ideological offensive against "spiritual pollution" in China. See chapter 6.

20. Ruan, *Lishi zhuanzhedian*, 47.

21. *BR* 23, 37 (September 15, 1980): 11–12.

22. *BR* 23, 47 (November 24, 1980): 8–9.

23. Support for Polish political and economic reform in this period was also seen as a way for China's leaders to help weaken the Soviet Union's grip on Poland. See Ruan, *Deng Xiaoping diguo*, 105–6.

24. Liao Gailong, "The '1980 Reform' Program of China," in *FBIS*, March 16, 1981, U1.

25. A revised draft of Deng's speech was first circulated among party cadres on September 11 as "Central Document No. 66 (1980)." Its text appears in *ICM* 3, 4 (April 1984): 2–11.

26. Promoted to take the place of the seven retiring vice-premiers at the NPC were three members of Deng's reform coalition, PLA Deputy Chief of Staff Zhang Aiping, Foreign Minister Huang Hua, and Minister of Nationality Affairs Yang Jingren. Replacing the several retiring senior members of the NPC Standing Committee, including PLA marshals Liu Bocheng and Nie Rongzhen, were another group of proreform leaders that included Guangdong Party First Secretary Xi Zhongxun, his deputy Yang Shangkun, Shanghai Mayor Peng Chong, and General Su Yu.

27. See *BR* 23, 36 (September 8, 1980): 7–8.

28. Ibid., 7.

29. *ZM* 33 (July 1980), in *FBIS*, July 9, 1980, U4–5; *DX* 23 (August 16, 1980), in *FBIS*, August 21, 1980, U1–3.

30. Following exposure of the Bohai cover-up, Yu Qiuli was forced to make a self-criticism and was transferred from his chairmanship of the State Planning Commission to a less important post as head of the new State Energy Commission; his place on the planning commission was taken by Chen Yun ally Yao Yilin. Kang Shi'en received a "demerit of the first grade" and was demoted from chairman of the State Economic Commission to minister of petroleum, his former post now occupied by another Chen Yun associate, economist Yuan Baohua. On the fate of the petroleum faction, see *FBIS*, July 9, 1980, U3–6; also Domes, *The Government and Politics*, 200–201; and Chang, "Chinese Politics," 15–16.

31. See *FBIS*, September 24, 1992, 31–33, cited in Fewsmith, *Dilemmas of Reform*, 81, n. 7.

32. Two collections of NPC deputies' comments and questions appear in *BR* 23, 39 (September 29, 1980): 33–36; and *ICM* 2, 11 (November 1980): 1–10.

33. *BR* 23, 39 (September 29, 1980): 33.

34. Ibid., 30. For discussion and defense of the abolition of the "four bigs" see *BR* 23, 40 (October 6, 1980): 22–29. For further analysis of the 1980 NPC session, see Kevin J. O'Brien, *Reform without Liberalization: China's National People's Congress and the Politics of Institutional Change*.

35. Hu Yaobang, "On Some Problems in Ideological and Political Work" (October 15, 1980), cited in Schram, "Economics in Command?," 422–23.

36. Liao, "The '1980 Reform' Program," U3.

37. See, e.g., *BR* 23, 36 (September 8, 1980): 23–25; *BR* 23, 45 (November 10, 1980): 15–19; and *BR* 23, 52 (December 29, 1980): 15–17.

38. *BR* 23, 44 (November 3, 1980): 15–17; *HQ* 17 (September 1980).

39. *BR* 23, 52 (December 29, 1980): 13–15.

40. *RMRB*, October 28, 1980; *BR* 23, 45 (November 10, 1980): 3–4; *BR* 23, 46 (November 17, 1980): 20–23.

41. See *Gongren ribao* (Workers' daily) (hereafter, *GRRB*), October 6, 1980; *BR* 23, 35 (September 1, 1980): 19–26; *BR* 23, 42 (October 20, 1980): 14–16; and *BR* 23, 50 (December 15, 1980): 5–6.

42. *BR* 23, 50 (December 15, 1980): 6–7; *BR* 23, 51 (December 22, 1980): 12–14.

43. *BR* 23, 46 (November 17, 1980): 24–25.

44. *BR* 23, 49 (December 8, 1980): 20–22.

45. Symposium participants included Bao Tong, a research fellow in the science policy research section of the State Council; Yan Jiaqi, a research assistant at the CASS Institute of Philosophy; Yu Haocheng, editor of the Qunzhong publishing house; Ruan Ming, assistant director of theoretical studies at the Central Party School; and Zhang Xianyang, a researcher at the CASS Institute for Marxism–Leninism–Mao Zedong Thought.

46. See XH, October 21, 1980; *ICM* 2, 12 (December 1980): 18–19.

47. See, e.g., *BR* 23, 8 (February 25, 1980): 11–19; *BR* 23, 28 (July 14, 1980): 4; *BR* 23, 34 (August 25, 1980): 3–4.

48. See, e.g., the remarks by Minister of Civil Affairs Cheng Zihua in *FBIS*, August 26, 1980, L9–12. On the implementation of the 1980 electoral reforms, see Brantley Womack, "Electoral Reform in China," 1–42 and passim.

49. The following discussion draws on Nathan, *Chinese Democracy*, chap. 10.

50. Cited in ibid., 213.

51. The text of a petition submitted by the striking students to the Hunan Provincial Party Committee on October 14, 1980, appears in *ICM* 2, 12 (December 1980): 16–17.

52. These events are described in Black and Munro, *Black Hands*, 63–73.

53. Ibid., 67, 71. Following the 1980 elections, Hu Ping, Wang Juntao, and Chen Ziming went on to become well-known political dissidents. In the mid-1980s Hu emigrated from China to the United States, where he attended Harvard University. In 1987 he became chairman of the Chinese Alliance for Democracy. Wang and Chen were arrested separately while trying to escape from China after the Tiananmen crackdown of June 1989. Both men were sentenced to thirteen-year prison terms for "inciting counterrevolution" (ibid., 296–313; see also chapter 12 below). Zhang Wei went on to become a successful reform politician in Tianjin, where he was slated to become deputy mayor in 1989. Following the June 4 massacre, however, he resigned from the municipal government in protest over the crackdown. After remaining unemployed for more than a year, Zhang emigrated to the United States. See *NYT*, November 2, 1990.

54. Liang and his American wife, Judith Shapiro, subsequently wrote three books together: *Son of the Revolution* (1984); *Cold Winds, Warm Winds: Intellectual Life in China Today* (1986), and *After the Nightmare: Inside China Today* (1987).

55. Nathan (*Chinese Democracy*, 220) reports that there were at least twelve known cases where prodemocracy activists contested local elections in the last half of 1980.

56. See, e.g., *RMRB*, December 5, 1980; and *BR* 23, 51 (December 22, 1980): 3–4.

57. A partial text of Wang's statement, issued in mid-January 1981, appears in *ICM* 3, 7 (July 1981): 17–18.

58. Deng Xiaoping put forward these descriptions in an important speech on December 25, 1980. See below.

59. Ruan, *Deng Xiaoping diguo*, 106–7.

60. Ibid., 108.

61. Ruan, *Lishi zhuanzhedian*, 50–51.

62. Ibid., 51–52. As indicated earlier, Deng Liqun was quite probably correct in this latter assessment.

63. Ibid., 52.

64. Partial texts of the December 1980 CC work conference speeches by Chen Yun, Zhao Ziyang, Li Xiannian, and Yao Yilin appear in *ICM* 3, 4 (April 1981): 15–20, see also *ZM* 40 (February 1981).

65. On the implementation of stringent readjustment measures, see XH, December 7, 1980, and February 28, 1981; *RMRB*, January 1, 1981, 1; *ICM* 3, 2 (February 1981): 1–10; and *ICM* 3, 4 (April 1981): 11–20.

66. "Implement the Policy of Readjustment, Ensure Stability and Unity," in Deng, *Selected Works*, 343.

67. Ibid., 352–53. Years later, Deng would effusively praise Poland's martial law authorities for their firmness in dealing with the 1980–81 Solidarity crisis. See chapter 8.

68. Ibid., 350.

69. *RMRB*, July 20, 1981; Domes, *The Government and Politics*, 222. In this same connection, a key section of Deng's original August 18 speech, in which he urged broad-gauged democratic reform, was deleted from official reproductions of the speech following the renewed outbreak of worker unrest in Poland in the winter of 1980–81. The passage in question was not officially restored to Deng's Gengshen speech until

the summer of 1986, when the question of democratic reform was once again placed on the national agenda. (I am indebted to Tony Saich for calling this to my attention.)

70. Deng, *Selected Works*, 350.

71. Ibid., 351–52.

72. Ibid., 353.

73. The following discussion draws on Baum, "From Feudal Patriarchy," 35–38.

74. A partial text of the indictments appears in *BR* 23, 47 (November 24, 1980): 12–17.

75. Government spokesmen minimized this issue, arguing that since almost all Chinese judicial experts had been subject to persecution during the Cultural Revolution, it would have been virtually impossible to find qualified judges who had not been mistreated.

76. These and other legal quirks in the trial are detailed in James C. Hsiung, *Symposium: The Trial of the Gang of Four and its Implication in China*, chap. 2 and passim.

77. For a list of high-level victims of Gang-inspired persecution, see *BR* 23, 48 (December 1, 1980): 11–12.

78. A partial transcript of Jiang's trial appears in *ICM* 3, 2 (February 1981): 14–17.

79. In 1983 Zhang Chunqiao and Jiang Qing had their death sentences commuted to life in prison, even though Jiang had steadfastly refused to repent. Suffering from cancer of the throat, Jiang Qing was allowed to leave prison, under guard, early in 1991; shortly thereafter she reportedly hanged herself.

80. *HQ* 24 (December 16, 1980).

81. *ZM* 40 (February 1981): 7–9, in *FBIS*, February 2, 1981, U1–6.

82. *CKYC* 17, 4 (April 1983): 82f, in Domes, *The Government and Politics*, 176. For additional information bearing on the Politburo's critique of Hua Guofeng, see Deng Liqun, "Answers to Questions," 35–36.

83. Domes, *The Government and Politics*, 176. See also *ZM* 39 (January 1981): 7–10, in *FBIS*, January 5, 1981, U1–8, and February 2, 1981, U1–6.

84. *Dongxifang* (hereafter *DXF*) 24 (December 10, 1980): 7–9. Lowell Dittmer, "China in 1981: Reform, Readjustment, Rectification," 33–34, recounts this incident.

CHAPTER 5
POLARIZATION AND PARALYSIS

1. According to one rather sensationalized account of this confrontation, published by Agence France Presse, Deng responded to General Xu's outburst with sarcasm, at which point Xu allegedly pulled a revolver and began firing in Deng's direction, wounding Deng's bodyguard. Xu himself was purportedly injured in this fracas as well. See *ICM* 2, 7 (July 1980): 14–15. According to a second, unrelated report, shortly after the Fifth Plenum Xu's disgruntled son, a pilot in the Chinese Air Force, allegedly hatched a plot to fly his MIG jet fighter from Zhejiang to Taiwan. His plan was exposed, however, and he was reportedly arrested and sent to prison. See *ICM* 6, 3 (March 1984): 16–17. While these stories may well be apocryphal, their revelation of severe strain in Deng's relations with the military tends to accord with other, more reliable sources. See, for example, Nethercut, "Deng and the Gun," 695–700.

2. Document of the CCP Central Secretariat (October 29, 1980), in *ICM* 3, 3 (March 1981): 1–2.

3. Ibid.

4. Ibid.

5. *ICM* 3, 3 (March 1981): 4–5. Among other worries, PLA leaders were said to be

concerned that a new round of rural reforms would make the job of military recruiting in the countryside more difficult, since (1) preferential collective welfare benefits for rural military dependents were being reduced (or even eliminated) under the household responsibility system; and (2) under conditions of agricultural decollectivization, the best and brightest rural youths were increasingly turning to entrepreneurial roles, rather than military service, to enhance their prospects for upward socioeconomic mobility.

6. See chapter 3.

7. *DX* 31 (April 16, 1981): 4–6, in *FBIS*, April 20, 1981, W1.

8. Ibid. Leftists had used Mao's phrase "Continuing the revolution under the dictatorship of the proletariat" as a rallying cry during the Cultural Revolution.

9. See Dittmer, "China in 1981," 41–42.

10. *JFJB*, January 4, 1981. The slogan was originally attributed to PLA model soldier Wang Jie.

11. *RMRB*, February 22 and 24, 1981; *BR* 24, 22 (June 1, 1981): 3.

12. See *RMRB*, March 19, 20, 21, 23, 24, and 26, 1981.

13. *RMRB*, April 24, 1981.

14. *JFJB*, April 26, 1981.

15. Huang's speech, which was originally delivered in October 1980, was not published until April 1981. See *BR* 24, 17 (April 27, 1981): 15–23. Insofar as Huang Kecheng had been imprisoned by Mao for twenty years for participating in Peng Dehuai's alleged "antiparty clique" in 1959, his endorsement of Mao carried special weight.

16. *FBIS*, August 12, 1979, P5.

17. *FBIS*, June 7, 1979, T4.

18. *FBIS*, April 25, 1979, L15–18.

19. *FBIS*, October 15, 1979, I1.

20. *FBIS*, November 5, 1979, Q2–3.

21. *RMRB*, November 11, 1980.

22. *FBIS*, December 7, 1979, O1.

23. *FBIS*, May 16, 1979, R2.

24. Ibid.

25. See Richard J. Latham, "The Rectification of 'Work Style': Command and Management Problems."

26. *FBIS*, October 24, 1979, L14–19; *ICM* 3, 2 (February 1980): 14–15.

27. *FBIS*, October 24, 1979, L14–19; also *ZM* 28 (February 1980): 20–21; and *Zhongguo zhisheng* 9 (n.d.): 5.

28. The complete text of *What if I Were Real?* appears in Link, *Stubborn Weeds*, 198–250.

29. Ibid., 249–50. The director considerably heightened the play's dramatic impact by using a clever "play without a play" involving the arrest of an "important guest" in the theater audience just prior to the opening curtain. The arrested guest, who is led away in handcuffs, is said to be a confidence man masquerading as the son of a high-level cadre. After witnessing this disturbing scene, the veracity of which it has no reason to question, the audience settles down to watch the play—about a young man arrested for impersonating the son of a high-level cadre. The collapse of the boundary between illusion and reality is completed when the young man arrested in the theater audience later appears as the play's central character.

30. See *RMRB*, March 19, 1980; *DX* 32 (May 16, 1981): 21–23.

31. The full text of *Unrequited Love* appears in *ZM* 44 (June 1981): 82–98. For a partial translation, see *ICM* 3, 6 (June 1981): 14–19.

32. *JFJB*, April 20, 1981, in *FBIS*, May 21, 1981, K6–K14. See also *ZM* 45 (July 1985): 11–13. The article was reportedly written by Liu Baiyu, director of cultural work in the army's GPD.

33. *ZM* 55 (May 1982), in *FBIS*, May 26, 1982, W1–2. Deng's negative reaction to *Sun and Man* was confirmed in his speech of July 17, 1981: "The movie gives the impression that the Communist Party and the socialist system are bad. It vilifies the latter to such an extent that one wonders what has happened to the author's party spirit. . . . A work of this sort has the same effect as the views of the so-called democrats" (Deng, *Selected Works*, 368–69).

34. "On Opposing Wrong Ideological Tendencies" (March 27, 1981), in Deng, *Selected Works*, 356–57.

35. *ZM* 55 (May 1982), in *FBIS*, May 26, 1982, W1–2; *ICM* 3, 9 (September 1981): 8–9; *ZM* 45 (July 1981): 11–13. For further analysis of the Bai Hua affair, see Richard Kraus, "Bai Hua: The Political Authority of a Writer," 191–93, 203–6; Merle Goldman, *Sowing the Seeds of Democracy in China: Political Reform in the Deng Xiaoping Era*, chap. 4; and Dittmer, "China in 1981," 41–44.

36. See Deng, *Selected Works*, 367.

37. *ICM* 3, 9 (September 1981): 8.

38. Wang Ruowang, *Hunger Trilogy*.

39. See Goldman, *Sowing the Seeds*, chap. 4; The text of Liu's essay appears in Perry Link, ed., *People or Monsters? and Other Stories and Reportage from China After Mao*, 11–68.

40. *ICM* 3, 9 (September 1981): 8–9.

41. See, for example, *RMRB*, August 18, 1981; *GRRB*, August 19, 1981; *BR* 24, 38 (September 21, 1981): 13–16; and *ICM* 3, 10 (October 1981): 4–9.

42. *BR* 24, 30 (July 27, 1981): 30.

43. Kraus, "Bai Hua," 193, n. 20.

44. "Concerning Problems on the Ideological Front" (July 17, 1981), in Deng, *Selected Works*, 367–71.

45. *FBIS*, December 15, 1981, K20.

46. See, e.g., *ZM* 46 (August 1981): 16.

47. Quoted in Liu Binyan, *A Higher Kind of Loyalty*, 245–46.

48. Ibid., 246.

49. *ICM* 3, 9 (September 1981): 9.

50. *BR* 24, 38 (September 21, 1981): 14.

51. See below.

52. *ZM* 55 (May 1982), in *FBIS*, May 26, 1982, W1–3; Wang Renzhong resigned from the Central Secretariat at the Twelfth Party Congress.

53. XH, August 30, 1981; *ICM* 3, 10 (October 1981): 1.

54. *FBIS*, November 30, 1981, V1. Later, Chen Yun would repeat his call for moderation and restraint in dealing with writers like Bai Hua and Ye Wenfu who had strayed across the line of acceptable opinion: "We must not overreact; we must not drag in too many people on account of some small matters," he cautioned in 1983. Noting that Bai Hua had been widely acclaimed as a genius, Chen reportedly urged his CC comrades to go see *Unrequited Love* for themselves. At a CC meeting in May 1983, Chen argued that Ye Wenfu's poem, "General, You Cannot Do This," had its positive side. "Why fly into a rage?" he asked. "Literature and the arts must not be treated like a war. . . . We mustn't start another literary inquisition." See *ICM* 6, 3 (March 1984): 15–17.

55. *BR* 24, 38 (September 21, 1981): 19.

56. Ibid., 13–16.

57. A translation appears in *ICM* 4, 2 (February 1982): 16–18.

58. *BR* 25, 2 (January 11, 1982): 29; Kraus, "Bai Hua," 193, 210; Dittmer, "China in 1981," 44.

59. See Goldman, *Sowing the Seeds*, chap. 4.

60. See Black and Munro, *Black Hands*, 68, 350–51n.

61. *Zhanwang* (hereafter *ZW*) 463 (May 16, 1981): 2, in *FBIS*, May 22, 1981, W5–6.

62. *Zhengming ribao* (hereafter *ZMRB*), July 5, 1981, in *FBIS*, July 9, 1981, W3.

63. Ibid., W4.

64. Ibid., W1.

65. *ZW* 463 (May 16, 1981), in *FBIS*, May 22, 1981, W6; *ZMRB*, June 27, 1981, in *FBIS*, June 29, 1981, W1–2. With Chen Yun's backing, Deng Liqun was named party propaganda director in April 1982, replacing Wang Renzhong. Later in the same year, at the Twelfth Party Congress, Little Deng was elevated to the Central Secretariat.

66. *BR* 24, 27 (July 6, 1981): 6–8.

67. *ZMRB*, July 5 and 7, 1981, in *FBIS*, July 9, 1981, W1–2, W5.

68. *BR* 24, 27 (July 6, 1981): 9.

69. "Resolution on Certain Questions in the History of Our Party since the Founding of the People's Republic of China," 26.

70. "Remarks on Successive Drafts," in Deng, *Selected Works*, 295.

71. "Central Document No. 23 (1981)," in *ICM* 3, 12 (December 1981): 1.

72. Ibid., 2.

73. Ibid.

74. Ibid., 2–3.

75. Deng Liqun, "Answers to Questions," 30–31.

76. "Remarks on Successive Drafts," in Deng, *Selected Works*, 291–92.

77. Ibid., 292.

78. Ibid., 282–83.

79. In February 1967, at a series of meetings of the Politburo and the MAC, a number of senior Chinese leaders, including Ye Jianying, Li Xiannian, Tan Zhenlin, Xu Xiangqian, Nie Rongzhen, Chen Yi, and Li Fuchun, had criticized the Leftist policies then being promoted by Lin Biao and Jiang Qing. Leftists subsequently attacked these critics for having churned up an "adverse current." The official verdict on the "February adverse current" was reversed in 1978.

80. "Remarks on Successive Drafts," in Deng, *Selected Works*, 288, 291, 296.

81. "Resolution on Certain Questions," 19–21, 23–24.

82. Ibid., 23.

83. Ibid., 23–24.

84. Ibid., 29–35.

85. Ibid., 35–37. In seeking to account for Deng's evident ambivalence in first embracing and then moving to restrict the campaign against bourgeois liberalism, it is possible that Deng's waffling may have been the product of a tacit quid pro quo between Deng and party/army conservatives. With the Central Committee about to issue its long-awaited assessment of Mao Zedong's historical record at the Sixth Plenum (see below), Deng may have traded his endorsement of the antiliberalism campaign for conservative acceptance of a critical evaluation of Mao's role in the last two decades of his life. See n. 90, below.

86. The "three supports" involved sending PLA work teams to areas where factional conflict had broken out, to give support to "Leftist" organizations, to industry, and to agriculture; the "two militarys" involved imposing military control in the worst trouble spots and giving military training to students.

87. *RMRB*, April 4, 1981.

88. Deng, *Selected Works*, 358.

89. Domes, *The Government and Politics*, 182, supports this interpretation.

90. "Remarks on Successive Drafts," in Deng, *Selected Works*, 293. Notwithstanding Deng's expression of personal satisfaction, his delicate balancing act on the question of Mao's historical record, viewed in conjunction with the vicissitudes of the ongoing campaign against Bai Hua and bourgeois liberalism, takes on the appearance of a classical political horse trade. See n. 85, above. I am indebted to Dorothy Solinger for suggesting the likelihood of such a trade-off.

91. "The Primary Task of Veteran Cadres Is To Select Young and Middle-Aged Cadres for Promotion" (July 2, 1981), in Deng, *Selected Works*, 361. For a detailed analysis of the campaign to rejuvenate party leadership, see Cabestan, *L'Administration Chinoise*, 111–31.

92. Deng, *Selected Works*, 364–65.

93. Ibid., 365.

94. *BR* 24, 51 (December 21, 1981): 35–36.

95. "Streamlining Organizations Constitutes a Revolution" (January 13, 1982), in Deng, *Selected Works*, 374–75.

96. Deng, *Selected Works*, 365.

97. Ibid., 378.

98. See Zhao Ziyang, "Report on Problems in State Council Reorganization," XH, March 8, 1952, in *ICM* 4, 4 (April 1982): 1–5.

99. Ibid.; see also *RMRB*, March 9, May 5, and August 24, 1982; and Cabestan, *L'Administration Chinoise*, 99–104.

100. Between 1982 and August 1985 only about one million veteran cadres—less than 25 percent of the eligible pool—went into retirement. See Cabestan, *L'Administration Chinoise*, 41–42. On measures adopted to induce old cadres to retire, see Ch'i, *Politics of Disillusionment*, 51–68. Melanie Manion, *Retirement of Revolutionaries in China: Public Policies, Social Norms, Private Interests*, traces the implementation of the new retirement policy and the various strategies employed by veteran cadres to circumvent it.

101. See *ZM* 53 (March 1982): 7–10, in *FBIS*, March 4, 1982, W3–5; and *Zhongbao yuekan* (hereafter *ZBYK*) (April 1982), in *ICM* 4, 5 (May 1982): 15–19.

102. *BR* 23, 14 (April 7, 1980): 18–19.

103. Chen, *Selected Works*, 245.

104. Anhui People's Broadcasting Station, October 7, 1981, in *ICM* 3, 12 (December 1981): 4–5.

105. See Ch'i, *Politics of Disillusionment*, 39.

106. For a sampling of cases, see *ICM* 3, 12 (December 1981): 5–8; *ICM* 4, 1 (January 1982): 14–15; *ICM* 4, 2 (February 1982): 18–20; *ICM* 4, 5 (May 1982): 20; *ICM* 4, 5 (May 1982) (Supplement): 14–19; and *ICM* 4, 6 (June 1982): 1–11.

107. XH, August 6, 1981, in *ICM* 3, 11 (November 1981): 9–10; *BR* 24, 43 (October 26, 1981): 5.

108. See *BR* 24, 48 (November 30, 1981): 3–4.

109. "Central Document No. 43 (1981)," in *ICM* 4, 6 (June 1982): 10–12. Hu Yao-bang had first alluded to the three crises of faith, belief, and trust in February 1980.

110. Ibid.

111. Ibid., 11.

112. *BR* 24, 51 (December 21, 1981): 33–34.

113. Chen Yun, *Chen Yun wenxuan (1956–1985)* (Selected works of Chen Yun), 245–46; Ch'i, *Politics of Disillusionment,* 37–40.

114. "Combat Economic Crime" (April 10, 1982), in Deng, *Selected Works,* 380–81.

115. Ibid., 381.

116. See, e.g., *JFJB,* January 18, 1982, in *ICM* 4, 5 (May 1982): 8.

117. On criticism of the SEZs, See Y. C. Rao and C. K. Leung, *China's Special Economic Zones: Policies, Problems, and Prospects.*

118. *HQ* (March 1, 1982), in *ICM* 4, 6 (June 1982): 1–10.

CHAPTER 6
DEFINING THE SPIRIT OF SOCIALISM

1. Deng Xiaoping, "Opening Speech at the Twelfth National Congress of the CPC" (September 1, 1982), *Selected Works,* 394–97. For further analysis of the Twelfth Party Congress, see Lowell Dittmer, "The 12th Congress of the Chinese Communist Party," 108–24; and *I&S* 18, 11 (November 1982): 14–62.

2. Deng, *Selected Works,* 396; *BR* 25, 36 (September 6, 1982): 5.

3. Deng, *Selected Works,* 348. A recurrent mistranslation of the phrase *jingshen wenming* (spiritual civilization) appears in the official English language edition of Deng's *Selected Works.* In translation, the Chinese phrase is repeatedly rendered—inaccurately—as either "civilization with a high cultural and ideological level" (p. 348) or "civilization which is culturally and ideologically advanced" (p. 396). It is conjectured that the translation was altered to avoid the religious connotation conveyed (in English) by the word "spiritual" (*jingshen*).

4. Ibid., 396.

5. *BR* 25, 38 (September 20, 1982): 4, 15.

6. See, for example, the statement by Vice-Premier Wan Li, in British Broadcasting Company (BBC), *Survey of World Broadcasts/Far East* (hereafter *SWB/FE*) 7109 (August 20, 1982).

7. Other elderly Politburo holdouts included Nie Rongzhen (eighty-three), Xu Xiangqian (eighty), Deng Yingchao (seventy-eight), and Ulanhu (seventy-eight).

8. *RMRB,* September 7, 1982. Though he remained on the Politburo Standing Committee until his death, Ye retired from the post of chairman of the NPC SC early in 1983, requesting that his name be withdrawn from consideration for reelection to the Sixth NPC. See XH, March 2, 1983, in *ICM* 5, 4 (April 1983): 5.

9. See "Constitution of the Communist Party of China," *BR* 25, 38 (September 20, 1982): 14–16.

10. *BR* 25, 38 (September 20, 1982): 4.

11. *JFJB,* August 28, 1982, cited in Domes, *Government and Politics,* 185.

12. Liao's election to the Politburo was purely honorific, as he was terminally ill at the time of the Twelfth Party Congress.

13. *JFJB,* August 28, 1982, cited in Domes, *Government and Politics,* 185.

14. *BR* 25, 38 (September 20, 1982): 14–16. For analysis of the 1982 Party Constitution, see Tony Saich, "The People's Republic of China."

15. Agence France Presse (hereafter AFP), August 23, 1982; Domes, *The Government and Politics*, 184.

16. On generational change in China's leadership in the early 1980s, see Hong Yung Lee, "China's 12th Central Committee"; and William deB. Mills, "Generational Change in China."

17. Hu Yaobang's speech is translated in *SWB/FE* 7125 (September 8, 1982).

18. Hu's speech appears in *BR* 24, 28 (July 13, 1981): 9–24.

19. The idea that class struggle continued to exist "within certain limits" had been incorporated into the text of the CCP's June 1981 "Resolution on Certain Questions."

20. *SWB/FE* 7125.

21. The text of the 1982 PRC Constitution appears in *BR* 25, 52 (December 27, 1982): 10–18. For analysis, see Hsin-chi Kuan, "New Departures in China's Constitution."

22. See Peng Zhen's comments on the draft constitution, in *BR* 25, 50 (December 13, 1982): 9–20.

23. Similar language had been invoked by ideological conservatives in their critique of ultrademocracy and extreme individualism since the spring of 1979.

24. *BR* 25, 52 (December 27, 1982): 10–11 (preamble).

25. Employing a typology of stages of development in postrevolutionary Leninist regimes proposed by Kenneth Jowitt, Hsin-chi Kuan, "New Departures," has characterized China's 1982 Constitution as "inclusionary" in nature, reflecting the party's desire to co-opt the active support of intellectuals and other relevant social forces without actually sharing power with them.

26. The following discussion draws on Shirk, *The Political Logic*, chaps. 11–12; Ruan, *Deng Xiaoping diguo*, 146–47; and Fewsmith, *Dilemmas of Reform,* chaps. 3–4.

27. On the relative benefits and burdens of these two schemes, see Shirk, *The Political Logic*, 231ff; and White, *Riding the Tiger*, 128–34.

28. Ruan, *Deng Xiaoping diguo*, 188.

29. Chen, *Chen Yun wenxuan*, 287. The earliest reference to the bird cage analogy appears in Chen's comments on economic planning dated January 25, 1982, in ibid., 278–80.

30. Ruan, *Deng Xiaoping diguo*, 146.

31. See chapter 9. In an ironic turn of events, Zhao Ziyang late in 1986 abandoned the *li gai shui* idea, which had proved difficult to implement, and endorsed instead a variant of Hu Yaobang's fixed remittance plan. See Fewsmith, *Dilemmas of Reform*, 209–11.

32. There is some controversy over the date of Zhao's letter. Although Ruan Ming, *Deng Xiaoping diguo*, 188, claims that the letter was written in 1984, others have suggested that it was more likely of later origin.

33. See David A. Kelly, "The Emergence of Humanism: Wang Ruoshi and the Critique of Socialist Alienation." For further analysis of the origins and development of the debate over socialist humanism, see Schram, "Economics in Command?," 433ff.

34. *WHB*, January 17, 1983. A partial translation of Wang's essay appears in *ICM* 5, 6 (June 1983): 7–8.

35. Zhou Yang's essay, entitled "Inquiry into Some Theoretical Problems of Marxism," appears in *RMRB*, March 16, 1983.

36. Su Shaozhi, "Develop Marxism Under Contemporary Conditions"; see also Schram, "Economics in Command?," 434–37.

37. The "double hundred" policy referred to the slogan "Let a hundred flowers blossom; let a hundred schools of thought contend."

38. *RMRB*, April 12, 1983; see Schram, "Economics in Command?," 436, n. 70.

39. Deng Liqun first used this term in a June 4, 1983, speech to the Central Party School in Beijing. See *ZM* 76 (February 1984): 6–11.

40. *BR* 26, 25 (July 4, 1983): XVIII–XIX.

41. Ibid., XX–XXI.

42. XH, September 2, 1983.

43. See *FEER*, November 10, 1983, and February 16, 1984; also Amnesty International, *China: Violations of Human Rights*, 54–55. For a collection of media reports concerning implementation of the 1983 anticrime campaign, see *ICM* 5, 10 (October 1983).

44. *HQ* 18 (September 16, 1983).

45. *HQ* 17 (September 1, 1983).

46. *Liaowang* (hereafter *LW*), September 1983, in *ICM* 5, 10 (October 1983): 7.

47. An unofficial transcript of Deng's address appears in *I&S* 20, 4 (April 1984): 99–111. The quotations below are all drawn from this transcript.

48. Liberal intellectuals, including Wang Ruoshui and others, had openly expressed doubts about Deng's four principles as early as 1979.

49. The text of the resolution on party consolidation appears in XH, October 12, 1983.

50. *Asiaweek* (hereafter *AW*) 43 (October 28, 1983): 13; *ICM* 7, 2 (February 1985): 20–21.

51. Thomas Gold, "'Just in Time!' China Battles Spiritual Pollution on the Eve of 1984," 942.

52. *Wenwei po* (hereafter *WWP*), June 25, 1989.

53. For further analysis of this controversy, see Schram, "Economics in Command?", Tony Saich, "Party Consolidation and Spiritual Pollution in the People's Republic of China"; and Colin Mackerras, "'Party Consolidation' and the Attack on Spiritual Pollution."

54. See, for example, *RMRB*, October 20, 23, 25, 31, and November 2, 1983. Selections of Chinese press articles and speeches attacking spiritual pollution of various types appear in *ICM* 5, 12 (December 1983): 5–10; *ICM* 6, 1 (January 1984): 4–19; and *ICM* 6, 2 (February 1984): 12–17.

55. Quoted in Yang, *Hu Yaobang*, 149.

56. Evidence to support the sibling rivalry theory of Deng Liqun's antagonism toward Hu Yaobang is explored in *ZM* 76 (February 1984) and 78 (April 1984). Whatever the validity of this theory, it is clear that from the outset of the spiritual pollution campaign in 1983 until Hu Yaobang was finally ousted from power in January 1987, Deng Liqun wasted no opportunity to embarrass Hu and undermine his base of support. See Richard Baum, "Deng Liqun and the Struggle against 'Bourgeois Liberalization,' 1979–1993"; and Ruan, *Deng Xiaoping diguo*, chaps. 8, 10–11, and passim.

57. XH, November 9, 1983, in *ICM* 6, 1 (January 1984): 6–7.

58. "Big Cannon" was a nickname given to the crusty, ill-mannered General Wang Zhen by Deng Xiaoping, who once remarked that while Wang "sometimes aims badly," he is "still a lovely cannon." See Liu, *"Tell the World,"* 93.

59. *RMRB*, October 25, 1983; *ICM* 5, 12 (December 1983): 2–3.

60. XH, January 1984, 4–5.

61. *ZM* 78 (April 1984), in *ICM* 6, 6 (June 1984): 20.

62. For a sampling of newspaper articles and radio broadcasts criticizing these and other manifestations of spiritual pollution, see *ICM* 6, 1 (January 1984): 8–11.

63. These developments are documented in *RMRB*, November 16 and 17, 1983; *FBIS*, November 3, 1983, Q2, T7; and Gold, "Just in Time!," 956–58.

64. Quoted in Liu, *A Higher Kind of Loyalty*, 173.

65. Quoted in Yang, *Hu Yaobang*, 148.

66. Quoted in ibid., 171. See also *RMRB*, January 27, 1984; and *ICM* 6, 4 (April 1984): 10–11.

67. *RMRB*, November 11, 1983; *BR* 26, 50 (December 12, 1983): 11–12; XH, October 11, 1983, in *ICM* 5, 12 (December 1983): 4–5.

68. *QSND* 12 (December 1983): 57–58.

69. Quoted in Yang, *Hu Yaobang*, 149.

70. *ZM* 76 (February 1984): 6–11, in *FBIS*, February 7, 1984, W1–W11.

71. *ZM* 78 (April 1984), in *FBIS*, April 6, 1984, W1–W8.

72. See Ian Wilson and You Ji, "Leadership by 'Lines': China's Unresolved Succession," 34.

73. See *China Daily* (hereafter *CD*), December 26, 1984.

74. On the phasing out of the campaign, see Liu, *A Higher Kind of Loyalty*, 173.

75. XH, December 23, 1983; *ICM* 6, 2 (February 1984): 12–13.

76. *FBIS*, November 14, 1983, K1; *ICM* 5, 12 (December 1983): 2. Liu Binyan, *A Higher Kind of Loyalty*, 73–74, details the dismissal of Hu and Wang.

77. Ruan, *Deng Xiaoping diguo*, 150.

78. Deng Liqun's tactical retreat is documented in Schram, "Economics in Command?," 453ff; see also Gold, "Just in Time!," 961–62.

CHAPTER 7
THE REBIRTH OF LIBERAL REFORM

1. On the predatory behavior exhibited by village cadres following the introduction of rural reforms, see Jean C. Oi, "Partial Market Reform and Corruption in Rural China."

2. On the nature and sources of rural opposition to post-Mao agricultural reforms, see David Zweig, "Opposition to Change in Rural China: The System of Responsibility and People's Communes," and Kathleen Hartford, "Socialist Agriculture Is Dead; Long Live Socialist Agriculture!: Organizational Transformations in Rural China." For analysis of emergent economic rivalries between interior and coastal regions, see Andrew H. Wedeman, "Bamboo Walls and Brick Ramparts: Uneven Development, Inter-Regional Economic Conflict, and Local Protectionism in China, 1984–91," chaps. 1, 3. See also Wedeman, ed., "Regional Protectionism," 3–8 and passim, and Dali L. Yang, "Reforms, Resources, and Regional Cleavages: The Political Economy of Coast-Interior Relations."

3. See *ZM* 78 (April 1984).

4. See, for example, the series of important editorials in *RMRB*, February 20, March 15, April 1, and April 23, 1984.

5. *CD*, April 13, 1984, 1.

6. Ruan, *Deng Xiaoping diguo*, 151.

7. Ibid.; also Hamrin, *China and the Challenge*, 82.

8. Ruan, *Deng Xiaoping diguo*, 160–61.

9. Ibid., 160.

10. Among the most important policy research groups providing ideas and support for Zhao Ziyang in this period were the Institute for Economic Structural Reform, known popularly as the Tigaisuo, under the direction of Chen Yizi, former head of the Rural Development Group, and the Beijing Association of Young Economists, headed by Zhao's secretary, Bao Tong. See Fewsmith, *Dilemmas of Reform*, 136–37.

11. In her analysis of the Third Wave phenomenon in China, Carol Hamrin credits the development strategist and reform-oriented CASS Vice-President Huan Xiang with convincing Zhao Ziyang, sometime in mid-1983, to promote an information-based Chinese "new technological revolution." See Hamrin, *China and the Challenge*, 75–80.

12. Ibid., 77.

13. *JPRS-Chinese Science and Technology* (hereafter *JPRS-CST*), July 8, 1985, 8–12; Hamrin, *China and the Challenge*, 78.

14. Notwithstanding the initial euphoria that surrounded the concept of a Third Wave information revolution, by 1985 it had become clear that the quick-fix approach advocated by Third Wave enthusiasts was excessively optimistic, as upwards of forty thousand newly imported microcomputers lay gathering dust in Chinese warehouses due to critical shortages of applications software, user manuals, trained operators, peripheral devices, spare parts, "clean" power supplies, and technical support. See Richard Baum, "DOS ex Machina: The Microelectronic Ghost in China's Modernization Machine."

15. See *MB*, December 6, 1984, in *ICM* 7, 3 (March 1985): 2.

16. *MB*, December 6, 1984.

17. Sources for the following discussion include *FBIS*, October 13, 1983, K2–7; XH, December 12, 1983, and August 11, 1988; *SWB/FE* 7685 (July 3, 1984); *SWB/FE* 7859 (January 26, 1985); *SWB/FE* 7868 (February 6, 1985); *I&S* 20, 8 (August 1984); *LW* 3 (1985); *ICM* 7, 4 (April 1985); *BR* 28, 10 (March 11, 1985); *Xue lilun* (Study theory) (April 1989); and David S. G. Goodman, "The Second Plenary Session of the 12th CCP Central Committee: Rectification and Reform."

18. See *SWB/FE* 7733 (August 28, 1984). On the changing emphasis of the consolidation campaign in this period, see *RMRB*, April 15 and 20, 1984.

19. See *RMRB*, March 23, 1984; Schram, "Economics in Command?," 450.

20. The pointed references to Western training were undoubtedly intended as a slap at the antipollutionists, who were highly critical of Western influences. See, e.g., *RMRB*, March 25, March 30, and April 12–16, 1984; also *GMRB*, March 16 and April 6, 1984.

21. Hu's interview, which was conducted on October 19, 1984, is serialized in *MB*, December 5, 6, and 8, 1984; a translation appears in *ICM* 7, 3 (March 1985): 1–2. The quoted passages from the general secretary's statement were very similar to statements made by Deng Xiaoping at a meeting of the CAC, also held in October 1984. Cf. *BR* 28, 9 (March 4, 1985): 15.

22. *RMRB*, June 12 and July 3, 1984. For analysis, see Kenneth Lieberthal, "The Political Implications of Document No. 1, 1984," 109–13.

23. *BR* 27, 29 (July 16, 1984): 9–10.

24. On the Moganshan conference and its aftermath, see Fewsmith, *Dilemmas of Reform*, chap. 4.

25. *WHB*, cited in *BR* 27, 29 (July 16, 1984): 30.

26. *BR* 27, 33 (August 13, 1984): 31.

27. *BR* 27, 29 (July 16, 1984): 19–23.

28. See, for example, ibid., 21.

29. *BR* 27, 33 (August 13, 1984): 32.

30. *BR* 27, 30 (July 23, 1984).

31. Thomas Bernstein, "China in 1984: The Year of Hong Kong," 38, notes that while media reports of managerial innovation proliferated in this period, large numbers of state enterprises, indeed whole industrial sectors, appeared to be entirely unaffected by such innovation.

32. The text of the October urban reform decision appears in *BR* 27, 44 (November 4, 1984).

33. For further analysis of the urban reform program, see Christine Wong, "The Second Phase of Economic Reform in China," 260–63.

34. *RMRB*, November 2, 1984, in *FBIS*, November 8, 1984, K2–7.

35. On this point, see Fewsmith, *Dilemmas of Reform*, 134–35.

36. Ibid.

37. *FBIS*, January 2, 1985, K1–6.

38. On the implementation of the 1984 enterprise reform drive and its effect on factory management, see Yves Chevrier, "Micropolitics and the Factory Director Responsibility System, 1984–87."

39. On this point see Shirk, *The Political Logic*, chap. 9. For analysis of provincial and local administrative responses to the 1984 urban reforms, see Cabestan, *L'Administration Chinoise*, 219–86.

40. Following the constitutional authorization of small-scale, supplemental private economic activity (*siying jingji*) in 1982, an internal party regulation, "Central Document No. 1 (1983)," tacitly encouraged local authorities to turn a blind eye to the practice of private individuals (and families) hiring more than the authorized limit of seven employees (two assistants and five apprentices) per enterprise. By 1984 the CCP's traditional ideological taboo against the private hiring of labor had been relaxed considerably. See Flemming Christiansen, "The Justification and Legalization of Private Enterprises in China, 1983–88," 80–85.

41. See Gold, "Urban Private Business," 90–92.

42. The appearance of a group of cadre-connected quasi-private entrepreneurs, though new to the PRC, was by no means unprecedented in China. In late imperial and republican times, entrepreneurial success was often a function of one's personal or family ties to officialdom. On the recrudescence of this phenomenon in the 1980s, see Dorothy Solinger, "Urban Entrepreneurs and the State: The Merger of State and Society."

43. See *I&S* 21, 4 (April 1985): 1.

44. On the genesis of the spiraling problem of redundant local enterprise growth, see Christine Wong, "Interpreting Rural Industrial Growth in the Post-Mao Period."

45. The following discussion draws on Richard Baum, "China in 1985: The Greening of the Revolution."

46. *Los Angeles Times* (hereafter *LAT*), February 4, 1985.

47. Zhao's address appears in *BR* 28, 16 (April 22, 1985): III–XV.

48. On the generic sources of clientelism and corruption in Leninist systems, see Kenneth Jowitt, "Soviet Neotraditionalism: The Political Corruption of a Leninist Regime."

49. For a comparison of pre- and postreform patterns of corruption in China, see

Connie Squires Meaney, "Market Reform and Disintegrative Corruption in Urban China"; and Dorothy Solinger, *Chinese Business under Socialism*, chap. 1.

50. *Zhongguo zhichun* (China spring; hereafter ZGZC) (December 1984), in *ICM* 7, 3 (March 1985): 4–7. For analysis of the design flaws inherent in the CC's October 1984 blueprint for a hybrid socialist commodity economy, see Jan S. Prybyla, "Why China's Economic Reforms Won't Work."

51. The Hainan scandal is examined in *FBIS*, August 6, 1985, 1–8; see also Ezra Vogel, *One Step Ahead in China*, 275–94. Despite a CDIC crackdown on the principal culprits involved in the Hainan case, it is by no means clear that flagrant violations of law were actually committed. The loans, foreign exchange transfers, import licenses, and commodity resale arrangements involved in the scheme, though clearly not proper, were apparently legal. This case illustrates how loopholes in reform laws, regulations, and policies enabled opportunistic, well-connected profiteers (often gaogan zidi) to manipulate the system to their advantage. A collection of press reports on the upsurge in cadre corruption and economic crime in this period appears in *ICM* 7, 6 (June 1985). 10–17.

52. Bo Yibo's various anticorruption commentaries appear in *SWB/FE* 7897, 7942, 7993, and 8085 (March 12, May 4, July 3, and October 18, 1985).

53. *SWB/FE* 8085 (October 18, 1985).

54. The case of Hu Shiying is examined in Liu, *"Tell the World,"* 97–98, and Link, *Evening Chats in Beijing*, 53–55.

55. Several years later, in an ironic reversal of form, Ye Fei affixed his signature to a letter jointly written by seven senior PLA generals urging the Chinese government not to employ force against student demonstrators at Tiananmen Square. See chapter 11.

56. On corruption and family politics in the reform period, see He Pin and Gao Xin, *Zhonggong "taizidang"* (China's Communist "princelings"); and Murray Scott Tanner and Michael J. Fedder, "Family Politics, Elite Recruitment, and Succession in Post-Mao China," 98–104. On the protection of high-level cadre children by their powerful parents, see Stanley Rosen, "China in 1986: A Year of Consolidation," 36–37. On the issue of intraparty resistance to legal accountability for CCP members, see James D. Seymour, "Cadre Accountability to the Law."

57. Li Peng reportedly scoffed at Zhao's offer, accusing him of "trying to put pressure on the old ones." See Liu, *"Tell the World,"* 36–37; also chapter 11, below.

58. Deng's statement was reportedly made at a meeting of the CAC in October 1984. See *NYT*, January 13, 1985.

59. Quoted in *NYT*, December 17, 1984.

60. Ibid.

61. For example, soon after the December 7 *RMRB* commentary, the Associated Press sent out an urgent dispatch from Beijing under the headline "China Abandons Marx." See also "Did Marx Fall, or Was He Pushed?" *The Economist*, December 15, 1984.

62. *RMRB*, December 8, 1984 (emphasis added).

63. *NYT*, December 11, 1984.

64. *ICM* 7, 1 (January 1985): 1–3.

65. *RMRB*, January 1, 1985.

66. See, for example, *BR* 28, 7 (February 13, 1985): 4; *NYT*, February 23 and March 31, 1985.

67. *BR* 28, 11 (March 18, 1985): 15–16.

68. *NYT*, December 31, 1984.

69. *Baixing* (hereafter *BX*) 138 (February 16, 1987): 4.

70. *ZM* 91 (May 1985), in *ICM* 7, 7 (July 1985): 1–10.

71. Ibid.; also *SWB/FE* 7927 (April 17, 1985).

72. *ZM* 91 (May 1985), in *ICM* 7, 7 (July 1985): 1–10.

73. *Yecao* (February 1984); in *ICM* 6, 10 (October 1984): 9.

74. See *I&S* 23, 5 (May 1987): 48–56.

75. Liu, *A Higher Kind of Loyalty*, 196–97.

76. Ibid., 197.

77. See Kyna Rubin, "Keeper of the Flame: Wang Ruowang as Moral Critic of the State," 249.

78. *BX* (June 1, 1985), in *SWB/FE* 7970 (June 6, 1985).

79. Ibid.; see also *ICM* 7, 8 (August 1985): 5–8.

80. *SWB/FE* 7973 (June 10, 1985).

81. *SWB/FE* 8005 (July 17, 1985).

82. Kyodo News Service (Tokyo), July 12, 1985.

83. See, for example, the five-part series "Reports from Shenzhen," in *BR* 27, 47 (November 26, 1984), through 28, 6 (February 11, 1985).

84. See, e.g., *FBIS*, April 15, 16, and July 15, 1985; also *BR* 28, 39 (September 30, 1985): 5.

85. *SWB/FE* 7986 (June 25, 1985); *FBIS*, July 8, 1985, K19.

86. XH, August 30, 1985. For analysis of the Shenzhen experience, see *ZM* 94 (August 1985), in *FBIS*, August 1, 1985, W1–7; also Joseph Fewsmith, "Special Economic Zones in the PRC," 78–85; and Vogel, *One Step Ahead*, 125–56.

87. *FBIS*, July 15, 1985.

88. *NYT*, August 4, 1985.

89. *NYT*, February 21, 1985.

90. Quoted in *BR* 28, 13 (April 1, 1985): 15.

91. See Nethercut, "Deng and the Gun." Contrary to the view expressed here, some observers credit Deng with having asserted effective control over the army by the late 1970s. See, e.g., Ellis Joffe, "Party and Military in China: Professionalism in Command," 56–63.

92. Quoted in *NYT*, March 6, 1985.

93. See, for example, *RMRB*, April 30, May 20 and October 9, 1984; *JFJB*, May 8 and 18, 1984.

94. See Alistair Johnston, "Party Rectification in the People's Liberation Army," 611n.

95. Ibid.; also *JFJB*, December 22, 1984; and *NYT*, December 30, 1984, and April 20, 1985.

96. *CD*, January 3, 1985. China's military budget for 1984 was estimated at RMB ¥18 billion (U.S. $6.4 billion), down from ¥22 billion in 1979, the year of the Sino-Vietnamese border war. See *NYT*, January 3, 1985.

97. *NYT*, April 20, 1985.

98. Ibid.; also *FBIS*, January 14, 1985.

99. XH, March 5, 1985; *NYT*, March 6, 1985.

100. Reuters (Wellington), April 19, 1985; *NYT*, April 20, 1985.

101. *BX* (June 1985), in *SWB/FE* 7970 (June 6, 1985). Verbal indiscretions such as this reportedly brought rebukes from several of Hu Yaobang's senior colleagues. When Hu was dismissed from office in January 1987, one of the reasons given was his penchant for talking off the cuff, without authorization. See chapter 9.

102. XH, June 11 and October 27, 1985; *NYT*, June 11 and 23, 1985; and *LAT*, October 28, 1985.

103. See Li Kwok Sing, "Deng Xiaoping and the 2nd Field Army," 40–41.

104. At the time of his retirement, Ye Jianying was too ill to attend meetings or conduct official business. He died a short time later.

105. For a somewhat different interpretation, see *I&S* 21, 12 (December 1985): 76–92.

106. In his October 1984 speech to recent retirees on the CAC, Deng had noted that "It is not easy to ask older comrades to give up their posts. But we must; and we must stay this course. If the old do not vacate their posts, . . . how can our cause thrive?" See *BR* 28, 9 (March 4, 1985): 15.

107. See *I&S* 21, 12 (December 1985): 25, 67.

108. See Tanner and Fedder, "Family Politics," 98–100.

109. *I&S* 21, 12 (December 1985): 23–24.

110. From interviews with former residents of Beijing.

111. *WHB*, September 19, 1985.

112. XH, September 22, 1985.

113. See Stanley Rosen, "The Chinese Communist Party and Chinese Society: Popular Attitudes toward Party Membership and the Party's Image," tables 1, 3, and passim.

114. Xu Shiyou reportedly spearheaded the army's opposition to Hu Yaobang. See *ZM* 110 (December 1986): 6–8; and Dreyer, "Deng Xiaoping: The Soldier," 549.

115. This incident is cited in Pang Pang, *The Death of Hu Yaobang*, 43.

116. The text of Deng's address appears in *Dangde jiaoyu* (Party education) (Tianjin) 5 (1985): 17–21; a partial translation, erroneously dated, appears in *ICM* 7, 11 (November 1985): 18.

CHAPTER 8
SOCIAL ORIGINS OF STUDENT PROTEST

1. Ma Ding's essay was published in *GRRB*, November 2, 1985; it is analyzed in *ZM* 103 (May 1986). Liu Zaifu's article appears in *ZM* 104 (June 1986), trans. in *FBIS*, June 12, 1986, W6–W13.

2. The impact of the 1985–86 literary and artistic renaissance is discussed in Bei Dao, "Terugblik Van Een Balling" (An exile looks back), 77ff.

3. On the role played by liberal media in the reform debates of this period, see Li Cheng and Lynn White, "China's Technocratic Movement and the *World Economic Herald*"; Kate Wright, "The Political Fortunes of Shanghai's 'World Economic Herald'"; and Seth Faison, "The Changing Role of the Chinese Media."

4. For analysis of the main intellectual currents of this period, see David A. Kelly, "The Chinese Student Movement and Its Intellectual Antecedents." On the emergence of an incipient civil society in China, see David Strand, "Protest in Beijing: Civil Society and Public Sphere in China"; see also Martin K. Whyte, "Urban China: A Civil Society in the Making?"; and "Symposium on Civil Society and the Public Sphere." Key speeches and writings of Liu Binyan, Fang Lizhi, Wang Ruowang, and Su Shaozhi from this period are translated in *CLG* 21, 2 (Summer 1988).

5. On the relationship between economic reform and the social mobilization of urban discontent in this period, see Halpern, "Economic Reform, Social Mobilization, and Democratization in Post Mao China." On the dysfunctional social effects of partial reform, see Zweig, "Dilemmas of Partial Reform"; James T. Myers, "China: Modern-

ization and 'Unhealthy Tendencies' "; and James C. Hsiung, "Mainland China's Paradox of Partial Reform: A Postmortem on Tiananmen," *I&S* 26, 6 (June 1990): 29–43.

6. See *ZM* 93 (July 1985) and *LW* 4 (1985).

7. For analysis of the sources of student unrest, see *Chaoliu yuekan* (hereafter *CLYK*) 1 (March 1987): 45–54; and *Zhong bao* (hereafter *ZB*), December 31, 1985, in *ICM* 8, 2 (February 1986): 4–6. Jeffrey N. Wasserstrom, "Student Protests and the Chinese Tradition, 1919–89," traces the history of student protest in China.

8. *ICM* 9, 1 (January 1987): 3–6.

9. For a selection of student posters from the 1985 protest demonstrations at Tiananmen Square, see ibid.

10. *ZM* (December 1985), in *FBIS*, December 23, 1985, W1–3.

11. Ibid.

12. Suzanne Pepper, *Deng Xiaoping's Political and Economic Reforms and the Chinese Student Protests*, makes a similar point.

13. See *I&S* 25, 2 (February 1989): 9–11.

14. African exchange students in China were frequently unhappy with their situation. Most were engineering or polytechnical students who had been sent to China by their home governments—often involuntarily—for extended periods of technical training at China's expense. Living on meager allowances in austere, segregated campus facilities, surrounded by an alien, often chauvinistic culture, facing up to five years of continuous study with little or no opportunity for home leave or other R&R, many African students displayed signs of depression, anger, and alienation.

15. As part of the "three supports and two militarys" campaign in the Cultural Revolution, PLA units occupied college campuses in many Chinese cities. In some cases, due to a chronic shortage of military housing, the soldiers remained on the campuses for as long as two decades. See chapter 6.

16. *ZB*, December 28, 1985, in *ICM* 8, 2 (February 1986).

17. See *ZM* 111 (January 1987), in *FBIS*, January 5, 1987, K9–10. The jailbreak incident (which allegedly included an attempt by the father of the incarcerated youth to free his son by force) is recounted in Benedict Stavis, *China's Political Reforms: An Interim Report*, 91.

18. These and other related survey research data are analyzed in Bruce Reynolds, *Reform in China: Challenges and Choices*, 59–63 and passim.

19. Stanley Rosen, "Youth and Students in China."

20. *FEER*, October 16, 1986, 69–70. Disaffection with the inequitable effects of reform also began to rise in the countryside in this period. Most rural complaints appeared to center on the proliferation of illegal businesses, cadre corruption, discrimination against private households, and envy of so-called ¥10,000 households. See, e.g., *LW* 45 (1985); *ZB*, December 18, 1985; and *ICM* 8, 2 (February 1986): 7–13. For analysis of the sources of rural discontent, see Oi, "Partial Market Reform."

21. See, e.g., *ZM* 94 (August 1985); *Faxue yanjiu* (hereafter *FXYJ*) 11 (November 1985) and 2 (February 1986); XH, December 19, 1985; *ICM* 7, 11 (November 1985): 25; and Lawrence R. Sullivan, "Assault on Reforms: Conservative Criticism of Political and Economic Liberalization in China, 1985–86," 209–12.

22. *LW* 33 (1985). Many of these new police recruits were ex-servicemen demobilized in the army reorganization of 1984–85.

23. In an unusual exception to the normal rule of exempting gaogan zidi from severe legal punishment, it was reported that a distant relative of President Li Xiannian was executed in 1986. Li was said to have become furious with Hu Yaobang when the Central Secretariat refused to intervene with the courts to prevent the execution.

24. *Shehui kexue* (Social sciences; hereafter *SHKX*) (1986), in *ICM* 8, 7 (July 1986): 15–20.

25. See Cabestan, *L'Administration Chinoise*, 338–40.

26. Ibid.; see also XH, January 10–11, 1986; *FEER*, January 23 and 30, 1986; and Rosen, "China in 1986," 37.

27. See *WWP*, July 21–22, 1986; also *ICM* 8, 9 (September 1986): 4–5.

28. *RR* 30, 20 (May 18, 1987): 14–15; *ICM* 8, 9 (September 1986): 5–6; also Rosen, "China in 1986," 38.

29. A useful collection of newspaper articles, essays, and documents pertaining to proposals for political reform in this period appears in *CLG* 20, 1 (Spring 1987).

30. Ibid.

31. *Shijie jingji daobao* (World economic herald; hereafter *SJJJDB*), June 2, 1986, in *CLG* 20, 1 (Spring 1987).

32. XH, August 14, 1986; *I&S* 22, 9 (September 1986): 4–7; and Rosen, "China in 1986," 39–40.

33. *FXYJ* 10 (October 1986), in *CLG* 20, 1 (Spring 1987).

34. *SHKX* 4 (1986), in *ICM* 8, 11 (November 1986): 1–4.

35. Feng Shengbao, "Preparations for the Blueprint on Political Restructuring Presented by Zhao Ziyang at the Thirteenth Party Congress," 2.

36. *ZM* 108 (October 1986), in *FBIS*, September 19, 1986, K20; *DGB*, September 17, 1986, in *FBIS*, September 29, 1986, K16.

37. For analysis of these developments, See Kelly, "The Chinese Student Movement," 135–38; and Stavis, *China's Political Reforms*, 51–59.

38. Feng, "Preparations for the Blueprint."

39. On the Beidaihe meeting, see *WWP*, August 8, 1986, in *SWB/FE* 8335 (August 12, 1986).

40. The text of the resolution appears in *BR* 29, 40 (October 6, 1986): I–VIII.

41. Ruan, *Deng Xiaoping diguo*, 185–86.

42. The argument over bourgeois liberalization at the Sixth Plenum is discussed in ibid. The text of Deng's address is in *BR* 30, 26 (June 29, 1987): 14; a slightly different version appears in *CLG* 21, 1 (Spring 1988): 22–23.

43. Ruan, *Deng Xiaoping diguo*, 185–86; *BR* 30, 26 (June 29, 1987): 14; *I&S* 23, 6 (June 1987): 17–18.

44. Ruan, *Deng Xiaoping diguo*, 186.

45. Ibid.

46. Feng, "Preparations for the Blueprint." The reform group's major activity in this period was to sponsor a series of academic panels and symposia on various aspects of political reform, in preparation for drafting a comprehensive reform plan to be introduced at the Thirteenth Party Congress.

47. *SWB/FE* 8407 (November 4, 1986).

48. Feng, "Preparations for the Blueprint," 2–4.

49. *RMRB*, January 15, 1987, in *FBIS*, January 16, 1987, K14.

50. *I&S* 23, 6 (June 1987): 17.

51. XH, November 26, 1986. Peng's definition of collective democracy restates the classical Leninist principle of democratic centralism.

52. Fang's speech appears in *ICM* 8, 12 (December 1986): 8–10.

53. *I&S* 23, 4 (April 1987): 124–42.

54. Stavis, *China's Political Reforms*, 92–95, gives a vivid account of these events.

55. XH, December 3, 1986, in *FBIS*, December 23, 1986, K18–19.

56. *SCMP*, January 12, 1987; *ZM* 111 (January 1987).

57. XH, November 15, 1986. The text of the amended electoral law appears in *FBIS*, December 8, 1986. Previously, democratic reform had only been applicable to elections at the county level and below.

58. *BR* 29, 8 (February 23, 1987): 17–18.

59. For analysis of the 1986 student demonstrations see Stavis, *China's Political Reforms*, 96–104; Julia Kwong, "The 1986 Student Demonstrations in China: A Democratic Movement?"; Lowell Dittmer, "Reform, Succession, and the Resurgence of Mainland China's Old Guard"; *ICM* 9, 1 (January 1987): 2–6; and *ICM* 9, 3 (March 1987): 27–28.

60. *SCMP*, December 24, 1986; Stavis, *China's Political Reforms*, 97.

61. XH, December 23, 1986, in *ICM* 9, 4 (April 1987): 3–4.

62. *RMRB*, December 25, 1986.

63. *ZM* 111 (January 1987), in *ICM* 9, 3 (March 1987): 24–26.

64. *SWB/FE* 8464 (January 13, 1987); *ZBYK* 2 (February 1987): 26.

65. Ruan, *Deng Xiaoping diguo*, 190.

66. Feng, "Preparations for the Blueprint," 8.

67. The text of Deng's talk was incorporated into "Central Document No. 1 (1987)," promulgated on January 6, 1987. This and other related documents from the antiliberalization campaign appear in *CLG* 21, 1 (Spring 1988): 18–21. My thanks to *CLG* editor James Tong for making available the original Chinese text of Central Document No. 1. Passages quoted below are from this source.

68. Deng's speech of December 30, 1986, was revised and abridged for publication three years later, after the Tiananmen crackdown of June 1989. In the altered version, all references to the Polish situation and to Wei Jingsheng were excised and a fresh "due process" clause was inserted, stating that "toward those whose main goal is to stir up trouble, and who violate criminal law, we shall deal with them according to the law." The revised text of Deng's speech appears in *Deng Xiaoping tongzhi lun jianchi si xiang jiben yuance fandui zichanjieji ziyouhua* (Comrade Deng Xiaoping on upholding the four cardinal principles and opposing bourgeois liberalization), 138–42.

CHAPTER 9
COMBATING BOURGEOIS LIBERALIZATION

1. *BX* 141 (April 1, 1987): 3. Other senior leaders who participated in the December 27 meeting included Yang Shangkun and Yu Qiuli.

2. Hong Kong sources report that the decision to sack Hu Yaobang had been made as early as November 1986—*before* the December student demonstrations—during a rancorous meeting of the Central Party Secretariat at which Hu and Deng allegedly got into a shouting match over the latter's repeated failure to step down as chairman of the MAC. See *ZM*, February 1, 1987, in *FBIS*, January 29, 1987, K2; and Goodman, *Deng Xiaoping*, 106. Ruan, *Deng Xiaoping diguo*, 187, claims that after the Sixth Plenum of September 1986, Deng urged Hu to step down as general secretary in order to take up the post of MAC chairman, which Deng intended to relinquish at the 13th Party Congress. If true, these claims suggest that Deng differed with conservatives mainly over the *timing* of Hu's removal, rather than the *necessity* thereof.

3. The document appears in *ICM* 9, 4 (April 1987): 1–2.

4. Kyodo, January 9, 1987; *SWB/FE* 8462 (January 10, 1987). The separate decisions to expel the three liberals were officially reported in XH, January 14 and 19, 1987, and *RMRB*, January 24, 1987.

5. See Wilson and Ji, "Leadership by 'Lines,'" 34.

6. *SWB/FE* 8467 (January 16, 1987).

7. Black and Munro, *Black Hands*, 107.

8. According to Ruan Ming, Chen Yun had Zhao Ziyang's 1984 letter (in which Zhao complained about Hu Yaobang's economic meddling) made available to participants at the January 16 Politburo meeting. Ruan, *Lishi zhuanzhedian*, further claims that Hu Yaobang was deeply shocked when he first learned, at the meeting, of the letter's existence and contents. Ruan's account of these events is partially contradicted by at least one knowledgeable Chinese source, who claims that Zhao never betrayed Hu Yaobang (personal communication, May 27, 1993).

9. In this connection, the document made explicit reference to the late U.S. Secretary of State John Foster Dulles, who once said that "the policy of the American government is to encourage liberalization in the Soviet Union and the countries of Eastern Europe." Apparently, Hu Yaobang was being judged guilty by association for having (unwittingly) advanced the aims of U.S. imperialism! Similar allegations, to the effect that China's liberal reformers were promoting Western schemes for the "peaceful evolution" (*heping yanbian*) of bourgeois democracy, later provided a significant part of the government's rationale for cracking down on student demonstrators in the spring of 1989.

10. The text of Central Document No. 3 appears in *ICM* 9, 5 (May 1987): 1–3.

11. *DGB*, April 9, 1987. The anti-Hu activities of CCP old-timers are examined in Ruan, *Deng Xiaoping diguo*, chap. 10.

12. *ICM* 9, 5 (May 1987): 2–3.

13. Ibid., 3.

14. *ICM* 9, 12 (December 1987): 34; and *China News Analysis* (hereafter *CNA*) 1342 (September 1, 1987): 4. See also Ruan, *Deng Xiaoping diguo*, 209–11. An account of Liu Binyan's expulsion from the party appears in Liu, *A Higher Kind of Loyalty*, chap. 18.

15. *ICM* 9, 5 (May 1987): 30.

16. Stavis, *China's Political Reforms*, 123.

17. See *SWB/FE* 8512 (March 10, 1987); *BX* 140 (March 16, 1987); and *ICM* 9, 5 (May 1987): 3–5, 10.

18. For further documentation and analysis of the 1987 antiliberalization drive, see *BX* 140 (March 16, 1987); *Jiushi niandai* (The nineties; hereafter *JSND*) 4 and 5 (1987); Kelly, "The Chinese Student Movement"; and Liu, *A Higher Kind of Loyalty*, chap. 18.

19. Liu, *A Higher Kind of Loyalty*, 262–63.

20. *ICM* 9, 5 (May 1987): 3–5, 10. The battle over the text of Document No. 4 (1987) is detailed in Ruan, *Deng Xiaoping diguo*, 205–7.

21. *BR* 30, 4 (January 26, 1987): 5. Zhao's "acting" designation was removed later in the year, when the Thirteenth Party Congress formalized his promotion.

22. *BR* 30, 5–6 (February 9, 1987): 6–7.

23. *Zhongguo qingnian bao* (China youth news; hereafter *ZGQNB*), February 12, 1987, in *ICM* 9, 5 (May 1987): 13–14.

24. A translation of Li Peng's address appears in *ICM* 9, 4 (April 1987): 5–6.

25. Ibid., 6. See also XH, February 2 and 16, 1987.

26. *DGB*, February 14 and March 29, 1987.

27. Zhao's report appears in *BR* 30, 16 (April 20, 1987): III–XX.

28. *RMRB*, March 4, 1987.

29. *BR* 30, 16 (April 20, 1987): XVI.

30. Chen Yizi, *Zhongguo shinian gaige yu bajiu minyun: Beijing liusi tusha de beihou* (China's ten years of reform and the 1989 democracy movement: Behind the Beijing massacre of June 4); Wilson and Ji, "Leadership by 'Lines,'" 34–35. See also Stuart R. Schram, "China after the 13th Congress," 180; and Tony Saich, "The Thirteenth Congress of the Chinese Communist Party: An Agenda for Reform?," 205.

31. Deng Xiaoping, *Fundamental Issues in Present-Day China*; see also *BR* 30, 20 (May 18, 1987): 14–17.

32. See *DGB*, April 9, 1987; and *BR* 30, 17 (April 27, 1987): 14–15. Despite Peng's recommendation, it was Yang Shangkun, not Deng Xiaoping, who remained on the Politburo as the lone old-timer following the Thirteenth Congress. In addition to Deng, Yang, and Peng, the other surviving "immortals" were Li Xiannian, Chen Yun, Deng Yingchao, and Bo Yibo.

33. *WHB*, August 8, 1989; Wilson and Ji, "Leadership by 'Lines,'" 35, n. 17.

34. Quoted in Michel Oksenberg, "China's 13th Party Congress," 15–16.

35. Feng, "Preparations for the Blueprint," 7.

36. Oksenberg, "China's 13th Party Congress," 15–16.

37. *DGB*, June 4, 1987.

38. *I&S* 23, 12 (December 1987): 96.

39. XH, August 28, 1987, in *SWB/FE* 8661 (September 1, 1987).

40. *SWB/FE* 8676 (September 18, 1987). The seven included six elderly veterans (Chen Yun, Li Xiannian, Peng Zhen, Hu Qiaomu, Xi Zhongxun, and Fang Yi) and one relative newcomer to the Politburo, Ni Zhifu.

41. *SWB/FE* 8684 (September 28, 1987).

42. The Thirteenth Congress is analyzed in Schram, "China after the 13th Congress"; Saich, "The Thirteenth Congress"; Oksenberg, "China's 13th Party Congress"; and *I&S* 23, 12 (December 1987): 12–99.

43. Saich, "The Thirteenth Congress," 204.

44. Oksenberg, "China's 13th Party Congress," describes this procedure; see also Wilson and Ji, "Leadership by 'Lines,'" 36.

45. Schram, "China after the 13th Congress," 184; Ruan, *Deng Xiaoping diguo*, 211–12. As stipulated in the Party Constitution, the Politburo was selected from among CC members.

46. *I&S* 23, 12 (December 1987): 95ff.

47. Deng also retained his concurrent chairmanship of the governmental MAC.

48. *ZM* 122 (December 1987), in *ICM* 10, 1 (January 1988): 9.

49. See chapter 11. Additional details concerning the nature of this arrangement appear in *ZM* 121 (November 1990).

50. Zhao's report appears in *BR* 30, 45 (November 9–15, 1987): I–XXVII.

51. Ibid., XXVI.

52. See *CNA* 1354 (February 15, 1988): 4.

53. *BR* 30, 45 (November 9–16, 1987): III–IV.

54. See Schram, "China after the 13th Congress," 177–78.

55. *The Guardian*, October 30, 1987, cited in Saich, "The Thirteenth Congress," 205.

56. *BR* 30, 45 (November 9–16, 1987): XI–XIV.

57. Ibid., IX.

58. Ibid., XV–XXI.

59. Ibid., XVI. On the attempt to separate party and government leadership at the

Thirteenth Congress, see Cabestan, *L'Administration Chinoise*, 340–42, and Tony Saich, "The Reform Decade in China: The Limits to Revolution from Above," 35–37.

60. On this point, see John P. Burns, "Chinese Civil Service Reform: The 13th Party Congress"; and Cabestan, *L'Administration Chinoise*.

61. *BR* 30, 45 (November 9–16, 1987): XIX.

62. *BR* 30, 50 (December 14–20, 1987): 16.

63. The idea of retaining strong authoritarian institutions throughout the inherently turbulent and destabilizing transitional processes of socialist modernization and reform was borrowed by Zhao's academic advisers from the work of American political scientist Samuel P. Huntington, *Political Order in Changing Societies*, chap. 1 and passim.

64. *BR* 30, 45 (November 9–15, 1987): VI, XV.

65. See *WWP*, December 24, 1987; *CNA* 1351 (January 1, 1988): 4.

66. These developments are documented in *I&S* 24, 2 (February 1988): 1; *WWP*, April 28, 1988; *RMRB*, May 2, 1988, 3; *CNA* 1360 (May 15, 1988): 4; and *Qiushi* (hereafter *QS*) 1 (July 1, 1988), in *JPRS* CAR-88–043 (August 4, 1988).

67. For further analysis see Lowell Dittmer, "China in 1988: The Dilemma of Continuing Reform," 13–15.

68. Tan Jian (research department chairman, CASS Institute of Political Science), in *WWP*, November 7–8, 1987; trans. in *ICM* 10, 1 (January 1988): 2.

69. Yu Haocheng (vice-chairman, Chinese Political Science Association), in ibid.

70. Gao Fang (professor of international politics, People's University), in ibid.

71. Ma Peiwen (former editor-in-chief, *Guangming Daily*; member of the governing council, Chinese Political Science Association), in ibid.

72. *BX* 155 (November 1, 1987).

73. *BR* 31, 1 (January 4–10, 1989): 4.

74. By the late 1980s these four luxury items, popularly known as the "four haves," had become prime status symbols in China's burgeoning consumer culture, replacing such previous benchmark products as the "three things that go round"—watches, bicycles, and sewing machines—as the standard yardstick of consumer affluence.

75. *NFRB*, May 3, 1988, in *ICM* 10, 7 (July 1988): 21.

76. *ICM* 10, 1 (January 1988): 26.

77. On economic overheating in 1987–88, see Cabestan, *L'Administration Chinoise*, 235–38; *WWP*, June 5, 1988; and *BR* 31, 1 (January 4–10, 1988): 4. The problem of rising prices is discussed in XH, January 12 and 14 and February 1, 1988, in *ICM* 10, 3 (March 1988): 12–18; and *JSND* (March 1988): 44–46.

78. *BR* 31, 37 (September 12–18, 1988): 29; *WWP*, September 4, 1988; and John P. Burns, "China's Governance: Political Reforms In a Turbulent Environment," 489.

CHAPTER 10
BITTERSWEET FRUITS OF REFORM

1. For useful accounts of the NPC proceedings, see *CNA* 1360 (May 15, 1988): 1–10; *FEER*, April 21, 1988, 12–13; and Dittmer, "China in 1988," 16–18.

2. *CNA* 1360 (May 15, 1988): 3–4.

3. Cabestan, *L'Administration Chinoise*, 249–55, examines interprovincial inequities in the collection and distribution of government revenues.

4. Shi Tianjian, "Role Culture and Political Liberalism among Deputies to

the Seventh National People's Congress." See also O'Brien, *Reform without Liberalization*.

5. Zhao's report to the Second Plenum is summarized in *BR* 31, 13 (March 28–April 3, 1988): 5–6. For Zhao's views on coastal development, see *BR* 31, 5 (February 1–7, 1988): 5.

6. Li's priorities are outlined in *BR* 31, 2 (January 11–17, 1988): 5. The differences between Li Peng and Zhao Ziyang are analyzed in Fewsmith, *Dilemmas of Reform*, 217–20.

7. Li's report appears in *BR* 31, 17 (April 25–May 1, 1988): 18–43. For analysis see *I&S* 24, 6 (June 1988): 12–18.

8. Cabestan, *L'Administration Chinoise*, 215–17, discusses the provisions and ambiguities of the bankruptcy legislation.

9. *FEER*, April 21, 1988, 13; *I&S* 24, 7 (July 1988): 9–11.

10. *WWP*, reported in *FEER*, November 3, 1988, 23; also *ICM* 11, 1 (January 1989): 15–16.

11. On the impact (real and anticipated) of housing reform, see *BR* 31, 46 (November 14–20, 1988): 14–18; *CNA* 1358 (April 15, 1988): 1–9; and *FEER*, May 26, 1988, 72–73.

12. *WWP*, July 4, 1988; and *CNA* 1370 (October 15, 1988): 1.

13. By 1989 the figure had risen to 10 percent. See Tony Saich, "Urban Society in China," 16.

14. *SWB/FE* 0234 (August 19, 1988); *ICM* 10, 12 (December 1988): 28–29.

15. *RMRB*, August 20, 1988.

16. *Jingji ribao* (Economic daily; hereafter *JJRB*) January 6, 1988, in *ICM* 10, 4 (April 1988): 14.

17. See Dorothy Solinger, "Capitalist Measures with Chinese Characteristics," 22–23.

18. In 1990 there were approximately sixty to eighty million floaters in China's urban areas. In some cities, the floating population was held responsible for up to one-third of all crime. In Beijing in 1988, forty or fifty floaters were arrested daily for petty larceny. See Dorothy Solinger, *China's Transients and the State: A Form of Civil Society?*, 10, 20, and passim; also Saich, "Urban Society," 20–23.

19. *FBIS*, February 1, 1989, 47; see also *LW* 36 (September 5, 1988): 18–19, in *FBIS*, September 14, 1988, 36; *CNA* 1359 (May 1, 1988): 1–8; *ICM* 10, 12 (December 1988): 28–33; and *SCMP*, September 3, 1988, in *FBIS*, September 6, 1988. On the rising incidence of labor unrest in the mid- and late 1980s, see Black and Munro, *Black Hands*, 114–21, and Saich, "Urban Society," 16–17.

20. See chapter 11.

21. The figures continued to rise in succeeding years. In 1990 police throughout the country handled two million criminal cases. See Central People's Broadcasting Station (Beijing), February 21, 1991, in *ICM* 13, 4 (April 1991): 18; cf. also *I&S* 24, 6 (June 1988): 30.

22. *FEER*, June 16, 1988, 22. In Beijing municipality more than 27 percent of the eleven thousand people investigated for committing economic crimes between 1982 and 1986 were members of the Communist Party.

23. *DGB*, April 12, 1988, in *ICM* 10, 6 (June 1988): 1.

24. XH, August 11, 1988, in *FBIS*, August 11, 1988, 18. Another 25,000 were expelled in 1988.

25. The data are presented in Rosen, "The Chinese Communist Party and Chinese Society," 30.

26. Survey data cited in ibid., 21, 49, 53.

27. Ibid., 28–29.

28. This incident, known as the "She'kou storm," was talked about in newspaper editorials and in letters to the editor for months afterward. See *CNA* 1374 (December 15, 1988): 2–4; and *FEER*, October 27, 1988, 41. Detailed analysis of the episode appears in Luo Xu, "The 'Shekou Storm': Changes in the Mentality of Chinese Youth Prior to Tiananmen."

29. AFP (Hong Kong), May 30, 1988.

30. *ICM* 10, 11 (November 1988): 4; *WWP*, September 13, 1988, 14; *CNA* 1371 (November 1, 1988): 2–3.

31. *I&S* 24, 1 (January 1988): 162; *RMRB*, June 8, 1988; *SWB/FE* 0172 (June 8, 1988); *FEER*, June 16, 1988, 18, and July 21, 1988, 19–21. Six people were subsequently arrested and tried for the murder of the Beida student.

32. *DGB*, August 6, 1988. For additional documentation on social unrest in this period, see Burns, "China's Governance," and Dittmer, "China in 1988."

33. Accounts of the "River Elegy" controversy appear in *FEER*, September 1, 1988, 40–43; *ICM* 11, 1 (January 1989): 1–10; *JPRS* CAR-89-004 (January 11, 1989): 6; and Woei Lien Chong, "Present Worries of the Chinese Democrats: Notes on Fang Lizhi, Liu Binyan, and the Film 'River Elegy.'"

34. *JSND* 11 (November 1988): 62–63, in *I&S* 25, 6 (June 1989): 29–30.

35. *ICM* 11, 1 (January 1989): 2.

36. On the economic debates of 1988, see Fewsmith, *Dilemmas of Reform*, chap. 7; and Gary Zou, "Debates on China's Economic Situation and Reform Strategies."

37. XH, May 19 and 24, 1988, in *FBIS*, May 19 and 26, 1988; *DGB*, July 26, 1988, in *ICM* 10, 9 (September 1988): 26; and *FEER*, November 9, 1988, 35–36.

38. See *WWP*, July 30 and August 1, 1988; and *DGB*, July 26, 1988, in *ICM* 10, 9 (September 1988): 26–28.

39. *ICM* 10, 9 (September 1988): 26–28; *I&S* 24, 9 (September 1988): 1–4; *FEER*, May 26 and August 4, 1988.

40. *FEER*, September 22 and 29, 1988.

41. A number of media reports about rising consumer complaints in this period appear in *ICM* 10, 10 (October 1988): 11–14, and 10, 11 (November 1988): 14–20.

42. Wilson and Ji, "Leadership by 'Lines,'" 35.

43. *ZM* 131 (September 1988), in *I&S* 24, 10 (October 1988): 1. The 1988 Beidaihe debates are chronicled in *JSND* 9 (September 1989): 16–19, in *ICM* 10, 9 (September 1988): 24–29; and Fewsmith, *Dilemmas of Reform*, 225–27.

44. On the spate of media rumors that circulated during the 1988 Beidaihe meetings, see *DGB*, August 14, 1988, in *ICM* 10, 10 (October 1988): 26–27.

45. See Wilson and Ji, "Leadership by 'Lines,'" 37.

46. *FEER*, September 22, 1988, 70–71.

47. *I&S* 24, 9 (September 1988): 4.

48. *Jing bao* (The mirror; hereafter *JB*) 11 (November 1988): 20–23, in *JPRS* CAR-89-007 (January 19, 1989): 10–11.

49. *RMRB*, September 27 and October 1, 1988; *CNA* 1370 (October 15, 1988): 4. Despite Zhao's fall from grace, he presented the political report to the Third Plenum. The text appears in *BR* 31, 46 (November 14–20, 1988): I–VIII.

50. *WWP*, October 11, 1988, 1; *CNA* 1371 (November 1, 1988): 4.

51. *FEER*, October 27, 1988, 38–42, and December 8, 1988, 60–61; *NYT*, December 11, 1988. On the causes, consequences, and political implications of diminishing central control over fiscal levers and resource allocations, see Barry Naughton, "The Decline of Central Control over Investment in Post-Mao China," and "Macroeconomic Obstacles to Reform in China"; Shirk, *The Political Logic*, chap. 9; and Christine Wong, "Central-Local Relations in an Era of Fiscal Decline: The Paradox of Fiscal Decentralization in Post-Mao China."

52. Qiao Shi's centrist views on party discipline and combating cadre corruption appear in *RMRB*, October 29, 1988, in *ICM* 11, 2 (February 1989): 2–3.

53. *BR* 31, 46 (November 14–20, 1988): II.

54. Kanghua reportedly had more than 170 subsidiaries.

55. See *FEER*, November 3, 1988, 23–25, and November 17, 1988, 90–92. On the high-level patronage networks that served to protect and nurture "private" companies, see Solinger, "Urban Entrepreneurs and the State."

56. *QS* 8 (October 16, 1988): 46–47, in *JPRS* CAR-89-001 (January 3, 1989): 41–42. For additional media accounts of the effects of guandao, see *ICM* 11, 2 (February 1989): 3–6.

57. Although Deng Pufang's name was widely linked to corruption, Harrison Salisbury has argued that the younger Deng was an innocent victim of unscrupulous associates within the Kanghua Corporation, who traded on his famous name to secure profitable business contacts. Based on sources close to the Deng family, Salisbury, *The New Emperors*, 420–22, claims that Deng Pufang was a genuine humanist who possessed "an idealistic and rather innocent mind."

58. See *ICM* 11, 1 (January 1989): 29–30.

59. Wu Jiaxiang, cited in Ma Shu Yun, "The Rise and Fall of Neo-Authoritarianism in China," 13–14 (emphasis added).

60. See Li and White, "China's Technocratic Movement."

61. On the tensions between neo-authoritarians and democrats, see Link, *Evening Chats in Beijing*, 283–90, and chapter 11 below.

62. *JB* 1 (January 1989): 29; *I&S* 25, 6 (June 1989): 30.

63. The proceedings of the conference are discussed in *JB* 137 (1988): 40–42, in *JPRS* CAR-89-018 (March 1, 1989): 12–16. Although Wang Ruoshui and Yu Haocheng had been invited to attend the decennial reform conference, the two men boycotted the proceedings in protest over the blacklisting of several of their colleagues, including political scientist Yan Jiaqi, who had been barred from attending.

64. *GMRB*, December 29 and 31, 1988. These events are analyzed in Lowell Dittmer, "The Tiananmen Massacre"; Wright, "The Political Fortunes"; and Faison, "The Changing Role of the Chinese Media."

65. Even before this particular incident, Hehai University had a rather long history of racial tensions. See *I&S* 25, 2 (February 1989): 9–11; and *ICM* 11, 2 (February 1989): 29.

66. *I&S* 25, 2 (February 1989): 9–11.

67. For a slightly different interpretation of the anti-African riots of 1988, stressing deliberate elite manipulation of the latent chauvinism of Chinese students, see Edward Friedman, "Permanent Technological Revolution and China's Torturous Path to Democratizing Leninism." On the political and cultural roots of racial tensions in contemporary China, see Michael J. Sullivan, "The 1988–1989 Nanjing Anti-African Protests."

68. See *FEER*, December 15, 1989, 38–39.

69. These events are examined in *JB* (April 10, 1989): 22–23; *I&S* 25, 3 (March 1989): 1, 4–6; *ZM* 137 (March 1989): 6–9; Orville Schell, *Mandate of Heaven*, 37–38; and Link, *Evening Chats in Beijing*, 260–61.

70. *I&S* 25, 3 (March 1989): 4–7; *ZM* 138 (April 1989): 6–9.

71. *ZM* 138 (April 1989): 6–9; *SCMP*, March 22, 1989; *I&S* 25, 6 (June 1989): 20.

72. Wilson and Ji, "Leadership by 'Lines,' " 38.

73. *ZM* 137 (March 1989): 6–9.

74. *I&S* 25, 3 (March 1989): 7.

75. Ibid., 5; *ZM* 137 (March 1989): 6–9; Dittmer, "The Tiananmen Massacre," 5.

76. *The Washington Post*, February 28, 1989. In addition to Fang, two other prominent liberal intellectuals, Liu Binyan and playwright Wu Zuguang, had also been invited to the February 26 presidential banquet in Beijing; however, neither man was prevented by the authorities from attending. The February 26 incident is discussed in detail in Link, *Evening Chats in Beijing*, 29–33.

77. *The Economist* (London), March 4, 1989, 67; Chong, "Present Worries of the Chinese Democrats," 3; and *AW*, July 7, 1989, 26–31.

78. The circumstances of Hu Yaobang's two heart attacks are discussed in Pang, *The Death of Hu Yaobang*, 2–10, 45–49; and Salisbury, *The New Emperors*, 439.

CHAPTER 11
THE BEIJING SPRING

1. *JB* (May 10, 1989): 2–6. A number of other rumors were also spread about the circumstances of Hu's initial heart attack. See *CLG* 23, 1 (Spring 1990): 56–57.

2. Commenting on the frequent use of mourning rituals as "cover" for the expression of political sentiments in Chinese culture, Lucian Pye, "Tiananmen and Chinese Political Culture: The Escalation of Confrontation from Moralizing to Revenge," 333, has written that "Funeral rituals provide one of the few opportunities Chinese have for publicly displaying emotion. . . . In Chinese culture, public grieving can legitimize the expression of sentiments that are only vaguely related to any sense of personal loss." Joseph Esherick and Jeffrey Wasserstrom, "Acting Out Democracy: Political Theatre in Modern China," 33, make a similar point.

3. In reconstructing the events of this period I have found the following sources particularly useful: Guojia Jiaowei Sixiang Zhengzhi Gongzuo Sipian, *Jingxin dongpode 56 tian* (The startling 56 days); Timothy Brook, *Quelling the People: The Military Suppression of the Beijing People's Movement*; Liu, *"Tell the World"*; Schell, *Mandate of Heaven*, part 1; "CND Interview with Gao Xin"; Tony Saich, "The Rise and Fall of the Beijing People's Movement"; Perry, "Casting a Chinese 'Democracy' Movement"; Andrew G. Walder and Gong Xiaoxia, "Workers in the Tiananmen Protests: The Politics of the Beijing Workers' Autonomous Federation"; Andrew J. Nathan, "Chinese Democracy in 1989: Continuity and Change"; Pye, "Tiananmen and Chinese Political Culture"; Corinna-Barbara Francis, "The Progress of Protest in China"; Frank Niming, "Learning How to Protest"; Ruth Cremerius et al., *Studentenprotest und Repression in China, April–Juni 1989: Analyse, Chronologie, Dokumente*; and *CLG* 23, 1 (Spring 1990), and 23, 2 (Summer 1990).

4. Guojia Jiaowei, *Jingxin dongpode 56 tian*, 21–31; *CLG* 23, 2 (Summer 1990): 17–18.

5. See chapter 8.

6. XH, April 27, 1989.

7. AFP (Beijing), April 26, 1989.

8. These events are chronicled in *CLG* 23, 2 (Summer 1990): 22–23.

9. *JB*, May 10, 1989, 22–26; Pye, "Tiananmen and Chinese Political Culture," 337.

10. *CLG* 23, 2 (Summer 1990): 31.

11. See Niming, "Learning How to Protest," 84–86; Walder and Gong, "Workers in the Tiananmen Protests"; and Perry, "Casting a Chinese 'Democracy' Movement."

12. Guojia Jiaowei, *Jingxin dongpode 56 tian*, 34–47.

13. For a survey of provincial reactions to the Tiananmen demonstrations, see Jonathan Unger, ed., *The Pro-Democracy Protests in China: Reports from the Provinces*.

14. See John H. Meier, "Tiananmen 1989: The View from Shanghai," 5.

15. See *CLG* 23, 1 (Spring 1990): 80.

16. Quoted in Unger, *The Pro-Democracy Protests*, 207.

17. *FEER*, May 11, 1989, 12.

18. There were unconfirmed reports that a few students were beaten—at least one badly—during the April 27 demonstration. See Brook, *Quelling the People*, 34.

19. This point is emphasized by Pye, "Tiananmen and Chinese Political Culture," 339–40. On student demonstrations as political theater, see Esherick and Wasserstrom, "Acting Out Democracy," 32–37 and passim.

20. This and other opinion surveys concerning public attitudes toward the student movement in April–May 1989 are reproduced in *China Information* 4, 1 (Summer 1989): 94–124.

21. *FEER*, May 11, 1989, 11–12.

22. Guojia Jiaowei, *Jingxin dongpode 56 tian*, 94; Rosen, "Youth and Students in China."

23. *MB*, May 26, 1989; *SCMP*, May 29, 1989.

24. *RMRB*, May 5, 1989; *ZM* 140 (June 1989): 6–10.

25. Saich, "The Rise and Fall," 190–93, discusses these developments.

26. On the growing rifts within both the democracy movement and the government itself, see Schell, *Mandate of Heaven*, chaps. 4–5; and Black and Munro, *Black Hands*, 171–77.

27. Two early declarations of principal formulated by the hunger strikers appear in *CLG* 23, 2 (Summer 1990): 50–53.

28. Ibid., 52–53; Francis, "The Progress of Protest in China," 912.

29. On May 14 Dai Qing urged the students in the square to stop their fast and "take into consideration the overall situation." The students responded by demanding "What kind of 'overall situation'? It must be the 'overall situation' of the government." See Liu, *"Tell the World,"* 50–51. Dai Qing's effort to mediate the conflict is chronicled in Li Honglin, "'Right' and 'Left' in Communist China: A Self-Account by a Theoretician in the Communist Party," 27–28.

30. *CLG* 23, 2 (Summer 1990): 52.

31. *FEER*, June 1, 1989, 12–18.

32. *CLG* 23, 1 (Spring 1990): 72.

33. *ZM* 140 (June 1, 1989): 6–10. Unofficial accounts of these events, given by Yang Shangkun and Li Peng, appear in *CLG* 23, 1 (Spring 1990): 69–87; see also Brook, *Quelling the People*, chap. 2.

34. Guojia Jiaowei, *Jingxin dongpode 56 tian*, 122.

35. Chong Woei Lien, "Petitioners, Popperians, and Hunger Strikers," 115, 121.

36. "CND Interview with Gao Xin."

37. These events are described in *CLG* 23, 1 (Spring 1990): 69–72; *FEER*, June 8, 1989, 14–18; *MB*, May 30, 1989; and Michael Fathers and Andrew Higgins, *Tiananmen: The Rape of Peking*, 69–71.

38. The hospital visit is described in *SWB/FE* 0462 (May 20, 1989).

39. Strictly speaking, Li's point was accurate, since it was Deng Xiaoping and other individual members of the Politburo SC and the CAC who had used the term "turmoil." Although the term also appeared in the April 26 *People's Daily* editorial, it had not, as of May 18, been incorporated into any official policy documents or directives.

40. *CLG* 23, 2 (Summer 1990): 46–54.

41. Wu'er subsequently developed something of a reputation for strategic fainting, a behavior he exhibited on more than one occasion in public appearances in 1989 and 1990. See Joseph F. Kahn, "Better Fed than Red."

42. For a colorful account of these events see Schell, *Mandate of Heaven*, 114–17.

43. See Liu, *"Tell the World,"* 36–37.

44. *MB*, May 29, 1989.

45. Quoted in *Huaqiao ribao* (Overseas Chinese daily), June 14, 1989.

46. Some army units reportedly failed to respond to orders issued by the martial law command to enter the city. See below.

47. Brook, *Quelling the People*, 48–54, describes the events of May 19–20, including sporadic outbreaks of violence.

48. On the effects of the May 20 martial law declaration on protest demonstrations in various Chinese cities, see Unger, *Reports from the Provinces*, 61–62, 71–73, 96–97, 134–35, 154–55, 175–76, and 193–94; also Guojia Jiaowei, *Jingxin dongpode 56 tian*, 150–51. The present author personally witnessed the events described in Shanghai and Nanjing.

49. An equally massive demonstration took place in Hong Kong on May 21, with approximately one million people marching in support of the Chinese students.

50. *FBIS*, May 22, 1989, 16. The letter's cosigners were former defense minister Zhang Aiping, former PLA chief of staff Yang Dezhi, former navy commander Ye Fei, and generals Xiao Ke, Chen Zaidao, Song Shilun, and Li Jukui. A full text of the letter, whose authenticity remains in doubt, appears in *The Solemn and Stirring Democratic Movement*, 42–43.

51. Similar rumors of an impending military crackdown circulated throughout Shanghai on Sunday evening, May 21. The rumors were quickly spiked by Shanghai municipal authorities, who made repeated broadcasts over the city's public loudspeaker system throughout the night to reassure the nervous populace that no troops would enter the city.

52. *CLG* 23, 1 (Spring 1990): 77.

53. See Brook, *Quelling the People*, 68–69.

54. *BR* 32, 29 (July 17–23, 1989): 10–11.

55. *SWB/FE* 0466 (May 25, 1989); also Hu Shikai, "Representation without Democratization: The 'Signature Incident' and China's National People's Congress."

56. Central People's Broadcasting Station (Beijing), May 22, 1989, cited in Brook, *Quelling the People*, 83–84.

57. Hu, "Representation without Democratization," 7–9.

58. Initially, Chinese sources reported that Deng's meeting with regional PLA commanders had taken place in Wuhan, but this has been strongly disputed by intelligence analysts, who claim that the meeting took place in Shijiazhuang. Still other sources

claim that Deng remained in Beijing throughout the entire period of the crisis. See Brook, *Quelling the People*, 46. Salisbury, *The New Emperors*, 519, n. 4, suggests that it may have been Deng Pufang, rather than his father, who traveled to Wuhan in late May, in connection with his work for the Chinese Handicapped Society.

59. Although General Yan's removal was said to be due to his advanced age, he was only sixty-seven at the time he stepped down. See Michael D. Swaine, *The Military and Political Succession in China: Leadership, Insitutions, Beliefs*, 216.

60. *FEER*, June 8, 1989, 16; *FEER*, September 21, 1989, 19–20; and *FEER*, February 1, 1990, 22. It was rumored that General Xu and other leaders of the 38th Group Army may have had children among the student protesters at Tiananmen Square.

61. At the time, Deng's only remaining official posts were as chairman of the two MACs.

62. *CLG* 23, 1 (Spring 1990): 80–81.

63. Ibid., 86–87.

64. *MB*, May 29, 1989, 2.

65. Hu, "Representation without Democratization," 7–9.

66. According to official sources, from May 16 to May 27 more than 170,000 out-of-town students had descended upon Beijing from the provinces. See *Beijing ribao* (Beijing daily), May 27, 1989. The decision to remain on the square was taken by show of hands on the part of three hundred representatives from various colleges and universities in Beijing and the provinces, meeting at Beijing Normal University on May 28.

67. Walder and Gong, "Workers in the Tiananmen Protests," 9, n. 2. Working-class distrust of college students was clearly reciprocated. Students generally insisted on maintaining the purity of their movement, eschewing open collaboration with the Workers' Autonomous Federation and even going so far as to deny the federation permission to move its headquarters onto Tiananmen Square. See ibid., 23–24, and Black and Munro, *Black Hands*, 159.

68. Walder and Gong, "Workers in the Tiananmen Protests," 9.

69. On the social and demographic characteristics of working-class supporters of the Tiananmen demonstrations, see Helena Pik-Wan Wong, "Worker Participation in the 1989 Democracy Movement in China."

70. Cited in Walder and Gong, "Workers in the Tiananmen Protests," 19. The reference to "feeling for stones as you cross the river" alludes to the ad hoc, improvisational style of economic experimentation and reform adopted by Deng Xiaoping (and later Zhao Ziyang) in the 1980s.

71. Zhu Houze had been reassigned to work at the ACFTU following his dismissal as party propaganda director in the spring of 1987. On the ACFTU's role in the events of April–May 1989, see Black and Munro, *Black Hands*, 182–83.

72. Walder and Gong, "Workers in the Tiananmen Protests," 24–25, note that Gongzilian members frequently chafed at the strict limits placed upon them by students. "The students wouldn't allow us to strike," complained one worker. "The[y] said, 'this is our movement, and you have to obey us.'" Another worker complained that "The students thought they were very powerful. We workers always felt we were subject to domination."

73. *LAT*, May 31, 1989; *Chicago Tribune*, May 31, 1989.

74. Personal communication, May 1992.

75. The other three strike leaders were Beijing Normal University lecturers Liu Xiaobo and Gao Xin and sociologist Zhou Duo.

76. Two days earlier police had detained eight student activists in suburban Daxing County, near Beijing, for allegedly attempting to break up a progovernment demonstration by four thousand "patriotic" citizens. Organized and orchestrated by local officials, participants in the rally chanted pro–Li Peng slogans and burned an effigy of Fang Lizhi. The eight student activists were accused of assaulting traffic police, inciting workers to strike, and rumor-mongering. As soon as word of their detention reached the student headquarters in Tiananmen Square, a Gongzilian picket team, aided by motorcyclists from the Flying Tigers brigade, drove to Daxing County and boldly snatched the eight students from custody. Before leaving the scene of the breakout, the workers and motorcyclists pelted the local public security bureau with rocks. Leaders of the jailbreak were reported to be among the fourteen nonstudent activists arrested on May 30. See *LAT*, May 31, 1989; *Chicago Tribune*, May 31, 1989; and Walder and Gong, "Workers in the Tiananmen Protests," 13.

CHAPTER 12
CRACKING DOWN

1. Walder and Gong, "Workers in the Tiananmen Protests," 24.
2. *FBIS*, November 10, 1989, 46–49.
3. *FEER*, August 23, 1990, 48.
4. *ZM* 165 (July 1991): 18, 23.
5. An incomplete, unofficial tally of eyewitness reports from eleven local hospitals (a small fraction of the total number of medical facilities in the Beijing area) revealed that these units received at least 478 dead bodies on the night of June 3–4. A careful attempt to assess the overall magnitude of the toll of dead and wounded, based on a variety of official and unofficial sources, appears in Brook, *Quelling the People*, 164–69.
6. In the following discussion I have relied extensively on Brook, *Quelling the People*; Robin Munro, "Remembering Tiananmen Square: Who Died in Beijing and Why?"; and Black and Munro, *Black Hands*, chap. 15. Other useful sources on the events of June 1989 include James Miles, *The Legacy of Tiananmen: China in Disarray*, chap. 1; Schell, *Mandate of Heaven*, chaps. 12–14; Mu Yi and Mark V. Thompson, *Crisis at Tiananmen: Reform and Reality in Modern China*; Suzanne Ogden et al., *China's Search for Democracy: The Student and the Mass Movement of 1989, Massacre in Beijing: China's Struggle for Democracy*; Amnesty International, *China: The Massacre of June 1989 and Its Aftermath*; George Hicks, *The Broken Mirror: China after Tiananmen*; Michael Duke, *The Iron House: A Memoir of the Chinese Democracy Movement and the Tiananmen Massacre*; Fathers and Higgins, *The Rape of Peking*; and Scott Simmie and Bob Nixon, *Tiananmen Square: An Eyewitness Account of the Chinese People's Passionate Quest for Democracy*.
7. Reuters (Beijing), June 2, 1989; *LAT*, June 2, 1989.
8. The first batch of several hundred combat troops reportedly entered the city from the southern suburbs as early as May 27. Transported in unmarked trucks dispatched singly at ten-minute intervals, the soldiers reached the Military Museum, five miles west of Tiananmen Square, without incident.
9. In support of this hypothesis it has been noted that PLA cameramen were out in force on the streets of Beijing on the night of June 2–3, shooting videotape of the army's peaceful, nonthreatening activities—and of the hostile reactions displayed by angry citizens. There have also been persistent, though unconfirmed reports that the

army and security police may have employed a substantial number of unemployed youths and working-class toughs, dressed in civilian clothes, to provoke acts of violence against martial law forces on June 2–3.

10. The group armies known to have participated in the June crackdown included six from the Beijing Military Region (24th, 27th, 28th, 38th, 63rd, and 65th), three from the Shenyang Military Region (39th, 40th, and 64th), and three from the Jinan Military Region (20th, 54th, and 67th). See Swaine, *The Military and Political Succession*, 80, 87, 92, 138. One analyst has reported that as many as 250,000 troops, representing from sixteen to eighteen group armies, took part in the crackdown. See Michael T. Byrnes, "The Death of a People's Army," 139.

11. Duke, *The Iron House*, 99. More than twenty of the injured were reportedly treated at a local hospital.

12. This incident is detailed in Reuters (Beijing), June 3, 1989; and *LAT*, June 3, 1989.

13. A detailed account of these events appears in Brook, *Quelling the People*, 109–20.

14. Ibid., 121–31. See also Schell, *Mandate of Heaven*, 139–41.

15. According to eyewitnesses, the army simply abandoned hundreds of military vehicles along Chang'an Boulevard in the course of the Saturday night debacle. By daybreak Sunday morning, June 4, angry crowds had set fire to most of the abandoned vehicles.

16. Brook, *Quelling the People*, 126–31, documents several acts of violence committed against soldiers.

17. The withdrawal of foreign journalists in the early morning hours of June 4 helps to explain the dearth of reliable eyewitness reports describing the unfolding of subsequent events, including the army's recapture of Tiananmen Square and the students' eleventh-hour evacuation.

18. "CND Interview with Gao Xin." See also Schell, *Mandate of Heaven*, chap. 13.

19. It was apparently these bursts of gunfire, seen ricocheting off the top of the monument, that triggered the subsequent rumors, spread by the mass media in Hong Kong and elsewhere, that soldiers had cold-bloodedly massacred rows of students sitting quietly at the base of the monument. Wu'er Kaixi, who had left the square sometime before the lights went out at 4:00 A.M., would later claim that many students had been killed in this early morning "assault."

20. Quoted in Munro, "Remembering Tiananmen Square." Notwithstanding the evident sincerity of this account, it is extremely difficult to conceive of anyone sleeping through all the commotion and excitement that surrounded the Heroes' Monument in the early morning hours of June 4, 1989.

21. "CND Interview with Gao Xin."

22. There are conflicting reports concerning the fate of Wang Weilin. Some assert that he was executed within minutes of the incident. Others claim he was placed under arrest. Although a government spokesman later denied that Wang was in jail, the organization Asia Watch has reported that Wang was sentenced to ten years' imprisonment. See Brook, *Quelling the People*, 177 and 248.

23. See June Teufel Dreyer, "The People's Liberation Army and the Power Struggle of 1989," 41–48.

24. The text appears in *SWB/FE* 0476 (June 7, 1989).

25. See Amnesty International, *China: The Massacre*, 58–67; and Karl Hutterer, "Eyewitness: The Chengdu Massacre," 4–5. On the violence in Shanghai, see Meier, "Tiananman 1989"; and Shelley Warner, "Shanghai's Response to the Deluge."

26. Cf. *China Update* 11, 2 (Summer 1991): 31; and *ZM* 170 (December 1991): 14, in *ICM* 14, 2 (February 1992): 13.

27. Hong Kong sources reported that a total of 28,600 people were detained for questioning after the disturbances. See *ZM* 170 (December 1991): 14; also Amnesty International, *People's Republic of China: The Continuing Repression*; and Asia Watch, *Repression in China since June 4, 1989*.

28. *RMRB*, July 7, 1989.

29. See Black and Munro, *Black Hands*, chap. 17. In 1992 it was reported that this underground network, reputedly code-named "Yellowbird Action" (*huangque xing-dong*), had received financial and logistical support from the U.S. Central Intelligence Agency. However, knowledgeable sources in Hong Kong and in the U.S. government vehemently denied the report. On the "Yellowbird Action" underground network, see Miles, *The Legacy of Tiananmen*, chap. 8.

30. These moves came shortly after U.S. National Security Advisor Brent Scowcroft paid a controversial, well-publicized visit to Beijing. On the release of prisoners, see *BR* 33, 5–6 (January 29–February 11, 1990): 5; and XH, June 6, 1990, in *FBIS*, June 6, 1990, 13.

31. *Toronto Globe and Mail* (hereafter *TGM*), April 3, 1991; *NYT*, January 27 and February 13, 1991. For a detailed account of the trials of Chen Ziming and Wang Juntao, see Black and Munro, *Black Hands*, chap. 19. Chen and Wang, suffering from the effects of chronic ill health, were released from custody in 1994 after serving only three years of their thirteen-year sentences. It was widely speculated that their release was timed to influence America's annual debate over renewing China's MFN status.

32. By September 1990 Amnesty International had recorded the names of more than fifty people sentenced to death for crimes allegedly committed in connection with protests against the military crackdown of June 3–4. See Amnesty International, *China: The Massacre*, 54–58.

33. The most detailed governmental account of the origins and development of the Tiananmen crisis was contained in a June 30 speech by Mayor Chen Xitong to the NPC SC. The text of Chen's speech appears in *CQ* 120 (December 1989): 919–46.

34. *NYT*, June 10, 1989; Byrnes, "The Death of a People's Army," 142.

35. Deng's speech appears in *BR* 32, 28 (July 10–16, 1989): 14–17. See also *FEER*, August 10, 1989, 13.

36. *China News Digest* (Shanghai), February 8, 1993, cited in Japan Economic Newswire (hereafter JEN), February 8, 1993.

37. Ibid.; also *Zhongguo qingnian* (China youth) 1 (January 1993): 4–5. The full significance of this terminological shift became clear in 1992, when the Fourteenth Party Congress reversed the 1989 formulation and approved China's transformation from a "socialist commodity economy" to a "socialist market economy." See chapter 14.

38. The communiqué of the Fourth Plenum appears in *CQ* 119 (September 1989): 729–31; for analysis, see David Shambaugh, "The Fourth and Fifth Plenary Sessions of the 13th CCP Central Committee."

39. *BX* 203 (November 1989): 19–22.

40. See AFP (Beijing), January 25, 1991, in *FBIS*, January 28, 1991, 27. Ying Ruocheng, China's most popular male screen actor, had portrayed a compassionate prison camp commander in Bernardo Bertolucci's award-winning film, "The Last Emperor."

41. *I&S* 26, 3 (March 1990): 13.

42. *SCMP*, July 25, 1990 (emphasis added).

43. *I&S* 25, 7 (July 1989): 1–4. For analysis of Jiang Zemin's role in handling student protest in Shanghai, see Meier, "Tiananmen 1989," 3–6 and passim.

44. *RMRB*, July 11, 1989; *CQ* 120 (December 1989): 894–95.

45. *WHB*, July 24, 1989; *FEER*, August 10, 1989, 13; *SWB/FE* 0518 (July 26, 1989). For a summary of charges leveled against Zhao in this period, see *CQ* 120 (September 1989): 900–901.

46. *BX* 206 (December 1990): 3, in *FBIS*, December 19, 1989, 16.

47. *WWP*, June 28, 1989.

48. In the spring of 1990 Deng signaled his willingness to allow Zhao to begin resuming some administrative responsibilities after first undergoing an extensive period of "investigation and research" in the provinces. See *SCMP*, July 24 and 25, 1990.

49. *SWB/FE* 0476 (June 7, 1989).

50. *ICM* 11, 9 (September 1989): 3–5.

51. On the privileged position of the gaogan zidi, see Chung Jae Ho, "The Politics of Prerogatives in Socialism: The Case of the *Taizidang* in China"; also He and Gao, *Zhonggong "taizidang"*; Tanner and Fedder, "Family Politics"; and *ICM* 14, 5 (May 1992): 3–13. Miles, *The Legacy of Tiananmen*, chap. 5, and Willy Wo-Lap Lam, *China after Deng Xiaoping*, 252–56, document the ineffectiveness of the party's 1989 strictures against nepotism and cadre privilege.

52. *JJRB*, July 31, 1989. According to a Chinese government report, there were 170 cases of physical assault against martial law forces, resulting in 21 deaths, in the three months following the Tiananmen crackdown. See Schell, *Mandate of Heaven*, p. 163.

53. This latter incident was related to the author by a member of the Beijing foreign press corps, who witnessed the event.

54. *ZM* 145 (November 1989): 12, quoted in *FBIS*, November 2, 1989, 15.

55. *BR* 32, 48 (November 27–December 3, 1989): 9.

56. See *SCMP*, November 9, 1989, in *FBIS*, November 9, 1989, 14.

57. *BR* 32, 49 (December 4–10, 1989): 18.

58. A third member of the Yang family, Yang Shangkun's daughter Yang Li, held a key post in the PLA's General Staff Department, while a fourth, son Yang Shaojing, held a responsible position on the National Defense Science and Technology Commission. A fifth reputed family member, Yang Baibing's son Yang Jianhua, was rumored to be a unit commander in the 27th Group Army (see Brook, *Quelling the People*, 46, 71). However, an informed source with reliable contacts inside the PLA has denied any knowledge of a "General" Yang Jianhua (personal communication, May 1993).

59. Jiang's speech appears in *BR* 32, 49 (December 4–10, 1989): 17–22.

60. See *BR* 32, 47 (November 20–26, 1989): 19.

61. The broad outlines of the Central Committee's thirty-nine-point economic program are given in the communiqué of the Fifth Plenum. See *BR* 32, 47 (November 20–26, 1989): 15–18. An abridged version of the final document appears in *BR* 33, 7 (February 12, 1990): I–XVI.

62. *BR* 32, 47 (November 20–26, 1989): 16–17.

63. For further analysis of this hybrid, middle-of-the-road strategy, see Barry Naughton, "The Chinese Economy on the Road to Recovery?"

64. *FBIS*, January 19, 1990, 16. On the impact of the fall of Communism in Eastern Europe on China's leadership and policies, see Miles, *The Legacy of Tiananmen*, chap. 2.

65. *NYT*, December 29, 1989.

66. *LAT*, December 28, 1989.

67. *ZM* 148 (February 1990): 6–8, in *FBIS*, January 16, 1990, 1–2; *SCMP*, January 8, 1990, in *FBIS*, January 8, 1990, 7–8.

68. *NYT*, December 29, 1989.

69. *ZM* 147 (January 1990): 9, in *FBIS*, January 2, 1990, 15.

70. *MB*, December 29, 1989, 2, in *FBIS*, December 29, 1989, 20.

71. *ZM* 156 (October 1990): 14–15, in *FBIS*, October 5, 1990, 14.

72. *SCMP*, December 28, 1989.

73. See David Shambaugh, "China in 1990: The Year of Damage Control," 40.

74. *NYT*, March 14, 1990; *JSND* 247 (August 1, 1990): 64–65, in *JPRS* CAR, September 21, 1990, 10–13.

75. *The Observer*, February 18, 1990. The performance of the PLA during and after the Tiananmen crisis is examined in Lam, *China after Deng*, chap. 4.

76. *FBIS*, June 6, 1989, 15–16, and June 24, 1989, 27–28.

77. *FEER*, June 14, 1990, 32; *Kaifang* (Opening up) 44 (August 15, 1990): 7–8, in *FBIS*, August 23, 1990, 35–37; and Harlan Jencks, "Party Authority and Military Power: Communist China's Continuing Crisis," 25–26.

78. *ZM* 156 (October 1990): 14–15, in *FBIS*, October 5, 1990, 14–15. On one occasion, in August 1990, Yang Shangkun reportedly threw a lavish banquet to soothe the ruffled feelings of around twenty of his senior military colleagues. Three-fourths of the invitees apparently refused to participate; several sent their personal secretaries in their stead. Interestingly, the discredited "whateverist" general, Chen Xilian, was one of the few high-ranking officers to attend the banquet. "If no one attends," remarked General Chen, "it will put [Yang] in an awkward situation. We had better go." (Ibid., 14.)

79. On the concept of peaceful evolution, see *FBIS*, October 18, 1989, 37, and February 23, 1990, 12–23; also *RMRB*, December 1, 1989; and *ICM* 13, 12 (December 1991): 1–8.

80. *FEER*, February 1, 1990, 22; Shambaugh, "China in 1990," 40.

81. *FBIS*, December 21, 1989, 20ff; *BR* 33, 12 (March 19 25, 1990): 9.

82. *ZM* 152 (June 1990): 14–17, in *FBIS*, June 1, 1990, 9–10.

83. *NYT*, February 15, 1990; *FEER*, March 1, 1990, 20.

84. On civil-military relations in the post-Tiananmen period, see Richard J. Latham, "China's Party-Army Relations after June 1989"; and Lam, *China after Deng*, chap. 4.

85. The following discussion draws on Richard Baum, "Political Stability in Post-Deng China: Problems and Prospects," 491–94.

86. Mary S. Erbaugh and Richard Curt Kraus, "The 1989 Democracy Movement in Fujian and Its Aftermath," 158. Neither Guangdong nor Fujian was among the provinces that experienced prodemocracy demonstrations in the first week following Hu Yaobang's death. The special economic zones were even more tardy. In the Xiamen (Fujian) SEZ, the first antigovernment rally took place only on May 4. In the Haikou (Hainan) duty-free port, the first rally occurred even later, on May 10. And in both the Zhuhai and Shantou (Guangdong) SEZs, the only recorded demonstrations occurred on May 18.

To attract significant numbers of nonstudent participants, student leaders in Guangzhou were forced to hold their rallies at night, after the city's bustling shops and markets closed their doors. Ironically, mass demonstrations against the Chinese government were considerably larger and more emotional in nearby British Hong Kong than in Guangzhou. Statistical data on dates, magnitudes, and frequencies of demonstrations in various Chinese cities appear in *Huo yü hsieh chih chen-hsiang* (The truth of fire and blood), sec. 3, 1–108; Guojia Jiaowei, *Jingxin dongpode 56 tian*; Wu

Mouren, *Bajiu Zhongguo minyun jishi* (Daily record of the 1989 Chinese people's movement); and Wong, "Worker Participation." I am indebted to James Tong, Helena Pik-Wan Wong, and Richard Siao for bringing these materials to my attention.

87. Personal observation, May 17–23, 1989.

88. In both the Romanian and Soviet cases, the failure of key military commanders to obey (or enforce) orders from above signaled the defection of important elements of the state's coercive apparatus, thus opening the door to effective popular resistance.

89. Since 1989 there has been a virtual explosion of literature on the subject of civil society in Communist systems. See, inter alia, Robert F. Miller, *The Development of Civil Society in Communist Systems*; Strand, "Protest in Beijing"; Whyte, "Urban China"; and "Symposium on Civil Society and the Public Sphere."

90. For further analysis of the stylized moral theatrics of the 1989 student demonstrations, see Pye, "Tiananmen and Chinese Political Culture"; Perry, "Casting a Chinese 'Democracy' Movement," 148–53; and Esherick and Wasserstrom, "Acting Out Democracy," 32–42.

91. See chapter 11.

92. Quoted in *SCMP*, July 7, 1990, in *FBIS*, July 9, 1990, 23.

93. Cf. Link, *Evening Chats in Beijing*, 222.

CHAPTER 13
PICKING UP THE PIECES

1. See, e.g., AFP (Hong Kong), February 7, 1990, in *FBIS*, February 7, 1990, 1.

2. See, e.g., *RMRB*, February 8 and 19, 1990, in *FBIS*, February 23, 1990, 23; also XH, February 8, 9, and 12, 1990, in *FBIS*, February 9, 1990, 8–9, and February 12, 1990, 14–18.

3. As remnants of the PRC's "new democratic united front" of the 1950s, the CPPCC and the eight democratic parties (sometimes called "flower vases" because of their decorative function) went into political eclipse during the anti-Rightist rectification movement of 1957. After Mao's death, the CPPCC reemerged as part of the reformers' effort to bolster the regime's sagging prestige among the masses. The text of the CC's "Opinions on Persisting in and Improving the System of Multiparty Cooperation and Political Consultation under the Leadership of the CPC" (December 30, 1989) appears in *FBIS*, February 7, 1990, 7–11.

4. *Dangdai* (Contemporary; hereafter *DD*), July 15, 1991, in *FBIS*, July 25, 1991.

5. Quoted in *ZM* 170 (December 1991): 22–23, in *ICM* 14, 2 (February 1992): 22–24.

6. See *JB* 171 (October 1991): 26–28, in *FBIS*, October 11, 1991, 15.

7. In September 1991 the author, accompanied by a member of the Beijing foreign press corps, visited the walled, gated residence at No. 6 Fuqiang Lane where Zhao Ziyang was said to be living under house arrest. Pausing at the front gate to look through its peephole, we were confronted by several uniformed security police, equipped with side arms and walkie-talkies, who emerged into the street from the houses on either side of No. 6. With their presence serving as a deterrent to further investigation, we left the scene without having confirmed Zhao's presence.

8. *MB*, December 29, 1989, in *FBIS*, December 29, 1989, 19.

9. *SCMP*, July 18, 1990, in *FBIS*, July 18, 1990, 8.

10. XH, July 31, 1990, in *FBIS*, August 1, 1990, 15; *SCMP*, July 24, 1990.

11. *SCMP*, April 26, 1990.

12. *DD*, May 12, 1990, 11–12, in *FBIS*, May 16, 1990, 19–20. The CIA was alleged to have offered indirect funding to a number of liberal Chinese think tanks, some of which were run by associates of Zhao Ziyang, for the purpose of "exerting a subtle and imperceptible influence on China's top-level leadership."

13. *SCMP*, September 4, 1990.

14. *SCMP*, September 7, 1990, in *FBIS*, September 7, 1990, 24.

15. *JB* 156 (July 1990): 37, in *FBIS*, July 9, 1990, 22.

16. *ZM* 164 (June 1991): 12–13. Although Yan Mingfu previously had been targeted for expulsion from the party, Yang Shangkun (who had been Yan's cellmate for eight years during the Cultural Revolution) and Politburo alternate member Ding Guan'gen (a regular member of Deng Xiaoping's bridge group) reportedly intervened to protect Yan's membership. See *SCMP*, September 6, 1990, in *FBIS*, September 6, 1990, 20.

17. Hu Qili was appointed vice-minister of machine building and electronics; Rui Xingwen and Yan Mingfu were appointed vice-ministers of state planning and civil affairs, respectively.

18. *BX* 206 (December 1989): 3, in *FBIS*, December 19, 1989, 16.

19. Ibid. See also Miles, *The Legacy of Tiananmen*, chap. 1.

20. Residents of Beijing and Shanghai related to the author numerous anecdotes concerning mutually protective behavior. For examples of the strategies employed by party members and cadres to avoid implicating others, see Link, *Evening Chats in Beijing*, 189–90, 228.

21. XH, October 22, 1992.

22. *SCMP*, September 6, 1990, in *FBIS*, September 6, 1990, 20. Zhu Houze was subsequently allowed to reregister, following a lengthy investigation of his case.

23. *MB*, June 10, 1990.

24. *SCMP*, June 25, 1991; *China News Digest (Global News)* (hereafter *CND*), April 18, 1991.

25. XH, October 22, 1992.

26. See *TGM*, September 4, 1990.

27. *RMRB*, August 31, 1992, cited in United Press International (hereafter UPI) (Beijing), August 31, 1992.

28. *BR* 26, 25 (July 4, 1983).

29. UPI (Beijing), December 4, 1990.

30. AFP, July 6, 1992. Miles, *The Legacy of Tiananmen*, chaps. 4–5, documents several major cases of corruption and fraud on the part of Chinese police.

31. *RMRB*, January 11, 1992; Reuters (Beijing), January 11, 1992.

32. Associated Press (hereafter AP) (Beijing), March 2, 1991; *FEER*, March 14, 1991, 18.

33. *SCMP*, October 21, 1991.

34. *RMRB*, February 23, 1992.

35. AP (Beijing), March 13, 1991; *CND*, March 13, 1991.

36. *RMRB*, February 23, 1992.

37. *SCMP*, March 26, 1992.

38. XH, October 22, 1992.

39. *SCMP*, September 8, 1990.

40. Chinese diplomatic source, personal communication, May 1991. Between late May and mid-June Chen Yun appeared to shift his ground on the question of the use of military force against students. In a televised address on May 26, he stated that "If we

do not suppress this chaos started by a small number of people, China will never enjoy peace. . . . We believe the party and the army have . . . the ability to control the chaos" (quoted in Reuters [Beijing], April 11, 1995). Shortly after the June 4 debacle, however, Chen Yun reportedly told his colleagues: "We must have a new verdict on the Tiananmen incident. While we old comrades are still around, we must clarify who is responsible for what. Otherwise, we will carry the stigma to our graves" (quoted in *SCMP*, September 5, 1990).

41. According to an internal PLA document circulated in Hong Kong in July 1991, Deng and other members of the party and military leadership watched the action on June 3–4 from their military headquarters in the Western Hills, near Beijing. The same document alleges that permission to open fire on the night in question had been given by an unnamed PLA officer who had been directing military operations from a helicopter hovering above Fuxing and Fuxingmenwai, a few miles west of Tiananmen. See *SCMP*, July 19, 1991.

42. *SCMP*, July 23 and 25, 1990. Notwithstanding this cynical interpretation, a senior party cadre with firsthand knowledge of this incident has credited Chen Yun with having had genuine humanitarian motives in defending the four liberals (personal communication, May 27, 1993).

43. *SCMP*, January 9, 1991, in *FBIS*, January 9, 1991.

44. Information provided by a Chinese informant. Although some observers have sought to downplay the seriousness of the schism between Deng and Chen, treating it as an artifact of a putative predisposition on the part of China watchers in Hong Kong and Taiwan to view Chinese politics as a never-ending series of personal power struggles and political intrigues (see Teiwes, "Politics, Purges, and Rectification," 28–33), the rift between China's two senior leaders nonetheless appeared to be real and growing. For additional examples of rivalrous conduct after the Tiananmen crisis, see *I&S* 28, 4 (April 1992): 109–10.

45. *FEER*, September 27, 1990, 13, November 8, 1990, 19–20, and December 20, 1990, 11.

46. *JB* 159 (October 1990): 28–31, in *FBIS*, October 11, 1990, 19.

47. *SCMP*, October 9, 1990, 12, in *FBIS*, October 9, 1990, 25–26.

48. *JB* 150 (January 1990): 48–51, in *FBIS*, January 19, 1990, 14–15.

49. *JB* 160 (November 1990): 38–39, in *FBIS*, November 15, 1990, 32–33.

50. *FBIS*, October 11, 1990, 19.

51. Ibid.; see also *FBIS*, December 3, 1990, 21.

52. *ZM* 158 (December 1990): 6–8, in *FBIS* December 3, 1990, 21–22.

53. Ibid., 22. One of the many obstructions created by conservatives in their drive to oppose Li Ruihuan in this period centered on Li's role in helping the noted Chinese "patriotic artist" Fan Zeng to secure permission to leave the country for a tour of Europe following the Tiananmen crackdown. Once in Paris, Fan Zeng denounced the Chinese government and sought political asylum, to the great embarrassment of his erstwhile sponsors in Beijing. Conservatives were only too eager to publicize Li Ruihuan's role in assisting Fan to leave the country.

54. On the causes for the delay, see *ZM* 157 (November 1990): 20, in *ICM* 13, 1 (January 1991): 2–3.

55. The communiqué of the Seventh Plenum appears in *BR* 34, 1 (January 7–13, 1991): 31–33.

56. The abridged text of the proposals for China's Eighth Five-Year Plan appears in

BR 34, 7–8 (February 18–March 3, 1991): 21–27.

57. *BX* 233 (February 1991): 3–4, in *FBIS*, February 1, 1991, 16.

58. Official Chinese sources list the number of people killed in the crackdown at 387, including both Tibetans and Chinese PAP forces. Tibetan sources have claimed that 450 Tibetans were killed. See *The Observer*, August 12, 1990.

59. *The Economist*, October 27, 1990. Miles, *The Legacy of Tiananmen*, chap. 10, examines the growth of ethnic unrest in China's far-western border regions.

60. AP (Beijing), April 25, 1990.

61. *SCMP*, June 20, 1990; AP (Beijing), September 18, 1990.

62. *CND*, November 11, 1990. On the reported prison torture of Tibetan political dissidents, including monks and nuns, see Amnesty International, *Torture in China*, 25–31.

63. AP (Beijing), March 22 and 26, 1991.

64. UPI (Beijing), May 16, 1991; AP (Beijing), May 19, 1991. Two years earlier, on the eve of the 1989 Tiananmen crisis, Zhao Ziyang had similarly chastised Western politicians and journalists for criticizing Chinese human rights abuses in Tibet. At that time, Zhao had claimed that such criticism served to endanger China's reforms and open policy.

65. UPI (Beijing), April 8, 1991; *FEER*, April 25, 1991, 18–19; AP (Beijing), May 16, 1991.

66. *SCMP*, September 24, 25, and October 15, 1991.

67. Official Chinese sources listed as killed six policemen, fifteen Uighur rebels, and one local Communist Party official. Local sources put the death toll considerably higher. According to one report, fifty civilians and eight policemen had been killed, along with two Chinese negotiators who had been sent into the besieged town to seek a truce. See *FEER*, May 3, 1990, 10–11; AP (Beijing), September 11, 1990; and *Baltimore Sun*, October 7, 1990.

68. *FEER*, May 3, 1990, 11.

69. *SCMP*, June 19, 1990.

70. *SCMP*, June 25, 1990.

71. *SCMP*, cited in *CND*, August 1, 1990.

72. Reuters (Beijing), November 5, 1991.

73. Asia Watch, cited in David Shambaugh, "China in 1991: Living Cautiously," 27.

74. Reuters (Beijing), October 25 and 29, 1991.

75. *Xizang ribao* (Tibet daily) (hereafter *XZRB*), October 7, 1991, cited in Reuters (Beijing), October 16, 1991.

76. Reuters (Beijing), March 24, 1992.

77. AP (Beijing), May 19 and 21, 1992.

78. *XZRB*, March 14, 1992, cited in Reuters (Beijing), March 24, 1992.

79. *SCMP*, October 14, 1991.

80. Reuters (Beijing), February 21, 1992.

81. Cited in Reuters (Beijing), April 7, 1992.

82. Wedeman, "Bamboo Walls and Brick Ramparts," and Yang, "Reforms, Resources, and Regional Cleavages," document and analyze these and other related types of provincial and local trade wars.

83. *WWP*, October 11, 1988.

84. On the sources and political implications of declining central control over mate-

rial and fiscal resources in the reform process, see Wong, "Central-Local Relations," and Jean C. Oi, "Local Government Response to the Fiscal Austerity Program, 1988–90."

85. *SCMP*, November 3, 1989, and January 13, 1990.

86. *Jingji yanjiu* (Economic research; hereafter *JJYJ*) (March 1990): 12–19, in *ICM* 12, 3 (March 1990): 4–5.

87. *Christian Science Monitor* (hereafter *CSM*), November 15, 1990.

88. *Asian Wall Street Journal* (hereafter *AWSJ*), December 3, 1990.

89. AP (Hong Kong), December 3, 1990, in *CND* (part II), December 3, 1990. The irony of Li Peng advocating a system pioneered by his old adversary, Zhao Ziyang, was striking.

90. One clear exception was in the Cultural Revolution, when provincial and local leaders in many areas ignored (or sidestepped) orders coming from the center.

91. See *SCMP*, May 9, 1991. Lam, *China after Deng*, 58–59, 117–18, examines the case of Ye Xuanping.

92. *FEER*, April 4, 1991, 21. On the perilous state of central-provincial relations in the early 1990s, see Wang Shaoguang and Hu An'gang, *Jiaqiang zhongyang zhengfu zai shichang jingji zhuanxingzhong de zhudao zuodong* (Strenghten the central government's leading function during the transition to a market economy); and Maria Hsia Chang, "China's Future: Regionalism, Federation, or Disintegration?"

93. The term new conservatism was first used at this conference by Xiao Gongqin, an associate professor of history at Shanghai Normal University. See Gu Xin and David A. Kelly, "New Conservatism: Ideological Program of a New Elite".

94. In the aftermath of the Tiananmen crisis, He Xin, a former Red Guard and college dropout, became Li Peng's most ardent apologist and intellectual paladin at CASS, where he was affiliated with the Institute of Literature. Endowed with a facile mind, a quick tongue, and seemingly unlimited self-confidence, He Xin eagerly endorsed the government's hard-line policies, in the process earning a reputation as a somewhat shameless political panderer. See *TGM*, July 11, 1991.

95. The new conservative agenda is analyzed in Gu and Kelly, "New Conservatism"; and Joseph Fewsmith, "Neoconservativism and the End of the Dengist Era." See also *DD*, January 15, 1992, 38–40, in *FBIS*, February 10, 1992, 20–22; and *BX* 260 (March 1992): 32–35, in *ICM* 14, 5 (May 1992): 6–13.

96. Gu and Kelly, "New Conservatism."

97. Zhongguo Qingnian Bao Sixiang Lilunbu, "Sulian jubian zhihou Zhongguode xianshi yingdui yu zhanlue xuanze" (Realistic responses and strategic choices for China after the Soviet coup), 35–39. The author of this essay was reported to be Pan Yue, son-in-law of PLA General Liu Huaqing. I am indebted to David Kelly for making available his translation of this important manifesto. A summary of the article appears in *FBIS*, February 10, 1992, 20–22.

98. *BX* 260 (March 1992): 32–35.

99. Ruan Ming, "Taizidang de Disandiguo meimeng" (The Third Reich fantasies of the taizidang), 39–41. Gu and Kelly, "New Conservatism," are skeptical of this latter claim because of the radically divergent and seemingly incompatible ideological premises and legitimacy claims that underpin new conservatism and Marxism-Leninism, respectively.

100. Deng Yingtao was the son of Deng Liqun; Chen Haosu was the son of the deceased former Chinese foreign minister, Chen Yi.

101. See Ruan, "Taizidang"; Chen Kuide, "Wangchao moride xinzheng" (New pol-

itics of a moribund dynasty); and Gu and Kelly, "New Conservatism."

102. See *SCMP*, June 25, 1991.

103. Poll results reported in Rosen, "Popular Attitudes."

104. *MB*, June 10, 1990.

105. *SCMP*, March 12, 1991.

106. *SCMP*, June 25, 1991 Zhao Ziyang had called for the dissolution of party cells in government organs at the Thirteenth Party Congress.

107. *ZM* 165 (July 1991), in *FBIS*, July 9, 1991, 36–37.

108. *ZM* 165 (July 1991): 24–25, in *FBIS*, July 8, 1991, 18–20.

109. The text of Jiang's speech appears in *BR* 34, 27 (July 8–14, 1991): 15–32. The genesis of the speech, and Deng's subsequent criticism of it, are discussed in *BX* 249 (October 1991): 3–4, in *FBIS*, October 8, 1991, 23.

110. *BR* 34, 36 (September 9–16, 1991): 10.

111. *SCMP*, September 4, 1991, in *FBIS*, September 4, 1991, 19–20. Underscoring the regime's concern with safeguarding internal security in the aftermath of the abortive Soviet coup attempt of August 1991, the PLA set up a secret committee charged with preventing future coups d'etat in China. Operating under the guise of a research institute on problems of Asian security, the group's mandate was to uncover "dissident rings" and other disgruntled elements within the military/state security system. See *SCMP*, August 14, 1992.

112. See *FBIS*, August 1, 1991, 35–37; August 6, 1991, 15; September 9, 1991, 4; and January 31, 1992, 25.

113. See *SCMP*, December 10, 1991, in *FBIS*, December 10, 1991, 23. Li Peng initially revealed the decision to cancel the 1991 Beidaihe conference on July 2. No reason was given for the cancellation, and no mention was made of Deng's illness. See *SCMP*, July 3, 1991, in *FBIS*, July 3, 1991, 13.

114. See, for example, *Toronto Star*, August 7, 1991, in *CND*, August 8, 1991; also *Xin bao* (hereafter *XB*), August 1, 1991.

115. *SCMP*, September 4, 1991, in *FBIS*, September 4, 1991, 19.

116. *JB* 170 (September 1991): 43, in *FBIS*, September 11, 1991, 19–20.

117. *RMRB*, September 1, 1991. Author of the article was Chen Yepin, former deputy director of the party's organization department.

118. *DD*, January 15, 1992, 35–37, in *FBIS*, February 11, 1992, 16.

119. Tony Saich, "Peaceful Evolution with Chinese Characteristics," 17–18, examines these developments in greater detail.

120. Quoted in *ZM* 170 (December 1991): 22–23, in *ICM* 14, 2 (February 1992): 22–24.

121. *GMRB*, October 23, 1991.

122. *RMRB*, October 23, 1991; *SCMP*, October 24, 1991.

123. *FBIS*, January 7, 1992, 24. In yet another angry outburst, Deng Liqun reportedly exclaimed, "Intellectuals who engage in liberalization . . . should be smothered to death!" See *BX* 249 (October 1991): 3–4, in *FBIS*, October 8, 1991, 22–23

124. For background on the Wenzhou experiment, see Alan P. L. Liu, "The 'Wenzhou Model' of Development and China's Modernization."

125. *JB* 174 (January 1992), in *FBIS*, January 7, 1992, 25.

126. *SCMP*, October 28, 1991; *BR* 35, 24 (June 15–21, 1992): 7–8.

127. See, e.g., *SCMP*, October 28, 1991.

128. *ZM* 169 (November 1991): 9–10, in *FBIS*, November 15, 1991, 28.

129. *SCMP*, December 5, 1991.

130. UPI (Beijing), October 31, 1991; *SCMP*, November 9, 1991. The contents of "Huang Fuping's" commentaries closely paralleled remarks made by Deng Xiaoping during a Lunar New Year visit to Shanghai in January 1991. According to the Beijing-based journalist James Miles, *The Legacy of Tiananmen*, chap. 3, the principal author of the March-April 1991 "Huang Fuping" commentaries was Zhou Ruijin, proreform party secretary of the *Liberation Daily*.

131. *China Education News*, October 31, 1991, cited in UPI (Beijing), October 31, 1991.

132. *The Standard* (Hong Kong), December 6, 1991, in *FBIS*, December 6, 1991, 18.

133. *DD*, December 1991, 16, in *FBIS*, December 17, 1991, 25.

134. *SCMP*, January 1, 1992, in *FBIS*, January 2, 1992, 25.

135. *JB* 172 (November 1991), quoted in ibid.

136. *SCMP*, October 2 and November 9, 1991; *ZM* 170 (December 1991): 6–8, in *FBIS*, November 29, 1991, 24.

137. *JB* 174 (January 1992): 30–33, in *FBIS*, January 7, 1992, 26–27.

138. Personal interview, May 1993. Hu Qiaomu spent the months of February and March 1989 in the United States, where he visited Pasadena, Ann Arbor, New York, Washington, D.C., and Boston. Several people who spent time with him during his visit, including the author, were struck by the sincerity of Hu's effort to comprehend postindustrial Western civilization and culture. Hu's "last testament," dictated shortly before his death in September 1992, confirmed his change of heart.

139. *ZM* 170 (December 1991): 6–8, in *FBIS*, November 29, 1991, 25.

140. *JB* 173 (December 1991): 31–32, in *FBIS*, December 12, 1991, 36–37.

141. *SCMP*, December 18, 1991, in *FBIS*, December 18, 1991, 42.

142. *JB* 174 (January 1992), in *FBIS*, January 10, 1992, 18–20.

143. Ibid.; *The Standard*, November 26, 1991; and *SCMP*, November 28, 1991.

144. *JB* 174 (January 1992), in *FBIS*, January 10, 1992, 18–20. The text of the communiqué of the Eighth Plenum appears in *BR* 34, 49 (December 9–15, 1991): 9–11.

145. The sole exception was the fourth point, concerning the need to purify the party and enhance its role as socialist vanguard. See *ZM* 171 (January 1992): 18–19, in *FBIS*, January 3, 1992, 22.

146. *ZM* 172 (February 1992): 9–12, in *FBIS*, January 27, 1992, 29.

147. *MB*, December 6, 1991, 8, in *FBIS*, December 6, 1991, 18; *JB* 175 (February 1992): 28–31, in *FBIS*, February 6, 1992.

148. *JB* 175 (February 1992): 42, in *FBIS*, January 30, 1992, 19–20.

149. *ZM* 172 (February 1992): 16–17, in *FBIS*, February 10, 1992, 19.

150. *JB* 174 (January 1992): 42–44, in *FBIS*, January 27, 1992, 34–35.

151. XH, January 25, 1992, in *FBIS*, January 27, 1992, 33–34.

152. *ZM* 172 (February 1992): 15, in *FBIS*, February 7, 1992, 30–31.

153. *MB*, March 6, 1992, 2, in *FBIS*, March 9, 1992, 27. One source claims that the letter was signed by thirteen CAC members, including Chen Yun (*SCMP*, May 13, 1992, in *FBIS*, May 13, 1992, 22). Although at least one CAC member subsequently denied personal knowledge of the letter or its contents, its existence was not disputed. See *Xin wanbao* (Evening news) (Hong Kong), March 24, 1992, 4, in *FBIS*, March 24, 1992, 35.

154. At one point Deng reportedly quipped that he would be completely unfit for leadership when he could no longer play bridge at all. Deng's bridge-playing habits and

partners are discussed in Min Li, "Deng Xiaoping de 'zhinantuan'" (Deng Xiaoping's "brain trust"), 40–41; see also Pye, "An Introductory Profile," 428; and Pang, *The Death of Hu Yaobang*, 38.

CHAPTER 14
DENG'S FINAL OFFENSIVE

1. A week before Deng's departure, Qiao Shi and Jiang Zemin, acting as his advance men, paid brief inspection visits to Guangdong and Shanghai, respectively. According to Hong Kong sources, three hundred plainclothes police and eighty special agents were detailed by the Guangdong provincial government to ensure Deng's personal safety during his southern visit. See *FBIS*, January 27, 1992, 30. A partial chronology of Deng's tour appears in Zhonggong Shenzhen Shiwei Xuanchuanbu, *Deng Xiaoping yu Shenzhen, 1992 chun* (Deng Xiaoping and Shenzhen, spring 1992), 15–16.

2. *ZM* 172 (February 1992): 9–12, in *FBIS*, January 27, 1992, 31; also *BX* 259 (March 1992): 26–27, in *ICM* 14, 5 (May 1992): 14–18.

3. An abridged transcript of Deng's major statements from his southern tour was first published on March 1, 1992, as "Central Document No. 2 (1992)." The text of this transcript appears in *Lien-ho pao* (United news; hereafter *LHP*), March 2, 1992, in *ICM* 14, 4 (April 1992): 6–13. Excerpts from Deng's various southern speeches also appear in Zhonggong Shenzhen Shiwei, *Deng Xiaoping yu Shenzhen*, 1–14. For analysis of Deng's tour and its political impact, see Miles, *The Legacy of Tiananmen*, chap. 3; Lam, *China after Deng*, 17–25 and passim; and Zhao Suisheng, "Deng Xiaoping's Southern Tour: Elite Politics in Post-Tiananmen China."

4. *ICM* 14, 4 (April 1992): 6–13.

5. Ibid., 9.

6. *DGB*, January 28, 1992; *SCMP*, January 31, 1992; *Sydney Morning Herald* (August 8, 1992).

7. *Xin shiji* (New century), cited in *SCMP*, February 17, 1992.

8. *LHP*, February 16, 1992, cited in *SCMP*, February 17, 1992.

9. *SCMP*, February 17, 1992.

10. Zhonggong Shenzhen Shiwei, *Deng Xiaoping yu Shenzhen*, 6. Miles, *The Legacy of Tiananmen*, chap. 3, claims that the controversial phrase "watch out for the Right, but mainly guard against the Left" was actually inserted into the transcript of Deng's southern speeches after the fact by Zheng Bijian, Hu Yaobang's former political secretary, who had been retained by Deng to edit "a big box of tapes" of Deng's remarks.

11. Ibid.; see also *MB*, March 7, 1992, in *FBIS*, March 9, 1992, 28. Deng's intended reference to Deng Liqun, Li Ximing, and Song Ping is reported in *SCMP*, April 3, 1992, in *FBIS*, April 3, 1992, 35; and *JB* 177 (April 1992): 32–36, in *FBIS*, April 3, 1992, 38.

12. *LHP*, March 2, 1992; *Zhuhai Special Zone Daily*, April 17, 1992, quoted in *SCMP*, April 27, 1992.

13. *ZM* 173 (March 1, 1992): 6–11, in *FBIS*, March 2, 1992, 26–27, 29–30. It was later suggested that Chen's pointed reference to "another center" had a second meaning as well, referring to his purported attempt to create a rival core leadership group within the party to counteract the formal authority of Jiang Zemin. See *ZM* 177 (April 1992): 8–11, in *FBIS*, April 2, 1992, 35–37.

14. On the hard-liners' attempt to suppress publication of Deng's remarks, see *SCMP*, March 31, 1992, in *FBIS*, March 31, 1992, 29–30.

15. China News Service, February 14, 1992, cited in *ICM* 14, 4 (April 1992): 90.

16. XH, February 18, 1992, in *ICM* 14, 4 (April 1992): 91.

17. *ICM* 14, 4 (April 1992): 91; also *SCMP*, February 17, 1992.

18. *MB*, February 14 and 21, 1992, in *FBIS*, February 14, 1992, 13–14, and February 21, 1992, 17. These events are discussed in Zhao, "Deng Xiaoping's Southern Tour."

19. Cited in *ICM* 14, 6 (June 1992): 8–9.

20. Cited in Reuters (Beijing), February 17, 1992.

21. Ibid.

22. *RMRB*, February 23, 1992, in *BR* 35, 12 (March 23–29, 1992): 18–20. On the bitter struggle for control over the editorial policy and content of *People's Daily* in this period, see *MB*, March 8, 1992, 13, in *FBIS*, March 9, 1992, 21–22.

23. *SCMP*, April 27, 1992; *ZM* 183 (March 1992), in *FBIS*, March 4, 1992, 16–18.

24. *MB*, April 10, 1992, 66, in *FBIS*, April 10, 1992, 20.

25. *DD*, May 1992, 24–25, in *ICM* 14, 7 (July 1992): 19–22.

26. *ZM* 177 (April 1992): 8–11, in *FBIS*, April 2, 1992, 35.

27. *ICM* 14, 7 (July 1992): 20.

28. Ibid., 21.

29. Ibid.

30. *SCMP*, April 3, 1992, in *FBIS*, April 3, 1992, 35.

31. XH, March 11, 1992.

32. *JB* 177 (April 1992): 41, in *FBIS*, April 7, 1992, 17.

33. *XB*, March 6, 1992, 17, in *FBIS*, March 9, 1992, 25; *SCMP*, March 9, 1992, in *FBIS*, March 10, 1992, 15.

34. See *SCMP*, March 9, 1992, in *FBIS* March 10, 1992, 15; *SCMP*, April 3, 1992, in *FBIS*, April 3, 1992, 35; *JB* 177 (April 1992), in *FBIS*, April 3, 1992, 40; *JB* 177 (April 1992): 41, 46, in *FBIS*, April 7, 1992, 17–18; and *ZM* 181 (November 1992): 8.

35. On the defection of Peng, Song, and Bo from the conservative camp, see *FBIS*, January 24, 1992, 15; April 2, 1992, 38; April 6, 1992, 38–41; April 7, 1992, 16–17; and April 10, 1992, 21; also *Jiefang ribao*, August 2, 1992; and *BR* 35, 35 (August 31–September 6, 1992): 7.

36. See, inter alia, *SCMP*, April 4, 1992 [*sic*], in *FBIS*, April 2, 1992; also *FBIS*, April 1, 1992, 15–17; AP (Beijing), April 3, 1992; and *BR* 35, 15 (April 13–19, 1992): 8. The full text of Li Peng's amended work report appears in *BR* 35, 15 (April 13–19, 1992): I–XVI.

37. See *SCMP*, March 27, 1992, in *FBIS*, March 27, 1992, 10–11; and April 3, 1992, in *FBIS*, April 3, 1992, 14.

38. XH, April 2, 1992; *SCMP*, April 3, 1992, in *FBIS*, April 3, 1992, 14–15

39. See *LAT*, April 4, 1992; XH, October 7, 1992.

40. The checkered history of the Three Gorges Dam project is examined in Lieberthal and Oksenberg, *Policy Making in China*, chap. 6; see also Luk Shiu-Hung and Joseph Whitney, *Megaproject: A Case Study of China's Three Gorges Project*; and the three-part series in *CSM*, July 18, 22, and 23, 1991.

41. These issues are examined in Luk and Whitney, *Megaproject*, 8–37 and passim.

42. Dai Qing's edited book, *Changjiang, Changjiang* (Yangzi River, Yangzi River), was later circulated in Hong Kong. Li Rui was spared expulsion from the party as a result of Chen Yun's eleventh-hour intervention on his behalf. See chapter 13.

43. See *The Wall Street Journal* (hereafter *WSJ*), January 19, 1993; and *China Rights Forum* (April 1993): 14–16.

44. See *WWP*, March 30, 1992; *BR* 35, 15 (April 13–19, 1992): 4–6, and 35, 16 (April 20–26, 1992): 4.

45. AFP, April 22, 1992. On the checkered history of the Shanghai and Shenzhen stock exchanges, see Orville Schell and Todd Lappin, "China Plays the Market."

46. *SCMP*, June 12, 1992. Zhu Rongji and Zou Jiahua had both been appointed vice-premiers in April 1991. Zou, son-in-law of Ye Jianying, was a moderately conservative reformer whose career had been closely associated with Yao Yilin in the State Planning Commission. At the time he was widely regarded as Zhu's principal rival for eventual succession to the premiership.

47. *RMRB*, May 8, 1992; *ICM* 14, 7 (July 1992): 23–24.

48. With so many high-level fence-straddlers hopping on the reform bandwagon in the spring of 1992, one can only assume that they must have concluded Deng was going to win his contest with Chen Yun and other old-guard conservatives. Analyzing the dynamics of bandwagoning in Chinese politics, Avery Goldstein, *From Bandwagon to Balance*, 14–15, makes the point that "The ability of actors to discern winners by attending to political cues is clearly central. . . . Those who prosper and come to predominate . . . are those who make the most of their cue-reading abilities. . . . The ambitious . . . [have] strong incentives to cultivate the cue-reading skills necessary to maximize their chances of being among the political vanguard."

49. *BR* 35, 22 (June 1–7, 1992): 7.

50. *BR* 34, 27 (July 8–14, 1991): 15–32.

51. On Jiang Zemin's change of heart, see *SCMP*, July 15, 1992.

52. *BR* 35, 25 (June 22–28, 1992): 7.

53. *MB*, March 26, 1992, 8, in *FBIS*, March 27, 1992, 11.

54. On Deng's reported preference for Zhu over Li, see Kyodo, March 22, 1992, in *FBIS*, March 23, 1992, 50.

55. XH, January 6, 1992, in *FBIS*, January 6, 1992, 40.

56. Li's conversion to the cause of accelerated reform apparently took shape in the autumn of 1991, when Deng Xiaoping urged him to cooperate with Jiang Zemin, hinting that such cooperation might help Li to get out from under the shadow of the Tiananmen debacle. See *JB* 174 (January 1992): 45, in *FBIS*, January 8, 1992, 23. On Li's belated endorsement of key features of Deng's reform programs, including the Shanghai stock exchange, see *SCMP*, March 26, 1992, in *FBIS*, March 26, 1992, 35–36; *BR* 35, 11 (March 16–22, 1992): 7; *BR* 35, 32 (August 10–16, 1992): 18; and *SCMPW*, January 16–17, 1993.

57. *SCMP*, April 1, 1992, in *FBIS*, April 1, 1992, 28.

58. *SCMP*, March 20, 1992.

59. *SCMP*, April 27, 1992.

60. For a collection of these materials, see Yuan Shang and Han Zhu, eds., *Deng Xiaoping nanxun houde Zhongguo* (China after Deng Xiaoping's southern tour).

61. Chen Yun's strong opposition to the idea of special economic zones had led to Shanghai's exclusion from the first round of SEZ experiments in 1978–79.

62. *BR* 35, 19 (May 11–17, 1992): 9.

63. Ibid. A short time later, Chen's supporters accused Shanghai city officials and the mass media of distorting their patron's remarks about the need for bold steps and emancipated thinking, thereby creating a false impression that Chen had fully endorsed Deng's policies.

64. The Chinese phrase conveying Chen's three conditions was "Jiang-Li budong; Song-Yao buxia; Shenzhen buxue" (Jiang and Li don't move; Song and Yao don't step down; Shenzhen isn't emulated). See *SCMPW*, February 6–7, 1993. A somewhat different version of Chen's three conditions appears in *Guai bao*, April 7, 1992, in *FBIS*, April 8, 1992, 22.

65. Saich, "Peaceful Evolution," 28.

66. *SCMP*, May 7, 1992.

67. Like Jiang, Li, and Qiao, Yang Baibing had lined up belatedly in support of Deng's reform offensive. See XH, March 31, 1992, in *FBIS*, April 1, 1992, 17; also *SCMP*, April 1, 1992. Following Tian Jiyun's speech, bootleg copies of a videotape of the speech were reportedly in great demand in Beijing. See Saich, "Peaceful Evolution," 29, n. 36.

68. A special five-part series praising the reform experiences of the Capital Iron and Steel Works appears in *BR* 34, 2; 34, 4; 34, 5–6; 34, 8; and 34, 11 (January–April, 1992).

69. AFP, July 7, 1992.

70. On Gao Di's ongoing efforts to sabotage Deng's reform initiative, see *SCMP*, March 27 and April 8, 1992, in *FBIS*, March 27, 1992, 33–34, and April 8, 1992, 21–22.

71. *ZM* 177 (July 1992): 15–16, in *FBIS*, July 1, 1992, 25–26. Early in 1995 a scandal surfaced at the Capital Iron and Steel Corporation, involving allegations of massive fraud and corruption by the long-time head of the company, Zhou Guanwu (who reportedly enjoyed a close personal relationship with Deng Xiaoping), and Zhou's profligate, high-rolling son, Zhou Beifang. See epilogue, below.

72. AFP (Beijing), July 10, 1992. Jiang Zemin later endorsed the concept of "survival of the fittest" in his work report to the Fourteenth Party Congress.

73. *DGB*, July 4, 1992, in *ICM* 14, 9 (September 1992): 48–49. Among the conference participants were Yu Guangyuan, Du Runsheng, Wu Jinglian, Dong Fureng, An Zhiwen, Tong Dalin, Wu Mingyu, and Sun Changjiang.

74. *BR* 35, 32 (August 10–16, 1992): 7.

75. *SCMP*, August 13, 1992. Persistent rumors of the impending dismissal of Wang, He, and Gao (among others) had been floating in Hong Kong since the conclusion of Deng's southern tour in mid-February. See, e.g., *FBIS*, March 6, 1992, 14; March 9, 1992, 21–22; and March 25, 1992, 34.

76. XH, August 10, 1992; *BR* 35, 34 (August 24–30, 1992): 7–9.

77. *BR* 35, 33 (August 17–23, 1992): 7–8.

78. *MB*, November 12, 1992, in *ICM* 15, 1 (January 1993): 15–16.

79. The following discussion draws from *BR* 35, 32 (August 10–16, 1992): 18–21; *Financial Times*, June 3, 1992; *AWSJ*, July 10, 1992; and Schell and Lappin, "China Plays the Market."

80. Schell and Lappin, "China Plays the Market," 732.

81. *BR* 35, 32 (August 10–16, 1992): 19.

82. Quoted in Schell and Lappin, "China Plays the Market," 742.

83. Ibid.

84. China News Agency, November 19, 1992.

85. *ZM* 179 (September 1992): 9–11, in *FBIS*, September 1, 1992, 25.

86. *ZM* 180 (October 1992): 6–8. See also Tony Saich, "The Fourteenth Party Congress: A Program for Authoritarian Rule."

87. *WSJ*, September 9, 1992. Notwithstanding the apparent seriousness of the newspaper's eyebrow-raising claim, the story may have been apocryphal, as numerous Western biographers and archivists have failed to uncover any evidence of Marx's alleged stock trades.

88. *BR* 35, 43 (October 26–November 1, 1992): 18, 20.

89. *CD*, November 20, 1992. The government promulgated a new set of uniform regulations in May 1993.

90. *SCMP*, September 10, 1992; *BX* 276 (November 16, 1992): 50–51, in *ICM* 15, 1 (January 1993): 34–35.

91. *ZM* 180 (October 1992): 14.

92. *BR* 35, 43 (October 26–November 1, 1992): 18–19.

93. Ibid.

94. See David Bachman, "The Fourteenth Congress of the Chinese Communist Party," 6. On the rise of hybrid forms of enterprise ownership and management in postreform China, see Victor Nee, "Organizational Dynamics of Market Transition: Hybrid Forms, Property Rights, and Mixed Economy in China," and Andrew G. Walder, "China's Trajectory of Economic and Political Change: Some Contrary Facts and Their Theoretical Implications."

95. *BR* 35, 43 (October 26–November 1, 1992): 29–30.

96. For a more detailed comparison of the two reports, see Saich, "The Fourteenth Party Congress."

97. *BR* 35, 42 (October 19–25, 1992): 10. By the fall of 1992 the government's translation of *dongluan* had undergone significant modification, from "turmoil" to mere "disturbance," reflecting the regime's attempt to blunt foreign criticism of the 1989 crackdown.

98. *ZM* 181 (November 1992): 18–19.

99. XH, July 22, 1992.

100. Quoted in UPI (Beijing), July 21, 1992. See also *SCMP*, July 23, 1992, and *DX* (August 1992): 44–46, in *ICM* 14, 10 (October 1992): 17–21.

101. As noted above, the announcement conveying the Ninth Plenum's decision to resolve Zhao Ziyang's case referred to the events of spring 1989 merely as a "political disturbance" (*zhengzhi dongluan*). In the initial drafts of Jiang Zemin's speech to the Fourteenth Congress, this relatively mild term was also used. In the final draft, which Deng Xiaoping reportedly had a hand in revising, the expression was retained, but with the addition of new, harsher terminology, as follows: "In late spring and early summer of 1989, *a political disturbance broke out*, and the party and the government, relying on the people, took a clear-cut stand against unrest. They quelled the *counterrevolutionary rebellion* in Beijing, defending the power of the socialist state and the fundamental interests of the people and ensuring the continued progress of reform, the opening up and modernization." *BR* 35, 43 (October 26–November 1, 1992): 14 (emphasis added).

102. Ibid., 17.

103. The term had first been used in 1984, gaining widespread currency in 1986. Prior to Jiang's report to the Fourteenth Congress, however, authorship of the term had never been attributed solely to Deng. See John Bryan Starr, "Redefinition of Chinese Socialism"; also *BR* 29, 38 (September 22, 1986): 4–7; and *BR* 30, 8 (February 26, 1987): 14–18.

104. *BR* 35, 43 (October 26–November 1, 1992): 11, 14, 16, 18. For official hagiog-

raphy on the emerging cult of Deng Xiaoping, see *BR* 35, 41 (October 12–18, 1992): 12–22; and Mao Mao (née Deng Rong), *Wo fuqin Deng Xiaoping, shangjuan* (My father Deng Xiaoping, vol. 1).

105. JEN, November 14, 1992. On Yuan Mu's role in drafting Jiang's work report, see *RMRB*, October 24, 1992.

106. See *BR* 35, 43 (October 26–November 1, 1992): 6.

107. *SCMPW*, February 20–21, 1993.

108. *BR* 35, 43 (October 26–November 1, 1992): 5–7; see also Saich, "The Fourteenth Party Congress," and Joseph Fewsmith, "Reform, Resistance, and the Politics of Succession."

109. Saich, "The Fourteenth Party Congress," n. 38.

110. Early in 1991 He Dongchang had criticized Deng Xiaoping for having "ideologically disarmed" the Chinese people by "blurring and confusing" the distinction between socialism and capitalism. See *JB* 174 (January 1992): 42–44, in *FBIS*, January 27, 1992, 35. He Dongchang had also reportedly backed publication by the State Education Commission of a conservative reference book attacking Deng's economic theories and principles. See *BX* 250 (October 1991), in *FBIS*, October 23, 1991, 37–38. In response to such attacks, He was removed from his post as chairman of the party committee of the State Education Commission on June 3, 1992—the third anniversary of the Beijing massacre.

111. Li Ximing, who was by far the youngest of the outgoing Politburo members, had come under strong reformist pressure to resign as a result, inter alia, of his having accused Hu Qili's supporters of whipping up a "Rightist tendency" in Beijing. See *ZM* 180 (October 1992): 9–12, in *FBIS*, October 5, 1992, 18–22.

112. The engineers were Jiang Zemin, Li Peng, Li Ruihuan, Zhu Rongji, Hu Jintao, Ding Guan'gen, Zou Jiahua, Wei Jianxing, Wu Bangguo, and Tan Shaowen; the scientists were Li Tieying (physics) and Wen Jiabao (alternate, geology). Ex-Soviet-bloc-trained members were Jiang Zemin, Li Peng, Liu Huaqing, Zou Jiahua, Li Lanqing, Li Tieying, Qian Qichen, and Wei Jianxing. See Bachman, "The Fourteenth Congress," 12–14.

113. The four were Liu Huaqing and Yang Baibing (PLA), Qiao Shi (party security specialist), and Wei Jianxing (minister of supervision and newly named head of the CDIC).

114. At forty-nine, Hu Jintao was the youngest Politburo SC member since Wang Hongwen's spectacular rise to the post of CCP first vice-chairman in the late 1960s. From 1988 to 1992 Hu served as party first secretary in Tibet, where he earned a reputation as a political authoritarian with reformist economic leanings. Prior to 1988 Hu had reportedly developed close ties with both Hu Yaobang (through service in the CYL) and Song Ping (in the Gansu provincial party organization).

115. Li reportedly received 1,892 votes (out of a possible 2,004) in the CC election, while Zhu received 1,998. See *SCMPW*, October 30–November 5, 1992, 8.

116. Wei Jianxing replaced Qiao Shi as head of the CDIC at the Fourteenth Congress.

117. *Dongfang ribao*, October 22, 1992, cited in Saich, "Peaceful Evolution," n. 33. Voting totals for the election to the new Politburo appear in *ZM* 181 (November 1992): 11.

118. *SCMPW*, January 16–17, 1993. For further analysis of the Yang Shangkun affair, see *FBIS*, October 27, November 5, and December 15, 1992; also Fewsmith, "Reform, Resistance, and the Politics of Succession."

119. Yan Kong, "Evolution of the Central Military Commission," 27–28. According to a former PLA officer, Liu Huaqing and General Wang Ruilin, deputy director of the CCP General Office (and Deng Xiaoping's personal secretary), first alerted Deng to the machinations of the Yang brothers. See Swaine, *The Military and Political Succession*, 196, n. 11. On Liu Huaqing's sudden rise to political and military prominence, see *SCMP*, July 15, 1992, and UPI (Beijing), January 27, 1993.

120. For further analysis of political implications of party and military personnel changes enacted during and immediately after the October Party Congress, see Li Cheng and Lynn White, "The Army in the Succession to Deng Xiaoping"; Fewsmith, "Reform, Resistance, and the Politics of Succession"; and Swaine, *The Military and Political Succession*, chap. 12.

121. *BR* 35, 43 (October 26–November 1, 1992): 32.

CHAPTER 15
THE LAST CYCLE

1. *SCMPW*, February 27–28, 1993; *Dongfang jibao*, January 14, 1993, in *FBIS*, January 14, 1993, 15. This interpretation is supported by the recent memoir of Xu Jiatun who, prior to his self-exile to the United States in 1990, had been head of the Chinese government's Xinhua bureau in Hong Kong. See *LHP*, August 31, 1993, in *FBIS*, September 17, 1993, 22.

2. *SCMPW*, February 27–28, 1993. The document in question was rumored to be the transcript of a tape recording, made on or about June 3, 1989.

3. Ibid.; *The Standard*, January 6, 1993.

4. *SCMPW*, January 16–17 and July 10–11, 1993; UPI, January 27, 1993. The military purge of autumn 1992 also reportedly served to weaken the political influence of Deng's former Second Field Army cohort. These events are examined in Fewsmith, "Reform, Resistance, and the Politics of Succession." See also Lam, *China after Deng*, pp. 227–31.

5. JEN, January 17, 1993; *SCMP*, January 26, 1993.

6. *SCMPW*, January 30–31, 1993.

7. Ibid.

8. JEN, January 27, 1993.

9. *SCMPW*, January 16–17, 1993.

10. AP (Beijing), March 17, 1993. An even larger defense budget increase—14.7 percent—was reported in *LAT*, March 17, 1993.

11. *SCMPW*, January 16–17, 1993. See also *DD* 21 (December 1992): 32–36, in *FBIS*, January 7, 1993, 12–14.

12. *SCMPW*, January 16–17, 1993.

13. Ibid.

14. The poem's colloquial translation at the head of the present chapter is from *NYT*, April 30, 1991.

15. See *SCMPW*, February 20–21, 1993; AFP (Beijing), February 1993.

16. *SCMP*, February 6, 1993.

17. *SCMPW*, February 20–21, 1993.

18. The extent of Rong Yiren's wealth was hinted at a few months later when his son, Larry Yung, acquired the fourteen-bedroom East Sussex family estate of the late British Prime Minister Harold MacMillan for an estimated purchase price of £5 million (U.S. $7.5 million). See JEN, July 4, 1993.

19. JEN, March 20, 1993.

20. *SCMP*, March 15, 1993.

21. *LAT*, March 23, 1993. Apart from these "converted" ex-cadres, 120,000 state employees reportedly quit their jobs in 1992–93 to go into business. Additional hundreds of thousands "took the plunge" on a part-time basis, moonlighting in the private sector after normal working hours and on weekends. By 1994, the xiahai craze had become so prevalent that it was not uncommon, for example, to find university faculty offices and government research facilities empty at peak daytime hours, as teachers and research personnel scrambled to supplement their meager, fixed incomes by "sunlighting" in the private sector. On the xiahai craze, see Miles, *The Legacy of Tiananmen*, chap. 4.

22. *CND*, March 24, 1993.

23. These developments are discussed in *LAT*, June 9, 1993; *MB*, July 11, 1993; and *SCMPW*, July 10–11, 1993.

24. This assessment, together with details about Hu Qiaomu's last testament, was provided by a knowledgeable Communist Party source (personal interview, May 1993). Deng Liqun's vastly diminished influence was confirmed late in 1994 when his left-wing propaganda journal, *Search for Truth*, discontinued publication.

25. Hu Jiwei, informal remarks on "China's Reforms and the News Media," UCLA, August 21, 1993.

26. My thanks to Tony Saich for sharing this anecdote.

CHAPTER 16
THE MANDATE OF HEAVEN

1. *CD*, February 27, 1993; UPI (Beijing), April 19, 1993; *SCMPW*, July 24–25, 1993; and *ICM* 17, 4 (April 1995): 15–16.

2. *DGB*, July 1, 1993, in *FBIS*, July 1, 1993, 48–50. I am indebted to Thomas Bernstein for calling this information to my attention.

3. In the interior provinces of Henan, Hubei, and Hunan, farmers suffered a reported average decline in real income of about 12 percent beginning in the late 1980s. On problems facing Chinese farmers in the 1990s, see Miles, *The Legacy of Tiananmen*, chap. 6; Edward Friedman, "Deng versus the Peasantry: Recollectivization in the Countryside"; and Jonathan Unger, "Life in the Chinese Hinterlands under the Rural Economic Reforms." Data on 1994 income differential are from *Beijing Review* 38, 14–15 (April 3–16, 1995): II.

4. The Renshou County riots are documented in *FBIS*, April 29, 1993, 10–12, and Miles, *The Legacy of Tiananmen*, chap. 6. The complaints of farmers are examined in *ICM* 15, 1 (January 1993): 56–59, and 15, 3 (March 1993): 28–40, 82–83; *FBIS*, March 9, 1993, 12–13; March 23, 1993, 83–84; and June 1, 1993, 69–70; and AFP, December 7, 1993.

5. *ZM* 202 (August 1, 1994): 28–29, in *ICM* 16, 10 (October 1994): 56–57. See also *ICM* 15, 3 (March 1993): 28–40.

6. Quoted in *SCMP*, March 22, 1993.

7. *JJRB*, March 2, 1993. This figure stands in marked contrast to the Ministry of Labor's official unemployment figures, which rose only slightly in the early 1990s— from 2.3 percent (13 million people) in 1990 to 2.7 percent (15.3 million) in 1994.

8. *CND* (Books and Journals Review), June 27, 1993.

9. Vice-Premier Jiang Chunyun, quoted in *CQ* 142 (June 1995): 653.

10. See *CQ* 141 (March 1995): 270. The government's decision to intervene to stabilize grain output and prices stemmed, in large measure, from a record 49 percent increase in the cost of grain in 1994. See *FEER*, June 1, 1995.

11. *ZM* 185 (March 1, 1993): 19, in *FBIS*, March 10, 1993, 14–15; and *CND*, June 1, 1995.

12. *CQ* 139 (September 1994): 863.

13. *GMRB*, July 7, 1993; *SCMPW*, August 14–15, 1993.

14. *ZM* 192 (October 1, 1993): 23, in *FBIS*, October 12, 1993, 26.

15. *SCMP*, March 26, 1992. The activities of triads in Guangdong are discussed in *SCMPW*, July 24–25, 1993. As one measure of the magnitude of the problem of organized crime, in 1993 Chinese police reportedly broke up 150,000 criminal gangs—a 25 percent increase over the previous year; in the last six months of 1994, authorities apprehended 277,000 gang members. See *WWB*, February 26, 1995; and *ICM* 17, 4 (April 1995): 94. Miles, *The Legacy of Tiananmen*, chap. 6, examines the problem of organized crime in the 1990s.

16. *GRRB*, July 27, 1993; *CD*, June 11, 1993.

17. Cf. *RMRB*, August 31, 1992, and XH, October 22, 1992.

18. The record was only slightly better at the county and municipal levels, where approximately 4,500 officials (an average of just over 2 per county) were caught and convicted in the same five-year period. See *BR* 36, 15 (April 12–18, 1993): 6.

19. Data cited in *Dignity* 9508 (March 26, 1995): 13–15. It was further estimated that in 1992 approximately ¥100 billion in public funds had been squandered by cadres on unwarranted feasting and entertainment.

20. *FBIS*, September 7, 1993, 42; Fewsmith, "Reform, Resistance, and the Politics of Succession."

21. *RMRB*, July 1, 1993; *CND*, October 23, 1993.

22. *SCMPW*, July 17–18, 1993. See also Ellis Joffe, "The PLA and the Chinese Economy."

23. A prime example was Deng Zhifang, second son of Deng Xiaoping, who was reported to be involved, among other things, in a major real estate development involving the construction of dozens of lush private villas on land owned by the PLA near the Shanghai airport. See *SCMPW*, July 17–18, 1993. The Baoli (Polytechnologies) Corporation, largest of the parastatal arms-merchandising companies established in China in the 1980s, counted among its officers several prominent gaogan zidi, including the sons-in-law of Deng Xiaoping (He Ping), Yang Shangkun (Wang Xiaochao), and Zhao Ziyang (Wang Zhihua). See Tanner and Feder, "Family Politics," 114–15; and Eric Hyer, "China's Arms Merchants: Profits in Command."

24. *RMRB*, July 26, 1993; see also *FEER*, August 12, 1993.

25. *The Times* (London), May 9, 1994; Lam, *China after Deng*, 231.

26. *BR* 36, 15 (April 12–18, 1993): 5–6.

27. *CD*, February 19, 1993; *WIID*, April 15, 1995. By comparison, Shanghai ca. 1930 had an estimated 25,000 prostitutes—four times as many as Paris.

28. *CD*, June 25, 1993.

29. Because of urban bias in the Yunnan population sample, it is likely that this 3.5 percent figure substantially overstates the rate of addiction for the province as a whole. The data appear in Dali L. Yang, "The State and 'Uncivil' Society: China's Growing Drug Problem in Comparative Perspective," 4–5.

30. Ibid.; *SCMPW*, July 17–18, 1993.

31. China News Agency, October 6, 1992; JEN, October 6, 1992.

32. Miles, *The Legacy of Tiananmen*, chap. 6, recounts the two-month siege at Pingyuan, which culminated in the arrest of 850 people and the seizure of 350 military rifles, 600 other assorted firearms, and nearly a ton of heroin. Seven of the accused traffickers—including leading local government officials—were ultimately sentenced to death.

33. On the new hedonism of urban youth, see Orville Schell, *Discos and Democracy: China in the Throes of Reform*, parts 2 and 6.

34. *FBIS*, July 7, 1993, 12–13; *SCMPW*, July 10–11, 1993.

35. *FBIS*, June 17, 1993, 26–27, and July 7, 1993, 12–13; *SCMPW*, July 10–11, 1993. Zhu later issued a tongue-in-cheek denial that he had ever used such graphic language.

36. For a discussion of Zhu Rongji's economic and fiscal reforms, see Lam, *China after Deng*, 84–94.

37. "Triangular debt" refers to the gridlock of uncollectible interenterprise business debts caused by a chain of interlinked credits leading from one enterprise to another to another—with each, in turn, unable to pay its creditors until receiving payment from its debtors. See CNS, April 23, 1994; Lam, *China after Deng*, 71–75, 346; *FEER*, February 23, 1995, 51; and Reuters, July 28, 1995.

38. Zhu's problems with enacting the bank law are detailed in *FEER*, March 30, 1995, 14–15.

39. *WWP*, August 23, 1993.

40. Later, it was reported that Deng had issued a brief statement during his New Year visit to Shanghai in which he expressed support for continued economic reform and urged new vigor in the campaign to combat corruption. See *BX*, February 1, 1994, 9, in *ICM* 16, 4 (April 1994): 7–8.

41. In January 1995, in an interview with Patrick Tyler of the *New York Times*, Deng Rong (who now went by the name of Xiao Rong) stated that her father's physical condition was deteriorating "day by day" (*NYT*, January 13, 1995). Though Chinese government spokespersons denied the accuracy of the quotation, the newspaper stood by its story.

42. Chen's terminal illness is discussed in *RMRB* May 29, 1995, in *FBIS*, June 9, 1995, 24–29.

43. Reuters (Beijing), April 12, 1995; *Time*, April 25, 1995; *FEER*, April 27, 1995, 14–15. Deng Xiaoping did not attend the memorial service.

44. The following discussion draws on Lam, *China after Deng*, chap. 4, and David Shambaugh, "China's Commander-in-Chief: Jiang Zemin and the PLA," 27ff.

45. This was the second batch of key military promotions supervised by Jiang since the ouster of the Yang brothers. See *JSND*, July 1994, 52–53, in *ICM* 16, 9 (September 1994): 72–74; and *ZM* 201 (July 1, 1994): 11–12, in *FBIS*, July 27, 1994, 38–39.

46. From 1992 to 1995, China's official defense budget rose from ¥25 billion to more than ¥63 billion. On an annual basis, the rates of increase were 12 percent, 16.2 percent, 20.9 percent, and 21.2 percent, successively (Shambaugh, "China's Commander-in-Chief," 37).

47. Quoted in Lam, *China after Deng*, 227.

48. On the rising potency of the Shanghai clique, see *I&S* 30, 10 (October 1994): 130–32; and *SCMP*, June 26, 1995, in *FBIS*, June 26, 1995, 30.

49. *SCMPW*, July 10–11, 1993, and July 31-August 1, 1993.

50. According to government statistics, more than 11,000 party and government officials came under investigation for economic crimes in 1994; in the same year,

judicial proceedings were instituted against 88 department or bureau-level cadres, 1,827 county-level cadres, and 4,007 judicial and law enforcement personnel, including 110 leading cadres. The latter figure was said to represent a 50 percent increase over 1993. See *ICM* 17,7 (July 1995): 35–36.

51. *NYT*, May 8, 1995; *MB*, May 8, 1995, 3, in *FBIS* May 15, 1995, 35.

52. Among Zhou Beifang's alleged improprieties was his unexplained accumulation of Hong Kong commercial assets worth an estimated U.S. $1.4 billion. Also under investigation was the 1993 purchase of Peru's largest tin mine by Zhou's Shougang holding company, for which an astronomical sum was paid that was said to be twice the actual market value of the facility.

Li Ka-shing had teamed with Deng Zhifang and Zhou Beifang in a series of Hong Kong business ventures in the early 1990s. Questions of impropriety arose in 1994, after Li's Cheung Kong holding company announced plans to erect an 850,000-square-meter, U.S. $1.2 billion high-rise commercial building—the Orient Plaza—on a prime piece of downtown Beijing real estate at the corner of Wangfujing Street and Chang'an Boulevard. To expedite issuance of the necessary construction permits and to secure eviction of the building site's current occupant—China's first (and reputedly the world's highest-volume) McDonald's restaurant—Li reportedly sought (and received) a friendly assist from Beijing municipal authorities. The problem was that McDonald's held a valid twenty-year lease on the coveted property. After receiving an eviction notice from the city, McDonald's demanded a formal inquiry into the matter. Following an official investigation, the Orient Plaza project was quietly redesigned and downsized, and McDonalds was permitted to continue operating on the disputed site. While the incident reportedly proved extremely embarrassing to the Deng family, no criminal charges were filed against anyone connected with the case. It was later rumored that Li Ka-shing had threatened to institute legal proceedings against anyone raising allegations of wrongdoing. On the Shougang and Orient Plaza cases, see *AWSJ*, February 22, 1995; *FEER*, March 2, 1995, 15–16, and March 23, 1995, 46–47; also *JSND*, March 1995; *Washington Post*, March 16, 1995; and *ICM* 17, 5 (May 1995): 13–17. On Ding Peng's alleged wrongdoing, see *Eastern Express* (Hong Kong), May 10, 1995, in *FBIS*, May 10, 1995, 17–18.

53. See *ZM* 211 (May 1, 1995): 23–26; and AP (Beijing), July 23, 1995. Although the official verdict was suicide, the nature of Wang's head wound made it unlikely, in the opinion of some commentators, that the wound was self-inflicted. It has also been conjectured that Wang may have been the conduit for bribes and kickbacks intended for higher-level officials, and that he was silenced to prevent him from informing on others. See *Eastern Express*, May 3, 1995, in *FBIS*, May 3, 1995, 16–17.

54. At first, Chen Xitong reportedly refused to step down, encouraging his subordinates to stonewall the anticorruption investigation. Thereafter, the Politburo solved the problem by peremptorily announcing Chen's resignation as a fait accompli. Unnamed Chinese sources, reputedly close to the official investigation, subsequently confirmed that at least some of Wang Baosen's graft "was Chen's doing," although these sources stopped short of accusing Chen of having Wang silenced (AP, July 23, 1995). On the Chen Xitong affair, see also *FBIS*, May 1, 1995, 13–24; *ZM* 212 (June 1, 1995): 15–18; *JSND*, June 1995, 35–37; and *NYT*, May 7, 1995.

55. See *FBIS*, May 19, 1995, 17. Yuan's post was taken over by Wang Mengkui, a speechwriter and reported adviser to Jiang Zemin.

56. Reportedly, Wei's chief competitor was State Council General Secretary Luo Gan, a protégé of Li Peng. See *SCMP*, April 29, 1995, in *FBIS*, May 1, 1995, 13.

57. The widening Beijing anticorruption probe is examined in *FEER*, April 27 and May 11, 1995; *The Economist*, May 6 and 20, 1995; *Businessweek*, May 15, 1995; *RMRB*, July 5, 1995; *CND*, July 19, 1995; and AP (Beijing), July 23, 1995.

58. *MB*, May 8, 1995, in *FBIS*, May 15, 1995, 35.

59. A public opinion poll released by CASS early in 1995 revealed that "punishment of corrupt officials" was regarded as China's second most pressing national problem (cited by 40 percent of all respondents), surpassed only by extreme consumer anxiety over rising prices (cited by 71 percent), and easily outdistancing the third most commonly cited problem, concern for the maintenance of social stability (25 percent). See *RMRB*, February 27, 1995; and *ICM* 17, 4 (April 1995): 94. A similar poll, commissioned by the Policy Research Center of the CCP Central Committee in December 1994, produced an even more striking result, with 3,393 of the 4,093 respondents— fully 83 percent—ranking "corruption and abuse of privilege" among cadres as the most urgent problem requiring party and government attention (ibid., 4).

60. The chronically ailing Peng Zhen, ninety-two, reportedly urged Jiang Zemin in a personal meeting not to "go too far" with the anticorruption probe. *MB*, May 10, 1995, in *FBIS*, May 15, 1995, 38.

61. After recovering from the heart problem that had necessitated his hospitalization in the spring of 1993, Li Peng resumed some of his former duties toward the end of that year, principally in the area of foreign affairs. However, he never recovered his lost influence over economic policy, the brief for which had been handed over to Zhu Rongji. When Li's two most powerful patrons, Yao Yilin and Chen Yun, died within a few months of each other early in 1995, his base of support was significantly weakened. Although Li Peng initially firmly endorsed the Beijing anticorruption drive in mid-February 1995, his enthusiasm apparently waned around the time of Wang Baosen's alleged suicide; thereafter, his power base was further weakened by the removal of Chen Xitong and Yuan Mu.

62. See *ICM* 16:4 (April 1994): 7. I am grateful to James Mulvenon for information concerning the physicians' affidavit.

63. *FBIS*, May 16, 1995, 18. In a fascinating sidebar to the Zhuo Lin drama, the Hong Kong stock market suffered a sudden, sharp sell-off at the end of April when local newspapers erroneously reported that it was Deng Xiaoping himself who had been hospitalized. Japanese sources subsequently claimed that the cause of Zhuo Lin's hospitalization had been a suicide attempt rather than a stroke, while Hong Kong journalists described Zhuo's ailment as a case of "nervous exhaustion." See *Tokyo shimbun*, May 5, 1995, in *FBIS*, May 5, 1995, 21; *MB*, May 10, 1995, in *FBIS*, May 15, 1995, 39; and *SCMP*, May 18, 1995, in *FBIS*, May 18, 1995, 18.

64. See *Eastern Express*, May 18, 1995, in *FBIS*, May 18, 1995, 15; and *SCMP*, July 8, 1995, 10, in *FBIS*, July 10, 1995, 26–27. The memorial plaque to Hu Yaobang reportedly contained an epitaph in Jiang's own calligraphy lauding Hu's "sincerity and honesty."

65. See *China Rights Forum*, June 1995, 10–14.

66. On Tian's NPC speech, see *ZM* 210 (April 1, 1995), in *ICM* 17, 6 (June 1995): 21–23.

67. I am indebted to Dimon Liu for calling this to my attention. On the NPC proceedings, see *FEER*, March 30, 1995, 14–15; and *ICM* 17, 6 (June 1995), 22–23. The high quotient of negative votes against Jiang Chunyun was reportedly a response to Jiang's widespread reputation for incompetence and to allegations that his wife had been detained by police on charges of corruption. See *FBIS*, May 18, 1995, 18.

68. *SCMP*, April 19, 1995, 17, in *FBIS*, April 19, 1995, 14–15.

69. The full text of this document, along with several other contemporaneous letters and appeals to the NPC requesting reversal of the June 4 verdict and amnesty for victims of the Tiananmen crackdown, appears in *China Rights Forum*, June 1995, 10–14

70. *FEER*, June 15, 1995, 15.

71. *SCMP*, May 18, 1995, in *FBIS*, May 18, 1995, 18.

72. See, e.g., *AFP* (Hong Kong), June 4, 1995, in *FBIS*, June 5, 1995, 20–21. In a move that was interpreted as a further sign of leadership anxiety over possible renewed political turbulence in Beijing, Jiang Zemin signed a decree giving the MAC and the PLA General Staff Headquarters sole authority to move troops within the nation's capital. See *XB*, May 12, 1995, in *FBIS*, May 12, 1995, 34.

73. See XH, August 2, 1995; and Reuters (Beijing), August 3 and 4, 1995. Altogether, 47,560 party members and cadres were disciplined for corruption in the first half of 1995, including 1,801 officials at the level of county magistrate, division chief, or higher—representing a significant year on year increase of 44.4 percent.

74. *CNS*, July 17, 1995; XH, July 18, 1995.

75. See *LAT*, July 21, 1995.

EPILOGUE
BURYING DENG

1. Estimates of GDP and per capita income vary widely depending on whether the official currency exchange rate or purchasing power parity (PPP) is used as the standard. The figures used here are denominated in PPP, generally regarded as a more accurate indicator of real economic equivalency.

2. Interestingly, the Chinese government in recent years has played down the country's aggregate economic accomplishments, giving scant publicity to any statistics that might tend to belie China's claim to be a poor, third world country. Such official modesty is evidently a function of China's twofold desire to secure international development credits and loans at the lowest possible rates and to enter the new World Trade Organization (WTO) on the more favorable terms extended to nonindustrialized countries.

3. See Wang and Hu, *Jiaqiang zhongyang zhengfu*; see also XH, July 29, 1993; Miles, *The Legacy of Tiananmen*, chap. 10; and Lam, *China after Deng*, 131.

4. *Viewing China through a Third Eye*, 29. While Wang Shan is widely regarded as the book's author, some observers have suggested that Pan Yue, Liu Huaqing's neo-conservative son-in-law, may have played a role in writing it.

5. Ibid., 18, 29–32, 83–86, 91, 110, and passim. Wang Shan's reputed ties to Chen Yuan are examined in *Kaifang* 94 (October 1, 1994): 20–23, in *FBIS*, January 12, 1995, 21–24. Wang's princeling connections are strongly suggested by his evasive, low-key analysis of the problem of China's profligate gaogan zidi: "The cadre children class is a relatively independent political and social community. They have played a fairly prominent role during the past thirty years . . . and have become a unique phenomenon in Chinese social life" (*Viewing China through a Third Eye*, 58). Tellingly, Wang Shan fails to treat official nepotism and guandao as serious problems requiring stringent countermeasures. Instead, he notes approvingly that most countries "adopt a policy of tolerance and letting bygones be bygones even when the cadres are caught red-handed" (ibid., 98).

6. Wu Dacheng, in *Jiangnan Academy Journal* (Nanjing) 3 (1994), cited in Lam, *China after Deng*, 391.

7. Cited in Miles, *The Legacy of Tiananmen*, chap. 9.

8. Ibid.

9. Poll results cited in *ICM* 17, 4 (April 1995): 3–4; and Miles, *The Legacy of Tiananmen*, chap. 10.

10. Quoted in *ZM* 202 (August 1, 1994): 16–17, in *ICM* 16, 10 (October 1994): 9.

11. Deng's instructions are reported in *XB*, July 29 and August 19, 1994. See also Lam, *China after Deng*, 385–86.

12. Deng's remarks on sources of instability are cited in *FEER*, February 2, 1995, 15. The last publicly released photo of the patriarch was taken on October 1, 1994. It showed Deng sitting motionless in an armchair, mouth slightly open, staring vacantly at a National Day fireworks display. Shortly thereafter, Deng reportedly was hospitalized for several weeks with an undisclosed ailment. See *SCMP*, May 18, 1995, in *FBIS*, May 18, 1995, 12.

• *R E F E R E N C E S* •

Books and Articles

Amnesty International. 1992. *Torture in China*. New York: Amnesty International ASA 17/55/92.

———. 1990. *China: The Massacre of June 1989 and Its Aftermath*. London: Amnesty International.

———. 1990. *People's Republic of China: The Continuing Repression*. London: Amnesty International, nos. 1–2.

———. 1984. *China: Violations of Human Rights*. London: Amnesty International.

Asia Watch. 1990. *Repression in China since June 4, 1989*. New York: Asia Watch.

Bachman, David. 1992. "The Fourteenth Congress of the Chinese Communist Party." New York: The Asia Society, Asian Update Series.

———. 1986. "Differing Visions of China's Post-Mao Economy: The Ideas of Chen Yun, Deng Xiaoping, and Zhao Ziyang." *Asian Survey* 26, 3 (March): 292–321.

———. 1985. *Chen Yun and the Chinese Political System*. Berkeley: University of California, Center for Chinese Studies.

Bachman, David, and Dali L. Yang, eds. 1991. *Yan Jiaqi and China's Struggle for Democracy*. Armonk, N.Y: M. E. Sharpe.

Barmé, Geremie, and John Minford, eds. 1988. *Seeds of Fire: Chinese Voices of Conscience*. New York: Hill and Wang.

Baum, Richard. 1995. "Deng Liqun and the Struggle against 'Bourgeois Liberalization,' 1979–1993." *China Information* 9, 4 (Spring): 1–35.

———. 1993. "The Road to Tiananmen: Chinese Politics in the 1980s." In Roderick MacFarquhar, ed. *The Politics of China, 1949–1989*, 340–471. New York: Cambridge University Press.

———. 1992. "Political Stability in Post-Deng China: Problems and Prospects." *Asian Survey* 32, 6 (June): 491–505.

———. 1989. "DOS ex Machina: The Microelectronic Ghost in China's Modernization Machine." In Denis F. Simon and Merle Goldman, eds., *Science and Technology in Post-Mao China*, 347–71. Cambridge: Harvard University Press.

———. 1986. "Modernization and Legal Reform in Post-Mao China: The Rebirth of Socialist Legality." *Studies in Comparative Communism* 19, 2 (Summer): 69–103.

———. 1986. "China in 1985: The Greening of the Revolution." *Asian Survey* 26, 1 (January): 31–53.

———. 1981. *Scientism and Bureaucratism in Post-Mao China: Cultural Limits of the "Four Modernizations."* Lund, Sweden: Research Policy Institute, University of Lund.

———. 1981. "From Feudal Patriarchy to the Rule of Law: Chinese Politics in 1980." In Robert Oxnam and Richard Bush, eds., *China Briefing, 1981*, 17–40. Boulder: Westview Press.

———. 1975. *Prelude to Revolution: Mao, the Party, and the Peasant Question, 1962–66*. New York: Columbia University Press.

Bei Dao. 1990. "Terugblik Van Een Balling" (An exile looks back). In *Het Collectieve Geheugen: Over Literatuur en Geschiedenis* (The collective memory: On literature and history). Amsterdam: De Balie/Novib.

Bernstein, Thomas. 1985. "China in 1984: The Year of Hong Kong." *Asian Survey* 25, 1 (January): 33–50.

Black, George, and Robin Munro. 1993. *Black Hands of Beijing*. New York: John Wiley & Sons.

Bonavia, David. 1989. *Deng*. Hong Kong: Longman.

Brodsgaard, Kjeld Erik. 1981. "The Democracy Movement in China, 1978–79: Opposition Movements, Wall Poster Campaigns, and Underground Journals." *Asian Survey* 21, 7 (July): 747–74.

Brook, Timothy. 1992. *Quelling the People: The Military Suppression of the Beijing Democracy Movement*. Oxford: Oxford University Press.

Burns, John P. 1989. "China's Governance: Political Reform in a Turbulent Environment." *The China Quarterly* 120 (December): 481–518.

———. 1989. "Chinese Civil Service Reform: The 13th Party Congress Proposals." *The China Quarterly* 120 (December): 739–70.

Butterfield, Fox. 1983. *China: Alive in the Bitter Sea*. New York: Bantam Books.

Byrnes, Michael T. 1990. "The Death of a People's Army." In George Hicks, ed., *The Broken Mirror: China After Tiananmen*, 132–51. Chicago: St. James Press.

Cabestan, Jean-Pierre. 1992. *L'Administration Chinoise après Mao: Les Réformes de l'ère Deng Xiaoping et Leurs Limites* (Chinese administration after Mao: The reforms of the Deng Xiaoping era and their limits). Paris: Éditions du Centre National de la Recherche Scientifique.

———. 1989. "The Reform of the Civil Service." *China News Analysis* 1383 (April 15): 1–10.

Cao Weidong. 1993. *Hongbing li* (Red medical record). Taiyuan: Shaanxi Renmin Chubanshe.

Chan, Anita. 1991. "The Social Origins and Consequences of the Tiananmen Crisis." In David S. G. Goodman and Gerald Segal, eds., *China in the Nineties: Crisis Management and Beyond*, 105–30. Oxford: Clarendon Press.

Chan, Thomas, E. K. Chen, and Steve Chin. 1986. "China's Special Economic Zones: Ideology, Policy and Practice." In Y. C. Rao and C. K. Leung, eds., *China's Special Economic Zones: Policies, Problems, and Prospects*, 87–104. Hong Kong: Oxford University Press.

Chang, Maria Hsia. 1992. "China's Future: Regionalism, Federation, or Disintegration?" *Studies in Comparative Communism* 25, 3 (September): 211–27.

Chang, Parris. 1980. "Chinese Politics: Deng's Turbulent Quest." *Problems of Communism* 30, 1 (January–February): 1–21.

Chen Kuide. 1992. "Wangchao moride xinzheng" (New politics of a moribund dynasty). *Zhongguo zhichun* 1 (January): 24–25.

Chen Yizi. 1990. *Zhongguo shinian gaige yu bajiu minyun: Beijing liusi tusha de beihou* (China's ten years of reform and the 1989 democracy movement: Behind the Beijing massacre of June 4). Taipei: Lien-ching Ch'u-pan Shih-yeh Kung-ssu.

Chen Yun. 1986. *Chen Yun wenxuan, 1956–1985* (Selected works of Chen Yun). 3 vols. Beijing: Zhongguo Renmin Chubanshe.

Chevrier, Yves. 1990. "Micropolitics and the Factory Director Responsibility System, 1984–1987." In Deborah Davis and Ezra F. Vogel, eds., *Chinese Society on the Eve of Tiananmen*, 109–33. Cambridge: Harvard University Council on East Asian Studies.

Chi Hsin. 1977. *The Case of the Gang of Four—With First Translation of Teng Hsiao-ping's "Three Poisonous Weeds."* Hong Kong: Cosmos Books.

Ch'i Hsi-sheng. 1991. *Politics of Disillusionment: The Chinese Communist Party under Deng Xiaoping, 1978–1989.* Armonk, N.Y.: M. E. Sharpe.

Chiu, Hungdah. 1980. "China's New Criminal and Criminal Procedure Codes." University of Maryland, School of Law, Occasional Papers in Contemporary Asian Studies, no. 6: 14–23.

Chong, Woei Lien. 1990. "Petitioners, Popperians, and Hunger Strikers." In Tony Saich, ed., *The Chinese People's Movement: Perspectives on Spring 1989*, 106–25. Armonk, N.Y.: M. E. Sharpe.

———. 1989. "Present Worries of the Chinese Democrats: Notes on Fang Lizhi, Liu Binyan, and the Film 'River Elegy.'" *China Information* 3, 4 (Spring): 1–20.

Christiansen, Flemming. 1989. "The Justification and Legalization of Private Enterprises in China, 1983–1988." *China Information* 4, 2 (Autumn): 80–85.

Chung Jae Ho. 1991. "The Politics of Prerogatives in Socialism: The Case of the *Taizidang* in China." *Studies in Comparative Communism* 24, 1 (March): 58–76.

"CND Interview with Gao Xin." 1991. *China News Digest (Global News)*, April 7–8.

Cremerius, Ruth, Doris Fischer, and Peter Schier, eds. 1990. *Studentenprotest und Repression in China, April–Juni 1989: Analyse, Chronologie, Dokumente.* Hamburg: Institute für Asienkunde.

Criminal Code of the People's Republic of China. 1982. Littleton: Frederick B. Rothman.

Dai Qing. 1989. *Changjiang, Changjiang* (Yangzi River, Yangzi River). Guiyang: Guizhou Chubanshe. English translation published by the International Rivers Network, San Francisco, 1991.

Davis, Deborah, and Ezra F. Vogel, eds. 1990. *Chinese Society on the Eve of Tiananmen.* Cambridge: Harvard University Council on East Asian Studies.

Deng Liqun. 1981. "Answers to Questions Concerning the 'Resolution on Certain Questions in the History of the Party since the Founding of the PRC' (July 30 and August 11)." *Chinese Law and Government* 19, 3 (Fall 1986): 12–55.

Deng Liqun et al. 1979. *FangRi huilai de sisu* (Thoughts upon returning from Japan). Beijing: Zhongguo Shehui Kexue Chubanshe.

Deng Xiaoping. 1989. *Deng Xiaoping tongzhi lun jianchi si xiang jiben yuance fandui zichanjieji ziyouhua* (Comrade Deng Xiaoping on upholding the four cardinal principles and opposing bourgeois liberalization). Beijing: Renmin Chubanshe.

———. 1987. *Fundamental Issues in Present-Day China.* Beijing: Foreign Languages Press.

———. 1984. *Selected Works of Deng Xiaoping (1975–1982).* Beijing: Foreign Languages Press.

Develop Marxism under Contemporary Conditions. 1983. Beijing: Institute of Marxism–Leninism–Mao Zedong Thought.

Dittmer, Lowell. 1990. "Patterns of Elite Strife and Succession in Chinese Politics." *The China Quarterly* 123 (September): 405–30.

———. 1990. "China in 1989: The Crisis of Incomplete Reform." *Asian Survey* 29, 1 (January): 25–41.

———. 1989. "The Tiananmen Massacre." *Problems of Communism* 38, 5 (September–October): 2–15.

———. 1989. "China in 1988: The Dilemma of Continuing Reform." *Asian Survey* 29, 1 (January): 12–28.

———. 1988. "Reform, Succession, and the Resurgence of Mainland China's Old Guard." *Issues & Studies* 24, 1 (January): 96–113.

Dittmer, Lowell. 1983. "The 12th Congress of the Chinese Communist Party." *The China Quarterly* 93 (March): 108–24.

———. 1982. "China in 1981: Reform, Readjustment, Rectification." *Asian Survey* 22, 1 (January): 33–46.

———. 1974. *Liu Shaoqi and the Chinese Cultural Revolution*. Berkeley and Los Angeles: University of California Press.

Dittmer, Lowell, and Yu-shan Wu. 1995. "The Modernization of Factionalism in Chinese Politics." *World Politics* 47, 4 (July): 467–95.

Domes, Jürgen. 1985. *The Government and Politics of the PRC: A Time of Transition*. Boulder: Westview Press.

Dreyer, June Teufel. 1993. "Deng Xiaoping: The Soldier." *The China Quarterly* 135 (September): 536–50.

———. 1989. "The People's Liberation Army and the Power Struggle of 1989." *Problems of Communism* 38, 5 (September–October): 41–48.

Duke, Michael S. 1990. *The Iron House: A Memoir of the Chinese Democracy Movement and the Tiananmen Massacre*. Layton, Utah: Gibbs Smith.

Erbaugh, Mary S., and Richard Curt Kraus. 1991. "The 1989 Democracy Movement in Fujian and Its Aftermath." In Jonathan Unger, ed., *The Pro-Democracy Protests in China: Reports from the Provinces*, 150–65. Armonk, N.Y.: M. E. Sharpe.

Esherick, Joseph W., and Jeffrey N. Wasserstrom. 1992. "Acting Out Democracy: Political Theatre in Modern China." In Jeffrey N. Wasserstrom and Elizabeth J. Perry, eds., *Popular Protest and Political Culture in Modern China*, 28–66. Boulder: Westview Press.

Faison, Seth. 1990. "The Changing Role of the Chinese Media." In Tony Saich, ed., *The Chinese People's Movement: Perspectives on Spring 1989*, 144–62. Armonk, N.Y.: M. E. Sharpe.

Fan Shuo. 1990. *Ye Jianying zai 1976* (Ye Jianying in 1976). Beijing: Zhonggong Zhongyang Dangxiao Chubanshe.

Fathers, Michael, and Andrew Higgins. 1989. *Tiananmen: The Rape of Peking*. London: Independent/Doubleday.

Feng Shengbao. 1990. "Preparations for the Blueprint on Political Restructuring Presented by Zhao Ziyang at the Thirteenth Party Congress." Paper presented to the Harvard University East Asia Colloquium (July).

Fewsmith, Joseph. 1995. "Neoconservativism and the End of the Dengist Era." *Asian Survey* 35:7 (July).

———. 1994. *Dilemmas of Reform in China: Political Conflict and Economic Debate*. Armonk, N.Y.: M. E. Sharpe.

———. 1994. "Reform, Resistance, and the Politics of Succession." In William A. Joseph, ed., *China Briefing, 1993*. Boulder: Westview Press.

———. 1986. "Special Economic Zones in the PRC." *Problems of Communism* 35, 6 (November–December): 78–85.

Fontana, Dorothy Grouse. 1982. "Background to the Fall of Hua Guofeng." *Asian Survey* 12, 3 (March): 237–80.

Forster, Keith. 1992. "China's Coup of October 1976." *Modern China* 18, 3 (July): 263–303.

Francis, Corinna-Barbara. 1989. "The Progress of Protest in China." *Asian Survey* 29, 9 (September): 898–915.

Fraser, John. 1980. *The Chinese: Portrait of a People*. New York: Summit Books.

Friedman, Edward. 1991. "Permanent Technological Revolution and China's Tortuous

Path to Democratizing Leninism." In Richard Baum, ed., *Reform and Reaction in Post-Mao China: The Road to Tiananmen*, 162–82. New York: Routledge.

Friedman, Edward. 1990. "Deng versus the Peasantry: Recollectivization in the Countryside." *Problems of Communism* 39, 5 (September–October): 30–43.

Garside, Roger. 1981. *Coming Alive: China after Mao*. New York: Mentor Books.

Gold, Thomas. 1991. "Urban Private Business and China's Reforms." In Richard Baum, ed., *Reform and Reaction in Post-Mao China: The Road to Tiananmen*, 84–103. New York: Routledge.

———. 1984. "'Just in Time!' China Battles Spiritual Pollution on the Eve of 1984." *Asian Survey* 24, 9 (September): 942–62.

Goldman, Merle. 1994. *Sowing the Seeds of Democracy in China: Political Reform in the Deng Xiaoping Era*. Cambridge: Harvard University Press.

———. 1991. "Hu Yaobang's Intellectual Network and the Theory Conference of 1979." *The China Quarterly* 126 (June): 219–42.

Goldstein, Avery. 1991. *From Bandwagon to Balance-of-Power Politics: Structural Constraints and Politics in China, 1949–1978*. Stanford: Stanford University Press.

Goodman, David S. G. 1994. *Deng Xiaoping and the Chinese Revolution*. London and New York: Routledge.

———. 1984. "The Second Plenary Session of the 12th CCP Central Committee: Rectification and Reform." *The China Quarterly* 97 (March): 84–94.

———, ed. 1981. *Beijing Street Voices*. London: Marion Boyars.

Gu Xin and David Kelly. 1993. "New Conservatism: Ideological Program of a New Elite." In David S. G. Goodman and Beverly Hooper, eds., *China's Quiet Revolution: New Interactions between State and Society*. Melbourne: Longman Cheshire.

Guojia Jiaowei Sixiang Zhengzhi Gongzuo Sipian. 1989 *Jingxin dongpode 56 tian* (The startling 56 days). Beijing: Zhongguo Dadi Chubanshe.

Halpern, Nina. 1991. "Economic Reform, Social Mobilization, and Democratization in Post-Mao China." In Richard Baum, ed., *Reform and Reaction in Post-Mao China: The Road to Tiananmen*, 38–59. New York and London: Routledge.

———. 1986. "Making Economic Policy: The Influence of Economists." In Joint Economic Commitee, Congress of the United States, *China's Economy Looks Toward the Year 2000*, vol. 1, 132–46. Washington, D.C.: United States Government Printing Office (May).

———. 1985. "Learning from Abroad: Chinese Views of the Eastern Europe Economic Experience, 1977–1981." *Modern China* 1: 77–109.

Hamrin, Carol Lee. 1990. *China and the Challenge of the Future*. Boulder: Westview Press.

Harding, Harry. 1987. *China's Second Revolution: Reform after Mao*. Washington, D.C.: The Brookings Institution.

Hartford, Kathleen. 1985. "Socialist Agriculture Is Dead; Long Live Socialist Agriculture!. Organizational Transformations in Rural China." In Elizabeth J. Perry and Christine Wong, eds., *The Political Economy of Reform in Post-Mao China*, 31–61. Cambridge: Council on East Asian Studies, Harvard University.

He Pin and Gao Xin. 1992. *Zhonggong "taizidang"* (China's Communist "princelings"). Taipei: Shih-pao Ch'u-pan Kung-ssu.

Hicks, George, ed. 1990. *The Broken Mirror: China after Tiananmen*. Chicago: St. James Press.

History of the Chinese Communist Party: A Chronology of Events (1919–1990). 1991. Beijing: Foreign Languages Press.

Hsiung, James C. 1990. "Mainland China's Paradox of Partial Reform: A Postmortem on Tiananmen." *Issues & Studies* 26, 6 (June): 29–43.

———, ed. 1981. *Symposium: The Trial of the Gang of Four and Its Implication in China*. Baltimore: University of Maryland, School of Law, Occasional Papers/Reprints Series in Contemporary Asian Studies, no. 3.

Hu Shikai. 1993. "Representation without Democratization: The 'Signature Incident' and China's National People's Congress." *The Journal of Contemporary China* 2, 1 (Winter–Spring): 3–35.

Hua Guofeng. 1977. "Political Report to the 11th National Congress of the Communist Party of China." *Peking Review* 20, 35 (August 26): 23–57.

Huntington, Samuel P. 1968. *Political Order in Changing Societies*. New Haven: Yale University Press.

Huo yü hsieh chih chen-hsiang (The truth of fire and blood). 1989. Taipei: Chung-kung Yen-chiu Tsa-chih She.

Hutterer, Karl. 1989. "Eyewitness: The Chengdu Massacre." *China Update* 1 (August): 4–5.

Hyer, Eric. 1992. "China's Arms Merchants: Profits in Command." *The China Quarterly* 132 (December): 1101–18.

Jencks, Harlan. 1990. "Party Authority and Military Power: Communist China's Continuing Crisis." *Issues & Studies* 26, 7 (July): 11–39.

Jin Chunming. 1984. "Guanyu Tiananmen shijian" (Concerning the Tiananmen incident). In *Zhonggong dangshi shehuizhuyi shiqi shuanti sunwenji (xiace)* (Special collection of papers on the socialist period in the history of the Chinese Communist Party, vol. 2). Hebei: Hebei Zhonggong Dangshi Yanjiuhui.

Joffe, Ellis. 1995. "The PLA and the Chinese Economy." *Survival* (forthcoming).

———. 1983. "Party and Military in China: Professionalism in Command." *Problems of Communism* 32, 5 (September–October): 56–63.

Johnston, Alistair I. 1987. "Party Rectification in the People's Liberation Army, 1983–87." *The China Quarterly* 112 (December): 591–630.

Jowitt, Kenneth. 1983. "Soviet Neotraditionalism: The Political Corruption of a Leninist Regime." *Soviet Studies* 35, 3 (July): 275–97.

Kahn, Joseph F. 1990. "Better Fed than Red." *Esquire* (September): 186–97.

Kau, Michael Y. M. 1975. *The Lin Biao Affair*. Armonk, N.Y.: M. E. Sharpe.

Kelly, David A. 1987. "The Chinese Student Movement of December 1986 and Its Intellectual Antecedents." *The Australian Journal of Chinese Affairs* 17 (January): 127–42.

———. 1987. "The Emergence of Humanism: Wang Ruoshui and the Critique of Socialist Alienation." In Merle Goldman, with Timothy Cheek and Carol Lee Hamrin, eds., *China's Intellectuals and the State: In Search of a New Relationship*, 159–82. Cambridge: Harvard University Council on East Asian Studies.

Kraus, Richard. 1986. "Bai Hua: The Political Authority of a Writer." In Carol Lee Hamrin and Timothy Cheek, eds., *China's Establishment Intellectuals*, 185–211. Armonk, N.Y.: M. E. Sharpe.

Kraus, Willy. 1982. *Economic Development and Social Change in the People's Republic of China*. New York: Springer.

Kuan, Hsin-chi. 1984. "New Departures in China's Constitution." *Studies in Comparative Communism* 22, 1 (Spring): 53–68.

Kwong, Julia. 1988. "The 1986 Student Demonstrations in China: A Democratic Movement?" *Asian Survey* 28, 9 (September): 970–85.

Lam, Willy Wo-Lap. 1995. *China after Deng Xiaoping.* Singapore: John Wiley & Sons.

Latham, Richard J. 1991. "China's Party-Army Relations After June 1989." In Richard H. Yang, ed., *China's Military: The PLA in 1990/91,* 103–23. Boulder: Westview Press.

——. 1983. "The Rectification of 'Work Style': Command and Management Problems." In Paul H. B. Godwin, ed., *The Chinese Defense Establishment: Continuity and Change in the 1980s,* 92–104. Boulder: Westview Press.

Lee, Hong Yung, 1992. "China's New Bureaucracy?" In Arthur L. Rosenbaum, ed., *State and Society in China: The Consequences of Reform,* 55–76. Boulder: Westview Press.

——. 1983. "China's 12th Central Committee." *Asian Survey* 23, 6 (June): 673–91.

Leijonhufvud, Goran. 1990. *Going against the Tide: On Dissent and Big-Character Posters in China.* Copenhagen: Scandinavian Institute of Asian Studies Monograph Series no. 58.

Li Cheng and Lynn White. 1993. "The Army in the Succession to Deng Xiaoping." *Asian Survey* 33, 8 (August): 757–86.

——. 1990. "China's Technocratic Movement and the *World Economic Herald*." Manuscript, Princeton University.

Li Honglin. 1994. "'Right' and 'Left' in Communist China." *The Journal of Contemporary China* 6 (Summer): 1–38.

Li Jian. 1993. *Deng Xiaoping sanjin sanchu Zhongnanhai* (Deng Xiaoping's three entrances and three exits from Zhongnanhai). Beijing: Zhongguo Dadi Chubanshe.

Li Kwok Sing. 1990. "Deng Xiaoping and the 2nd Field Army." *China Review* (Hong Kong) 3, 1 (January): 40–42.

Liangci Tiananmen shijian (The two Tiananmen incidents). 1989. Hong Kong: Tianhe Publishing Company.

Li Zhisui. 1994 *The Private Life of Chairman Mao.* New York: Random House.

Liao Gailong. 1981. "The '1980 Reform' Program of China." *Qishi niandai* 134 (March 1, 1981): 38–48. Trans. in *FBIS,* March 16, 1981, U1–19.

Lieberthal, Kenneth. 1985. "The Political Implications of Document No. 1, 1984." *The China Quarterly* 101 (March): 109–13.

Lieberthal, Kenneth, and David M. Lampton, eds. 1992. *Bureaucracy, Politics, and Decision Making in Post-Mao China.* Berkeley and Los Angeles: University of California Press.

Lieberthal, Kenneth, and Michel Oksenberg. 1988. *Policy Making in China: Leaders, Structures, and Processes.* Princeton: Princeton University Press.

Link, Perry. 1992. *Evening Chats in Beijing: Probing China's Predicament.* New York: W. W. Norton.

——, ed. 1983. *People or Monsters? and Other Stories and Reportage from China after Mao.* Bloomington: Indiana University Press.

——, ed. 1983. *Stubborn Weeds: Popular and Controversial Chinese Literature after the Cultural Revolution.* Bloomington: Indiana University Press.

Liu, Alan P. L. 1992. "The 'Wenzhou Model' of Development and China's Modernization." *Asian Survey* 32, 8 (August): 696–711.

Liu Binyan. 1990. *A Higher Kind of Loyalty.* New York and Toronto: Random House.

——. 1989. *"Tell the World": What Happened in China and Why.* With Ruan Ming and Xu Gang. New York: Pantheon Books.

Luk Shiu-Hung and Joseph Whitney, eds. 1993. *Megaproject: A Case Study of China's*

Three Gorges Project. Armonk, N.Y: M. E. Sharpe.

Luo Xu. 1995. "The 'Shekou Storm': Changes in the Mentality of Chinese Youth Prior to Tiananmen." *The China Quarterly* 142 (June): 541–72.

Ma Shu Yun. 1990–91. "The Rise and Fall of Neo-Authoritarianism in China." *China Information* 5, 3 (Winter): 1–19.

MacFarquhar, Roderick. 1993. "The Succession to Mao and the End of Maoism, 1969–82," 248–339. In Roderick MacFarquhar, ed., *The Politics of China, 1949–1989*. New York: Cambridge University Press.

Mackerras, Colin. 1984. " 'Party Consolidation' and the Attack on Spiritual Pollution." *The Australian Journal of Chinese Affairs* 11 (January): 175–86.

Manion, Melanie. 1993. *Retirement of Revolutionaries in China: Public Policies, Social Norms, Private Interests*. Princeton. Princeton University Press.

Mao Mao (née Deng Rong). 1993. *Wode fuqin Deng Xiaoping, shangjuan* (My father Deng Xiaoping, vol. 1). Beijing: Zhongyang Wenxian Chubanshe.

Massacre in Beijing: China's Struggle for Democracy. 1989. New York: Warner Books.

McCormick, Barrett. 1990. *Political Reform in Post-Mao China: Democracy and Bureaucracy in a Leninist State*. Berkeley and Los Angeles: University of California Press.

Meaney, Connie Squires. 1991. "Market Reform and Disintegrative Corruption in Urban China." In Richard Baum, ed., *Reform and Reaction in Post-Mao China*, 124–43. New York: Routledge.

Meier, John H. 1990. "Tiananmen 1989: The View from Shanghai." *China Information* 5, 1 (Summer): 1–13.

Miles, John. 1996. *The Legacy of Tiananmen: China in Disarray.* Ann Arbor: University of Michigan Press (forthcoming).

Miller, Robert F., ed. 1992. *The Development of Civil Society in Communist Systems*. Sydney: George Allen and Unwin.

Mills, William deB. 1983. "Generational Change in China." *Problems of Communism* 32, 6 (November–December): 16–35.

Min Li. 1992. "Deng Xiaoping de 'Zhinantuan' " (Deng Xiaoping's "brain trust"). *Jing bao* 174 (January 1992): 40–41.

Mu Yi and Mark V. Thompson. 1989. *Crisis at Tiananmen: Reform and Reality in Modern China*. San Francisco: China Books and Periodicals.

Munro, Robin. 1990. "Remembering Tiananmen Square: Who Died in Beijing, and Why?" *The Nation* (June 11).

Myers, James T. 1989. "China: Modernization and 'Unhealthy Tendencies.' " *Comparative Politics* 21, 2 (January): 193–214.

Nathan, Andrew J. 1989. "Chinese Democracy in 1989: Continuity and Change," *Problems of Communism* 38, 5 (September–October): 17–29.

———. 1985. *Chinese Democracy*. New York: Alfred A. Knopf.

———. 1973. "A Factionalism Model for CCP Politics." *The China Quarterly* 53 (January–March): 34–66.

Naughton, Barry. 1993. "Deng Xiaoping: The Economist." *The China Quarterly* 135 (September): 491–514.

———. 1992. "The Chinese Economy on the Road to Recovery?" In William A. Joseph, ed., *China Briefing, 1991*, 77–95. Boulder: Westview Press.

———. 1990. "Macroeconomic Obstacles to Reform in China." Paper presented at the Southern California China Colloquium, UCLA (November).

———. 1987. "The Decline of Central Control Over Investment in Post-Mao China."

In David M. Lampton, ed., *Policy Implementation in Post-Mao China,* 51–80. Berkeley and Los Angeles: University of California Press.

————. 1986. "Sun Yefang: Toward a Reconstruction of Socialist Economics." In Carol Lee Hamrin and Timothy Cheek, eds., *China's Establishment Intellectuals,* 124–54. Armonk, N.Y.: M. E. Sharpe.

Nee, Victor. 1992. "Organizational Dynamics of Market Transition: Hybrid Forms, Property Rights, and Mixed Economy in China." *Administrative Science Quarterly* 37: 1–27.

Nethercut, Richard D. 1982. "Deng and the Gun: Party-Military Relations in the People's Republic of China." *Asian Survey* 22, 8 (August): 691–704.

Niming, Frank. 1990. "Learning How to Protest." In Tony Saich, ed., *The Chinese People's Movement: Perspectives on Spring 1989,* 83–105. Armonk, N.Y.: M. E. Sharpe.

O'Brien, Kevin. 1994. "Implementing Political Reform in China's Villages." *Australian Journal of Chinese Affairs* 32 (July): 33–60.

————. 1990. *Reform without Liberalization: China's National People's Congress and the Politics of Institutional Change,* New York: Cambridge University Press.

Ogden, Suzanne, Kathleen Hartford, Lawrence Sullivan, and David Zweig, eds. 1992. *China's Search for Democracy: The Student and the Mass Movement of 1989.* Armonk, N.Y.: M. E. Sharpe.

Oi, Jean C. 1991. "Local Government Response to the Fiscal Austerity Program, 1988–90." Paper presented at the UCLA China Seminar (March).

————. 1991. "Partial Market Reform and Corruption in Rural China." In Richard Baum, ed., *Reform and Reaction in Post-Mao China: The Road to Tiananmen,* 143–61. New York: Routledge.

Oksenberg, Michel. 1987. "China's 13th Party Congress." *Problems of Communism* 36, 6 (November–December).

Oksenberg, Michel, and Sai Cheung-yeung. 1977. "Hua Guofeng's pre–Cultural Revolution Hunan Years, 1949–66: The Making of a Political Generalist." *The China Quarterly* 69 (March): 3–53.

O'Leary, Greg, and Andrew Watson. 1982. "The Production Responsibility System and the Future of Collective Farming." *The Australian Journal of Chinese Affairs* 8 (July): 1–34.

Onate, Andres D. 1978. "Hua Kuo-feng and the Arrest of the 'Gang of Four.'" *The China Quarterly* 75 (September): 540–65.

Paltiel, Jeremy. 1985. "The Interaction of Party Rectification and Economic Reform in the CCP, 1984." Manuscript.

Pang Pang. 1989. *The Death of Hu Yaobang.* Manoa: University of Hawaii, Center for Chinese Studies.

Pepper, Suzanne. 1986. *Deng Xiaoping's Political and Economic Reforms and the Chinese Student Protests.* Indianapolis: Universities Field Staff International Reports, no. 30.

Perry, Elizabeth J. 1992. "Casting a Chinese 'Democracy' Movement: The Roles of Students, Workers, and Entrepreneurs." In Jeffrey N. Wasserstrom and Elizabeth J. Perry, eds., *Popular Protest and Political Culture in Modern China,* 146–64. Boulder. Westview Press.

Petracca, Mark, and Mong Xiong. 1990. "The Concept of Chinese Neo-Authoritarianism: An Exploration and Democratic Critique." *Asian Survey* 30, 11 (November): 1099–1117.

Prybyla, Jan S. 1989. "Why China's Economic Reforms Won't Work." *Asian Survey*

29, 11 (November): 1017–32.

Pye, Lucian W. 1993. "An Introductory Profile: Deng Xiaoping and China's Political Culture." *The China Quarterly* 135 (September): 412–43.

———. 1990. "Tiananmen and Chinese Political Culture: The Escalation of Confrontation from Moralizing to Revenge." *Asian Survey* 30, 4 (April): 331–47.

———. 1981. *The Dynamics of Chinese Politics*. Cambridge, Mass.: Oelgeschlager, Gunn & Hain.

Qing Ye and Fang Lei. 1993. *Deng Xiaoping zai 1976, shangce: Tiananmen shijian* (Deng Xiaoping in 1976, vol. 1: The Tiananmen incident). Shenyang: Chunfeng Wenyi Chubanshe.

———. 1993. *Deng Xiaoping zai 1976, xiace: Huairentang shibian* (Deng Xiaoping in 1976, vol. 2: The incident at Huairen hall). Shenyang: Chunfeng Wenyi Chubanshe.

Quan Yanchi. 1992. *Canzhuo shangde Zhonggong lingxiu* (Chinese Communist leaders at the dinner table). Hong Kong: Cosmos Books.

Rao, Y. C., and C. K. Leung, eds. 1986. *China's Special Economic Zones: Policies, Problems, and Prospects*. Hong Kong: Oxford University Press.

Renminde daonian (The people's grief). 1979. Beijing: Beijing Cubanshe.

"Resolution on Certain Questions in the History of Our Party since the Founding of the People's Republic of China" (June 27, 1981). *Beijing Review* 24, 27 (July 6, 1981).

Reynolds, Bruce, ed. 1987. *Reform in China: Challenges and Choices*. Armonk, N.Y.: M. E. Sharpe.

Rosen, Stanley. 1991. "The Rise (and Fall) of Public Opinion Research in Post-Mao China." In Richard Baum, ed., *Reform and Reaction in Post-Mao China: The Road to Tiananmen*, 60–83. New York: Routledge.

———, ed. 1990–91. "The Debate on the New Authoritarianism." *Chinese Sociology and Anthropology* 23, 2 (Winter).

———. 1990. "The Chinese Communist Party and Chinese Society: Popular Attitudes toward Party Membership and the Party's Image." *The Australian Journal of Chinese Affairs* 37 (July): 51–92.

———. 1990. "Youth and Students in China." In Winston Yang and Marcia Wagner, eds., *Tiananmen: China's Struggle for Democracy*. College Park: University of Maryland School of Law.

———. 1987. "China in 1986: A Year of Consolidation." *Asian Survey* 27, 1 (January): 35–55.

Ruan Ming. 1992. "Taizidang de Disandiguo meimeng" (The Third Reich fantasies of the princelings). *Zhongguo zhichun* 10 (October): 39–41.

———. 1991. *Deng Xiaoping diguo* (The empire of Deng Xiaoping). Taipei: Shih-pao Ch'u-pan Kung-ssu.

———. 1991. *Lishi zhuanzhedianshangde Hu Yaobang* (Hu Yaobang at the turning point in history). River Edge, N.J.: Ba Fang Wenhua Qiye Gongsi.

Rubin, Kyna. 1987. "Keeper of the Flame: Wang Ruowang as Moral Critic of the State." In Merle Goldman, with Timothy Cheek and Carol Lee Hamrin, eds., *China's Intellectuals and the State: In Search of a New Relationship*, 234–50. Cambridge: Harvard University Council on East Asian Studies.

Saich, Tony. 1993. "Peaceful Evolution with Chinese Characteristics." In William A. Joseph, ed., *China Briefing, 1992*, 9–34. Boulder: Westview Press.

———. 1992. "The Fourteenth Party Congress: A Programme for Authoritarian Rule." *The China Quarterly* 132 (December).

———. 1992. "The Reform Decade in China: The Limits to Revolution from Above."

In Marta Dassù and Tony Saich, eds., *The Reform Decade in China: From Hope to Dismay*, 10–73. London: Kegan, Paul International.

Smith, Tony. 1990. "The Rise and Fall of the Beijing People's Movement." *The Australian Journal of Chinese Affairs* 24 (July): 181–208.

———. 1990. "Urban Society in China." Paper presented to the International Colloquium on China, Saarbrucken (July 3–7).

———. 1988. "The Thirteenth Congress of the Chinese Communist Party: An Agenda for Reform?" *Journal of Communist Studies* 4, 2 (June): 203–8.

———. 1984. "Party Consolidation and Spiritual Pollution in the People's Republic of China." *Communist Affairs* 3, 3 (July): 283–89.

———. 1984. "The People's Republic of China." In W. B. Simons and S. White, eds., *The Party Statutes of the Communist World*, 83–113. The Hague: Martinus Nijhoff.

Salisbury, Harrison. 1992. *The New Emperors: China in the Era of Mao and Deng*. Boston: Little, Brown.

Schell, Orville, 1994. *Mandate of Heaven*. New York: Simon & Schuster.

———. 1989. *Discos and Democracy: China In the Throes of Reform*. New York: Doubleday.

Schell, Orville, and Todd Lappin. 1992. "China Plays the Market." *The Nation* (December 14): 727–42.

Schoenhals, Michael. 1991. "The 1978 Truth Criterion Controversy." *The China Quarterly* 126 (June): 243–68.

Schram, Stuart R. 1988. "China after the 13th Congress." *The China Quarterly* 114 (June): 177–97.

———. 1984. "'Economics in Command'? Ideology and Politics since the Third Plenum, 1978–84." *The China Quarterly* 99 (September): 417–61.

Schroeder, Gertrude E. 1979. "The Soviet Economy on a Treadmill of 'Reforms.'" In Joint Economic Committee, Congress of the United States, *Soviet Economy In a Time of Change*, vol. 1, 312–40. Washington, D.C.: U.S. Government Printing Office.

Seymour, James D. 1989. "Cadre Accountability to the Law." *The Australian Journal of Chinese Affairs* 21 (January): 1–27.

———, ed. 1980. *The Fifth Modernization: China's Human Rights Movement, 1978–1979*. Stanfordville, N.Y.: Human Rights Publishing Group.

Shambaugh, David L. 1995. "China's Commander-in-Chief: Jiang Zemin and the PLA." Paper presented at the Sixth Annual AEI Conference on the People's Liberation Army, Coolfont, VA (June).

———. 1993. "Deng Xiaoping: The Politician." *The China Quarterly* 135 (September): 457–90.

———. 1992. "China in 1991: Living Cautiously." *Asian Survey* 32, 1 (January): 19–31.

———. 1991. "China in 1990: The Year of Damage Control." *Asian Survey* 31, 1 (January): 36–49.

———. 1989. "The Fourth and Fifth Plenary Sessions of the 13th CCP Central Committee." *The China Quarterly* 120 (December): 852–62.

———. 1984. *The Making of a Premier: Zhao Ziyang's Provincial Career*. Boulder: Westview Press.

Shi Tianjian. 1989. "Role Culture and Political Liberalism among Deputies to the Seventh National People's Congress, 1988." Paper presented at the annual meeting of the Association for Asian Studies, Washington, D.C. (March).

Shirk, Susan L. 1993. *The Political Logic of Economic Reform in China*. Berkeley and Los Angeles: University of California Press.

————. 1990. "Cycles in the Process of Reform: The Economic Consequences of Chinese-Style Economic Reforms." Manuscript (June).

————. 1990. "The Political Price of Reform Cycles: Elite Politics in Chinese-Style Economic Reforms." Manuscript (June).

————. 1989. "The Political Economy of Chinese Industrial Reform." In Victor Nee and David Stark, eds., *Remaking the Economic Institutions of Socialism: China and Eastern Europe*, 328–64. Stanford: Stanford University Press.

Simmie, Scott, and Bob Nixon. 1989. *Tiananmen Square: An Eyewitness Account of the Chinese People's Passionate Quest for Democracy*. Seattle: University of Washington Press.

Skinner, G. William, and Edwin A. Winckler. 1969. "Compliance Succession in Rural Communist China: A Cyclical Theory." In Amitai Etzioni, ed., *Complex Organizations: A Sociological Reader* (second edition), 410–38. New York: Holt, Rinehart, and Winston.

The Solemn and Stirring Democratic Movement. 1990. Hong Kong: Ming Bao Publishing House.

Solinger, Dorothy J. 1993. *China's Transition from Socialism: Statist Legacies and Market Reforms, 1980–1990*. Armonk, N.Y.: M. E. Sharpe.

————. 1992. "Urban Entrepreneurs and the State: The Merger of State and Society." In Arthur L. Rosenbaum, ed., *State and Society in China: The Consequences of Reform*, 121–42. Boulder: Westview Press.

————. 1991. *China's Transients and the State: A Form of Civil Society?* Hong Kong: Chinese University of Hong Kong, Institute of Asia-Pacific Studies, USC Seminar Series no. 1.

————. 1989. "Capitalist Measures with Chinese Characteristics." *Problems of Communism* 38, 1 (January–February): 19–33.

————. 1984. *Chinese Business under Socialism*. Berkeley and Los Angeles: University of California Press.

————. 1982. "The Fifth National People's Congress and the Process of Policy Making: Reform, Readjustment, and the Opposition." *Asian Survey* 22, 12 (December): 1238–75.

————. 1981. "Economic Reform via Reformulation in China: Where Do Rightist Ideas Come from?" *Asian Survey* 21, 9 (September): 947–60.

Starr, John Bryan. 1984. "Redefinition of Chinese Socialism." *Current History* (September): 265–68.

Stavis, Benedict. 1988. *China's Political Reforms: An Interim Report*. New York: Praeger.

Strand, David. 1990. "Protest in Beijing: Civil Society and Public Sphere in China." *Problems of Communism* 39, 3 (May–June): 1–19.

Su Shaozhi. 1983. "Develop Marxism under Contemporary Conditions." *Selected Studies in Marxism* 2 (February): 1–39.

Sullivan, Lawrence R. 1988. "Assault on Reforms: Conservative Criticism of Political and Economic Liberalization in China, 1985–86." *The China Quarterly* 114 (June): 209–12.

Sullivan, Michael J. 1994. "The 1988–1989 Nanjing Anti-African Protests." *The China Quarterly* (forthcoming).

Swaine, Michael D. 1992. *The Military and Political Succession in China: Leadership,*

Institutions, Beliefs. Santa Monica: The Rand Corporation.

———. 1990. "China Faces the 1990s: A System in Crisis." *Problems of Communism* 39, 3 (May–June): 20–35.

"Symposium on Civil Society and The Public Sphere." 1993. *Modern China* 19, 2 (April).

Tan Zongji. 1984. "Shiyiju sanzhong quanhui shi jianguo yilai dangde lishide weida zhuanzhe" (The Third Plenum of the 11th Central Committee is a great turning point in our party's history since 1949). In *Zhonggong dangshi shehuizhuyi shiqi zhuanti lunwenji (xiace)* (Special collection of papers on the socialist period in the history of the Chinese Communist Party, vol. 2). Hebei: Hebei Zhonggong Dangshi Yanjiuhui (November).

Tanner, Murray Scott, and Michael J. Feder. 1993. "Family Politics, Elite Recruitment, and Succession in Post-Mao China." *The Australian Journal of Chinese Affairs* 30 (July): 89–120.

Teiwes, Frederick C. 1992. "Politics, Purges, and Rectification since the Third Plenum." Manuscript.

Ting Wang. 1980. *Chairman Hua: Leader of the Chinese Communists.* Montreal: McGill-Queens University Press.

Tong, James, ed. 1981. "Underground Journals in China." *Chinese Law and Government* 14, 3 (Fall).

———, ed. 1980–81. "Underground Journals in China." *Chinese Law and Government* 13, 3–4 (Fall–Winter).

Tretiak, Daniel. 1979. "China's Vietnam War and Its Consequences." *The China Quarterly* 80 (December): 740–67.

Tsou, Tang. 1986. "Political Change and Reform: The Middle Course." In Tang Tsou, ed., *The Cultural Revolution and Post-Mao Reforms: A Historical Perspective*, 219–58. Chicago: University of Chicago Press.

Unger, Jonathan, ed. 1991. *The Pro-Democracy Protests in China: Reports from the Provinces.* Armonk, N.Y.: M. E. Sharpe.

———. 1990. "Life in the Chinese Hinterlands under the Rural Economic Reforms. *Bulletin of Concerned Asian Scholars* 22, 2 (April–June), 4–17.

Viewing China Through a Third Eye. 1994. Foreign Broadcast Information Service Daily Report (Supplement): China. FBIS-CHI-95-075 (April19).

Vogel, Ezra. 1989. *One Step Ahead in China.* Cambridge: Harvard University Press.

Walder, Andrew G. 1993. "China's Trajectory of Economic and Political Change: Some Contrary Facts and Their Theoretical Implications." Paper presented at the Conference on Chinese and East European Transitions: Divergent Roads?, UCLA (June).

———. 1992. "Urban Industrial Workers: Some Observations on the 1980s." In Arthur L. Rosenbaum, ed., *State and Society in China: The Consequences of Reform*, 103–20. Boulder: Westview Press.

———. 1989. "The Political Sociology of the Beijing Upheaval of 1989." *Problems of Communism* 38, 5 (September–October): 30–40.

Walder, Andrew G., and Gong Xiaoxia. 1993. "Workers in the Tiananmen Protests: The Politics of the Beijing Workers' Autonomous Federation." *The Australian Journal of Chinese Affairs* 29 (January): 1–30.

Wang Hongmo et al. 1991. *Gaige kaifang de licheng* (The course of reform and opening up). Vol. 4 of *1949–1989 nian de Zhongguo* (China in the years 1949–1989). Henan: Renmin Chubanshe.

Wang Ruowang. 1991. *Hunger Trilogy*. Armonk, N.Y.: M. E. Sharpe.

Wang Shaoguang and Hu An'gang. 1993. *Jiaqiang zhongyang zhengfu zai shichang jingji zhuanxingzhong de zhudao zuoyong* (Strengthen the central government's guiding role in the shift to a market economy). Liaoning: Renmin chuban she.

Wang Shu-shin. 1982. "Hu Yaobang: New Chairman of the Chinese Communist Party." *Asian Survey* 22, 9 (September): 801–22.

Warner, Shelley. 1991. "Shanghai's Response to the Deluge." In Jonathan Unger, ed., *The Pro-Democracy Protests in China: Reports from the Provinces*, 215–31. Armonk, N.Y.: M. E. Sharpe.

Wasserstrom, Jeffrey N. 1990. "Student Protests and the Chinese Tradition, 1919–1989." In Tony Saich, ed., *The Chinese People's Movement: Perspectives on Spring 1989*, 3–24. Armonk, N.Y.: M. E. Sharpe.

Wedeman, Andrew H. 1994. "Bamboo Walls and Brick Ramparts: Uneven Development, Inter-Regional Economic Conflict, and Local Protectionism in China, 1984–1991." Ph.D. dissertation, University of California, Los Angeles.

———, ed. 1993. "Regional Protectionism." *Chinese Economic Studies* 26, 5 (Fall).

Weil, Martin. 1982. "The Baoshan Steel Mill." In Joint Economic Committee, Congress of the United States, *China under the Four Modernizations*, part 1, 365–91. Washington, D.C.: U.S. Government Printing Office.

White, Gordon. 1993. *Riding the Tiger: The Politics of Economic Reform in Post-Mao China*. London: Macmillan.

Whyte, Martin K. 1992. "Urban China: A Civil Society in the Making?" In Arthur L. Rosenbaum, ed., *State and Society in China: The Consequences of Reform*, 77–102. Boulder: Westview Press.

Wilson, Ian, and You Ji. 1990. "Leadership by 'Lines': China's Unresolved Succession." *Problems of Communism* 39, 1 (January–February): 28–44.

Womack, Brantley, ed. 1982–83. "Electoral Reform in China." *Chinese Law and Government* 15, 3–4 (Fall–Winter).

Wong, Christine. 1991. "Central-Local Relations in an Era of Fiscal Decline: the Paradox of Fiscal Decentralization in Post-Mao China." *The China Quarterly* 128 (December): 691–715.

———. 1988. "Interpreting Rural Industrial Growth in the Post-Mao Period." *Modern China* 14, 1 (January): 3–30.

———. 1985. "The Second Phase of Economic Reform in China." *Current History* 84, 503 (September): 260–63.

Wong, Helena Pik-Wan. 1993. "Worker Participation in the 1989 Democracy Movement in China." UCLA Department of Political Science.

Wright, Kate. 1990. "The Political Fortunes of Shanghai's 'World Economic Herald.'" *The Australian Journal of Chinese Affairs* 23 (January): 121–32.

Wu Mouren et al. 1989. *Bajiu Zhongguo minyun jishi* (Daily record of the 1989 Chinese people's movement). New York: private publication.

Xiao Lan, ed. 1979. *The Tiananmen Poems*. Beijing: Foreign Languages Press.

Yan Jiaqi. 1979. *Siwu yundong jishi* (A true record of the April 5 movement). Beijing: Renmin Chubanshe.

Yan Jiaqi and Gao Gao. 1989. *Wenhua Dageming shinian shi* (A ten-year history of the Cultural Revolution). Partial manuscript photocopied in Hong Kong.

Yan Kong. 1993. "Evolution of the Central Military Commission." UCLA Department of Political Science.

Yang, Dali L. 1993. "The State and 'Uncivil' Society: China's Growing Drug Problem in Comparative Perspective." Univ. of Chicago, Department of Political Science.

Yang, Dali L. 1991. "Reforms, Resources, and Regional Cleavages: The Political Economy of Coast-Interior Relations." *Issues & Studies* 27, 9 (September): 43–69.

Yang Zhongmei. 1988. *Hu Yaobang: A Chinese Biography.* Armonk, N.Y.: M. E. Sharpe.

Yeung Yue-man and Xu-wei Hu. 1992. *China's Coastal Cities: Catalysts for Modernization?* Honolulu: University of Hawaii.

Young, Graham. 1984. "Control and Style: Discipline Inspection Commissions Since the 11th Congress." *The China Quarterly* 97 (March): 24–52.

Yuan Shang and Han Zhu, eds. 1992. *Deng Xiaoping nanxun houde Zhongguo* (China after Deng Xiaoping's southern tour). Beijing: Gaige Chubanshe.

Zhang Yunlun, ed. 1988. *Zhongguo jigoude yange* (The evolution of Chinese organizations). Beijing: Zhongguo Jingji Chubanshe.

Zhao Suisheng. 1993. "Deng Xiaoping's Southern Tour: Elite Politics in Post-Tiananmen China. *Asian Survey* 33, 8 (August): 739–56.

Zhonggong Shenzhen Shiwei Xuanchuanbu. 1992. *Deng Xiaoping yu Shenzhen, 1992 chun* (Deng Xiaoping and Shenzhen, spring 1992). Shenzhen: Haitian Chubanshe.

Zhongguo Qingnian Bao Sixiang Lilunbu. 1992. "Sulian jubian zhihou Zhongguode xianshi yingdui yu zhanlue xuanze" (Realistic responses and strategic choices for China after the Soviet coup). Reprinted in *Zhongguo zhichun* (China spring) 1 (January): 35–39.

Zhongkan: Kang Sheng pingzhuan (Pleasing to the eye, bitter to the taste: A critical biography of Kang Sheng). 1982. Beijing: Hongqi Chubanshe.

Zou, Gary. 1989. "Debates on China's Economic Situation and Reform Strategies." Paper presented to the annual meeting of the Association for Asian Studies, Washington, D.C. (March).

Zweig, David. 1989. "Dilemmas of Partial Reform." In Bruce Reynolds, ed., *Chinese Economic Policy*, 13–40. New York: Paragon House.

———. 1983. "Opposition to Change in Rural China: The System of Responsibility and People's Communes." *Asian Survey* 23, 7 (July): 879–900.

———. 1981. "The System of Responsibility: National Policy and Local Implementation." Paper presented at the SSRC Conference on Bureaucracy and Rural Development, Chicago (August 26–30).

PERIODICALS AND NEWS AGENCIES

Agence France Presse
Asian Survey
Asian Wall Street Journal
Asiaweek
Associated Press
Australian Journal of Chinese Affairs
Baltimore Sun
Beijing Review
Beijing ribao
Caiwu yu kuaiji (Beijing)
Chaoliu yuekan (Hong Kong)
The China Quarterly

China Daily (Beijing, in English)
China Education News
China Information (Leiden)
China News Agency (Hong Kong)
China News Analysis (Hong Kong)
China News Digest (Books and Journals Review) (Internet on-line)
China News Digest (Global News) (Internet on-line)
China News Digest (Shanghai, in English)
China News Service (Beijing)
China Record (London)
China Review (Hong Kong)
China Update (New Haven)
Christian Science Monitor
Chung-kung yen-chiu (Taipei)
Chung-kuo jih-pao (Taipei)
Dagong bao (Hong Kong)
Dangdai (Hong Kong)
Dangde jiaoyu (Tianjin)
Dongfang ribao (Hong Kong)
Dongxiang (Hong Kong)
Dongxifang (Hong Kong)
The Economist (London)
Far Eastern Economic Review
Faxue yanjiu (Beijing)
Financial Times (London)
Gongren ribao (Beijing)
Guai bao (Hong Kong)
Guangming ribao (Beijing)
Hongqi (Beijing)
Hsinhua Weekly (Beijing, in English)
Huaqiao ribao (New York)
Issues & Studies (Taipei)
Japan Economic Newswire (Tokyo, in English)
Jiefangjun bao (Beijing)
Jiefang ribao (Shanghai)
Jing bao (Hong Kong)
Jingji ribao (Beijing)
Jingji yanjiu (Beijing)
Jiushi niandai (Hong Kong)
Joint Publications Research Service
Kaifang
Kyodo (Tokyo)
Liaowang (Beijing)
Lien-ho pao (Taipei)
Los Angeles Times
Ming bao (Hong Kong)
Nanfang ribao (Guangzhou)
The Nation
Newsweek (Asia edition)

The New York Times
The Observer (London)
Peking Review (Beijing, in English)
Qishi niandai (Hong Kong)
Qiushi (Beijing)
Renmin ribao (Beijing)
Reuters
Shehui kexue (Beijing)
Shijie jingji daobao (Shanghai)
South China Morning Post (Hong Kong)
South China Morning Post Weekly (Hong Kong)
The Standard (Hong Kong)
Survey of World Broadcasts/Far East (BBC)
Sydney Morning Herald
Time (Asia edition)
Toronto Globe and Mail
Toronto Star
United Press International
Wall Street Journal
The Washington Post
Wenhui bao (Shanghai)
Wenwei po (Hong Kong)
Xin shiji
Xin wanbao (Hong Kong)
Xin bao (Hong Kong)
Xinhua (New China News Agency, Beijing)
Xizang ribao (Lhasa)
Xue lilun
Yecao (Guangzhou)
Yomiuri shimbun (Tokyo)
Zhanwang (Hong Kong)
Zhengming (Hong Kong)
Zhengming ribao (Hong Kong)
Zhong bao (Hong Kong)
Zhongbao yuekan (Hong Kong)
Zhongguo qingnian (Beijing)
Zhongguo qingnian bao (Beijing)
Zhongguo zhichun (New York)
Zhuhai Special Zone Daily

Administration: reform of, 88, 137–38, 139, 144, 151, 193–94, 196, 214, 220, 326, 327–28, 361, 374. *See also* Civil service; *Nomenklatura*; Personnel system

"Adverse current" of 1979, 83

African students: racial incidents involving, 191, 239–40, 434n

Agriculture: reform of, 52, 64, 66, 68–69, 86, 164, 169, 266, 338, 377–78, 379, 421n, 428n. *See also* Responsibility systems

"Alienation under socialism": debate on, 5, 133–54, 157, 159, 161, 189, 190–192

All-China Federation of Trade Unions, 272

Alliance in Support of the Patriotic Movement in China, 290. *See also* "Yellowbird Action"

Amnesty International, 240

An Zhiwen, 295, 462n

Anarchism, 81, 92, 102, 113, 127, 195, 310. *See also* "Extreme individualism"; "Ultrademocracy"

"Another center": theory of, 13, 14, 339, 346. *See also* Chen Yun

Anti-Rightist Rectification Campaign (1957), 62, 87, 93, 135

Asia Watch, 448n

Asian Development Bank, 254

Assembly: freedom of, 89, 112. *See also* "Four big freedoms"

"Back door" connections, 108, 174–75. *See also* Clientelism; Nepotism

Bai Hua, 127–30, 136, 153, 160, 316, 422n, 424n. *See also* "Unrequited Love"

Bank of China, 326, 328, 382; corruption in, 382; excessive loans by, 224; reform of, 383, 388

Bankruptcy, 96, 229, 356; law on, 227–28. *See also* Enterprises

Bao Tong, 210, 214, 215, 238, 253, 256, 270, 274, 295, 362–63, 413n, 418n, 429n

Baoshan Iron and Steel Complex, 55, 105, 112

Bao Zunxin, 290, 389

Bei Dao, 241

Beidaihe, 171, 197, 215, 232–35, 253, 369

Beijing: corruption in, 385

Beijing Coking Plant, 272

Beijing Languages Institute, 41

"Beijing Massacre." *See* Tiananmen crisis (1989)

Beijing Normal University, 253, 255

"Beijing Spring." *See* Tiananmen crisis (1989)

Beijing Students' Autonomous Federation (BSAF), 250, 251, 253, 254, 267

Beijing Transistor Research Institute, 37

Beijing University (*Beida*). *See* Peking University

Beijing Workers' Autonomous Federation (*Gongzilian*), 250, 254, 271–74, 276, 286–87, 310, 446n, 447n

Bernstein, Thomas, 430n, 466n

Bertolucci, Bernardo, 449n

Bingshang. See Military commerce

Black market, 382

Bo Xicheng, 365

Bo Yibo, 4, 28, 67–69, 86, 115, 147, 158, 168, 196, 206, 213, 222, 241, 242, 247, 293, 321, 334, 336, 339, 348; and cadre corruption, 176; his criticism of Mikhail Gorbachev, 314; and Hu Yaobang, 208; and party rectification, 194; rehabilitation of, 62; and student demonstrations, 204

Bohai Gulf oil rig disaster, 55, 56, 104, 105

Bonuses. *See* Incentives

"Bourgeois democracy," 98, 199, 204–5, 221, 306, 313. *See also* "Bourgeois liberalization"

"Bourgeois influence." *See* "Bourgeois liberalization"

Bourgeois intellectuals, 62, 297. *See also* Intellectuals

"Bourgeois liberalization," 5, 11, 20, 97, 123, 127–30, 136, 140–42, 147–49, 155, 167, 181–82, 188, 196, 198, 199, 204, 206, 208, 212, 213, 222, 239, 241, 247, 248, 250, 254, 293, 294, 296, 302, 304, 306, 319, 328, 331, 332, 335–37, 339, 342, 346, 355; campaigns against, 8, 128–30, 159, 179, 181, 197, 209–11, 213, 214, 249; criticism of, 112–13, 126, 140–42, 159–60, 197–99, 204–5, 328–30, 333, 353, 382; linked to crime wave, 156; in special economic zones, 165, 342

"Briefcase companies" (*pibao gongsi*), 176, 236

British Broadcasting Corporation (BBC), 335

Budget: balancing of, 302; deficits, 68, 110–11; of People's Liberation Army, 88, 121

Bulgaria, 303

Bureaucracy, 174, 194, 220. *See also* Administration
"Bureaucratism": critique of, 73, 101, 138, 221; and Polish crisis of 1980–81, 103
Bush, George, 242, 323

Cadres: corruption of, 126, 139–42, 155, 174–77, 193, 229, 230, 236–38, 332, 338, 378, 379–80, 428n, 467n, 468n, 471–72n; dismissal of, 98; lifetime tenure of, 97, 100, 106; recruitment of, 138, 168–69, 194; rehabilitation of, 44; retirement of, 100, 137–39, 144–47, 168–69, 213, 215, 331, 424n
Cao Siyuan, 268
Capital accumulation, 96
Capital construction: excessive rate of, 55, 87, 223, 225, 377; mismanagement in, 105; wastefulness and redundancy in, 224
Capital investment. *See* Capital construction
Capital Iron and Steel Corporation, 272, 353, 385, 462n, 469n
Capitalism, 23, 49, 173, 179–80, 213, 239, 351; critique of, 99, 101, 102, 113, 123, 182, 381–82; and Deng Xiaoping, 178–79, 336; and market reforms, 334, 336, 342; and "peaceful evolution," 306, 337; and "peaceful evolution," borrowing from, 239, 345, 351; restoration of, 49, 52, 122, 170, 172, 179, 331, 334–35, 337; Zhao Ziyang on, 219
"Capitalist roaders," 35, 44
Capital punishment, 84, 155, 193
Carter, Jimmy, 73, 81
Catholic Church, 309
Ceausescu, Nicolae, 303–4, 309, 313
Central Advisory Committee (CAC). *See* Chinese Communist Party
Central Arts Academy, 273
Central Committee. *See* Chinese Communist Party
Central Discipline Inspection Commission (CDIC). *See* Chinese Communist Party
Central Intelligence Agency (CIA), 315
Central Military Affairs Commission (MAC). *See* People's Liberation Army
Central Party Secretariat. *See* Chinese Communist Party
Central planning, 9, 55, 152, 332; Chen Yun and, 171, 320; and market regulation, 94–95, 171, 175, 337, 342; reduced scope of, 95–96, 170, 355, 361
Chai Ling, 254, 258, 271, 286, 290
Chaos: fear of, 5, 20, 89, 110–11, 221, 307, 310, 330, 342, 359
"Charter '77," 309

Chen Boda, 27
Chen Duxiu, 97
Chen Erjin, 130
Chen Haosu, 330
Chen Jun, 241
Chen Muhua, 226
Chen Pixian, 148
Chen Xiaotong, 386
Chen Xilian, 27, 33, 34, 35, 36, 59, 61, 62, 90, 92, 131, 451n
Chen Xitong, 204, 260, 276, 289, 300, 347, 364, 365, 449n; alleged corruption of, 386, 469n
Chen Yi, 423n
Chen Yigang, 74
Chen Yizi, 68, 213, 232, 238, 290, 411n, 429n
Chen Yonggui, 27, 35, 64, 100, 146, 410n
Chen Yuan, 328, 330, 338, 364, 471n
Chen Yun, 4, 8, 9, 10–11, 28, 45, 50, 64–69, 82, 84, 87, 100, 105, 107, 115, 117, 132, 133, 138, 145, 147, 148, 151, 153, 158, 160, 185, 186, 194, 208, 215, 216, 218, 241, 293, 295, 296, 315, 322, 328, 332, 336, 337, 339, 341, 344, 348, 360, 363, 365, 371, 375, 410n, 422n, 454n, 458n, 462n; and Bai Hua, 130, 422n; "bird cage" analogy of, 152, 171, 236, 302, 426n; and "bourgeois liberalization," 111, 130, 160, 197, 239, 339, 353; and cadre retirement, 138, 145, 168; and Cultural Revolution, 62; death of, 383; declining health of, 20, 321, 352, 354, 375; and Democracy Wall, 82; and Deng Liqun, 11, 216, 217, 321, 423n; and Deng Xiaoping, 10–11, 13, 45, 67–68, 107, 111, 165, 319–20, 332, 339, 340–42, 344, 345–46, 352–54, 354–55, 359, 454n, 461n; and economic crime, corruption, 140–41, 155, 317, 319, 332; and economic readjustment (1979), 66–68, 84, 86, 112, 320 (*see also* "Readjustment, restructuring, consolidation, and improvement"); and Gang of Four, 40, 404n; and Mikhail Gorbachev, 304; and Hu Qili, 364; and Hu Yaobang, 147–48, 149, 152, 207, 407n; and Hua Guofeng, 45, 48, 66, 67, 68; and Jiang Zemin, 296, 332; and leadership succession, 138, 336–37, 339, 353; and Mao Zedong, 400n; and Marxism-Leninism, 332; and "new conservatism," 330; on opposing "Rightism," 339, 344, 355, 359; on party discipline, 140, 194; and "peaceful evolution," 334, 337, 339; and Peng Zhen, 414n; and petitioners' movement, 78–79; and Polish crisis, 111; reform strategy of, 4, 10, 107, 320, 322, 355, 411n; retirement of,

139, 145, 215; and secret protocol of 1987, 208, 218, 257; *Selected Works* of, 111, 168; and special economic zones, 165, 337, 341–42, 353, 359, 461n; and "spiritual pollution," 159; and "stock market fever," 359–60; and "theory of another center," 13, 14, 339, 459n; and Tiananmen crisis (1989), 258, 453–54n; and Tiananmen incident (1976), 62; and Vietnam campaign, 80; and Wei Jingsheng, 82; and Boris Yeltsin, 332, 333; and Zhao Ziyang, 152, 153, 172, 211, 239, 241–42, 270, 437n; and Zhu Rongji, 333

"Chen Yun Thought," 320, 321

Chen Zaidao, 128, 305, 409n, 445n

Chen Zheng, 287

Chen Zihua, 418n

Chen Ziming, 287, 290, 291, 388, 402n, 412n, 419n, 449n

Chi Haotian, 319, 367

Chiang Ching-kuo, 187

China Economic Development Corporation, 237, 299

China Futures Society, 166

China Handicapped Association, 267. *See also* Deng Pufang

China Human Rights League, 73, 81

China International Trust and Investment Corporation (CITIC), 36, 96, 237, 299

China Merchants' Steamship Navigation Company, 67

China Rural Trust and Development Corporation, 299

Chinese Academy of Social Sciences (CASS), 53, 60, 79, 239; and administrative reform, 193–94; and political reform, 195; and Tiananmen crisis (1989), 266

Chinese Communist Party (CCP)
—Central Advisory Committee (CAC), 17, 100, 144–45, 217, 222, 257, 258, 293, 297, 321, 322, 334, 336, 338–40, 345–46, 348, 360, 362, 368, 371; abolition of, 21, 368; and Deng Xiaoping, 17, 345–46, 359; and Tiananmen crisis (1989), 275, 293
—Central Committee work conference: (November 1978), 62–63; (April 1979), 83, (December 1980), 122, 138; (January 1980), 89
—Central Discipline Inspection Committee (CDIC), 64, 91, 92, 138, 140, 141, 145, 158, 177, 194, 237, 298, 316, 319, 345–46, 378
—Central Party School, 65, 111, 374
—Central Secretariat, 69, 90, 147–48, 366, 410n

—collective leadership in, 64, 66, 91, 101, 147
—conference on theoretical work (1979), 79–81
—Constitution of, 48, 49, 101, 136, 144, 145, 147, 149, 186
—corruption in, 91, 126, 176, 237, 298, 317–18, 319, 385–87
—discipline problems in, 48, 50, 101, 140, 148, 308, 316, 330
—electoral reform in, 91
—"fine tradition and style of work" in, 12–13, 50, 53, 59–60, 91
—"Guiding principles of inner-party political life," 91, 92, 93, 97, 100, 140, 197, 236, 239, 257
—and intellectuals, 187, 217, 241
—morale problems in, 147, 276, 307, 308, 315–18, 331, 369
—National Party Conference (1985), 186, 188, 191, 194
—public image of, 141, 229–31, 237, 253, 300, 330
—recruitment policies of, 187, 330, 331
—"rectification and consolidation" of, 99, 140, 144, 149, 157–59, 161, 167–68, 168, 177, 179, 194, 207, 230, 315–16, 317–18
—reform of leadership in, 97, 99, 101, 106, 144–46, 194–96, 214, 220, 237, 331
—Yan'an spirit, 144
—Tenth National Congress (1973), 29
—Eleventh Central Committee: Third Plenum (1978), 6, 45, 62, 63–66, 68, 83, 123, 144; Fourth Plenum (1979), 64, 86–88, 107; Fifth Plenum (1980), 90–93, 97, 100, 105, 107, 121, 140; Sixth Plenum (1981), 117, 128, 131–34
—Eleventh National Congress (1977), 49
—Twelfth Central Committee, 146, 185; Second Plenum (1983), 157–59; Third Plenum (1984), 170–72; Fourth Plenum (1985), 185, 186; Fifth Plenum (1985), 186; Sixth Plenum (1986), 197–99
—Twelfth National Congress (1982), 142–50, 156, 216, 398n
—Thirteenth Central Committee, 216, 217; Second Plenum (1988), 226; Third Plenum (1988), 235, 236; Fourth Plenum (1989), 241, 295–96, 362; Fifth Plenum (1989), 300–302, 322, 326; Seventh Plenum (1990), 215, 320, 321, 322, 327; Eighth Plenum (1991), 336, 338; Ninth Plenum (1992), 362
—Thirteenth National Congress (1987), 186, 198, 208, 214–16, 218, 221, 222, 225–26

Chinese Communist Party (*cont.*)
—Fourteenth Central Committee, 364–65
—Fourteenth National Congress (1992), 20, 21, 316, 330, 338, 349, 352, 353, 359, 360–62, 364, 366, 368, 449n
Chinese People's Political Consultative Conference (CPPCC), 306, 313, 321, 328, 373, 452n
Chinese University of Science and Technology (CUST), 201
Chinese Writers' Association, 128
Civic Forum, 309
Civil service: reform of, 194, 221. *See also* Administration; *Nomenklatura*; Personnel system
"Civil society," 20, 189–90, 192, 273, 307, 309, 433n
Class struggle, 87, 89, 113, 135, 142, 149, 156, 329, 332, 334
Clientelism, 9, 174. *See also* Corruption; Factionalism; *Guandao*
Coastal development strategy, 226, 235. *See also* Special economic zones
Collective ownership. *See* Enterprises
Command economy, 16, 60, 61, 65, 112. *See also* Planned economy
Communist Youth League (CYL), 60, 61, 112, 169, 230
"Complete Westernization," 201, 203, 207, 213, 232
Confucianism, 13, 231, 329
Conservative faction, 161, 178–79, 182, 187, 361; attack of, on liberalism, 199, 200, 213, 332; and Hu Yaobang, 198–200, 206, 208, 211; revival of, 178, 179, 182. *See also* "Leftism"
Constitution. *See* Chinese Communist Party; People's Republic of China
Constitutional reform. *See* Legal reform
Corruption, 16, 18, 91, 102, 105, 113, 139–42, 168, 174–77, 179, 190, 193–94, 200, 223, 229–31, 236, 237, 271, 297, 318, 331, 332, 338, 359, 379, 385–87, 389, 390, 431n, 434n, 468n, 470n, 471n; and *gaogan zidi*, 174–75, 177, 431n, 467n, 471–72n; and military commerce, 370, 380; in People's Liberation Army, 123–24; and Polish crisis of 1980–81, 103; in rural areas, 378, 434n; and Shenzhen stock market riot, 358, 359; and student demonstrations, 202; and Tiananmen crisis (1989), 251, 253, 298, 317–18. *See also* Crime; *Guandao*
Crime: and "bourgeois liberalization," 156; crackdown on, 155–56, 193, 381, 465n; and

drug abuse, 381; economic, 102, 139–41, 144, 155, 168, 174–77, 179, 194, 199, 229, 318, 344, 380, 468n; rising rate of, 113, 155–56, 229, 317–18, 379–80, 440n; in urban areas, 189, 193, 229; violence and, 231, 318, 379. *See also* Corruption; Legal system
Criminal code of 1979, 84, 86, 114, 150, 414n
"Crisis of faith," 3, 86, 91, 144, 381. *See also* "Three crises of faith"
"Crossing the river by groping for stepping stones," 17, 272
Cult of personality, 17, 21, 51–52, 98, 106, 117, 132, 363
Cultural Revolution, 3, 4, 8, 9, 10, 12, 27–29, 31, 43, 48–49, 60, 62, 68, 70, 74, 76, 86–87, 89, 101, 114, 122, 123, 127, 135, 136, 270, 332; abuse of cadres in, 4, 114–15; anarchy in, 84, 105, 167, 310; Mao Zedong and, 3, 44, 87; reversal of verdict on, 30, 35, 62, 331, 332
Cycles: and reform. See *"Fang/shou* cycles"

Dai Qing, 256, 349, 408n, 444n, 460n
Dalai Lama, 323
"Dare to die brigades," 272
Darwinism, social, 355
Dazhai brigade, 410n, 411n
Dazibao. See Democracy Wall; Wall posters
Decentralization. *See* Administration; Economic system; Fiscal reform
"Decision on Reform of the Economic Structure" (1984). *See* Urban reform
De-Maoization, 121, 123. *See also* Mao Zedong
Democracy Wall, 69, 71–75, 77, 80–83, 88, 89, 102, 130, 205, 240; crackdown on, 78, 79, 81, 82, 126. *See also* Wall posters
Democratic centralism, 13, 72, 87, 435n
"Democratic consultation and mutual supervision": as alternative to bourgeois democracy, 220–22, 313–14
Democratization, 7, 61, 72–74, 77, 81–82, 91, 102, 104, 106–7, 195–97, 198, 200–201, 203, 221, 294, 329. *See also* "Bourgeois democracy"; Leadership system; Political system; "Socialist democracy"
Deng Liqun, 9, 11, 13, 40, 57, 68, 69, 77, 80, 111, 129, 131, 144, 148, 154, 155, 161, 162, 165, 179, 181, 187, 189, 196, 210, 211, 215, 216–17, 295, 320, 322, 331–33, 336, 337, 344, 364, 375, 423n, 427n, 466n; and "bourgeois liberalization," 179–81, 196, 198, 210, 332; and "capitalistic reform," 335; and Chen Yun, 11, 111, 160, 216, 217, 320, 321;

and Deng Xiaoping, 11, 30, 37, 180, 334–35, 337, 339, 340, 346–47, 403n; and Hu Qiaomu, 9, 37, 69, 80, 144, 165, 198, 295, 332, 333, 336–37, 364; and Hu Yaobang, 11, 134, 152–53, 159, 161–63, 180–81, 198, 206, 211, 427n; and humanism debate, 154–55; and intellectuals, 180; and Li Ruihuan, 335; and "Mao Zedong craze," 339; and "open policy," 181, 334; and "peaceful evolution," 332, 334; and People's Liberation Army, 371; and reform cycles, 5–7; and special economic zones, 160, 165; and "spiritual pollution," 155, 159–63, 417n; and student demonstrations, 204; and Wang Zhen, 331–32, 339, 371, 375; and Yan Jiaqi, 214; and Yang Shangkun, 21; and Yu Guangyuan, 131; and Zhao Ziyang, 161–62

Deng Nan, 341, 365

Deng Pufang, 162, 213, 237, 341, 364, 442n, 446n

Deng Rong, 353, 468n

Deng Xiaoping, 4, 9–11, 14, 20, 22, 28, 30, 31, 39, 42, 43, 45, 47, 48, 51, 53, 56–58, 61, 63–65, 73, 77, 83, 88, 92, 93, 106, 111, 115, 117, 129, 132–34, 142, 146, 148, 153, 166, 169, 172, 185, 192, 194, 208, 211, 249, 256, 275, 293, 304, 310, 315, 321, 330, 334–37, 338, 360, 409n, 419n, 433n, 436n; and "black cats, white cats" theory, 29, 35, 96, 144, 258; and "bourgeois liberalization," 77, 99, 128, 140–41, 143, 158, 167, 198–99, 204–5, 213, 294, 423n; bridge-playing habits of, 21, 69, 458–59n; and cadre corruption, 102, 140–42, 298, 317, 466n; and Capital Iron and Steel Works, 353, 354; and capitalism, 99, 101, 102, 113, 178–79, 198, 294, 342–43; and Central Advisory Committee, 17, 100, 145, 321, 322; and Chen Yun, 13, 67–68, 107, 165, 215, 319–22, 337, 341–42, 354, 454n, 461n; and commercialization of art, 157, 159; and Democracy Wall, 71–73, 75, 78, 81, 83, 89, 102, 412n; and Deng Liqun, 159, 163, 335, 337, 339, 403n; and economic reform, 16–18, 63–64, 66–67, 68–69, 111–12, 141–42, 143–44, 161–62, 178–79, 182–83, 232–33, 234, 235, 236, 294–95, 320–21, 334, 340, 341–44, 353–54, 391–92; and factionalism, 7, 13, 15, 157–59, 185, 188, 211; and Fang Lizhi, 204–5, 240, 242; and "feudal influence," 97–98, 99, 100; and "four big freedoms," 82, 89, 92; and "four cardinal principles," 80–81, 89–90, 113, 128, 293–94, 344; and Gang of Four, 4, 30–31, 37, 49, 71, 117; and

Mikhail Gorbachev, 304; health of, 21, 333, 354, 363, 383, 387, 392, 468n, 472n; and Hu Qiaomu, 337, 403n; and Hu Yaobang, 11, 65, 80, 83, 152, 179, 187, 206, 207, 235, 249, 463n; and Hua Guofeng, 42–43, 46, 49, 51, 52, 67, 90, 93, 116–18, 131–32; and humanism, 157–58; and Jiang Zemin, 295–96, 332, 351, 371; last instructions of, 394; and leadership reform, 88, 97, 99–102, 137–39, 143, 186–87, 194–95, 215, 331, 419n; and "Leftist" threat, 20, 334, 344–48, 370–71; legacy of, 22, 341, 370, 391, 394; and Li Peng, 321, 322, 375; and Li Ruihuan, 336; and Li Weihan, 417n; and Mao Zedong, 28–29, 30, 31, 35, 46–47, 56, 58–59, 71, 73, 81, 101, 121, 132–36, 137; and "open policy," 57, 63, 96, 164–65, 182, 191; and "peaceful evolution," 334, 336, 343, 370; and People's Liberation Army, 17, 29, 88, 117, 121–23, 132, 136, 183–85, 187, 188, 217, 258, 269, 293–94, 320, 370, 400n, 432n, 445n; and personality cult, 17, 21, 363–64; and petitioners' movement, 79; and Polish crisis (1980–81), 102–3, 205, 250, 275, 436n; and price reform, 16, 17–18, 232–34; purge of, 5, 35–37, 50; reform coalition of, 4–5, 10, 19, 22, 67, 77–78, 107, 121, 143; rehabilitation of, 4, 8, 29, 42, 44–46, 48, 49, 63, 117, 408n; retirement of, 16, 100, 139, 145, 185, 214–15, 217, 301; and "Right deviationist wind" (1975), 39, 44, 49, 135; role of, as political balancer, 13, 15–16, 83, 89–90, 99, 143, 157–59, 185, 188, 211; and "second Chinese revolution," 9, 47; and secret protocol of 1987, 208, 218, 257; and "seek truth from facts" debate, 58–59; and "socialism with Chinese characteristics," 16; and "socialist spiritual civilization," 16, 143–44, 148, 188; "southern tour" of (1992), 8, 14, 20, 341–45, 349, 350, 352; and special economic zones, 20, 67, 141, 142, 165, 182, 340, 341–44; speeches at: Army Political Work Conference (1978), 58, 59; Eleventh Party Congress, 50; National Education Conference (1978), 57; National Party Conference (1985), 188; National Science Conference (1978), 57; Twelfth Party Congress, 143–44; speeches of: March 16, 1979, 78; March 30, 1979, 80–81, 83; August 18, 1980, 99–102; December 25, 1980, 112, 113; and "spiritual pollution," 73, 102, 157–59, 161, 198, 250; and "stability and unity," 16, 21, 63, 79, 81, 89, 112–13, 134, 342, 394; and stock markets, 342–43, 357, 359;

Deng Xiaoping (*cont.*)
  and student demonstrations (1985–86), 202,
  204, 242, 249; succession to, 16, 151, 381;
  and "theory of one center," 13, 144, 344,
  347; and "third echelon," 16, 185, 194; and
  "three poisonous weeds" (1975), 29–30, 52,
  56, 60, 67; and "three supports and two militarys" (1967), 136; and Tiananmen crisis
  (1989), 19, 21–22, 249–51, 253–54, 256–
  58, 261–62, 269–70, 275, 293–301, 314,
  369–70, 454n; and Tiananmen incident
  (1976), 4, 22, 34–37, 43, 45–46, 135–36,
  370; and Vietnam campaign (1979), 80; and
  Wang Ruowang, 205; and Wang Zhen, 321,
  340; and Wei Jingsheng, 10, 73–74, 80–81,
  205; and "Whatever" faction, 58–59; and
  Xu Shiyou, 122, 147, 420n; and Yang
  Shangkun, 21–22, 225, 369–71; and Zhao
  Ziyang, 11, 211, 234–35, 241, 253, 254,
  258, 261, 269, 297, 298, 300–301, 308, 315,
  450n; and Zhu Rongji, 333, 350, 351
"Deng Xiaoping Thought," 351, 363
Deng Yingchao, 4, 20, 40, 64, 185, 186, 368,
  425n
Deng Yingtao, 68, 330, 364
Deng Zhifang, 390, 467n, 469n
de Pompadour, Mme., 20
Ding Guan'gen, 296, 365, 366, 453n, 464n
Ding Peng, 385
Ding Shisun, 299
Dissidents, 13, 111, 240. *See also* Human
  rights
Dittmer, Lowell, 398n
Domes, Jürgen, 401n, 415n
Dong Furen, 462n
"Double August" (*renbayue*), 390
Drug abuse, 335, 343, 380, 381, 467n, 468n.
  See also Corruption
Du Runsheng, 295, 319, 462n
Dulles, John Foster, 437n

Eastern Europe: collapse of communism in,
  19, 276, 303–4, 307. *See also* "Gentle revolution"
"Eating from the same big pot," 95
Economic construction: central task of, 143,
  198, 218, 344. *See also* "One center": theory
  of
Economic growth, 96, 223, 340, 351, 352, 377,
  391, 471n; excessive rate of, 111, 223, 302,
  307, 342, 355, 359, 360, 373, 377
"Economic methods." *See* Market regulation
Economic readjustment. *See* "Readjustment,
  restructuring, consolidation, and improvement"

Economic system, reform of, 5, 7, 14, 21, 57,
  60, 63, 72, 94, 96, 97, 149, 164, 169–72,
  211, 232, 302, 303, 320, 334, 350; acceleration of, 166, 169, 341, 342, 345; and corruption, 141, 177, 178, 191; criticism of, 182,
  210, 213, 334, 336–37, 345; effects of, 164,
  307, 340, 391–92; irreversibility of, 9, 22,
  375, 398n; and "new conservatism," 329;
  objectives of, 165, 226; and political reform,
  193–95, 197; slowdown of, 112, 121, 174;
  and Tiananmen crisis (1989), 19, 294, 302–
  3. *See also* Enterprises; Market regulation;
  Structural reform; Urban reform
Education: reform of, 57, 247. *See also* Universities
"Eight-character charter." *See* "Readjustment,
  restructuring, consolidation, and improvement"
"Eight immortals," 438n
Elections, local, 85, 107–10, 112, 372
Electoral system: reform of, 84–86, 91, 102,
  107–8, 110, 201, 223, 374. *See also* Democratization; Political system
"Emancipate thinking," 61, 63, 80, 81, 86, 95,
  97, 107, 226, 335, 336, 352
Engels, Friedrich, 63
Enterprises
—collective, 173, 361
—private, 170, 227, 334, 348
—state-owned, 95, 96, 171, 175, 179, 361;
  bankruptcy of, 227–29, 356; contract workers in, 228; management of, 60, 95, 151,
  171, 214, 223, 226–28, 321; profit, remittance by, 151–53, 171; reform of, 112, 169–
  70, 172, 175, 227–28, 232, 233, 302, 338,
  353, 355–56; restructuring of, 169, 350,
  355; stock transactions in, 360; taxation of,
  151, 171, 228; unemployment in, 228, 229;
  violations of law by, 223
Entrepreneurship, private, 96, 164, 169–70,
  173, 178, 193, 232, 238, 331, 430n. *See also*
  Enterprises; *Getihu*
Everbright Corporation, 237, 299
"Extreme individualism," 92, 102, 113, 127,
  156. *See also* Anarchism; "Ultrademocracy"

Factionalism, 3, 7–12, 15, 91, 149, 157, 168,
  199
Factory manager responsibility system. *See*
  Responsibility systems
Fan Zeng, 454n
Fang Lizhi, 190, 196, 200–201, 209, 238, 239–
  40, 289, 290; and George Bush, 242; and
  "complete Westernization," 201, 203; criticism of, 201, 204, 210; and Deng Xiaoping,

240, 241; expulsion of, from CCP, 207, 209; and Hu Qiaomu, 200; and Wan Li, 201; and Zhao Ziyang, 223

"*Fang/shou* cycles," 5–9, 15, 19–21, 23, 82, 89, 94, 107, 112, 113, 150, 163, 165, 178, 190, 298, 357, 375, 397n, 398n

Fang Yi, 215, 416n

Fang Zhiwen, 109

Farmers: declining incomes of, 377, 378, 466n; protests by, 378; and Tiananmen crisis (1989), 266, 308. *See also* Agriculture

"February adverse current" (1967), 135, 423n

Feng Lanrui, 413n

"Feudal autocracy." *See* "Feudal influence"

"Feudal influence," 11, 13, 17, 74, 97–101, 106–7, 136, 195, 220

"Feudal prince economy," 326–27. *See also* "Independent kingdoms"

"Fifth Modernization," 73. *See also* Wei Jingsheng

"Fine tradition and style of work": debate over, 12–13, 53, 59, 60, 91. *See also* Chinese Communist Party

Fiscal reform, 151, 302, 326, 382, 442n, 455–56n. *See also* Enterprises; *Li gai shui*

"Five-Anti" campaign," 142

"Floating population" (*liudong renkou*), 229, 250, 292, 378, 392, 440n. *See also* Unemployment

"Flying Tiger brigades," 265, 274, 278, 447n

Foreign Exchange Certificates (FEC), 382

Foreign investment, 67, 96, 165, 169, 182, 226, 303, 342, 353, 359, 374. *See also* Joint ventures; Special economic zones

Foreign trade, 55–56, 67, 174–76, 234, 237, 303, 350

Forster, Keith, 404n

"Four big freedoms," 54, 70, 82, 89, 92, 105. *See also* Democracy Wall

"Four cardinal principles," 14, 16, 22, 79–81, 83, 85, 86, 88, 89, 92, 107, 110, 111, 113, 123, 127, 128, 136, 149, 150, 157, 159, 195, 197, 198, 207, 212–14, 218, 241, 293, 296, 325, 332, 344, 346, 356, 363

"Four little dragons," 166, 342, 344

"Four modernizations," 54–55, 66, 73, 81, 88, 400n

Fraser, John, 71

Fu Quanyou, 367

Fu Yuehua, 76, 77, 82, 415n

"Gang of Five," 322, 335–36, 364

Gang of Four, 4, 27, 31, 32, 36, 37, 39, 40–45, 49, 53–54, 56, 61–63, 70, 72–73, 84, 87, 97, 110, 113, 136, 156, 191, 401n; arrest of, 4,

37, 41–42, 45, 404n; crimes of, 41, 44, 49, 50, 57, 406n; and Deng Xiaoping, 31, 34–35, 37, 71; and Hua Guofeng, 34–36, 39; trial of, 113–18; and "Whatever" faction, 50–51

Gao Di, 322, 336, 347, 350, 352, 354, 356, 364

Gao Gao, 290

Gao Xin, 286, 290, 446n

Gaogan zidi, 173, 185, 191, 247, 298, 328, 364–65, 431n, 434n, 467n, 471n; and economic crime, corruption, 174–77, 190, 236–37, 380. *See also* Corruption; *Guandao*

Ge Yang, 210

"General, You Cannot Do This," 124–26, 128, 422n. *See also* Ye Wenfu

Geng Biao, 122, 146

Gengshen reforms (1980). *See* Leadership system; Political system

"Gentle revolution" of 1989, 19, 303, 307, 309, 310

Getihu, 173, 193, 228, 265. *See also* Entrepreneurship

Glasnost, 234, 303

"Goddess of Democracy," 273, 275, 288

Goldman, Merle, 413n

Goldstein, Avery, 461n

Gong Xinhan, 385

Gong Yuzhi, 356

Gongzilian. See Beijing Workers' Autonomous Federation

Gorbachev, Mikhail, 238, 255, 258, 273, 304, 313–14; criticism of, 304, 313, 314–15, 334; visit of, to China (1989), 218, 241, 258, 261

Grain: rationing of, 379

"Greater China," 392

Great Leap Forward, 29, 55, 60, 87, 96, 135, 348

Guan Weiyan, 209

Guandao, 236–38, 248, 256, 259–60, 261, 471n. *See also* Corruption; *Gaogan zidi*

"Guiding principles for inner-party political life." *See* Chinese Communist Party

Gulag Archipelago, 73

Guo Jianmin, 385

Guo Luoji, 210

Hainan Island, 168, 175, 227, 343, 431, 451n

Halpern, Nina, 398n

Han Dongfang, 271, 290

Han Guang, 409n

Hao Jianxu, 187

He Dongchang, 204, 253, 364, 464n

He Jingzhi, 322, 336, 337, 346, 356, 364

He Long, 44, 405n
He Ping, 476n
He Xin, 328, 352, 456n
Heavy industry: priority of, 54–55, 66–67
Hirohito, 242
HIV (human immunodeficiency virus), 240
Hong Kong, 142, 160, 181, 225, 315, 345, 374, 380, 445n, 470n
Hong Kong Commission for Human Rights, 240
Hong Xuezhi, 306
Hou Dejian, 273, 274, 286, 287, 290, 291
Household responsiblity systems. *See* Responsibility systems
Housing: privatization of, 228
Hu An'gang, 392, 393
Hu Fuming, 408n
Hu Jintao, 169, 365, 366, 409n, 464n
Hu Jiwei, 60, 77, 154, 160, 161, 179, 210, 375, 413n; and freedom of press, 179; and petition drive of May 1989, 268–69, 296; reassignment of, 163
Hu Keshi, 409n
Hu Ping, 109, 419n
Hu Qiaomu, 4, 9, 13, 60, 64, 68, 77, 80, 98, 111, 115, 129, 131, 134, 144, 146, 148, 177, 185, 206, 239, 295, 332, 333, 336, 337, 375, 408n, 409n, 416n; and "bourgois liberalization," 97, 101, 204, 210, 337; death of, 14, 20, 364, 368; and Deng Liqun, 180; and Deng Xiaoping, 30, 37, 177, 337, 403n; and economic reform, 14, 60, 69, 94, 411n; and Fang Lizhi, 200; and Hu Yaobang, 176, 198; and information revolution, 166; last testament of, 14, 458n, 466n; and "open policy," 182; and Polish crisis of 1980–81, 111; and special economic zones, 165; and "spiritual pollution" campaign, 417n; visits United States, 458n; and Zhou Yang, 160, 189
Hu Qili, 60, 148, 169, 181, 186, 188, 196, 204, 215, 216, 236, 239, 242, 249, 251, 256, 259, 293, 364, 453n; criticism of, 270, 295, 296; and freedom of press, 179; and political reform, 195; rehabilitation of, 315; and "River Elegy," 232; and Tiananmen crisis (1989), 251, 256, 259, 269, 270, 293; and Zhao Ziyang, 256, 269
Hu Sheng, 80, 242
Hu Shiying, 176–77
Hu Yaobang, 9, 11, 13, 16, 51, 58, 60, 61, 64–66, 76, 90, 91, 97, 98, 111, 115, 117, 129, 131, 132, 133, 146, 148, 149, 152, 153, 161–63, 164, 166, 167, 177, 179, 184–86, 198, 204, 208, 216, 222, 225, 226, 315, 319,

407n, 408n, 410n, 416n, 432n; and Bai Hua, 130, 149; and "bourgeois liberalization," 98, 129, 148–49, 152, 179–80, 198, 206–9; and Chen Yun, 148–49, 152, 207, 407n; and "crisis of faith," 91, 416n, 425n; death of, 7, 19, 242–43, 247, 248, 316; and Democracy Wall, 75, 82, 89; and Deng Liqun, 11, 159, 161–63, 180, 181, 211, 217; and Deng Xiaoping, 11, 30, 133–34, 152, 199, 436n; and "feudal influence," 97; and "four cardinal principles," 198; and freedom of the press, 179, 356; and Hu Qiaomu, 176; and Hu Qili, 186; and Hua Guofeng, 131; intellectual network of, 77, 80, 83, 89, 101; and Marxism, 178; and party rectification, 149; and People's Liberation Army, 122, 132, 147, 184, 187–88; and petitioners' movement, 76; and Polish crisis, 103; resignation of, 11, 206–9, 211, 213, 239, 241, 436n; and "spiritual pollution" campaign, 161–63; and structural reform, 4, 151, 164, 171; and student demonstrations of 1986, 207–8; and theory conference of 1979, 79, 413n; and "theory of one center," 198; and "theory of productive forces," 144; and "third echelon," 168, 194; and Tiananmen incident (1976), 62; and "Total Westernization," 207; "turning point" speech of (1980), 106, 107; verdict on, 247, 249, 251, 254; and "Whatever" faction, 51; and Ye Jianying, 417n; and Zhao Ziyang, 11, 150–52, 153, 161, 207, 398n, 437n
Hua Guofeng, 4, 8–12, 22, 27, 31, 36, 39–45, 48–50, 53, 55, 56, 58, 61, 64, 66, 69, 77, 84, 92, 93, 94, 105, 131–33, 145, 217, 296, 405–6n, 407n, 416n; and Chen Yun, 45; and Deng Xiaoping, 42–43, 46, 49, 51, 53, 93, 116, 131, 132; and economic readjustment (1979), 87; fall from power of, 50, 51, 63, 66, 72, 89, 90, 92, 93, 99, 100, 104, 116–18, 131–33, 146, 387; and "flying leap" (*see* ten-year economic plan); and Gang of Four, 4, 35–37, 39, 42, 49, 117–18, 404n; and Hu Yaobang, 131; and intellectuals, 52–53; and Mao Zedong, 3, 37–39, 41, 93; and People's Liberation Army, 59, 92–93, 117, 122; personality cult of, 51–52, 117, 363; and Tangshan earthquake, 38–39; ten-year economic plan of, 52, 54–56, 67–68, 88, 320; and Tiananmen incident (1976), 33–36, 43, 50, 62, 116; and "two whatevers," 219
Huan Xiang, 429n
"Huang Fuping," 458n
Huang Hua, 417n

Huang Huoqing, 409n
Huang Ju, 385
Huang Kecheng, 123, 127, 409n, 421n
Huang Xiang, 81, 389
Huang Yongsheng, 400n
Humanism, socialist: debate over, 5, 153–56, 157, 161, 189, 198. *See also* Alienation
Human rights, 73, 81, 231, 242, 271, 278, 336, 389; in Inner Mongolia, 325; in Tibet, 323; United States and, 339
Hunan Teacher's College, 108, 109
Hungary: model of market socialism in, 171
Hunger strike: of May 1989, 255–62, 265, 271, 273. *See also* Tiananmen crisis (1989)
Huntington, Samuel P., 439n

Ideology. *See* "four cardinal principles"; "Mao Zedong Thought"; Marxism-Leninism
Iliescu, Ion, 304
Incentives: material, 63, 68, 95, 105, 169, 174, 182, 223–24, 234. *See also* Enterprises; Workers
Income: per-capita, 391; urban-rural gap in, 378. *See also* Farmers; Workers
"Independent kingdoms," 29, 326–28. *See also* "Feudal prince economy"
Industrial democracy, 102, 104, 106, 112. *See also* Labor unions; Workers
Industrial reform. *See* Enterprises; Urban reform
Inflation, 16–18, 22, 55, 105, 110, 174, 190, 192, 223–24, 226, 228, 229, 232, 235, 297, 302, 359, 377; and economic instability, 223; fear of, 172, 190; and student demonstrations, 202; surge in rate of, 174, 233, 382; and Tiananmen crisis (1989), 250, 253, 307
Information revolution. *See* "Third Wave"
Intellectuals, 153, 154, 180, 193, 398n; creative freedom of, 129–30, 193, 198; Deng Xiaoping and, 204; Hu Yaobang and, 77, 80, 83, 89, 101, 129; Hua Guofeng and, 52; policy toward, 5, 127–30, 135, 165, 189, 196, 209, 331; political activism of, 240, 241, 388, 412n; recruited into CCP, 187; role of, 57, 190; and Tiananmen crisis (1989), 254; Zhao Ziyang and, 155, 242
"Iron rice bowl," 68, 95, 169, 172, 226, 228, 379

Japan, 54, 55, 57–58, 161, 162, 190–91, 240
Ji Dengkui, 27, 62, 64, 90, 92, 131
Jiang Chunyun, 365, 388, 470n
"Jiang-Li axis," 353, 375, 462n

Jiang Qing, 27, 30, 31, 35, 40, 42, 44, 71, 132, 401–2n, 420n; arrest of, 404n; and Hua Guofeng, 38–39; and Mao Zedong, 3–4, 31; suicide of, 420n; and Tiananmen incident (1976), 33–34; trial of, 113, 115, 116. *See also* Gang of Four
Jiang Zemin, 13, 21, 216, 243, 251, 270, 295–96, 301, 302, 304, 306, 315, 332–34, 336, 337, 345, 352, 353, 366, 370, 384–85, 459n, 464n; and "bourgeois liberalization," 296, 302, 332; and Chen Yun, 296, 332, 360; on corruption, 386–87; criticism of, 321, 333, 353; and Deng Xiaoping, 345, 347, 350–51, 362, 363, 387; and economic reform, 350–51, 360–61, 363; and "four cardinal principles," 363; and Hu Yaobang, 388, 470n; and Mikhail Gorbachev, 304; and Military Affairs Commission, 301, 367; and military commerce, 384; and "peaceful evolution," 302, 332; and Peng Zhen, 470n; and People's Liberation Army, 384, 471n; and "rule by core" faction, 388; self-criticism of, 347; and "Shanghai clique," 384; speech at Fourteenth Party Congress, 361–63, 463n; speech on seventieth anniversary of CCP (1991), 332; and student demonstrations, 202, 204, 302, 450n; succession strategy of, 384–87; and Zhao Ziyang, 296, 300, 361–62; and Zhu Rongji, 350; and Zhuo Lin, 389
"Jiang-Zhu axis," 375
Joint ventures, 84, 142, 337, 350

Kang Sheng, 27, 30, 62
Kang Shi'en, 55, 67, 104, 105, 418n
Kang Youwei, 330
Kanghua Development Corporation, 237, 299, 442n
"Key" schools, 57
Korea (North), 249, 251
Kornai, Janos, 96
Kuan, Hsin-chi, 426n
Kuomintang, 89

Labor unions: democratic reform of, 104, 106, 111, 112; party control of, 207, 229. *See also* Beijing Autonomous Workers' Federation; Industrial democracy; Workers
"Law of value," 52, 64
Leadership system: reform of, 99–101, 104, 107, 109–11, 116, 137–39, 144–45, 146, 186–87, 194–97, 214–15, 364. *See also* Democratization; Political system
"Lean to one side," 72
Lee Kuan Yew, 232

"Leftism," 15, 56, 123, 183, 334, 336, 339, 342, 344, 346, 351, 353, 359, 370; critique of, 159, 167–68, 349, 356; danger of, 165, 334–36, 344, 345, 347, 348, 351, 352, 354, 370; Hua Guofeng and, 132

Legal system: reform of, 54, 61, 64, 66, 84, 85, 102, 106

Lei Feng, 123, 180, 306

Lenin, V. I., 58, 97, 201

"Leninger, Dr." *See* Wang Shan

Leninism. *See* Marxism-Leninism

Leninist systems, 16; corruption in, 174, 430n

Li Chang, 319

Li Desheng, 183–85, 199, 305

Li Fuchun, 423n

Li gai shui, 151, 153, 171, 172, 327, 382, 426n. *See also* Fiscal reform

Li Guixian, 382

Li Honglin, 195, 210, 413n

Li Jingquan, 28

Li Jukui, 445n

Li Ka-shing, 385, 469n

Li Lanqing, 365, 464n

Li Lisan, 97

Li Lu, 254

Li Peng, 13, 14, 21, 169, 186, 204, 212, 215, 216, 236, 238, 259, 292, 296, 302, 304, 320, 322, 326, 327, 348, 353, 364, 375, 387, 388, 464n, 470n; and Chen Xitong, 470n; and Chen Yun, 470n; criticism of, 256, 348, 353, 372, 375; and Deng Xiaoping, 320–21, 345, 350–52; and economic reform, 226–27, 233, 235, 320–21, 322, 327, 348, 351–52, 355, 360, 372–73; and "four cardinal principles," 212; heart attack of, 375; report of, to Seventh National People's Congress, 227; report of, to Eighth National People's Congress, 373; and special economic zones, 302, 371–72; and Three Gorges Dam, 348, 349; and Tiananmen crisis (1989), 248–49, 256, 259–63, 269, 271, 292–93; and Zhao Ziyang, 233–35, 239, 269, 297, 456n; and Zhu Rongji, 470n; and Zou Jiahua, 352

Li Qiyan, 386

Li Rui, 168, 319, 349, 460n

Li Ruihuan, 203, 216, 296, 321, 322, 335, 345–46, 364, 366, 373, 388, 454n, 464n; on art and literature, 356; his critique of "Leftism," 339, 340, 356; and Deng Liqun, 335; and Deng Xiaoping, 336, 345; and "River Elegy," 335; and student demonstrations of 1986, 203

Li Shoucheng, 126

Li Shuxian, 289, 290

Li Tieying, 216, 260, 364, 373, 417n, 464n

Li Weihan, 97, 98, 147, 364, 417n

Li Xiannian, 28, 40, 45, 48, 54, 64, 100, 105, 112, 115, 132–33, 145, 146, 185, 194, 208, 213, 215, 225, 241, 258, 293, 296, 297, 321, 331, 345, 373, 401n, 423n; death of, 20, 368; declining health of, 321; and Deng Xiaoping, 42, 408n; and Gang of Four, 42; and Hu Yaobang, 434n; and Hua Guofeng, 61, 63; and political reform, 197; retirement of, 215; and Tiananmen incident (1976), 34

Li Ximing, 204, 216, 253, 337, 339, 344, 347, 364, 365, 464n

Li Yinhe, 61

Li Yining, 232

Li Yizhe [pseud.], 74

Li Zhengtian, 74

Li Zhisui, 401n, 402n

Liang Heng, 108, 110

Liang Qichao, 330

Liang Xiang, 318

Liang Xiao [pseud.], 40

Liao Chengzhi, 146

Liao Gailong, 65, 83, 103, 106, 107, 111, 112, 215, 220, 413n

Liberalism. *See* "Bourgeois liberalization"; "Rightism"

"Liberated cadres" faction. *See* "Rehabilitated cadres" faction

Lifetime tenure: for cadres. *See* Cadres

Light industry: role of, 66, 152

Lin Biao, 29, 31, 71, 87, 90, 123, 124, 136, 400n

"Lin Biao clique," 110, 113–16

Lin Chun, 61

Lin Hujia, 82

Lin Yanzhi, 346

Link, Perry, 399n

Literature and art, 189, 211

"Little Dragons": of East Asia, 23, 392

"Little gang of four," 90, 131. *See also* "Whatever" faction

Liu Baiyu, 422n

Liu Binyan, 128, 180, 190, 196, 207, 209–10, 238, 443n

Liu Bocheng, 400n, 417n

Liu Fuzhi, 379

Liu Guoguang, 320

Liu Huaqing, 301, 365, 370, 380, 384, 464n, 465n

Liu Ji, 385

Liu Shaoqi, 11, 28, 87, 90, 98, 115, 365, 400n, 407n, 409n

Liu Xiaobo, 286, 289, 291, 389, 446n

Liu Xinwu, 210

Liu Yuan, 365

Liu Zaifu, 189, 210
Liu Zhengwei, 385
Long March, 400n
"Loyalist" faction, 3–4, 27, 41, 43, 44, 45, 46.
    See also Hua Guofeng; "Whatever" faction
Lu Dingyi, 198
Lu Jianhua, 393
Lu Jiaxi, 209
Lu Keng, 181, 184
Lu Xun, 129
Luo Gan, 469n
Luo Ruiqing, 408n

Ma Ding [pseud.], 189
Ma Hong, 69
Ma Tianshui, 116
Macao, 225
MacDonald's restaurant, 469n
Manion, Melanie, 424n
Mao Mao. See Deng Rong
Mao Yuanxin, 30, 34–35, 36, 41, 61, 116
Mao Zedong, 8, 12, 29, 31, 33, 40, 41, 44, 46,
    51, 56, 58, 59, 81, 90, 101, 109, 117, 118,
    184, 199, 201, 223, 273, 300, 339, 342, 348,
    414n; and class struggle, 23, 135, 332, 415n;
    criticism of, 62, 70–73, 87, 91, 98, 107,
    134–36; and Cultural Revolution, 3, 44,
    135, death of, 3, 8, 39–40; declining health
    of, 34, 37, 50, 402n; and Deng Xiaoping,
    28–29, 30, 31, 35, 56, 71, 101, 121, 132–35,
    136, 137, 199, 414n; fallibility of, 44, 45,
    46, 60, 70–72, 87, 134–36; funeral of, 27–
    28; and Gang of Four, 3–4, 30–31; and
    Great Leap Forward, 60; and Hua Guofeng,
    3, 31, 38, 49, 51, 93, 405n; legacy of, 4, 46,
    47, 101, 121, 123, 136; and Lei Feng, 123;
    official assessment of, 86, 132, 134–36; per-
    sonality cult of, 17, 98; Selected Works of,
    41; and Tiananmen incident (1976), 34–36,
    135–36
"Mao Zedong craze," 339
"Mao Zedong Thought," 46, 48, 58–59, 83, 87,
    101, 135, 136, 232, 332, 339, 363
Market reform. See Economic system; Market
    regulation; Urban reform
Market regulation, 4, 5, 18, 20, 22, 68, 165,
    175, 295, 337, 342, 355–56, 374, 375; and
    capitalism, 171, 336; and central planning,
    171, 342; economic discipline of, 95–96,
    171, 213, 295, 337, 361
Martial law, 112, 253, 258, 262–69, 271, 296,
    305, 316, 319; termination of, 291; in Tibet,
    323
Marx, Karl, 58, 360, 463n
Marxism, 178, 361, 363. See also Marxism-

Leninism
Marxism-Leninism, 5, 72, 107, 108, 149, 153,
    154, 157, 314, 328, 332; contemporary rele-
    vance of, 178, 189, 210
Marxism-Leninism-Mao Zedong Thought, 40,
    79, 150, 332. See also "Four cardinal princi-
    ples"
May 4th Movement (1919), 241, 253
Miles, James, 458n, 459n
Military Affairs Commission (MAC). See Peo-
    ple's Liberation Army
Military commerce (bingshang), 183, 370,
    380, 384
Moganshan: conference at (1984), 169
Monetary policy, 22, 55, 173–74, 223–24,
    233–35, 302, 326, 377
Money supply. See Monetary policy
Mongolia: collapse of communism in, 324
Most-Favored Nation (MFN), 291, 323

Nakasone, Yasuhiro, 190
Nanxun. See Deng Xiaoping, "southern tour"
    of
Nathan, Andrew, 398n, 399n
National Conference on Administrative Re-
    form (1985), 193
National Conference on Education Work
    (1978), 57
National Historical Institute, 371
National People's Congress (NPC), 52–54,
    105, 213, 330, 374
    Fifth Congress, 52–54; Second Session
    (1979), 67, 84, 85; Third Session (1980), 98,
    99, 104–6, 110, 111; Fourth Session (1981),
    138, 141
—Sixth Congress: First Session (1983), 155;
    Third Session (1985), 174
—Seventh Congress, 225–27; approves Three
    Gorges Dam, 348; and Tiananmen crisis
    (1989), 247, 268–71
—Eighth Congress: First Session (1993), 330,
    372–75, 378, 380; Third Session (1995),
    388–89
National Science Conference (1978), 56, 57
Naughton, Barry, 399n
"Neo-authoritarianism," 18, 21, 206, 220–22,
    226, 238–39, 256, 328, 361
"Neoconservatism," 328–30
Nepal, 323
Nepotism, 91, 92, 176, 195, 230, 236; in Peo-
    ple's Liberation Army, 123–24. See also
    Corruption; Gaogan zidi; Guandao
"New authoritarianism." See "Neo-authoritari-
    anism"
"New conservatism." See "Neoconservatism"

"New Democracy," 219, 452n

New Economic Policy (NEP), 97

Nie Rongzhen, 4, 40, 41, 51, 80, 185, 209, 267, 305, 400n, 417n, 423n, 425n

Nomenklatura, 73, 134, 220–21, 361. *See also* Administration; Civil service; Personnel system

Novak, Robert, 71

Nuclear weapons: testing of, 192

"One center": theory of, 13–14, 21, 144, 198, 218, 321, 334, 339, 344, 347, 348, 363, 373

"One center and two basic points." *See* "One center": theory of

Open cities, 341. *See also* "Open policy"; Special economic zones

"Open policy," 56, 57, 63, 96, 142, 149, 153, 164–65, 168, 169, 181–83, 211, 213, 303, 329, 334, 336, 341, 342, 350; expansion of, 143, 165, 166, 169, 345; negative by-products of, 102, 141–42, 156, 340; opposition to, 7, 142, 164, 182, 191, 210, 213, 320, 334, 344. *See also* Special economic zones

Orient Plaza, 469n

"Ossified thinking": criticism of, 88, 91, 107, 188

Panic buying, 233–34. *See also* Inflation

Pan Yue, 471n

Party cells, 220, 331, 361. *See also* Chinese Communist Party

Party discipline, 19, 101, 140–42, 157, 176, 194, 199, 220, 230, 308. *See also* Chinese Communist Party

Party rectification. *See* Chinese Communist Party

"Patriarchy": critique of, 97–98, 100

"Peaceful evolution," 302, 306, 328–34, 336, 337, 339, 340, 343–44, 346, 352, 370, 437n

Peasants. *See* Farmers

Peasants' associations, 106

Peking University, 59, 109, 200, 222, 227, 231, 255, 299–300, 304, 346–47; 1980 election at, 109–10

Peng Chong, 146, 148, 197, 417n

Peng Dehuai, 62, 400n, 405n, 421n

Peng Zhen, 4, 28, 62, 64, 84, 86, 105, 115, 145, 177, 185, 186, 206, 225, 227, 258, 293, 296, 298, 320, 321, 409n, 411n, 470n; and "bourgeois liberalization," 199; and Chen Yun, 355; and Deng Xiaoping, 348, 409n, 414n; and Hu Yaobang, 208; and petition movement of May 1989, 268; and political reform, 197; retirement of, 168, 214, 215; and

"spiritual pollution" campaign, 159–60; and Zhao Ziyang, 297

People's Armed Police (PAP), 183, 276, 278, 282–83, 306, 323–24

People's Bank of China. *See* Bank of China

People's congresses, local, 102, 195, 201–2, 214, 372. *See also* Elections; National People's Congress

People's courts. *See* Legal system

People's democratic dictatorship, 113, 150, 156, 238, 362. *See also* "Four cardinal principles"; Proletariat: dictatorship of

People's Liberation Army (PLA), 19, 58–59, 58, 60, 93, 121–23, 136, 183–84, 306, 367; 27th Group Army of, 286, 288, 292, 299, 305, 366, 367; 38th Group Army of, 248, 282, 283, 288, 305; Second Field Army of, 400n, 465n; Unit 8341 of, 41, 64; Air Force (PLAAF), 199; budget of, 88, 121, 183, 305, 370, 380, 468n; commerce in, 183, 370, 380, 384; corruption in, 123–25, 183, 380; and Deng Xiaoping, 17, 29, 88, 117, 121–23, 132, 183–85, 187, 188, 217, 258, 269, 293–94, 320, 370, 432n, 445–46n; "fine tradition and style of work" in, 58–60; force reductions in, 183–84; and Fourteenth Party Congress, 364, 366; and Gang of Four, 42; General Logistics Department (GLD), 184; General Political Department (GPD), 93, 123, 147, 162, 184; and Hu Yaobang, 122, 132, 188; and Hua Guofeng, 92–93; and Jiang Zemin, 371, 384; leadership changes in, 384; "Leftism" in, 122, 183; and Lei Feng campaign, 123, 305–6; Military Affairs Commission (MAC), 17, 29, 42, 43, 80, 92, 122, 132, 270, 306; modernization of, 17, 183–84; morale and discipline in, 122, 289, 304–7, 308–9; and rural reforms, 421n; reform of, 88, 121–23, 183–85, 305, 370; restoration of rank and insignia in, 184; retirement of officers in, 183–85; and Soviet Coup attempt (1991), 457n; and Thirteenth Party Congress, 216, 217; and "three supports and two militarys" campaign (1967), 136; and Tiananmen crisis (1989), 17, 20, 262–71, 276–89, 292–94, 308–9, 367, 454n; and Vietnam campaign (1979), 80; and "Yang Chengwu affair," 124–25; and "Yang family generals," 301, 305–6, 367; and Zhao Ziyang, 217

People's Republic of China (PRC): Constitution of, 53–54, 61, 96, 97, 105, 149–50, 373–74, 413n, 426n

Personnel system: reform of, 100, 220–21. *See*

also Administration; Civil service; *Nomenklatura*

Petitioners' movement (1978–79), 76–79, 89. *See also* Democracy Wall

"Petroleum clique," 9, 54–56, 67, 83, 104, 105, 162

Planned economy. *See* Central planning

Pluralism, 18, 222, 294, 313, 362, 393

Poland: crisis of 1980–81, 7, 102–4, 110–11, 112, 205, 250, 257, 275, 314, 419n, 436n

Political participation, 102–3, 107, 221. *See also* Democratization; Electoral system; Political system

Political prisoners. *See* Dissidents; Human rights

Political system: reform of, 72, 77, 99, 102–7, 108, 111–12, 121, 193–99, 202, 214–15, 220, 226, 313, 314, 321, 361. *See also* Democratization; Electoral system; Leadership system

Polytechnologies Corporation, 467n

Pornography, 102, 159–60, 182, 381. *See also* "Spiritual pollution"

"Practice" faction, 10, 11, 66, 68, 71, 86, 89, 90, 92, 103, 165. *See also* "Rehabilitated cadres" faction

"Practice is the sole criterion for testing truth," 9, 58, 59, 65, 86, 132, 356

Press: freedom of, 89, 106, 109, 112, 179, 209–10, 247, 356

Price reform, 16, 18, 68, 69, 95, 171–74, 190, 224, 226, 227, 232–36, 303. *See also* Economic system

"Primary stage of socialism," 218–19, 221, 223

"Princelings," 102, 141, 328, 330, 364, 365, 471n. See also *Gaogan zidi*

Private ownership. *See* Enterprises; Entrepreneurship; *Getihu*

Production responsibility systems. *See* Responsibility systems

"Productive forces": theory of, 57, 96, 218–19, 321, 356, 363. *See also* "One center": theory of

Professional societies. *See* "Civil society"

Profiteering. *See* Corruption; *Guandao*

Proletariat: dictatorship of, 49, 72, 79, 81, 85, 90. *See also* "Four cardinal principles"; People's democratic dictatorship

Property rights, 69, 227

Prostitution, 182, 229, 334, 344, 380, 381

Protectionism, local, 326

Public opinion, 221, 253, 255, 330–31, 394, 470n

Public ownership. *See* Enterprises

Public security. *See* Crime; Legal system; People's Armed Police

Pye, Lucian, 12, 398n, 443n

Qian Qichen, 365, 464n

Qiao Shi, 186, 194, 216, 236, 249, 259, 267, 269, 296, 298, 303, 318, 322, 324, 345, 350, 351, 352, 353, 366, 370, 373, 383, 386, 388, 459n

Qin Benli, 239, 242, 251

Qin Jiwei, 136, 216, 270, 305, 365, 367

Qingming incident. *See* Tiananmen incident (1976)

Qinshihuang, 32, 62, 401–2n

Racial discrimination, 191, 239–40

"Readjustment, restructuring, consolidation, and improvement," 66–68, 84, 86–87, 112

"Red-eye disease," 164

Reform. *See* Administration; Economic system; Leadership system; Political system; Price reform; Structural reform

Reform cycles. See "*fang/shou* cycles"

Reform through labor, 74, 110, 130

Regionalism: growth of, 392, 394

"Rehabilitated cadres" faction, 8, 9, 28. *See also* "Practice" faction

Religion, 106, 331

Renbayue. See "Double August"

Renshou County: riots in, 378

Ren Jianxin, 366

Ren Wanding, 81, 82, 240, 289, 291

"Resolution on Certain Questions in the History of Our Party" (1981), 132, 134–36, 137, 219, 332

Responsibility systems, 4, 28, 52, 63, 303; in agriculture, 68, 122, 165, 170, 182, 389; in industry, 151, 169, 227

Retirement: of cadres. *See* Cadres; Leadership system

"Right deviationist wind" (1975), 39, 44, 49, 135. *See also* "Three poisonous weeds"

"Rightism": critique of, 80, 83, 87, 88, 92, 93,

"Rightism" (*cont.*)
123, 128, 148, 159. *See also* "Bourgeois democracy"; "Bourgeois liberalization"

"River Elegy" (*Heshang*), 231–32, 335, 441n

Romania, 303–5, 309, 452n

Rong Yiren, 96, 373, 465n

Ru Xin, 153
Ruan Ming, 413n, 418n, 436n, 437n
Rui Xingwen, 295, 296, 315, 364, 453n
"Rule by core" faction, 388, 389, 390
"Rule by law" faction, 388, 390
Rural Development Research Group, 68

Sakharov, Andrei, 73
Salisbury, Harrison, 31
Samizdat, 74, 75
San Xia. *See* Three Gorges Dam
Schram, Stuart R., 399n
Scientific research, 56–57
Scowcroft, Brent, 449n
"Seek truth from facts," 47, 50, 51, 52, 58, 59, 61, 63, 73, 107, 158, 162
Self-reliance, 52, 54, 56
"Self-strengthening movement," 57
"Sent-down youths," 76, 412n
Sha Yexin, 126, 128
"Shanghai clique," 385, 468n
Shanghai Communiqué (1972), 135
Shantou Special Economic Zone, 67, 165, 451n
Shapiro, Judith, 419n
Shcharansky, Anatol, 73
"She'kou storm," 230, 231, 441n
Shenzhen Special Economic Zone, 67, 160, 165, 181–82, 342, 345, 353, 357–60, 371–72, 388
Shirk, Susan, 6–7
Shougang. See Capital Iron and Steel Corporation
Sideline production: household, 52. *See also* Entrepreneurship
"Socialism with Chinese characteristics," 16, 322, 363, 374
"Socialist democracy," 54, 61, 64, 80, 81, 85, 86, 105–7, 150, 195, 200
"Socialist humanism." *See* Humanism
"Socialist legality," 84–86, 101, 149, 150, 220
"Socialist market economy," 361, 363, 374, 449n. *See also* Market regulation
"Socialist modernization," 63, 143, 144, 213. *See also* "Four modernizations"
"Socialist planned commodity economy," 96, 171, 361
"Socialist spiritual civilization," 5, 16, 143, 148, 188, 219, 346. *See also* "Spiritual civilization"
Solidarnosç, 7, 205, 309. *See also* Poland
Solinger, Dorothy, 399n, 424n
Song Ping, 215, 216, 296, 336, 344, 347, 353, 365, 388

Song Renqiong, 64, 115, 145, 146, 148, 185, 339, 348, 416n
Song Shilun, 445n
Song Zhenming, 55, 104, 105
Soviet Union, 72, 149; attempted coup in (1991), 314, 328–29, 333, 452n, 457n; collapse of communism in, 7, 8, 19–20, 307, 310, 313, 324, 325, 330, 332, 334–36, 341, 347. *See also* Gorbachev, Mikhail; Yeltsin, Boris
Special economic zones (SEZs), 16, 20, 67, 141–42, 160, 164, 165, 175, 181–83, 303, 337, 340–44, 371, 373
Specialized households. *See* Entrepreneurship; *Getihu*
Speech: freedom of, 61, 71, 74, 79, 81, 82, 89, 92, 106, 107, 109, 150, 196, 247, 356. *See also* "Four big freedoms"
"Spiritual civilization," 88, 144, 148, 198, 425n. *See also* "Socialist spiritual civilization"
"Spiritual pollution": campaign against, 5, 8, 154, 155, 156–62, 164, 165, 167, 168, 170, 179, 188, 189, 198, 199, 207, 208, 209, 239, 241, 247, 250, 398n
"Stability and unity": after Deng Xiaoping's death, 393; appeal for, 63, 77, 79, 81–82, 107, 108, 112–13, 134, 221, 301, 329, 342
Stalin, Joseph, 55, 101, 112, 201
State Council, 29, 138–39; Economic and Trade Office of, 350; reorganization of, 139
State Economic Commission, 54, 151
State enterprises. *See* Enterprises
State Planning Commission, 151, 350
Stock market, 342, 348, 350, 352, 357–60
Stone Corporation, 266, 268
Strikes, 112, 193, 207, 379. *See also* Labor unions; Workers
Structural reform, 4, 16, 99, 107, 121, 174, 198, 213, 226; Deng Xiaoping and, 16, 30; freeze on, 18, 112. *See also* Economic system; Market regulation; Urban reform
Student demonstrations, 106, 112, 253, 275; of 1985, 190–92, 200; of 1986, 200–204, 206, 207, 208, 209, 211, 213, 230, 240; of 1988, 227–28, 230–31; of 1989, 7, 20, 229, 238, 239, 247–51, 255, 256, 272, 275, 296, 307, 309. *See also* Tiananmen crisis (1989)
Su Shaozhi, 154, 155, 178, 190, 195, 196, 209, 210, 214, 219, 238–39, 241, 242, 413n
Su Xiaokang, 290
Su Yu, 417n
Su Zhenhua, 40, 41, 404n
Subsidies: to consumers, 18, 171–72, 228, 234

Succession: origin of, 3, 8, 15, 31, 39, 41, 100, 118, 137, 151, 333, 334, 337, 339, 367, 383–85, 392–94

"Sun and Man," 422n. *See also* "Unrequited Love"

Sun Changjiang, 209, 408n, 462n

Sun Yat-sen, 348

Sun Yefang, 68, 94, 411n, 416n

"Survivors" faction, 9, 10, 28, 30, 40, 43, 48, 64, 90, 122

"Tail of capitalism," 337

Taiwan, 142, 187, 188

Taizidang. *See* "Princelings"

Tan Shaowen, 365, 464n

Tan Zhenlin, 28, 78, 147, 423n

Tangshan: earthquake in (1976), 38–39, 333

Tao Sen, 108, 110

Tao Zhu, 62, 409n

Taxation. *See* Enterprises; Fiscal reform; *Li gai shui*

Technocrats, 365. *See also* "Neo-authoritarianism"; "Third echelon"

Technology: role of, in economic development, 57, 67; transfer of, 54, 55, 69, 165, 303, 345

Teiwes, Frederick, 399n, 407n

"Third echelon," 8, 13, 16, 21, 138, 168, 169, 185, 186, 193, 194, 225, 296, 321, 333, 364

"Third Wave," 166, 429n

"Three-anti" campaign, 142

"Three crises of faith," 91, 139, 140. *See also* "Crisis of faith"

"Three disorders," 317

Three Gorges Dam, 348–49, 460n

"Three kinds of people": rectification of, 157–59, 161, 168, 177

"Three poisonous weeds" (1975), 29–30, 31, 37, 52, 56, 60, 67

"Three supports and two militarys" campaign (1967), 136, 424n, 434n

Tian Jiyun, 169, 186, 195, 196, 353, 364, 373, 378, 388–89, 462n

Tiananmen crisis (1989), 7, 8, 10, 11, 19, 177, 202, 247–98, 303, 315, 319, 330, 342, 349, 362, 364, 471n; aftermath of, 292–95, 298–300, 307, 438n; anniversary of, 390; crackdown on, 250, 253, 255, 275–89, 448n; fatalities in, 276, 283–84, 447n; labeling of, 292, 314, 315, 330, 362, 463n; origins of, 18–19, 239–42, 252; reassessment of, 21, 22, 314, 341, 352, 362, 369, 370, 388, 389, 454n. *See also* Hunger strike; Student demonstrations

Tiananmen incident (1976), 4, 22, 32–37, 43, 45, 46, 50, 59, 62, 71, 81, 82, 109, 117, 127, 132, 135, 136, 402n; and Deng Xiaoping, 4, 22, 34–37, 43, 136; labeled "counterrevolutionary," 36; reconsideration of, 43, 45, 51, 61–62, 70, 116; suppression of, 33–37, 402n

"Tiananmen massacre." *See* Tiananmen crisis (1989)

Tiananmen Poems, the, 32, 70, 402n

Tibet: unrest in, 226, 323–25, 455n

Toffler, Alvin, 166

"To get rich is glorious," 174

Tong Dalin, 166, 389, 462n

"Total Westernization." *See* "Complete Westernization"

Trade Unions. *See* Labor unions; Workers

Triads, 379, 467n

"Triangular debt," 382, 468n

Trotsky, Leon, 304

Turn-key projects, 54, 55, 112

"Two whatevers," 9, 43, 46, 83, 116, 132, 218, 219, 405n. *See also* "Whatever" faction

Tyler, Patrick, 468n

Ulanfu, 185, 425n

"Ultrademocracy," 80–82, 86, 89. *See also* Anarchism; "Extreme individualism"

"Ultra-Leftism," 78, 86, 91, 95, 127, 149, 157, 158, 165, 177, 406n

"Undeveloped socialism," 219. *See also* "Primary stage of socialism"

Unemployment, 71, 96, 228, 229, 378, 466n. *See also* "Floating population"; Workers

United Nations Commission on Human Rights, 240

United States, 72, 81, 162; and human rights, 339; and Most-Favored Nation (MFN) debate, 291, 323; relations of, with China, 63, 73, 77; visit to, by Deng Xiaoping (1979), 77, 80; visit to, by Zhao Ziyang (1983), 162, 166

Universities: political climate in, 110, 212, 299. *See also* Student demonstrations; Tiananmen crisis (1989)

"Unrequited Love," 126–30, 136, 422n. *See also* Bai Hua

Urban reform: of 1984, 169–72, 219. *See also* Economic system; Enterprises

Urban unrest, 190, 192–93, 224, 228, 232, 250

Vietnam: attack on (1979), 80, 82, 88

Viewing China through a Third Eye, 392, 393, 398n

Voice of America (VOA), 108, 163, 265, 335

Wade, Nigel, 42
"Waiting for work." *See* Unemployment
Wall posters, 51, 59, 69–73, 74, 78, 127, 139.
    See also Democracy Wall; "Four big free-
    doms"
Wan Li, 9, 68, 69, 92, 115, 148, 196, 204, 216,
    225, 292, 302, 321, 322, 345, 355, 366, 369,
    388, 411n, 416n; and Fang Lizhi, 201; re-
    tirement of, 365, 373; and Tiananmen crisis
    (1989), 249, 268–69, 270–71, 292
Wan Runnan, 266, 290
Wang Baosen: suicide of, 385, 469n
Wang Dan, 260, 261, 271, 290, 291, 388, 389
Wang Daohan, 69
Wang Dongxing, 27, 37, 40, 41, 45, 46, 48, 51,
    60, 62, 64, 90, 131, 408n, 410n
Wang Ganchang, 389
Wang Hongwen, 27, 33–30, 31, 35, 40, 42,
    401n, 404n
Wang Huning, 385
Wang Jun, 365
Wang Juntao, 109, 110, 290, 291, 402n, 412n,
    419n, 449n
Wang Meng, 189, 295, 364
Wang Mengkui, 469n
Wang Renzhi, 209, 239, 322, 336, 337, 339,
    340, 347, 356, 364
Wang Renzhong, 20, 64, 69, 90, 97, 100, 111,
    115, 123, 127–29, 142, 148, 154, 416n,
    423n
Wang Ruilin, 384, 465n
Wang Ruoshui, 77, 153–55, 160, 161, 163,
    189, 209, 210, 239, 389, 413n, 427n, 442n
Wang Ruowang, 128, 180, 190, 196, 205, 207,
    209, 210
Wang Shan, 392, 393, 471n
Wang Shaoguang, 392, 393
Wang Weilin, 289, 448n
Wang Xiaochao, 467n
Wang Xizhe, 74, 130, 389
Wang Zhaoguo, 169, 186, 194, 195
Wang Zhen, 4, 9, 13, 28, 40, 44, 45, 64, 100,
    108, 109, 115, 145, 159–60, 161, 165, 198,
    199, 206, 225, 226, 241, 293, 296, 297, 321,
    322, 325, 331, 332, 336, 337, 339, 346, 368,
    371, 375, 427n; and "bourgeois liberaliza-
    tion," 159–60; and capitalism, 332, 334; and
    Chen Yun, 45; death of, 20, 375; and Deng
    Xiaoping, 36, 336, 339–40, 346; and
    Mikhail Gorbachev, 304; and Hu Yaobang,
    198; and humanism, 159; and intellectuals,
    297; and leadership succession, 335–36; and
    "peaceful evolution," 331, 332, 336, 339; re-

tirement of, 168, 185; and "River Elegy,"
    232; and special economic zones, 165; and
    "spiritual pollution," 159–60; and student
    demonstrations of 1986, 204; and Tian-
    anmen crisis (1989), 258; and Zhao Ziyang,
    297
Wang Zhihua, 467n
Wei Guoqing, 28, 36, 45, 88, 93, 123, 127,
    146, 147, 162, 177
Wei Jianxing, 366, 386, 464n
Wei Jingsheng, 10, 73–74, 78, 80–81, 82, 205,
    209, 210, 240–42, 414n, 415n, 436n
Wen Jiabao, 366, 464n
Wen Yuankai, 210, 413n
"Wenzhou model," 334
Westernization, 56–57, 102, 142, 201, 232,
    239. *See also* "Complete Westernization"
"Whatever" faction, 4, 8–10, 45, 46, 47, 50–
    51, 55, 58–61, 62, 63–65, 67, 70, 72, 83, 88,
    89, 90, 92, 100, 145, 177, 363. *See also*
    "Loyalist" faction; "Two whatevers"
What if I Were Real?, 126, 128, 421n
"White slips," 377
"Wind" faction, 353, 366
Witke, Roxane, 31
Workers: and Tiananmen crisis (1989), 250,
    271–72, 275, 446n; unrest among, 103, 112,
    193, 207, 228–29, 379; wages of, 55, 171,
    174, 182, 223, 302. *See also* Industrial de-
    mocracy; Labor unions; Strikes
Workers' militia, 35, 36, 41, 402n
"Workers' picket corps," 272
Work style: rectification of. *See* Chinese Com-
    munist Party; "Fine tradition and style of
    work"
World Bank, 166
World Economic Herald, 190, 210, 238, 239,
    242, 251
World Trade Organization (WTO), 471
Wu Bangguo, 365, 385, 464n
Wu De, 27, 33–35, 43–45, 59, 61, 62, 70, 90,
    131
Wu Hu luan Hua, 409n
Wu Jiang, 96, 408n
Wu Jinglian, 232, 462n
Wu Mingyu, 462n
Wu Shuqing, 299, 335, 347
Wu Xueqian, 186
Wu Yu-shan, 398n
Wu Zhong, 402n
Wu Zuguang, 209, 210, 389, 443n
Wu'er Kaixi, 253, 254, 260, 261, 267, 271,
    290, 445n, 448n

Wuhan Steel Rolling Mill, 105

Xi Zhongxun, 64, 67, 74, 124, 131, 146, 148, 207, 215, 268, 417n
Xiahai ("taking the plunge"), 374, 466n
Xiamen (Amoy) Special Economic Zone, 67, 165, 182, 451n
Xiang Shouzhi, 305
Xiao Gongqin, 456n
Xiao Ke, 445n
Xiao Rong. *See* Deng Rong
Xiaozibao, 76. *See also* Wall posters
Xidan Wall. *See* Democracy Wall
Xie Fei, 365
Xinjiang: ethnic unrest in, 323–25, 455n
Xu Jiatun, 465n
Xu Liangying, 210, 389
Xu Qinxian, 269, 446n
Xu Shiyou, 28, 33, 36, 41, 45, 88, 121, 146, 147, 415n, 420n, 433n
Xu Weicheng, 322, 328, 336, 346
Xu Wenli, 130
Xu Xiangqian, 100, 122, 185, 267, 305, 400n, 423n, 425n
Xue Muqiao, 68, 94–95, 171, 411n, 416n

Yan Fu, 330
Yan Jianhong, 385
Yan Jiaqi, 195, 196, 214, 215, 220, 238, 242, 251, 290, 402n, 413n, 415n, 418n, 442n
Yan Mingfu, 195, 209, 253, 257, 258, 260, 295, 296, 315, 364, 453n
Yan Tongmao, 446n
Yang Baibing, 217, 301, 305–7, 338, 353, 365, 366, 367, 464n
Yang Chengwu, 40, 124
Yang Dezhi, 146, 148, 183, 185, 215, 305, 416n, 445n
Yang Dezhong, 64
"Yang family generals," 21, 301, 305–7, 366, 367, 384. *See also* Yang Baibing; Yang Shangkun
"Yang Jianhua," 450n
Yang Jingren, 417n
Yang Li, 450n
Yang Rudai, 364
Yang Shangkun, 28, 62, 74, 86, 115, 146, 185, 216, 225, 249, 256, 257, 263, 293, 302, 304, 305, 307, 309, 334, 336, 345, 388, 417n, 436n, 438n, 450n, 451n, 453n; and Deng Xiaoping, 21, 257, 270, 347, 369, 409n; and Military Affairs Commission, 217, 241, 301; retirement of, 21, 338, 365, 373; and

special economic zones, 67, 371; and "theory of one center," 334; and Tiananmen crisis (1989), 249, 251, 256–58, 263, 269–70, 293, 314, 369–70; and Zhao Ziyang, 269, 270
Yang Shaojing, 450n
Yang Xiguang, 413n
Yang Yong, 148
Yao Mingde, 126
Yao Wenyuan, 27, 35, 37, 40, 42, 62, 404n
Yao Yilin, 64, 67, 68, 115, 186, 213, 215, 216, 235, 236, 238, 249, 296, 297, 302, 303, 320, 321, 322, 326, 336, 347, 353, 365, 383, 416n, 418n, 461n
Ye Fei, 147, 177, 431n, 445n
Ye Jianying, 10, 28, 29, 33, 36, 40, 44, 48, 51, 53, 54, 58, 64, 90, 98, 106, 115, 122, 132–33, 144, 145, 146, 153, 185, 186, 231, 328, 402n, 413n, 423n; and Cultural Revolution, 49, 87; and Deng Xiaoping, 36, 42, 45, 404n, 408n; and Gang of Four, 41, 42; and Hu Yaobang, 131, 417n; and Hua Guofeng, 45, 49, 131, 132–33, 406n; and Liu Shaoqi, 91, 416n; and Mao Zedong, 87–88, 101; retirement of, 145, 185, 425n; speech of, at Fourth Plenum of Eleventh Central Committee (1979), 86–88; speech of, at PLA work conference (1978), 59; and "spiritual civilization," 88
Ye Qun, 400n
Ye Wenfu, 124, 128, 130, 160, 422n
Ye Xuanping, 231, 327, 328, 364
Ye Zhefeng, 177
"Yellowbird Action," 449n
Yeltsin, Boris, 332, 333
Ying Ruocheng, 295
Youth: crime rate among, 379; crisis of faith among, 381
Yu Guangyuan, 53, 61, 69, 77, 95, 96, 131, 166, 210, 239, 319, 413n, 415n, 462n
Yu Haocheng, 196, 238, 290, 413n, 418n, 442n
Yu Qiuli, 55, 67, 84, 105, 148, 162, 215, 418n, 436n
Yu Shuo, 287
Yu Yongbo, 367, 384
Yuan Baohua, 418n
Yuan Mu, 253, 289, 298, 304, 328, 337, 363, 386
Yugoslavia: breakup of, 392
Yung, Larry, 465n

Zeng Peiyan, 385

Zeng Qinghong, 385
Zhang Aiping, 305, 417n
Zhang Baifa, 200, 386
Zhang Chunqiao, 27, 30, 31, 33, 35, 40, 42, 61, 71, 116, 404n, 420n
Zhang Jingfu, 69
Zhang Pinghua, 51, 64, 80
Zhang Tingfa, 185
Zhang Wannian, 305, 367
Zhang Wei, 109, 419n
Zhang Xianyang, 209, 210, 413n, 418n
Zhang Yimou, 356
Zhang Zhen, 367, 380, 384
Zhao Dajun, 177
Zhao Erjun, 177
Zhao Nanqi (Cho Nam Gi), 367
Zhao Ziyang, 9, 10, 16, 68, 69, 74, 86, 90, 92, 112, 132, 133, 141, 146, 151, 152, 164, 167, 171, 177, 185, 186, 204, 213, 215, 216, 219, 222, 225, 236, 249, 254–56, 258, 259, 263, 272, 273, 293, 308, 318, 319, 327, 356, 388, 411n, 426n, 455n, 463n; and Bao Tong, 238, 255–56, 362; and "bourgeois liberalization," 155, 211, 213, 221, 239; and George Bush, 242; and Chen Yun, 10, 111, 172, 211, 241; and coastal development strategy, 226, 235; and crackdown on crime, corruption, 140, 141, 155, 236, 261; criticism of, 234, 239, 295, 297; and Deng Liqun, 161–62; and Deng Xiaoping, 10, 68, 152, 211, 213, 253–54, 258, 261, 297, 308, 315; and economic reform, 4, 68–69, 151, 218–20, 226, 232–36, 302; fall from power of, 12, 19, 177, 211, 235, 241, 269, 270, 295, 296, 316; fate of, 13, 21, 300–301, 314, 315, 322, 362–63, 369, 452n; and "four cardinal principles," 213; and Mikhail Gorbachev, 218, 257; and Hu Yaobang, 11, 150–53, 161, 207, 211, 248, 249, 398n, 437n; and inflation, 174; and intellectuals, 241, 242, 429n; and Li Peng, 227, 233–35, 239, 262; and "neo-authoritarianism," 18, 220–22, 226, 238, 328; and People's Liberation Army, 217; and political reform, 196, 214–15, 218–22; and price reform, 219, 220, 232–34; and "primary stage of socialism," 219; report of, to Fourth Session of Fifth National People's Congress (1981), 138, 141; report of, to Thirteenth Party Congress (1987), 218–22, 361; and "River Elegy," 232; and secret protocol of 1987, 218, 257; and "spiritual pollution" campaign, 161–62; and "theory of one center," 218, 334; and "theory of productive forces," 218–19; and "third echelon," 194; and "Third Wave," 166; and Tiananmen crisis (1989), 13, 208, 248–49, 251, 253–63, 270, 293, 295–98; visit of, to North Korea, 249, 251, 253; visit of, to United States, 162, 166
Zheng Bijian, 171, 459n
Zheng Liangyu, 358, 359
Zhongnanhai, 76, 77, 127, 247, 248, 279, 404n
Zhou Baifang, 385, 462n, 469n
Zhou Duo, 286, 290, 389, 446n
Zhou Enlai, 3, 29, 30, 31, 32–33, 35, 37, 44, 45, 76, 98, 118, 144, 186, 348, 400n
Zhou Guanwu, 385, 462n
Zhou Gucheng, 226
Zhou Hui, 409n
Zhou Jiannan, 388
Zhou Ruijin, 458n
Zhou Weizhi, 130
Zhou Yang, 129, 154, 157, 160, 161, 189
Zhou Yibing, 305
Zhu De, 103, 400n
Zhu Houze, 181, 189, 195, 196, 209, 316
Zhu Muzhi, 51, 186
Zhu Rongji, 333, 338, 350, 351, 355, 360, 365, 366, 372, 373, 375, 382, 385, 386, 388, 461n, 464n, 468n
Zhuhai Special Economic Zone, 67, 165, 342, 371, 372, 451n
Zhuo Lin, 387, 389, 470n
Zou Jiahua, 338, 350, 352, 364, 365, 373, 461n, 464n